SMALL BUSINESS ENTREPRENEURSHIP

An Ethics and Human
Relations Perspective

SMALL BUSINESS ENTREPRENEURSHIP

An Ethics and Human Relations Perspective

Lavern S. Urlacher

Prentice Hall
Upper Saddle River, NJ 07458

Library of Congress Cataloging-in-Publication Data

Urlacher, Lavern S.
    Small business entrepreneurship : an ethics and human relations perspective / Lavern S. Urlacher.
      p.   cm.
    Includes index.
    ISBN 0–13–636408–X
    1. Small business—Management.   2. Small business—Moral and ethical aspects.   I. Title.
    HD62.7.U75   1999
    658.02`2—dc21   98-30843
                                                                         CIP

Acquisitions Editor: Elizabeth Sugg
Editorial Assistant: Maria Kirk
Director of Production and Manufacturing: Bruce Johnson
Managing Editor: Mary Carnis
Editorial/Production Supervision and Interior Design: Tally Morgan, WordCrafters Editorial
Services, Inc.
Cover Design: Miguel Ortiz
Manufacturing Buyer: Ed O'Dougherty
Marketing Manager: Danny Hoyt

© 1999 by Prentice-Hall, Inc.
Simon & Schuster/A Viacom Company
Upper Saddle River, New Jersey 07458

Printed in the United States of America

10 9 8 7 6 5 4 3 2 1

ISBN 0-13-636408-X

Prentice-Hall International (UK) Limited, *London*
Prentice-Hall of Australia Pty. Limited, *Sydney*
Prentice-Hall Canada Inc., *Toronto*
Prentice-Hall Hispanoamericana, S.A., *Mexico*
Prentice-Hall of India Private Limited, *New Delhi*
Prentice-Hall of Japan, Inc., *Tokyo*
Simon & Schuster Asia Pte. Ltd., *Singapore*
Editora Prentice-Hall do Brasil, Ltda., *Rio de Janeiro*

To my wife, Joyce Muggli Urlacher, for her support and encouragement, and to my children: Brian, who provided much needed computer technical support; Wyatt, whose artistic talent was put to use in drawing the bridge model; and Janna, who sacrificed time with her dad so that this book could be written.

I would also like to acknowledge every teacher who ever looked into the eyes of a student and saw the promise of a better tomorrow. I would especially like to thank those teachers who gave me hope, who strived to build me up and not tear me down.

Contents ●●●●●●●●●●●

Part III. Monitoring Information and the Greater Environment

Preface ● ● ● ● ● ● ● ● ● ● ● ●

A Letter to the Student· · · · · · · · · · · · · · · ·

It is my profound hope that this book will have a positive impact on your life. If you or anyone else had asked me if I would ever write a book, much less a textbook, I would have answered "never in a million years." In the end I wrote this book because I thought it needed to be written. I wrote it out of frustration. As a adjunct professor, I was teaching a class in small business management, and was frustrated with the textbook.

Partially, this was because of my experience with small businesses. I spent fifteen years as a small business owner and as a manager in three different types of businesses before attending graduate school to pick up an advanced degree. After graduation I worked part time as an adjunct professor and full time as an unemployment tax representative for the state of South Dakota. I worked exclusively with businesses and wound up doing a lot of coaching and consulting with new proprietors. One day I walked into a new establishment and visited with the new entrepreneur. As I was helping this person set up her payroll and handing her the appropriate forms for both state and federal filing requirements, I discovered that she had just graduated from college with a degree in accounting. She had been taught a lot about accounting, but not from a practical how-to, small business perspective. She had never seen the forms and did understand the steps required to get a business off the ground from a legal-requirement point of view.

It is my intent in this book to fill in many of those gaps. I discuss what forms must be filed when and with whom. You will find the forms to file income tax and payroll in an appendix at the end of Chapter 10. You will find the forms to file a loan request with the SBA. I have included a format to form a franchise, buy a business on a contract for deed, and to deal with many with similar concepts. You will find an interview with a lender and two formats with which to file a business plan as well as an in-depth look at marketing research prior to the marketing plan format. In this type of course, more than any other in a typical business degree curriculum, the focus should be on a step-by-step, how-to framework. The only problem is that in a small business the steps are rarely sequential. It often seems that everything progresses at the same time, or remains stagnant.

I have developed a bridge model, which the book elucidates. This model was the outcome of an attempt to demonstrate to my students how the functional areas are integrated into a small business system. The model confirms that business is supported by people and systems that must generate an acceptable level of quality in the products and services that are produced. The model demonstrates that successful long-term business endeavors must be grounded in honesty and integrity—that a business must be grounded in ethical conduct if it intends to be successful. The ethical conduct a business engages in is most evident within the human relationships that support the business and also in the products and services the business produces. The model demonstrates that small businesses make decisions as an ongoing process. To make good-quality decisions, good information systems must be an integral part of the business structure.

In this book I have used many of my own experiences and have made extensive use of interviews with small business owners and with people in firms that tend to work with and support small business. I used this format to demonstrate how similar small businesses are but how unique they are in bringing their products or services to the marketplace. Although their problems and challenges are similar, they require very different approaches. It is my hope that the generosity of these people in sharing their life and business experiences will inspire readers not only to learn from them but to really gain an aptitude for creative problem solving.

The businesses that I chose to profile are truly entrepreneurial endeavors. These are not the sons and daughters of wealthy people who were groomed in the family business to take over when their parents retired. These are everyday working people who had a dream and possessed the ability and courage to pursue that dream. That doesn't mean they found the gold at the end of the rainbow. The process of running their businesses goes on in a very daily sort of way. These people were willing to share their hopes, fears, successes, and failures with the hope that you might learn from them. In the telling, take what you can and leave the rest. I am very grateful to those who opened their doors to me to share with us.

The focus of this book is not the SBA's definition of small business, which for most of us is big business, but on a much smaller scale. The intent is not to preclude or limit the size of the prospective entrepreneur's dream, only the size of the beginnings. I have a special appreciation for the fact that starting a small business involves an extensive search for information. Starting and running a small business often seems to be a continuous quest for solutions to ever-changing problems. To help simulate that process, I added a number of outside-the-classroom activities, to involve you in your communities in the search for firsthand information.

In small business management so many of the decisions that need to be made are financial in nature that I felt it particularly important that readers have a thorough understanding of the time value of money concepts. Included is a segment intended to expand your understanding of that concept, with a special focus on the capital budgeting process, which is what a business plan is really all about.

I hope that this book will act as a resource for you after this class has ended. It is my hope that the information contained in the book teaches lessons that are larger than just an exercise in academics. I would also like to thank you for allowing me to share in this part of your educational experience.

A Note to the Instructor·················

This text is written to be used with a very hands-on approach. Although I believe there are several ways in which this course could be taught using this text, in one sense the content resembles a bell curve, with the more general information at the very beginning of the book, in Part I, and also at the end, in Part III. If the book is used in a 17-week semester-length course, my recommendation would be to spend no more than a week each on the three chapters in Part I, to spend approximately 12 weeks in Part II, and to finish with a week each on the two chapters in Part III.

One suggested method of teaching the course using this text would be with the use of a class project that attempts to simulate the starting of a new business. I have found it useful to divide the class into teams of three to five, depending on the size of the class. I have allowed approximately one hour a week of class time, of which I float between the groups to lend support and ideas. The intent is to have the students come up with a workable small business concept and to prepare a business plan, which includes a marketing plan, on a small business proposal. Once complete, I have the groups present their business plans to a peer loan committee for approval. Peer grading may be incorporated. Once the loan committee approves the business plan, I will run the students through the SBA loan guarantee process, which includes obtaining an SBA loan package for a 7(a) loan. I generally set a target date of around week 12 for the project to reach this point, and the completion of Chapter 9. If you are teaching under a quarter system, this process will have to be accelerated. The time frame may vary depending on the groups as well, but with the start of Chapter 10, I follow the project with small business accounting principles. From the pro forma income statements I will have the groups set up a check register, prepare a schedule C and form SE, and file a 1040. Once the income tax process is complete, I run the students through the payroll process, starting with the SS-4 federal identification number application and all the federal and state forms to complete a full year's payroll. Nearly half of the federal government's budget comes from the payroll tax. From personal experience I know many businesses that fail because of gaps in knowledge of these expenses. I have included all the forms in the appendix to Chapter 10, with the exception of state-specific forms. The South Dakota forms that are included as samples could be assigned to demonstrate the general use of state forms.

Because small business management is heavily involved in making financial decisions, in Chapter 7 I address ratio analysis, time value of money, and capital budgeting. In the time value of money discussion we use present and future value tables exclusively. The answers to the worksheet, work problem, and minicase-type problems are given at the end of the chapter. This chapter could be handled by students through self-study, but they may need a little guidance. I have found that few students understand the concepts well enough to get through the problems on their own; they usually need a few pointers along the way. I have also found that most students are very appreciative of the knowledge and skills they obtain in this segment, because the applications are so universally applicable. The capital budgeting process can be emphasized as well. Most students have been exposed to that process in a finance class, but I have found that few students know how to apply a sensitivity analysis to a capital budgeting process. I leave it up to the instructors's discretion whether to cover this material.

Another approach to teaching small business management or entrepreneurship using this book would be to use the outside-the-classroom exercises extensively, either in addition to a project or in lieu of a project. At the end of some of the chapters are suggested outside activities to get the students involved in information seeking and problem solving processes. It has been my experience that as a small business owner, a constant search for information from primary sources is a requirement. These activities are intended to get students involved in actively seeking out resources and experiences that emulate the activities of a small business manager.

I believe this text could also be used to teach small business management in a very traditional way. I have included end-of-chapter questions that attempt to force the student back into the chapter to identify the main points. A video series such as *Growing a Business* could also be used to support the text. Additional video recommendations are provided in the instructor's manual.

A central theme of the book is the bridge model, which I developed after years of personal experience owning and managing several small businesses and after many years of consulting with small business owners as an unemployment tax representative. The bridge model was actually developed for the classroom while I was teaching small business management as a adjunct professor. I needed a tool that would attempt to demonstrate the interrelatedness of the functional areas in which a small business owner must perform. The bridge model is also intended to emphasize and prioritize the critical element of management: the premise that small business, actually all business, must be grounded in ethical conduct. A position of honesty and integrity will provide a foundation that allows a business to survive over the long haul. I attempted to emphasize with the pillars that business success comes from people. The quality of the internal and external relationships influence whether a business succeeds or fails. The model demonstrates that the quality of human relationships also affects the quality of products and services that a business produces, and that quality is a major pillar of support for any business. The functional areas, which are each important, must be supported by the human systems and quality pillars, and all are tied together with information. Thus the girders of management and customer information systems make the business complete. The bridge model also demonstrates that we operate in a larger environment as well.

Within this book are a number of entrepreneurial profiles. I wanted to include real stories of real people to demonstrate the similarities and uniqueness of each business venture. I also felt it would lend credibility to the book and to the bridge model to relate these entrepreneurial stories, including my own. I believe the challenges of small business ownership are best described by the people currently experiencing those challenges. The advice and lessons given in the entrepreneurial profiles are intended to represent and emphasize the functional areas. For example, Hurly's Candies' primary constraint is the production process, whereas Prairie Gardens is faced with a huge marketing dilemma. In support of almost every major topic, I conducted interviews with people in that line of business. The book is supported heavily with primary research and personal examples.

Thank you for selecting this book; I hope it serves you well.

Vern Urlacher

Acknowledgments ● ● ● ● ● ● ● ● ● ● ● ● ● ● ●

Thank you to every expert, both corporate and academic, who contributed to the content of this work. Special recognition goes to Rebecca Legleiter of Tulsa Community College; Patti L. Wilber, Ph.D., Northwestern Oklahoma State University; and Cal Taillefer, Crestwood, Ontario.

I would also like to extend a special thanks to Dana Lee Meltzer of Prentice Hall for assisting me with this project. Without her unwavering support and encouragement, this text would never have been written.

SMALL BUSINESS ENTREPRENEURSHIP

An Ethics and Human
Relations Perspective

1 Entrepreneurial • • • • • • • • • •
Beginnings

Chapter Objectives

- To provide a bridge model overview that will allow the student to visualize and prioritize the functional areas of a business.

- To assist in building an appreciation for the interrelationships between the functional areas in the management of a small business.

• THE BRIDGE MODEL ·················

This book is based on a bridge model premise (Figure 1–1). A number of marketing research firms and small business owners that were interviewed seemed in general agreement that this model makes sense. The bridge model was the outcome of a decade or so of my experience owning and managing several small businesses and nearly a decade of working with small business owners. The model was developed for a course that I was teaching in small business management, for which I needed a way to tie together and prioritize the critical functions of managing a small business. I believe this model would be valid for many large corporate entities as well.

At a very basic level, for a business to remain successful, it must be grounded in honesty. The model uses the term *ethics,* because it encompasses a broader horizon. In plain language, though, a business must obtain the basic trust of its customer base to remain healthy. Businesses demonstrate this by presenting themselves to the public in the form of their products and services as being honest and worthy of customers' trust. The issue of ethics extends beyond the realm of a firm's customer base; it should also be reflected in the relationships the business establishes, including relationships with the larger community. A successful business should strive to be a good neighbor and a responsible citizen.

The bridge model is just that—a model. It is not a proven law of business conduct. It does not suggest that exceptions do not exist or that an economically successful enterprise cannot be created that violates the principles of the model, particularly the ethics foundation. The truth of the matter is that many exceptions exist. If a violation of ethical standards were a guarantee of failure, the number of unscrupulous business owners would be on the decline. Similarly, the number of legal actions taken to correct a wrong or a harm caused by a company's products or services would also be on the decline. We would have little need for a state's department of revenue or the federal Environmental Protection Agency, Occupational Safety and Health Administration, and/or any other regulatory agency empowered by a state or the federal government to protect the rights of the public, because everyone would do what is ethically right. I'm not that altruistic, nor am I naive enough to believe that such is the case.

Still, with the combined experience of those firms represented in this book, I believe that a high degree of correlation exists equating small business success to the bridge model. I maintain that a solid foundation on which to build a successful business is obtaining the trust of customers as well as all others who are associated with the business. Those relationships are grounded in ethical behavior. It would be interesting to do a study of businesses that failed and those that succeeded and attempt to correlate those results to this model.

Somewhat similar to the concept of grounding a business in ethics rest two sets of pillars that support the functional areas of the business. The first set of pillars deals with human relationships. The premise is that organizations, in this case small business organizations, are not simply made up of physical assets such as building and equipment, but are made up of people. The essence of what makes a small business a success and/or a failure depends on the people who are affiliated with that business and the quality of their relationships between each other. The premise suggests that high-quality output is a function of the quality of the human relationships both internal and external to the business.

Internal relationships relate to business manager and employee relationships. This implies that each person has unique skills and abilities, but it is the quality of the relationships, based on mutual trust, respect, and commitment, that

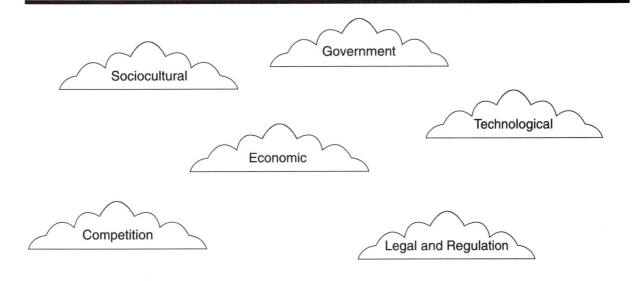

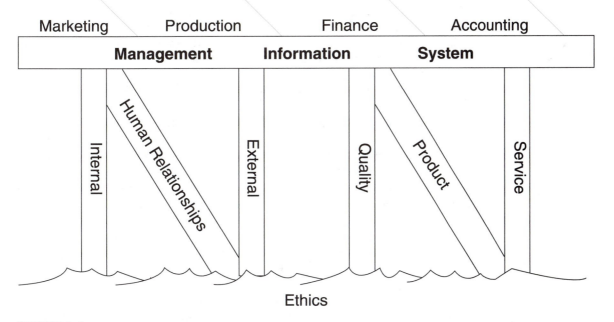

FIGURE 1–1

allows or supports high levels of performance. It is the people within an organization who can maximize the potential of the organization by utilizing the human and financial resources available. The performance of an organization is linked to the total performance of the people within the organization.

Much has been said and written about employee involvement and empowerment, and in many respects many businesses, both large and small, have gone a long way toward achieving that. It is almost a given that high levels of performance have become a requirement for success in a highly competitive global environment. Major corporations have recognized this for a long time, demonstrated in part by the types of ads for employment which all seem to be seeking team players. The premise, then, is that successful small businesses are managed and run by closely knit groups or teams, which in turn are built on mutual trust, respect, and commitment.

As you read this book, especially the interviews with small business people and others associated with small businesses, look for those relationship elements as well as all the other elements of the bridge model buried within the interviews that are scattered throughout the book. I don't want you to hear these concepts from me as much as from people who are currently in the trenches. What small business is, and how small business is conducted, represent a patchwork of many people's small business experience.

The external relationship pillar is similarly important. Successful small businesses have built personal human relationships outside their walls. Those human relationships are also based on mutual trust, respect, and commitment. The health and survivability of a business depend on the quality of those external relationships as well. Vendors, creditors, customers, and others are critical to supporting the ongoing activity of a small business. The banker relationship is a prime example. A bank does not lend to a business; it lends money to a person who owns a business. The same types of relationships exist in sales. A customer does not buy from a company or a business (they do to a degree, depending on the product or service), but the customer generally buys from a person. The sale is the outcome of a relationship between one person and another. Every business is supported by a network of these one-on-one human relationships.

The critical placement of the human relationship pillars is designed to bring home the point that if those critical relationships are violated, the business will crumble and fall. This concept is not itself new. Now as in the past, how successful small businesses treat people relates back to such things as the golden rule: Treat others the way you want to be treated. This is not a new concept at all, and certainly there are exceptions to almost every rule, but the premise—an ideal if you will, but just plain good advice—is to build a business grounded in honesty and ethical behavior and to develop solid human relationships, both internally and externally. This will give you the foundation to stay in business for the long haul. I challenge you to find a multigenerational business or major corporation that can violate the principles of this model and not be affected adversely and or have its survival put in jeopardy.

The bridge model implies that the next step in the building of a solid small business is to put in place the other two pillars, which are based on a high-quality product and/or a high-quality service level, both of which are outcomes of high-quality human relationships. The premise here is that people develop the systems that produce the products and deliver the services only in an environment where open communication exists, which is best exemplified by a closely knit group whose accepted goal is to produce high-quality products or services. Such a group accepts the premise that the business is operating in a highly competitive environment and that success depends on achieving an acceptable level of sales and profit performance. The premise is that the business survives based on the level of acceptance that customers bestow on a particular business product or service. A critical part of a customer's acceptance of a product or service in the marketplace is directly dependent on the quality of the firm's products or services.

This concept is somewhat incomplete: The quality of a product and service itself is not enough. The firm must be meeting the needs of the customer base with the right products and the right services, which implies that these quality pillars of success need to be supported and tied into the other elements that make a business workable. The bridge model demonstrates that the pillars of business success are supported by the functional areas of the business and by the girders of customer information systems and management information systems. The quality pillars have been placed within the model to signify that a violation of the principles of quality will eventually lead to the collapse of the business structure. Quality is critical to long-term health and survivability. For many small businesses the quality component is their niche. For many small business firms, quality in product or service is the one way they can differentiate themselves from the competition, which in turn allows them to price their products or services at a premium in the marketplace.

As mentioned above, the quality factors of a business are supported by human relationships and by the information gathered. In one sense you can reduce the concept of small business success down to and equate it with the quality of the decisions made by the people managing and running the business. Stop and think about the concept of decision making. Every person is influenced by and makes decisions based on the total of their past experience, which has been influenced by the person's educational experience, religion, nationality, the family and the neighborhood the person grew up in, and so on. The total of all the things that make each of us unique will influence our decisions, which sometimes are just as unique as the person making them. Past experience is half of the decision-making equation; the other half is based on the information at hand now or at the time the decision is made.

Good, accurate, reliable, timely information supports good decision making. To tie the functional areas together, I have placed two girders in the bridge model which support and are supported by the critical pillars of success. The customer information system is designed to obtain information about customer wants and needs: to measure the level of acceptance that customers are granting a business's products or services and to feed that information to the management team to support good decision making. With good customer information, management and other members of an organization can make those minor or major changes that maintain quality and maintain the product mix or service components that the customer wants. The customer information system is also not a stand-alone component, embedded solely in the marketing function but is also, although to a lesser degree, a part of other functional areas. The entire organization should be sensitive to, and constantly gathering, customer information.

Management information is the other information girder that ties an organization together and supports good decision making. The information gathered is critical to the survivability of a firm. The scope of a good management information system is much broader than the customer information system. It is designed to scan the wider environment of the organization. The political and social, legal and technological, as well as economic and competitive environments must be monitored. The management information system gathers information internally from the functional areas. Information concerning cost, quality, and customer satisfaction levels and other information generated internally all act to support decision making. Information concerning production processes, scrap, rejects, returns, and sales performance by customer, territory, and sales representatives are other examples of information generated internally. Additional information derives from measuring and monitoring employee performance. Measures of cost, profit, performance, quality, and levels of service that lead to changes in the way a firm does business is what information systems are all about.

I cannot overemphasize the importance of constantly attempting to improve the information systems of an organization. The information system put in place should attempt to identify why customers are using a firm's products or services. It should be able to tell the firm's managers why they are successful and to help identify the firm's strategic success variables: In short, if the firm continues to do such and such an activity, it will be successful. This type of information guides and directs the future activity of a firm. A good management information system will also monitor those elements that pose a threat to the future survivability of a firm. In many respects a management information system tells small business owners what they should measure, what activities are critical, and to some degree what should be rewarded in their businesses.

Internal information concerning costs, quality, and customer acceptance in the form of sales, returns, repairs, and so on, also helps the small business manager make decisions that relate to capital budgeting expenditures, market research, product development, expansion, and so on. This type of information is more specific to the customer information system, which is an equivalent but specialized part of the management information system. However a business organizes the information-gathering function, the results are the same. Poor information will support poor decision making. Misinformation will produce incorrect assumptions, causing errors to be made in the decision-making process. Accuracy and timeliness are both requirements for success.

The pillars of success and the girders of success support the functional areas of the firm. Each represents a very important component of the completed bridge structure. In my years as a unemployment tax auditor I saw hundreds of business failures. Each specific reason for failure could be traced back to failures in one or more of the functional areas. The intent with regards to the placement of functional areas in the bridge model design is to demonstrate that if a small business disregards a functional area or fails to perform a function adequately, the bridge will be left with a huge gap, rendering it useless. In the same way, a small business that fails to master a critical functional area, especially in the big four—accounting, finance, marketing, and production—will be rendered inept and useless, and be bound to fail.

In the interviews that I conducted for this book, I attempted to get entrepreneurs to identify critical elements of success in their businesses. A consensus exists, which supports the premise that for a small business to be successful a business owner must know the numbers. In my auditing experience, time after time I saw businesses fail because they could not relate costs and revenue components. Is that strictly an accounting function failure, or is it part of the management information system? I think it is a failure of both. I have included in this book a small business view of the accounting function, supported with state and federal tax forms, in an attempt to raise your awareness of the mandates of the accounting function. I have also attempted to place in that chapter a streamlined approach to revenue and cost relationships.

When you read the interviews, look for the emphasis the entrepreneurs place on the numbers. Both the accounting and finance functions deal with the numbers, especially at the beginning of a business, when the quest for financing gets the most attention. Without it, an entrepreneurial dream dies on the vine. This function is also often the most frustrating and the most difficult. I have given this topic major emphasis.

Look for the ethical issues brought out by the financial community when evaluating a loan applicant. In this book we take a step-by-step approach to obtaining financing, especially a Small Business Administration–guaranteed loan, with information on alternative financing. Since many people choose to go into business through the route of a franchise, we take an in-depth look at franchising. Included are both a franchise offering circular and the opposite perspective, offered by the American Association of Franchisees and Dealers, which looks at the darker side of franchising.

In the functional area of finance the decisions that are made generally can be reduced to an understanding of time-value-of-money concepts. It is critical to understand the concepts of mortgage amortization and discounting cash flows, on which the financial industry is based. I have found that most students do not have a complete understanding of the time-value-of-money concepts, which would enable them to make the leap to real-world applications. As a small business owner, I feel that these concepts are critical to making informed decisions. Worksheets are included in Chapter 7 for those who would like another look at these concepts.

The marketing function, beginning with marketing research and interwoven with the customer information system, is one of the other critical functional areas. In the interviews with small business owners featured in this book, I found that they keep coming up with the same critical functional areas, although I was not surprised to see that happen. Marketing is one of those critical areas. It doesn't matter what type of business you are in—a failure to sell what you make, or more accurately, to make what will sell—will wipe a business out. Part of the marketing function is dependent on location. Look for that element, especially in the interview about the Burlington Restaurant, to bring home that concept. The marketing research firms interviewed address this same issue.

We will look at the marketing function from the perspectives of marketing research firms as well as advertising media firms. We also blend in the perspectives of several small business entrepreneurs and attempt to address their specific challenges. Unlike finance and accounting, where a step-by-step process can be looked at and followed, marketing is more unique to the individual firm; thus the way marketing concepts are taught is more general in nature. Although the concepts taught in most marketing courses are valid and useful concepts, marketing seems to be a constant challenge for most small business owners. It seems that for most small business owners there is a never-ending search to discover what will work for their businesses cost-effectively and the elimination of what won't work. Marketing is a search for a cost-effective way to build a customer base, although as the marketing research firms will tell you, the customer base is always changing. A business gains new customers and loses other customers as part of the natural ongoing business process, which is why advertising and marketing are so important, especially in a competitive world. More than any other function, marketing is dependent and supported by the quality pillars.

The final function that my interview process brought out as a critical element was the production function. In my years as a unemployment tax auditor, the reason most people went into business for themselves was because they were good at a particular service. The new business venture often boiled down to quality issues of the production of whatever product or service the entrepreneur was selling. This is the baseline for success in a small business venture. Yet I did see many small business fail simply because the quality of their service or the workmanship of their product, which by definition is the production function of their business, was simply not acceptable to the majority of their customers. When customers say "no," you either have to find another customer or go out of business.

One of the best examples I can think of concerning poor service quality causing the demise of a business was a lady who started a computer service business in the territory that I covered. She was selling word processing, payroll, and other bookkeeping services. She had only one employee but could not keep up with her own reporting requirements. I used to stop at her business on a quarterly basis to pick up her payroll report, which was delinquent. It would take her several hours to pull this payroll information on her one employee from her database. We're talking about information from six paychecks. I would stand around her business or go run other errands and then stop back as she struggled to set the proper parameters in her computer program to print the information I needed—all of which could have been done manually in about 3 minutes. I often wondered if her performance was this substandard for her clients, as payroll reporting was one of the services she provided to the public. It was not a great surprise to me when she finally closed the door on the business. From the start this business was simply not workable, due to a number of fundamental functional area flaws, of which the worst was the production function. A small business can buy time to fix some of the functional areas that need to be improved. This is common; many firms struggle constantly to improve one aspect or another of their operation, and the transition is rarely smooth. Yet a certain level of competence in the production area must always be maintained or the customers will turn their backs on the business and walk away, never to return. That is what happened in the case of this computer service business; the customers could not accept the level of service they were getting.

This book does not specifically address the function of production outside the quality of product and/or service pillar approach, because in small business, production is so business specific. It also assumes that before an entrepreneur goes into a particular business, the ability to produce a product or service is inherent. Still, in reading the interviews you should be able to pick up on how intensely most of the entrepreneurs pursue the production function. Most entrepreneurs seem to be engaged in a constant search to maintain and/or improve the quality of their products. They are also constantly searching for ways to improve the efficiency of what they are doing. A learning curve exists with most production activities, so that with experience and time in a business, the production function normally will continue to be improved and to evolve. Without the learning curve to instigate gains and improvements in the production process, many successful firms would have been left by the wayside.

Production and marketing tend to be closely intertwined, because as technology changes and as customer tastes change, a successful business must be able to adapt to and follow the change. In fact, it is better if a business is on the cutting edge and is ahead of the curve, to lead customers in the process of change, but that is rarely the case. Most firms are racing to catch up and to stay somewhat current in a rapidly changing competitive environment. To stay still is to die on the vine of obsolescence, and the production function is a part of that process of change.

In lieu of the production function, I chose to write a section on management to address some of the special issues faced by small business managers. In my experience as a business owner and as a consultant during my tax-auditing years, I saw many situations that either did, or could, put a business in jeopardy. I chose to address management issues such as accelerated business growth and the business downturn cycle, risk management, and other topics.

The bridge model would not be complete without addressing some issues that operate outside the control of the small business manager. To a large extent these are issues that must be incorporated in the management information system to measure and monitor the initiating elements of change: the technological, government or political, legal, socio-economic, and competitive environments. All of these can create opportunities or barriers to success, so we devote a short segment to each of these elements.

A small business does not operate in a vacuum; the events that are going on around the manager often affect the business directly. Ignorance as to the significance of an event, or even lack of awareness of an event, will not change and does not lessen the impact that event can have on the small business. Staying informed by forming and accessing good information sources that provide valid, reliable, and timely information is a critical function. This is easier said than done—developing a good information network can be an overwhelming challenge in light of the information explosion in our society. We can reach information overload very early in the game, and for the small business owner, other matters often seem more pressing. The entrepreneur does, after all, have a business to run.

The bridge model puts existing concepts in a new perspective, so that the reader can develop an appreciation for the many roles that the small business manager must perform. It is also my hope that the bridge model perspective will assist the future entrepreneur to prioritize and visualize more fully the interrelationships among the functional areas of a business. The model should demonstrate to the entrepreneur the importance of doing the right thing: being fair and honest with employees and with businesses and customers who work with you in the pursuit of a better life for all concerned.

• WHY START A BUSINESS?· · · · · · · · · ·

Each year thousands of new businesses are born. Each new proprietor has a dream that his or her idea will work out and that all dreams will come true. People start businesses for many different reasons. For the budding entrepreneur it is important that the motivation to start a business stems from the right reasons and that the wrong reasons can be identified and avoided. Consider the following reasons together with some precautionary notes.

1. *I want to be my own boss because I find it hard to work for my current boss. He or she is such a jerk!* You might want to ask yourself about your other relationships with people: family, co-workers, friends. Do you really like people, and do you really get along well with people? If the answer is "no," how do you propose to deal with all those internal and external relationships? Your customers will be your boss—so will your banker and/or other creditors. If you fail to satisfy customers, your revenue source will dry up. You must deal with employees if you have any. You must deal with suppliers, creditors, governmental agencies, and many others. Business is first and foremost a people enterprise and requires good human relations skills.

2. *I want to be my own boss so that I don't have to work so hard. I don't want to punch a clock—I want the freedom to come and go as I please.* When I bring this concept up among small business owners, the response I often get is a very loud laugh. If free time is your goal, unless the enterprise is highly structured in the sense of limiting the demands it will place on you, small business ownership is probably not your best choice. In a discussion with Jeff Alvey, a banker, one of the

main reasons he stated for business failures was that owners were not willing to work hard enough.[1] The implication is that the boss is generally the first person at work and the last person to leave. Not only must the routine work get done, but also special projects such as repairs, construction, maintenance, or a special order, which may demand that you work evenings, weekends, and even holidays.

You know the old saying, "Make hay while the sun shines." Farmers know that they must plant or harvest or make hay even if it means very long days, because those favorable conditions will not last forever. The same is true in a small business: When conditions are favorable, you do that income-producing activity even if it means very long days. The founders of Ben & Jerry's ice cream were once asked if they had any advice for someone starting a new business. The response was: "get a lot of sleep before you start."[2]

3. *I want to start a business to make a lot of money.* Well, everyone in the United States would like to make a lot of money. It is a reason, but not a reason that can stand on its own. To go into business just to make money is not something customers will accept. They will not use your product or service just so that you can make money. There must be something else that provides real value to the customer.

The reality is often the opposite as far as making a lot of money is concerned, at least at first. The owner is not only the last one to go home at night but is usually the last one to get paid. Everybody else demands to get paid first. To maintain the credibility of your internal and external relationships, everyone else must be paid first. Normally, the employee relationships are the most critical, so they are paid first, then the government, creditors, and suppliers. If any money is left, you get paid. The good news is that if a lot of money is left, you can get paid a lot provided that you do not need the money for expansion: new equipment, fixtures, inventory, and so on. Most businesses generally require a long time to grow.

If you were to take a drive through the main business district or strip in your town and speak to the owner of some of the seemingly successful small businesses, you might discover that some of those firms are second or third generation, although there are some relatively new firms that grew very fast. They are exceptions to the general rule.

4. *I'm going to start a business because I can't find a job that pays what my old job paid.* Many victims of the corporate downsizing going on in the past few years have had a tough time finding a job that is at or near the level of the one they lost, leaving them angry and frustrated. Their response is to buy themselves a job in the form of owning their own small business. Whether this strategy makes sense depends on the fundamentals. For the strategy to work, the person must be able to meet the demands of the marketplace by providing a product or service that enough people want, in order to generate an adequate level of profit. I know of an instance where a former executive started a food service business. The man had 30 years of experience as a corporate executive but no experience in food service. He invested his life's savings, which included cashing out a substantial company retirement. He refinanced his house and put everything into his business. Two years later he was broke and was facing bankruptcy. What will he now do about retirement? In hindsight he would have been far better off to invest his retirement funds in corporate bonds and taken even a minimum-wage job. On the other hand, many seniors own and run successfully campgrounds, trailer parks, tourist novelty shops, and a host of other types of businesses. The key here is to limit one's risk and to know what you are getting into. Experience in the type of business venture you are starting is even more important at age 55 than it is at age 25, because of the limited time left to recover and prepare for retirement income.

Some small business ventures fit the profile of a job. An in-home daycare center, which can be very structured, with specific hours and days of operation, has low startup costs and little risk. The nature of this type of business is very much like a job.

5. *I'm a creative person and will find self-expression in running my own business.* This is valid as long as the proprietor does not get lost in this creativity to the exclusion of such mundane things as paperwork and management. The marketplace rewards creativity. Free enterprise is constantly looking for the proverbial better mouse trap. A unique product or service that is difficult to duplicate can leave a business in a niche by itself. If cash inflow is adequate and expenses are controlled, this type of business has a good chance of success. The key to success here is often the implementation of good management practices, which entails some degree of discipline and the maintenance of good records.

The idea that someone can do a better job, do it faster, or cheaper, or improve, enhance, modify, or find a way to be more efficient is often the stimulus that leads to the eventual launching of a new enterprise. A state of dissatisfaction often results in a decision to launch a new venture.

6. *I want to be in control and I like making decisions. If I run my own business I can make all the decisions.* Most existing small business owners enjoy the control and the decision making. Just remember that all small business owners are responsible for the decision making, whether they enjoy it or not. The entrepreneur will be held responsible even if he or she fails to make decisions. Failure to make decisions or act on critical information can be the worst decision of all. The desire to own a business for control purposes can be a valid reason if the desire stems from dissatisfaction of the way the marketplace is currently meeting a need. This may also inspire a sense of personal confidence that you can do a better job. If your skills, training, and experience exceed your current level of responsibilities, you may be ready to go it alone. Success will depend on how well you really are equipped to handle those responsibilities, as well as your response to the many variables over which you have no control.

Some people choose to run a business as a way to prepare for retirement, not just in the sense of having something to occupy their time but in the sense of preparing financially for retirement. This group tends to run sideline businesses on a part-time basis, such as a lawn care or cleaning service. Other businesses tend to be seasonal, such as a bait shop or a painting service. Often, the intent is to remain part-time or seasonal, to supplement income and build a nest egg for retirement. Some invest in real estate as a vehicle to build equity and diversify financial holdings away from the stock market. Others start a business to give them something to do; still others consider running a business as a form of tax shelter. The first group is going to be concerned with limiting their risk. One does not risk life savings because of boredom. This type of business tends to be primarily a hobby. A limit is also placed on the amount of time the business will demand. A campground or tree-moving service is seasonal in nature and has limited demands, so that retirement can still be enjoyed. Those concerned with the tax benefits of a small business are looking for a business that will allow them to depreciate assets while the value of the business appreciates. In addition, the expense write-offs associated with vehicles, cellular phones, and office equipment can often lead to a tax loss, which can be used to offset other income. The Internal Revenue Service (IRS) tends to scrutinize closely some of these outside businesses, such as say a horse ranch owned by a heart surgeon.

One principle of small business management is that a proprietor must assess a situation at a particular time and in a particular place and perceive an opportunity. That opportunity may stem from a unique set of circumstances, possibly an unserved or underserved market, or a new technology that creates a window of opportunity. If the assumptions surrounding a business opportunity are valid at a particular point in time and the decision is made to purchase the inputs required to take advantage of the perceived opportunity, the proprietor will expend his or her capital. In accounting terms, the funds are *sunk,* meaning that these assets are no longer liquid—that a capital commitment has been made. In other words, the entrepreneur is locked into a financial commitment, and to a very large degree financial flexibility has been lost.

If you could take a photograph in time, to view the circumstances surrounding a financial decision and then compare those circumstances with a point in the future, you will probably notice that the situation will have changed considerably. What was a glowing opportunity at one point may well evaporate in the near future. We live in a very dynamic, constantly changing environment. Change is the one constant in business that you can count on.

The successful small business manager must be adaptable to those changes, which create the real challenges and often create tremendous adversity which the small business manager must overcome to survive. The proprietor must be able to recognize those shifts in the environment and react correctly. Sometimes, such a reaction is difficult because the entrepreneur is locked into a set of expenditures that has been sunk into assets purchased from the perspective of a previous set of circumstances. This is the control the new proprietor assumes with the decision to enter into business for himself or herself. The proprietor is responsible for the outcome of those decisions, be they positive or negative. It requires a certain strength of character to live with such uncertainty and the pressures that accompany it.

It is one of those ironies in business life that in a sense the dynamic nature of the world around us creates those windows of opportunity that bring many small business ideas to fruition. Those same dynamics are a major cause for creating an environment that can also cause the failure of many of those same small businesses.

7. *Corporate America is a cold, cruel place to work in, with no compassion for people, only a desire for more and more profit. I'm so stressed that I want out, and the best way to do this is to start my own business.* Think about this carefully; be sure you are running to something and not away from something. The costs of a failed business far exceed job dissatisfaction. I have worked with business owners who were so depressed they could barely function, completely devoid of the ability to implement creative solutions to save their failing enterprises. In one extreme case, such a depression resulted in a suicide. Even a successful enterprise will create stress. If you have a family it is difficult to isolate that stress and keep family and business separate. It takes a strong marital relationship to survive a business failure. It takes a tremendous emotional toll on the entrepreneur, and failure can take a big bite out of the person's self-image and self-confidence. Past failures can make the entrepreneur a lot more conservative and a lot more tentative in successive ventures. Sometimes people learn from their past; sometimes they are controlled by their past.

Why should the customer choose your product or your service? The answer to this question is the real reason why you should start your own business. Therein also lies the answer to the question of what kind of business you should start. Your business will almost always be a natural extension of yourself: to capitalize on who you are, especially your gifts and special talents.

PROFILE IN ENTREPRENEURSHIP: ARDEN BARLOW, THE BURLINGTON RESTAURANT[3]

Having answered in a broad sense why people go into business, it is useful to look at a profile of a typical entrepreneur. A number of studies have been done that attempt to build a profile of a typical entrepreneur, but people who start small businesses are as distinct as the businesses themselves. Yet some common characteristics do appear.

In the course of writing this book, I visited with a number of small business owners, the first of whom was Arden Barlow, who owns and manages the Burlington Restaurant in Sioux Falls, South Dakota. The Burlington is located on 41st Street in Sioux Falls, a prime location in this city of more than 100,000 people.

In part I wanted to visit with Mr. Barlow to discover why he was successful while so many others who attempted to make it in the restaurant business failed on that same street. I personally knew of several restaurant business failures within a two-block radius of the Burlington. I asked Mr. Barlow to share his success story and hoped to glean some recipe for success to pass on to you.

Mr. Barlow, currently in his early 60s, purchased the building that is now the Burlington Restaurant with a partner in 1984. He purchased that building because he felt, and was later proved correct, that the site had great potential. In fact, he indicates that hardly a week goes by when a real estate agent doesn't inquire whether the building is for sale. To which Mr. Barlow's favorite response is: "Everything I have is for sale, for the right price, except my wife."

When I asked Mr. Barlow why he thought he became successful in the restaurant business, his response was: "A lot of things; the most important is having a good deal of experience and knowing what your doing. You have to know every position in the business because you never know when someone is not going to show up, and then you have to fill in." People get sick, they quit, they don't show up, and that usually happens at the worst possible moment. You have to be able to fill in or the customer suffers.

Mr. Barlow did have a lot of experience prior to purchasing the building, the former Sambo's Restaurant, which he remodeled into the Burlington. His first restaurant experience came after he had spent about 16 years working in a locker plant, where he learned the meat-cutting trade. He signed on in what was then a partnership arrangement with the Sambo's Restaurant chain. That experience dates back to 1974.

Sambo's offered an intensive training program. They would put together a class of what they called partners and send them off to Santa Barbara, California, to work in one of their busiest restaurants. At Santa Barbara the new partner would start out as a dishwasher then move up and train in every other position within the restaurant. The idea was to train prospective managers who were grounded in all the day-to-day operational aspects of the restaurant business.

Mr. Barlow reflected back on his class of prospective partners, indicating that they came from quite a mix of backgrounds. They were the sons of lawyers, bankers, businesspeople, and blue-collar workers. Mr. Barlow says that as he looks back at the class photograph and picks out people who made

(*continued*)

(*continued*)

it and those who didn't, there doesn't seem to be any logic in why one made it and another did not. In many cases it seemed that those who appeared to be least likely to succeed actually did succeed, while others who you think should succeed, failed.

Sambo's management would put these partners through the hoops in the day-to-day operation of a restaurant and would complement that hands-on training with classroom training. The experience was designed to be very intense. A favorite technique used was that after an already grueling day, trainees were called back to the restaurant at about 2:00 A.M. to help out, due to the unexpected arrival of a busload of customers.

Management wanted to make certain that their new partners understood that to own and manage a successful restaurant was going to take long hours in a fast-paced environment. The training was designed to train restaurant managers who would operate an outlet for three or four years and then be promoted to a district management position. As a district manager they would then oversee five or six other restaurants in an assigned territory.

Mr. Barlow managed a Sambo's outlet for about four years before being sent on the road as a district manager, where he spent a little over three years in that capacity. In late 1979 the company, which at that time had nearly 1100 outlets, shut down. Mr. Barlow said that the irony of it all was that the person who terminated him was one of his classmates from the Sambo's company school in Santa Barbara. A few weeks later that manager was himself terminated. The company completed its store closings by early 1980.

Unemployed after his termination from Sambo's, Mr. Barlow fell back on some of his past experiences and went to work for awhile for a local grocery store. A few months later he was hired as a district manager for Country Kitchen, a restaurant chain based in Minneapolis, Minnesota. With Country Kitchen, Mr. Barlow's duties were greatly expanded. He had 21 restaurant outlets to oversee and covered a territory extending over the Dakotas, part of Minnesota, and into Saskatchewan, Canada.

Mr. Barlow stayed with Country Kitchen as a district manager for a little over three years, until 1984, when he purchased the Burlington site. He said that all through those years he saw a number of the old Sambo's restaurant sites which were still sitting vacant. The one on 41st Street in Sioux Falls, South Dakota had been stripped of fixtures back in 1979 when it was closed and had just sat vacant all those years. Mr. Barlow kept telling a friend that they should buy one of those sites. He said that he probably never would have done it on his own, but one day his partner said, "Well, if you want to buy one, let's do it." So they each put up 50 percent of the money and along with an SBA loan purchased the site in Sioux Falls. The remodeling concept was to use a train-car-like decor—thus the name Burlington—which opened the door for business in 1984.

With a little hindsight it's fairly easy to see why Mr. Barlow was successful. If you were the banker 1984, would you have gone with this SBA loan on the Burlington? Probably most of us would have. Why? Well, for one thing, the man had the experience. He had worked in a restaurant, had managed a restaurant, and had acted as a district manager overseeing multiple operations—all a big, big advantage in favor of increasing his odds of success. The second strong supporting issue was that both the price and the location were right. Sioux Falls had a population of around 80,000 people and was growing fast. In 1997 it had a population of around 120,000, with no end of growth in sight. During the early 1980s most people in the community expected strong growth. The community's growth prospects were a very positive force supporting the chances of success for the Burlington and for Mr. Barlow.

That's not the whole story. On its grand opening in 1984, the Burlington still had to convince the local public it was a place to patronize. The business had to be managed so that the quality of service and the quality of food were such that customers would want to return.

The Burlington is a full-service, full-menu restaurant. The clientele varies but is supported by a strong base of regulars. Many seniors like the Burlington; they enjoy the breakfast buffet and are also heavily represented as evening patrons. Working-class people often patronize the Burlington because of the food and service. It's a nice sit-down type of restaurant, a place where you can relax to eat. The street is usually busy, so many of the patrons are drop-in trade. From a marketing standpoint, location is undoubtedly the restaurant's biggest advantage. In fact, Mr. Barlow needs to do little advertising. Location, word of mouth, and repeat customers are enough to keep the restaurant operating near capacity.

The key to management success in a restaurant is, first, to have enough customer volume to make the place financially healthy. For Mr. Barlow his location met that requirement. The second requirement is to establish a standard of quality in the food and service that will retain the customers who do patronize the establishment. The third element of success is to maintain food and labor costs that are acceptable within the design of the establishment, to meet projected profit levels. Successful management of a restaurant entails all those elements, plus the implementation of systems to train and supervise employees and to monitor smooth operation of the business on a day-to-day basis. These elements must be developed and in place to operate a controlled operation that runs smoothly, efficiently, and profitably.

I asked Mr. Barlow what his management style was. He responded; "You could call my management style that of a family. I try to hire people who are honest, and I tell them that with honesty you can build trust." Then he went on to tell me a story about seeing an Oprah Winfrey program on which Kelsey Grammer from *Frasier* was a guest. Oprah asked Kelsey how he got into show business, and Kelsey explained that he was working as a dishwasher at a restaurant when an opportunity to audition for a part came up. Kelsey asked his boss for the afternoon off, but his boss said no, he needed him. Kelsey took the afternoon off anyway, and when he returned, the boss called him into the office and informed him that he was letting him go because Kelsey just didn't seem to fit into this family-type operation. Both Oprah and Kelsey laughed at this story, thinking it funny that anyone would or should take a dishwashing job seriously.

It was obvious to Mr. Barlow, that neither Kelsey Grammer nor Oprah Winfrey have ever managed a restaurant. Neither had a clue as to the importance of everyone working together to maintain a high-quality food product along with good service. Nor did they understand how one missing component interrupts the smooth flow of activity. They did not understand

(*continued*)

(continued)

that Kelsey Grammer's boss actually did need him that day. To Oprah and Kelsey the concept that anyone would need a dishwasher was a joke.

Someone once asked me my opinion of what it was like to run a restaurant based on my experience. I responded by asking them if they had ever had guests over for a Thanksgiving meal. I indicated that running a restaurant was like having 300 people over for a special meal three times a day every day. To do a good job you need the dishwasher, the cook, and everybody else in the organization.

In visiting with Mr. Barlow, it was easy to tell that he not only believed but practiced that family management philosophy. Sioux Falls has a current unemployment rate below 3 percent. Food service help is hard to find in this city, yet Mr. Barlow's Burlington, with only 13 employees, has three employees who have been with him for over 10 years. Employee turnover is very low at the Burlington. Mr. Barlow frets over the fact that he cannot pay his people more than he does and that he cannot afford some of the fringe benefits that he would like to provide for his employees. When you visit with Mr. Barlow's employees, you can read in their eyes and in their voices that they think a lot of their boss.

I asked Mr. Barlow how he keeps his labor costs in line. He explained that his labor ratio is a little higher than it should be, but goes on to explain that South Dakota has had a hard winter and there are days when weather affects his business. He said, "I look at my records from last year and use them to make sales volume projections. From those projections I do my scheduling. With the way this winter has been, I know I should send some of the help home, or not bring them in at all on bad days, but they have bills to pay as well, so I bite the bullet a little bit."

I asked Mr. Barlow how many hours he puts in a week himself at the restaurant. He told me usually around 100 hours. I asked him if he has always done that, and he said, "Yes. I guess that's my control system is being here." I asked Mr. Barlow if his wife also worked in the business, and he told me that she is a schoolteacher and teaches at a school in Sioux Falls.

I explained to Mr. Barlow that in my own restaurant one of the reasons I got out of the business was burnout. The long hours were putting pressure on my family life, especially when I had small children at home. I asked Arden if that was an issue for him. Mr. Barlow's response was that he would never do this with children at home.

There seems to be a trend in the small business world that entrepreneur types often come from families where one or both parents were self-employed, so I asked Mr. Barlow about his background. Was his father or mother self-employed? He then told me part of the story of his formative years. Mr. Barlow said his father died when he was 5. His mother was left in 1939 with seven children: no life insurance, no social security, nothing. He said: "We were very poor, so poor in fact that we would not have had heat had not some farmer dropped off a load of corncobs in the yard which we could burn for heat." One of his jobs after school was to take a pail and walk the railroad tracks picking up pieces of coal that fell off train cars. He said, "I don't like to talk about this much, especially to these young kids I hire. They think it's some kind of story and can't imagine anything like that. Growing up like that makes you appreciate everything, though; after that, nothing seems very hard."

In looking at a business like Mr. Barlow's Burlington we realize that his is just one story among many, but some common and recognizable characteristics are present that contributed heavily to the success of the Burlington. In this story and others that follow it, one of the key elements is experience. Not just experience, but the right kind of experience. In the Burlington's situation, as with most retail businesses, location is of utmost importance. Mr. Barlow possesses a demonstrated understanding of the numbers. He understands where his food costs should be and where they actually are. He understands where his labor costs should be and where they are. He understands the equipment and its operation. Mr. Barlow understands the production function and the relationship that the quality of product and service have on the continual profitability of the business.

Mr. Barlow knows who his customers are and why they patronize his establishment. It's not that he designed a building to take on the atmosphere of a railroad car; that's just part of the overall presentation of the product and service. What is offered on the menu, the price, the portion size and quality of the food, and the level and quality of service provided by the wait staff all play a part in the marketing component for the Burlington. Location does make the Burlington readily accessible to customers, which reduces the need for advertising, but without supporting that location with a quality food product and good service the Burlington could easily go out of business like so many others have. It is Mr. Barlow's ability to make it all happen that is the key to his success, and that ability is firmly grounded in experience.

Even with Mr. Barlow's background, I sensed an element of uncertainty in him about starting this business. He felt confident enough to start the business, and felt he could make it work, but he also understood that it would take a lot of effort. He understood that the work was never over, that to be successful would take constant diligence, and that providing high levels of product and service was an ongoing event—so much so that Mr. Barlow was spending 100 hours a week to make it happen. That's commitment.

Your business should be something you want to do, something you are passionate about. If you start a business, you will spend thousands of hours each year pursuing that activity. If it consumes the lion's share of your time and energy, that time is best spent in an activity that you truly enjoy. At a very basic level, that activity needs to be fun lest it becomes work and eventually degrades into drudgery. A sense of fun can permeate an entire organization. Fun creates an atmosphere that your customers want to be a part of, and keeps them coming back. It creates an environment that your employees enjoy and want to be part of as well. Enjoying your work helps you maintain your creative energies, which will be required to solve the myriad of problems that arise.

• QUESTIONS FOR DISCUSSION·······

1. The bridge model implies that for a small business to be successful over the long haul, it must be grounded within a broad definition of ethics. Do you accept or reject this hypothesis? Explain your reasoning.

2. In your opinion, what is the most valid reason for going into business for yourself?

3. Some of the wrong reasons for going into business for oneself were outlined in the text. In your opinion, do you think a wrong reason could lead a small business to failure? Explain your reasoning.

4. How did Mr. Barlow describe his management style?

5. Does Mr. Barlow's management style fit the bridge model? Explain your position.

2 Entrepreneurial Qualities · · · · · · · · · · ·

Chapter Objectives

- To provide an appreciation of the complexities and demands placed on the small business owner.

- To begin to build insight as to the uniqueness of each small business by exposing readers to the entrepreneurial experience through small business profiles.

- To assist in realizing the importance of teamwork in managing a successful enterprise and to provide insight and tools that students can use to develop a cohesive team.

For an entrepreneur to be successful, certain qualities need to be present. Successful entrepreneurs are as diverse as any group of people, but some common characteristics are present.

• CHARACTERISTICS OF A SUCCESSFUL ENTREPRENEUR

Entrepreneurs tend to be self-motivated. They have the ability to set the alarm clock to a relatively early hour to begin the day's work. In their minds they feel the need to get going because they have so many things that need to be done. A good day ends with "Boy, did I get a lot done today!" Not all are workaholics, but many are. In part, this tendency stems from inner drive: by definition, self-motivation.

An entrepreneur will tend to have a somewhat unique perspective on the world. Corporations seek a top management team that is visionary in nature. Such a team can evaluate the environment around them, gather the right information to assess a situation, predict the direction a market or new market will take, then formulate a course of action. From the standpoint of the firm's resources and capabilities, they lead the firm into the future, to maximize returns for investors. To some degree, entrepreneurs do the same thing, but they do it alone and on a microscale. To call entrepreneurs visionary is correct, but to call them opportunistic may sometimes be more accurate.

One implication is that the entrepreneur is a leader. Not all are. To be a leader, you must have followers. To have followers generally requires a strong personality and a good many people skills. Entrepreneurs often have strong personalities and an unshakable belief in themselves and in their abilities. They will need this to succeed. To start a new business from the ground up, especially in an area where something has never been tried before will take a great deal of resolve. People around them will often think them a little crazy. Typical comments might include: "You're going to do what?" "I can't imagine attempting something like that." "Boy, that takes guts." "My wife would divorce me if I tried something like that." The ability to live with comments like these require a great degree of self-confidence. An entrepreneur's sense of self-worth tends to come from within, not from the outside validation that others provide. Entrepreneurs tend to be able to stand by themselves. In a sense many are loners, but often loners with people skills, some to the point of being manipulators. They get what they want. Regardless, they must be able to withstand a certain amount of societal pressure.

Entrepreneurs often value going it alone, being independent, and being in charge. Like everybody else, they obtained their system of values through their socialization process. That is why many entrepreneurs have a father or mother who was self-employed in a business or profession. Or, from an early age, they learned to stand on their own or go it alone. Out of necessity, many had to develop a sense of self-reliance. They depend on themselves to take care of themselves.

The entrepreneur tends to be intelligent, and now more than ever, educated. Education is becoming more and more of a requirement, due to the complexity of the society in which we live, but many exceptions exist. The entrepreneur must be somewhat organized. To gather the right type of information for the decision-making process, obtain financing, muster the resources, purchase and install the equipment, hire personnel, market the product or service, and maintain the records required takes a high degree of organizational skills.

My father, himself an entrepreneur, owned a farm and ranch in western North Dakota, and I would often hear him complain about his hired men, and often about his sons as well, with this statement: "I don't know, they just can't see work." What he meant by that statement was that the entrepreneur in a way sees the big picture, yet can also be very detail oriented. They know what needs to be done and in what sequence. They have the ability to organize and the ability to prioritize. Without the ability to organize resources and activities, nothing gets done. By definition, a business organizes the resources to produce a product or service which the public needs and does so at a profit. At the end of a good day the entrepreneur feels a sense of "Boy, did I get a lot done today!" Another good day may end in the statement "We sure made some money today." The last statement validates the entrepreneur's management and organizational skills, as well as confirming that his or her vision was correct.

The successful entrepreneur generally has a certain degree of self-discipline and certainly the ability to delay gratification. In part this stems from the ability to prioritize. Not only does the small business manager need to know what needs to get done, and in what order, but a prioritized list of inputs needs to be developed as well. Those inputs need to flow into the organization at the right time. The entrepreneur is usually stretching financial resources to the limit. Not everything that is wanted can be had. Sometimes not even everything that is needed can be afforded. To overspend can jeopardize the firm's financial future and the ability to meet current financial demands. The entrepreneur needs to be able to delay gratification—a skill arising from a personality or character trait stemming from self-discipline.

From a personal standpoint the ability to delay gratification means that certain things cannot be afforded. The nice home, right car, right clothing, entertainment, big boy or big girl toys may have to wait until the business can afford to pay its owner-manager a sufficient wage. It is even more difficult to delay gratification for the owner of a small business, because often the cash flow is sufficient. It is easy to delay for two weeks the sales tax owed and use that couple of thousand to make a down payment on a new car.

As a small business owner-manager the very survival of the business may depend on the entrepreneur's ability to delay gratification in the form of financial self-discipline. It would be nice to have a new pickup truck, new office furniture, and/or new equipment to work with. Yet the expenditures could well overload the business's ability to remain healthy.

An entrepreneur needs the ability to problem-solve. Various roadblocks will obscure the entrepreneur's vision. The ability to be flexible and adaptable, to find another way, is a requirement. The entrepreneur is generally competitive and at the least very tenacious. *Quit* is a word that does not set very well. If entrepreneurs are to overcome the inevitable obstacles, they must have the ability to stick with something to the end. This requires a bit of personal courage and strength of character, sometimes to a fault. In other words, some entrepreneurs won't quit when they should, and throw good money after bad in an attempt to see the thing through or somehow make it work.

Successful entrepreneurs tend to be very knowledgeable in specific areas. That's often why they started their particular businesses in the first place. This knowledge may stem from a skill that has been developed. Many entrepreneurs are perfectionists. This knowledge base often is fueled by an unquenchable desire to learn every little detail they can about something. I mentioned before that many business ideas are an outcrop of a person's passion to do something, to be creative. Many entrepreneurs are creative; they think in new and different ways. Maybe this trait is why some people in our society look at the true entrepreneur almost in awe.

Entrepreneurs are just people striving to get their needs met, and they do so through owning a small business.

As you probably gathered by reading thus far, a perfect entrepreneurial profile does not exist. No magic formula or combination of personality traits can make someone successful. You cannot take a personality or preference test, with a result telling you that you have the ideal traits and personality makeup of an entrepreneur. In fact, sometimes it may seem that a contradiction exists. The successful entrepreneur doesn't seem at all like the type. As Mr. Barlow said: "You know, when I look back at the photograph of all those prospective partners in that Sambo's class, the ones who made it and those who failed doesn't make a lot of sense. The ones you would have expected to succeed didn't and some of those you would think didn't have a chance, made it."[1] Sometimes the difference between success and failure can be minuscule—like the difference in speed between those who finish first and second in a 100-yard dash. That last little bit of effort and determination can sometimes make the difference.

I was discussing the topic of small business success with the part owner of a local marketing research firm. As we discussed the changes in the business makeup of our community, Paul Schiller said, "I don't care what anybody says: part of what you need to make it in business is a little luck."[2] That statement took me back to an incident in my own life. During the early 1980s at the peak of the oil boom in the Rocky Mountain region, I owned Sentry Safety Inc., an oil field safety service company, a small firm employing four or five men but quite successful. I had just purchased a nice home and was having a painter in to do some painting. I was at the kitchen table trying to finish some paperwork before I hit the field. The painter turned to me and said, "You're sure lucky." It took me a moment to figure out what he meant, and then I responded: "You know from the outside looking in it sure looks like I'm one lucky fellow. Like I just fell into this thing, with a new home, a fleet of new pickups, successful business, and all. Did you know that I work seven days a week, 365 days a year? Did you know that I risked everything I had and everything I could borrow to start this business? Did you know that I risk my life and have people who are willing to risk their lives working with poison gas and sometimes oil well blowouts? Did you know that when the phone rings it usually means being gone on a job for two or three days straight? That means 24 hours a day, trying to catch a nap in the pickup when the situation allows, and eating out of a lunch pail."

All the painter said was "Oh." But the painter was right in a sense, and so was Paul Schiller. Beyond that "ain't I great attitude," a degree of luck must exist for a business to be successful. There must be a market for your product or service. A change in that market could deny your business before you get it off the ground. If a key competitor moves in and/or targets your firm, you could be driven out of business before you are up and running. It takes the cooperation of others even to allow you the opportunity to try: people like bankers, suppliers, customers, employees, and others. Everyone involved risks something to one degree or another so that you and your business can have a chance. Luck does play a part: the right product at the right time, or being in the right place at the right time. Not everything in life is planned.

I started out talking about persistence, and as long as I'm on Sentry Safety stories, let me share with you how I made our first sale. Financially we were down to about two weeks of existence due to a number of unforeseen delays. My first sale came from the last call on a day that started at 5:00 A.M. I had covered over 300 miles that day and was driving past a refinery at 9:00 at night, tired and frustrated. The lights were on, I pulled in, and as luck would have it, the operations engineer was on duty. It just so happened that we provided a service he needed and a project to clean their oil storage tanks was on his itinerary. A deal was made to provide the safety equipment, and we were on the job site at 6:00 A.M. the following morning. Would we have gone under without that particular job? I don't know, but time was running out fast. Determination, tenacity, luck, destiny—in the end it doesn't really matter which. Success is often a little of each, and failure a possibility around the next corner. Success can only be measured in the past tense; it must be projected and earned in the future tense.

Entrepreneurs must have a personality that enables them to adjust to uncertainty. It generally takes a long time to reach a level of comfort about that uncertainty. Personally, I hate going to the bank to ask to borrow money. I think most people have a similar dislike of that until a business is mature enough and has established itself, particularly in the sense of establishing some security and cushion in the balance sheet. A sense of financial unease tends to prevail for most entrepreneurs. Entrepreneurs need to be able to live with a degree of uncertainty. Some entrepreneurs are more comfortable with debt than others. Each entrepreneur's level of comfort with debt and financial uncertainty is translated into how fast he or she is willing to grow the business. Be aware, though, that growth or lack of it is almost always thrust upon a small business owner and is somewhat difficult to control. Unplanned growth is more prevalent in the early stages of a business than at a later stage. By this I mean that in the beginning months and years a new proprietor is attempting to carve a niche out of the market, and revenue from almost any source is welcome. This sometimes leads to product or service offshoots that were not originally planned on. After a business has established itself, the focus tends to become narrower and more specialized. The business is less able to and less willing to step outside the box, so to speak. Growth tends to be more planned and less sporadic. Success and the confidence of past success enables the business owner more easily to say no to jobs or sales that do not fit into the overall strategy.

A small business is most at risk during that critical first year, after a concept is formulated in the mind of an entrepreneur and finally put on paper. This concept stems from the entrepreneur's evaluation and assessment of the current variables around him or her. The financing is somehow obtained, and the organization, planning, and implementation evolve into the production of a good or service in the marketplace. The level of acceptance by customers determines the firm's level of productivity. From that point forward, as long as market conditions do not change, the entrepreneurial process is more one of management than one of creation. The risk factor drops precipitously. Good management in a somewhat stable environment can take a business into the next generation or next phase of growth, as many have. Most entrepreneurs are uncomfortable in this initial phase. A small group thrive on the excitement and challenge of the startup phase, which can create an adrenalin rush. For some entrepreneurs once the excitement of the startup phase is over, they can become complacent and bored. Some entrepreneurs will tend to sell their business after the startup phase is complete and move on. Occasionally, the personality of the entrepreneur will lead him or her to make decisions that will cause the business to self-destruct or the person will create some type of crisis that requires his or her creative abilities to survive, providing that excitement again. Such personality profiles are best left to the psychology department, but many of us can recognize people and or businesses that appear to fit this profile.

At first glance it would seem that to be an entrepreneur, one must like to assume risk or they would not risk it all, everything they have, and all that they can borrow to launch a venture. I believe that most entrepreneurs are actually risk adverse. It appears to others that they are taking an awful chance. Entrepreneurs often actually attempt to eliminate the risk of the unknown. They do so originally from the perspective of being very confident in themselves and their abilities, and through a thorough investigation that leads them to make decisions based on knowledge or at least based on reliable information. Entrepreneurs generally have some experience in what they are attempting. They may try to eliminate financial risk by limiting debt in their structure, by growing a part-time business, or by preselling a customer base. On occasion, all they have and all they are is laid on the line, but few like that position. They do what they do because that's who they are.

In the course of writing this book and visiting with entrepreneurs I would often walk away from an interview with feelings of gratitude that I was not still in business for myself. Yet I can't help but feel a twinge of nostalgia and admiration for the people I met who were attempting to make their dreams come true. For entrepreneurs to succeed it seems that sometimes it is only their dreams that sustain them: their dreams and the faith they have in themselves that they can make their businesses work. In fact, I think the combination of faith and/or confidence in themselves, and a dream worth fighting for, is a requirement for success. That commitment must be strong enough to sustain the entrepreneur, and drive him or her onward to persevere over the obstacles that will inevitably befall them. The desire to realize their dreams must be strong enough to make the work, the long hours, and the personal sacrifices worth it. Generally, entrepreneurs must place a high personal value on being in business for themselves or else they would simply get frustrated and quit.

I would like to expand on the concept of placing a high personal value on owning a small business. If the entrepreneur is married, it is often critical that the spouse share this value, and share it to reasonably the same degree, for the business to succeed. Without this shared value, when the business reaches those points of peak demand on time, energy, and resources at extreme levels, a less than fully committed spouse will have feelings of resentment and begin to push for concessions from the spouse. At the point where the commitment to run a small business becomes just not worth it to the spouse, it becomes very difficult for the entrepreneur to sustain the desire for both. A choice will soon have to be made unless some compromise or middle ground can be found where both the relationship and the business can continue.

Some spouses work together in a business, which creates its own set of problems. For other couples, only one works the business, while the other provides support, moral or financial. It is rare, if not impossible, to separate business and family. The demands and the stress of starting and managing a small business tends to spill over into the entrepreneur's personal life. The greater the extent to which joint decision making is used, the more likely both spouses will share in the ownership and consequences of those decisions, thus minimizing resentment between spouses. On the other hand, attempting to share decisions in the same functional area can be fertile ground for disagreement. In the end, marital relations in a small business environment must be resolved by the couples themselves. How one couple resolve differences and share responsibilities and exert a span of control will not necessarily work for the next couple.

If a prioritized list were to be created concerning the personal qualities required for an entrepreneur to be successful, the list would probably be created most accurately from the perspective of hindsight. If I were to prioritize that list for myself, based on my personal businesses experiences, I would list the spousal support first. I mentioned that to a small business owner friend of mine and he concurred. I also asked a banker how important the support of one's spouse was in a loan consideration, to which he responded, "big."

Let me propose an analogy: Not having the support of your spouse is like showing up for a fight with one hand tied behind your back. My wife once told me that having a husband in small business was like putting up with a mistress. All my time, energy, and money went to support this business mistress and not my spouse. The above are major contributing reasons why I am teaching and writing about small business management rather than actually running a small business.

One other point that you may find interesting and perhaps a trifle frightening. Throughout my years as a tax auditor and in the process of writing this book I visited with and personally know many small business owners. On a number of occasions almost out of the blue, the proprietor would begin to talk about his or her business life and would often make a statement like, "If I had to do this over again, I don't think I'd do it." I think many of these people felt they could confide in me since I had been in their shoes. To some degree the entrepreneur was looking at my life from the outside in much the same way that most of you are doing with the entrepreneur. Entrepreneurs would see a government employee, working a 40-hour week, someone who could go home at the end of the day and leave the job behind, or even leave the job for another. This all looked good to them, at least for a moment. I think in part they wanted to talk to someone because they were lonely. The gentlemen that comes to mind as I write this was surrounded by as many as 100 employees but was still lonely because his job as a small business manager carried with it certain expectations. The small business owner has many lonely moments, many of which require a decision. It is difficult for them to find someone who understands what they are going through; it is also difficult for them to find someone they can confide in. Fortunately, there seems to be a trend toward peer groups, where business owners share experiences and even financial data with each other.

• WHAT TYPE OF BUSINESS TO START · · · ·

A good starting point in deciding what type of business you should start, or if you should consider starting a business, begins with understanding who and what you are. In a society such as ours, few people understand themselves—a fact borne out by the number of counselors and psychiatrists employed. Most people are running to satisfy expectations and demands placed on them from the outside. They never stop long enough to spend time with themselves to get to know that person inside. To get to know that person inside generally requires a degree of isolation and quiet. Our world is one of overstimulation, where most people hide from themselves, constantly in a state of overstimulation. Surrounded by people and noise even when alone, the television, stereo, or radio are on: something, anything, to drown out the quiet.

A period of reflection and meditation in solitude to acquire a degree of personal understanding is often required before making life-altering changes. Without a sense of self, the tendency exists to continually chase that "something out there." "I want to go into business to get rich." "I want to make a lot of money." Such reasoning is dangerously superficial. Begin with the right reason for you; go into business if doing so will bring a sense of fulfillment to you.

Every person brings himself or herself into a business. Personal strengths and personal weaknesses within the context of a level of skill and talent will tend to create for the entrepreneur a realm of opportunity and a realm of constraints. One's personal strengths need to be strong enough on which to base a workable business concept, and personal weaknesses must not be such that they could cause the business to fail. For some people, as in the case of the following small business profile, the entrepreneurs always knew the type of business they wanted to start.

PROFILE IN ENTREPRENEURSHIP: JAN AND PAT GARRITY,
PRAIRIE GARDENS[3]

Pat Garrity met his future wife, Jan, while attending South Dakota State University. During the 1970s, both Jan and Pat were studying horticulture and had a particular interest in orchards. That interest was sparked in large part by a professor and by some field trips they took to visit apple orchards in Minnesota.

The 1970s spawned a certain degree of romanticism, of which running an orchard seemed to fit the romantic back-to-nature lifestyle. After graduation the Garritys moved to the state of Washington, where they were both employed on a 100-acre orchard, working initially as apple pickers and eventually managing that orchard. I asked Jan how important that experience was in eventually operating their own orchard. Jan indicated, "very beneficial, except the only thing I can say is that we were going to run our place so much differently than it was run by the boss we were working for. Ours was going to be so much better. Now we kind of know where he was coming from." Neither Pat nor Jan came from a farm or agricultural background at all. Pat is the son of a banker, and while Jan's parents lived on a farm, Jan's father actually made his living as a writer and author.

Pat said that "in moving to Washington we really learned a lot about the industry, about how much work it is, and how dedicated you have to be to make it. One of the things we didn't realize, especially since we were not raised on a farm, was the lack of guarantees that existed in agriculture. You could do everything right, from a marketing and production perspective, you can have all your ducks in a row, but if the good Lord say's your only going to get 1200 bushels of apples this year, then that's all your going to get. You have nothing to back up your marketing efforts with; if you buy product, you begin to lose the concept. That is something we probably could have adjusted to a little easier had we been raised on a farm."

For the Garritys, getting used to the unpredictable weather was a big adjustment. Jan said: "In Washington the weather is ideal for apples; it's like raising corn here in South Dakota. It took us several years to get used to the unpredictability of the weather." The unpredictability associated with the weather has forced the Garritys to rethink and modify their original production-based marketing strategy.

According to Pat: "We really do need to maintain the perception that everything is a piece of cake, because our whole concept is based on entertainment farming. If you want to keep that entertainment aspect in it, you have to make it appear that this is the greatest thing in the world—it is so romantic—when in reality the behind-the-scenes events can be kind of gut wrenching."

Jan went on to explain that in Washington, although that experience was really helpful, it was limited to the production concept—not unlike agriculture in the rest of the country, which is production based and production oriented in the sense that profitability is attained in a commodity environment by producing quantity. Success is achieved by producing huge generic quantities with small profit margins. That avenue was essentially closed to the Garritys, who were trying to create a successful orchard with some 3000 apple trees on their 55 South Dakota acres. This limited production capability forced the Garritys into a new concept. Pat indicated that it took a long time to come out of that mentality. "We were very much production oriented. We came out of college production oriented, we went to Washington production oriented, we came back home production oriented. The entire industry is that way, almost all agriculture is conducted in that way. You go to the agricultural banks to get your loans and they are production oriented; everything is context back to the concept that if you can get the product, you can get the income. It took us a long time to understand that if you can't get the product, you need to come up with another way to still come up with the income."

The Garritys began that search for another way through trade magazines and direct marketing associations, and began to look at what people were doing in other states. Some time in the early 1980's the Garritys began to develop the concept of entertainment farming as it would apply to Prairie Gardens: "that if we were only going to get so many apples at least we can remove the price part of the commodity; we can at least control the price." Pat said; "The pick-your-own concept was a given from the beginning, but it was hard to envision that after spending 80 hours a week in the field, someone else would consider those same chores as entertainment. When we finally began to understand that the farm atmoshpere was entertainment, at that point we really began to sell it as such." Once Pat and Jan realized the concept of entertainment farming, they began to carry that concept to the next step, which was to begin building tradition into the concept through annual pumpkin and apple fests. "It became something to do; the families continue to come back until the kids grow up. We're at a point now where we are hoping those kids who have grown up start bringing their kids, starting this whole thing over again."

I asked the Garritys how they began to market the you-pick-it or pick-your-own concept. Jan said: "We do advertise in the local shopper and the

(*continued*)

(continued)

daily paper and in some of the regional papers. Another aspect that we pursue, that we kind of grew into after studying some of those direct marketing conferences, was that a lot of orchards use a brochure or pamphlet, and when I saw that I thought, this is perfect, because my sister owns and manages two newspapers. So she and I laid that out and publish a mini-newspaper that we print up once a year, which we give out to everyone who comes into the store; or if we have a booth somewhere or mail out a gift box, we put one in there. That publication gets in the hands of many people. A lot of people will call or write for a catalog and that acts as our catalog. It's a little four-page newspaper."

Pat expressed the importance of continuity: "just being there, and doing your darndest to be consistent. People have a very difficult time understanding how little control we have over the product: how many berries there are, and how big they are, and how far apart they are. People have a hard time realizing that the weather and the season itself have such an impact on the product. If we can stay consistent for several years in a row, you can see the sales and the customer traffic going up and up, but then if you have a bad year, volume drops back and you have to rebuild that customer base back again. The customer wants the product and the conditions perfect. The one saving grace is that if a customer goes to a competitor thinking things will be better over there, they usually find that the competitor is having the same weather-related problems as we are. Once customers realize that, they usually come back to us."

Jan explained that they do some marketing through various open-air farmers' markets, one of the major ones in the region being in Sioux Falls, which is the only Metropolitan Statistical Area in eastern South Dakota. Pat said: "We do pretty well because we come in with such a specialized product. We don't sell as much as we anticipated, because of the large population base, but we do okay. One of the things we are learning in our business is that consistency goes a long way. We have gone to what we call satellite markets, of which Sioux Falls is just one. We have found that if we go to one of those markets in a given year we sell x number of dollars, but if we go the next year we sell 20 percent more, and if we go the following year we sell 30 percent more, and after a few years you can look back and you realize that your sales are 100 percent above the point you started at. You find that the consistency and continuity builds a customer support base. It's like the customer is waiting; they may see you in the market for three years and never buy from you and then one day decide that what your doing must be right and then they start buying from you. Every year we get these brand-new customers, so when we look back we have never gone backwards in any year unless the weather created a total disaster."

Word of mouth has something to do with this. Tradition and credibility has helped to build this growing customer base for Prairie Gardens. Jan said: "I've had people tell me 'Oh we've lived out here for years and we've wanted to come out but have just never made it.'" Pat explained: "When those types of people finally do come out to become customers, they often become some of our biggest fans and will spend a tremendous number of dollars out there. One thing that we have discovered is that we have tremendous customer support within the a relatively close geographical area, and although that constitutes a relatively large number of square miles, it only represents about 100,000 potential customers. That limited customer base will only generate a limited amount of revenue. We really do well within that customer base, but we need to try to reach beyond that base."

The Garritys began to approach the challenge of reaching that broader customer base by marketing through grocery wholesalers. Pat explained: "The local grocers are very supportive, but many of the larger grocery store chains are very difficult to break into. The major chains are so large that they want not only tremendous volume but they want expediency. It is easy for those produce managers just to buy from their distribution system. It doesn't matter that you can beat their distribution system on quality or even on price. The corporate mentality is such that it is just easier to call for a truckload of whatever. Many of those produce managers are not very receptive to the idea of ordering smaller quantities from a diverse network of suppliers. We did have excellent luck with the Hy Vee Food Stores, though, which is a regional grocery chain currently operating in seven states. Hy Vee is based in Cherokee, Iowa." According to the Garritys it is little wonder that the Hy Vee stores are leaders in their industry. Pat said he found them to be great to work with and found that they were very receptive to marketing locally grown produce.

I asked the Garritys how they got started. Both Pat and Jan laughed. Pat said, "You talk about people starting with nothing, we started on an absolute shoestring. We saved about $5000 dollars for a sprayer and then asked the banker to buy in with us." The 55-acre farm that Prairie Gardens was started on belonged to Jan's father, who offered it to them if they wanted to move back to South Dakota. "We used a lot of debt to start. Our strengths, though, are that we managed to be very innovative, and we have always managed to come up with ways to overcome obstacles."

Having started on a financial shoestring, it was nearly impossible for Prairie Gardens to make the Garritys a living and support the debt, so Pat took a job in Yankton, a nearby town with a population of around 14,000. Pat first worked for a firm that did light manufacturing and later went to work for a mail-order garden seed company. Pat eventually rose to a management position with the mail-order firm and has left them to work full time in his own business only three years ago. All during that time Jan was managing and operating Prairie Gardens with some seasonal part-time help. Pat extended his week by working evenings and weekends at the orchard. From the onset the Garritys knew and understood that the orchard was going to take about seven years for the trees to begin producing at a respectable rate.

Jan said: "After a while, though, we began to weigh what was more important: the stable income from Pat's salary or the labor load that was really mounting, and the yields were rising from the apple crops. It was requiring a great deal of energy to continue."

I asked the Garritys, how important, in hindsight, that outside income was in the survival of their venture. Jan indicated, "I wish we would have swum a little bit more on our own." Pat agreed: "In the context of that type of product, obviously it was going to take a while for our investment in apple trees to kick in. I think working a job for five years was a good idea, but rather than working another job for another five years, I wish we had told ourselves to stop and think. I believe that had I quit the job at that time, those

(continued)

(*continued*)

creative energies would have kicked in and we would have come up with the solutions we eventually found, but it would have happened a lot earlier. We probably would have started doing our jams way back then, with necessity being the mother of invention. I think that the things we're thinking of now, we would have had under our belt five years earlier. If you are really intent on making a business survive, sooner or later you are going to have to swim on your own."

Pat explained: "I quit my job in 1993; that year we had 2000 fewer bushels of apples than we had grown the year before, and we wondered how we were going to make it. By year's end we had made $2000 more than we had the year before, counting my job, and that was a management salary. We made up that entire amount by me being at home, with both of us focusing on marketing. That is when we started going to Sioux Falls, that is when we started doing satellite marketing, that is when we really started realizing that we are the ones who have to do this, that the safety factor is no longer there— and we haven't gone back since. We haven't always jumped ahead with the gains we think we should have reached, but we have never gone backward. We weren't making those gains while I was working. One thing we tried to do while I was working is that we kept trying to find somebody like us to help us, to take our place. We never could find that person, because that person was me. That somebody was not out there some place, and it wasn't until we finally realized that fact that we were finally able to really move ahead."

The Garritys added to their finances with a rural development loan, which the local bank and the South Dakota Department of Agriculture participated in. Pat praised and talked about how supportive the bank was. "One problem the bank has with this type of loan is that they don't have anyone to really compare us to. That is also true for us; that is difficult, and so it is our vision that is going to make the place fly. Bankers can listen and act as a sounding board but they really can't offer us anything other than their support."

Pat went on to explain: "We believe that to really put some financial stability in our business we must get away from the commodity end of the business and concentrate more on the value-added part of the business." The value added comes from Garritys branded products such as their jams, jellies, and apple cider. "We also have a bakery that does really well; our bakers are the grandmother types, who like to bake and make homemade jam. We also do gift boxes and are attempting to build a corporate client base. The cider is really good for name recognition, and it is a good outlet for our number 2 grade apples, but the profit margins are not that great on apple cider."

I quizzed the Garritys on their pricing strategy, to which they responded that in many ways they have been very hesitant about going into grocery stores. Pat indicated: "We have been very cautious about how we are marketing ourselves, and it's been a tough area for us. We may have held ourselves back by a year or two because of this transition that we've been going through in our minds as to how we should get the job done. It wasn't until we realized that we needed to really go with the value-added concept that the business really began to take off."

The Garritys built a new building in 1991 at Prairie Gardens, which houses the bakery and apple washing and grading equipment and also has temperature-controlled storage units for the produce and apples. This structure is the center of Prairie Gardens, which supports the value-added concept. Guests tend to congregate in and around this facility to watch the apples being washed and graded, and to browse and sample the products during the apple fest.

The Garritys talked about the intensity of their business and discussed how important planning was to them if they were to maintain some semblance of creativity. Pat called it stepping outside the box. For the Garritys January is an important month, because it's that one month where things slow down a little so that they not only can rest and recharge, but can step back from the business to do some creative thinking.

Jan described their annual calendar. "January is our downtime, February is when the trees are pruned and any major mechanical maintenance is done on equipment or buildings, March and April get into the planting season, and we do spraying during May. The retail store opens in June with strawberry season." The Garritys also start their satellite marketing and put on workshops throughout the summer. "July is cherry season, along with raspberries and apricots. August brings the second crop of raspberries, and we also bring in peaches from Colorado; this fills a void in our production calendar and adds to our product mix. We get a lot of calls from people looking for really good peaches. We also raise sweet corn and market our homegrown sweet corn all throughout the summer as well, primarily wholesale. September brings on the beginning of the apple crop, and the Indian corn, gourds, squash, and pumpkins are ripe as well. October is the busiest month at Prairie Gardens, with the full apple crop in season. Each weekend we host our apple fest, which offers hay rides, musical festivities, and other events. October is also a big month for hosting tours for schools as well as for banking groups and other business groups. November starts the Christmas rush, with gift baskets and boxes, as well as the season for Christmas trees."

Pat discussed the division of labor and responsibility between himself and Jan for Prairie Gardens. They break the organization down into four main functional areas: finance, marketing, production, and personnel. Jan takes care of personnel while Pat handles production and finance, which includes bookkeeping, and they share the marketing responsibilities. In the ideal atmosphere Pat feels that they should not share any of those responsibilities because as a married couple it becomes difficult to leave the business and not bring it into the house and into the relationship. Pat says that even in January they work 60 hours a week, and during the busy season it's 80 hours a week and more. Pat, like many of the entrepreneurs I have visited, says that when you own your own business there is a different mentality about work and about hours. "Don't ever think that owning your own business is easier, less stressful, or has fewer hours and demands than working a job. The appearance and the reality of owning your own business are two different things."

Jan added: "When we started out, we never dreamed the things we are doing now; we were just going to grow fruit. We were going to grow it by the bushel and sell it by the basketful and people were going to flock to us. We had no idea what it was going to take to get the product to those customers."

(continued)

(continued)

I asked Jan if she knew then what she knows now whether she would still be willing to undertake this business venture, and her response was doubtful. Pat's response was similar but then he qualified that statement: "If I knew then what I know now, so that I wouldn't have had to go through all the ups and downs, I would say, yes, I'd do it in a minute, but I would do a lot of things differently."

Jan has worked in this business 10 years longer than her husband has, but Pat has had the experience of working two different jobs during that time. According to Pat: "I haven't seen anything out there that is a smooth sail. I don't think our environment is much worse than that of many other jobs. If I have to work to earn a living, I would do this. If Prairie Gardens were to shut down this year, I would still go out and work for an orchard. Jan may not, but I love this kind of work." Jan added: "When it's good it's really good, it is a wonderful way to live. It's a great way to raise a family. When you stop and list what our jobs are, we are both a jack of all trades, and we take a lot of pride in that. I was thinking about what our jobs are. We are mechanics, entomologists, chemists, marketers, designers, accountants, producers, and a lot of other things, and that is pretty amazing. It is quite an accomplishment." Pat affirmed Jan's statement by adding: "People come up to me all the time and ask me what I'm spraying on my trees. You don't just go out and spray your trees without knowing who your enemy is. You have to be an entomologist; you have to know what you are spraying for; you do not want all that spray on your apples. The days of just doing something are over and have been over for a long time."

I asked the Garritys to expand on the depth of knowledge required to be in their business. Jan indicated that she had just read an article in a trade journal emphasizing the fact that to be successful in the orchard business, one had to live, eat, drink, and sleep the orchard. "For us we have at times reached the point where we wished we could just take a break from it for a few months, but I don't think we can ever do that; it's just not realistic." Pat added: "January, February, and March, which are our slower months, are our creative times. For us to make anything possible and for this diversified program to work, we've got to be thinking creatively during these times. There is no one to copy from. For us to make this thing work, we've got to be thinking creatively during this time, because once April starts, the creativity is gone; all that is left is implementation. I used to fight this idea of never being able to shut down. What you have to do in business today is to sit down and come up with goals—whether they are yearly goals or long-term goals—but you must set your goals. You then must come up with your strategy or your action plan as to how you are going to accomplish those goals. Your action plan is how you are going to get the job done; that's your implementation. Your strategy is part of your creativity. You've got to get those two things done, but once you've got your action plan in motion, it is tough to go back to being creative."

Pat explained that even though you plan, things don't always work out that way. "This year we planned on doing really well in our store. November and December are not slow months, they are very good months, but when the sleet storms began our customer base dropped off to almost nothing, because people couldn't get through on the roads. Our entire action plan to do well in the store at Prairie Gardens went out the window. We decided to move our business into the mall, and that worked well for us. We did this as an afterthought. We are beginning to realize that we need a plan B. If the weather is going to throw us a curve ball so that our original plan doesn't work, we need to have another plan in place beforehand. It is so hard to make those types of decisions on the spot. I've talked to other people and they tell me that this is nothing new; this is reality. You need a contingency plan on paper and in your mind because there is too much at stake just to fly by the seat of your pants. I don't think there is any business out there any more that you can operate by the seat of your pants."

I asked the Garritys why things were this way. Pat laughed and said, "You have so much invested." Jan explained: "We talked about this with the banker last year, and people have a different mentality today. Customers have a Wal-Mart mentality; they are less loyal than they used to be; customers like to do all their shopping in one place." Pat added: "A major impact in business today is Wal-Mart. You can cuss about it, but it is still there. The key to success and failure is answering the question of how you are going to compete with that. Even a business like ours competes against Wal-Mart. The trap is to cuss it and blame the customer for going to Wal-Mart. The key is to figure out a way to differentiate from them. Too many business owners operate a lifestyle type of business, and even though they are losing money, they fail to change that lifestyle to recognize the changes occuring in the industry, and continue on just as they were until the day they lock the door."

I asked the Garritys if they were to identify the key principles associated with success, what they would be. Pat's response was: "You must have structure; you must define and assign your critical areas, such as your personnel, finance, production, and marketing. The people assigned those tasks must know what they are doing. Another key area is the planning: from the goals to the strategy to the action plan in a structured environment. This plan does not need to be an elaborate multipage document, but it should be written down. You must have established goals, and you must have a way to get those things done. Having an action plan in place helps keep your focus; you do not have time to be going in 10 different directions. Know your market—that means know your product and know who you are selling those products to. Know your business. Very few are successful who don't really know their business."

How difficult is it for a husband and wife to work together in the same business? Jan responded by explaining how it takes discipline not to bring the business into the house. "You know we're worrying about weather, and looking out the window it's staring you in the face. It's hard to shut it off. Sam is our barometer; when things get too intense, Sam lets us know." Sam is the Garritys' 5-year-old son.

Pat indicated that one of the things they are hoping to do is to get involved in the Small Business Family Initiative, which is a group sponsored by the University of South Dakota School of Business. The intent of this organization is to work with families who are in business, not so much to address business issues but to address family concerns. "One of the things that really scared us was a couple that we knew and looked to for inspiration, who got a divorce a couple of years ago—that nearly blew us away. They had an

(continued)

(continued)

operation that we thought was doing quite well, but every frustration that they were dealing with, we are dealing with. Now that we have visited them, we discovered that they are going through the same types of problems that we are going through. They also are doing some value-added things in their operation. The family issues are something that you really have to watch, because problems can come up faster than you realize, and you need to be careful."

The Garritys have extended their search for outside support to include business issues as well as family issues. Pat went on to explain another area of outside support they are pursuing. "A positive relationship with your banker is good, but a banker is not a consultant; they are for the most part just a vendor of money. Bankers are people you can bounce ideas off, but they generally cannot act as visionaries for your business. One of the things we did was set up a board of directors. We were able to bounce things off this group, and they were coming up with things that worked great. We also contacted the Small Business Development Center of the University of South Dakota, which put us in touch with a small business consultant. This organization is helping us set up a five-year marketing plan and a five-year business plan. We already had much of this, but now we have it written down. What we realized is that some things we can't do for ourselves, our customers can't do for us, nor can our banker—we need someone from the outside looking in. If I were to do things over, this is a process that I would have started a lot earlier. If I were to give advice to someone starting a business, it would be to have a board of directors: to get outside help and to set up a network of support."

If one were to contrast the two small businesses profiled here and in Chapter 1, it would be difficult to find much similarity; they are very different. If a truism exists for small businesses and their owners, it is that each is so very unique. Yet each produces a product or service and must deliver that product or service profitably to customers.

The Garritys are presented with a particularly difficult set of circumstances in that their location is remote, an advantage that Mr. Barlow's Burlington has that they don't have. The Garritys must somehow convince their customers to come to them, or to somehow get their product to the customers. The Garritys are also faced with weather-related production problems, which causes inconsistency in the quality and quantity of product produced.

The Garritys are an example of how important creativity is in small business. This business started on a financial shoestring. It began with a dream and was implemented and supported by hard work and creativity. Each time a business stopping barrier was encountered, the Garritys seemed to come up with a solution. Like many small business entities, Prairie Gardens evolved into what it is today, but that evolution and growth took place in synchronization with Pat and Jan's internal understanding of their business: in the sense of who and what they were and how they fit into the local and regional economy; an understanding of who their customers were, what those customers wanted, and how to reach them.

Like Mr. Barlow, the Garritys really know their business. They understand the functional areas and have a high degree of competency in those areas. I think that demonstrates a baseline for the would-be entrepreneur—a minimum requirement. The Garritys are a tremendous example of resilience and adaptability. A small business manager must have the ability to change with the times. The Garritys demonstrate the importance of planning and contingency planning in a successful operation. Planning helps take some of the bumps out of the road and gives you a starting point to react to the "what if's."

The Garritys teach us the importance of continuity and consistency. Their customers want to know first that Prairie Gardens will be there, and second, that the product they buy will be what they expect. For the Garritys their customers are looking not only for product quality but quality that includes an element of experience. In so doing the Garritys have a product differentiation and positioning strategy that is hard for competitors to duplicate. This is a cornerstone of Prairie Gardens' success.

Another lesson we can learn from the Garritys is that reality is often far different than that envisioned in our dreams. "We were just going to grow apples, grow them by the bushels and by the basketfuls." Maybe what the Garrity story is really about is commitment: first to a dream and a vision, and second, about a commitment to each other and to the Garrity family.

The story of Prairie Gardens also demonstrates how complicated life has become, especially life as a small business owner. It is intense, and complex. The Garritys also teach us that you don't have to have all the answers yourself—you can get help from the outside. Pat ranks setting up a board of directors as an early priority in his advice to other would-be entrepreneurs.

• ELEMENTS OF SMALL BUSINESS MANAGEMENT ·

As indicated in Chapter 1, this book is built around the bridge model. In writing this book a number of business owners were interviewed, some of whose stories are shared in the book. If the business experience of just those small business owners featured in this book were totaled, they would easily add up to over 100 years of small business ownership experience. In the search for a common thread, a number of the same themes kept coming up over and over. Each proprietor would have a slightly different version, but they all had much in common. Their experiences, along with my small business experience, helped to formulate the bridge model. In attempting to teach small business management I have found visualization of a bridge model to be an easy way to grasp the interrelationships of the elements that go into small business management. This model represents a prioritization of those elements.

Ethics

As indicated earlier, the bridge model of business is grounded in ethics. Without ethics or standards of conduct, the entire structure would be unstable and would not last. Ethics provides the foundation—as basic and as fundamental as economic activity is to the building of a society. In every society we have rules of conduct, expected ways of behaving. Some of these rules are informal—it is just the way things

JOTTINGS FROM JAN[4]

It ain't been easy
"If it were easy, everyone would be doing it!" Those are the words uttered by Jan and Pat Garritys' former boss, Harold, in Washington state, where the Garritys managed Keystone Ranch, a 100-acre apple and pear orchard. "Back then, I did not fully understand the true meaning of those words, but you can believe that I do now! Pat and I are proud to be entering our thirteenth year at Garrity's Prairie Gardens. And in reference to Harold's words, it ain't been easy!"

It would have been easy if . . .
"In our very first spring, in 1984, it had not rained cats and dogs, as much as 3 inches in a half-hour during planting season. This postponed the planting season to the point where during the month of June we finally had to mud most of the plants and trees into the ground."

It would have been easy if . . .
"There had been no drought from 1985 through 1987. Fortunately, we installed a complete drip irrigation system, which kept the plants and trees alive, but the extreme heat coupled with hot, dry winds was not conducive to growing young fruit trees and other plants."

It would have been easy if . . .
"We had been educated on advertising during our first strawberry season in 1985. We felt confident on how to grow the short-seasoned red berries, but we did not know how to sell them until it was almost too late. Fortunately, a dear friend pointed us toward the direction of local marketing."

It would have been easy if . . .
"The herds of deer inhabiting the nearby Jim River valley did not move into the orchard every winter and munch on the tender new growth on every apple tree to reduce our future crop. Fortunately, with the help of the state, we are erecting a high deer fence to eliminate the annual nibbling."

Yes, it would be easy if . . .
"It never hailed, if temperatures did not plummet before the trees were dormant, if mechanical equipment never broke down, if supplies would come in on time when ordered, if it had not flooded in 1992 and 1993, and on and on. Pat and I are obviously not quitters. With determination, hard work, some tears, and help from family and friends, Pat and I have reached our thirteenth anniversary. Facing these challenges and more, we have paved the way to establish a way of life in South Dakota for ourselves and our son that we are proud of. But, hey, who said it would be easy? Thank you, Harold, for those profound words. We truly know why everyone is not doing this."

are done. Yet each of us at one time or another has said the wrong thing at the wrong time. The consequence of such behavior is embarrassment. Why? Because everyone else present also knew that it was the wrong thing to say. That is why the moment was embarrassing. To take this a step further, if you were continually to say the wrong thing, members of the group would distance themselves from you. People would not talk to you or sit by you, or want to be seen by you, lest they, through association, be thought of in the same light. You did not break any laws other than to violate the expected way of behaving. That expected way of behaving is defined by the group.

In business there are expectations also: expectations in the way business is conducted and how people treat each other. Most of those are not written down, unless in a company manual or credo, but for small business that is usually not the case. The consequences of violating those expected ways of behaving is the same as in the larger society. People begin to distance themselves. If the people who distance themselves happen to be the people who are your customers, you soon will be out of business.

Defining expected ways of behaving for a business begins at a very basic level with the fact that people expect to be treated with a degree of trust, respect, and honesty. That is not to say that businesses are all honest and act that way. It is to say that we all want and expect businesses to treat us fairly and honestly.

Let me attempt to define this expected way of behaving from the perspective of a vignette. A number of years ago I had done an extensive home remodeling project and had spent several thousand dollars at a retailer of home improvement goods. The store manager knew me by name. At this time I was working for a company based in Midland, Texas. My boss called me up on a Saturday afternoon and asked me to pack up for a job in western Wyoming. My supervisor couldn't tell me how long this job would take, only that I should leave as soon as I could pack. This was before instant cash machines were available, and the banks were closed on weekends.

Needing cash, I drove over to a home improvement store, walked up to the manager, and inquired what time he was closing. I then asked him how much cash he had in the till. He promptly lifted the change drawer and counted the cash. I told him I wanted to write him a personal check for that cash, explaining my situation. He said, "stop back 10 minutes before closing and you can have it all if you want it."

What happened in that short exchange can be explained this way. The proprietor recognized his customer. In addition, he trusted that customer because trust had been built over a period of months by the process of the exchange relationship. I gave him a personal check in exchange for home improvement goods. The retailer wanted to continue to enter into those exchange relationships. As an expression of good faith, this retailer was willing to extend service beyond the usual customary range of service, due to extenuating circumstances. In return, I, the customer, owe the retailer and reciprocate through customer loyalty and extended goodwill. None of this was discussed; it just was part of those unwritten rules of behavior. If either party violates those rules, the relationship is in jeopardy. A insufficient-funds check any time within the course of this business relationship could easily have resulted in a different outcome.

Relationships

In speaking with other business owners about their experiences, the word *honesty* came up many times. People look for honesty in their employees and from their customers, suppliers, and everybody else within the context of both business and human relationships. The first set of pillars that support the functional areas attempt to define those human relationships. Business is a people business no matter what you are selling.

Internal relationships take two forms. The first is the relationship between management, usually the small business owner, and the employees. The second internal relationship exists among the employees themselves. A direct correlation exists between the quality of those internal human relationships and the quality of the products and/or services delivered to the customer. A breakdown in those relationships can jeopardize the stability of the enterprise, which is why they are represented by one of the pillars in the model presented.

In general, if you ask small business owners to describe the type of relationship they want to develop with their employees to form a successful enterprise, most proprietors look to gain the trust and respect of their employees. In the small business profile on the Burlington Restaurant, Mr. Barlow described his management style as that of a family. What is a family? It is by definition a tight-knit social group whose members usually are of common ancestry. In a healthy family setting you are free to be yourself and are accepted as yourself. You are allowed to express your feelings freely without fear of reprisal. In a family, the members are concerned about each other, support each other, and are willing to help each other out. Emotional bonds of love and affection are present. Family members stick together to maintain and build the success of the unit.

This is not such a strange concept. If you look in the employment section of almost any newspaper, you will discover that many help-wanted ads are seeking someone who can become a team player. What is a team? It is a close-knit social unit sharing a common purpose. If the team has a name like the Green Bay Packers, we seem to understand what they are about. What gives a team its power and its ability to accomplish their intended purpose is the unity among its members. The whole group can often accomplish things that individually they could not, because the members support each other and their skills are complementary. The more tightly knit the group—the more motivated—the more intensely they share a common purpose and the better the group performs. In the world of athletics this concept is easy to measure. They put a score up in lights for all to see. In the world of business, measurement is not always so clearcut. Yet unity alone will not guarantee a championship; it also takes skill among the members and leadership. The reverse is also true, a championship is not guaranteed to a team made up of members chosen based on their skill alone.

A highly effective team requires dynamic leadership; the tone or climate of a small business is influenced by the sum of the personalities of its members but is influenced most by the personality of the small business owner. The members will automatically look to the owner for cues as to what is expected. It takes time for trust to be built between the members and the leadership. At one level the members require that the leadership be competent. After all, they may have given up a secure job to sign on with your firm, or signed on due to the promises that were made. The first step in building the trust of team members is to be competent. They need to understand and believe that you know what you are doing and have the ability to recognize what must be done. As a business owner you are the formal leader, which means that you must possess the ability to organize resources and activity to get the job done. For any team to become tight-knit, the followers must believe in their leader.

To make the analogy to a football game, the other 10 players look to the quarterback to be able to read the defense and call the right play. The other 10 must believe that their quarterback can deliver the ball to the right person at the right time and in the right place to be successful. The old adage that nothing breeds success like success is true. What that adage is really saying is: Prove it to us and we will believe in you. The strength or intensity of the members' belief will influence what they, as individuals, will be willing to sacrifice in the attempt at success. Lack of belief will result in a substandard performance and substandard results. A strong belief coupled with a strong commitment will result in a 100 percent effort by every member, which will automatically greatly enhance the chance for success. A particular player may raise his or her level of performance to a higher-than-normal level to accomplish the task because that player was called on by the group to deliver. That performance is a result of the trust shown to the leader, and the commitment to the purpose and to the other members.

In the small business environment, the members will only trust a leader in whom they believe. As a manager you will be called on to prove yourself constantly. Being competent is only one part of the team building equation. The second part of team building from the perspective of the relationship between the entrepreneur and the employees stems from the level of commitment in the organization or for the purpose of the organization. Stop and think about this for a moment. What is the purpose of a small business? What is it that the small business owner wants? Generally to make money, right? How? Some people believe that it's on the backs of the employees. What business advertises for in personnel ads is for team members who will give 100 percent of effort, in the form of working late, coming early, power lunches, short coffee breaks, sacrifices in their personal lives, and family time—to do what? To make their employer lots of money? To do the work equivalent of throwing a cross-body block, so that a business belonging to someone else can make money? I don't think so. The commitment shown in such a structure is one sided, it is extracted commitment, not commitment that is freely given. The performance of such a team will reflect the level of commitment. To varying degrees many firms in this country are managed with extracted commitment and remain profitable. The teams that are running these organizations are often loose-knit work groups, whose performance is adequate to keep things running. People need jobs to survive.

For commitment in an organization to be complete, like trust it must be reciprocal. I have explained what management wants. What does the employee team member want? I recently posed that question to an employee of a manufacturing firm who had applied for a supervisory position. The response was: "I want a better life." He went on to explain what that meant to him: better pay so that he could provide more of the good life for his family. Others want different things. As individuals we define success as achieving or obtaining the things we want. Those things are varied but can be broken down into a number of groups.

In the context of a small business, the owner cannot always offer what it is that employees want. A starting point in the screening process begins with identifying what it is that the prospective team member wants. If what you are offering is not even close, it is unlikely that this person will be willing to throw the equivalent of that cross-body block for you and your business so that you can achieve the goals that you have set for your business. Each small business is unique and must act within certain parameters, but if you can build a team around you that wants what you have to offer, it becomes much easier to build a high level of commitment, and a high level of intensity can be achieved as well. In other words, a high level of team performance can be achieved if the members believe in the leadership, and if they believe that in performing, they will obtain what it is that they want.

One other critical point in building the trust of the team members. The degree to which employees trust you, and the degree to which you do what you say you say you will do, form the foundation for a long-term trust relationship. The old adage that nothing breeds success like success can be altered to read that nothing breeds trust like demonstrating trustworthiness.

The process of obtaining team members' trust and commitment begins with clear explanations, that is, clear communication of what is expected, how it is measured, and how it is rewarded. A violation of those expectations is viewed as a broken promise and begins to erode the level of trust between members and the leadership of the team. A part of the trust-building process must include information sharing. Another part of the process is a clear relationship between an action desired by the employer and an outcome desired by that employee. The closer that relationship is, the more intense the action on the part of the employee.

An example of reinforced trust building which demonstrates that an action causes an outcome can best be demonstrated by a story regarding the commission structure of a car dealership. I performed an audit on an outlet for a chain of used-car automobile dealerships. In this business there were approximately 15 employees. When I asked for and was given the payroll register, I received a computer printout file that was approximately 6 inches thick. In running a sample to follow one person's payroll through the year, I discovered that one employee received over 300 paychecks in a single year. What was going on was that management was making it perfectly clear what type of behavior was rewarded. The action and outcome were undeniable and reinforced immediately. An elaborate quota system was set up, and bonuses were issued for achieving a daily, weekly, or monthly sales quota not only for autos sold but also for the service sector. For example, if the dealership set a quota of three car sales a day, when a salesperson exceeded that quota the idea was to impress on everyone in the organization that this was a really big event. A bonus check was cut for that salesperson and for the other team members as well. The idea was to instill excitement through this instant reward.

The hype should carry forward to the next sale. If a fourth and fifth sale was made that day, the commissions were increased with each sale, each followed by increasing levels of hype in an attempt to drive the intensity of the team to higher and higher levels. The net effect was a highly motivated team. Within two years of opening this dealership the owners had outgrown their original facility and were expanding through construction.

Part of this firm's success stems from the fact that the team members are made aware of the operating costs of this operation. They understand the markup structure, they realize the impact that each sale has on the overall profitability picture. They are made to feel that as team members, they are a part of the business, which demonstrates that partnership through a realistic share in the firm's profits. By providing a commission structure that allows everyone to share, the members also know that they are in this business together and thus support each other's efforts. In this type of structure everybody wins.

The opposite of this scenario is also true. As a payroll auditor I experienced a number of situations where the owners of a firm would hustle me into a room, lock the door, and impress on me the necessity of confidentiality. These types of owner-managers were absolutely paranoid that information regarding officer compensation and/or company profitability would leak to the employees. Such company information was a deep, dark secret because if profit levels were known, management feared that their employees might want to share.

One of the most extreme cases that I happened to see was in a medium-sized business where payroll totaled some $1.3 million, with slightly over 100 employees or, more accurately, over 100 W-2 forms. In counting W-2's, employee turnover is included. The two key officers took compensation of $1 million; the other $300,000 or so was distributed among the other 100 or so W-2's. I couldn't believe how repressive this firm's wage scale was, so I went back and discovered that fewer than five W-2's showed total compensation over $10,000.

No surprise that employee moral was low, as was performance. Turnover was high. This was a sewing operation in a small rural community which was forced to close its doors a year or two later.

It may at first appear that a closed system such as the one above is maximizing profitability. In reality there is little loyalty and little incentive for the workforce to go the extra mile. Information in such an organization tends to flow one way, and that is down. In such a system the owner-manager must possess all the answers to survive, because solutions to problems will not come up from the bottom. A team effort to increase profitability or to overcome a threat will not be available. That was the situation this firm was in. As soon as a situation arises that management cannot solve, the company is often forced to lock the door—as this firm did. There was no incentive, there was no trust, there was no way that a unified stand could be made that might have utilized the creative energies and/or human resources of this business.

Team Dynamics

One critical task that small business managers are charged with is building a team around themselves. In small businesses more than in large firms, a single employee has a larger impact on the overall success and failure of the organization. The starting point for small business owners building a team is to hire team members who have similar values, attitudes, and belief systems that they have themselves. In addition, the employees hired must have the basic skills to be competent at the job as well as possessing the motivation to do the job well, which brings us back to hiring people who already possess the attitudes, values, and belief systems that we ourselves possess—or in simpler terms, hiring people who want the same things that our businesses can offer employees.

This is no small task. In part what this statement is saying is that as a small business owner it is not worth the time and energy that is required to change someone's belief systems so that the person can fit into the organization, cold as that may sound. It is an easier path to find someone who already has the desired values and/or traits. That new employee should enhance the team concept, not detract from it.

Some elaboration is probably in order concerning people's attitudes and belief systems. What the small business manager is really concerned about is the behavior that the employee exhibits on the job—that employee's level of commitment, intensity, and skill level demonstrated in the performance of his or her duties. The entrepreneur is generally not concerned with the person's religious, political, or other beliefs, but attitudes and beliefs that affect behavior in the workplace are a major concern to the entrepreneur.

Consider a prospective employee who wants to be part of something (your business organization) because of what your business represents, which hopefully is honesty, integrity, quality of workmanship, and quality of service. But some employees just want to put in their eight hours and don't really care about what they are doing because it's just a job and if they don't get this one, they'll get another one next week. Compare that attitude with the attitude that "my parents always told me to do the best job that I can and to treat people the way I would want to be treated." If you knew nothing else about two employee applicants, which of the two applicants would you hire?

Unfortunately, prospective employees are not labeled with tags identifying skill level, attitude, and belief systems. You have to find that out on your own, which is both difficult and hard work. If I could give you three easy steps to screen applicants, evaluate them, and select the right ones, I would do so. In truth, of the over 100 employees I've hired during my small business management career, I never fully mastered this process, although many of my employees were excellent. I could recognize a good employee when I had one and did all in my power to reward and retain such a person. In my own business experience, the degree to which I failed to hire a person who did not fit into my firm's team defined the level of turnover in the organization.

Let me approach this concept from another direction. Every business large or small that survives does so for a reason. They fill a niche in the marketplace, and the market says yes to this business in the form of a purchase often enough or to a level that keeps the business healthy. It is the job of the manager or small business owner to develop an information network that can tell the entrepreneur why the business is successful: in other words, why the customer is using your product or service. This is the essence of the customer information system, explained more fully in Chapter 8. The clearer this information is to the entrepreneur, the closer he or she is to developing products or services that meet customer needs. It also tells the small business manager how they can best utilitze their resources, both human and financial, to perform those activities that will keep the business successful. These are the strategic success variables that tell the manager what to measure.

From the perspective of developing a team, the mission of that team is to perform the critical activities that keep the business ongoing. The entrepreneur must hire people who can best facilitate the performance of those activities. In a large organization this is broken down into job descriptions and job requirements defining the range of duties and the realm of responsibility. In a small business the same functions occur but are managed a lot closer to the hip. A policy manual and an employee handbook are usually not written until a new enterprise has progressed a long way down the road.

One constant challenge with which the entrepreneur is faced is matching the right person to the right job. In part, that process begins with an employee search in an attempt to induce the right types of applicants to apply for positions. The search is followed by a screening process designed to identify the best applicants based on a match between the job description and an applicant's skills and personal traits, of which values, beliefs, and attitude are a part. The level of job performance that an employee will demonstrate is in part influenced by the accuracy of the match between their skill level and personality traits. If the job duties are too simplistic, they do little to allow the employee to use their creative talents and skills. The result is often a substandard performance and a dronelike attitude, which does not do good things for employee retention, either. The employee becomes frustrated and sooner or later will probably quit. On the other end of the continuum, if employees are given duties and responsibilities that go beyond their capabilities, that is frustrating as well, and sooner or later they will quit. In fact, the sooner their level of incompetence is brought to light, the sooner people will leave a position. High pay may entice them to stick around longer, but the job is frustrating and performance will be substandard. Both situations are under the control of the business manager, and either end of the continuum does not enhance performance or job satisfaction, nor does it meet the need to produce high-quality products or service.

A case in point: On a particular audit that I conducted for a state department of labor, a construction company was delinquent on a report. Every time I called the firm I was transferred to the bookkeeper, who kept telling me that the report was in the mail. I finally forced the issue by issuing an audit notice. The audit was to be performed on a Monday. When I walked into the business I was informed that the bookkeeper had resigned the previous Friday. I talked to the owner and informed him that I was auditing the firm, bookkeeper or not. He was at first upset about being audited, but I explained that in fact I was doing him a favor because I sensed problems. Several hours into the audit I called the owner's attention to some serious issues and suggested a full outside audit by a reputable CPA firm, since the scope of my audit was limited to payroll issues. As it turned out, there were some serious issues, which caused the business financial hardship, and later was in part the cause of the business closing its doors.

At first glance one would want to blame the employee, but that person's incompetence was only part of the problem. Underlying that issue was a manager who was not monitoring the critical issues. This firm's mistake was the attitude that the real work of a construction firm is to build things and that those in the organization who do the building deserve the highest pay. Bookkeeping was deemed to be the work of a woman and since the bookkeeper was a woman, she could therefore keep books. In reality, this poor woman had only minimal training in accounting and had full-charge accounting duties thrust upon her for a firm doing a business of several million dollars a year. She was being paid receptionist wages, while more and more duties were piled on which were beyond the limit of her abilities. The end result was frustration, and when her incompetence was forced into the light, she did the only thing she could—she quit.

I saw the same situation happen in a Fortune 500 company with sales in the billions. Double-digit growth in the accounting function caused a living nightmare in the accounting department. The scope of the duties soon outran the abilities of many of the accounting personnel, including many of those at very senior levels. The result was frustration and employee turnover.

I belabor this point because frustration caused by exceeding employee abilities can cause great harm to a firm. It should underscore the importance of establishing good information systems and good control systems to monitor a firm's critical issues. It should also underscore the importance and need for employee training and supervision and how important it is to maintain good lines of communication grounded in trust. Had these employees been able to trust management, they would not have been afraid to say, "I can't do this job alone."

This book makes the assumption that the critical activity revolves around and depends on the quality factors of product and service. The customer information system will identify those factors in any business, but I am confident that a high degree of correlation exists. If this is the standard by which your customers are measuring your firm, then as a business manager it begins to define what you as a manager will use to measure the activity of your team. It also defines the types of skills that your team members must possess to accomplish the critical tasks.

The next logical step in developing a highly functional team that demonstrates exceptional responsiveness to the customer service needs of your customer base is to articulate and communicate the connection between your team's activities and the success of the organization. In no uncertain terms your employees should be made aware of how their performance on their assigned task and range of duties affect the success of the firm. Feedback is imperative. This is the premise of the measurement control systems of your organization. It should also be the premise of your employee reward systems and compensation packages. It is imperative, though, that the connection between your reward systems and compensation structure and the success-generating activity be accurate. A mistake here will cause you to lead the firm off course. Everyone will be rushing around doing things that are not what the customer wants. If the level of performance of your team improves, the result should be an improvement in the bottom line.

My recommendation is that such an improvement in performance resulting in an improvement in the bottom line be shared by those who made it happen. The information should be shared so that the progress can be seen and recognized by all. But why should the employees care if all that is seen is more money in the boss's pocket? They will feel that they have a right to share in this additional profit. To withhold it will decrease the employee's level of trust, commitment, and intensity. It will contribute to employee turnover. Yet not all rewards need be paid out in dollars and cents; there are many rewards other than monetary. Demonstrating your appreciation and articulating that directly to your employees will go a long way toward building a tight-knit team.

Teams are nothing other than a close-knit social unit. Like a family, every member plays a role in the success of the unit. Each member knows the other members; they know each other's strengths and shortcomings. In the performance of a task each member knows what to expect from the other members. They learn to depend on each other. Close-knit units, which are built on a system of trust and commitment, will generally be able to outperform units loosely thrown together. The reason that professional football players report to camp is to become a cohesive unit so that their level of performance will exceed the sum total of each member's individual talent.

The implication for the business manager is that turnover kills the cohesiveness of the unit. Every time a member leaves the group and is replaced by another, the dynamics of the group is changed and the team must rebuild. Sometimes the transition is smooth, but a continual change of members will generally degrade the team's performance.

It is sometimes difficult to design job duties that enable employees to utilize their skills and allow for the implementation of creativity to avoid frustration through boredom while avoiding frustration through overload. The job itself often dictates the duties, which does not lend itself to a lot of team building. We are not putting together football teams that go out into an arena filled with screaming fans and television cameras to perform. The world of work is a lot less dramatic. Yet teams built on trust, honesty, and mutual respect will tend to stick together and to outperform groups that are not cohesive. Teams are based on shared goals, which means that the members have common values, beliefs, and attitudes. Highly effective teams share responsibility and the members assume roles to maintain the group's effectiveness. In the workplace this means that a person may work outside the boundaries of a specific job description because the group needs someone to fulfill a role.

Imagine for a minute a group of people thrown together to perform a task. If a number of high school students are called at random to build a float for the homecoming parade, at first everyone just stands around wondering what to do. Out of that group will come an informal leader, and as group cohesiveness builds, so does their efficiency. The members begin to assume roles, duties, and responsibilities. If the group melds together, they can have fun, be creative, and do a great job. If the members of the group do not meld together, infighting and role confusion occur. The job gets done, but usually not as well as it could have been done, nor was it fun. In the end the group went along and did the job halfheartedly just to get it over with. In the world of work this is just getting through the day, getting to the paycheck.

As a small business owner, you become the formal leader, but hopefully also the informal leader. You put the group together by selecting the members, or at least approving their selection. The tone, attitudes, and values are very much top down but are influenced by every member of the group. You can build a cohesive group in part through successive and frequent interaction, which leads to successful outcomes. For the entrepreneur a successful outcome is profitable. For the employees a successful outcome is fun, creative, rewarding, and all those things we call incentives. A paycheck is the norm, but monetary incentives such as profit sharing help build that cohesiveness. These demonstrate shared values, which results in shared outcomes.

I indicated earlier that not all incentives need to be monetary. People want to belong to certain groups and be with certain people. The workplace can be a place where your employees want to be, not just because of the pay but because of the people and because it's a good place to work: knowing that they are appreciated; being treated as part of the group, not just a production unit; recognizing and rewarding good ideas and good performance. Every team is unique because of the makeup of its members. As a team leader one truism exists and that is that you cannot be someone you are not, so the team will often reflect the small business owner's personality.

Human relationships are also based on expected ways of behaving. Most of us expect to be treated with a degree of respect: respect for who we are as human beings and what we do in the work world. That respect should be mutual between employer and employee. Trust goes hand in hand with respect, both of which have their roots in honesty. Honesty is the base on which the other two are built. If you begin any relationship, but specifically an employer-employee relationship, with honesty, trust and respect, the earned outcome will be honest behavior. The same holds true for relationships between employees.

• QUESTIONS FOR DISCUSSION · · · · · · · ·

1. Explain why the Garritys' Prairie Gardens has a more difficult marketing situation than Arden Barlow's Burlington Restaurant.

2. What suggestions would you give Pat and Jan Garrity as to generating new markets or new sources of revenue?

3. What is the greatest challenge facing the Garritys?

4. Do you agree or disagree with the premise that a close-knit team is essential to high levels of performance in a small business? Explain.

5. Identify and discuss the key elements in building a cohesive team in a small business.

6. I suggested that small business owners share the wealth with those employees who helped create it. Do you agree or disagree? What percentage of profits is fair?

7. What is the key element in building trust between a small business owner and his or her employees?

8. I have suggested that a small business owner is very much alone, and in fact is lonely. Do you agree with that statement? Explain.

9. It was suggested that a small business needs a degree of luck to succeed. Do you agree? Why or why not?

10. If you were to draw a profile of an entrepreneur, what personality traits or qualities and what skills would you think would be most important to enhance the entrepreneur's chances of success?

3 Ethics: A Foundation You Can Build On

• • • • • • • • • • • • •

Chapter Objectives:

- To provide an appreciation for the concept that ethical behavior is good business.

- To provide the experience of people reaching out to people.

- To provide a model for a code of conduct that attempts to balance the sometimes conflicting needs of all stakeholders in a small business.

My opening statement concerning the inclusion of a section on ethics is: Why? It won't do much good to attempt to teach ethics in the classroom, especially at this level. The ethical conduct and ethical standards of each person have for the most part been firmly rooted and established long before entering a postsecondary institution of higher learning. It is doubtful that change will occur as the result of reading a chapter or even taking a course in ethics.

• ETHICAL CONDUCT • • • • • • • • • • • • • •

Let's use as a definition of *ethics* doing what is right instead of what is wrong. We do not learn our ethics from what is written in books. Our ethical conduct is written and/or imprinted inside us, written on the hearts and in the minds of humankind. It got there through the socialization process and was influenced by family or lack of family, friends, school, neighborhood, religion or lack of religious upbringing, as well as a myriad of other factors that make us who and what we are today.

Sometimes, though, people change; sometimes their behavior is changed by an act of kindness or by a monumentous event in their lives. Sometimes people are inspired to do good things for other people when they see or hear the goodness of others. Acts of kindness begin with a person's ability to see others outside themselves and to feel compassion or empathy for others, which leads to action—thus an act of kindness. Ethics is more than kindness or goodness, but such acts are visible and somewhat measurable (not that somebody needs to keep score). The action itself does not guarantee that the person doing the good deed is a moral and/or ethical person, but one would expect a correlation to exist. If nothing else, those who benefit are affected regardless of their benefactor's motive.

As a people, Americans are noted for generosity and caring for those in need. It is part of our heritage. This reminds me of a story I heard or read, I can't remember where. Shortly after the end of World War II, Berlin was blockaded by the Russians. The United States responded with an unprecedented warlike effort during peacetime to keep West Germany from falling into the hands of the Soviets. West Berlin was kept alive and supplied with the necessities of life through a massive airlift.

At first the Berliners didn't know what to make of all those planes flying over and into their city. Many Germans were filled with fear and mistrust. These were the same Americans who only recently had been dropping bombs on them with many of those same planes. Yet those planes were now their lifeline. As with any massive relief project, distribution bottlenecks and glitches were bound to occur, and the Berlin airlift was no exception. Many of those who most needed food and other necessities were not getting them, and as generally is the case, those who are hurt the most are the children. Many of these kids were fatherless from the war, innocent victims of politics and war.

One day Captain Gail Halverson, a pilot who was flying over the city of Berlin with a load of relief supplies, looked down on the city and began to think about those kids. The more he thought about them, the more it bothered him. His heart went out to them, and he wished there was something he could do to help on a personal level other than just flying in supplies, most of which were bottlenecked near the runway. He mentioned this to other members of the flight crew, and somebody came up with the idea of air dropping their own relief in the form of bundles attached to miniature parachutes. They took some rags and made up several bundles consisting of chocolate bars, chewing gum, and the like. They then made makeshift parachutes to use to drop their gift bundles safely. The next time they made their landing approach over West Berlin they opened up the window of the cockpit and threw these little bundles out.

When this crew got back to base, some of the other pilots who saw these tiny parachutes float to the streets below wanted to know what this crew was doing. After hearing about this air crew's project, many decided to join in. Soon other crews began making up their own bundles to toss out the window to the children below, and as time went on, the sky became filled with miniature gifts, all floating to the children below on tiny parachutes: tokens of peace, love, and friendship from unknown, unseen airmen to children below in the beleaguered city of West Berlin.

The other side of this story is the children. When these packages first arrived, the parents were horrified. First these hateful Americans helped to kill their menfolk in war, leaving them widows. Now they wanted to kill their children with poisoned chocolate bars. They must know how desperately hungry many of these children are and how vulnerable they would be to such a dirty trick. It took some time for the adults of West Berlin to accept the fact that these were packages of good will falling from the skies above their city. It took some time before the children were allowed to run the streets in search of these precious little bundles of cargo, which were expanding beyond chocolate to include other desperately needed but difficult-to-get items. The drone of a plane engine now sent the children scurrying out into the streets looking for falling treasure rather than racing for a basement or other makeshift bomb shelter. A lot of healing occurred over the skies of Berlin for both the children on the ground and the former bomber pilots in the sky.

To understand ethics begins with an opening of one's eyes and a softening of one's heart. Goodness begins with one human being reaching out to another with an act of kindness. Such acts create a change of heart, which often does more good for the giver than for those who receive. It often gives to the giver new meaning and purpose in life.

Could you imagine what it must have been like for many of those pilots? They had just finished a war. They had forced themselves to look upon the German people as an enemy. For many that concept had escalated into a personal hatred for the German people, fueled by the loss of friends and comrades. Now they were supposed to fly again to save these people. Why? They wanted to go home. Most of these pilots and crews were sick of flying. They must now fly mission after mission of relief flights, with overworked crews and overworked equipment, trying to do what had never been done before.

Yet for many, with each little bundle that floated to those kids below, a part of that anger and hatred could melt away. A new purpose and a new energy was created. To watch the children scramble for those packages must have brought great joy to those pilots. It gave them a reason to fly. Think also what it did for them when they got home. They could live in peace and joy, and as they embraced their wives and children, they could remember not the bombs they dropped, but the relief and the joy they had dropped on the children of Germany.

The Berlin airlift took place some 50 years ago. You might think that it was a different time and that people are different today. It might seem that the worst of times sometimes brings out the best in people, at least that has been said. The Berlin airlift demonstrates that even when people have been surrounded by the evils of war, goodness can prevail—that people will rise up out of the ashes and do things that are extraordinary. People have always been intrigued by the seeming contradiction displayed by human behavior, especially the struggle between good and evil, which seem to coexist within all of humankind.

So what does this have to do with business, specifically with operating a small business? Ethics, goodness, or whatever you want to call it or however you want to define it is reflected in your behavior. As a small business owner, your ethical code will determine how or if you have the ability to see outside yourself and what if anything you are going to do about it. As a small business owner your scope or span of influence will extend farther than before. Your ethical standards will dictate what you are willing to do, in both a positive sense and a negative sense. Your ethical standards will determine what you are unwilling to do, that is, how far you will go in many areas either to make a buck or to sacrifice that dollar to do the right thing. Your ethics, in fact, define for you what the right thing is.

Will you be a good neighbor, good employer, good supplier, good creditor, and so on, or will you take what you can any way you can? I am saying that being a ethical person and running an ethical business is "good business." It is the way to stay in business; it is also the way to maintain your own self-respect and dignity.

PROFILE IN ENTREPRENEURSHIP: CAROLYN DOWNS, THE BANQUET[1]

I want to demonstrate to you that some people, and some businesses, are trying to do the right thing, that many are searching for the goodness that is within each of us. I also want to demonstrate that expressing "goodness" within a business organization, in an attempt to be a good neighbor by meeting the needs of the surrounding community, is something that goes on all the time. Such acts are rarely written up by the media. In most communities goodness gets a lot less attention than any evil that goes on. I firmly believe that the number of acts of kindness still far outweigh the number of harmful acts that occur in our country; they just don't draw as much attention. I would also argue that when a community reaches the point where goodness and human kindness do not outweigh acts of evil, such a community is no longer a very good place to live.

The business community can do a lot to take the lead in setting the ethical, good-neighbor tone for a community by setting an example and by encouraging their employees to reach out to those in need in the community. However, the baseline for the goodness that one human being expresses to another human being begins at the individual level.

In the community of Sioux Falls, South Dakota, whenever one thinks on the level of human kindness, several agencies or groups come to mind, but almost always in that list is the Banquet, which is a community and regional outreach to the poor of that community. The Banquet was founded in 1985 by an ecumenical group of people, which included a bishop, a former governor, and a number of clergy, lay ministers, and professional people who came together to assist the poor and the homeless with a feeding ministry. The Banquet has a very unique approach, though, in that their target ministry is not the poor but the volunteer, who in turn ministers to the guest. Those served are primarily those who are living with a very limited means, those who are lonely, and those who are homeless. This involves a wide cross section of people, and most who have worked as volunteers seem to be amazed at how many children and families are present.

Carolyn Downs, the director, says: "The number of volunteer groups who come to serve is so varied. It is wonderful; that is the best part of this job. The next best part of the job is watching these volunteers come together with those they have often perceived to be lazy, to not want to help themselves, or who were using the system. It is wonderful to see the realization of one another, and that is a two-way street—there has to be a realization by both the volunteer and the guest. They both need to realize that we are so much alike even though their lives are worlds apart. Watching them come together and to see that understanding come about is a wonderful part of this job. We call it the Miracle on Main, since we are appropriately located on Main Avenue. I think it is a miracle to see patience and understanding happen every night."

According to Carolyn: "The people who founded the Banquet ministry on the premise of focusing on the volunteer were really wise. They had tremendous insight. They had a belief that the community would respond. The concept "banquet" came about after a lot of prayer and a lot of work, which included some hands-on. Members went to visit a place, which was ministering to people in a similar way. They went to Milwaukee, Wisconsin and spent several days in a consortium of ministries there. After $2\frac{1}{2}$ days of working there the minister in charge, who happened to be an Episcopalian priest, sat down with them. He asked them to tell him who their target ministry will be, and when they named the homeless, the lonely, the elderly, and the single parent, the priest responded, 'no.' "If you found your ministry on that premise, you will fail in what really needs to happen. Your target ministry is the volunteer."

It was a wonderful concept. It was a real awakening as to why that would be the focus. Carolyn indicated that she had worked in programs in San Francisco, Portland, Phoenix, Colorado, Minneapolis, Washington, D.C., and in other places, and she said she has never been in a place that has that focus. All these places use volunteers, they are thankful for volunteers, but they are not targeted as their ministry.

When the founding group returned to Sioux Falls, they determined that the board of directors and the staff at the Banquet would minister to the volunteer through total involvement. The volunteer group would plan the menu, the staff would work with them to make sure that the numbers were right, that adequate food was prepared, that the equipment was functioning, and that the facility was clean and decent for the guests. The staff's job was to coordinate the effort; the staff's job is not to feed the hungry—that is the job of the volunteers. The staff works with the volunteers, enabling them to be prepared to meet and minister to the guests.

The volunteer groups come to develop a real sense of loyalty to the Banquet, because they have so much invested. When they leave they have come to realize that their most important part has been their interaction with the guests. The volunteer groups come with the food, or have it delivered. They have by some means raised the funds to purchase what they will need. They bring volunteers in to prepare the food as well as to serve it.

It takes between 28 and 35 people to minister by serving a meal at the Banquet. For some groups that number of volunteers is too many for their organization. For those situations Carolyn will merge two small groups to accommodate and facilitate their ability to participate. Carolyn indicated that the Banquet will make all kinds of concessions to allow volunteers to participate. I asked Carolyn if she ever gets a group that cancels. "Occasionally; the most challenging is when that occurs at the last minute, but I have

(continued)

(continued)

learned over the years when we are in trouble to call upon the youth. They have no qualms about doing extraordinary things. They are wonderful. With college back in session it will take one call and we will have our group. I just received a call from a group of choir students who want to get involved. It is really exciting."

"The youth of today fill me with such hope. We have many of the area colleges and universities involved, with student associations, fraternities, sororities, and student councils all getting involved. That is why I have so much hope, not only for this place but for the future. I think this generation is going to make a big difference. They are asking questions that are going to cause change."

The Banquet serves a meal six days a week, Monday through Friday evenings, and a meal on Saturday at noon. The average guest count runs about 350 people. With that tight a schedule, Carolyn indicated that there is very little recovery time between meals. "This ministry begins with the volunteers' commitment to come to prepare and serve the food. The staff has an orientation period, during which they minister to the volunteers. After the meal has been served and cleanup is complete, there is a closing session. The staff will spend a half-hour of orientation with the volunteers before they open the door as a means of preparing them to welcome the strangers. The emphasis is to go way beyond the food, to be with the guest at this mealtime, to serve themselves as well as the food." Carolyn likes to explain that with each person who comes through their door there are two guests, the body and the soul. It is easy to feed the body; it is much more difficult to feed the soul, which can only come by being with people.

"During orientation the staff attempts to make the volunteers feel comfortable in ministering to the guests; to make them feel needed and to help the volunteers realize what an integral part of the process they are. The volunteers are the crux of this ministry. Most groups serve once a year; a few will serve twice, but it takes a lot of volunteers to run this program. We have over 20,000 volunteers registered with us; we have over 500 groups that support us from a three-state area. It is phenomenal; the volunteer information center says that we are probably the largest volunteer organization in the upper midwest. It is amazing: We receive no state, no federal, no city, no United Way monies. We operate strictly on personal donations. We do one fund raiser a year; we send out letters only to past supporters and to the business community. We have never needed to solicit our total mailing list."

"As I said, the orientation session is to prepare the volunteer to meet the guest. The closing session is the time where we can throw facts and figures at the volunteers. It is a time when they can ask questions back. Having been involved with a meal, and after having sat down and visited with the guests over a meal, many have questions. It is a time the volunteers can express their likes and dislikes and can express what they are feeling. One of the most common comments relates to the waste—that after a meal the trash can is half-full of wasted food. It is hard for many to realize that even in such a program as the Banquet, there will be waste after a meal served to 350 people. If you have worked in a restaurant, you know that the waste would be much greater, but it is a revelation, especially when they realize that bananas have peels. Also 20 percent of the guests are children, and they are not always going to clean their plates. It is a realization that doesn't always come naturally."

"What the experience does for the volunteer is it really bridges the gap between the guests and themselves. It puts a face on the guest and humanizes the situation. The volunteer experience does much to dispel myth and prejudice. Yes, a few of the guests could be considered just lazy, but most are not. One of the goals of this ministry is to bridge the gap that exists between the haves and the have-nots in this and the surrounding community."

A story Carolyn likes to tell is one involving Citibank, a major employer in this community. When the bank's employees were serving as volunteers, the CEO flew in from New York and stopped down at the Banquet. He sat and ate with the guests. He sat across from a guest who was reading the *Iliad*. He was amazed; he commented: "I wouldn't enjoy reading the *Iliad;* I don't think I could read it if I had to." Shortly after he left, the guest commented to Carolyn: "Do you know who I sat with tonight? That guy is the head man over at Citibank. Who would think I would ever sit with someone so important." As Carolyn said: "Those who come to serve need to feel a little humility and come to the realization that what we share with each other is humanity—that the guest needs to be treated with dignity. The guests, on the other hand, need to realize that they are not alone—that people do care, that many are willing to and want to help. That this is not a cold and sullen world. Most people just need to bridge the gap as to what the needs are, and many good people exist who will respond."

"In this community the business community was slow to respond; it was individuals who went back to their churches, and it was the church membership that drew the business community in. When the business community does get involved, a tremendous bonding takes place between employees who participate as volunteers. Serving others brings people together." Carolyn then told the story of a local businessman who has long been a supporter of the Banquet, who just purchased a flower wholesale business. "He told us that if you ever need flowers for your table, you call and we'll get you flowers. We have called and they have sent us flowers. He finally brought his employees from the flower business down to the banquet to serve as volunteers. They were astounded, they brought red roses down to put on the tables and for the guests. One volunteer just cried; she said: 'Did you see that little girl walk out clutching that rose? That little girl told me that it's for her grandmother's grave. Anytime you need flowers, you just call and we'll make sure you get some.' She was really touched by that experience."

Carolyn said: "These guests deserve roses, too. Do you think they ever have flowers at home on their tables? I doubt it, and roses to top it off. That lady who works in the flower business never once thought that the roses she worked on would end up in a soup kitchen, much less in the hands of a little girl who will place one on her grandmother's grave. Hearts were touched and hearts were opened with that experience. It is experiences like that which need to happen. When she goes back to work that lady will tell the rest of the employees, and in turn they will respond by wanting to come down here again. In coming down they will begin to draw closer together. This place brings meaning to life for many people and they are not just guests."

In a state like South Dakota, which ranks at or near the bottom in average income, many of the guests are simply underemployed. In a community

(continued)

(continued)

like Sioux Falls, the unemployment rate is currently one of the lowest in the nation. Underemployment is the bigger problem: people with low level skills who are attempting to make ends meet on minimum-wage jobs. As Carolyn puts it: "What many of the Banquet's guests must do is make choices. The first choice is to put a roof over their family's heads. The next choice is utilities; with the cold winters in the north country, they cannot fall behind on their utilities or they will go without. Clothes are purchased at Good Will centers, but the only real discretionary income they have in their budget is food. When the money runs out, the Banquet acts as a safety net. Most of the guests do not have health or dental insurance. Still, they have medical bills. Most do not have a car; still, if they work, they have transportation expenses. The money just isn't there to meet all those needs. So the Banquet acts to help pick up the slack when the money runs out.

"If all we needed was people to serve food, we would only need about six volunteers. We serve a lot more than food. There is a fellowship and a hospitality also served. To facilitate that we send volunteers outside, before the doors are open, meeting and greeting the guests. The volunteers serve hot apple cider in the winter and cold fruit juice in the summer. In this way the guests have been served hospitality even before they enter the building. We also have people standing at the front door handing out tickets and greeting the guests. The tickets are actually cards, which is simply a way to keep a count of the number of guests who have been served." Carolyn indicated that the tickets say nothing except for their hours of operation, and the function itself could easily be replaced by a staff person at the door with a mechanical counter, clicking off numbers as the guests come through the door. The purpose is to allow for more human interaction between the volunteers and the guests. Farther down the line are two more volunteers who collect the tickets, again meeting guests and welcoming them to the Banquet.

Carolyn says that when she tells others about how the Banquet functions, they are astounded. She says that she has been in soup kitchens around the country and the most you might see, as far as staff is concerned, is one or two at the door. "The usual case is a couple of burly men in uniform whose jackets say security—like you are entering a danger zone, which in some cases you are. Here at the Banquet we also occasionally have trouble, but people are generally a lot more gracious than they are given credit for. It is not a danger zone when you serve in a hospitable way."

Another unique feature of the Banquet is the children's room. "That was a concept we borrowed from a church in Frogtown, Minnesota. Some students came in and set up a little table to provide a place for the children to draw on. We created a special room that is well equipped. We offer the children planned activities such as crafts. The children's room provides an opportunity for volunteers to interact with the children. It also allows the children a chance to show the volunteers what they can do by showing off their talent, and it makes them feel special. Beyond that lies another reason for the children's room. At a place like the Banquet, we have a very mixed crowd that come as guests. They can be very edgy around children: Some of the guests may have mental health problems, others simply don't like children. The children, who are forced to wait in line for a period of time, can get very antsy and can get out of order. It works a lot better if we can bring them in out of the line to a place where they can play until their parents come in. At that time they can go through the line and eat together as a family. The children's room relieves a lot of the anxiety.

"As you can see a lot of careful thought has gone into the planning and the creation of the Banquet. I just admire those who founded this ministry."

• ETHICS IN THE EXCHANGE RELATIONSHIP· · · · · · · · · · · · · · · · · · · ·

When you yourself need a service, who do you seek out? Is it not someone who is good at what they do in that particular type of service? Is it not also someone in whom you can trust? Trust to do what? Trust to do a good job at a fair price. Trust that you won't be taken advantage of in your ignorance or in your inability to perform that service yourself. Is this not ethical behavior? It is the foundation on which you can build a business. It is the foundation on which business in the United States has traditionally been built on. Ethics is more than just the foundation of this book. It is the place to start—the beginning. You begin to build your business by first building relationships with a core group of contacts, and anchoring those relationships in mutual trust.

I recently had a former student come to me for advice and assistance in starting an at-home bookkeeping service. We discussed her goals and aspirations and began a discussion of marketing. I agreed to mentor her to the best of my ability, but before we parted I asked her to do me a favor. I asked her to spend no less than one day in a quiet place thinking about ethical issues: thinking primarily about what she would be willing to do and what she would not be willing to do in the course of running her bookkeeping business. I asked her to decide for herself what her definition of right and wrong was and what her response will be when her personal values are challenged. She asked why she should do this. My response was because she will be challenged ethically, and when that challenge comes, a response will be required. I suggested that it was better to have developed her values and her position beforehand rather than attempting to develop a policy manual concerning ethics on the spot, so to speak.

We parted but stayed in contact by phone and met at least weekly for a cup of coffee or a Coke. She was not two or three weeks into her business—in fact, it was over her very first client—when she called me with an ethical dilemma. My response was that I could not tell her what to do, but that my advice was always to do the right thing. To add to the irony, I also worked as a tax investigator in the area and would regularly perform audits based on payroll claimed but not reported, which in turn led me full circle on this issue right to the door of the former student and her client. I was not aware that this investigation involved her client until the moment I walked in the door, only to discover my former student sitting there to represent this employer.

After conducting my audit investigation I did not have to wait long before receiving a phone call from my former student. The first thing she said: "Do you remember that conversation we had about ethics? Well, boy, were you ever right!" I knew she would be challenged ethically, but I really didn't expect it to happen to her so soon. As we both went on to discover, her ethics were to be challenged quite frequently, which was especially disturbing to me because she had only four clients at the time. It is unfortunate that right and wrong is rarely so well defined as it is in a bookkeeping business, which parallels so closely what is legal and what is illegal.

• ETHICS AND MORALITY • • • • • • • • • • • •

By definition, ethical behavior has to do with morality. *Morality*, by definition, has to do with rightness or wrongness. In business, rightness of behavior is closely associated with honesty and being trustworthy, being a man or woman of your word, committed to doing the right thing or to treating the customer right. When you stop and think about this for a moment, it is not such a strange concept. The marketing concept is not far from the definition of ethics: to give customers what they want. What does the customer want? They want to be treated fairly. They do not want to be deceived concerning price, product quality, or timeliness and quality of service. They do not want to pay for something they did not receive. In short, they don't want to be ripped off. Treating the customer right has for years been the mantra of business in the United States. We have developed truisms in our culture so that we don't forget the importance of treating the customer right. These sayings also help to convey the importance of this concept to others, especially employees. Thus we have "the customer is always right," "the customer is king," and other such sayings.

The relationship between a business and a customer requires that these conditions be reciprocal. That is, the customer is also expected to be ethical, to be honest and trustworthy, a man or woman of his or her word. As a customer we guard against unscrupulous and unethical businesses that attempt to prey upon us and the rest of the trusting public. The reverse is also true, and when we become a business owner, we must guard against unethical and unscrupulous customers.

The types of unethical behavior exhibited by a firm's customers is varied. The types of unethical customer behavior your firm will be exposed to will depend in part on the type of business you are in. If you run a retail establishment or any type of business where you have inventory, external theft from shoplifters is always a threat.

Retail establishments have gone to great lengths to protect themselves from shoplifters. Many stores employ security or train their staff in security. If you go into a department store, more and more you see some type of electronic detection machine that patrons must pass through in order to exit the store. Manufacturers are working with retailers to reduce theft through the use of electronic or magnetic tags that activate an audio alarm if not removed or disabled at the checkout counter.

If you examine the merchandise layout and displays used by most major retail stores you will find that many stores actually use chains or cables to prevent a more expensive piece of clothing from being removed without the assistance of a store clerk. Most retailers who sell expensive items that are small generally display them in a locked display case which requires the assistance of a store clerk prior to customer examination.

Many stores use video cameras that scan the store and display on a bank of screens monitored by security personnel or which simply store the visual scan on tape to be viewed at will. Other stores incorporate observation windows. Many older retailers especially would build the office space above the retail floors so that store employees could look down to observe customers on the floor. I'm sure the original intent of such a design was multifaceted. The store manager wanted to be able to observe customers in part for customer information purposes as well, but the location of the elevated office space was meant to act as a deterrent to shoplifting. The elevated office also provided the store manager a view of the employees as well, both to observe work behavior and to monitor when they needed additional help during peak demand periods.

Any establishment that has inventory that is readily removable will have cause to guard against the threat of shoplifting. Customer fraud and dishonesty go far beyond mere shoplifting. In cases where a warranty or return policy is associated with products, a window of opportunity exists for deceit as well. The possibility of someone, say, buying a dress for a party, wearing the dress, and then returning it the next day is an example. Through ignorance, customers may damage or destroy a product or piece of equipment, intentionally or unintentionally, and then return it for an exchange or to get their money back. Either way it costs money.

In the restaurant business customers may walk out without paying; customers have driven off without paying for gas; and in the grocery business, a customer's groceries may be stolen by someone else. My point is that blind trust is not always feasible. Trust generally is something that must be earned, and trust must be reciprocal. In part the degree of customer trust that can be granted may depend on the region of the country or the type of client base that you have. Another way of looking at the situation is to the degree to which you must guard against customer deceit. It also depends on the type of product or service you are providing.

I remember a conversation I had with a restauranteur who explained that he didn't mind so much if once in awhile someone ate at his place of business and wrote him a rubber check, because all he was really beaten out of was the food cost. What really upset him was a person who wrote the check out for more than the purchase, because then it took the next five customers to make up for the loss created by the bad customer. If such a problem persists, the proprietor has no choice other than to change the business's policy, usually by tightening up what is acceptable. In my restaurant checks were generally accepted if we knew the customer well; there were no restrictions. I considered a policy of accepting checks for the amount only because insufficient funds checks were beginning to be a problem. In the end it is really the ongoing relationship that your business has with your customers which dictates the degree of trust that can be extended. The willingness of the proprietor to extend trust to the customer in the form of credit, a return, a warranty policy, or other means is influenced by the business's exposure to loss within that transaction as well as the firm's history of those transactions.

The best example I can think of to exemplify this concept comes from my parents. As old as I am, and with as much education and business experience as I have, I am continually amazed at the business savvy that my parents demonstrate. My parents, who are retired from farming and ranching, own a trailer court with a campground and small antique store just north of Bowman, North Dakota, which is located in the extreme southwestern corner of the state. In part because they do not want to be tied down to this enterprise too closely, my father erected a sign and a put up a mailbox at the entrance to their campground. The sign simply directs patrons to park themselves and identifies which sites have both water and sewer hookups and which have just electricity. The sign directs the patrons as to what the nightly rates are, and requests that they just put the money in an envelope and leave it in the mailbox. The mailbox is left unlocked.

Bowman lies on U.S. highway 85, which is used by many Canadian tourists who are travelling south into the United States. The Black Hills of South Dakota, particularly the Mount Rushmore National Monument, which lies about 160 miles to the south of Bowman, is an attraction that brings tourists up and down highway

85. Many of the tourists who come with their campers and travel trailers just shake their heads in amazement at the level of trust and hospitality offered them. My parents will often leave the area for several days at a time to visit their children or other relatives, only to return and find cash and checks in the mailbox, often along with some very nice letters. They do, though, have a neighbor who will kind of watch the area for them in their absence, but for the most part the campground is a business based almost entirely on customer trust.

My father explains that most people are basically honest, especially the types of customers he has. He indicates that most are retired people who have a little money; otherwise, they could not afford to be driving what they are driving or afford to be on vacation. He points out that his rates are lower than most these people are used to paying, and furthermore, that his rates do not represent a financial hardship. Most of his patrons appreciate the fact that his campground is there, is neat and clean, and is well protected by trees. My parents will readily admit that they are sure that a few people drive off without paying but that the percentage doesn't warrant them staying there 24 hours a day to ensure that they don't lose a dollar or two. The campground is operating at a profit. I'm sure that if their livelihood hinged on the revenue generated by the campground, controls would need to be tightened up a bit, but I did want to demonstrate that for the most part, people have the ability to rise to the level of expectations. Caution must always prevail, but it is refreshing to see this type of business prosper in the marketplace. It shouldn't be such a surprise that a business like my parents' campground can survive, because that really is just an example of the legacy of the way business has been conducted in this country.

• A LOOK BACK · · · · · · · · · · · · · · · · · ·

The heritage that we share in this nation is grounded in moral principles. Ours is a story of a people who were willing to sacrifice for others. The last paragraph of the Declaration of Independence reads: "And for the support of this Declaration, with a firm reliance on the protection of divine Providence, we mutually pledge to each other our Lives, our Fortunes and our sacred Honor." By word and pen these men were bound to the death to perform what they set out to do. U.S. history is rich with tales of men and women who put principle before personal gain. It is what made this nation great.

The United States was founded by people who settled here for religious freedoms. These people lived life from a religious perspective and conducted their business affairs the same way. To gain personally at the expense of another was generally not done. Society ran more closely to the Golden Rule (Do unto others as you would have them do unto you), which has its roots in scripture: "Teacher, which commandment of the law is the greatest? Jesus said to him: You shall love the Lord your God with your whole heart, with your whole soul and with all your mind. This is the greatest and first commandment. The second is like it: You shall love your neighbor as yourself. On these two commandments the whole law is based, and the prophets as well" (Matthew 22:36–40).

The greatest commandment had and continues to have a huge impact on the lives of many believers. One other verse has had a similar impact: "What profit would a man show if he were to gain the whole world and destroy himself in the process" (Matthew 16:26, Mark 8:36, Luke 9:25). For people of Judeo-Christian heritage who believe in a life after death and who believe in a final judgment, those verses have significance. At some level every person grasps the concept that we are not immortal and that death is inescapable. That point comes home to us most poignantly when we bury a loved one. At that time, whether a believer or not, the realization that you cannot take your accumulated wealth with you upon death becomes vividly apparent. The question then is not whether we will die, but when. More important, how will we live? What principles guide our life's actions?

In the society in which we currently live, much is done to deny the reality of death. Television and other forms of media focus primarily upon youth. The ads are filled with beautiful people filled with life and vitality. Age and the aging process is something much of the media leads us to believe should be considered as very undesirable. Cosmetic firms sell billions of dollars' worth of products that are designed to help deny the aging process. Other ads tell us to "do it," live fast and hard and reach for the pleasure that their products will bring. Millions of people believe and respond to these ads, and in so doing our societal beliefs, attitudes, and values have been changed somewhat. Our culture has changed.

Sociology defines a *norm* as an accepted way of behaving. Society, or more accurately a group in society, defines what is acceptable and what is not acceptable. Before television, radio, and other forms of mass media, values and norms were established primarily by family, extended family, and the community, of which the church was often the central institution. Little wonder that the Golden Rule was the norm. In addition, beyond a generation or two ago, most people lived their entire lives in or near the community they grew up in, and because everybody knew everybody else, a powerful incentive was present to maintain the norms. A violation of the normative standards of behavior could cause a reputation to be ruined, which in turn could easily cause one's business to be ruined as well. Societal pressure, along with religious convictions and perceptions, were strong elements in defining how people would conduct their business affairs.

Let me add one more thread to this line of thought on how life used to be. People lived a lot closer to life and death, resulting in a different sense of reality, an acceptance that life was very temporary. Childbirth occurred in the family home, generally with the assistance of a midwife. Death also occurred in the home. Nursing homes did not exist, the extended family filled that function, and thus the children and grandchildren were present to witness the decline and death of the parents and grandparents. Society was also more agrarian; people not only raised the animals they ate but did the slaughtering and processing themselves. People were also very close to nature not only in the sense of the crops they raised, which were so dependent upon the weather, but also in a larger sense. They recognized and understood nature. The young buck would challenge the old monarch and would be defeated until time and age caused the natural transition to occur again. In the same way a man turned the farm or the family business over to his son or daughter. It was the acceptable way of doing things. The natural cycle of birth, youthful exuberance growing into mature strength, then wisdom, and finally declining to the feebleness of old age, to be followed by death, was and still is the law of nature. This perspective of life, coupled with a religious heritage, has influenced and been a part of the way business affairs have been conducted in this country for a long time. It has been only in the last 50 years or so that these traditions have been challenged seriously in our society. This system of doing business as though everyone is your neighbor, because in reality the business owner probably was your neighbor, took this country from the wilderness to a position of global power by the end of World War II.

The best story I can think of to illustrate how business was often conducted in the past is one my father-in-law told me as he described his life. In the retelling it might be helpful to have a little background. Glen Ullin is a small farming community located in west central North Dakota. Like many others in North Dakota, this town was formed when in 1879 the Northern Pacific Railroad laid its tracks across the North Dakota prairie. Towns just sprang up along those tracks. Generally, they were created at a distance of 6 miles apart, which was roughly the distance that a steam-powered locomotive could travel before it had to take on water. These became convenient stops for mail pickup and dropoff points, followed by a post office, and then the rest of the small town followed naturally. If you travel the interstate highway system through the midwest, you can sometimes still notice the regularity of exits into small towns every 6 miles. When the exits are 12 miles apart it is usually because a town has died out over the years. Glen Ullin is one of those towns. It was named after a piece of English literature, *Lord Ullin's Daughter*. The word *Glen* stems from the fact that the town lies in a valley.

In my wife's family lineage were two brothers, Anton and Lucas Muggli, originally from Cold Springs, Minnesota, who moved to Glen Ullin in 1905 to manage the local roller mill. The Muggli brothers had learned their trade from their father, who owned a flour mill near Cold Springs. After moving to Glen Ullin they managed the local mill and later bought controlling interest in the same mill. Anton married Susie (Theisen) Muggli, and together they raised 13 children, of which Ewald, my father-in-law, was the ninth child. Ewald grew up around the mill helping his father and four older brothers. Anton also had extensive land holdings, so there was also farming and livestock to take care of. The depression years of the 1930s took its toll on the family fortunes, but they retained the mill.

In 1942 Ewald was drafted into the army. He served as a radio operator for General Patton's 90th Division of Field Artillery. In 1945 he was discharged and began his long journey home to Glen Ullin. One of his first stops after returning home was to stop in at the mill, where he found his father Anton at work. "The old man looked up kind of surprised to see me home, and said, 'Oh you're back. Well, what do you plan on doing now?'" Ewald indicated that he would like to farm. Anton offered him a quarter section (160 acres) north of town and also offered to provide any seed or fertilizer needed, which could be taken from the mill. After checking around town, Ewald discovered that a farmer just south of town a few miles was retiring and had seven quarter sections of land for sale. Ewald sought this man out, negotiated a price, and informed him he wanted to buy him out, but he didn't have any money. After some discussion the retiring farmer offered to let Ewald farm the ground and make a payment to him in the fall after the harvest was in. (He did not even specify what the payment should be.) And so it was agreed. Ewald then went back to Glen Ullin to visit with the farm equipment dealer, telling him of his recent purchase and that he needed a full line of farm machinery and had no money, but could he carry him until fall, until after the harvest was in, at which time he would make a payment? Again with a handshake, these terms were accepted. A final stop was to the fuel dealer, and credit was granted with payment postponed until after the harvest. In two years with two good crops and fair prices, the farm and the machinery were paid off. (This farm remains in the family to this day.)

Amazing as this story seems, it was not uncommon for those times. In part the previous generation believed in making room economically for the current generation. Bear in mind, though, that the majority of farmers and merchants were small proprietors, not corporate chains. In part also, they were willing to take a financial risk on one who was willing to risk life and limb in the fight against tyranny and for freedom. They also believed Ewald and others like him to be men of their word, and the agreement entered into bound both parties by their word.

The position of this author's business model takes the view that ethics is the foundation upon which American business is grounded. It is what people expect and are looking for. It is the way to do business and the way to stay in business today just as in the past. Technology and automation have changed business enormously, but the human element remains essentially the same. What do customers want? They want to be treated fairly: a fair price and good service. In short, customers want to do business with someone they can trust today just as in yesteryear.

Unfortunately, the reality of today doesn't always read quite like the Waltons or the Mugglis. I have over the years developed an adage: Wherever there is money there is corruption; wherever there is big money, there is big corruption. To the degree that corruption becomes pervasive in our society and in our business dealings, to that same degree does it begin to erode the foundation of our nation's businesses and economic structure. Just as a nation cannot last long under a system of anarchy, a nation cannot maintain a healthy economy in an environment of corruption.

• CODE OF ETHICS · · · · · · · · · · · · · · · ·

Every person has adopted a personal code of ethics which guides that person's behavior. Each of us believes that our own system of values is correct. Our behaviors and actions reflect that internal value system. We do not universally share the same value system, nor do we share the same code of ethics. As a nation and as a people we share some similarities, but there is a broad variation between persons.

One of the fundamental determinants of a person's personal ethical standards stems from the person's attitude toward money, which in turn can sometimes be tied to the person's beliefs concerning life and death. In our society money is more than a medium of exchange; it is a measurement tool. Wealth is a primary measure of success and status. If you were to eavesdrop on a conversation between two people who have just met, say, at a Christmas party, the conversation might go something like this: "Hi! My name is Joe So and So. I don't think we've met." "No we haven't, I'm Pete So and So. Pleased to meet you." "So Pete, what line of work are you in?"

The exchange is small talk, but it also demonstrates what the parties are interested in. Their line of work is their measure of success, which equates to a measure of earning power, which in turn acts as a measure of wealth, which in turn is a measure of status. Within the context of our society, money and wealth are given a measure of status. The importance of that status symbol depends upon the participants and the importance they place on it. So in the example above, Joe says, "I'm a specialist in heart surgery," and internally everyone goes, "Oh, big house, big money, high status."

Money is not the only status symbol in our society, but it is a major status symbol. The person who places the acquisition of wealth above all else can more readily justify any means of acquiring wealth. Any means unless that person's behavior is acted upon and constrained by some other value set which acts to modify the person's behavior.

Where you draw the line personally equates with where your ethical standards lie within the continuum. On one extreme, wealth can be obtained by any means. Murder, extortion, child pornography, cocaine and other illegal drug sales, as well as a host of other activities, both legal and illegal, can generate wealth. Society has laws prohibiting many of those activities, but such laws do not prevent such activities from happening. Those who participate do so for profit. If such activity is personally repulsive to you, it is repulsive because of your personal system of beliefs.

Most people can readily agree that child pornography is a bad thing and that the sexual exploitation of children should be illegal. At some basic level most of us agree on what is right and what is wrong, but as we move down the ethical continuum of what is defined as ethical and what is not ethical, we soon enter a gray realm. For instance, what about the sexual exploitation of adults for profit? The debate begins to widen into issues of consent, freedom of expression, and so on. Where you place this issue on the continuum of ethical standards depends on you and your value system.

A real dilemma exists in our society concerning ethics and ethical standards. On one hand, there seems to be broad agreement that morality and ethics are on the decline in the nation. The problem begins with the definition of a standard code of ethics. We have one set of standards that has been instituted by government, which tells us what behavior is legal and what is not legal. That is not to say that what is legislated is automatically ethical or moral. It is simply what is legal under current legislation.

How can government legislate morality or ethics? The President and Congress decree that something is legal and therefore ethical and right, and something else is illegal and therefore wrong and unethical. To decree something does not make it so, just as management cannot decree that quality will exist and have it appear automatically. So government cannot decree that ethical conduct shall exist. If government could make that decree, we would not need prisons to house those who violate the law. Government is even less able to legislate a standard of conduct, due to the cynicism with which the public regards many government agents. To further depress the government's credibility, the government itself is rife with its own ethical problems.

Society raises its voice in anger and frustration over this decline in ethics. With each political and business scandal, society's awareness deepens, but the decline in ethical standards seems to continue. The newspaper and television media are filled with stories about how the elderly were bilked out of thousands of dollars through one scam or another, how insurance companies and manufacturers are being sued for one thing or another, how financial fraud is worsening—and the list goes on and on. Society's response is that the problem exists because we are not teaching our young people about ethics.

The truth is that our nation's young people are being taught ethical standards. The standards that they are being raised on are not the same standards that their parents' generation was raised on. Present-day standards of behavior would be almost unrecognizable compared to what most children's grandparents were raised on, but then so would the moral and ethical challenges be almost unrecognizable to this generation's grandparents. The real question is who or what is influencing the standards of behavior of the current generation, and who is responsible for instilling the "proper values" and standards of behavior.

The answer to the first question is multifaceted. The current generation has been reared in the information age. Their parents were the first generation raised with a television set in the home. Programming was limited and was heavily censored. Vulgarity and sexual content were strictly forbidden. Violence was tolerated but was often surreal. Television shows often had a moral to the story. The good guy almost always won, and the hero and heroine often literally wore white hats to make them recognizable. Good triumphed over evil. Not so in today's programming, where media competition seems to continually push the limits, in sexual content, violence, gay themes, and so on. Evil is often thrust into the limelight, and today there often are no good guys, and evil often triumphs.

The same problems exist with the media today as in yesteryear. People know that what goes on in a television show or movie is not real. Children are less able to make that distinction. To a large extent the television is so commonplace that children are not always coached in television's unreality and so are left more vulnerable to television's influence on their behavior and value formation. With the constraints being taken off this form of media, negative things are bound to happen, such as copycat crimes—murder as the result of play that mimics television.

Children's values are heavily influenced by the television programs and movies they see. The current V-chip is a small step toward industry recognizing that impact and is a token response to it. Yet is it the television and movie industries' total responsibility to provide only positive moral programming? Someone is allowing children to watch programming filled with vulgarity, violence, and sexually explicit content. That someone is generally the parents of those children, and is it not the parent's responsibility to impart a set of socially and morally "right" set of values and standards of behavior in their children?

It would seem that parents are failing in their job as parents. If so, why? Again there is no simple answer, nor is there a single answer. Television and the media may be a contributing factor. Peer pressure certainly has some influence. Parents are not parenting in part because they are working. Parents are not parenting in part because they are parenting alone. Parents aren't parenting because they are exhausted. Parents aren't parenting because it's too much work; it requires tremendous amounts of energy. Parents aren't parenting because they want to enjoy themselves. Parent's aren't parenting because they don't know how; they did not have good role models when they were growing up. The list goes on and on, but the fact remains that many children are not being raised with the "right" values, and society is not helping.

One solution: Get schools to teach ethics in the classroom. If, for instance, all the business schools in the United States taught ethics in the classroom, then upon graduation business students would act and behave more ethically in the working world of business. I don't think so. It's too late in a person's developmental stage for a business school to have much of an impact on personal values. Every person is already acting from his or her own set of values. Studying another set will not initiate a change in behavior unless a person wants to adopt a new set of values. The study of ethics, then, is really only an academic exercise, but still one that can raise awareness. If a higher degree of awareness is the beginning of change, so be it, but people often only hear the message they want to hear. Communication models tell us that individuals filter information to fit their existing belief systems—a course in ethics will do little to alter a system of beliefs.

If ethics is to be taught in a business school, what standard of ethics will be taught? The standard of ethics this country was founded on is under attack. The standard I'm referring to is the Judeo-Christian Mosaic law, the Ten Commandments. Due to pressure from special-interest groups and through legislation, a separation of church and state exists. Strong arguments have been made that such separation is good. If I were a non-Christian, I would resent being forced by the state to accept Christian values, but the question concerning ethics broadens. If not the Christian version of morality and ethics, then what standard should be taught? Second, who should teach it? The church itself historically has not been without its own ethical problems. Yet the ethical standards most of us refer to have been influenced strongly by Christianity and Christian principles. Many of our laws reflect a Christian influence as well. Thou shalt not kill, steal, bear false witness, and variations of those commandments are reflected in our laws concerning murder, battery, assault, and so on.

• ETHICAL BUSINESS BEHAVIOR · · · · · ·

It is not our intent in this book to identify and solve the problems associated with childrearing and parenting. The behavior of those children who have become adults and are entering the world of business is, however, a concern. How does this issue of ethics affect a business's chance of success? What is ethical business behavior?

The answer to the first question is in part the premise of this book. It is my belief that the customer is more likely to accept a product or service from a firm that the customer perceives to be ethical. In short, customers want to do business with someone they can trust. The answer to the second question gets a little more complicated. What is ethical depends on your perspective and the value structure of all the participants. It is almost a forgone conclusion that the participants, that is, the stakeholders of a business, will have varying sets of values. To meet everyone's expectations completely will be almost impossible. The best outcome could be would an equilibrium between the stakeholders.

Part of the ethical problems associated with big business in the United States stems from the perspective of how we measure success and whose perspective or position is protected within the context of the stakeholders. A fiduciary responsibility exists between management and the stockholders of a corporation. It is management's job to make decisions that are in the best interests of the stockholders. We teach that in corporate finance in every business school in the country. The primary objective of the financial manager is to maximize wealth to the stockholder; in so doing you maximize the utility to everyone.

The stockholder stakeholder in a company has had an even louder voice with the advent of pretax retirement funds over the past 20 years or so. Managed 401(k)'s have pumped trillions of dollars into their combined portfolios, with billions of additional dollars pouring into those funds every month. Fund managers are scrambling to be the fund of choice by demonstrating higher and higher rates of return. Pressure to perform is brought to bear on corporate management by fund managers, who control huge blocks of voting stock. The quest for short-term profits to support high rates of growth has to a large extent caused decisions to be made almost exclusively for the stockholder stakeholder and often at the exclusion of all other stakeholders.

Perspective and loyalty to a specific group can create a bias in what is deemed ethical. With the current perspective, management will often strive to widen profit margins through personnel cuts. The correct term is *downsizing*. With downsizing in place, management can often create an atmosphere where those who remain will be willing to go without pay increases, and in some cases, pay cuts. One could understand these types of concessions if a joint decision were being made to save a company from financial ruin. Yet at the same time that this trend in downsizing is occurring, corporate profits have helped drive the Dow Jones averages to record levels, even while supporting huge pay increases for top executives. Is this an issue of ethics, or free-market forces at work?

Fear of plant closings, or the threat of having the company move a plant to Mexico or the Pacific Rim, has pressured some communities into providing economic assistance and tax breaks to keep a firm in their backyard, to protect the city's economic base. Is such behavior ethical? Is this even a question of ethics? Does a company have a responsibility to treat their employees fairly? If they do, what is fair? They are, after all, providing employment.

Consider a moment what would happen if the company took the perspective of the employee: that management's loyalty is first to the employee and all else was secondary. Wages and benefits would be as high as the company could withstand without actually going under economically. Such a thought is absurd. What right does the worker have to all the economic rewards? No one would invest in such a company. Yet what right does the company have to reap record financial rewards on the backs of their employees, often at the expense of the other stakeholders?

The same argument could be made for each stakeholder within the realm of the corporation. If decisions were made for the best interests of the customer, prices would be lowered to the lowest levels possible that would still keep the company in business. Product quality would be at a very high level, and product safety would have one of the highest priorities.

We do live in a free-market system; few would dispute that the business of business is to make a profit. Yet we do not live in a totally free-market system; government involvement exists at all levels, regulating access to markets and access to funds, and legislation erects many barriers of entry while providing economic assistance and technical assistance to others. Protected monopolies existed for generations, allowing firms to build financial empires which at the stroke of a pen became deregulated to let the free market prevail. This is not a free-market system.

This argument is not a cry against profit, or that the quest for profit is bad and unethical; it is not. It is an attempt to bring to attention and to make the point that profit is the result of many factors and the actions of many of the stakeholders. Should not the distribution of that profit take into account those same stakeholders? Thus customers have the right not to be price gouged and to be given a reasonable assurance that the products they buy are safe. The community that provides water, sewer, roads, and an educational system to train current and future employees acts to support the firm's income-producing activities. In so doing the firm should ethically assume a responsibility not to pollute or cause harm in any way to the community. The firm should be a good neighbor and help to support that community. They should pay a fair wage and should pay their share of local, state, and federal taxes.

Ethical conduct is doing the "right" thing, and not because the law forces that action. Some semblance of balance should exist between meeting the needs of those stakeholders who participate in the activity of bringing a product or service to the marketplace. The balance of power is such that the initiator of the "right" actions generally rests with top management. It is by nature a top-down concept. If we could accept that premise as true, shouldn't the same standard be applied to small businesses, and to individuals as well?

For the small business owner it is a good idea to spend some time thinking about how our personal values and ethics will be challenged by the process of going into business. The new entrepreneur will cast a much wider net as far as ethical issues are concerned than they did prior to going into business. As an employee, most individuals' actions and behavior is to a large extent subservient to the ethical standards of the employer. Most employees will adhere to their employer's standards as long as their personal values are not violated too far. In a situation where a person's values are severely challenged, the person will be forced at some point to make a choice as to whether he or she will terminate his or her position or compromise his or her personal ethics. At some point it just simply isn't worth it for the person to continue. When the individual employee reaches that point, the person will quit.

As an entrepreneur, ethical issues become more complex. As a business owner the entrepreneur has entered into an array of financial commitments as well as interpersonal relationships and commitments. Expectations and pressure to perform are generally associated with those commitments. It may at times lead a business owner to act in ways that violate the entrepreneur's personal ethical standards. The loyalties associated with the commitments made may cause the entrepreneur to set aside his or her personal values and justify unethical actions because it's all "for the good of the company" or for "the good of the business."

When a person subordinates personal values to something or someone else, they generally experience a degree of stress. The amount of personal stress felt by the person will have some correlation with how far that person has compromised his or her values. As an entrepreneur, you can prevent much of the stress buildup due to ethical issues simply by creating a code of ethics to which you yourself, your business, and your employees can adhere. It is best if that code of ethics is articulated in writing and made available to everyone in the company.

It goes without question that the ethical conduct demonstrated by a firm is top down, that employees will attempt to emulate and synchronize with management's ethical standards. It is also helpful if the ethical standards that are articulated and the ethical standards that are demonstrated through behavior are the same. Dual standards just create confusion and further conflict for individuals and the organization.

Ethical standards begin to emerge within the context of the firm's mission statement. Ethical conduct is formulated within the policies established by the firm. Ethical standards are validated and confirmed by the actions of top management. It is the owners' actions and attitudes that will be emulated by the employees.

The following is an example of a code of ethics that attempts to balance the rights of all stakeholders.

Code of Ethics

1. **No harm.** This company adopts a policy of *do no harm*. We pledge to do no harm to the environment, we will not knowingly pollute the air, water, or the soil, through the production, distribution, or any ongoing activity of this firm.

    We pledge to do no harm to our customer. We will follow generally accepted industry standards in the production, distribution, and service of our products. We will not put the personal safety of our customers ahead of profit. We will meet and exceed the safety standards established by industry and governmental agencies.

    We pledge to do no harm to our employees. The personal safety of our employees has the highest priority. We will not put our employees at risk in the production, distribution, and service of our products.

2. **Integrity.** We pledge to be a firm of integrity. This company pledges and adopts a policy of honesty and truthfulness, to be reflected in billing procedures, payroll, accounting, and tax reporting. This company will pay its creditors on a timely basis. We shall always act from a position of honesty: to our customers, to our suppliers, to our creditors, to our employees, and to all others we deal with or interact with in the course of our business operation.

    We pledge our commitment to treat our customers and our employees with dignity. We will not tolerate any form of employee harassment. We will adhere to and support fair hiring practices; we will not discriminate due to age, gender, race, religious belief, disability, or for any other reason. Our

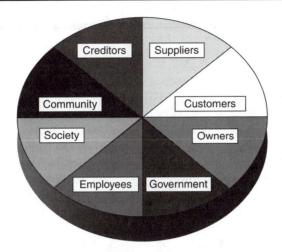

FIGURE 3–1   Stakeholders of a business

aim is to maintain a highly efficient and highly effective customer-oriented, quality-driven organization. Our team members will reflect those values and that commitment. Our compensation will meet and exceed any mandates. We are committed to fair compensation practices that reflect the achievement of our goals in the marketplace.

We pledge to honor customers' legitimate complaints and will accept reasonable product returns and exchanges. This company will do everything in its power to correct any customer problem, and to reduce the number of customer product or service problems through a quest for improvement in our production and process methods.

3. **A good neighbor.** We pledge to be a good neighbor in our community and to be a good citizen of our state and of our nation. We will support our community's efforts to make this a good place to live, first by being a good employer, and second, by backing and supporting the efforts of our community.

We pledge to be a good citizen of our state, first by obeying the laws and regulations that apply to our business and our industry, and second, by paying those taxes that are owed to the state government and/or regulating bodies. We extend the same pledge to the federal government.

4. **A good investment.** We pledge to do everything within our power to honor the commitment made to us by our investors and creditors. We will best meet those interests by providing a high-quality product and service which meets the needs of the customer, and by maintaining the trust and commitment that customers have placed in us. We pledge to keep our technological process in a competitive position and to monitor those variables that will cause us to make decisions that will lead us to continued prosperity. We pledge to make decisions that are for the good of the company, and will not tolerate decisions that result primarily in the personal gain of any officer or management personnel. We will not tolerate gratuities and or kickbacks from suppliers or customers. Our commitment and our loyalty are pledged to those stakeholders who make this company possible.

A code of ethics will be somewhat specific to the type of business and the industry that you are in. It stands to reason that some similarities might exist, especially in such areas as the treatment of customers and employees. It also stands to reason that the code of ethics and the firm's mission statement would correlate closely.

• QUESTIONS FOR DISCUSSION · · · · · · · ·

1. Do you agree or disagree with the discussion in the text which suggests that ethics cannot be effectively taught in the classroom?

2. Do you agree that the best way to stay in business is to run a business that is ethical? Explain your position.

3. Do you agree or disagree that the business community can take the lead in setting the "good neighbor" tone for the community?
   (a) If so, how?
   (b) Does the business community have an ethical obligation to take such a lead?
   (c) Why should they? Or why shouldn't they?

4. Is it important to set a written ethical policy prior to going into business? Why or why not?

5. How can you possibly know what ethical issues you will be confronted with prior to going into business?

6. *Ethics* and *morality* are words often used interchangeably. Are ethics and morality the same thing?

7. In the section "A Look Back" we discussed the issue of how life and business were a few generations ago.
   (a) Do you think people in general are more or less ethical than they were in your grandparents' time? Why?
   (b) Do you think it is easier or more difficult to grow up in current society versus that of your grandparents' time and still maintain your family value system?

9. Do you think it is ethical for the government to impose itself as a stakeholder in your new business? Why or why not?

10. In enacting legislation, do you think the federal government has helped advance ethical conduct by the business community, or do you think such legislation has helped detract from ethics in general? Explain your position.

4 Financing Your Business • • • • • • • • • •

Chapter Objectives

- To provide an appreciation of financial institutions through a 5 C's screening process.

- To provide a model from which to develop a business plan.

- To aid in addressing the complex issue of developing a revenue forecast and to introduce the application of sensitivity and scenario analyses in refining that forecast.

- To communicate the importance of contingency planning for small business managers not only to acquire financing but also to avoid disaster by planning for the unexpected.

Once a proprietor has made a decision to start a small business venture, a logical next step is somehow to obtain the capital to make that decision a reality. For most people that entails some type of financing. If a guarantee could be given here, it would be that this phase is one of the most frustrating and trying phases of a new business startup. Obtaining financing is hard. It is also hard to make money and it is equally difficult to hang onto money once you have made it. A degree of humility is required. It is also important to maintain a perspective that the financial institutions have seen hundreds of applicants like you and have a degree of competence in spotting trouble before it starts. It is also imperative to maintain the perspective that a bank's principal priority is to make money. If you are an acceptable fit from the bank's position, you will be granted a loan based on the bank's conditions. It is also helpful to realize that rejection is not the end; it is only a temporary setback. Persistence and adaptability will help you prevail.

I have mentioned before and will mention again that after the idea-generation phase, multiple steps in the business concept are progressing simultaneously. This development is constrained by the availability of capital, and unless acceptable levels of financing can be obtained, all previous expenditures are often wasted. The financing stage is therefore most critical.

For most emerging entrepreneurs one of the first stops in the quest for financing is at the local bank. My own experience involved visiting several banks before finding one who was willing to assist in an SBA-guaranteed loan. In light of that experience, I felt it would be helpful to retrace my steps. I contacted one of the major commercial lenders in Sioux Falls, South Dakota, First National Bank, whose loan portfolio consists of roughly 65 percent small business loans. First National Bank actively pursues small business loans; thus the probability of finding an ear receptive to the possibility of financing your dreams is much greater at this type of financial institution.

In an interview with Jeffery Alvey,[1] one of the bank's vice presidents, I was not surprised that his response, which was representative of the bank's position, took me back to the foundation of the bridge model presented throughout this book. Mr. Alvey stated that the bank views all loan applicants from the perspective of five C's:

1. Character
2. Collateral
3. Cash flow
4. Capital
5. Competence

The bank views these five C's as a screening process and rejects some 75 percent of the applications received.

• THE FIVE C's PERSPECTIVE · · · · · · · · ·

Character

The first C, *character,* is given the heaviest weight. To quote: "If we are not comfortable with the applicant's character, nothing else matters. We believe the bank cannot make a bad loan to a good person, nor can it make a good loan to a person of poor character."[2]

To become a productive member of the business community means being a person of your word: being able to manage the resources at your disposal to fulfill the commitments you have made to those around you. If you we were to view a small business or a major corporation from the perspective of their stakeholders, we can go back to those internal and external relationships: internally, the employees, including management; externally, customers, suppliers, creditors, stockholders, governmental entities, and the community at large. The firm maintains it's character and credibility by fulfilling the commitments made. If payday is established as being on the 15th and 30th of the month, from the employees' perspective it is not acceptable for payday to be on other days. A lack of trust begins to ensue if financial commitments are not kept. It is no different for the small proprietor. When a person walks into a financial institution and asks for a loan of $1 million, the bank will not take the request lightly. The bank also has made financial commitments to their stakeholders; the bank is a for-profit institution. They loan money to make money; therefore, they loan money only to those from whom they can reasonably expect repayment. The bank community generally will only loan to people of high moral character.

Collateral

The second C is *collateral*. The bank must protect its own interest first and will require that you have sufficient collateral to cover the loan. What is sufficient depends on the institution and the specific situation. In a general range the bank will usually require that you have at least a 25 percent equity stake in your venture. In my first venture the bank wanted 40 percent equity. In my interview with Mr. Alvey I was quoted 25 percent to 30 percent equity, but then had that figure qualified by a case where 50 percent equity was required. The amount of equity required will depend on the bank's degree of confidence in a particular venture. If the financial institution is comfortable with this loan, it will tend to be on the lower end of the spectrum. Other factors will play into this scenario, but in the end if a loan is granted, the equity required will depend on the bank's comfort level with that type of loan in that type of industry or enterprise.

My first venture, which was launching a startup oil field safety firm in the middle of livestock and wheat country, made the bank very uncomfortable. The bank was skeptical to loan in an area with which they had no experience; thus 40 percent equity was requested from the first financial institution approached. Having raised the 40 percent requested and having it available in cash as requested, I met with the loan officer who had originally set the parameters, only to have the loan denied. In this case the loan officer was less than credible. He arbitrarily set a high equity stipulation to discourage further pursuit of this venture. Having met the bank's request, the loan officer seemed at first surprised and then irritated that I was back. My initial loan request did not even make it to the loan committee stage; the loan request was rejected immediately. The bank simply was not interested in making that type of loan. Fortunately, the next bank down the street happened to be an SBA-approved lender and was able and willing to grant my loan request contingent upon an SBA guarantee.

A valuable lesson was learned and never forgotten concerning bankers and banking institutions. First and foremost, the small business entrepreneur needs a good banker. Second, when dealing with bankers and banks, a personal relationship must be developed. The banker needs to know you and your business and needs to feel comfortable that you are, indeed, serious, credible, and trustworthy. Third, the bank is a for-profit institution and the loan officer will always operate from a perspective of what's best for the bank. A personal note: Ironically, the bank that initially turned down my loan request sent a loan officer to call on me several years later in an attempt to solicit my business account. Obviously, this occurred after my business was established and had proven itself. The bank was then comfortable with granting a loan. That seems to be typical: that when you don't need a loan, it's easy to get one. From the bank's perspective I suppose it's the reverse of the issue. When they are ready to grant a loan to a business, the business doesn't seem to want one. In the same way, the loan officer mentioned met with little success in granting a loan to my business. It was too late; the account remained with their competitor.

If the bank were forced to call a loan, the type of assets and the liquidity of those assets are prime determinants concerning the level of debt the bank will allow a business to carry. Single-purpose highly specialized equipment will require more equity than a generic piece of equipment such as a pickup truck. The bank can sell a pickup truck to recover monies owed, but if an asset pledged as collateral is something like a olive pit–extracting machine, the amount of money they can recover will be limited. Thus the loan limits associated with that type of firm will reflect that liquidity limitation.

For existing businesses that are looking for financing or additional financing, accounts receivables can be pledged as collateral and are usually granted as a loan value of about 75 percent. However, an accounts receivable aging list may be required, which in turn may reduce the loan value if collection problems exist. In my own experience, I had a line of credit on my accounts receivable. The bank set loan limits of 90 percent on those aged 30 days or less, 80 percent on receivables that were 30 to 60 days old, and 70 percent on receivables 90 to 120 days old; the bank was not much interested in accounts receivable older than 120 days. There will be some variations between banking institutions, but generally speaking, their policies will be similar. Inventory is usually granted about a 50 percent loan value, as are depreciated assets. First Bank was looking for a 1:1 debt/equity ratio based on the assumptions above. This will vary between banks, but I think a 1:1 debt/equity ratio is generally representative. It should also be noted that this ratio is in reference to a conventional loan. An SBA guaranteed loan would normally be more liberal in their collateral requirements.

Cash Flow

The third C is *cash flow*. According to Mr. Alvey, after character, collateral and cash flow are the most critical stages in the loan screening process. The cash flow phase is where a detailed business plan is imperative, backed by a marketing plan with realistic obtainable forecasts and projections. You must demonstrate unequivocally to the financial institution that you can repay the debt. That means answering questions concerning whether a market exists for your product or service, how big that market is, and how much of that market you can reasonably expect to obtain. The second part of the question requires that you demonstrate that you can make a profit. For the small business owner, this becomes a much larger issue. In corporate America, a particular product or market is one of many. Corporations are supported by experts in all the functional areas, have greater access to capital, and can afford to wait for a product or market to develop.

The sole proprietor often must hit the ground running, so to speak. Unless they have an outside source of income, the window of opportunity closes very rapidly. Time becomes a vicious enemy when cash inflows are not adequate. The proprietor must not only make a profit, but the profit must be large enough to live on, repay the debt, and grow the business. A tall order indeed. If a small business starts out with $100,000, of which $25,000 is equity, an ROE (return of equity) of 100 percent is hardly adequate. I have developed an adage: "It is not the cost of capital but the cost of living" which is the greatest obstacle to overcome for small business owners. I need to be careful of my definition of small business. A firm with assets of $5 million would be considered small by the SBA's definition. I am speaking of those with assets of less than $500,000 and indeed many with assets under $50,000.

The financial institutions are keenly aware of this dilemma. Outside income can be a major consideration in a bank's decision as to whether or not to grant a loan. This raises yet another question. Should one start a business on a part-time basis? Having done both myself and not being convinced of the best course, I posed these questions to Mr. Alvey. His response was not in support of a part-time venture, the biggest reason being that the proprietor demonstrates a lack of commitment and a lack of focus. "It is easy to quit"; therefore, the enterprise is not given the effort required to make it successful. My personal experience has been that returns are substandard because one cannot devote the time and energy required to make things work properly. This has been true particularly in my livestock-raising endeavors, where not being there has cost me money on more than one occasion.

The business plan must be well thought out. It needs to be realistic and achievable. The pro-forma income statements must demonstrate the health of the enterprise. The bank will scrutinize these projections closely. Help is available in putting together a good business plan from the Small Business Development Centers, which are funded through the SBA and are available throughout the nation. It should be noted that in my interview with First National Bank I was told that of the 70 to 75 percent of the loan requests rejected, most were rejected because the entrepreneur had a poor business plan. Even if your idea is good, it must be presented in a format acceptable to the financial institutions.

One of the most challenging aspects of putting together a good business plan is developing realistic pro-forma financial statements for a new startup firm where no history exists. The single most difficult task, as well as the most critical task in putting your business plan together, is generating a forecast that is accurate. The startup firm will generally develop a forecast based on several criteria and/or approaches. A starting point is a market analysis. What is the market size in your prospective trade area? How much of that market can you expect to corner based on the current levels of competition, your marketing effort, and your investment in plant and equipment? If a market exists for your product or service, one can compute a level of production based on your production capability stemming from your investment in plant and equipment. One can also use industry standards and do a comparison analysis. Your final forecast tends to be a blend of all the above.

In my own experience of the loan process, the most difficult aspect was the preparation of a five-year pro-forma set of financial statements. In my case the market was certainly adequate to absorb a new entrant, and market share did not appear to be a problem. The key constraint would be the availability of equipment and personnel, which in turn was limited by the amount of capital I could raise based on my current financial position. Total revenue, then, would be a function of the efficiency and the level of equipment utilization. I calculated a price list for equipment rental rates that was competitive in the marketplace, then multiplied that by a utilization rate to establish an initial forecast.

This initial forecast became a benchmark and management tool to monitor and control our sales activity. The annual forecast was broken down into monthly forecasts. Jobs were posted and analyzed by their revenue-creating capability, duration, and the amount of equipment and personnel required. Sales activity could be increased or decreased based on the level of equipment utilization projected for the near months. Having established an initial forecast, and having established a projected profit and loss statement stemming from that level of activity, I could calculate a rate of growth financed by the retained earnings that would flow through subsequent years' financial statements to complete a five-year forecast.

The reality of operation is almost always different from the original forecast; a degree of flexibility is required. A level of cash reserve for the unknown and unexpected would be advisable. In my situation I ran into an unexpected roadblock in the form of a delay in obtaining the needed liability insurance, which in turn was a requirement to be placed on an approved vendors list of many of my major potential clients. This caused a three-month delay in the firm's cash flow, which created a critical cash shortage problem. It is nearly impossible to foresee every event, but it is possible to plan for the unforeseen in the sense of factoring in reserve.

Capital

For a business to operate, it must have capital. We are not talking about collateral—we are referring to cash and/or liquid assets. The current asset portion of the balance sheet is what is used to pay the current liability portion of the balance sheet within the current period. The bank is concerned that adequate cash is available to meet those current obligations. From the perspective of the small business bridge model, a lack of current assets will cause a business to begin to violate both internal and external relationships by not meeting the fiduciary commitments to employees, creditors, suppliers, and others. Yours would not be the first business to go broke with orders on the desk. To meet the financial obligations adequately on a day-to-day basis, the small business owner needs an operating budget. The year's projected cash inflows and outflows are broken down into a month-by-month budget. This operating budget facilitates planning and provides a basis for making decisions concerning purchases, inventory levels, equipment purchases, employee hiring and scheduling, sales activity, and short- and intermediate-term cash management.

The bank is going to be very concerned with your break-even analysis and your ability to repay. You, on the other hand, must also be concerned with being able to make a living. You must factor in cash flow requirements for growth. Growth can severely strain a firm's financial resources. You can, in fact, go broke. The demands on cash from purchasing new equipment, expanding inventory, increasing payroll and the accompanying increase in payroll taxes, and increasing accounts receivables can all drive up your operating expenses and can quickly outstrip your ability to raise cash. If you are out of cash and simultaneously exceed your ability to borrow, the entire firm will come screeching to a halt. Growth is good but must be planned and managed growth. The budget helps control and monitor cash flows so that the firm's current financial position does not become critical.

Competence

The bank or any other lender will not loan money to someone unless they feel confident that this person has the capability to operate this business. The fifth C, then, is *competence*. In short, they are going to want to see a demonstrated ability to manage this type of business. The financial institution is going to be very interested in your past experience. As a small business owner, you are responsible for all the functions of the enterprise. Experience goes well beyond the ability just to perform the work, so to speak, or the production function. It entails the marketing, accounting, pricing, personnel, sales, finance, risk management, and every other issue the fledgling enterprise encounters.

One cannot overemphasize the importance of experience. In my work with a state department of labor I have often been involved in the early stages of a startup business. Unfortunately, I have often been involved in the final stage, when some of these businesses failed. Many times I have heard the proprietor say: "If I only knew then what I know now; I have learned so much." What they really are saying is that if they had the experience they acquired while operating the business before they started, they might not have failed.

During the mid-1980s I had the opportunity to attend a seminar hosted by several federal agencies, including the Department of Energy and the Small Business Administration. The focus of the seminar was on obtaining federal loans and/ or federal grant money. One of the key points brought out by the SBA representative at the conference was the importance of experience, but not just experience— the right kind of experience. The speaker explained it this way: If you are entering a business in a particular industry, you enter into a field that is first, filled with competition, and second, one that has been littered with the corpses of failed businesses. Those who succeed do so for a reason. You can get experience in a particular field by obtaining an education and by working for someone in that industry. If you want the best kind of experience, seek out the best in the industry in your region and work for this person. In fact, go to that person, tell them of your aspirations, and ask them if they will mentor you and train you—even if you worked for nothing, even if you had to pay the business owner to acquire this type of experience. It would be worth it to avoid the "If I only knew then what I know now" and to retain and apply the "I have learned so much." To say that such experience is invaluable would be an understatement. Such experience could well be the difference between success and failure or possibly make the difference between moderate success and great success.

I closed my interview with Mr. Alvey by posing the question of what he considered to be the main reasons for business failure in his experience. His response was twofold. First, business failed because the proprietor did not have a sense of business savvy, and second, because they were unwilling to get some help. To elaborate on this aspect of business savvy, in part it has to do with going broke while making money. In brief, though, it implies cash flow problems: perhaps too much inventory, poor control over accounts receivable, or a lack of financial discipline, spending funds that should be marked for other financial commitments. Mention was also made that people enter into business with unrealistic expectations; specifically, they did not realize fully the demands the business would place on them. Many are unwilling to work hard. The business may demand 80 or 100 hours a week. The final aspect discussed concerning this business savvy was in the area of failure to plan. Not that the proprietor did not have a business plan or a forecast, but if the forecast was for $250,000 and actual revenue is only $180,000, a contingency plan for the unexpected shortfall needs to be implemented to maintain some semblance of the original profit projections. Failure to react will tend to lock in a loss.

Mr. Alvey's second reason concerning why new firms go broke centers around the client's refusal to seek help when help is required, which is most closely related to the accounting function. Mr. Alvey indicated that many of his clients have a difficult time distinguishing between cash flow and profit. Demands on cash in the early stages of a business is generally great. This lack of understanding goes beyond just a lack of financial aptitude, and also implies a lack of financial discipline. The danger is that the entrepreneur spends cash that should be committed to financial obligations incurred. A new pickup truck or new office equipment is purchased because cash seems to be available. Often the business owner doesn't realize that other current obligations have already been incurred, which will take that cash. The owner looks in the checkbook and spends the money he thinks he has. The next thing he knows he must file a sales tax return, or make a payroll deposit or workers' compensation premium, and is completely surprised by these expenses. This type of business owner is operating financially blind and cannot make good, informed decisions.

Having once been stung by the unexpected, the entrepreneur compounds his mistake by failing to recognize or admit his limitation. He does not seek help. When he is finally forced to get help, it is too late. The accrued financial obligations have wiped out his equity and the bank will not extend credit to satisfy the multitude of creditors who are exerting pressure for payment. As it turns out, profit was not what the proprietor thought, and the doors swing shut on yet another business startup. "If only I knew then what I know now."

Having concluded my interview with the bank, the next logical step in the loan process is to refine the business concept in your mind and to begin to prepare a business plan to present back to the financial institution. It only makes sense to prepare a business plan in the format that is most conducive to the bank's loan requirements—in the case of First Bank, a format that addresses the five C's.

In a series of interviews with some of the major regional financial institutions, the five C's criteria were repeated over and over, although not in the same words. Concerns were expressed over the applicant's experience and management capabilities, credit history, level of capitalization and collateral, cash flow, business plan or the quality of the plan, business concept, and the personal history of the applicant. A good business plan with the five C's format would have addressed the concerns of all the financial firms interviewed. It could safely be assumed that a five C's format would need little or no modification to address the major concerns of most banks in the country. A guarantee that a loan will be granted based on a good business plan cannot and does not exist, but without a workable business plan, obtaining financing will be difficult indeed.[3]

• BUSINESS PLAN OUTLINE: EMPLOYING THE FIVE C's APPROACH · · · · · · · · · · · · · ·

Cover Sheet

Include the following on the cover sheet of your business plan: the business's name and the firm's logo if one has been developed; and the names, addresses, and phone numbers of all the principals involved in the business and the percent of ownership associated with each.

Considerable time and energy go into choosing a name and designing a business logo. You will position and market your business based on that name and logo. If you are a service firm, this can be especially important. You might want to consider a color or color combination, not unlike your school colors. Your name design and colors can be reflected in your building, vehicles, equipment, signs, and invoices to convey a message that all helps to present your image to the public. You know a Dr. Pepper truck the instant you see one because it is distinctive. The color of all Dr. Pepper trucks is maroon, while a Coke truck is red with white letters. Your firm's name, design, and colors should begin to take form during the idea generation or business conception phase. Demonstrating that name, logo, and colors throughout your business plan implies a well-thought-out, total marketing concept and a thorough business concept. Try to be distinctive, creative, recognizable, and memorable.

Business Abstract

In a paragraph or two, identify and explain in brief your business concept, and the type and form of business you plan to start. Explain that this is a startup, expansion, or purchase of an existing firm. Describe the types of products or services your business provides and the approximate size of this operation. Describe some of the key input factors, such as equipment, raw materials, and labor required. Explain your existing status and your physical location or proposed physical location. Briefly explain why the business is needed and what it offers the community.

Character References

The bank will run a routine check on your credit and possibly check for a criminal record. You need to demonstrate that you are a person of good character and worthy of the institution's trust. It is difficult to blow your own horn, but a statement of your character supported by personal and business references should be provided. In addition to the letters of reference, a list of other personal and business references can be provided that the bank can follow up on if they wish. If your credit or personal record is less than spotless, an honest statement of the circumstances and an explanation of why you are still loanworthy may be required. A demonstration of personal fiduciary responsibility can back up your statements.

Collateral

One of the first things the bank will require of you is a personal financial statement. Even if you have prepared a personal financial statement, it is highly likely that the bank officer will ask that you to complete another one using the bank's forms. You could request the bank's form, or since you probably will have met with a bank officer on a number of occasions prior to submitting a business plan, one probably will already have been provided. Either way the loan request will eventually go to a committee and the bank will want you to use their format. Most financial institutions have an integrated software package which helps them compute key ratios from their desktop, and your financials need to fit into their format. At any rate, use the bank's financial statement forms and include it in your business plan as an exhibit of your collateral section. If appropriate, include a schedule in which you separate business assets from personal assets. Most financial institutions have a commercial loan application format, where the financial statement format separates and categorizes those assets.

Provide a schedule in which you show the amount of cash, equity, and type of equity you will put into your business. Prepare a pro-forma balance sheet incorporating the loan proceeds. Define your shopping list, a detailed account of what the loan proceeds will be used for. If used equipment is being purchased, provide an explanation.

Once a concept emerges from the idea stage, and while issues concerning the firm's name, logo, and colors are being defined, a mental vision of what you want your business to be should begin to emerge. A part of that concept development entails a visualization of the business's day-to-day operations, out of which a detailed list of fixtures and equipment is put together. This list of equipment must be found and priced comparatively to be presented in a schedule or as part of the balance sheet presented in the collateral section.

Cash Flow

The first part of the cash flow section will deal with the market analysis. Is there a market? How big is the market? What market share can you expect to obtain? Support your forecast with market research and market area statistics.

Market analysis is the most difficult and the most critical element in the business plan. No one will be able to give you an adequate guesstimate. Considerable effort needs to be expended in developing your forecast. Typical market research begins by breaking the marketing information sources into two components, starting with public information. Public information tends to be broad in nature. Your marketing research should probably begin at the local library, seeking sources of information such as a marketing atlas or trade journals may provide. Look into the industry through a register of industry standards and investment publications. Use governmental agencies such as the Small Business Administration, Small Business Development Centers, state and local economic development groups, and contact the chamber of commerce. The U.S. Department of Labor keeps statistics on the number of employers in a given industry and the makeup of the labor force. The state department of revenue collects statistics on sales tax receipts by industry sector from which a county or regional market breakdown can be calculated if not provided. Once the public information has been compiled and analyzed, prepare a synthesis to include in your market analysis. Public information should be able to identify the size of the total market in a particular industry.

The second phase of your market research will comprise primary information, the type of information that is not available to the public. You will be required to obtain primary information on your own. Marketing research firms are available, but many small businesses will have difficulty in being able to afford or justify the cost. At this juncture in your marketing plan phase, at least go talk to a local marketing research firm if one is available; they may be willing to advise you how to conduct your own research. Your primary marketing research will attempt to define your realistic share of the local market with a specific location and specific trade area defined. You may need to identify key traffic patterns and volume of traffic, if applicable. You will want to identify key competitors and analyze the competition. It might be a good idea to interview suppliers of your key equipment or inputs for their insights and opinions. Local job service managers, business insurance agents, unemployment tax representatives, sales tax revenue agents, and worker's compensation representatives can provide some insights. Define your customer and develop a specific customer profile. Prepare and conduct an informal survey, if applicable. Estimate your potential market share and make a preliminary forecast. Based on your investment in plant, equipment, and the level of personnel you have available, define your capacity. Predict a level of capacity or set a target level of capacity and adjust your preliminary forecast.

Once you have completed your forecast it would be a good idea to again contact your local Small Business Development Center representative for their input. When you have reached a level of comfort with your forecast, synthesize the information and present the results in the business plan. A description of the market and an analysis of market trends and market projections should also be included. Growth in the market can be factored into income statements, which are projected over the next three to five years.

With the forecast completed, a financial analysis can begin. Knowing what the industry averages are, by doing a comparative analysis one can develop a projected income statement based on your stated level of volume. Income statements should be developed to cover a three- to five-year forecast. From the projected balance sheet created under the collateral section and with the projected income statements, one can create projected balance sheets for the next three to five years. The projected income statement can be broken down into quarterly, monthly, and weekly forecasts.

A quarterly and annual budget will need to be made up, and provisions will need to be made in the loan request to address any operating cash short falls and to meet cash requirements for growth. A provision creating a reserve for unexpected contingencies should also be addressed.

Sensitivity Analysis

Your projected financial statements are just that, projections. If one were to predict outcome concerning a forecast, the highest probability would be that the outcome will be something other than what you had projected, be it higher or lower. Reality rarely emulates a paper forecast, at least not without a prior history. A sensitivity analysis helps to attempt to address the range of probable outcomes and allows for contingency plans to be built in.

The first step in conducting a sensitivity analysis would be to identify the critical elements in the revenue formula. For example, for an excavating business or backhoe service, revenue is a function of how many feet the machine can dig per hour, how many hours the machine will be employed during the year, and rate per foot the proprietor will be able to charge. The number of feet per hour the machine will be able to dig depends on soil types, soil conditions, weather conditions, the experience of the operator, the maintenance and performance of the machine, and a few other minor variables. Using heuristic data if available, or through the use of test trials, a probability distribution can be established. From the distribution, a range can be established above and below the expected rate so that by applying standard deviation methods, a degree of probability can be assigned to the range. In this way one can assign, say, an 80 percent probability that the outcome will fall within a specific range.

Sensitivity analysis applies a range by varying the numbers of critical variables in the revenue equation, which in turn measures the outcome of those changes above and below the expected value and calculates the effect on revenue. Sensitivity analysis changes one variable at a time, leaving the other variables constant but in turn changing each element in the revenue equation according to the range of that variable's probability distribution. A sensitivity analysis applied to the excavating business mentioned above would look something like the following:

revenue = variable 1 (the number of feet the machine can dig per hour) ×
variable 2 (the number of hours the machine will work per year) ×
variable 3 (the price charged per foot)

A baseline revenue forecast begins with the following assumptions. Given the assumption of 50 feet per hour × 1200 hours per season × $1.35 per foot = $81,000. That is what we expect, but assume a change in the number of feet the machine can dig of plus or minus 10 feet per hour. That change in the number of feet the machine can trench in an hour is a function of the variables mentioned earlier. Things like soil condition, weather, operator experience, and the like all can act to create an outcome greater or less than we normally would expect. Plus or minus 10 feet per hour creates a range in which, say, 90 percent of all outcomes would fall. The probability of those outcomes are based on field tests or historical data.

We apply that range to the number of feet trenched in an hour as follows. Note that this figure is the only variable changed in the first set of equations; we hold the other variables constant.

Variable 1 (Feet per Hour)

(50 ft + 10 ft) × 1200 hours × \$1.35 per foot = \$97,200.

Base case: 50 ft × 1200 hours × \$1.35 = \$81,000 (this is our original forecast)

(50 ft − 10 ft) × 1200 hours × \$1.35 per foot = \$64,800

Variable 2 (Hours per Season)   A plus or minus 200 hours represents the range. Note again that the only variable we are changing is the hours per season variable; the other variables remain constant.

50 ft × (1200 hours + 200 hours) × \$1.35 = \$94,500

Base case: 50 ft × 1200 × \$1.35 = \$81,000

50 ft × (1200 − 200) × \$1.35 = \$67,500

Variable 3 (Rate Charged per Foot)   Assume a range of 0.25. Note again that only variable changed is the rate charged per foot; all the other variables remain constant.

50 ft × 1200 × (\$1.35 + 0.25) = \$96,000

Base case: 50 ft × 1200 × \$1.35 = \$81,000

50 ft × 1200 × (\$1.35 − 0.25) = \$79,200

Note that variable 1 is the most sensitive variable. It is useful for the proprietor to recognize which variable is the most critical. When bidding a job, soil type and soil conditions are more important than the price charged per foot in determining the revenue outcome. This remains true even in light of the fact that a larger percentage change occurs in price.

Scenario Analysis

Having completed a sensitivity analysis, a scenario analysis can quickly be calculated. The sensitivity analysis provided us with a range of outcomes given variations in the key variables. Reality is often such that when things are going well, everything seems to work out that way, and when one thing is bad, everything is bad. For instance, in our excavating business example, a long, wet spring could severely affect the number of hours the machine could operate; in addition, the wet conditions could negatively affect the number of feet per hour the machine could dig. Such conditions could create additional expenses that would have the same results as a lower price per foot. From this hypothetical example you can see the effects of a best-case or worst-case scenario. The positive or negative effects are measured in the scenario analysis. The best-case scenario takes the best possible outcome of each of the variables used in the sensitivity analysis above and reflects them in a new revenue outcome, as shown below. The worst-case scenario does the same thing with the poorest outcomes.

Best case: (50 ft + 10 ft) × (1200 + 200) × (\$1.35 + 0.25) = \$134,400

Base case: 50 ft × 1200 × \$1.35 = \$81,000 (our original forecast, if everything goes as planned)

Worst case: (50 ft − 10 ft) × (1200 − 200) × (\$1.35 − 0.25) = \$44,000

It should be noted that the expected outcome is the base case. The probability that the worst case will occur should be roughly equal to the probability that the best case will occur. Our business plan is based on the outcome expected with the base case. It is, however, helpful to develop a contingency plan in event of a worst-case scenario. If the best case materializes, the impact is nothing but beneficial, but if the worst case arises, the impact can be terminal to your business. A contingency plan demonstrates to the financial institution that your planning is thorough, as it should be. One final note: The inclusion of sensitivity and scenario analyses supported by a worst-case contingency plan will add a dimension of complexity to your overall business plan. It creates a danger that the banking representative could get lost in the numbers. It is my recommendation that the business plan not just be dropped on some loan officer's desk but that you request an opportunity to present the plan. In many respects a similarity exists between the loan process of a small business and the capital budgeting process of many major corporations.

Using the worst-case scenario figures as a revenue input figure, recompute the projected income statement. The result will probably show a loss, or at best a nominal profit. This figure, along with the break-even analysis, is the basis for developing a contingency plan should things not turn out as anticipated. A contingency plan will demonstrate to the financial institution that your business plan has been well thought out. Your contingency plan should provide some revenue-enhancing alternatives and some bare-bones cost-cutting procedures to keep the business alive should it fall on hard times.

A contingency plan created from a scenario analysis implies that we can predict what might go wrong in our business operations. It does not address the unknown, the unforeseen, or the unexpected. Still it begins to address those issues surrounding a defensive strategy. If you were already five years into your business, it would be much easier to develop a contingency plan because you would have a more realistic idea of what could go wrong.

A final schedule, which could just as easily be the first schedule, in the cash flow section of the business plan should address any sources of outside income available. As indicated earlier, it is not just the cost of capital and the cost of doing business that strains the financial resources of a fledgling firm, but the budding entrepreneur must also bear the cost of living. If one has savings or the financial support of a spouse, the burden is lessened considerably. This can sometimes make the difference in whether or not a loan is granted.

Capital

The capital portion is somewhat redundant, as cash flow was addressed with the annual budget. A schedule of the annual budget can be used with an explanation of how cash flow issues will be addressed during that critical first year of operation. A contingency plan for an expanded growth rate should be added, as well as a plan for meeting operational shortfalls. If your operational budget indicates some seasonal cash shortages, due to the nature of your operation, or if accounts receivables will be substantial and create uneven cash flows, a line of credit may be in order. These issues can be elaborated on here and a general agreement for a credit line worked out. Customer credit policies should be explained here, also collection procedures for accounts receivables if applicable.

Competence

In the competence section of the business plan, the applicant must demonstrate the ability to manage the firm he or she is setting out to create. A statement of the background and pertinent experiences of the principals is in order, not altogether different from a job application letter. Define the past experiences that qualify you to manage this business. If a gap exists in your background that poses a problem, propose a training development program. In addition, this would be a good place to identify those professionals who will be assisting you, and the scope of their involvement. If an (SBA) SCORE representative is being used as a mentor, mention of this is positive.

• CONVENTIONAL BUSINESS PLAN OUTLINE · · · · · · · · · · · · · · · · · · ·

The key function of any business plan is just that, planning. The business plan should demonstrate that the business concept is well thought out. A more traditional approach is laid out in outline form below. What one format has over the other is presentation. My original premise remains: Give to the financial institution what they want as far as format is concerned.

1. *Executive summary.* Here you can describe the business, the product or services offered, a brief description of the uniqueness of your business, and why the product or service is needed. You will want to identify the principals involved in the business and their qualifications. Identify the market segment aimed at and describe in brief how you will obtain your proposed market share.

2. *Background.* Identify the growth trends in the industry, the key competitors, consumer buying behavior, and the like. Identify how you will enter this segment, your company image, position, and competitive advantage.

3. *Objectives.* Identify both short- and long-term objectives for the business.

4. *Product and/or services.* Identify the benefits to your customer; include a description of the uses, unique characteristics, patents, company logo brand, and so on. You can identify your warranty policy and address product liability issues, if appropriate.

5. *Marketing strategy.* Identify your market segment, the size of the segment, your distribution channel, your market share, and forecast. You might want to project your market share for several years and compare your market share with that of your competitors. Identify your pricing strategy here also.

6. *Selling tactics.* Describe the methods expected to be used to promote and sell your products and/or services. Include a sample of any promotional or sales literature that you have developed. Identify your promotional and advertising budget and any advertising plan that you have developed.

7. *Plan of operation and organization.* Your legal structure should be identified and any organizational chart, if applicable. Identify your personnel needs, training, and compensation plans. Identify your equipment wish list, facilities requirements, and facilities layout.

8. *Projected financials.* At a minimum, project income statements and balance sheets for the first three years. It would be advisable to have developed an operations budget and cash flow statement for at least the first year. Identify issues of cash flow projections and capital requirements. Identify your expected business cycle and cash flow turn around. Identify your expected accounts receivable status. Identify your capital inputs in the form of owner's equity. Include a schedule of equity inputs in the form of cash equipment and real estate, if applicable.

This outline should identify the key points. As I indicated earlier, one format over another is not the issue as long as the business plan submitted is thought through thoroughly. The bank will in the end use their internal loan approval process in evaluating your plan as to feasibility. In the end the bank will probably apply a 3C, 5C, or 7C criteria analysis in evaluating your business plan.

• QUESTIONS FOR DISCUSSION · · · · · · · ·

1. Mr. Alvey of the First National Bank stated that the first and most important factor considered in any loan application was the applicant's personal character, but when the business plan is submitted, it appears that the greatest emphasis is placed on the cash flow capabilities of the firm. How do you explain this apparent contradiction?

2. Do you agree that character should be the bank's primary concern? Why or why not?

3. Collateral requirements were cited as ranging roughly between 20 and 50 percent of the loan request. Explain this broad range.

4. Since cash flow is so important to financial institutions, many consider a source of outside income a major factor in granting a loan. Discuss the advantages and disadvantages of a part-time business venture, which allows the new entrepreneur to keep his or her job to support the fledgling enterprise.

5. Would you recommend that the new entrepreneur take a part-time job to support a full-time business instead of trying to maintain a full-time job to support a part-time business?

6. How would you recommend that a budding entrepreneur obtain the "right experience" before launching a new venture of his or her own?

7. How long would you recommend that a person work for others before trying to run a business of his or her own?

• QUESTIONS FOR REVIEW · · · · · · · · · · ·

1. What are the 5 C's?
2. What are the major elements of the business plan's cash flow projections?
3. (a) What is a business logo? (b) Why is a logo important, or is it important? (c) Explain how and where a logo is used.
4. Why is a sensitivity analysis important? Explain what it does.
5. Why is contingency planning important? How does a scenario analysis help in contingency planning?

5 SBA Services and Loan ••••••• Programs, Venture Capitalists, Owner Financing, and Other Methods of Creative Financing

Chapter Objectives

- To introduce the various loan programs and services offered by the SBA.

- To introduce the contract for deed, owner financing process, and various valuation techniques in valuing a business.

- To expose readers to some critical questions that need to be answered prior to purchasing a business.

- To introduce several financing options for the prospective small business owner.

• THE SMALL BUSINESS ADMINISTRATION: BACKGROUND AND OVERVIEW

The United States is in many areas the envy of the world. Our standard of living and our position of world dominance is to a large degree held up and supported by our free-enterprise system. Free enterprise is the vehicle by which people express their creativity by producing a better product or service, to obtain a better life for themselves. The premise of free enterprise is that in doing that activity, the person advances to the good of all. In a sense, small business acts as a national product and idea incubator out of which often grow major corporate structures. The national government has recognized the importance and the contribution of small business to the nation and has provided an agency, the Small Business Administration (SBA), to assist and promote small business.

The SBA vision statement reads as follows: "The U.S. SBA was created in 1953 as an independent agency of the federal government to aid, counsel, and assist and protect the interests of small business concerns, to preserve free competitive enterprise, and to maintain and strengthen the overall economy of our nation. Small business is critical to our economic recovery, to building America's future, and to helping the United States compete in today's global marketplace."[1]

From an economic perspective, small business contributes heavily to the nation's economic well-being. Over 22 million nonfarm small businesses exist in the country. Small businesses employ approximately 53 percent of the U.S. workforce. That percentage is growing; in 1994, of the 3.3 million new jobs created, 62 percent were created by small business. Small business contributes about 50 percent of the nation's gross domestic product.[2]

The SBA was created in part because the U.S. economy has not adequately provided a mechanism for venture capital. Banks are for-profit concerns and are under no obligation to loan money for new ventures. To acquire a direct unassisted bank loan, a bank is most comfortable with a business with a history. If a history does not exist, an even larger equity position will be required to collateralize the loan adequately. Without the SBA, most new business loans would not be granted.

Capital availability is much easier for corporate America. Should a large corporation require capital for expansion into new a product area or into new markets, an investment banker can readily assist in an initial public offering, be it a debt instrument in the form of a bond offering or an equity offering in the form of additional common stock. The person generally does not have access to Wall Street, especially for a startup venture. The Small Business Administration is undoubtedly the most important source of venture capital in the nation. It should be noted here that the SBA does not make direct loans but provides loan guarantees, without which most startup loans would be rejected or at least become much more restrictive. The SBA is also one of the best sources of information, assistance, and management help.

A personal note: Like any governmental agency, the SBA is a bureaucracy; therefore, the quality of service you receive will depend on the people with whom you deal. If your needs are not being met, seek out another representative. This agency is there to assist small businesses, but it does require effort on your part to fully realize and benefit from the resources available. The following is a partial summary of the programs and services available through the SBA.

Access to Information

SBA Answer Desk

The Answer Desk is a toll-free information center that answers questions about starting or running a business and how to get assistance. A computerized telephone message system, the desk is accessible 24 hours a day, seven days a week. Answer Desk operators are available Monday through Friday 9:00 A.M. to 5:00 P.M. ET by calling 800-8ASK-SBA.

SBA OnLine

SBA OnLine is an electronic bulletin board that provides concise and current information about programs and services that can assist in starting and running a business. It also includes many SBA publications. Accessed by modem (9600, n, 8, 1), it operates 23 hours a day, seven days a week, and is updated daily. To access SBA OnLine, dial 800-697-4636 or 900-463-4636. The SBA OnLine number for the D.C. metro area is 202-401-9600.

SBA on the Internet

The SBA home page offers detailed information on SBA and other business services, access to SBA OnLine, and links to outside resources on the World Wide Web. To access, use uniform resource locators (URLs):

> SBA home page: http://www.sba.gov
>
> U.S. Business Advisor: http://www.business.gov
>
> SBA gopher: gopher://gopher:.sba.gov

For more information, see the SBA publication *Programs & Services*.[3]

At the time of this writing, the U.S. Business Advisor is still being developed. The intent is to provide a one-stop electronic link to all business information and services the federal government provides. The idea is that with one contact, one can access the applicable laws and regulations stemming from other agencies, and departments. They will also have the capability to download forms, saving the individual much time and energy to remain in compliance.

Management-Assistance Aids

The SBA produces and maintains a library of management-assistance publications and videos, which are available at nominal costs. A complete list is available in the Resource Directory for Small Business Management. Available through your SBA field office, the SBA Answer Desk, or possibly through the SBA OnLine 900 number.

Business Counseling and Training

Service Corps of Retired Executives (SCORE)

Some 12,400 or so SCORE volunteers in nearly 400 chapters provide expert advice, based on their many years of firsthand experience and shared knowledge, on virtually every phase of business. SCORE counselors are located at SBA field offices, business information centers, and some SBA small business development centers. The quality of the counseling provided by the SCORE volunteer often depends on the person and the quality of the relationship developed. An attempt will be made to match you with a volunteer who has run a similar type of business. Sometimes that match is close, sometimes it isn't.

Small Business Development Centers (SBDCs)

Funded and administered by the SBA, SBDCs provide a variety of management and technical assistance to small businesses and would-be entrepreneurs. They are a co-operative effort among the SBA, the academic community, the private sector, state and local governments. They can help you prepare SBA loan applications. Over 900 SBDCs, located primarily at colleges and universities, are in all 50 states. To find the closest SBDC to you, contact the SBA office in your area.

Like any other governmental agency, the quality of service you receive will depend on the personnel in your nearest office. Primarily what the SBDCs are good at is to assist you in developing your business plan, which in turn is dependent on your marketing plan and ultimately, your forecast. The operative word here is *assist*. In a recent visit with a representative from my nearest SBDC the words *assist* and *personal empowerment* were stressed. They are an excellent resource as you begin to gather market information and begin to develop your business plan, but they cannot and will not do the work for you.

As you will see later, the SBA application is a fairly simple process. As stated previously, the SBA acts to guarantee loans. The real hurdle will be the bank; your business plan must pass their scrutiny and standards. The SBDCs can assist, but the bulk of the footwork will be your own.

Lending Programs

7(a) Loan Guaranty

This is the SBA's primary business loan program. Under 7(a) the SBA guarantees loans to small businesses that cannot obtain financing on reasonable terms through other channels, such as direct bank loans. This program generally is used to meet the varied short- and long-term needs of small businesses. Lenders, not the SBA, approve and service the loans and request SBA guaranties. The guaranties reduce risks to the lenders, expanding their ability to make small business loans.

Loan proceeds from the 7(a) program may be used for business startups, expansions, equipment purchases, working capital, inventory, or real estate acquisitions. Generally, the SBA can guarantee up to $750,000 of a private-sector loan; as much as 80 percent on loans of $100,000 or less and 75 percent on loans of more than $100,000. The interest rate may not exceed 2.75 percent over the prime lending rate except for loans under $50,000, where rates may be slightly higher. A recent interview with an SBA representative cited about a 2 percent premium on those types of loans; check with your local lender for specifics. Maturities can extend 10 years for working capital and 25 years for fixed assets. For additional information, contact your local SBA office. Note also that these programs are subject to change, but this or a similar program has been around for years.

Low-Documentation Loan (LowDoc)[4]

For small business loans of $100,000 or less, the LowDoc loan program features a one-page SBA application, cutting the paperwork burden for both small businesses and the lending institutions. Once the applicant has satisfied the lender's requirements, the lender and applicant together complete the SBA's one-page guaranty application. If approved, the SBA guarantees up to 80 percent of the loan, with a quick turnaround to the lender.

Eligibility   You are generally eligible if:

- You are starting a new business.
- Your business has average annual sales for the preceding three years not exceeding $5 million and 100 or fewer employees, including affiliates.
- Your business satisfies other 7(a) program criteria.

Interest Rates

- Loans of less than seven years: up to 2.25 percent over prime
- Loans of seven years or longer: up to 2.75 percent over prime

Loans under $50,000 may be subject to slightly higher rates.

Maturity   Length of time for repayment depends on:

- Your ability to repay
- The use of the loan proceeds

Maturity generally is five to 10 years; up to 25 years for fixed-asset loans.

Collateral   You must pledge sufficient assets to secure the loan, but loans generally are not declined where inadequate collateral is the only unfavorable factor. Normally business assets are pledged, and occasionally, personal assets. Personal guaranties of the principals are required.

CapLines

CapLines offers five types of loans to finance the short-term, cyclical working-capital needs of small businesses. Under this program, loan proceeds generally will be advanced against a borrower's existing or anticipated inventory and/or accounts receivable.

MicroLoans[5]

Under the MicroLoan Program, a small business can borrow up to $25,000 from an intermediary lender, which also provides management and technical assistance designed to help ensure success.

Eligibility   Virtually any type of for-profit small business is eligible for the Micro-Loan Program. It must, however, meet the SBA's size standards at the time of application.

Use of Loan Funds   MicroLoan funds may be used for working capital or to purchase inventory, supplies, furniture, fixtures, machinery, and/or equipment. These funds may not be used to purchase real estate, to provide a down payment on a project in excess of $25,000 in value, or with limited exceptions, to refinance existing debts.

Loan Terms   The MicroLoan program has a maximum loan amount of $25,000. The maximum term allowed for a loan is six years; however, loan terms vary according to the size of the loan, the planned use of funds, the requirements of the intermediary lender, and the needs of the small business borrower.

   Interest rates vary depending on the intermediary lender. Rates are generally competitive. MicroLoan applicants must meet the credit requirements of their local intermediary lender. Generally, however, applicants will be expected to demonstrate good character, a strong commitment to their business idea, and a credit history that demonstrates a reasonable assurance that the loan will be repaid. In addition, applicants should have some management expertise or be willing to participate in training designed to strengthen management skills. Collateral requirements will be set by the local lending intermediary.

This is by no means an exhaustive and complete description of the SBA programs and services available, but it does highlight the main services applicable within the context of this book. Two other programs deserve mentioning here, the Women's Prequalification Loan and the Minority Prequalification Loan. At the time of this writing, no direct SBA loans are available, including those to women and minorities. The programs do exist, but funding is not available and probably will not become available. The prequalification loan programs simply prequalify to the lender the loan guarantee. It doesn't matter; the lender must first approve the loan, then seek the SBA's approval. The fact that a particular loan is preapproved provides little advantage; prequalification is mostly symbolic.

Loan Application Procedure

As you read through the literature the SBA issues regarding its various loan programs, you will probably notice screening criteria somewhat similar to those established by First National Bank. It is not just a coincidence that the qualification criteria for the MicroLoan Program sound vaguely familiar and correlate closely with the lending philosophy of First National Bank. The SBA considers the smaller 7(a) loans, LowDoc, and MicroLoan programs all to be basically character loans. In any SBA loans it is commonplace that a credit check will be run on the applicant, the ideal result being that it is returned spotless. Since the loan is based largely on the person's character and integrity, they would hope this applicant has been fiscally responsible and trustworthy in his or her financial dealings to date. They may well check for a criminal record, and particularly with the 7(a) loan program, file form 4506 with the IRS, which is a request for a copy or transcript of the applicant's income tax forms for the past three years. This to identify false statements made on the application and to ensure compliance with the IRS.

Following are the credit requirements and steps in applying for a loan that have been established by the Small Business Administration.[6] A loan applicant must:

1. Be of good character.
2. Demonstrate sufficient management expertise and the commitment necessary for a successful operation.
3. Have enough funds, including the SBA-guaranteed loan plus personal cash, to operate the business on a sound financial basis.
4. Show that the past earnings record and probable future earnings will be sufficient to repay the loan in a timely manner.

The steps in applying for a loan are as follows:

1. Prepare a current balance sheet. Prepare a balance sheet as of the day the business is to start; indicate the principals' investment.
2. Prepare profit and loss statements for the current period and for the most recent three fiscal years if available. Business startup applicants should prepare a detailed projection of earnings and expenses for at least the first year of operation. A monthly cash flow projection is also recommended.

3. Prepare a current personal financial statement of the proprietor or of each partner or stockholder owning 20 percent or more of the corporate stock in the business.

4. List collateral to be offered as security for the loan, along with an estimate of the present market value of each item and the balance of any existing liens.

5. State the amount of the loan requested and the purposes for which it is to be used.

6. Take this material to your lender. If the lender is unable or unwilling to provide the financing directly, explore the possibility of using the SBA-guaranteed loan program.

Failure or less than satisfactory results in any of those measures of the applicant's character may not immediately disqualify the applicant, but it will certainly raise questions and put the application in jeopardy.

As the bridge model that this book is based on suggests, issues of ethics and trust between the participants of the organization, both internally and externally, are pervasive. Trust and commitment must be maintained for a firm to survive in the marketplace. Both the banking community and the SBA are sending the message that if you are not trustworthy, they will not allow you access to capital.

• VENTURE CAPITALISTS···············

Venture capitalists may well be more restrictive than banks as a source of capital. Not unlike the bank, the venture capitalist is concerned with the background and experience of the entrepreneur. The venture capitalist is much more restrictive, in the sense that the size of the project must also meet their parameters. What they are looking for is a small company with a good track record and a history demonstrating geometrical growth. The ideal candidate will need money to fuel this growth for several years, after which time the firm will be able to go public through an initial public offering of common stock, which provides a vehicle for the venture capitalist to bail out and realize a sizable profit. A direct sale or a merger with a publicly traded company, which would result in a common stock deal, would accomplish the same thing for the venture capitalist, who in turn would look for other candidates in which to reinvest.

Who and what is a venture capitalist? They often are a form of limited partnership, which is backed by huge financial resources. The financial backing may come from the banking industry, which has an arm or a branch in the venture capital sector. Other financial giants, such as pension funds or insurance companies, may participate as well.

What does the venture capitalist want? One perspective to take would be that the venture capitalist enters a limited partnership with monies that are deemed investments in a higher risk bracket, but at the same time they are not looking for risk. They want to make investments that will return inordinately high rewards; for those rewards they will accept a higher-than-normal level of risk. Their goal is achieved if your firm can go public in the near to intermediate future. That means that your company must have enormous market potential. To put a dollar figure on your potential sales level, it must be in the tens of millions or even the hundreds of millions of dollars.

An example of a good venture capitalist candidate would be a high-tech firm, which could have the potential of being a component supplier to the major PC manufacturers or to have developed software that would have a similar potential.

With the venture capitalist capital and management connections, they would like to see you and your team develop this company from humble beginnings to a multi-million-dollar firm, and they would like that growth to occur almost overnight.

Having been in a high-growth firm myself, and trying to visualize the stress and energy that it would take to take a firm to that level, I can't imagine anyone wanting to walk that road. It should be fairly obvious that unless your product or business concept is of a very exceptional nature, the venture capitalist is just not going to be interested in a startup venture.

The venture capitalist fills a niche in the financial community, but the initial startup is generally not something they're looking for. If your startup venture has a meteoric start, the venture capitalist may be an intermediary step for you in becoming a publicly traded company. Initially, though, it is doubtful that the venture capitalist will be interested in launching your venture. Keep them in mind for the day when your profile fits their requirements. On that day a decision will have to be made as to how big is big enough, or like the venture capitalist, should you realize your profits from this meteoric growth and move on to something else?

Take the perspective of the venture capitalist for a moment. One of the key elements that a venture capitalist will be concerned about is the size of the firm they are looking to finance. Consider that their intention is to take this firm public in a few years or to be purchased by a larger firm that is already publicly traded. It should be obvious that the candidate they will want to deal with is a firm that has an asset base in the millions or tens of millions of dollars. The venture capitalist is a for-profit entity. They want not only a profit but huge returns on their capital, and they want you and your firm to deliver that profit. You have to ask yourself if it is worth it.

I once ran an advertisement in the *Wall Street Journal* in search of a suitor interested in investing in or buying out my oil field enterprise. I received several interested responses, one from a venture capitalist who was interested in a business in the oil field service sector. When I called this firm, they wanted to know what our gross sales were and how large an entity we were. I was told that the bare minimum they were looking for at the time was existing sales in the low millions of dollars range. What they really were interested in was a firm that was multiregional, with management in place to take the business to a national or even an international level, with need of a cash infusion to do that. Given the impact of inflation, that same venture capitalist would be talking about a firm with existing revenues in the tens of millions.

If you will notice the size of the public offerings that are published in the financial pages, you will notice that those offerings are rarely in the low tens of millions of dollars. They are very often in the hundreds of millions and billions of dollars. For a firm to be listed on Nasdaq requires a substantial asset base. Stop and think for a moment about where the venture capitalist wants a business in which they invest to be at and the time frame they are looking at to get there. It should be evident that they are not really talking about small business, at least not in the same context that this author is visualizing small business. The size and the financial assets required to take a company public require a very substantial asset base. It requires a substantial sum of money just to undergo the expense associated with a public offering.

I alluded to the fact that many venture capitalists target or specialize in certain industries. They may be interested in the computer software or hardware industry, for example, so having a successful enterprise in that industry would make your business attractive to venture capitalists who specialize in that sector. If you or your business are in search of a venture capitalist, it makes sense to identify those who are interested in a business in the same developmental stage as your enterprise. It also makes sense to create a detailed business plan that fits more into the venture capitalist profile than a traditional business plan does. Earlier we went through the five C's approach to a business plan. I doubt that such a format would be appropriate for venture capitalists. They would be looking for firms that have demonstrated large market potential, accelerated growth, and managerial ability to take a company to the business level expected. Those are the elements that should be emphasized in any business plan developed for the venture capitalist market.

If you are interested in pursuing a business relationship with a venture capitalist, it would be advisable to put together a team of professionals to assist you. I doubt that this type of venture is something that the average person wants to pursue on his or her first business venture. The world of venture capitalists and public offerings is a very technical, highly sophisticated, and high-finance style of capitalization. When swimming with such large fish, extreme caution is required so as not to get eaten.

• ANGELS·······················

What are financial angels? In many respects they are a new breed of venture capitalists. Some come from the aftermath of a venture capital experience. Many come from the high-tech world, where the company they started or were a major player in was bought out or went public. Many of these people are new millionaires from this process. Many chose to exit the corporate world due to burnout.

Imagine going through the intense process of developing a firm to the point of going public, and then trying simply to walk out the door and quit. I believe the solace of solitude might last a week, two at best. This type of personality would probably be hungry for another challenge but one not quite so intense.

I believe this best describes what and who an angel is: someone who is looking to assist, to participate, and be involved in a new business venture. Angels will probably be looking to get involved in businesses similar to those they left, because that is their area of expertise. In essence, they are choosing to become mini-versions of venture capitalists. They do not necessarily want to become intensely involved in the business enterprise they are seeking; as often as not, an advisory or consultant position is more suitable for them. You can also expect that if you are contacted by such a person, he or she will also be interested in making a substantial profit through the involvement. It also stands to reason that an angel is going to be more interested in an existing business than in a startup venture. This concept is fairly new, but it is my opinion that those involved will evolve to something that is very similar to what a venture capitalist is today.

One other twist to this concept. Within every community are people who have wealth. Some might be interested in financing a local business. In the area where I grew up, the oil industry brought many new millionaires whose new wealth stemmed from owning the mineral rights associated with oil wells that were drilled. I know of at least one such person who was concerned about the local community and wanted to see that community prosper. This person would be willing to finance certain ventures as long as he perceived the business to be a benefit to the community. Such people are rare, but they do exist. It's the motive that is important.

• CONTRACT FOR DEED···············

The availability of startup capital is a major hurdle for most budding entrepreneurs. This poses a problem as well for the prospective seller of an existing business. The number of potential buyers becomes limited by the availability of capital. Similar to the housing market, as the price rises the number of potential buyers shrinks.

Unlike the housing market, the level of equity that a potential buyer must put up is substantially larger. Unlike the housing market, lenders are much more reluctant, due to the risk involved, to finance the purchase of a small business. This quandary creates a situation in which the seller may be forced to become a lender in order to sell an existing business. For the potential buyer the seller then becomes a potential source of capital, provided, of course, that the terms and conditions can be agreed upon.

The most difficult aspect almost always will be price, and a number of valuation techniques should be employed. The correct price lies somewhere between the high end, at or near the asking price, and the low end, the highest price the market will bear at or above the liquidation value of the assets less selling costs. Some difficult questions need to be answered, including the following:

- Is this a successful business, and if so, why?
- Why is the seller really selling? (Look beyond the standard answers: "due to ill health" or "to pursue other interests.")
- What is the character and reputation of the seller?
- What is the reputation of the business?
- Will the business remain healthy with a change of ownership?
- Will the business be able to make you a living, as well as supporting the additional debt?
- Who are the customers?
- What is the image of the business?
- Are the customers loyal to the owner or current personnel, or are they loyal to the business?
- Is revenue rising or falling? Why?
- Will the sales trends continue?
- Can you enhance revenue? How?
- Who is the competition?
- How strong are the competitors?
- Are new competitors moving in?
- Are there potential zoning law changes?
- Are highway construction or street construction projects pending to change traffic patterns or interrupt traffic patterns?
- Are there any environmental problems with this business?
- In your trade area, are there environmental or other issues that would hinder your location or hinder your customers?
- Are there supplier problems?
- Are there legal problems, such as pending lawsuits?
- What is the condition of the physical structure?
- What is the condition of the electrical, plumbing, heating, and air-conditioning systems?
- What is the condition of the equipment?
- Will the equipment need repair, replacing, maintenance, or updating?
- Can you remain competitive with the existing structure and equipment?
- Will you need to expend capital to rectify any of these situations, and if so, how much?
- Are there any personnel problems, such as liability suits?

- How is employee morale?
- What has employee turnover been?
- Will you keep or terminate the existing staff?
- How critical are the existing employees to the continued success of this enterprise?
- How critical is the existing management to the success of this enterprise?
- Can you replace the existing owner from a managerial point of view?

The answers to these and other questions will determine your chances of success. If you find that the character of the seller is questionable, the best course of action is to terminate negotiations immediately. In the course of attempting to answer these questions you have a right to examine whatever records you deem necessary. You would probably want to see tax returns for at least the past three years. This will take you beyond the point where the proprietor was thinking of selling.

- Has profit been overstated in the past year or two to make the business appear more profitable than it really is?
- Can you verify sales by cross-checking them with sales tax returns?
- How do the financial ratios compare to previous years?
- How do the financial ratios compare to industry averages?
- How well has this business been managed?
- Can you identify management errors?
- Can you correct those management errors, or do they stem from flaws in design or layout?
- Can you create a new profit and loss statement incorporating additional debt, with corrected ratios from projected sales?
- What potential exists for growth?

If the seller refuses to produce the records, terminate the offer. If the records are bogus, terminate the offer. If the records cannot be verified, this reduces the value of the assets to their liquidation value, because you cannot make a correlation to profitability.

I once was pursuing the purchase of a listed business. In visiting with the listing realtor, I asked for the records noted above. His response was: "Well, I could get them for you, but they wouldn't do you much good because (wink, wink) he doesn't report his real income to Uncle Sam, but he's doing such and such for volume. It's a hell of a good business." My response was: "Then what you are telling me is that this man is lying to the government for his own financial gain." To which the realtor could only reply with an affirmation. "What do you suppose the odds are then that he would lie to me in his profit and personal gain?" The answer is obvious, and unless the seller is willing to sell for liquidation value and the buyer is willing to jump into this enterprise blind, the negotiations are over. If you cannot trust the person or his or her records, you have nothing credible on which to base a purchase decision. One needs to take a very skeptical position when auditing the seller's records.

I suppose in a situation such as I just described one could try to estimate what sales volume really is by conducting an investigation comparable to what the IRS or the state department of revenue would conduct. They may interview the suppliers of this business and obtain records of input purchases from which a markup or some other ratio could be calculated, backed up by using comparable financial statements or industry averages.

Proper records will give you a historical record of income and expenses. One can apply Pareto's law and identify the 20 percent of items that account for 80 percent of revenues, apply the same to the expense side, and then seek to verify those numbers. The check register and canceled checks will help identify the suppliers, and you could visit with a couple of them to seek their opinion and to verify that collection problems do not exist. You can also verify several of the expense categories against the entries on the tax return. It would be advisable to contact the state department of revenue to verify that the account is current and that the license is transferable. Do the same with the state department of labor.

You are not necessarily looking for a business that has been managed perfectly. In this type of business there is little room for improvement. A much better scenario is a business that has excellent sales revenue which appears to be stable but shows low profitability due to correctable mistakes. You are looking for a situation to capitalize on. It may be that a business has the potential to expand its customer base but for some reason hasn't recognized or pursued that expansion. You may be able to grow the business by expanding services. What you are looking for is adequate sales revenue, or at least the potential of good volume. What you are not looking to do is get locked into a financial commitment where due to low sales volume you are required to work 80 hours a week to break even. You do not want a sweatshop environment.

If your findings appear to be satisfactory and legitimate, it would be advisable to obtain the services of an accounting professional to review your findings and make recommendations. You may have overlooked something or made an error in some material way. Your level of fear, uncertainty, and anxiety will be eased a little by a competent second opinion. If at this time you feel you wish to pursue an offer, it would also be advisable to contact an attorney to bring into the loop along with the accountant. Your accountant can assist in helping you identify a reasonable valuation. Your attorney may be of great help in assisting with the negotiations. It is at the offering and counteroffering points that negotiations generally become the most stressful and often get bogged down, with a gap between the offering and selling prices. An understanding of amortization techniques or the present value of annuities can be helpful in narrowing that gap. If the seller is adamant about price, there may be maneuvering room concerning terms.

For example, suppose that the seller is demanding $150,000 for the business with 20 percent down, which amounts to $30,000, with the remaining $120,000 to be amortized over 15 years at 12 percent. This calculates to be $120,000/6.811 = $17,618.55 annually or $1468.21 per month.

Suppose that the buyer makes an offer of $125,000 accepting the same terms. $125,000.00 × 20 percent down = $25,000 down and the remaining $100,000 amortized over 15 years at 12 percent = $100,000/6.811 = $14,682.13 annually or $1223.51 per month.

Suppose that a counteroffer was made, accepting the seller's price but dropping the interest rate to 8 percent, which changes the calculations to $125,000/8.560 = $14,602.80 annually or $1216.90 per month. The $5000 additional down payment can be made up in part by lower monthly payments, and also by having a higher depreciable basis in the business. Reality may lie somewhere in between, but it gives the buyer another approach to bridge the gap over price.

If an agreement on valuation can be reached and an offer is submitted and accepted, the final stage in the purchase process involves the terms of the contract itself. Most contracts for deeds follow a fairly standard format but are modified by the particulars of each transaction. It would be advisable to have your attorney prepare the contract. Hiring your attorney to prepare the contract means an additional expense on your part, but if you are the buyer, have your attorney prepare the contract. If you are the seller, have your attorney prepare the contract. The language used in the contract tends to be more beneficial to the party doing the contract preparation. For example, a standard clause will address the event of a foreclosure. Your attorney will attempt to be less restrictive in the wording, allowing, say, a minimum of 30 days' notice before foreclosure proceedings begin and possibly allowing for some type of recovery, whereas the seller's attorney might only require a 14-day notice and foreclosure would be immediate, with the forfeiture of all the assets purchased and possibly the inclusion of inventory, fixtures, and additions in the sense of replaced equipment that have been made since the time of purchase. Your attorney will choose which clauses and covenants are put into the contract, and the number of restrictions will at least originally be less.

Once the contract has been prepared, it is forwarded to the second party in the agreement, in this case the seller. The seller will review the contract and accept the terms and conditions by signing, or require modifications to be made to the contract before acceptance. In the normal course of events, the seller would hire an attorney to read the contract and render an opinion as to modifications, deletions, and/or additions of covenants, or restrictions. The seller's attorney is concerned that the contract is not lopsided and that the interests of the client are fairly represented. It would be rare that modifications are not made; however, much of the original form of the contract should remain intact. Thus your interests (the buyer) are protected and not unduly hindered. The net effect should be a contract a little more balanced in your favor.

If you have taken a course in business law, you will recall the elements of a contract. A contract is an agreement between competent parties, the agreement must be for a legal purpose, and consideration must be involved. A contract for deed contains those elements, but just those elements are insufficient to define the agreement adequately. A typical contract for deed sales agreement will be somewhat like the following. Most attorney's use some form of template when preparing such contracts.

Contract for Deed: Sales Agreement

The first part of the agreement will usually identify the date, time, and place that the agreement was entered into. It will also identify the parties entering into the agreement, often include their addresses, and will often identify each as hereafter referred to as the buyer or the seller.

1. *Sale*. This section will say something to the effect that the buyer agrees to buy and the seller agrees to sell, and identify what it is that is being bought and sold. It may refer to a schedule, a bill of sale, or list a legal description of the real estate involved.

2. *Purchase price*. Here the price that the buyer is paying the seller is stated. The price will often be referred to as *consideration*. This section may break down the price into components (e.g., real estate, equipment, supplies, etc.), defining how the purchase price was arrived at.

3. *Payment*. Sometimes this section will be referred to as *terms*; it defines what is to be paid as a down payment, and how much is to be amortized and under what interest rate. The payment section will often refer to an *amortization schedule*, which will be attached to the contract. The day of the month, place, and amount of the payment will be defined. Payment is often made to an escrow agent, such as a bank. If so, it may be defined here or be defined

as a separate element. A grace period can be addressed as well as late-payment penalties.

It would be advisable to insist that an escrow account be set up and used for payment purposes. This is especially important in event of the death of either party. An escrow account provides for an intermediary to make payment to. Should relations with the seller break down, you will not have to deal physically with the other party to make payment, nor will you have to worry about the mail being delivered promptly. The bank will have accurate, undisputable records that payments were made and that they were made in a timely fashion. This could become critical should a dispute arise concerning foreclosure issues.

4. *Warranties of seller.* This section of the contract identifies and explains the warranties or representation that the seller makes to the buyer. Your attorney can insist that certain conditions or warranties be included and granted to you in this part of the contract, to protect your interests. These can be very important and very critical.

   (a) The seller will usually be required to make a warranty that they do in fact have the right to sell whatever it is that they are selling, that in so doing they are not breaching any other previously binding contract or mortgage agreement. Language to the effect that the assets are free of encumbrances and liens may be used. If real estate is involved, a title search and opinion may be required and/or title insurance provided.

   (b) A warranty should be required to the effect that all taxes and assessments have been paid on the real estate, if involved; similarly, that no taxes are owed to any governmental agency by the seller, and that the buyer is not responsible for past tax obligations or any taxes stemming from the seller's activities.

This book is written from the perspective of sole proprietorships, but I want to digress here to elaborate and expand on this issue. If the seller has been operating as a corporation and the seller wishes to sell you the corporation's stock and allow you to continue the corporate entity—don't. I strongly recommend that you buy the assets and only the assets. If you want a corporate structure, form a new corporation and bring the purchase of those assets into the new corporate structure.

Why? Because by the very nature of a corporation, the corporation is a perpetual entity, often described as being like a third person. The problem with purchasing such a structure is that this entity has a past history for which it is forever responsible. On the positive side, that may have created tremendous goodwill; on the negative side, all contingent liabilities are the responsibility of the corporation. The warranty set forth in item 4(b) will not protect you, the buyer, because from a legal perspective, in all likelihood this entity will be reviewed as a continuation—the sale was just a stock swap. If you buy stock in GM, nothing changes at GM. If you bought controlling interest in General Motors stock, the corporation does not change; you just control the corporation. The same thing is true in buying a small business that is operating as a corporation.

If the corporation has not paid payroll taxes nor paid suppliers in three years, changing stockholders does not relieve the corporation of those obligations. The same would be true for worker compensation claims, product liability claims, and so on. The IRS will seize the assets of the corporation to satisfy any obligations not met. Your corporation will be liable. You must then attempt to recover damages from the seller. Why put yourself in jeopardy by assuming someone's corporate structure? The very wording of the warranties implies that you, as buyer, desire to begin with a clean slate.

(c) A bulk sales agreement warranty will usually be required, which addresses the issue that all suppliers of goods and services to the business have been paid up to the date of closing. It also ensures that should past obligations arise, the buyer is not responsible for those obligations.

(d) A warranty that the seller owes no brokerage fees or commissions, and that the agent selling this property has been paid by the seller. No charges can be levied against the buyer.

(e) A warranty that the seller can guarantee a good and marketable title, that the sale will not be encumbered and will be free of all liens and charges. It may also require a warranty to the effect that the seller has not entered into an agreement to sell the same entity to another party at the same time.

(f) A warranty may be included stating that the seller affirms to the buyer that in entering into this agreement, the buyer is not assuming any contracts of the seller. This may pertain to agreements the seller entered into concerning the rent of a sign, or commitments made to advertising agencies, for radio or television spots, or any other type of contract.

(g) The buyer may want to include a warranty or condition that restricts the seller from going into competition with the buyer. Such a warranty may restrict the seller from opening a similar business in a certain geographic region, or set a time restriction. This is especially important if a element of goodwill was part of the purchase.

(h) "Time is of the essence" warranties may be included, indicating that the agreement will be entered into and carried out with some degree of expedience.

(i) Statements may also be included indicating that the warranties set forth are material in nature, which implies that a violation of the warranty would materially violate the contract, and provides an escape, or conditions of redress, for the buyer.

The warranties made by the seller to the buyer act as an inducement for the buyer to accept the contract. The buyer must also make some warranties to the seller to induce the seller to accept the offer and enter into the agreement.

5. *Warranties of the buyer.* The buyer will make certain warranties to the buyer in this section of the contract. Some of the warranties may be placed or required by the seller or the seller's attorney.

(a) A statement or warranty will be made that the buyer has the legal right and authority to enter into this agreement, that he or she is, in fact, a competent party.

(b) The buyer must grant the seller the right to enter. That is the right to come onto the property or business to inspect the property or equipment. Conditions may be expressed that proper notice be given before doing so.

(c) The seller may require a warranty from the buyer that proper insurance be maintained and that a binder be submitted, and that the seller be named as the insured to the extent of their insurable interest.

(d) The seller will require a warranty that taxes and licenses be maintained, if applicable.

(e) The seller will require a warranty clause that real estate, equipment, and or other assets be maintained in as good condition as when purchased, or that proper repairs and maintenance be done.

(f) A clause concerning improvements may be added. The seller may require the buyer to forfeit any improvements in event of foreclosure.

(g) The seller will usually restrict the buyer from assigning the contract without prior written permission from the seller. In many cases the buyer may set a condition that the sale of the business or assets, or any part of the assets, will cause the contract to be terminated, and the full amount owed becomes due and payable in a set number of days. Similar restrictions may be placed on subletting the premises or property.

(h) The seller may require the buyer to serve notice to the seller under certain circumstances and/or events. For example, if the seller allows the subletting of the property, the buyer will require notice of such an arrangement and may require prior approval.

(i) The conditions initiating forfeiture or foreclosure proceedings will be set forth in this clause. A grace period may be addressed here or separately or not at all. Most contracts define the number of days a payment can be late before proceedings can be initiated. This clause will address what, how, and in what manner foreclosure and forfeiture will occur.

6. *Possession.* This part of the agreement will define what the buyer will be taking possession of and at what time and place. If customers or clients are part of the course of business, that will usually be addressed also. A date and time of closing will be set forth specifically or a statement made to the effect that upon a mutually agreed upon time, closing and possession will occur.

At the time of closing, certain conditions may be set. For example, the buyer may be required to bring a cashier's check in the predetermined amount. At that time the seller will deliver a bill of sale. Inventory items may be counted and assigned at that time as well. At the closing the seller may enter into and sign a noncompete agreement.

7. *Partial invalidity.* A disclaimer or clause will often be added stating that if one or more of the conditions, warranties, or restrictions set forth in the contract violates some type of legal ordinance, that part of the contract becomes null and void, but the body of and intent of the agreement remain in force, and such a violation does not invalidate the contract itself.

8. *Captions not controlling.* A clause will often be added which states that the warranties, restriction, and captions are for convenience only, that in essence, the contract need not be deemed a contract of entity. That is, if something material was forgotten or left out, the intent of the parties prevails, not just the limitations of the agreement.

9. *Benefit.* This section states that the agreement is binding on both parties. It will usually state that this agreement is extended to the heirs, successors, and assignees of the parties involved. Sometimes a separate clause regarding successors and heirs is included.

10. *Attorney fees.* It is often a part of the agreement as to who pays the attorney fees.

11. *In witness whereof.* As a final section of the agreement, the parties will sign the agreement. Their role as seller or buyer is usually identified beneath the signatures. The signatures are usually witnessed and notarized by a notary public, and the seal is affixed to the contract.

Both parties will receive copies of the contract, and the contract is often registered with the county at the register of deeds office.

This is not intended to serve as a template of a contract or sales agreement format. It will, however, be representative of many sales agreements. Other warranties or conditions may be added to require performance, restrictions, or guaranties pertaining to pertinent elements within the agreement. The contract is often unique to the situation. It should be easy to recognize how easily language and conditions can be tilted in either the seller's or buyer's favor. It is why I recommend that you have your attorney write the contract, even if it means that you agree to pay the attorney fees. If the other party writes the contract, hire your own attorney and amend the contract with language and warranties more favorable to you.

• VALUATION TECHNIQUES·············

Valuation is difficult at best. Often, multiple valuation methods are computed to provide a range of values. Occasionally, two or more methods arrive at a similar price. In the end it boils down to how bad the seller wants to sell and how far the seller is willing to compromise on price and terms as compared with how badly the buyer wants to buy the business. If the seller has more than one prospective buyer, he or she will be less likely to make huge concessions. If the business has been listed for six months or a year and has generated little interest or if several offers have been rejected, the seller may begin to realize that the asking price is too high.

Following are six key factors in determining a business's value:

1. The firm's recent profit history
2. The general condition of the firm (condition of the facility and equipment, completeness and accuracy of the books, employee morale, etc.)
3. The market demand for this particular kind of business or the business's products.
4. Economic conditions, especially interest rates and availability of capital.
5. The ability of the business to transfer goodwill
6. Future profit potential

Valuation is an imperfect art. The following are some commonly used approaches[7]:

1. Liquidation value
2. Replacement cost
3. Sales or earnings multiples
4. Return on investment
5. Discounted cash flow

Liquidation Value

As indicated earlier, if the business is showing little or no profit, or if the records are not deemed to be valid, your offer may be that of liquidation value only. In this case you would want to do a complete physical inventory of all equipment and fixtures. Setting a correct value on equipment and fixtures may not be easy either. You could contact an auction house for an estimate; auctioneers often have books similar to the blue book for pricing automobiles. You could offer to pay a reputable auctioneer to prepare an estimate from the equipment and fixtures list and to make a physical inspection. Contact an equipment dealer to price certain used equipment or to price certain items. Your bank may be able to provide some assistance. Contact the SBA to see if they are having any liquidation auctions of a similar type of business and plan to attend.

An ongoing business is generally worth a premium over liquidation value. Other things to consider and possibly add to the price are the cost of delivery and installation of the equipment and fixtures. If this were a startup business, a lag time exists from the time capital is expended for equipment and fixtures until the door is opened for business. A premium could be added for this lag time. The amount of money you pay over and above the actual value of assets is often called *blue sky*, or *goodwill* in accounting terms. The business name, location, image reputation, and so on, may have a positive value for the new proprietor and be worthy of a premium.

Replacement Cost

A starting point is the equipment and fixtures list you obtained from a physical inventory. The replacement cost approach basically calculates what it would cost you if you were to start this business from scratch. This does not imply that you need everything on that list, but it acts as a reference as to what the seller considered necessary to operate the business. You create your own wish list and obtain prices for each item, and add up the total. You will also need to consider delivery and installation expenses.

Compare the cost of the startup with the asking price of the business. This does not suggest that they should necessarily be equivalent. The seller is trying to sell you used equipment, probably not all of which you need or want. The seller is also offering those features identified as goodwill and a value must be associated with them also.

Compare the replacement cost with the liquidation value and with the asking price. I would begin to feel uncomfortable if the asking price were much more than the replacement cost figure unless there was some compelling reason why it should claim that much of a premium.

Sales or Earnings Multiples

A key assumption being made is that sales volume and/or net income are going to continue as they have been, or improve. Two perspectives are present when viewing earnings multiples. The first perspective stems from using the seller's net income figure. If the business has been well managed and net income relatively high, the original asking price was probably derived by using a multiple of net income. Calculate that multiple.

The second perspective obviously stems from your own pro-forma income statement, having estimated the additional costs associated with the purchase and those profit-enhancing implementations. Apply your multiple to your projected net income figure and compare to the previous valuation computations.

Another method is to use the gross sales figure and attempt to derive a value from that. In effect, it is similar to using net income, except that the multiple is lower. If industry standards were applied to a forecast, one could project net income. Ratio analysis can also be applied, specifically that regarding profitability, to again estimate net income. The business in question has a history and thus the forecast should be fairly accurate, although a change of ownership and management may affect sales adversely. Is customer loyalty associated with the current management?

Return on Investment

Regardless of the method used, the return on your investment must be acceptable. You should also consider the value of your wages when calculating return on investment (ROI). As a broad rule of thumb, a return of 15 to 20 percent is an acceptable return from a small business. The implication is a multiple of five to seven times net income after subtracting fair market value for personal wages. An opportunity cost always exists; those dollars could be invested in high-grade corporate bonds or in mutual funds while you work the equivalent of 80 hours a week on two jobs, perhaps even at minimum wage.

Discounted Cash Flow

Discounted cash flows are used frequently by major corporations in evaluating competing capital expenditure proposals. The principal advantage in using this type of technique is that adjustments are made for the timing of cash inflows, and the cash inflows are risk adjusted. The principal disadvantage of the use of this type of technique stems from the fact that cash inflows are still estimates. A material change in input values can render the process meaningless. If net income projections are accurate, this is a very useful technique.

Projections that are extended out more than five to seven years begin to become meaningless, due to the difficulty of most projects to make projections accurately that far out. Discounted cash flow methods reduce the impact on far-out projections. Another way of handling that issue is to terminate the projections with a liquidation value five or seven years down the road.

1. Determine net income projections (in this example over seven years). This is a critical number and care should be taken to ensure as much accuracy as possible. As in the ROI example above, some adjustments may be required for reasonable management wages.
2. Determine a required discount factor that should be your required rate of return on this business investment.
3. Determine an estimate of the resale value or salvage value of the business at that point in the future where this projection ends. Another option would be to extend this project through the expected life of the investment.
4. Set up a format to calculate the projections in present value terms (as the following example demonstrates).

Example

Assume a $10,000 cash inflow over seven years with a $50,000 salvage or resale value and a required rate of return of 15 percent.

YEAR	CASH INFLOW	DISCOUNT FACTOR	PRESENT VALUE
1	$10,000	0.87	$8,700
2	10,000	0.756	7,560
3	10,000	0.658	6,580
4	10,000	0.572	5,720
5	10,000	0.497	4,970
6	10,000	0.432	4,320
7	10,000	0.376	3,760
7	50,000	0.376	18,800
			$60,410

Based on the assumptions above, this example would support a purchase price of $60,410.

• RECOMMENDATIONS FOR THE BUYER TO CONSIDER ························

Some recommendations to keep in mind when purchasing a business:

1. Keep the inventory as a separate item; do not include unless it is advantageous to take the entire inventory. You do not need to start out with an obsolescence problem or to have too much capital tied up in inventory. Purchase what you need; the rest is the seller's problem.

2. Do not take the seller's accounts receivables. They (along with the collection problems associated with them) belong to the seller.

3. Purchase the assets of the business, not a corporation's stock. A stock purchase leaves you as the majority stockholder in a perpetual entity. The corporation brings with it its history and any and all contingent liabilities. If the corporation did not pay its income or payroll taxes for the past two years, for example, it is the corporation that is liable for them. The IRS will seize the corporation's assets to settle the liability. Liability suits can follow. If you want a corporate structure, form a new corporation and purchase the assets with the new corporate structure.

4. Have your attorney draw up the contract for deed. The seller will have his or her attorney read the contract and challenge conditions not to the seller's advantage. Your attorney will use language that will be more favorable to you in case of default. Your attorney is more likely to include favorable conditions and minimize restrictions.

5. Do not assume any accounts payable. Insist on a bulk sales agreement clause to release you from any liens or encumbrances or liabilities from the prior owner's inability or unwillingness to pay past bills.

6. Have payments made into an escrow account if a contract for deed is being used. This will protect you from having someone standing in your doorway collecting a payment each month. An escrow may be especially appreciated in the event that the personal relationship between the parties breaks down. The purchase and sale of a business can be an emotionally charged experience for both parties. Both parties may appreciate the interpersonal distance afforded by an escrow account. In addition, in the event of the death of either party, an escrow account is already in place for the estate, facilitating a smooth continuation of the contract.

7. The closing date will be a time when utilities and licenses will be switched over. A time will be set to complete and purchase the inventory.

This is not intended to be a complete list. The professionals involved will be able to identify and rectify any gaps and or additions associated with your particular situation.

Some Advantages to Buying an Existing Business

There are some advantages to buying an existing business. The principal advantage is that the level of acceptance of the enterprise has been established in the marketplace. The business has a financial history; thus the revenue forecast is likely to be more accurate. The expenses have also been established in an existing business. If a question arises concerning the level of expense associated with utilities, last year's expense figures will be an accurate starting point in computing this year's expense. Operating systems have been established and are in place. Management consists of identifying errors in the existing operating systems and correcting them, and also implementing changes that will capitalize on the growth potential identified during the purchase analysis.

When starting a business project it is difficult to anticipate all the expenses in getting the project off the ground. It is inevitable that cost overruns develop; sometimes the overruns are very substantial. In purchasing a business, that type of thing is somewhat minimized. For example, suppose that you rented a building to start a convenience store. You need four compressors to run your coolers. When the electrician arrives he indicates that your electrical service can't handle that kind of load; you need to rewire for a new service. In the process you move a wall, escalating a budgeted expense of $2000 for four compressors to $12,000. These kinds of things can always happen when purchasing a business but they are more apt to happen in a new startup.

When purchasing an existing business, you are, in fact, purchasing a complete line of used equipment. The actual purchase price may be less than the replacement cost. In addition, all this equipment is installed and should be operational. On the next business day your cash flow begins, unlike a new startup, where lag time exists between equipment expenditures and revenue generation. The business already has a customer base to build on.

Some Disadvantages to Buying an Existing Business

You inherit all past decisions concerning name, location, layout and design, inventory, image, pricing structure, equipment, and every other facet of the business. Not all of these are easily or cheaply corrected.

You may have had to pay more than replacement cost for used equipment. You were forced to take all the existing equipment, some of which you simply will not use or need. You may be forced to pump in additional monies to change the layout or to install replacement equipment.

Your customers may associate the business with the previous owner and keep asking for that person. The changeover can cost you customers and money. The employees may resist change; they may keep telling you that the previous owner didn't do it that way. The same goes for your suppliers; they, too, will keep comparing you to the former owner. It will take some time for everyone involved to make the transition—and they will; it is just a question of how much it will cost you.

• UNCONVENTIONAL TYPES OF FINANCING ·

When seeking financing for a business venture, plans must often be altered due to the fact that the financial institution will not approve the loan request at the original level. A degree of flexibility within the realm of financing needs to be maintained. Sometimes, cost overruns create a situation where original plans cannot be carried out as structured. Flexibility and adaptability are thrust upon us. Sometimes it just doesn't make good sense to add any more debt to our financial structure. As investment goes up, revenue must also go up to keep profitability ratios in line. If an increase in revenue is not reasonably expected and the additional investment does not reduce expenses, additional expenditures may not be acceptable. Many small business owners are faced with finding alternative, sometimes creative ways to find additional financing.

Home Equity Loan

The easiest source of money available in the United States is for vehicles and homes. You may be required to have a 25 percent equity minimum to finance a small business venture, but you can often buy a vehicle costing $20,000 or more for little or nothing down and often at very attractive interest rates. The reason, of course, is that the vehicle finance companies have a vested interest in keeping their parent companies production lines operating at capacity if possible. Thus they are willing to make credit and financing concessions.

The housing industry is supported by powerful political lobbies in the form of the National Association of Realtors (NAR). The NAR is backed and supported by thousands of local real estate groups. Their agenda is to make sure that Washington is aware of the importance of the housing industry to the well-being of the national economy. Residential home building is considered a major economic indicator. Homeownership in a larger sense represents the American dream. A combination of these forces have created mechanisms to make home ownership possible, and to a large extent affordable. Financing is facilitated through a number of programs, such as the Government National Mortgage Association (GNMA) loans, known as Ginnie Maes; the Federal National Mortgage Association (FNMA) loans, or Fannie Maes; and federal home loans such as those of FMHA, backed by home mortgage insurance. Like vehicle financing, these programs allow individuals access to relatively large amounts of capital with little or nothing down. For many people the equity position they have in their homes, acquired through debt reduction and home value appreciation, represents the bulk of their personal net worth. This net worth can represent a source of capital to fund a business enterprise if you are willing to risk putting that equity into a business venture.

Home Refinancing Loan

To refinance a home is the equivalent of financing a new home purchase, less the involvement of the realtor to facilitate the purchase. The lender will review your financial history, not only from the perspective of credit worthiness but also to verify your ability to pay. The mortgage lender is going to be concerned that they are dealing with a person of good character. The mortgage lender will also be concerned that the loan is adequately collateralized.

To confirm your credit standing, the mortgage banker will order a credit report from a credit bureau. The lender will require documentation that you can make the mortgage payments. You will usually be required to bring in your last two year's tax returns, along with copies of your W-2's. The lender will require you to bring in your most recent pay stub, showing earnings year to date. The lender may require you to sign a form granting authorization for the bank to contact your current employer for confirmation of employment. In addition, the lender will want you to somehow document all the monthly bills you currently have and how much is owed each creditor. In this way the lender can establish your ability to pay using a predetermined formula. An industry norm uses a formula that allows roughly 28 percent of the borrower's gross pay to be the maximum allocated for a house payment. Thus a monthly income of $2,500 will be required to support a house payment of $700 per month. The lender will usually set another parameter, which will restrict the borrower to a total debt/income ratio of about 36 percent. In the example above, an income of $2500 per month would support total debt obligations of $2500 × 36 percent = $900. If the borrower wanted to finance a house payment of $700, then $200 would be the maximum allowed to finance other obligations. If this person's other monthly debt obligations exceeded $200, it would tend to begin pushing the allowable home payment down. Some variation exists, especially if a loan guarantee can be provided by an agency such as the Veterans Administration.

If you are married, the lender will want to see wage verification for both spouses but will consider joint incomes in authorizing a loan. If you have a second job, those pay stubs will also be required. Documentation to verify other sources of income will also be required. The process is to verify that your income is what you say it is and to verify that your income is stable. This raises another issue; if you are quitting a job to pursue a business venture, you will probably want to do your refinancing well ahead of your employment termination. Lenders are very wary of the self-employed. If you are self-employed, the lender will use the net income figure on your schedule C for wage-verification purposes.

The lender is also concerned about your ability to meet your home mortgage obligations in light of your other financial commitments. The lender will want to see documentation concerning all your debt obligations: vehicle payments, credit card obligations, student loans, and so on. These commitments will be evaluated in light of your income to make a decision to qualify you for a loan payment amount.

The lender will next attempt to establish that you are creditworthy through a credit check. A credit bureau will be contacted to obtain your abstract. If there are credit issues in your background, it would be best to contact the credit bureau yourself. You may be allowed to attach a written explanation to your file citing the circumstances surrounding the issue.

The lender will next require that the home mortgage be collateralized adequately. To do so will generally require an appraisal by a certified appraiser. You will be charged for the appraisal. The appraised valuation is important; the interest rates will be a function of the percentage of the valuation that you are borrowing. Most lenders will require that the loan amount be not more than 80 percent of the appraised value to obtain their best rate. Many lenders will, however, loan up to 100 percent of appraised valuation, and some newer programs allow for a loan of as much as 125 percent of appraised valuation. Interest rates are graduated upward to compensate the lender for the added risk associated with these types of loans. At the 125 percent level rates can begin to approach credit card rates. One other consideration before refinancing at 90 percent or more of your home appraisal is that it will be some time before you would acquire enough equity in your home to consider refinancing in the future. The main issue here is that if interest rates were to drop from the time you refinanced your house, it may be difficult to refinance again, due to a lack of home equity.

If you qualify for a loan guarantee such as through the Veterans Administration, which currently will guarantee up to $36,000 on a home mortgage, you may qualify for a lower interest rate. The interest rate charged is not only a function of your equity position, it is also a function of how long the mortgage will run and whether you buy the rate down through points. The starting point for the interest rate you will pay relates to current market conditions for home mortgage rates. The rate you will pay on your home loan will usually be at least three percentage points less than you would pay on a business loan and could easily be as much as five percentage points less, assuming, of course, the lender's business loan rate.

Before refinancing your home as a loan source, be sure you understand what the costs are going to be. As far as normal refinancing goes, a rule of thumb is that if you can save one percentage point, it is generally worthwhile to consider refinancing. If you cannot save that percentage point, a second mortgage or a line of credit may be a better source of business capital.

An appraisal of the property will be required by one of several certified appraisers that the lender uses. Some lenders will substitute a driveby appraisal if credit and loan percentages are at 80 percent or less. This will vary with the lender; some lenders will substitute a driveby appraisal only if they hold the original loan, but an appraisal will still be required. Following is a estimate of the general refinancing costs based on a $100,000 mortgage. Some variation will exist between lenders, and some terminology may differ, but they will in essence be the same.

Loan origination fee (sometimes called points; currently, one point but may be as high as four points or more)	$1000.00
Appraisal fee	318.00
Credit report	50.00
Tax service fee (a search to make sure that property taxes have been paid)	59.00
Underwriting fee	150.00
Settlement or closing charges (fees charged by the title company)	212.00
Title insurance premium	440.00
Recording fee (the mortgage is recorded at the register of deeds office)	25.30
Survey (the property is surveyed to ensure that the boundaries are correct)	95.00
Flood zone certification	19.50
Total	$2368.80

In addition, any discount or buy-down points can be added. There will also be some prorated prepaid escrow expense settlements for taxes, insurance, and so on.

Refinancing is an expensive proposition, but if, for example, the borrower were able to save one percentage point on the loan outlined above, the refinance charges will be recovered in roughly two years. If $30,000 of equity is used to finance a business venture, and that equity saves 5 percent over a conventional loan, the refinance charges will be recovered in approximately a year and a half.

Most mortgage lenders will have very similar loan requirements, due to the fact that they will generally package your loan together with similar home loans to sell in the secondary market. Therefore, home mortgage loans must be uniform and meet preestablished guidelines and requirements set by the secondary market.[8]

Second Mortgage Home Equity Loans

A second home mortgage leaves your original home loan intact and does what the name implies—adds a second home loan to the first. You do not even need to go to the same lender. The second lender will file a lien on your home, but that lien is subordinate to the first mortgage lien. A second mortgage is a home equity loan. Historically, these were used primarily for home improvements, but with the changes in the IRS interest rate deduction rules, home equity loans have been used for everything from buying cars and vacations to financing a new business venture.

The chief advantage of a second mortgage stems from the fact that the majority of the refinancing expenses are avoided. The mortgage company will require an appraisal, which the borrower will pay for at the closing. If a recent appraisal has been done, it may be waived. If you are dealing with the same lender, a cheaper, driveby appraisal may be done. In some cases the valuation can be established by using the real estate tax assessment valuation. In addition, a title search may be required and title insurance may need to be increased. The second mortgage will be recorded and an appropriate charge will be assessed. The costs associated with a second mortgage can range from a low end of virtually nothing to hundreds of dollars, but few should approach $1000.

The mortgage lender is loaning on the equity of your home. They have the right to file a mortgage lien but are subject to the first lienholder's claim on that property. In so doing the lender is accepting a higher degree of risk; to be compensated the lender will charge a higher rate of interest. At the time of this writing a home loan with an 80 percent equity position could be financed for 30 years with a rate of around $7\frac{1}{2}$ percent. A second mortgage could be obtained for a maximum of 15 years with a five-year fixed rate of around $9\frac{1}{2}$ percent. A five-year fixed rate allows the lender a rate window to raise the rate should interest rates rise. The rate charged is a function of the prime rate plus $1\frac{1}{4}$ percent. Variable-rate loans are also available, but on most second mortgages or home equity loans the loan payment is set up on a 15-year amortization. Second mortgages of this type usually cannot exceed 90 percent of the home's valuation. Although some lenders will allow second mortgages of up to 125 percent of a home's valuation, rates will reflect this added risk.[9]

Home Equity Line of Credit

A home equity line of credit is essentially the same as a second mortgage. The lender sets up a line of credit based on the equity in your home. Suppose that you have a home valued at $100,000. Your current payoff is, say, $59,000. The lender using the 90 percent valuation criterion could set up a $31,000 line of credit: $90,000 − $59,000 = $31,000. The borrower is supplied with checks to write on this line of credit, or a telephone transfer can be made into the borrower's account. The rate charged is usually a variable rate based on the prime rate plus $1\frac{1}{2}$ percent. In the case of a line of credit, the loan is not amortized; only the interest is billed on a monthly basis. This type of loan is becoming very popular.

Note: The home equity line of credit and the second mortgage should not be confused with the most recent trend in consumer finance. It appears that as many Americans are approaching the maximum on their personal credit cards or as it becomes more difficult for banks to issue additional credit cards due to the saturation of the market, a new tactic for high-interest-rate loans has been developed. Various financial institutions now offer home equity credit, made easy with just a signature and an authorization card by return mail. If you calculate the rate of interest on these offers, you soon discover that the interest rates associated with this type of credit are at or near credit card rates.

Suppliers and Dealers

Almost every business is supported by an array of vendors. It is worthwhile to cultivate personal relationships with a chosen few. These people work within your industry and know scores of similar businesses within their respective territories. They know their clients' businesses from a certain perspective. They are excellent sources of information and could well be aware of pieces of equipment lying in a storage building at the regional office or in a customers' storage that could be utilized by your business. Once located it could often be purchased for pennies on the dollar—the one person's junk adage.

In the restaurant industry, suppliers will gladly place new or nearly new equipment into your business with an understanding that subsequent purchases be made from that company. For example, a soft drink vending machine will be installed by a food supplier with the requirement that the syrup be purchased from them. This example is industry specific but the concept is not. If equipment is required, separate financing can often be provided by the equipment dealer. A lease-to-buy option on new and used equipment from many dealers and suppliers is also available. If you make your needs known to your suppliers and vendors, many of these people will look out for you. It is in their best interests to keep you in business.

Subcontractors and Competitors

Your startup budget may not allow you to purchase all the equipment you need. In some situations you may be limited to the size of the job you can pursue, due to a lack of equipment or personnel. Depending on the type of business you are in, subcontracting out portions of the job to someone else can expand your capabilities and facilitate revenue generation.

Occasions may arise where your existing equipment or capacity is at 100 percent. If this situation exists, you know you are profitable and the marketplace is accepting your product or service. A dilemma exists, in that demand must be met or sales and market share will be permanently lost; on the other hand, growth must be controlled. In this type of situation some of the work can be subcontracted out. In this way your capacity is expanded without expending additional capital. It may at first seem counterproductive to contact your competitor, but a degree of cooperation can be helpful in expanding your capacity without capital expenditures. Your competitors have equipment and inventory similar to yours. A working relationship with the competition may create a situation where equipment could be rented on a short-term basis or an equipment exchange could be arranged.

Credit Cards

I am somewhat reluctant to mention the use of credit cards and recommend only limited use, due to the potential for serious problems. I am aware of one successful small business owner who financed his firm on credit cards. The business was started on a part-time basis but was now ready to go full time. Equipment was in place, but additional financing for production inventory was required. The bank rejected the plan. The proprietor presold his output, then used credit cards to finance the inputs and paid off the cards when the accounts receivable were realized. This was continued until enough profit was generated to operate almost strictly on cash.

A common characteristic among entrepreneurs is their undying belief in themselves and their business ideas. This carries over into what they are willing to do to get a business off the ground and keep it going once the enterprise is launched. Meeting customer demands by unconventional and sometimes creative means is part of what being in business is all about. At times this means applying that creativity in the area of financing.

Partnerships and Joint Ventures

By definition, one of the chief advantages of the formation of a partnership is the bringing together of two or more partners for the purpose of conducting a for-profit business. Each partner shares management responsibilities, and each partner shares in the arrangement by providing capital. If you do not have enough capital to start a business venture on your own, maybe by pooling your resources with someone else you can raise the necessary capital.

Suppose that as in most startup loans, a minimum of 25 percent equity is required. Suppose you have the 25 percent equity required but your loan is still rejected. If you were to find three other people like yourself, you could start this enterprise without a loan. By pairing up with one other person who had an equal equity position and applying jointly for a loan, you would enter the business with a 50 percent equity position. The lender would be much more likely to grant a loan to a business which was capitalized that well.

Certain advantages and disadvantages are inherent in a partnership. One critical consideration is that if both partners are going to be working in the business and both are going to attempt to make a living at the enterprise, the volume of business or level of revenue must be enough to meet those needs.

Early in the agreement and in writing, the relationship between the partners should be spelled out, especially relating to the types and rates of compensation of the partners. It is rare that partners enter a partnership agreement with exactly the same capital inputs. It is also unlikely that both partners have the same degree of skill or experience to contribute to the partnership.

One suggestion for handling those inequities associated with the human element is to value each partner's contribution in labor by an hourly rate. This compensation can be given priority in the agreement, and partners are paid first for their labor. The second element of inequity stems from the level of financial contribution each partner brings into the agreement. If a value is placed on each asset, an appropriate rental rate or rate of return can be assigned. In this way much of the assets can be held outside the partnership. Once the labor rate has been taken in a draw, the rental payments can be made, and finally, profits from the partnership can be distributed or reinvested. If the assets are to be maintained within the partnership, a greater share can be distributed to the partner contributing the most.

If you have little in the way of assets but have the ability to contract work due to your business contacts, experience, or particular expertise, it may be possible to solicit a partner for a joint venture: that is, find a contractor or someone in your line of business, even a competitor, with whom you could enter into an agreement to complete a single project jointly. Define up front what the compensation in this arrangement will be, draw up a contract, perform the project jointly, and share in the profits. In this manner you will gain not only capital but experience, both of which can be applied to the next project, until you are in fact on your own.

• QUESTIONS FOR DISCUSSION········

1. If you were starting a business and needed $20,000, which SBA loan would be most appropriate?
2. What if the loan amount were $100,000? Which SBA loan program would be most appropriate for that loan?
3. What type of business is the venture capitalist most interested in?
4. You are considering the purchase of a quickie mart type of gas station priced at $200,000. The seller is offering a contract for deed. Identify and define the conditions that you would want included in the contract for deed.
5. Discuss some ways in which the suppliers of a business can help an entrepreneur with financing.

6. How can you use your home equity to finance your business venture? Which would be the most advantageous way to use that home equity?

7. Discuss the advantages and disadvantages of forming a partnership to launch a small business.

8. Discuss some of the major questions when considering the purchase of an existing business.

9. What types of records would you want to examine prior to making an offer on a business?

• QUESTIONS FOR REVIEW · · · · · · · · · · ·

1. What services does SCORE provide? What do those services cost?

2. What is the purpose of the SBDCs? Who funds them?

3. Identify the elements that the SBA indicates influence the value of a small business.

4. When purchasing a business, what are the main valuation techniques?

5. Explain the difference between a home refinance and a second mortgage.

6. Identify the major advantages of buying an existing business.

7. Identify some of the major disadvantages associated with purchasing an existing business.

6 Franchises and Franchising Opportunities

Chapter Objectives

- To provide a detailed outline of what the Franchisor must disclose in a Uniform Franchise Offering Circular, before offering the franchise to the public.

- To provide a source of information, and a source of assistance through the AAFD and the FTC in identifying key questions as to what to look for before purchasing a franchise.

The fact that the topic of franchising is placed in this part of the book does not imply that franchising is a source of startup capital. It is not, at least generally it is not a source of capital, although some of the major franchisors will provide some assistance in obtaining capital. In part I chose to place this topic here because many people believe that the franchisor is a source of capital, like a car dealer providing financing mechanisms for car purchases right at the car lot. For the majority of franchise agreements, you will be required to find financing on your own should you wish to enter into an agreement. You, however, are a source of capital for the franchisor—do not forget this fact. The franchisor needs the franchisee as a source of expansion capital and as a means to expand sales and increase profit. The franchisor chose franchising as a mechanism, to finance rapid growth. The issue, then, is what the franchisor is offering the franchisee in this arrangement. Ideally, the franchise agreement should be mutually beneficial.

The first name that comes into people's minds when you say the word *franchise* is McDonald's. True, McDonald's is a franchise, but it is nearly impossible to acquire a McDonald's franchise unless you already own one of their franchises and a new outlet is desired in your territory. McDonald's has undoubtedly been very successful and has been good for many of its franchisees. The franchise industry will often refer to their's as the next McDonald's, but the industry is not what it was, and many franchisors are not what they appear to be. Caution is the watchword here, as in buying any business. Perhaps even a higher degree of caution is required because you as an individual are often dealing with professionals or a team of professionals. If the franchisor sets up the franchisee to be a part of his profit center through the sale of franchises, the buyer had best beware.

• FEDERAL OVERSIGHT OF THE FRANCHISE INDUSTRY · · · · · · · · · · · · · · ·

The Federal Trade Commission (FTC) oversees the interstate activities of the franchise industry. If the franchisor engages in illegal activity, the FTC is the regulatory arm that can take action. The FTC does not guarantee that the franchisor is playing fair or that the franchise offer is a good deal for the prospective buyer. Not unlike the Securities and Exchange Commission (SEC), they do not make investment recommendations to investors; they only attempt to provide some oversight in the industry to protect the public. The fact that these agencies exist validates the point that problems exist, that problems have existed in the past, and that problems are expected to exist in the future. The Federal Trade Commission can be contacted through the office of the FTC Franchise Program Advisor, Division of Marketing Practices, Bureau of Consumer Protection, Pennsylvania Avenue at 6th Street N.W., Washington, DC 20580, or by telephone at 202-326-2968.

The FTC is the regulatory agency at the federal level. Currently, about half the states have regulations governing franchise agreements. The department of securities under the secretary of state's office will usually be the regulatory arm at the state level. States that do have oversight requirements usually require that a uniform franchise offering circular be submitted for approval and may require additions to the circular. For information concerning specific requirements in your state either to become a franchisor or a potential franchisee, contact your department of securities office of the secretary of state in your state.

Under the Franchise Rule, the FTC require franchisors to disclose all essential information in the form of a uniform franchise offering circular (UFOC). Most states that require filing of franchise information by a prospective franchisor have accepted the Franchise Rule as the standard for franchisor regulation filings. Following is a sample outline of a UFOC. It is not complete but presents the key points.[1]

1. *The franchisor, its predecessors and affiliates.* This section of the circular provides the name of the franchisor, its predecessors, and its affiliates; the name under which the franchisor does or intends to do business; and the principal business address of the franchisor, its predecessors, and its affiliates, and the franchisor's agents for service of process. In addition, the business form of the franchisor must be given, including the state of incorporation or business organization.

2. *Business experience.* This part of the disclosure lists the names and positions of directors, trustees, and/or general partners; and the principal officers and other executives of the franchisee offered by this offering circular. All franchise brokers must be listed, stating each person's principal occupations and employers during the past five years.

3. *Litigation.* Disclosure must be provided as to the franchisor, its predecessor, a person identified in item 2, or an affiliate offering franchises under the franchisor's principal trademark. In addition, disclosure is required concerning any administrative, criminal, or material civil action that is pending. If during the 10-year period immediately preceding the date of the offering circular, anyone in item 2 has been convicted of a felony or pleaded nolo contendere to a felony charge, this must be disclosed. The intent is to bring to light those franchisors whose past practices have caused them to be sued or taken to court by their franchisees to seek satisfaction. Litigation should signal caution in proceeding and would certainly give cause to investigate the franchisor thoroughly before entering into an agreement.

4. *Bankruptcy.* Disclosure must be made if during the 10-year period prior to the circular offering the franchisor, its predecessors, or its affiliates, officers, or general partners were engaged in a bankruptcy proceeding. Disclosure is required of the person or company that was the debtor under the bankruptcy code, the date of the action, and any material facts.

5. *Initial franchise fee.* An explanation must be provided concerning the initial fees paid by the franchisee, the timing of those payments, and any refunding or nonrefunding provisions.

6. *Other fees.* Disclosure of other recurring or isolated fees or payments that the franchisee must pay to the franchisor or its affiliates or that the franchisor or its affiliates impose or collect in whole or in part on behalf of a third party must be revealed, including the formula used to compute these fees and payments. If any fee is refundable, the conditions when each fee or payment is refundable must be stated. An explanation of all other fees that the franchisor will charge the franchisee must be disclosed. Examples of those fees include a royalty on sales, renewal fees, training fees, transfer fees, accounting or assistance charges, or any other type of fee.

7. *Initial investment.* The franchisor must disclose the following expenditures, stating to whom the payments are made, when payments are due, whether each payment is refundable, and the conditions when each payment is refundable. If part of the franchisee's initial investment in the franchise is financed, an estimate of the loan repayments, including interest, must be provided.
   (a) Real property, whether purchased or leased, must be disclosed. If neither estimable nor describable by a low–high range, a description of the requirements must be provided concerning property type, size, and location.

(b) Equipment, fixtures and other fixed assets, construction, remodeling, leasehold improvements, and decorating costs must be disclosed, whether purchased or leased.

(c) Inventory requirements must be disclosed.

(d) Security deposits, utility deposits, business licenses, and any other prepaid expense must be disclosed.

(e) A disclosure is required concerning any additional funds required of the franchisee before operations may begin, including the initial phase of operations.

(f) Other payments that the franchise must make to begin operations must be disclosed. This requirement was added as a kind of catch-all phrase to prevent the franchisor from hiding a fee not addressed specifically in the disclosure requirements.

This section spells out an estimate of all the fees the franchisee will pay to actually get into business and begin operating. It will estimate the type of expense or fee, the amount and method of payment (such as lump sum or ongoing as incurred), when the expenditure will be due, and to whom it will be payable.

8. *Restrictions on sources of products and services.* Any restrictions must be disclosed. The franchise industry has a history of problems in this area, where the franchisee is required to buy input materials and supplies from the franchisor. The franchisor would add a markup on those purchases to generate profits at the expense of the franchisee. Any restrictions on the purchase of supplies and services by the franchisee must be disclosed here. Disclosure must be made requiring the franchisee's obligations to purchase or lease from the franchisor, its designee, or from suppliers approved by the franchisor or under the franchisor's specifications. Each obligation must be disclosed concerning the following:

(a) The goods, services, supplies, fixtures, equipment, inventory, computer hardware and software, or real estate relating to establishing or operating the franchised business.

(b) The manner in which the franchisor issues and modifies specifications or grants and revokes approval to suppliers.

(c) Whether and for what categories of goods and services the franchisor or its affiliates are approved suppliers or the only approved suppliers.

(d) Whether, and if so, the precise basis by which the franchisor or its affiliates will or may derive revenue or other material consideration as a result of required purchases or leases.

(e) The estimated proportion of these required purchases and leases to all purchases and leases by the franchisee of goods and services in establishing and operating the franchised business.

(f) The existence of purchasing or distribution cooperatives.

9. *Franchisee's obligations.* This section of the disclosure spells out the principal obligations of the franchisee under the franchise and other agreements after signing the franchise agreement. A table itemizes areas of obligation and performance. A guarantee of performance is required of the franchisee.

10. *Financing.* This part of the circular generally informs you that you are on your own to obtain financing. It will usually include a disclaimer indicating that the franchisor is not responsible for nor guarantees your note, lease, or any other financial obligation. If any type of financing is available, the terms and conditions are disclosed here.

11. *Franchisor's obligations.* The reason you would be willing to enter into a franchise agreement should be defined in this part of the circular. The franchisor is required to disclose such commitments as training and support services. The franchisor must state the obligations to be met during operation of the franchise business, including assistance in the following areas:

(a) Products or services to be offered by the franchisee to its customers

(b) Hiring and training of employees

(c) Improvements and developments in the franchised business

(d) Pricing

(e) Administrative, bookkeeping, accounting, and inventory control procedures

(f) Operating problems encountered by the franchisee

In addition, disclosure concerning the franchisor's advertising program for the product or services must be spelled out, as well as other pertinent areas of support.

12. *Territory.* A description of any exclusive territory granted the franchisee should be spelled out in this section. Rights concerning the franchisee's location must be disclosed; also whether the franchisor has established or may establish another franchisee who may also use the franchisor's trademark; also whether the franchisor has established or may establish a company-owned outlet or other channels of distribution using the franchisor's trademark; also whether the franchisor or its affiliate has established or may establish other franchises or company-owned outlets or other channels of distribution selling or leasing similar products or services under a different trademark; also whether or not continuation of the franchisee's exclusive territorial rights depend on the achievement of a certain sales volume, market penetration, or other contingency and under what circumstances the franchisee's territory may be altered.

13. *Trademarks.* The rights the franchisee has to use and operate under the trade name will be described in this section of the circular; also the disclosure of those principal trademarks to be licensed to the franchise.

14. *Patents, copyrights, and proprietary information.* If the franchisor owns rights in patents or copyrights that are material to the franchise, a description of these patents and copyrights and their relationship to the franchise need to be included, as well as their duration and whether the franchisor can and intends to renew the copyrights. To the extent relevant, disclosure is required concerning patents and copyrights.

15. *Obligation to participate in the actual operation of the franchise business.* This section may establish restrictions or specifications as to who is authorized to actually run or manage the franchise operation. It may further restrict the franchisee with covenants concerning nondisclosure and noncompete agreements.

16. *Restrictions on what the franchisee may sell.* If restrictions on the sale of goods and services is required by the franchisor, they should be included in this section, including conditions imposed by the franchisor. If restrictions or conditions are imposed to limit the customers to whom the franchisee may sell those goods or services, disclosure is also required.

17. *Renewal, termination, transfer, and dispute resolutions.* This part of the circular spells out under what terms and conditions the franchise agreement is renewed or terminated, and the conditions under which a sale or transfer is

authorized and the fees associated with it. Dispute resolutions, and arbitration and grievance procedures are also addressed in this section.

18. *Public figures.* If a public figure is used to promote the franchise, that relationship must be disclosed in this section, including the following:
    (a) Compensation or other benefit given or promised to a public figure arising from the use of the public figure in the franchise name or symbol or the endorsement or recommendation of the franchise to prospective franchisees
    (b) The extent to which the public figure is involved in the actual management or control of the franchisor
    (c) The total investment of the public figure in the franchisor

19. *Earnings claims.* If claims are made, they must be disclosed. An earnings claim made in connection with an offer of a franchise must be included in full in the offering circular and must have a reasonable basis at the time it is made. If no earnings claim is made, item 19 of the circular must contain the negative disclosure prescribed in the instruction: something to the effect that they do not furnish or authorize any information concerning sales or profit figures and that results will vary from location to location based on market demand, competition levels, and the management ability of the local franchisee.

20. *List of outlets.* The franchisor must disclose how many franchise outlets exist and where those outlets are located. The franchisor must disclose the following:
    (a) The number of franchises of a type substantially similar to those offered and the number of franchisor-owned or franchisor-operated outlets as of the close of the last three years.
    (b) The names of all franchisees and the addresses and telephone numbers of all their outlets. The franchisor may limit its disclosure to all franchisee outlets in the state unless the total of all franchise outlets is less than 100.
    (c) The estimate of the number of franchises to be sold during the one-year period following the close of the franchisor's most recent fiscal year.
    (d) The number of franchisee outlets in the following categories for the three-year period immediately before the close of the franchisor's most recent fiscal year have:
        (1) Transferred controlling ownership
        (2) Been canceled or terminated by the franchisor
        (3) Not been renewed by the franchisor
        (4) Been reacquired by the franchisor
        (5) Been reasonably known by the franchisor to have otherwise ceased to do business in the system
    (e) The name and last known home address and telephone number of every franchisee who has had an outlet terminated, canceled, not renewed, or otherwise voluntarily or involuntarily ceased to do business under the franchise agreement during the most recently completed fiscal year or who has not communicated with the franchisor within 10 weeks of the application date.

21. *Financial statements.* The franchisor must disclose recent audited financial statements. These statements must be prepared in accordance with generally accepted accounting principles. These financial statements must be audited by an independent certified public accountant. Some concessions are made for unaudited interim-period reports.

22. *Contracts*. A copy of all agreements proposed for use in regarding the offering of a franchise, including the franchise agreement, leases, options, and purchase agreements must be made available and disclosed.

23. *Receipts*. The last page of the offering circular is a detachable document acknowledging receipt of the offering circular by the prospective franchisee. It must contain specific statements and must be provided 10 days prior to the signing of the agreement. Basically, it states that the prospective franchisee has been given a copy of the UFOC and all appendices and exhibits. The franchisee signs a receipt to that effect and must be given a minimum of 10 days to examine those documents. This acts as a cooling-off period and allows the franchisee to escape from any agreement within the 10-day period.

Exhibits

1. *State administrators*. Generally, the administrator is the department of securities in the secretary of state's office.
2. *Franchise territory*. Defines the exclusiveness or the geographical or market size of the franchisee's protected territory.
3. *Agent for service of process*. The attorney or CPA involved; the person who is authorized to receive all services of process in the event of a legal action brought against the franchisor.
4. *Guarantee of performance*. Documents and guarantees the performance of the franchisor.

• THE FRANCHISOR–FRANCHISEE RELATIONSHIP ·

The real dangers inherent in franchising stem from an imbalance of power. Initially, at least, all the power rests with the franchisor. They make the rules. The franchise agreement is a legally binding contract. In the section on the contract for deed sales agreement, an argument was made that you and your attorney write the contract so that the language and conditions are more favorable to you. In a franchise agreement the contract is already written, and you are expected to sign on the dotted line. Whose interests do you think the language, warranties, covenants, and restrictions will be written to protect? The franchisor will absolutely protect its own interests. In fact, many have years of experience with franchisees, so that issues that have come up and caused contracts to evolve and modifications to be made further protect the interest of the franchisor. You can rest assured that the contract you are about to sign has been tried and tested on other franchisees.

A second element in the favor of the franchisor rests with the way legislation is enacted at federal, state, and local levels. In Washington, whenever an issue concerning an industry arises, the industry storms the capital with lobbyists to ensure that their side is heard. When legislation is drafted, the committee doing the drafting will consult industry members for input. Thus the legislation voted on and enacted is written in favor of the industry giants, not in the favor of the individual or consumer. Add issues of campaign finance into the picture and the interests of the industry group are protected even further.

A third element in favor of the franchisor stems from the way in which statistics are reported on the success rates of franchisees.[2] The U.S. Department of Commerce (DOC) reports statistics on the success rates of franchisees. The results reported indicate about a 95 percent success ratio. There is an old adage which says that if something sounds too good to be true, it probably isn't true. That certainly holds true for DOC statistics. As in most governmental agencies, those in control must continue to justify their existence to assure continued funding of their agency. In fact, attempts are made to expand the agency, thus advancing the careers of those with a vested interest. The agency's cause is furthered by demonstrating to legislative bodies and to the general public positive statistics that demonstrate the effectiveness of the agency, validating their continued existence. For example, the U.S. Department of Labor keeps statistics on job placements through their local job service offices. For unemployment and placement statistics, an executive who loses his $50,000 per year job, but out of boredom accepts a position as a movie theater ticket taker one evening a week for minimum wage is considered placed in a job. The same type of statistical distortion occurs with the Department of Commerce. If a franchise is sold and the proprietor goes under but the business is taken over by another franchisee or by the franchisor, it is not counted as a failure for statistical purposes.

Having done some work in marketing research and having participated in research studies, I have become quite cynical about accepting statistics at face value. Before looking into the actual mechanics of a study, I always want to know who did the study: who paid for the study and who will benefit by a specific outcome. Problems with validity and reliability in research are difficult to overcome. Anytime that someone with an agenda performs a study, the results should be scrutinized very carefully before being accepted as fact.

For the entrepreneur wishing to enter business for themselves but not wanting to go it alone, the prospect of a franchise can look very appealing. The key is to find a franchise relationship that is fair and equitable to both the franchisor and the franchisee. In an attempt to offset the apparent advantages that the franchisor holds over a franchisee, many franchisees have banded together and have begun to form associations to help protect the interests of franchisees. One such organization is the American Association of Franchisees and Dealers, formed in May 1992 with the mission of bringing fairness to franchising. The AAFD is a national nonprofit trade association representing the rights and interests of franchisees and independent dealers throughout the United States. The following is an excerpt from the AAFD Member Guide[3]:

Bringing Fairness to Franchising

The American Association of Franchisees and Dealers (AAFD) has come into existence for the purpose of providing a counterbalance in the franchising industry. With the AAFD's mission of Bringing Fairness to Franchising, the Association intends to bring the franchising marketplace back into balance. The AAFD acts to educate the public regarding fair franchise practices, quality franchise opportunities, and to expose the unethical practices that have too long existed in the franchising industry. The AAFD believes balance can be achieved through a process of educating the public and helping franchisee groups to organize into strong collective bargaining units. By creating a level of playing field in which franchisors and franchisees can negotiate fair and equitable franchise agreements, and franchise relationships, the AAFD expects to help the franchising industry heal itself and achieve its enormous promises.

Over the past 50 years the method of product and service distribution known as franchising has exploded to become an industry of enormous power and influence promising to deliver the American Dream of business ownership to millions of Americans. The franchising industry has been heralded to represent over 600 billion dollars in annual sales. This represents almost 40 percent of all retail sales in the United States.

The logic behind the success of franchising is flawless. Take a proven, predictable product or service combined with a well-known, respected trademark or trade name and license the business to a local business owner who invests his own capital and sweat equity to insure success at the retail level. Clearly, the success of franchising has been repeated time and again under appropriate circumstances creating successful local business and multi-millionaires out of franchisors.

Unfortunately there is a dark side of franchising. A side as predictable as the axiom that breeds it, "absolute power corrupts absolutely!" The success of the franchising format of small business ownership has led to a significant imbalance in the relative bargaining power of franchisors and franchisees. Armed with (now questionable) Department of Commerce statistics which suggest that 95 percent of all franchised businesses are successful, the franchising industry has sold franchising as a surefire path to success in business. As an attorney for the Federal Trade Commission recently commented, "There is a buying frenzy in franchising. Virtually anything will sell."

As the franchising industry has experienced explosive growth, franchisors have learned they need promise very little in order to attract buyers. The modern day franchise agreement is a mere shell of its equivalent of 40 or 50 years ago. In the not too distant past, franchise owners were truly independent business owners who agreed to represent a franchisor's trademark and product line for a fixed period of time. Franchisees routinely received exclusive territories, and when the franchise terminated, the franchisee was free to continue in his chosen trade or profession as an independent, or under a new name. Franchisors made substantial promises and provided valuable perks in order to attract franchisees. Franchisors promised substantial marketing support, training and economic inducements to gain the commitment of their franchised affiliates.

Today, the modern franchise frequently provides no exclusive territory, restricts the activities of the franchisee as an independent businessman, provides that the franchisor controls the franchise location and restricts the franchisee from continuing in the business upon termination of the franchise. Indeed, frequently the modern day franchisee is merely a license to operate the business on behalf of the franchisor for the term of the franchise. Some franchisees specifically state that the franchisee owns no equity in the business, and that the business really belongs to the franchisor. Moreover, most modern franchise agreements promise very little required services and support from the franchisor.

A seller's market in franchising has led to a serious decline in the quality of franchise opportunities. The franchising marketplace is seriously out of balance, and there has been no significant market correction over the past 50 years. Although there were efforts during the 1970s to curb fraud in franchising practices, the enormous unbridled power of the franchising industry was able to influence legislative efforts so that a franchiser could cure any deficiency in its franchise practices by merely disclosing the abuses.

Unfortunately, current laws which purport to regulate franchising effectively legalize rather than restrict abusive franchising practices. As long as the franchisor discloses the details of its practices, the practices are enforceable. There are no minimum legal standards of fairness to protect the legitimate interests of the franchisees.

The problems in franchising are all directly related to the inability of the marketplace to recognize unfair franchising practices, and to demand better product from franchisors. The franchising industry has literally controlled public education, as well as the legislative agenda in franchising, such that the public is given only a steady diet of franchise success stories.

The AAFD is dedicated to marketplace solutions to the current imbalance within the franchising community. In 1996, the AAFD introduced its Fair Franchising Standards, the first ever comprehensive guidelines for balanced franchise relationships. The AAFD's Fair Franchising Standards are a negotiated "work in process" of the AAFD's Committee on Standards and Accreditation. This committee, made up of franchisors, franchisees, and franchise legal counsel, has been charged with the task of developing standards of franchising practices which balance the legitimate interests of franchisors and franchisees to achieve Total Quality Franchising! The AAFD now offers its Fair Franchising Seal to franchise systems which embrace the AAFD's Standards.

The AAFD has established a lofty goal of creating an effective independent franchisee association affiliated as an AAFD Trademark Chapter for every franchise system in America. The Association targets the 500,000 franchised businesses and the approximately 500,000 independent dealerships to become voting members. Membership is also open to millions of Americans who have an interest in owning a franchised business, and the many hundreds of thousands of companies who seek to do business with franchisees.

Building a strong, vibrant trade association is a self-fulfilling prophecy. As franchisees gain economic power, franchisees will achieve the ability to educate the public, influence legislation, expose abusive franchising practices, and honor and reward exemplary practices.

The AAFD seeks to serve the franchising community, promote that which is good and healthy, and excise that which is exploitative and unscrupulous. Although only in its sixth year of existence, the AAFD has seen a remarkable shift in the currents in the franchising community. We welcome your support and assistance in our goal of Bringing Fairness to Franchising!

The AAFD can be reached at 1420 Kettner Boulevard, Suite 415, P.O. Box 81887, San Diego, CA 92101. They can be reached by calling 800-733-9858 or 619-235-2565. On the Internet their address is http://www.aafd.org; e-mail Benefits@AAFD.org.

AAFD Goals of Service[4]

The American Association of Franchisees and Dealers has established four goals of service:

1. Market support services
2. Legal and financial support services
3. Legislative support services
4. General member benefits

Market Support Services The primary goal of the AAFD is to help franchisees. The center of that issue is to assist franchisees in negotiating leverage so that fair and equitable relationships can be developed between the franchisor and the franchisee. A key component in developing those equitable relationships is understanding the elements of a fair deal as far as franchise agreements are concerned. Two of the key educational tools which AAFD has developed are the Franchisee Bill of Rights and Eight Things to Look For in a Franchise Opportunity.

The Franchisee Bill of Rights

The franchisees of America, representing the best of the American entrepreneurial spirit, hereby recognize and demand a basic minimum of commercial dignity, equity and fairness. In recognition thereof, the franchisees of America do proclaim this Franchisee Bill of Rights as the minimum requirement of a fair and equitable franchise system.

- The right to an equity in the franchised business
- The right to engage in a trade or business
- The right to the franchisor's loyalty, good faith, and fair dealing, and due care in the performance of the franchisor's duties, and a fiduciary relationship where one has been promised or created by conduct
- The right to trademark protection
- The right to market protection

- The right to full disclosure from the franchisor
- The right to initial and ongoing training
- The right to ongoing support
- The right to marketing assistance
- The right to associate with other franchisees
- The right to representation and access to the franchisor
- The right to local dispute resolution and protection under the laws and the courts of the franchisee's jurisdiction
- The reasonable right to renew the franchise, and the right not to face termination, unless for cause
- The reciprocal right to terminate the franchise agreement for reasonable and just cause
- The post-termination right to compete

Eight Things to Look for in a Franchise

1. Select a franchising company that is primarily interested in distributing products and services to ultimate consumers. Although this rule may seem obvious, many (if not most) franchising companies are primarily interested in selling franchises and less concerned with the quality of the products and services they are theoretically in business to sell.
2. Your franchising company should be dedicated to franchising as its primary mechanism of product and service distribution. Avoid the franchisor with a large number of company-owned stores, or who distributes its products through other channels, such as supermarket or discount stores.
3. Your franchising company should produce and market quality goods and services for which there is an established market demand. The value of franchising emanates from the value of the franchisor. Too many prospective franchisees cannot qualify for a widely recognized franchise and settle for a lesser known system thinking the franchise concept is more important than the product and trade name.
4. Select a franchisor with a well-accepted trademark.
5. Evaluate your franchisor's business plan and marketing system. A well-established, well-designed marketing system promises substantial and complete training and overall franchisee support.
6. Your franchisor should have good relationships with its franchisees. Likewise, the franchisee should have a strong franchisee organization which has negotiating leverage with the franchising company. A franchisor who does not permit its franchisees to organize is a sure sign of trouble ahead. Strong franchisee associations, on the other hand, will pave the way to successful and cooperative franchising systems.
7. Only deal with franchising companies that provide sales and earnings projections which demonstrate an attractive return on your investment. Do not believe franchisors who claim they are forbidden by law to provide earning projections and evidence of actual performance. To the contrary, all state and federal laws regulating franchising encourage franchisors to provide earnings claims to prospective franchisees.
8. Select a franchisor that supports the AAFD's Franchisee Bill of Rights and agrees to respect these rights as they apply to your franchise.

Legal and Financial Support Services The AAFD has established a network of experienced franchisee counsel throughout the United States to represent the interests of franchisees and prospective franchisees. Currently, the Franchisee LegaLine operates in more than 40 states, offering free initial consultations to AAFD members and valuable special member programs, including initial franchise opportunity reviews, initial franchise dispute reviews and special member pricing.

The AAFD has also developed a Speakers and Experts Bureau as a source of notable speakers and to provide resources to franchisee counsel when the need for expert witnesses arise. A new Mediation and Arbitration Panel will help members take advantage of alternative dispute resolution methods.

The Franchisee FinanciaLine is modeled on the AAFD's successful LegaLine program. The Franchise FinanciaLine provides a range of invaluable financial services, including bookkeeping, accounting, tax advice, and lending services. Most FinanciaLine members offer AAFD members a special fiscal Physical to evaluate the members' fiscal health and develop a plan to boost cash flow and management. New in 1997 is the new AAFD Lenders Network of banks and small business lending and investment companies interested in doing business with AAFD members on a preferential basis.

Legislative Support Services   As a national trade association, the AAFD has an exceptional opportunity to speak out on issues of concern to franchisees in the various legislative areas. The Association is active in Congress and state legislatures, promoting franchisee supportive legislation. The AAFD is establishing its own legislative agenda, which includes establishing minimum standards for franchise relationships and encouraging collective bargaining in franchise negotiations.

Due to recognizing the reputation and experience of some AAFD founders, and because there has been a complete void of franchisee advocates available to the legislative branch of government, the AAFD has achieved immediate access to legislative offices at both the state and federal level. The Association was invited by Congressman Hohn LaFalce (D-NY) to comment on proposed franchise legislation before it was introduced to Congress two years ago. More importantly, several of the AAFD's legislative proposals were incorporated in the LaFalce legislation prior to its introduction.

As important as developing grass root support for franchisee causes, the AAFD represents a philosophy that fair franchising is good business. The Association's political agenda is based upon the fundamental philosophical premise that a balanced marketplace will of its own develop equitable and mutually prosperous franchise relationships.

General Member Benefits and Dues   As a national business trade association, the AAFD endeavors to provide the full array of general member benefits one would expect from a broadly based trade association. Some of the AAFD's current and planned member benefits are as follows:

- All members are entitled to AAFD member discounts and networking opportunities, a subscription to the Franchisee Voices Newsletter and a copy of the annual Member Guide, with a $100.00 minimum dues contribution.

- Members paying minimum annual dues receive a voucher for a free consultation with a *LegaLine* attorney or *FinancialLine* accountant. New members also receive a free one-year subscription to *The Franchise Times*. From time to time the AAFD's membership department offers special dues-incentive packages that offer even more benefits and value for new and renewing members. Franchise members paying annual dues are eligible to participate in Trademark Chapters.

- AAFD members paying $500.00 per year, at the time of this writing, receive all of the above, plus the right to market their goods and services through the AAFD, and the right to participate in the AAFD's professional services panels if they offer special member pricing.

- Life membership is available for those who pay one-time dues of $5,000.

Example of a Poor Franchising Experience

The following is a personal experience with a franchise agreement that was very one-sided and would have resulted in a personal disaster had I entered into it. This experience and similar experiences shared by thousands of others underscore the need for an association like the American Association of Franchisees and Dealers.

I received a phone call one day from a real estate agent who was representing a franchisor of a food service business chain. As it turned out, the franchisor had entered into a relationship with a franchisee. The franchisee's outlet had failed and the agent was looking for someone with management experience to take it over. It just so happened that I was looking for an opportunity in the food service business, so I requested a copy of the franchise agreement and made an appointment to inspect the facility.

The offer to sell was for $50,000. I was told that the franchisor just wanted someone in the facility to take over, and this was a very lucrative deal. The facility was about 1600 square feet, fully furnished with equipment and fixtures. It had seating for about 40 people, but most of its business was carry out and catering. This franchise was located in a metropolitan area, with only one other outlet in the area, which was in this community's sister city across the river. The population base was about 75 percent in the other city, 25 percent or about 15,000 people in the community where this franchise opportunity existed. The volume projected for this outlet sounded substantial.

As I read the franchise agreement I discovered that the franchisee did not own the building or real estate, and that the real estate was leased to the franchisee from the franchisor. I was further informed that the franchisor's brother owned a second corporation which owned the sign adjacent to the outlet and that a mandatory monthly lease fee was assessed for that advertisement. A 4 percent franchise fee was assessed on gross sales volume. The franchisee was restricted from buying any supplies from the outside except for certain perishables. All equipment and fixtures were to be purchased from the franchisor. All paper products and raw inputs were to be purchased from the franchisor. Any product not sold the day it was prepared was the responsibility of the franchisee. All product sold was prepared in advance but on the same day. That meant very long days, beginning at a very early hour. In short, the franchisee was positioned so that fixed and variable costs were almost locked in. The only way this enterprise could be profitable was through volume. I estimated the break-even volume to be in the $400,000 range, depending on how many hours of labor I could squeeze out of my family.

This franchise agreement created a very difficult situation for the franchisee. It was great for the franchisor. Yet not one item in the agreement was or is illegal. It may be representative of some of the abuses that go on in the franchise industry. As long as the conditions are disclosed, there is little a franchisee can do except band together with other franchisees and demand more equitable treatment. Know who you are dealing with and read and understand the agreement before signing on as a franchisee.

Disadvantages of Franchise Ownership

The disadvantages stemming from owning a franchise would be an inverse of the advantages.

1. The franchisee never really owns the business. He or she only owns the franchise, which often has a limited life and must be renewed continually.
2. The franchisee never really has complete control of the business; he or she is always subject to the franchisor in regard to the restrictions and obligations imposed under the franchise agreement.
3. The franchisee is required to pay a franchise fee, royalty, and other fees imposed by the franchisor. It is at times like operating with a handicap. It sometimes seems that the franchisor is using the franchisee as a profit center, by selling the franchisee supplies and materials at a premium and by assessing other fees.

4. The franchisee must comply with the restrictions imposed under the agreement regardless of whether or not the franchisee agrees with those restrictions.

5. The support that the franchisee receives may not turn out to be what was envisioned originally.

Advantages of Franchise Ownership

What the prospective franchisee is seeking in a franchise agreement is as follows:

1. The franchisee wants to be in business for himself or herself but still have the support of the franchisor. The franchisee would like that support to be ongoing but not overbearing or restrictive.

2. The franchisee wants the marketing muscle and name recognition of the franchisor.

3. The franchisee is seeking the security of a proven system.

4. The franchisee would like a proven accounting system with computer support.

5. The franchisee wants to sell a high-quality product or service.

6. The franchisee wants to earn a respectable profit and build equity in a business he or she owns.

Things to Look for in a Franchisor

Most things to look for relate to the objectives of the franchisee. You want to know the character of the franchisor. You can do this best by visiting a number of franchise outlets and visiting with the franchisee. Be sure that these are not company-owned outlets but outlets owned by individual franchisees. You are looking for a history of good relationships and equitable treatment. You would want to verify that a proven history of success exists or that if relatively new, the franchisor has developed a good business concept and produces high-quality products and services. Get an attorney and a CPA involved, and do some homework on this franchisor. Check out all 23 points in the UFOC. What you must define for yourself is the quality and overall equitableness of the agreement.

The small business bridge model of this book could be used to establish a standard to gauge the quality of the franchise agreement, together with the 5 C's loan evaluation criteria. In the end the equitableness features will hinge on the character of those franchisors who are initiating the agreement. If character or ethics become an issue, abandon your pursuit of a relationship with people who are of questionable character. In visiting with existing franchisee outlets, you should be able to identify the quality of the relationship established between the franchisor and their various franchisee partners. Ask yourself if you would like to be a part of that team. Once the character issues and the quality of relationship issues are resolved, a thorough financial analysis and marketing analysis should follow before a decision is made to sign on as a franchisee.

Franchising Standards

Prior to entering a franchise agreement, you should do all that you can to verify the quality of relationship you are about to enter into. Help is available through the AAFD (American Association of Franchisees and Dealers). One of the services available to members is a free initial franchise opportunity review. Why not take advantage of that service?

The scope of the mission for the AAFD was to publish a set of fair franchising standards. As of this date in 1997, those standards are in print, although not in final form and therefore subject to refinement and revision, but the general framework has certainly been established. Those standards represent a foundation from which to evaluate and ascertain a franchisor's position of fairness. Following is an outline of the 18 standards set forth by the AAFD.

Chapter 1. Accreditation

Standard 1.1   Criteria for Accreditation
Standard 1.2   Benefits of Accreditation
Standard 1.3   Term of Accreditation; Renewal
Standard 1.4   Provisional Accreditation

Chapter 2. Mutuality of rights and equity

Standard 2.0   General Standard
Standard 2.1   Franchisor's Ownership Rights
Standard 2.2   Franchisee's Ownership Rights
Standard 2.3   Independent Contractor
Standard 2.4   Right of Association
Standard 2.5   Right to Use Franchisor's Trade Name
Standard 2.6   Right to Associate with Other Associations
Standard 2.7   Right to Collectively Bargain
Standard 2.8   Right to Air Grievances

Chapter 3. Territorial rights

Standard 3.1   Reasonable Market Protection
Standard 3.2   Franchisor's Right to Maximize Market

Chapter 4. Intellectual property

Standard 4.0   General Standard
Standard 4.1   Copyright Ownership
Standard 4.2   Ownership of Patents
Standard 4.3   Reasonable Market Protection (as it applies to the use of patents)
Standard 4.4   Costs of Patent Modifications
Standard 4.5   Cost of Trademark Modifications
Standard 4.6   Confidential Information and Trade Secrets
Standard 4.7   Protection of Confidential Information
Standard 4.8   Cost of Trade Dress Modifications
Standard 4.9   Cost of Computer Software and Technology Modifications
Standard 4.10   Computer Software Technology
Standard 4.11   Computer Software Technology Updates

Chapter 5. Term and renewal

Standard 5.0   General Standard
Standard 5.1   Initial Term

Chapter 16. General releases

Chapter 17. Real estate issues

Chapter 18. Miscellaneous provisions

This outline of the fair franchising standards established by the American Association of Franchisees and Dealers should provide a very good idea of the breadth of issues that the prospective franchisee can encounter. Granted that not every standard is a major concern or issue within the context of a specific franchisee agreement, but certainly these standards have evolved due to issues that have risen from past conflicts within franchise agreements.

It is useful to contrast these standards along with the Franchisee Bill of Rights and compare them with the uniform franchise offering circular that the franchisor has submitted. The fair franchising standards act as a counterbalance and can be contrasted almost point by point from the two viewpoints. The goal is fairness. If a situation does not exist where both parties to the franchise agreement can win, it is very likely that the participants should not enter into that agreement.

The franchise agreement is a contractual agreement. Prior to entering into such an agreement, the prospective franchisee would want to make every effort to ensure that the provisions within the contract are such that they enhance the entrepreneur's chances of success and do not act as a barrier to that success. It is difficult to identify every contingent problem area of a contractual and business relationship, but the 18 standards and other support material offered by the AAFD can go a long way toward the evaluation of the franchise offering circular.

The other side of this issue is this. If you were to move in the direction of becoming a franchisor, prospective franchisees would be looking at your franchise offering circular wondering if it is "fair." If you could offer a stamp of approval from the AAFD in the form of accreditation, that would put most prospective franchisees at ease with the knowledge that fairness exists within your franchise offering. Many franchisors seek to obtain accreditation from the AAFD for those very reasons.

It may sound as though I am labeling all franchisors and franchise agreements as bad. I am not, and in fairness I will attempt to present a franchisor who I believe to be offering a fair and equitable agreement.

PROFILE IN ENTREPRENEURSHIP: BERNARD SCHRAMM AND DARLA
LARSEN, PARK-IT MARKET[5]

A franchise called Park-it Market has been operating for about six years, primarily in Sioux Falls, South Dakota. Park-it Market has only recently been authorized to become a franchisor. The principals are Bernard Schramm and his wife, Darla Larsen. I've known Mr. Schramm professionally for about six years and am beginning to know him personally as well. I've watched from the sidelines as Park-it Market has battled city hall and the state legislature to gain authorization to conduct business. The concept of Park-it Market is for a nominal fee, to facilitate and be a medium to allow people who have personal vehicles they want to sell to park their vehicles in a central location where buyers can view them without being hassled by a high-pressure salesmen. The interested buyer contacts the seller by phone. The seller lists his or her phone number and the asking price on a sticker taped to the inside of the car window. Negotiations are between the buyer and seller, and the actual purchase is from the buyer directly to the seller. Park-it Market acts only as a marketing medium to provide a central location.

The legal battles that ensued were probably initiated by others in used-vehicle sales businesses in the region who did not want to see a new form of competition move in. Mr. Schramm was successful in large part because he is a former corporate attorney. The legal costs for someone else would probably have been cost prohibitive. Access to the court system and knowledge of the law were paramount in the success of this venture due to the fact that the sale of motor vehicles is closely regulated in every state.

The first Park-it Market was in Sioux Falls. The idea to start this business originated with Mr. Schramm's wife Darla. A number of years ago, like many other people, Mr. Schramm and Darla Larson had an extra car to sell. So they went down to the local drugstore and bought several "For Sale by Owner" signs. Sticking this in the car window, they parked the car in a highly visible location, a local mall parking lot. Mr. Schramm had to leave town on business, so his wife was left to take all the calls from prospective buyers and arrange to meet these strangers, usually at night, to show his car. To make matters worse, one late October evening when Darla Larson was meeting a prospective buyer, it began to sleet, and when she arrived at the parking lot, a towaway sticker was attached to the windshield of the car. Darla's response to Mr. Schramm upon his arrival back home was that there should be an easier way for people to sell their vehicles legally.

Thus the impetus for the concept of Park-it Market. Mr. Schramm began to do legal research, and after a month or two determined that there was a way to do this but it involved walking a very fine line. The project entailed a number of possible legal problems. Park-it Market wanted to avoid actually interfacing themselves into the buyer–seller relationship. So Park-it Market is very careful in these regards, and this is a basis for some of the franchisee training. According to Mr. Schramm, this is a legally intensive business. Mr. Schramm indicated that many prospective franchisees have asked why they couldn't just go out on their own and do the same type of thing. Mr. Schramm indicates that they could but it would probably cost them at least as much for legal fees as they would spend on a franchise fee, and they would still not have any other support.

(continued)

(continued)

Mr. Schramm indicated that they did not want to start offering the franchise until they had developed the system to the stage where Park-it Market could do for franchisees what they say they will do for them. Mr. Schramm indicated that many new franchisors are being more careful. Many franchisors have gotten themselves into some real legal trouble through violating their franchise agreements. Violating franchise agreements brings on the threat of class-action lawsuits by the franchisees, and some relatively well-known franchisors are currently embroiled in such suits. Violations of franchise agreements are also a way of inviting more state and federal regulations and oversight. Currently, over half the states do not require a franchisor to file an offering circular with the state.

The positive attributes of Park-it Market's franchise offering stem from its low initial investment. Park-it Market offers a high-profit business with a low initial investment and low overhead (item 7 in the UFOC). The initial franchise fee for an urban lot runs only $6000, with an estimated initial investment of somewhere between $10,000 and $16,000 for total startup costs. A larger metro lot has total estimated startup costs under $30,000 (item 8), imposes no restrictions, and does not designate suppliers. However, if you do purchase materials from the franchisor, the materials will be marked up only 20 percent above cost to cover shipping and handling. Items 11 and 12 do guarantee an exclusive territory. Item 11 identifies key support functions for acquiring and negotiating a lease for the franchise and providing legal assistance to your local attorney to help comply with local ordinances and city codes, obtaining the required conditional use permits, and so on. In addition, item 11 indicates that training will be provided at no expense other than your travel and living expenses while in Sioux Falls, where training usually takes place.

The initial Sioux Falls outlet now averages approximately 140 cars a day on their lot with about a one-third turnover each week. A unique feature about Park-it Market is the way leases are arranged. The lease is flexible; the more cars that are on the lot, the more rent that is paid. Such a rental agreement surprises many retailers, who are used to negotiations to minimize rent with increases in volume. This is good for the retail location, and the franchisee is making money as well. This is indicative of the type of relationships that Bernard Schramm tries to establish. It is also why this business was selected to describe in this book. Success in small business is built on ethical human relationships. A system where everybody wins will effect a high standard of performance.

Contrast this lease agreement with the franchise offer example earlier in this chapter, and the difference is clearly great. Ask yourself which franchisor you would be more willing to trust with a business partner relationship.

What Park-it Market really has to offer its franchisees is the legal counsel and support to get the concept legalized in the franchisee's trade area and assistance in negotiating a lease with a well-known and reputable retailer. Negotiations are under way for a relationship with a national retailer, a proven standardized accounting system with software and marketing support to educate the public to the Park-it Market concept.

On the negative side, Park-it Market does not yet have an extended history of franchised outlets. In fact, the three outlets that operated in 1996 were all company owned; 1997 will be the first year of franchisee operations. There currently is good interest in Park-it Market franchises. Time will tell how fast this franchise grows.

• QUESTIONS FOR DISCUSSION·········

1. Explain the advantages of purchasing a franchise.
2. Explain some disadvantages of purchasing a franchise.
3. Before purchasing a franchise, explain how a prospective franchisee can obtain the information required to evaluate the franchisor.
4. What information should a prospective franchisee seek out prior to making a commitment to enter into a franchise agreement?
5. What is the AAFD, and what support services do they offer their members?
6. Who has oversight authority and responsibility over the franchise industry?
7. What are the fair franchising standards?
8. Explain why the balance of power in franchise agreements has been so one-sided.

• BEYOND THE CLASSROOM: RECOMMENDED ACTIVITIES············

1. Identify three main equipment or fixture inputs required in your business plan. Using *Thomas's Business Directory*, identify three main suppliers, along with their addresses and phone numbers, for each input. Write or call one in each category and request a price list.
2. Call the SBA Answer Desk at 800-8ASK-SBA.
3. Visit the SBA on the Internet.
4. Visit your regional SBA office.
5. Attend a business liquidation auction in your area.
6. Interview one or more of the following:
   (a) A local business banker
   (b) An auctioneer
   (c) A business real estate broker
   (d) An SBA representative
   (e) A small business owner
   (f) A sales tax representative
   (g) A Department of Labor unemployment insurance tax representative
   (h) Your local Job Service Office manager
   (i) A business insurance agency
   (j) A local franchisee

7 Evaluating Financial Statements, Time Value of Money, and Capital Budgeting

Chapter Objectives

- To provide a review of some critical financial concepts which go into financial decision making.

- To provide financial tools to evaluate and manage a small business.

- To introduce the student to the basic concepts of ratio analysis.

- To reintroduce the student to sensitivity and scenario analysis and provide extensive exercises in the time value of money concepts.

• EVALUATING FINANCIAL STATEMENTS USING RATIOS ·················

In Chapter 6 the use of valuation techniques was discussed. If you are evaluating the financial statements of someone else, as in the case of a potential business purchase, care must be taken to verify that the numbers provided on the financial statements are accurate. In the case of an audit, your accountant may well recreate the financial statements from the original source documents, primarily the canceled checks and original invoices. The auditor will also be concerned that all expenses and revenues were reported and that they were reported in their proper period to prevent an over- or understatement of revenue or expenses. Other issues will be how many accounts payable were left out of the statement and how accurate the inventory count was at the time of the statement.

In evaluating your own financial statements, the key issue is that you are accurate and consistent in preparing your financial statements. All revenue and all expenses should be reported in the proper period, and the inventory count needs to be accurate. The goal is to begin with financial statements that are accurate and reliable and that the financial statements reflect what they are supposed to reflect. The financial statements should be somewhat unique to the type of business you are in and should reflect as much detail as you need to assist in decision making.

Once the format and accuracy issues are settled and the financial statements completed, reflect each line on the income statement as a percentage of total revenue. You can compare your profit and loss (P&L) statements with your previous income statements, with other businesses P&L statements, or with industry averages. In this way you can identify areas of expense that tend to be out of line or where an advantage exists. The greatest benefit is to identify expense creep, which seems to occur naturally with time. Discipline and diligence are required to maintain and control your percentages.

The use of ratios, specifically profitability ratios, will obtain similar results, but my personal preference is to use percentages, because they are a bit more fine tuned and seem more meaningful in evaluating the income statement. The next logical step would be to compute and conduct a ratio analysis.

The purpose of financial analysis is to assist in decision making and to measure how the business is doing. Measurement implies a comparison with the past and with projections. It is advantageous to compare a business with its key competitors and with the industry at large. The universal tool is through the use of financial ratios, but for the sole proprietor not all the ratios apply due to the business's structure. The following is a quick summary of the applicable ratios.

Liquidity Ratios

Liquidity ratios are concerned with answering questions concerning the business's ability to meet its short-term financial obligations. The time frame is one year.

Current Ratio

$$\text{Current ratio} = \frac{\text{current assets}}{\text{current liabilities}}$$

Current assets normally are cash, accounts receivables, inventories, anything that will be converted to cash within the next year. *Current liabilities* are generally accounts payable, short-term notes, the current portion of any long-term notes or mortgages, accrued taxes, and expenses, including accrued labor and payroll taxes associated with labor, accrued sales tax, and income taxes not deposited.

What is a good or acceptable current ratio? The traditional answer is at least a 1, meaning that the business's current assets are equivalent to their current liabilities. What is good depends on the business cycle of the business, which in turn depends on the type of business. A bakery that deals in perishables will tend to have very little inventory. The expenses they incur are mainly day-to-day and month-to-month expenses, such as utilities, labor, and inventory. A firm like this still should have a current ratio of 1.0 or better when viewed on an annual basis, but if they have roughly 90 days' worth of cash or very liquid assets, they are probably in no danger of not meeting their current obligations. It would be a different story if they were, say, an automotive parts store or a manufacturing firm, where inventory tends to be much heavier. For this type of firm, a 1.0 current ratio might not be adequate, because so much of those current assets are tied up in inventory.

Quick Ratio

$$\text{Quick ratio} = \frac{\text{current assets less inventory}}{\text{current liabilities}}$$

This is another measure of a firm's ability to meet their current obligations and is most pertinent to firms with substantial levels of inventory. The implication is that inventory is or can be the least liquid of the current assets. A forced liquidation may result in deep discounts of the inventory's stated value.

In the bridge model the two pillars consisting of those internal and external human relationships have a special significance here. They remain intact by maintaining a level of trust between the business owner and employees, suppliers, creditors, and so on, who deal with the firm. Adequate cash flow is a requirement to maintain the integrity of those relationships. Failure to pay on time or to meet the firm's financial commitments will undermine those relationships. Violate those relationships continually and you will be out of business. The liquidity ratios are a measure of a firm's ability to maintain those relationships financially. This is not to say that the relationships are adequately maintained if they are not violated financially, but it is one criterion.

Management Ratios

Management ratios attempt to measure how well management is using the assets under their control or in their employ. They are significant measures for the sole proprietor.

Inventory Turnover

$$\text{Inventory turnover} = \frac{\text{sales}}{\text{inventory}}$$

What is deemed good depends again on the business; a restaurant or a bakery will have a higher turnover ratio than that of a automotive parts store. The results can identify problems with obsolescence: inventory levels that are too high; inventory that is not moving; inaccurate inventory counts due to pilferage or damaged goods. The principle value of using ratios is that they raise questions. Management's job is to identify the cause and take corrective action.

Days Sales Outstanding

$$\text{Days sales outstanding} = \frac{\text{accounts receivables}}{\text{average sales per day}}$$

What is good depends on your billing cycle and how much of your sales is based on credit. The restaurant will probably have very little in the way of accounts receivable whereas the automotive parts store may have a substantial number of charge accounts. The key issue is: Are accounts receivable growing? Are accounts receivables growing at a faster rate than sales? If the answer is yes to the latter, you may have collection problems and/or are carrying uncollectibles on the books. Examine your accounts receivable aging report. This is your money; you have a right to go after it. The collection process begins with a phone call. You may identify bottlenecks or delays in your billing procedures. Again the ratios can make you aware that problems exist; management must find the cause and provide the solutions.

Fixed-Asset Turnover

$$\text{Fixed-asset turnover} = \frac{\text{sales}}{\text{net fixed assets}}$$

This ratio is a measure of how well management is using the equipment at their disposal. Ratios can be misleading if the equipment is mostly new or mostly depreciated. Inflation, depreciation, and valuation can play a big role in ratio outcomes. The best comparative measure is with prior years' ratios.

Total Asset Turnover

$$\text{Total asset turnover} = \frac{\text{sales}}{\text{total asset base}}$$

This ratio measures the total asset turnover: how good a job is management doing with the asset base. Outcomes are influenced by level of sales and by how and where the assets are distributed. Problems in inventory, accounts receivables, and excessive expenditures in plant and equipment will affect this ratio. Total asset turnover has the most meaning compared with previous years' ratios.

The asset management ratios also support the bridge model. The human relations pillars are based in part on trust. Trust must be reciprocal, which includes the trust between the customer and the business. Trust should not be blind. Not everyone is trustworthy; credit policies and procedures should reflect this. A customer whom you cannot trust is not worth keeping as a customer. The poor-credit customer costs money. Such customers deteriorate and detract from the level of trust and commitment that you can provide your good customers.

The other two pillars, which pertain to quality of product and service, are also affected. Credit is part of total quality service, which should not be allowed to be impeded by deadbeat accounts. Those customers need to be terminated or put on a cash basis to protect and maintain the integrity of the relationships with your good customers. A second component of the quality of service is maintained by having adequate inventory levels to meet customer demands. Failure to meet this demand due to poor inventory management, obsolescence, pilferage, or damaged goods is a violation of that quality of service on your part.

Debt Management Ratios

Debt ratios are important for several reasons. First, creditors are interested, to ascertain if sufficient collateral is available to provide loan security. It is important that the business not become so overextended that it loses its financial flexibility, which would impair its ability to meet a financial challenge, or preclude it from taking advantage of an opportunity. The firm needs to maintain a position of adequate cash and/or cash flow to meet current demands and to take advantage of short-term cash management techniques. Debt structure can enhance net profit or dilute net profit depending on the relationship between the cost of debt and the return on capital.

Debt Ratio

$$\text{Debt ratio} = \frac{\text{total debt}}{\text{total assets}}$$

Total debt includes current liabilities, accounts payable, accrued taxes, and so on; add both short- and long-term debt.

Times Interest Earned

$$\text{Times interest earned} = \frac{\text{EBIT}}{\text{interest charges}}$$

The creditor is not too concerned with this ratio as long as the firm is meeting its financial obligations. Times interest earned is of more interest to a bond investor or a rating agency in a major corporation. In a sole proprietorship the important issue is simply whether this business make its payments.

Debt ratios tie into the bridge model in the sense that financial commitments must be maintained so as not to violate those relationships with creditors, as discussed in the liquidity ratio section.

Profitability Ratios

Profitability ratios reflect the cumulative effect of all the business decisions made by a firm's management to date. Those decisions determined the asset mix, personnel choices, product and/or service choice, control systems, information system, marketing efforts, and a litany of other decisions, within the context of a greater environment that brought the firm to its current position. If good decisions were made within a friendly or at least a receptive environment, the firm has thrived. Profitability ratios measure how those decisions affected the business today or at in a recent time period.

Profit Margin on Sales

$$\text{Profit margin on sales} = \frac{\text{net income}}{\text{sales}}$$

Net income is computed after interest and taxes. The result shows a percent of net profit on sales. This percentage has already been calculated if as indicated earlier you took your income statement and calculated all items as a percentage of sales or revenue.

Basic Earning Power and Return on Total Assets

$$\text{Basic earning power} = \frac{\text{EBIT}}{\text{total assets}}$$

$$\text{Return on total assets} = \frac{\text{net income}}{\text{total assets}}$$

Both these ratios demonstrate a return on the asset base and reflect how well management is employing those assets in income-producing activity. Decisions have been made as to asset allocation; therefore, if market conditions change, it may be difficult, if not impossible, for the manager to alter or influence outcomes. The basic earning power ratio reflects the real earning power of the business before the impact of interest expenses and tax rates on the return on assets.

The return on assets ratio can answer some questions regarding expansion. If the return on the asset base is higher than the cost of debt, and if an expanded asset base can be employed and not dilute returns, an increase in debt will result in an increase in net income. Financial leverage can be employed. The return must be great enough to warrant the added risk of an increased debt ratio.

Several other issues arise out of this line of questioning. First, is there an ideal size for your business? Will expansion cause the quality of your product or service to decline? Do you have the systems in place to train personnel and handle that expansion? Will an expansion create some economies of scale that will, in fact, enhance net income beyond the benefits of financial leverage? Will expansion create synergies?

Return on Equity

$$\text{Return on equity} = \frac{\text{net income}}{\text{owner's equity}}$$

Return on equity measures exactly that—the return on the owner's equity. Is that return adequate to compensate the owner for his or her risk? A broad rule of thumb is to return 20 to 25 percent on a small business investment, depending on the business. Are you being compensated adequately for your labor? There is a big difference between a firm that is a closely held corporation where the owner is taking a salary that is expensed and a sole proprietorship where salary is considered a draw and included in net income.

Profitability is a requirement that all businesses must meet to remain operative. Profitability is essential to maintain the internal relationships in the bridge model. If the small business owner is to remain an employer, and if any future increases in pay or internal career opportunities are to be offered to existing employees, they must stem from current and future profits.

If the business is to fulfill its responsibilities to their external relationships, profitability must exist. For the community to benefit from the business's community involvement and support, it will require profit. To retain a level of trust among the firm's suppliers, creditors, and customers, profit must obviously exist. Profit is, after all, a primary goal of the free-enterprise system.

• TIME VALUE OF MONEY · · · · · · · · · · · · · · ·

Time-value-of-money concepts are applied in many areas of small business. An understanding of these concepts enables the user to make informed decisions concerning such issues as buy-or-make decisions and buy-or-lease decisions. Time-value-of-money concepts are the foundation of insurance and mortgage contracts as well as of retirement planning. The business plan is like a stand-alone risk component in the capital budgeting process. Time-value-of-money concepts allow for a discounted cash flow analysis with appropriate hurdle rates adjusted for risk. Time-value-of-money concepts can be used to evaluate almost any financial decision.

As a college professor teaching in the area of finance and investments, experience has taught me that few of my students have a working understanding of these concepts. I have found that teaching a single method (the use of the future value and present value tables) through the use of progressive worksheets and case problems has proven itself to be beneficial in gaining a working and transferrable understanding of the concept of the time value of money.

The key to understanding the time value of money is first to know how to use each of the tables, then understand what type of problem or equation each table addresses. The final step is to acquire the ability to look at a problem or situation and ask the right question to relate it back to the appropriate table. Sometimes real-life situations require that a problem be broken down into several elements before an answer can be calculated. Real-life situations are often complex and compound problems. Practice and persistence are required to master any skill. The use of time-value-of-money concepts is no different.

Future Value of a Dollar

Table A7–1, future value interest factors for $1 (see the appendix to this chapter), often referred to as a *compounding table,* is the easiest concept to grasp, probably because people are generally familiar with the concept of the compounding of money. We use this table to calculate any type of compounding problem. I suggest you write on top of the table the types of problems it will solve.

It is important to understand how these tables are calculated. A critical element in the use of all these tables is the assumption that interest paid flows in at the end of the period. The tables are annual tables, so the interest is paid in at the end of the period. In reality, interest is compounded daily. Over time it will alter the numbers. Similarly, the tables assume that any interest is reinvested at the same rate immediately. Reality is rarely like that.

The use of a calculator or computer software will generate a more accurate answer. I like to teach use of the tables because students today are pushed so fast through the use of technology that they often do not grasp an understanding of the numbers. The use of time-value concepts requires that you understand the output.

Technology-based solution procedures will generate values quickly even when an input error or assumption error exists, but you need to be able to understand whether that output value is correct. In this area I think it pays to slow down and grind through an understanding of the use of the tables. They are a powerful tool, and having an understanding of this concept can change your financial future regardless of whether or not you run your own business.

WORKSHEET 1:

Using Table A7–1 (p. 162), Future Value Interest for $1

Use Table A7–1 any time you have a sum of money to be put into a savings account where interest will be paid at a constant rate over a period of years. Computing straight compounding problems is easy. Just multiply the sum by the factor found in Table A7–1 by matching the number of years with the appropriate interest rate. Thus the answer to line A is calculated as follows: $1000 \times 1.191 =$ a value of $1191. (Check your answers at the back of the chapter.)

LINE	SUM	PERIOD (YR)	INTEREST RATE (%)	FACTOR	VALUE
A	$1,000	3	6	_____	_____
B	1,000	10	8	_____	_____
C	1,000	20	10	_____	_____
D	5,000	5	8	_____	_____
E	5,000	15	8	_____	_____
F	5,000	20	8	_____	_____
G	10,000	20	12	_____	_____
H	10,000	30	8	_____	_____
I	10,000	40	8	_____	_____

You have probably heard of the *Rule of 72,* which states that you can tell how long it will take for a sum to double its value by dividing the interest rate return into 72. For instance, for an interest rate of 8 percent divide 8 into 72; you get a sum of 9. Notice in the table that nine years at 8 percent equates to a factor of 1.999, which is very close.

So how can this knowledge help the prospective small business owner? You're probably thinking that it will take years before you have capital to invest in savings accounts to sit around and draw interest. I hope not; I hope that you will be funding an IRA or some other type of retirement fund. A more immediate application and concern is putting together pro-forma income statements and projections in the form of a forecast. The banks usually want three- to five-year projections even when you have little or nothing to base them on. The use of compounding will help.

Your original forecast was based on some interrelationship of numbers: a return on investment, level of equipment capacity, or some other relationship. A level of investment was utilized and a level of profit was predicted. Much of that profit will be reinvested in the business, which in turn should expand sales revenue and establish a rate of growth. Once that rate of growth is established, you can use the principles of compounding to identify key inputs into a projected financial statement. For example, if you expect sales revenue to grow at a rate of 15 percent and your initial sales forecast is $270,000, what will sales be in three years? A factor of 1.521 multiplied by $270,000 will give you a third-year forecast of $410,670.

Future value interest factors (FVIF) tables can also be used to calculate historical rates of growth. Using basic arithmetic rules, one can compare past results to present and calculate a historical rate of growth. This gives us the ability to look backward and forward from a historical point of view. Suppose that Bill's Backhoe service did $125,000 of revenue in 1986; 10 years later he was doing $425,000 of volume. Answer two questions. What was his historical rate of growth in sales or gross revenue? What would you predict his sales level to be in five years assuming a similar rate of growth? Using the information available, we know that a 10-year time span exists. 1996 − 1986 = 10 years. We know that revenue in 1996 was 425,000. If we divide that figure by the original revenue figure of 125,000, we know that revenue has grown by a factor of 3.4. If you look at Table A7–1 and go down to the 10-year time frame, then slide your finger across the factors until you come to a factor at or close to 3.4, then correspond that factor with a percentage rate, you will find that the 10-year factor at 13 percent is 3.395. Thus Bill's Backhoe service has had slightly over a 13 percent rate of growth in gross revenue. Projecting ahead five years, the factor at 13 percent is 1.842. If we multiply the current revenue figure of $425,000 by the five-year factor of 1.842, we can project revenue to be $782,850 five years from now.

Some limitations exist for calculating rates of growth. For one thing, companies tend to grow in steps because expansion in plant and equipment is generally not purchased in small increments. Also, growth is often constrained by market demand and/or some other limiting factor. It is extremely difficult to maintain high rates of growth over extended periods of time. Nonetheless, it is a very useful tool. It might be helpful to note on top of Table A7–1 as a future reference that this table is used to calculate historical rate of growth problems.

The next type of problem this table can solve is very similar to calculating rates of growth. We will calculate rates of inflation historically and can project replacement costs into the future. I enjoy doing this exercise with my students. We send everyone home with an assignment to talk to parents, grandparents, uncles, aunts, and so on, with the idea of searching their memories for the price of something they remember purchasing when they were young. The student must then price that item today so we can begin to build a shopping basket of goods and services. This is basically how the Consumer Price Index is computed. Once gathered, we calculate the rate of inflation on each item and project the price of that item to your retirement age.

For example, my father farmed in southwestern North Dakota. In 1967 he purchased a new pickup truck. It was navy blue with a white top, two-wheel-drive, and had most of the amenities available at that time. The total purchase price was about $2800. A similar truck would sell today for about $18,000. The calculations are the same as historical rates of growth: 1997 − 1967 = 30 years. The 1997 figures of $18,000 divided by the 1967 figure of $2800 yields a factor of 6.4286, which would lie somewhere between 6 and 7 percent. If I were to retire in 20 years and wanted to purchase a similar pickup truck, assuming a 6 percent rate of inflation, I would use a factor of 3.207 and multiply it by the current vehicle price to project a future vehicle cost of $57,726. If you were to retire in 40 years and wanted one of those trucks to go fishing in or travel on vacation with, it would cost you, assuming the same rate of inflation, $18,000 × a factor of 10.285, for a total projected price tag of $185,130.

Is that possible? Talk to your family and do some of the same calculations. These calculations have serious consequences for your future. From the perspective of small business management, they have implications concerning replacement costs of plant and equipment. The good news is that in the recent past, inflation has been held down to a modest level, but that depends on what you're buying, including education.

One final thing to remember about the use of the FVIF tables is that the table is always dealing with a single sum: a savings deposited one time, or a pickup truck that cost $2800—it doesn't matter if we are dealing with a cash savings deposit or some other singular number. This table computes future values of that number, assuming a constant rate of return on the original value.

Future Value of an Annuity

The next logical step is to address those instances where single sums are not used. Most people don't save by dropping a large sum into some type of savings account. Most people save a little at a time, generally on a monthly or bimonthly basis. Table A7–2 (future value interest factors for a $1 annuity; see the appendix) deals with those types of problems. These tables are also annually based. The revenue is considered to flow into the annuity at the end of the year. Notice the factor for year 1. It does not matter what the rate of return is; the first-year factor is always 1.0, because no time has been allowed for the sum to generate interest revenue. This assumption will tend to create values less than they normally would be; on the other hand, this table assumes that interest revenue is reinvested immediately at the same rate, which is not always feasible—an element that will tend to overstate the value of such an investment.

The term *annuity* is defined as any equal annual cash inflow or outflow invested at a constant rate over the life of the investment—not to be confused with an insurance annuity, although insurance contracts are based on the same general principles.

WORKSHEET 2:

Using Table A7–2 (p. 163), Future Value Interest Factors for a $1 Annuity

> Table A7–2 is used for problems in which you are saving a sum of money on a regular basis and investing it at a constant rate for a period of time. If you are investing monthly, remember to multiply that sum by 12 because the tables are drawn up on an annual basis. The future value of an annuity problem is also referred to as a sum of annuity problem. The annual sum is multiplied by a factor derived from the table. The factor will increase based on the time frame—thus the time-value-of-money concept. An increase in the interest rate will also have a positive bearing on the factor. Thus for line B, a 10-year period with a 9 percent return equates to a factor of 15.193, which we multiply by the $100 annual savings for a value of $1519.30, of which $900 is accumulated principal and the remainder is accumulated interest.

LINE	SUM	PERIOD (YR)	INTEREST RATE (%)	FACTOR	VALUE
A	$ 100	1	5	_____	_____
B	100	10	9	_____	_____
C	100	10	5	_____	_____
D	1200	10	8	_____	_____
E	1200	10	10	_____	_____
F	1200	20	10	_____	_____
G	1200	30	10	_____	_____
H	1200	40	10	_____	_____
I	1800	8	12	_____	_____
J	1800	20	5	_____	_____

K. More realistically, we save by the month. If I ask you how much you might expect to have saved if you put $75 a month away for five years invested at 9 percent, you must first calculate your annual savings rate, then use the table. You would have saved _____.

L. If you save $60 per month for a period of six years invested at 7 percent, at the end of that period your savings would have grown to _____.

M. If you save $150 per month for a period of nine years invested at an 11 percent rate, your savings would accumulate to _____.

Present Value of a Dollar

The time-value-of-money concept is based on the premise that a dollar received today is worth more than a dollar received tomorrow or some time in the future. A dollar received today can be invested to return interest income. A dollar received a year or more from now forgoes that interest-earning opportunity. One method to account for that lost opportunity is to discount the value of those cash inflows.

The principles of capital budgeting will discount cash flow by a predetermined rate. The discount rate could be at the cost of capital. Discount rates are also used as hurdle rates to evaluate projects, with differing degrees of risk.

The easiest way to understand the concept of the present value of a dollar is with real-life applications. Most states offer some type of lottery to raise revenue. Did you ever wonder why the lottery commission pays out the proceeds to the winner over 20 years? The answer is obvious. A dollar received today is worth more than a dollar received in the future. Those future dollars are therefore worth less. They are discounted by the opportunity rate of return.

In Worksheet 3 we calculate the present value of a $1,000,000 lottery payout over 20 years, discounted at an estimated corporate bond rate of 8 percent. Notice that the factor is multiplied by the annual sum just as in the future value calculation. It may seem odd that the answer for the first year is not $46,000 ($50,000 × 0.08 = $4000). If you would return to Table A7–1, the future value of $1 table, and multiply the factor for one period at 8 percent, you have 1.080 × $46,300. You will notice that the result is very close to $50,000. The present value of a dollar table is the inverse of the future value of a dollar table.

WORKSHEET 3:

Using Table A7–3 (p. 164), Present Value Interest Factors for $1

LINE	PERIOD (yr)	CASH INFLOW	FACTOR	PRESENT VALUE
A	1	$50,000	0.926	$46,300
B	2	50,000	_____	_____
C	3	50,000	_____	_____
D	4	50,000	_____	_____
E	5	50,000	_____	_____
F	6	50,000	_____	_____
G	7	50,000	_____	_____
H	8	50,000	_____	_____
I	9	50,000	_____	_____
J	10	50,000	_____	_____
K	11	50,000	_____	_____
L	12	50,000	_____	_____
M	13	50,000	_____	_____
N	14	50,000	_____	_____
O	15	50,000	_____	_____
P	16	50,000	_____	_____
Q	17	50,000	_____	_____
R	18	50,000	_____	_____
S	19	50,000	_____	_____
T	20	50,000	_____	_____
Total		$1,000,000		

This problem demonstrates that a dollar received today is worth more than a dollar received tomorrow if inflation was at 8 percent throughout the 20-year period. The problem above would define the purchasing power or decline of purchasing power of that $1 million winning.

Suppose that this 20-year stream of cash inflows was saved in an interest-bearing account yielding 8 percent (use Table A7–2). At the end of the 20 years, to what would that annuity have grown? 50,000 multiplied by a factor of (a) _____ = (b) _____.

Take this scenario one step farther. Suppose that instead of 20 years of equal payments, the lottery commission paid out the $1 million up front in a single sum. Suppose also that this sum was placed in an interest-bearing account yielding 8 percent and left there for 20 years. At the end of that period the original $1 million would have grown to (use Table A7–1). $1,000,000 multiplied by a factor of (c) _____ = (d) _____.

This is why the lottery commission does not pay out the total sum up front. It is also the financial principle behind cash-value life insurance policies. The risk component of a financial loss due to death is built into the premium. The cash-value component is a separate issue.

Suppose that a 20-year-old looking for a life insurance program agreed to pay a premium that included a savings component of $100 per month for 20 years. After paying premiums for 20 years, the insurance company agrees to pay a death benefit of $50,000 for the life of the policy. If no death benefit is paid out, the insurance company will pay $100,000 for the surrender of the policy at age 70.

The insurance company would calculate the premium based on a 20-year term policy and then add the savings component of $100 per month. This policy offers a $100,000 cash payout to the insured at age 70. Is this a good deal? View this policy from two viewpoints, first from the view of the insurance company. They are receiving a stream of cash inflows of $1200 for 20 years. Assume an interest rate of 8 percent (achievable through investments in corporate bonds) using Table A7–2. $1200 multiplied by a factor of (e) _____ = (f) _____. That takes us 20 years down the time line; from this point forward no additional premiums are paid in, so the insurance company will invest the sum in (f) for the remaining 30 years. Using Table A7–1, the sum in (f) is multiplied by a factor of (g) _____, which will grow to a total of (h) _____ by the end of this 50-year period.

Now view the policy from the perspective of the investor. First the policy was purchased in part to provide retirement income, although insurance companies claim they are selling protection, not retirement income plans. If inflation averaged even a modest 3 percent, the $100,000 cash payout would have the purchasing power of (i) _____ (using Table A7–3). What the insurance company paid was roughly 3 percent on the 20-year stream of cash inflows (using Table A7–2): $1200 multiplied by a factor of (j) _____, which equals (k) _____, which in turn was compounded for 30 years at roughly 4 percent; thus (k) is multiplied by a factor of (l) _____ (using Table A7–1), which equals (m) _____, which is close to the $100,000 figure offered in the policy.

The scenario above was not intended to be a representation of any particular insurance policy. Insurance products are varied and have changed dramatically over the years. At the time of this writing one major insurance company just closed a class-action lawsuit brought by disgruntled policyholders, and another major insurance company is currently engaged in a class-action lawsuit that is very similar in nature. Knowledge of the time-value-of-money principles will empower you to analyze any type of financial program.

The use of Table A7–3 is most applicable to the small business manager in preparing a capital budgeting analysis. The topic of capital budgeting is addressed later in this chapter. Another use of the PVIF table is to calculate the yield on zero-coupon corporate bonds. Zero-coupon bonds pay no interest; they are sold at a discount to be redeemed at par upon maturity. Par value for corporate bonds is 100 points or $1000. For example, an ABCzr09 which closed at 40 $\frac{1}{8}$ is a bond that matures in the year 2009 and is selling for a price of $401.25. One can calculate the price of a bond by turning the quote into a decimal. Thus 40 $\frac{1}{8}$ becomes 0.40125. Multiply this decimal by $1000, the par value of a bond, which will equal $401.25. Another way to calculate the bond's price is to realize that bonds are quoted on 100 basis points; thus one point is equal to $10. Break the one point into fractions and match a dollar value to each fraction; thus $\frac{1}{2}$ point is equal to $5, $\frac{1}{4}$ point is equal to $2.50, and $\frac{1}{8}$ point is equal to $1.25. The quote of 40 $\frac{1}{8}$ represents 40 multiplied by $10 or $400. Add the $\frac{1}{8}$ point or $1.25, for a total value of $401.25.

Using Table A7–3, determine the number of periods in years you are dealing with. At the time of this writing, 1997 is subtracted from the maturity date of the bond, 2009, which is 12 years. From the 12-year line, read across until you find the factor closest to 0.40125 (the decimal representing the bond quote), then read the corresponding discount rate at the top of the column. In this case a factor of 0.397 is closest, representing an interest rate near 8 percent.

You can check your result using the inverse of this process. Invest $401.25 at 8 percent for 12 years. You will find a factor of 2.518 in Table A7–1 which equals a sum of $1010.35, which is close to the $1000 par value of the ABC bond to be received at maturity.

Present Value of an Annuity

The most common application of Table A7–4 (present value interest factors for a $1 annuity; see the appendix) is to calculate amortization schedules, such as those required in a mortgage loan. In this case a loan amount which is a present value sum, discounted at a particular interest rate, is paid off in a mortgage of a stated number of years. The tables assume a constant rate of interest and that payment is made at the end of the period. Table A7–4 is also an annual table. It is important to remember that the use of an annual table will result in an annual mortgage payment; thus dividing by 12 will give an approximate monthly payment. In reality, we tend to make payments monthly, which would in effect either pay the mortgage off more quickly or lower the monthly payment.

The small business owner will apply this information in computing payments on vehicles, equipment, and real estate, particularly office or shop buildings, retail outlets, or any other situation where amortization will be used. Individuals have need of this skill in computing amortization schedules, primarily for homes and vehicles.

This is a typical scenario: A person walks onto a car lot looking for that special set of wheels. That sporty red one catches his or her eye. The dealer walks up and asks if he can help you. "Yeah; what are you asking for this one?" The salesman says: "For you, just for today, $16,999—a special dealer discount—but you better act fast because this one won't last long." You respond, "No, I mean how much, you know, a month." "Oh," the salesman says, "come into my office and we'll figure it out."

You don't have to go into that guy's office or anyone else's. Just find out how much that car's total price is and decide how long you want those payments to run. Call your finance company and find out what the interest rate will be. Use Table A7–4 and figure out those payments for yourself. When we're done with this segment, you'll be able to do amortizations backward. That way you can set a payment first, based on an interest rate and a time frame, and can calculate how much you can pay for a vehicle for a given payment. This type of knowledge will leave you in a much stronger negotiating position.

One final point: When computing amortizations you divide the present value sum by the factor. In the other three tables you were multiplying the factor by some other number.

WORKSHEET 4:

Using Table A7–4 (p. 165), Present Value Interest Factors for a $1 Annuity

Compute the following mortgage or amortization schedules. The answer to line A is calculated as follows:

$$\frac{\$13,000}{3.993} = \$3255.69$$

$$\frac{\$3255.69}{12} = \$271.31$$

LINE	PERIOD (YR)	SUM	INTEREST RATE (%)	FACTOR	ANNUAL PAYMENT	MONTHLY PAYMENT
A	5	$13,000	8	3.993	$3255.69	$271.31
B	3	13,000	8	_____	_____	_____
C	7	18,000	7	_____	_____	_____
D	10	32,000	9	_____	_____	_____
E	15	60,000	8	_____	_____	_____
F	20	60,000	8	_____	_____	_____
G	30	60,000	8	_____	_____	_____
H	15	95,000	7	_____	_____	_____
I	20	95,000	7	_____	_____	_____
J	30	95,000	7	_____	_____	_____
K	10	75,000	12	_____	_____	_____
L	15	75,000	12	_____	_____	_____
M	20	75,000	12	_____	_____	_____
N	30	75,000	12	_____	_____	_____

Most individuals as well as most small business owners are on some type of budget. The individual knows how much he or she can afford per month for a payment on a particular piece of equipment or piece of real estate. Suppose, for example, that a proprietor is paying $1300 per month for a retail space. This person is considering buying instead of renting. The question at hand is how much can he or she pay for a building for that kind of money? If taxes and insurance run $300 per month, then $1000 per month or $12,000 per year would be available for principal and interest payments ($1300 − $300 = $1000 × 12 = $12,000). If a 20-year mortgage is being sought, and if mortgage interest is 8 percent, the factor being 9.818, then a $12,000 annual payment would support a mortgage of $117,816 ($12,000 × 9.818 = $117,816).

Compute the sum that could be amortized given the following parameters:

LINE	MONTHLY PAYMENT	ANNUAL PAYMENT	INTEREST RATE (%)	PERIOD (YR)	FACTOR	MORTGAGE
A	$215	$2580	9	5	_____	_____
B	320	3840	7	3	_____	_____
C	600	7200	7	30	_____	_____
D	800	9600	8	15	_____	_____
E	550	6600	9	30	_____	_____
F	275	3300	10	3	_____	_____
G	150	1800	18	5	_____	_____

Having gone through all four tables, what is now required is the ability to apply those skills to situations. The trick to applications is to determine what type of question is being asked, then break the problem down and apply the correct table to the problem. Practice will internalize the use of the time value tables for you. Practice, preferably with numbers that have meaning to you personally: your own retirement plan, school loans, car loans, and so on. I believe that the concept of time value is a skill you will want to take with you when you leave college, and will use those concepts throughout your life, even if you do not own your own business.

I have taught time-value techniques to hundreds of students. Most students readily grasp the concepts, some almost immediately; others take awhile. To help students internalize the concepts, I have written a number of minicases or word problems that force the student to jump from one table to another. The minicases are designed to increase in complexity progressively. Once you are comfortable with the academic applications, real-life applications should be a natural extension.

WORKSHEET 5: APPLICATIONS

Mary Jones

Mary Jones is a 24-year-old college graduate with a degree in elementary education. Mary recently signed a teaching contract which offered her an annual base salary of $26,000 to teach the fourth grade. Mary has stated that her investment goal is to be able to retire comfortably, and she would like to own her own home. Mary also indicated that she abhors debt. She is asking you for some help in analyzing the following scenarios.

As a teacher, Mary is required to put 5 percent of her gross salary into a teacher retirement program. This fund is managed by the state and is mandated to pay a minimum interest rate of 5 percent. Mary doubts that the state will ever pay over that rate. She would like to know how much she will accumulate if she stays with this school system for 20 years. Do not figure any pay increases. Five percent of $26,000 translates into an annual sum of (a) _____ multiplied by a factor of (b) _____, which will equal a sum of (c) _____.

Mary doesn't have a lot of confidence in anything the government does, so she decided to hedge her bets with a supplemental 401(k) pretax savings program. She is interested in a bond fund which has historically returned 9 percent. She intends to invest $80 a month in this fund for 20 years as well. You tell her that this savings program should accumulate as follows. An annual sum of (d) _____ multiplied by a factor of (e) _____ should equal (f) _____ by the end of 20 years.

Since this is Mary's first job, she is on a tight budget. Mary does, however, need some form of economical and dependable transportation. She shopped around for a new car but just didn't think she could handle the payments. Mary checks out the newspaper ads and finds a used Geo Metro. Her mechanic advises her not to pay over $4500, and after some tough haggling she makes the deal. Her credit union tells her that three-year loans are the maximum they will offer on a used vehicle and offer her a three-year loan at 9 percent. Mary's payments figure out to be: $4500 divided by a factor of (g) _____ equal annual payments of (h) _____ and monthly payments of (i) _____. These payments she can handle.

Affordable housing is Mary's other major concern. She wants to budget 20 percent of her gross pay for housing. That amounts to $5200 a year or $433.33 a month. She has a couple of choices, but after doing some checking around, Mary finds another young first-year teacher who is looking for a roommate. Not finding an adequate apartment, Mary decides on a 14 ft. × 70 ft.

mobile home, which she pays $28,000 for and finances for 8 percent over 10 years. The payments are calculated as follows: $28,000 divided by a factor of (j) _____ equals annual payments of (k) _____ and monthly payments of (l) _____. Her roommate offers to pay for the lot rent and utilities.

Ten years later Mary's mobile home is paid off. She still wants a house, so she sells her mobile home to another teacher for $21,000 on a 10-year CFD (contract for deed). Mary accepts $1000 as a down payment and finances the remaining $20,000 for 10 years at 9 percent. Mary will receive monthly payments based on the following calculations: $20,000 divided by a factor of (m) _____ equals annual payments of (n) _____ and monthly payments of (o) _____.

Mary buys herself that house she has always wanted. She had to borrow $95,000 but was able to obtain a 7 percent 30-year loan. Her monthly payments calculate out to be (p) _____, but with her mobile home CFD payments she thinks she can handle her new mortgage, even without a roommate.

Mary likes her job, and she likes the community, and since Mary has purchased a house of her own, she would like to stay in the community and teach until her retirement. Assume that Mary has been teaching for 20 years already and is considering teaching another 20 years, until she reaches retirement age. Mary asks you about her bond fund, the value you projected in (f). If she discontinues making her $80 a month contributions, what will that fund be worth assuming that it continues to grow at a rate of 9 percent (q) _____? What would her bond fund be worth if she continues to fund it at the current rate of $80 per month for a full 40 years? Assume a 9 percent bond yield on this as well (r) _____.

Willie Winkle

Willie wondered how so many of his friends could afford to buy homes and drive new cars, while he just rented. Willie asked you to help him out. After some discussion you discovered that Willie was paying $600 a month for apartment rent. You figure that if he could use that $600 a month to buy a house he could afford $7200 a year for mortgage payments. You check with a mortgage company and they tell you rates are around 7 percent. You calculate that with a 20-year mortgage Willie's $7200 rent money could finance (a) _____. With a 30-year mortgage Willie could afford a (b) _____ mortgage. Not bad, but escrow in the form of real estate taxes and insurance will eat up about $2000 per year, so Willie really only has $5200 to work with.

You call the mortgage company back. They tell you about this first-time home buyer program. They can offer this 5 percent 30-year loan program for first-time home buyers. Willie qualifies; now his $5200 will finance (c) _____. Willie buys a house and moves in.

A week later Willie calls again. Now he's worried that if he's hit with a big repair bill he won't be able to handle it. You talk Willie into letting your sister Millie move in with him, and she agrees to pay $400 a month to Willie for rent. Willie agrees but just for the time being. Willie takes this $400 a month and invests it in an equity mutual fund. Five years later the fund, which averaged 12 percent, has grown to a hefty (d) _____. Even after Millie moved in, Willie was worried. To be on the safe side, Willie took an evening job at the local theater: free movie tickets, free popcorn, and $32 take-home pay for a Wednesday night at the movies. Willie does this 50 weeks a year for five years. He sticks this cash reserve into a money market mutual fund yielding 6 percent. At the end of this five-year period this fund is worth (e) _____.

Guess what? Willie married Millie and they have a daughter, Shellie. Now Willie is really worried. He knows college will start for his daughter in 18 years. Willie calls you again, wondering if he quit his job at the movie theater but kept this money market mutual fund in savings at 6 percent for another 18 years what it would be worth. You calculate the figure found in (e) to grow to (f) _____. Willie gives up the movie theater work. He can't stand the smell of popcorn and wants to spend some time with Shellie.

If college costs are $10,000 a year when Willie and Millie's daughter is born, and if college costs increase at a rate of 5 percent a year for 18 years, her freshman year will cost (g) _____. Willie is worried again; he knows he will need some additional savings if he plans to pay for his daughter's college. Willie calls you again; this time he wants to know what his house would be worth by the time his daughter goes to college. You call the realtor; he projects a 6 percent rate of real estate appreciation. You take the mortgage figure in (c) and appreciate that figure by 6 percent for 23 years, which calculates to an estimated value of (h) _____. Willie is no longer worried about college costs; he feels he can supplement his cash savings with an equity loan.

You get another phone call. This time it's Millie; she is worried. She and Willie were trying to do some retirement planning. The idea of Willie saving the $400 a month rent she gave him for those five years seemed like a good retirement plan. Millie was wondering if they kept that savings level up for another 35 years, and if their fund averaged 12 percent, what it would be worth at the end of that 40-year period. You estimate it to be worth roughly (i) _____. Millie isn't sure they can maintain that savings. She is wondering if they just left the sum in (d) in the mutual fund, and again assuming a 12 percent rate of growth, what it would be worth in 35 years. You estimate the value to be (j) _____. You caution them that the purchasing power of those dollars will not be equivalent to today's purchasing power. You figure inflation will average 4 percent a year over those same 40 years. If Willie and Millie want to replace $30,000 a year of purchasing power, they will need (k) _____ a year to do it. You explain that another way to view this purchasing power thing would be to take the sum in (i) and reduce it by the present value of 4 percent over 40 years. Thus 40 years from the start of this savings program, those dollars saved would have a purchasing power of only (l) _____ cents compared to the value of a dollar today, and the sum in (i) would have the purchasing power of (m) _____ in today's dollars.

Lyle and Nyla

It was one of those whirlwind romances. It started out in one of those line-dance routines down at Borrowed Bucks Roadhouse. By the time they played Boot Scoot Boogie, things between Lyle and Nyla were getting hot. It was one of those cowboy-type weddings, most of which had to be financed by borrowed bucks—credit card type.

The good news was that Nyla had been in a finance class or two (lucky for Nyla). Even better news was that Nyla actually paid attention in class (lucky for Lyle). It was agreed that Nyla would handle the finances, and this saga is about Nyla's financial strategy. Their goal was a place in the country. Lyle knew that he just had to have a horse.

Nyla had arranged to be apartment manager, which provided a free apartment in exchange for management duties. This arrangement saved them $700 a month that they had been paying for rent. Nyla figured five years of rent savings invested in a 8 percent bond fund would accumulate to

(a) _____ for a down payment on that place in the country. Nyla also knew that two incomes are better than one and with a little budgeting was able to save another $300 a month out of Lyle's paycheck which she invested in a 6 percent money market fund, which would add (b) _____ to their down payment five years down the road.

The acreage they eventually bought cost $182,000 less the funds available in (a) and (b), which they use for their down payment. Nyla calculates a 20-year mortgage assuming a 7 percent loan to cost them (c) _____ per month, while a 30-year 7 percent mortgage would run them (d) _____ a month. They decide on the 30-year loan.

Nyla is a self-employed financial consultant. She decides to set up an IRA for herself and plans to fund $2000 annually for 40 years. If she can maintain a 10 percent return, that IRA will grow to a value of (e) _____ by the end of that period. Lyle has a 401(k); with his employer match he expects to fund $3200 annually for 30 years. Lyle conservatively hopes that this fund will return 9 percent. Nyla figures that Lyle will accumulate (f) _____ by the time he takes early retirement to raise horses.

Lyle and Nyla expect to put a lot of work into their acreage. Nyla expects that property to appreciate by 6 percent a year. She figures that in 40 years it will be worth (g) _____, and in 50 years it will be worth (h) _____, at which time she and Lyle will sell it and move into an apartment.

Nyla's biggest concern is the loss of purchasing power of their retirement income due to inflation. She calculates that if they needed an additional $25,000 a year on top of social security in today's dollars to finance a comfortable retirement, 40 years from now, assuming a 5 percent rate of inflation they will need (i) _____, and 50 years from now they will need (j) _____ assuming the same rate of inflation. That means that if Lyle needed a two-horse trailer to haul his horses in and that trailer costs $3200 today, 40 years from now that trailer would cost (k) _____, but if inflation rose, say, by only 3 percent over those 40 years, that horse trailer would cost (l) _____ and the price of everything else would go up by that factor as well.

Monty Markowitz

Monty was the only child of a machinist from Maine. Monty's father and mother knew that Monty had miserly qualities even as a child. Monty's grandmother gave Monty $15,000 for college when he was 8 years old. Monty put his money in an interest-bearing account that yielded 7 percent, and he knew that in 10 years that account would have grown to (a) _____, which would, along with his summer jobs, be enough to get by on.

When Monty was 18 and in college, he decided to take a part-time job to replace the savings that were being spent on his education. He worked as a mechanic after school and on weekends. His average earnings was around $200 a week, of which Monty saved $100. Monty kept this up 52 weeks a year for four years. Monty had this savings in a mutual fund yielding an average of 14 percent. By graduation Monty had accumulated (b) _____.

Monty was proud of what he had accumulated. Monty calculated that if he never added another cent to that fund but just left it to appreciate for 40 years, that fund would at a 10 percent rate of growth be worth (c) _____. If he could maintain a 12 percent rate of growth, it would be worth (d) _____, and a 14 percent rate of growth would increase the fund's value to (e) _____.

After college Monty took a job and rewarded himself with a new car. GMAC was offering 6 percent financing on new cars. His $17,000 five-year car loan cost him (f) _____ per month. Monty next bought himself a town-house. His $78,000 7 percent 30-year mortgage gave him monthly payments of (g) _____.

Monty's employer set up a 401(k) retirement plan. Monty's contribution and his employer's matching funds would fund $4800 a year into an aggressive growth fund that should yield at least 10 percent. Monty figures that if he stays with the company 10 years he will be vested and the fund should be worth (h) _____. If he stays 20 years, that fund will grow to (i) _____, and if he stays 40 years, that retirement could grow to (j) _____ at those rates.

It was just a few weeks later that Monty lost his grandmother. She left him her house, which was worth $80,000. Monty decided to sell this home on a contract for deed, accepting 20 percent down, and carrying the mortgage at 8 percent for 15 years. If Monty saved the down payment in an 8 percent interest-bearing account, that figure would grow to (k) _____ in 40 years. The other 80 percent, or $64,000, which was carried as a contract for deed at 8 percent, would generate a monthly stream of revenue of (l) _____ for 15 years. If Monty were to save this entire stream of cash inflows for the entire 15 years, and assuming that he, too, could get an 8 percent return in corporate bonds, that value would amount to (m) _____ at the end of 15 years, after which Monty will decide between selling his townhouse and adding the appreciation to the sum in (m) to buy a home in the country for a price of $300,000, or keep his townhouse and leave the sum in (m) for 25 years.

If Monty leaves the sum in (m) in an 8 percent interest-bearing account for another 25 years, that account will appreciate to a value of (n) _____. If he buys this $300,000 house in the country and if real estate appreciates at the rate of 5 percent a year, in 25 years that house will have appreciated to a value of (o) _____.

If Monty buys the house he calculates his retirement to be funded by the total in (c), (j), and (k). Monty calculates that if this total were invested in corporate bonds at 8 percent, it would generate a annual revenue of (p) _____, which would leave the principal intact for his estate. If he were to try spend all his cash in 25 years, assuming 8 percent amortization, it would generate an annual revenue of (q) _____, which along with his social security income should finance a cruise or two.

Ben Banks

Ben Banks was born the son of a wealthy banker from Boston. His father was determined to teach Ben the art of saving. Ben's first lesson began at birth. Ben's grandfather deposited $50,000 in a fund for Ben's future education. Invested at a constant rate of 7 percent and leaving it compound for 18 years, this education fund would grow to a total of (a) _____ by Ben's first year of college. Ben's father put Ben on the bank's payroll when Ben achieved age 8. A total of $500 per month had to be invested in a preferred savings account yielding 8 percent. Ten years of investing at this rate gave Ben a balance of (b) _____.

College costs were estimated to be about $6000 a year the year Ben was born, but they were rising at an annual rate of 8 percent. By the time Ben was to start college, it would cost him around (c) _____ a year.

Ben enjoyed banking, and he knew he had a bright future in it. When Ben looked back at the bank's records he noticed that the year he was born, bank deposits were $18 million. The year Ben started college, bank deposits had risen to $85 million, which represented a (d) _____ percent rate of growth in deposits during that 18-year period. He also calculated the growth in net earnings, which had risen from $1.2 million the year he was born to $9,228,000 some 18 years later. This growth in net earnings represented a (e) _____ rate of growth.

The area Ben enjoyed most at the bank was the trust department, where the retirement funds were managed. In the trust department one of the bank's clients had invested $200 per month for 40 years and had achieved a 9 percent return, which represented a value of (f) _____. Remarkable as that was, the bank had another client who had managed a 15 percent rate of return over 30 years on her $2500 annual contribution, which left her with a total of (g) _____. The lesson Ben learned from the time-value-of-money concepts was that the higher the rate of return, the faster funds accumulate and that real growth can be accomplished by maintaining those returns over long periods of time.

Ben also liked the home mortgage department. Ben noticed that a client of the bank's was wrestling with a home mortgage problem. Ben calculated that a $70,000 mortgage with an 8 percent interest rate would produce monthly payments on a 10-year loan of (h) _____, a 15-year mortgage a monthly payment of (i) _____, a 20-year mortgage monthly payments of (j) _____, and a 30-year mortgage monthly payments of (k) _____. The client indicated that he and his wife had only $550 per month available for principal and interest payments. Ben explained that he thought interest rates would drop to 7 percent in the next six months. Ben explained that with a $550 monthly payment a 20-year mortgage would finance (l) _____ and a 30-year mortgage would finance (m) _____. The client decided to wait for interest rates to drop.

One day Ben ran across a bank customer who had invested in zero-coupon bonds. Ben noticed that the bonds, purchased for 25 $\frac{3}{4}$ points and matured in 20 years, were actually yielding around (n) _____. That same client indicated that he had bought the zero-coupon bonds because he also had a single-premium life insurance policy, for which he had paid a one-time premium of $10,000, and which matures in 20 years and pay him $20,000. Ben explained that this life insurance contract was paying slightly less than a (o) _____ percent return. Ben explained that had $10,000 been invested in 8 percent corporate bonds, at the end of 20 years they would have been worth (p) _____.

Hopefully, these minicases, became easier as you went along. Once you have a level of comfort with the tables, the next step is real-life application. Next we use time-value-of-money concepts to address several wealth accumulation strategies applied to an average person or situation.

WORKSHEET 6: WEALTH ACCUMULATION STRATEGIES

In our example we use John Q. Public and his wife, Ann. Both have average jobs and are able to own a modest house. Homeownership is generally the largest single investment most people make in their lives and is at the core of these strategies. We will assume that this couple can handle a $800 monthly house payment.

Strategy 1 is to buy as large a house as you can and let inflation do your work for you. We assume a $200 per month escrow and a $600 per month principal and interest payment. We assume an attractive 7 percent interest rate on the mortgage. Thus a 30-year mortgage at 7 percent produces a factor of 12.409 using the PVIFA tables. Multiply this factor by $600.00 × 12 months to finance a maximum mortgage of $89,344.80. What this will buy depends on where you live in the United States.

Many states offer first-time home buyers a reduced mortgage through the sale of bonds that offer some tax incentive to the investor. Suppose that one of these loans is available at a rate of 6 percent. Calculate the maximum 30-year mortgage that $7200 will support: $7200 multiplied by a factor of (a) _____ will finance a mortgage of (b) _____.

Strategy 1 is like borrowing this sum and putting it into the real estate inflation bank for 30 years while you are making payments on the loan to pay it off. In this scenario, by the time the mortgage has been paid off, the home's value has appreciated with inflation. Suppose a rate of inflation or a rate of appreciation of 5 percent for 30 years: $89,344.80 multiplied by a factor of 4.322 FVIF table equals $386,148.22. Assume the same original price but appreciate that price by 4 percent: $89,344.80 multiplied by a factor of (c) _____ equals (d) _____. If the home appreciated by 6 percent, the value would be (e) _____.

This strategy makes sense for those who are stable enough to live in the same community most of their lives, which is easier said than done. It also implies that the community will have stable employment and an economic base that will support real estate price appreciation. Buyers must have the ability to make ever-increasing mortgage payments. Those payments are a function of price and interest rates. Rising mortgage interest has a detrimental effect on real estate prices because people are increasingly priced out of the market. Strategy 1 is heavily dependent on future increases in real estate prices.

Strategy 1 allows homeowners to leverage their home equity into larger and larger homes, by selling and moving up. This allows for a larger principal sum to be deposited in the real estate inflation bank.

Strategy 2 spins off from strategy 1. The cheapest money available to most people is home mortgage money. The mortgage banking industry, Wall Street, and the real estate industry have all lobbied hard to provide the mechanisms to finance individual homeownership. Homeownership supports stable communities, and home building is important to the nation's economic health. That said, a person can use a home mortgage to his or her financial advantage.

Take the scenario in strategy 1, where a home was financed for 30 years and it is now 10 years into that period. Answer these questions: What is the value of this home if it has appreciated by 5 percent a year? What is the mortgage payoff at the end of 10 years? The answer to the first question is easy: $89,344.80 multiplied by a factor of 1.629 (FVIF) equals $145,542.68. The second question is probably a little harder. Notice that the PVIFA factor for 30 years at 7 percent is 12.409, and notice how those factors become progressively smaller as you move from year 30 to year 25 to year 20, where the factor is 10.594. If you recall, the maximum mortgage that $600 × 12, or $7200, would support was found by multiplying $7200 by 12.409; thus the figure of $89,344.80 was found. To calculate the payoff, multiply 10.594 by $7200; thus the payoff is $76,276.80, which represents only $13,068 of principal being paid off in 10 years. What will the mortgage payoff be 15 years into the mortgage? (f) _____. How about 20 years into the mortgage? (g) _____. Then calculate the payoff 25 years into the mortgage. (h) _____. Notice how principal payments are accelerated the closer you get to the end of the mortgage.

The original question in strategy 2 was how much equity does this person have in his home after 10 years of mortgage payments? $145,452.68 ($89,3440.80 × 1.629) less a payoff of $76,276.80, for an equity position of $69,175.88. The second part of this strategy equation deals with tapping that equity to better the borrower's financial position. This works best if the homeowner has an opportunity to refinance at a lower interest rate. The homeowner must decide if an increase in mortgage payments can be withstood or if he or she wants them to remain the same. Refinancing will require that mortgage payments are again stretched out to 30 years. Assume that they just take out the $13,068 of principal with no increase in payments. Assume that they invest this $13,068 in a tax-deferred 401(k) or supplemental retirement fund, and let it accumulate at 12 percent. The premise here requires forced savings. A second part of the premise is that the returns are greater than the rate of mortgage interest. A benefit also exists in lowering taxable income through increased pretax savings and increased home mortgage interest deductions. FVIF for 30 years produces a factor of 29.960 multiplied by $13,068.00 equals $391,517.28.

If homeowners are to take full advantage of the equity appreciation in their homes due to a reduced principal balance and the appreciation of the property value, they must be able to support the larger payments through an increase in their personal earnings. Assume a 4 percent increase in wages over the 10-year period, which also allows for an increase in the $7200 available for a mortgage payment to grow at an annual rate of 4 percent; thus $7200 multiplied by a factor of (i) _____ equals (j) _____, which in turn would finance a 30-year mortgage. Assume an interest rate of 7 percent; then (k) _____, which allows the homeowner to pull out (l) _____ of equity to be invested, preferably by channeling into a pretax savings account for 25 years with an estimated annual rate of growth of 12 percent, would accumulate to (m) _____. This scenario works best for a person who has a difficult time saving, where forced savings in the form of a house payment is the only way they seem to be able to save. The danger in this program lies in getting that equity into a pretax savings plan which is tax deferred. That type of retirement income is difficult to access once it is in place. Professional help may be needed to help facilitate this program.

I stretched this equation to 40 years. Had they stayed on track, they would have paid off their house in 30 years, after which time they could use the $7200 a year to fund a 401(k) at the estimated 12 percent for the next 10 years (year 30 to year 40). This equates to $7200 multiplied by a factor FVIFA of 17.549, or $126,352.80. Under either of the situations above, the value of the home would have appreciated to $628,987.39 ($89,344.80 multiplied by a 40-year 5 percent FVIF factor of 7.040).

By utilizing home equity, whenever an advantage can be achieved through refinancing, especially when interest rates drop, an opportunity arises not only to increase the homeowner's overall wealth, but to diversify the source of that wealth.

Scenario 3 involves purchasing a more modest home with an accelerated payoff, then financing a retirement plan more fully after that mortgage is paid off. The same $7200 would finance a 15-year mortgage of (PVIFA factor of 9.108) $65,577.60, after which $7200 would be invested in a retirement plan annually for the remaining 25 years. Thus $7200 multiplied by a factor of 133.333 FVIFA equals $959,997.60 plus an appreciated home value of $461,666.30 ($65,577.60 multiplied by 7.040 FVIF). The danger inherent in this strategy stems from the homeowner's ability or inability to actually use the former home mortgage payment for savings. It is very easy to justify funding other needs.

It is probably obvious to you by now that using the tables does offer some limitations. We have been constrained to the use of whole percentage points in calculating returns or computing mortgages. That is, however, as far as I am going to take you in the time-value-of-money concept. The next step is for you to master the use of a financial calculator. Many good manuals are available on the use of financial and business calculators.

• CAPITAL BUDGETING ·················

Next, we revisit a problem discussed in the business plan. The very nature of most startup small business ventures can be viewed from the perspective of a stand-alone project. In this brief summary of the capital budgeting process, we employ time-value-of-money concepts and discounted cash flow techniques. Capital budgeting, sensitivity analysis, and scenario analysis provide mechanisms to compare capital outlays with cash inflows under varying conditions. The capital budgeting process using discounted cash flows, with accompanying sensitivity and scenario analyses, address that contingency element that bankers tend to be concerned about. This process helps deal with the what-if projections should they not turn out the way you expected, thus helping you firm up the forecasts in your business plan.

The accuracy of input estimate numbers is critical to meaningful output. It does not matter how sophisticated the computer model or spreadsheet analysis used if the cash inflow and expense projections are erroneous. To the best of your ability, assumptions should be verified. As a measurement of time and effort in the capital budgeting process, 99 percent of your efforts should be expended in verifying the numbers, the other 1 percent in presenting them. Here we demonstrate the 1 percent, but I do this because your banker probably will want to see a presentation of the projections in your business plan. Let's look at an example of this process.

Budgeting Example: Bob's Backhoe Service

Bob is starting a trenching business. He plans to lease a shop, lease a service vehicle, and hire a truck to transport his backhoe from job site to job site, but he wants to purchase the backhoe, which he has priced at $130,000. The equipment dealer will grant the loan and finance the machine for an assumed 12 percent interest rate. Bob calculates his fixed cost to run the backhoe at $55,600 a year. Bob also calculates his variable costs to run $21 per hour. Bob estimates that with a good operator, the machine can trench 50 feet per hour. Bob also expects to be able to charge $1.30 per foot of trenching, and he expects to be able to log 2000 machine hours per season of trenching. (These assumptions are the basis for Bob's revenue forecast). 2000 hours × 50 feet × $1.30 per foot equals $130,000 per year.

Bob expects to operate this machine for five years before trading it off on a new backhoe. At that time Bob expects the backhoe to have a salvage value of $45,000. The first analysis will run this project through the five-year period without any consideration for income tax. The cash outflow represents the cost of the machine, and the cash inflow represents the net income figure from the pro-forma income statement (2000 hours × 50 feet per hour × $1.30 per foot trenched = $130,000 gross revenue). We then subtract the $55,600 of fixed costs and subtract $42,000 of variable costs ($21 per hour × 2000 machine hours). Thus we have a sum of $130,000 less $97,600 of total expenses, for an annual net revenue inflow of $32,400. If we use a discount rate of 12 percent, which is the rate charged by the equipment dealer, and multiply the PVIF factor (Table 7A–3) for each of the five years, we can compute the present value of those discounted cash flows to determine if the costs can be recovered. The following example addresses this issue.

YEAR	CASH OUTFLOW	CASH INFLOW	DISCOUNT FACTOR	VALUE
Now	$130,000		1.0	($130,000.00)
1		$32,400	0.893	28,933.20
2		32,4000	.797	25,822.80
3		32,4000	.712	23,068.80
4		32,4000	.636	20,606.40
5		32,4000	.567	18,370.80
5	Salvage value:	45,0000	.567	25,515.00
				12,317.00

The $12,317 represents a return on this project in excess of 12 percent. The internal rate of return (IRR) method would raise the discount rate until the result is zero, which identifies the exact return on the project. The implication inherent in the IRR method is that the inputs are exact, which is generally not possible in any forecast.

The second analysis incorporates an income tax savings element. An assumption of a 15 percent federal tax bracket and a 7 percent state income tax is applied—thus a total 22 percent tax rate. Depreciation is based on a seven-year useful life and straight-line depreciation. It should be noted that any application of a tax benefit incorporated in an analysis makes the assumption that taxable profits exist throughout the duration of the project and that those profits are large enough to achieve the full tax benefit. It also assumes that the tax rates remain constant. Those assumptions become invalid should the firm post a loss. This analysis treats the tax savings as a cash inflow, whereas in reality they represent a reduction in taxes paid.

YEAR	CASH OUTFLOW	DEPRECIATION	CASH INFLOW	DISCOUNT FACTOR	VALUE
Now	$130,000			1.0	($130,000.00)
1		$18,571.43	$ 4,085.71	0.893	3,648.54
1			32,400.00	0.893	28,933.20
2		18,571.43	4,085.71	0.797	3,256.31
2			32,400.00	0.797	25,822.80
3		18,571.43	4085.71	0.712	2,909.03
3			32,400.00	0.712	23,068.80
4		18,571.43	4,085.71	0.636	2,598.51
4			32,400.00	0.636	20,606.40
5		18,571.43	4,085.71	0.567	2,316.98
5			32,400.00	0.567	18,370.80
5			45,000.00	0.567	25,515.00
5		(7,857.15)	(1,728.57)	0.567	(980.11)
		$85,000.00			$26,066.06

Sensitivity Analysis

The next phase of evaluating a project is to reevaluate the critical assumptions used to generate the initial forecast. In Bob's Backhoe Business revenue was a function of the number of feet per hour that his machine could trench in a given hour, the number of hours the machine would work in a year, and the price per foot that could be charged given the demand for those services and the competitive environment in which Bob must operate. Sensitivity analysis isolates those assumptions into separate variables.

Variable 1, the number of feet per hour that Bob's machine can trench, is a function of a number of factors. The experience of the operator will have an effect. The performance and operating condition of the machine itself will have an effect. Certain soil conditions, such as clay, will slow the trenching operation; sand will speed it up. Weather conditions will have an impact: Dry would be best; frozen soil or mud would slow trenching operations. Impediments such as existing electrical or water lines would also slow the trenching operation. Given these factors, it is difficult to make an accurate, uniform estimate of this critical variable. In reality what is created is a range of performance, based on the above-mentioned factors and conditions.

It should be easy to recognize how even a small change in this or any of the key variables can translate into a large change in gross revenue and ultimately, net income. It is this fact that also concerns financial institutions, and that is why they are so concerned that a proprietor have some hard experience in the business he or she is going into. The banker is going to want to know what your degree of confidence is in your forecast. Your ability to demonstrate that degree of confidence could make the difference between obtaining financing or rejection.

Historical documentation would be best. If yours is a startup, historical records do not exist. Records are available through the use of test trials. Industry standards can be used. Your competitors, suppliers, and trade journals may be other sources of information. If test trials are used, results can be plotted. The use of standard deviation techniques can be applied, or the results can simply be graphed within a range where, say, 70 percent of the results lie, then 80 percent, then 90 percent. In Bob's case an initial estimate of 50 feet was used. Then 30 test trials were run. If we add and subtract 5 feet from the initial estimate, yielding a range of 45 to 55 feet per hour, and if 21 results lie within that range, a 70 percent degree of confidence can be applied to that range assuming that the tests were valid and reliable. If a 90 percent degree of confidence is desired, 27 of the results must fall within the range. Suppose that widening the range each direction 3 feet per hour accomplishes that. Thus 27 results or 90 percent of the outcomes will fall in a range of plus or minus 8 feet of Bob's original estimate: 90 percent of the results will fall within the range of 42 to 58 feet per hour.

Sensitivity analysis changes one variable at a time and leaves the other variables constant to measure the effect on net income from changes in that variable.

Variable 1 (Feet per Hour)

(base + 8 feet) × 2000 hours × $1.30 per foot = $150,800 − $97,600 = $53,200

Base: 50 feet × 2000 hours × $1.30 per foot = $130,000 − $97,600 = $32,400

(base − 8 feet) × 2000 hours × $1.30 per foot = $109,200 − $97,600 = $11,600

Variable 2, hours per year, is a function of demand. Weather conditions (e.g., wet, early frost, late spring) can affect how much trenching can be done. The level of competition can have an effect. General economic conditions will influence demand. Other variables also exist to influence the number of hours the machine will operate. For the purpose of this exercise, let us assume that 90 percent of the outcomes fall in a range of plus or minus 400 hours per year.

Variable 2 (Hours per Season)

50 feet × (base + 400 hours) × $1.30 per foot = $156,000 − $106,400 = $49,600

Base: 50 feet × 2000 hours × $1.30 per foot = $130,000 − $97,600 = $32,400

50 feet × (base − 400 hours) × $1.30 per foot = $104,000 − $89,200 = $14,800

Variable 3 (Price per Foot)   Assume plus or minus 0.15.

50 feet = 2000 hours × (base + 0.15) = $145,000 − $97,600 = $47,400

Base: 50 feet × 2000 hours × 1.30 per foot = $130,000 − $97,600 = $32,400

50 feet × 2000 hours ×(base − 0.15) = $115,000 − $97,600 = $17,400

Of the three variables it is relatively easy to see that feet per hour is the most critical. It is good to be able to recognize this. Bob could be more price competitive under conditions where trenching is relatively easy.

Scenario Analysis

The final phase of a project analysis is to recognize that things tend to happen in a scenario. It often seems that everything either works or it doesn't. For Bob's Backhoe Service and similar businesses, an economic recession could cause lots of projects to be delayed or canceled, in turn creating a lot of overcapacity in the industry. Work would be hard to get and hours of operation would be cut. Competition would cause price pressure. All that would be needed to complete the set of woes would be bad weather or poor trenching conditions and the stage is set for a worst-case scenario. An economic expansion or boom period could just as well create an opposite scenario, where trenching firms would have to scramble to keep up to demand, which in turn would create an upward pressure on price. Selective job choice could complete a best-case picture for Bob's business. A scenario analysis puts numbers to those perspectives. Best case takes the best outcomes from each variable, while worst case takes the worst outcomes within the range identified previously.

Best case: 58 feet per hour × 2400 hours × $1.45 per foot =
$201,840 − $106,000 = $95,840

Base case: 50 feet per hour × 2000 hours × $1.30 per foot =
$130,000 − $97,600 = $32,400

Worst case: 42 feet per hour × 1600 hours × $1.15 per foot =
$77,280 − $89,200 = ($11,920)

A contingency plan can be addressed in event of a worst-case scenario. Somehow that $11,900 loss must be made up and payments to the equipment dealer sustained. In all probability the manager Bob would lay off his operator and run the machine himself to cut his fixed costs. Other steps could also be addressed. The bank will be more inclined to extend a loan if the contingencies of a worst case have been addressed. As a businessperson it is prudent to have expended some energies in creating plan B.

Still another step can be applied in the capital budgeting process. From historical or industry data, a series of probabilities could be assigned to the likelihood of each possible series of events or outcomes. In the sensitivity analysis an underlying assumption is that the probability of outcomes resembles a normal curve, when in fact those variables may be skewed to one extreme or the other. In such a case, where historical data support such a conclusion, a decision tree can be formulated to assigned the likelihood of each event occurring and then calculating a weighted average of the outcomes.

TABLE A7-1 Future-Value Interest Factors for One Dollar Compounded at k Percent for n Periods: $FVIF_{k,n} = (1 + k)^n$

Period	1%	2%	3%	4%	5%	6%	7%	8%	9%	10%	11%	12%	13%	14%	15%	16%	20%	25%	30%	35%
1	1.010	1.020	1.030	1.040	1.050	1.060	1.070	1.080	1.090	1.100	1.110	1.120	1.130	1.140	1.150	1.160	1.200	1.250	1.300	1.350
2	1.020	1.040	1.061	1.082	1.102	1.124	1.145	1.166	1.188	1.210	1.232	1.254	1.277	1.300	1.322	1.346	1.440	1.562	1.690	1.822
3	1.030	1.061	1.093	1.125	1.158	1.191	1.225	1.260	1.295	1.331	1.368	1.405	1.443	1.482	1.521	1.561	1.728	1.953	2.197	2.460
4	1.041	1.082	1.126	1.170	1.216	1.262	1.311	1.360	1.412	1.464	1.518	1.574	1.630	1.689	1.749	1.811	2.074	2.441	2.856	3.321
5	1.051	1.104	1.159	1.217	1.276	1.338	1.403	1.469	1.539	1.611	1.685	1.762	1.842	1.925	2.011	2.100	2.488	3.052	3.713	4.484
6	1.062	1.126	1.194	1.265	1.340	1.419	1.501	1.587	1.677	1.772	1.870	1.974	2.082	2.195	2.313	2.436	2.986	3.815	4.827	6.053
7	1.072	1.149	1.230	1.316	1.407	1.504	1.606	1.714	1.828	1.949	2.076	2.211	2.353	2.502	2.660	2.826	3.583	4.768	6.275	8.172
8	1.083	1.172	1.267	1.369	1.477	1.594	1.718	1.851	1.993	2.144	2.305	2.476	2.658	2.853	3.059	3.278	4.300	5.960	8.157	11.032
9	1.094	1.195	1.305	1.423	1.551	1.689	1.838	1.999	2.172	2.358	2.558	2.773	3.004	3.252	3.518	3.803	5.160	7.451	10.604	14.894
10	1.105	1.219	1.344	1.480	1.629	1.791	1.967	2.159	2.367	2.594	2.839	3.106	3.395	3.707	4.046	4.411	6.192	9.313	13.786	20.106
11	1.116	1.243	1.384	1.539	1.710	1.898	2.105	2.332	2.580	2.853	3.152	3.479	3.836	4.226	4.652	5.117	7.430	11.642	17.921	27.144
12	1.127	1.268	1.426	1.601	1.796	2.012	2.252	2.518	2.813	3.138	3.498	3.896	4.334	4.818	5.350	5.936	8.916	14.552	23.298	36.644
13	1.138	1.294	1.469	1.665	1.886	2.133	2.410	2.720	3.066	3.452	3.883	4.363	4.898	5.492	6.153	6.886	10.699	18.190	30.287	49.469
14	1.149	1.319	1.513	1.732	1.980	2.261	2.579	2.937	3.342	3.797	4.310	4.887	5.535	6.261	7.076	7.987	12.839	22.737	39.373	66.784
15	1.161	1.346	1.558	1.801	2.079	2.397	2.759	3.172	3.642	4.177	4.785	5.474	6.254	7.138	8.137	9.265	15.407	28.422	51.185	90.158
16	1.173	1.373	1.605	1.873	2.183	2.540	2.952	3.426	3.970	4.595	5.311	6.130	7.067	8.137	9.358	10.748	18.488	35.527	66.541	121.713
17	1.184	1.400	1.653	1.948	2.292	2.693	3.159	3.700	4.328	5.054	5.895	6.866	7.986	9.276	10.761	12.468	22.186	44.409	86.503	164.312
18	1.196	1.428	1.702	2.026	2.407	2.854	3.380	3.996	4.717	5.560	6.543	7.690	9.024	10.575	12.375	14.462	26.623	55.511	112.454	221.822
19	1.208	1.457	1.753	2.107	2.527	3.026	3.616	4.316	5.142	6.116	7.263	8.613	10.197	12.055	14.232	16.776	31.948	69.389	146.190	299.459
20	1.220	1.486	1.806	2.191	2.653	3.207	3.870	4.661	5.604	6.727	8.062	9.646	11.523	13.743	16.366	19.461	38.337	86.736	190.047	404.270
21	1.232	1.516	1.860	2.279	2.786	3.399	4.140	5.034	6.109	7.400	8.949	10.804	13.021	15.667	18.821	22.574	46.005	108.420	247.061	545.764
22	1.245	1.546	1.916	2.370	2.925	3.603	4.430	5.436	6.658	8.140	9.933	12.100	14.713	17.861	21.644	26.186	55.205	135.525	321.178	736.781
23	1.257	1.577	1.974	2.465	3.071	3.820	4.740	5.871	7.258	8.954	11.026	13.552	16.626	20.361	24.891	30.376	66.247	169.407	417.531	994.653
24	1.270	1.608	2.033	2.563	3.225	4.049	5.072	6.341	7.911	9.850	12.239	15.178	18.788	23.212	28.625	35.236	79.496	211.758	542.791	1342.781
25	1.282	1.641	2.094	2.666	3.386	4.292	5.427	6.848	8.623	10.834	13.585	17.000	21.230	26.461	32.918	40.874	95.395	264.698	705.627	1812.754
30	1.348	1.811	2.427	3.243	4.322	5.743	7.612	10.062	13.267	17.449	22.892	29.960	39.115	50.949	66.210	85.849	237.373	807.793	2619.936	8128.426
35	1.417	2.000	2.814	3.946	5.516	7.686	10.676	14.785	20.413	28.102	38.574	52.799	72.066	98.097	133.172	180.311	590.657	2465.189	9727.598	36648.051
40	1.489	2.208	3.262	4.801	7.040	10.285	14.974	21.724	31.408	45.258	64.999	93.049	132.776	188.876	267.856	378.715	1469.740	7523.156	36117.754	163433.875
45	1.565	2.438	3.781	5.841	8.985	13.764	21.002	31.920	48.325	72.888	109.527	163.985	244.629	363.662	538.752	795.429	3657.176	22958.844	134102.187	*
50	1.645	2.691	4.384	7.106	11.467	18.419	29.456	46.900	74.354	117.386	184.559	288.996	450.711	700.197	1083.619	1670.669	9100.191	70064.812	497910.125	*

Using the calculator to compute the future value of a single amount

Before you begin, make sure to clear the memory, ensure that you are in the correct mode, and set the number of decimal places that you want (usually two for dollar-related accuracy).

SAMPLE PROBLEM You place $800 in a savings account at 6 percent compounded annually. What is your account balance at the end of five years?

Hewlett-Packard HP 12C, 17 BII, and 19 BII[a]

Inputs: | 800 | | 5 | | 6 |
Functions: | CHS | PV | | n | | i | | FV |
Outputs: [1070.58]

Texas Instruments BA-35, BAII, BAII Plus[b]

Inputs: | 800 | | 5 | | 6 |
Functions: | +/− | PV | | N | | %i | | CPT | | FV |
Outputs: [1070.58]

[a] For the 17 BII and 19 BII you would use the | +/− | key instead of the | 2nd | key instead of the | CHS | key, the | N | key instead of the | n | key, and the | I%YR | key instead of the | i | key.

[b] For the Texas Instrument BAII you would use the | %i | key instead of the | %i | key. When using the Texas Instruments BAII Plus, make sure that your calculator is set to 1 *payment per year* | I/Y | key to work with annual compounding.

TABLE A7-2 Future-Value Interest Factors for a One-Dollar Annuity Compounded at k Percent for n Periods: $FVIFA_{k,n} = \sum_{t=1}^{n} (1 + k)^{t-1}$

Period	1%	2%	3%	4%	5%	6%	7%	8%	9%	10%	11%	12%	13%	14%	15%	16%	20%	25%	30%	35%
1	1.000	1.000	1.000	1.000	1.000	1.000	1.000	1.000	1.000	1.000	1.000	1.000	1.000	1.000	1.000	1.000	1.000	1.000	1.000	1.000
2	2.010	2.020	2.030	2.040	2.050	2.060	2.070	2.080	2.090	2.100	2.110	2.120	2.130	2.140	2.150	2.160	2.200	2.250	2.300	2.350
3	3.030	3.060	3.091	3.122	3.152	3.184	3.215	3.246	3.278	3.310	3.342	3.374	3.407	3.440	3.472	3.506	3.640	3.813	3.990	4.172
4	4.060	4.122	4.184	4.246	4.310	4.375	4.440	4.506	4.573	4.641	4.710	4.779	4.850	4.921	4.993	5.066	5.368	5.766	6.187	6.633
5	5.101	5.204	5.309	5.416	5.526	5.637	5.751	5.867	5.985	6.105	6.228	6.353	6.480	6.610	6.742	6.877	7.442	8.207	9.043	9.954
6	6.152	6.308	6.468	6.633	6.802	6.975	7.153	7.336	7.523	7.716	7.913	8.115	8.323	8.535	8.754	8.977	9.930	11.259	12.756	14.438
7	7.214	7.434	7.662	7.898	8.142	8.394	8.654	8.923	9.200	9.487	9.783	10.089	10.405	10.730	11.067	11.414	12.916	15.073	17.583	20.492
8	8.286	8.583	8.892	9.214	9.549	9.897	10.260	10.637	11.028	11.436	11.859	12.300	12.757	13.233	13.727	14.240	16.499	19.842	23.858	28.664
9	9.368	9.755	10.159	10.583	11.027	11.491	11.978	12.488	13.021	13.579	14.164	14.776	15.416	16.085	16.786	17.518	20.799	25.802	32.015	39.696
10	10.462	10.950	11.464	12.006	12.578	13.181	13.816	14.487	15.193	15.937	16.722	17.549	18.420	19.337	20.304	21.321	25.959	33.253	42.619	54.590
11	11.567	12.169	12.808	13.486	14.207	14.972	15.784	16.645	17.560	18.531	19.561	20.655	21.814	23.044	24.349	25.733	32.150	42.566	56.405	74.696
12	12.682	13.412	14.192	15.026	15.917	16.870	17.888	18.977	20.141	21.384	22.713	24.133	25.650	27.271	29.001	30.850	39.580	54.208	74.326	101.840
13	13.809	14.680	15.618	16.627	17.713	18.882	20.141	21.495	22.953	24.523	26.211	28.029	29.984	32.088	34.352	36.786	48.496	68.760	97.624	138.484
14	14.947	15.974	17.086	18.292	19.598	21.015	22.550	24.215	26.019	27.975	30.095	32.392	34.882	37.581	40.504	43.672	59.196	86.949	127.912	187.953
15	16.097	17.293	18.599	20.023	21.578	23.276	25.129	27.152	29.361	31.772	34.405	37.280	40.417	43.842	47.580	51.659	72.035	109.687	167.285	254.737
16	17.258	18.639	20.157	21.824	23.657	25.672	27.888	30.324	33.003	35.949	39.190	42.753	46.671	50.980	55.717	60.925	87.442	139.109	218.470	344.895
17	18.430	20.012	21.761	23.697	25.840	28.213	30.840	33.750	36.973	40.544	44.500	48.883	53.738	59.117	65.075	71.673	105.930	173.636	285.011	466.608
18	19.614	21.412	23.414	25.645	28.132	30.905	33.999	37.450	41.301	45.599	50.396	55.749	61.724	68.393	75.836	84.140	128.116	218.045	371.514	630.920
19	20.811	22.840	25.117	27.671	30.539	33.760	37.379	41.446	46.018	51.158	56.939	63.439	70.748	78.968	88.211	98.603	154.739	273.556	483.968	852.741
20	22.019	24.297	26.870	29.778	33.066	36.785	40.995	45.762	51.159	57.274	64.202	72.052	80.946	91.024	102.443	115.379	186.687	342.945	630.157	1152.200
21	23.239	25.783	28.676	31.969	35.719	39.992	44.865	50.422	56.764	64.002	72.264	81.698	92.468	104.767	118.809	134.840	225.024	429.681	820.204	1556.470
22	24.471	27.299	30.536	34.248	38.505	43.392	49.005	55.456	62.872	71.402	81.213	92.502	105.489	120.434	137.630	157.414	271.028	538.101	1067.265	2102.234
23	25.716	28.845	32.452	36.618	41.430	46.995	53.435	60.893	69.531	79.542	91.147	104.602	120.203	138.295	159.274	183.600	326.234	673.626	1388.443	2839.014
24	26.973	30.421	34.426	39.082	44.501	50.815	58.176	66.764	76.789	88.496	102.173	118.154	136.829	158.656	184.166	213.976	392.480	843.032	1805.975	3833.667
25	28.243	32.030	36.459	41.645	47.726	54.864	63.248	73.105	84.699	98.346	114.412	133.333	155.616	181.867	212.790	249.212	471.976	1054.791	2348.765	5176.445
30	34.784	40.567	47.575	56.084	66.438	79.057	94.459	113.282	136.305	164.491	199.018	241.330	293.192	356.778	434.738	530.306	1181.865	3227.172	8729.805	23221.258
35	41.659	49.994	60.461	73.651	90.318	111.432	138.234	172.314	215.705	271.018	341.583	431.658	546.663	693.552	881.152	1120.699	2948.294	9856.746	32422.090	104134.500
40	48.885	60.401	75.400	95.024	120.797	154.758	199.630	259.052	337.872	442.580	581.812	767.080	1013.667	1341.979	1779.048	2360.724	7343.715	30088.621	120389.375	*
45	56.479	71.891	92.718	121.027	159.695	212.737	285.741	386.497	525.840	718.881	986.613	1358.208	1874.086	2590.464	3585.031	4965.191	18280.914	91831.312	447005.062	*
50	64.461	84.577	112.794	152.664	209.341	290.325	406.516	573.756	815.051	1163.865	1668.723	2399.975	3459.344	4994.301	7217.488	10415.449	45496.094		*	*

Using the calculator to compute future value of an annuity

Before you begin, make sure to clear the memory, ensure that you are in the correct mode, and set the number of decimal places that you want (usually two for dollar-related accuracy).

SAMPLE PROBLEM You want to know what the future value will be at the end of five years if you place five end-of-year deposits of $1,000 in an account paying 7 percent annually. What is your account balance at the end of five years?

Hewlett-Packard HP 12C, 17 BII, and 19 BII[a]

Inputs: `1000` `5` `7`

Functions: `CHS` `PMT` `n` `i` `FV`

Outputs: `5750.74`

Texas Instruments BA-35, BAII, BAII Plus[b]

Inputs: `1000` `5` `7`

Functions: `+/-` `PMT` `N` `%i` `PV` `CPT` `FV`

Outputs: `5750.74`

[a] For the 17 BII and 19 BII you would use the `+/-` key instead of the `CHS` key, and the `N` key instead of the `n` key, and the `I%YR` key instead of the `i` key.

[b] For the Texas Instrument BAII you would use the `CPT` key, for the Texas Instruments BAII Plus you would use the `2nd` key instead of the `CPT` key. When using the Texas Instruments BAII Plus, make sure that your calculator is set to *1 percent per year* `1/Y` key to work with annual compounding.

TABLE A7-3 Present-Value Interest Factors for One Dollar Discounted at k Percent for n Periods: $PVIF_{k,n} = \dfrac{1}{(1 + k)^n}$

Period	1%	2%	3%	4%	5%	6%	7%	8%	9%	10%	11%	12%	13%	14%	15%	16%	17%	18%	19%	20%	25%	30%	35%
1	.990	.980	.971	.962	.952	.943	.935	.926	.917	.909	.901	.893	.885	.877	.870	.862	.855	.847	.840	.833	.800	.769	.741
2	.980	.961	.943	.925	.907	.890	.873	.857	.842	.826	.812	.797	.783	.769	.756	.743	.731	.718	.706	.694	.640	.592	.549
3	.971	.942	.915	.889	.864	.840	.816	.794	.772	.751	.731	.712	.693	.675	.658	.641	.624	.609	.593	.579	.512	.455	.406
4	.961	.924	.888	.855	.823	.792	.763	.735	.708	.683	.659	.636	.613	.592	.572	.552	.534	.516	.499	.482	.410	.350	.301
5	.951	.906	.863	.822	.784	.747	.713	.681	.650	.621	.593	.567	.543	.519	.497	.476	.456	.437	.419	.402	.328	.269	.223
6	.942	.888	.837	.790	.746	.705	.666	.630	.596	.564	.535	.507	.480	.456	.432	.410	.390	.370	.352	.335	.262	.207	.165
7	.933	.871	.813	.760	.711	.665	.623	.583	.547	.513	.482	.452	.425	.400	.376	.354	.333	.314	.296	.279	.210	.159	.122
8	.923	.853	.789	.731	.677	.627	.582	.540	.502	.467	.434	.404	.376	.351	.327	.305	.285	.266	.249	.233	.168	.123	.091
9	.914	.837	.766	.703	.645	.592	.544	.500	.460	.424	.391	.361	.333	.308	.284	.263	.243	.225	.209	.194	.134	.094	.067
10	.905	.820	.744	.676	.614	.558	.508	.463	.422	.386	.352	.322	.295	.270	.247	.227	.208	.191	.176	.162	.107	.073	.050
11	.896	.804	.722	.650	.585	.527	.475	.429	.388	.350	.317	.287	.261	.237	.215	.195	.178	.162	.148	.135	.086	.056	.037
12	.887	.789	.701	.625	.557	.497	.444	.397	.356	.319	.286	.257	.231	.208	.187	.168	.152	.137	.124	.112	.069	.043	.027
13	.879	.773	.681	.601	.530	.469	.415	.368	.326	.290	.258	.229	.204	.182	.163	.145	.130	.116	.104	.093	.055	.033	.020
14	.870	.758	.661	.577	.505	.442	.388	.340	.299	.263	.232	.205	.181	.160	.141	.125	.111	.099	.088	.078	.044	.025	.015
15	.861	.743	.642	.555	.481	.417	.362	.315	.275	.239	.209	.183	.160	.140	.123	.108	.095	.084	.074	.065	.035	.020	.011
16	.853	.728	.623	.534	.458	.394	.339	.292	.252	.218	.188	.163	.141	.123	.107	.093	.081	.071	.062	.054	.028	.015	.008
17	.844	.714	.605	.513	.436	.371	.317	.270	.231	.198	.170	.146	.125	.108	.093	.080	.069	.060	.052	.045	.023	.012	.006
18	.836	.700	.587	.494	.416	.350	.296	.250	.212	.180	.153	.130	.111	.095	.081	.069	.059	.051	.044	.038	.018	.009	.005
19	.828	.686	.570	.475	.396	.331	.277	.232	.194	.164	.138	.116	.098	.083	.070	.060	.051	.043	.037	.031	.014	.007	.003
20	.820	.673	.554	.456	.377	.312	.258	.215	.178	.149	.124	.104	.087	.073	.061	.051	.043	.037	.031	.026	.012	.005	.002
21	.811	.660	.538	.439	.359	.294	.242	.199	.164	.135	.112	.093	.077	.064	.053	.044	.037	.031	.026	.022	.009	.004	.002
22	.803	.647	.522	.422	.342	.278	.226	.184	.150	.123	.101	.083	.068	.056	.046	.038	.032	.026	.022	.018	.007	.003	.001
23	.795	.634	.507	.406	.326	.262	.211	.170	.138	.112	.091	.074	.060	.049	.040	.033	.027	.022	.018	.015	.006	.002	.001
24	.788	.622	.492	.390	.310	.247	.197	.158	.126	.102	.082	.066	.053	.043	.035	.028	.023	.019	.015	.013	.005	.002	.001
25	.780	.610	.478	.375	.295	.233	.184	.146	.116	.092	.074	.059	.047	.038	.030	.024	.020	.016	.013	.010	.004	.001	*
30	.742	.552	.412	.308	.231	.174	.131	.099	.075	.057	.044	.033	.026	.020	.015	.012	.009	.007	.005	.004	.001	*	*
35	.706	.500	.355	.253	.181	.130	.094	.068	.049	.036	.026	.019	.014	.010	.008	.006	.004	.003	.002	.002	*	*	*
40	.672	.453	.307	.208	.142	.097	.067	.046	.032	.022	.015	.011	.008	.005	.004	.003	.002	.001	.001	.001	*	*	*
45	.639	.410	.264	.171	.111	.073	.048	.031	.021	.014	.009	.006	.004	.003	.002	.001	.001	.001	*	*	*	*	*
50	.608	.372	.228	.141	.087	.054	.034	.021	.013	.009	.005	.003	.002	.001	.001	.001	*	*	*	*	*	*	*

*$PVIF$ is zero to three decimal places.

Using the calculator to compute the present value of a single amount

Before you begin, make sure to clear the memory, ensure that you are in the correct mode, and set the number of decimal places that you want (usually two for dollar-related accuracy).

SAMPLE PROBLEM   Calculate the present value of $1,700 to be received in eight years, assuming an 8 percent opportunity cost.

Hewlett-Packard HP 12C, 17 BII, and 19 BII[a]

Inputs:	1700		8		8	

Functions:	CHS	FV	n	i	PV

Outputs:				918.46

Texas Instruments BA-35, BAII, BAII Plus[b]

Inputs:	1700		8		8	

Functions:	+/−	FV	N	%i	CPT	PV

Outputs:				918.46

[a] For the 17 BII and 19 BII you would use the +/− key instead of the CHS key, the N key instead of the n key, and the I% YR key instead of the i key.

[b] For the Texas Instrument BAII you would use the 2nd key instead of the CPT key; for the Texas Instruments BAII Plus you would use the %i key instead of the %i key. When using the Texas Instruments BAII Plus, make sure that your calculator is set to 1 payment per year (UY key) to work with annual compounding.

TABLE A7-4 Present-Value Interest Factors for a One-Dollar Annuity Discounted at *k* Percent for *n* Periods:

$$PVIFA_{k,n} = \sum_{t=1}^{n} \frac{1}{(1+k)^t}$$

Period	1%	2%	3%	4%	5%	6%	7%	8%	9%	10%	11%	12%	13%	14%	15%	16%	17%	18%	19%	20%	25%	30%	35%
1	.990	.980	.971	.962	.952	.943	.935	.926	.917	.909	.901	.893	.885	.877	.870	.862	.855	.847	.840	.833	.800	.769	.741
2	1.970	1.942	1.913	1.886	1.859	1.833	1.808	1.783	1.759	1.736	1.713	1.690	1.668	1.647	1.626	1.605	1.585	1.566	1.547	1.528	1.440	1.361	1.289
3	2.941	2.884	2.829	2.775	2.723	2.673	2.624	2.577	2.531	2.487	2.444	2.402	2.361	2.322	2.283	2.246	2.210	2.174	2.140	2.106	1.952	1.816	1.696
4	3.902	3.808	3.717	3.630	3.546	3.465	3.387	3.312	3.240	3.170	3.102	3.037	2.974	2.914	2.855	2.798	2.743	2.690	2.639	2.589	2.362	2.166	1.997
5	4.853	4.713	4.580	4.452	4.329	4.212	4.100	3.993	3.890	3.791	3.696	3.605	3.517	3.433	3.352	3.274	3.199	3.127	3.058	2.991	2.689	2.436	2.220
6	5.795	5.601	5.417	5.242	5.076	4.917	4.767	4.623	4.486	4.355	4.231	4.111	3.998	3.889	3.784	3.685	3.589	3.498	3.410	3.326	2.951	2.643	2.385
7	6.728	6.472	6.230	6.002	5.786	5.582	5.389	5.206	5.033	4.868	4.712	4.564	4.423	4.288	4.160	4.039	3.922	3.812	3.706	3.605	3.161	2.802	2.508
8	7.652	7.326	7.020	6.733	6.463	6.210	5.971	5.747	5.535	5.335	5.146	4.968	4.799	4.639	4.487	4.344	4.207	4.078	3.954	3.837	3.329	2.925	2.598
9	8.566	8.162	7.786	7.435	7.108	6.802	6.515	6.247	5.995	5.759	5.537	5.328	5.132	4.946	4.772	4.607	4.451	4.303	4.163	4.031	3.463	3.019	2.665
10	9.471	8.983	8.530	8.111	7.722	7.360	7.024	6.710	6.418	6.145	5.889	5.650	5.426	5.216	5.019	4.833	4.659	4.494	4.339	4.192	3.570	3.092	2.715
11	10.368	9.787	9.253	8.760	8.306	7.887	7.499	7.139	6.805	6.495	6.207	5.938	5.687	5.453	5.234	5.029	4.836	4.656	4.486	4.327	3.656	3.147	2.752
12	11.255	10.575	9.954	9.385	8.863	8.384	7.943	7.536	7.161	6.814	6.492	6.194	5.918	5.660	5.421	5.197	4.988	4.793	4.611	4.439	3.725	3.190	2.779
13	12.134	11.348	10.635	9.986	9.394	8.853	8.358	7.904	7.487	7.013	6.750	6.424	6.122	5.842	5.583	5.342	5.118	4.910	4.715	4.533	3.780	3.223	2.799
14	13.004	12.106	11.296	10.563	9.899	9.295	8.745	8.244	7.786	7.367	6.982	6.628	6.302	6.002	5.724	5.468	5.229	5.008	4.802	4.611	3.824	3.249	2.814
15	13.865	12.849	11.938	11.118	10.380	9.712	9.108	8.560	8.061	7.606	7.191	6.811	6.462	6.142	5.847	5.575	5.324	5.092	4.876	4.675	3.859	3.268	2.825
16	14.718	13.578	12.561	11.652	10.838	10.106	9.447	8.851	8.313	7.824	7.379	6.974	6.604	6.265	5.954	5.668	5.405	5.162	4.938	4.730	3.887	3.283	2.834
17	15.562	14.292	13.166	12.166	11.274	10.477	9.763	9.122	8.544	8.022	7.549	7.120	6.729	6.373	6.047	5.749	5.475	5.222	4.990	4.775	3.910	3.295	2.840
18	16.398	14.992	13.754	12.659	11.690	10.828	10.059	9.372	8.756	8.201	7.702	7.250	6.840	6.467	6.128	5.818	5.534	5.273	5.033	4.812	3.928	3.304	2.844
19	17.226	15.679	14.324	13.134	12.085	11.158	10.336	9.604	8.950	8.365	7.839	7.366	6.938	6.550	6.198	5.877	5.584	5.316	5.070	4.843	3.942	3.311	2.848
20	18.046	16.352	14.878	13.590	12.462	11.470	10.594	9.818	9.129	8.514	7.963	7.469	7.025	6.623	6.259	5.929	5.628	5.353	5.101	4.870	3.954	3.316	2.850
21	18.857	17.011	15.415	14.029	12.821	11.764	10.836	10.017	9.292	8.649	8.075	7.562	7.102	6.687	6.312	5.973	5.665	5.384	5.127	4.891	3.963	3.320	2.852
22	19.661	17.658	15.937	14.451	13.163	12.042	11.061	10.201	9.442	8.772	8.176	7.645	7.170	6.743	6.359	6.011	5.696	5.410	5.149	4.909	3.970	3.323	2.853
23	20.456	18.292	16.444	14.857	13.489	12.303	11.272	10.371	9.580	8.883	8.266	7.718	7.230	6.792	6.399	6.044	5.723	5.432	5.167	4.925	3.976	3.325	2.854
24	21.244	18.914	16.936	15.247	13.799	12.550	11.469	10.529	9.707	8.985	8.348	7.784	7.283	6.835	6.434	6.073	5.746	5.451	5.182	4.937	3.981	3.327	2.855
25	22.023	19.524	17.413	15.622	14.094	12.783	11.654	10.675	9.823	9.077	8.422	7.843	7.330	6.873	6.464	6.097	5.766	5.467	5.195	4.948	3.985	3.329	2.856
30	25.808	22.396	19.601	17.292	15.373	13.765	12.409	11.258	10.274	9.427	8.694	8.055	7.496	7.003	6.566	6.177	5.829	5.517	5.235	4.979	3.995	3.332	2.857
35	29.409	24.999	21.487	18.665	16.374	14.498	12.948	11.655	10.567	9.644	8.855	8.176	7.586	7.070	6.617	6.215	5.858	5.539	5.251	4.992	3.998	3.333	2.857
40	32.835	27.356	23.115	19.793	17.159	15.046	13.332	11.925	10.757	9.779	8.951	8.244	7.634	7.105	6.642	6.233	5.871	5.548	5.258	4.997	3.999	3.333	2.857
45	36.095	29.490	24.519	20.720	17.774	15.456	13.606	12.108	10.881	9.863	9.008	8.283	7.661	7.123	6.654	6.242	5.877	5.552	5.261	4.999	4.000	3.333	2.857
50	39.196	31.424	25.730	21.482	18.256	15.762	13.801	12.233	10.962	9.915	9.042	8.304	7.675	7.133	6.661	6.246	5.880	5.554	5.262	4.999	4.000	3.333	2.857

Using the calculator to compute the present value of an annuity

Before you begin, make sure to clear the memory, ensure that you are in the correct mode, and set the number of decimal places that you want (usually two for dollar-related accuracy).

SAMPLE PROBLEM You want to know what the present value will be of an annuity of $700 per year at the end of each year for five years, given a required return of 8 percent.

Hewlett-Packard HP 12C, 17 BII, and 19 BII[a]

Inputs:	700	5	8		
Functions:	CHS	PMT	n	i	PV
Outputs:					2794.90

Texas Instruments BA-35, BAII, BAII Plus[b]

Inputs:	700	5	8		
Functions:	+/-	PMT	N	%i	CPT
Outputs:					2794.90

[a]For the 17 BII and 19 BII you would use the +/- key instead of the CHS key, the N key instead of the n key, and the I% YR key instead of the i key.

[b]For the Texas Instrument BAII you would use the 2nd key instead of the CPT key; for the Texas Instruments BAII Plus you would use the I/Y key instead of the %i key. When using the Texas Instruments BAII Plus, make sure that your calculator is set to 1 payment per year I/Y key to work with annual compounding.

• ANSWERS TO THE WORKSHEETS·····

Note: Answers will vary slightly due to rounding or depending on the present and future value tables used.

Worksheet 1

LINE	FACTOR	VALUE
A	1.191	$ 1,191
B	2.159	2,159
C	6.727	6,727
D	1.469	7,345
E	3.172	15,886
F	4.661	23,305
G	9.646	96,460
H	10.062	100,620
I	21.724	217,240

Worksheet 2

LINE	FACTOR	VALUE
A	1.0	$ 100.00
B	15.193	1,519.30
C	12.578	1,257.80
D	14.487	17,384.40
E	15.937	19,124.40
F	57.274	68,728.80
G	164.490	197,388.00
H	442.580	531,096.00
I	12.300	22,140.00
J	33.066	59,518.80
K	[5.985]	5,386.50
L	[7.153]	5,150.16
M	[14.164]	25,495.20

Worksheet 3

LINE	FACTOR	PRESENT VALUE
A	0.926	$ 46,300
B	0.857	42,850
C	0.794	39,700

Worksheet 3 (continued)

LINE	FACTOR	PRESENT VALUE
D	0.735	36,750
E	0.681	34,050
F	0.630	31,500
G	0.583	29,150
H	0.540	27,000
I	0.500	25,000
J	0.463	23,150
K	0.429	21,450
L	0.397	19,850
M	0.368	18,400
N	0.340	17,000
O	0.315	15,750
P	0.292	14,600
Q	0.270	13,500
R	0.250	12,500
S	0.232	11,500
T	0.215	10,750
Total		490,750

(a) 45.762
(b) $2,288,100
(c) 4.661
(d) $4,661,000
(e) 45.762
(f) $54,914.40
(g) 10.062
(h) $552,548.69
(i) $22,800
(j) 26.87
(k) $32,244
(l) 3.243
(m) $104,567.29

Worksheet 4

LINE	FACTOR	ANNUAL PAYMENT	MONTHLY PAYMENT
B	2.577	5,044.63	420.39
C	5.389	3,340.00	278.35

Worksheet 4 (continued)

LINE	FACTOR	ANNUAL PAYMENT	MONTHLY PAYMENT
D	6.418	4,985.97	415.50
E	8.560	7,009.35	584.11
F	9.818	6,111.22	509.27
G	11.258	5,329.54	444.13
H	9.108	10,430.39	869.20
I	10.594	8,967.34	747.28
J	12.409	7,655.73	637.98
K	5.650	13,274.34	1,106.20
L	6.811	11,011.60	917.63
M	7.469	10.041.50	836.79
N	8.055	9.310.99	775.92

	FACTOR	MORTGAGE
A	3.890	$10,036.20
B	2.624	10,076.16
C	12.409	89,334.80
D	8.560	82,176.00
E	10.274	67,808.40
F	2.487	8,207.10
G	3.127	5,628.60

Worksheet 5

Mary Jones

(a) $1300
(b) 33.066 (Table A7–2)
(c) $42,985.50
(d) $960
(e) 51.159 (Table A7–2)
(f) $49,112.64
(g) 2.531 (Table A7–4)
(h) $1,777.95
(i) $148.16
(j) 6.170 (Table A7–4)
(k) $4,172.88
(l) $347.74

(m) 6.418 (Table A7–4)

(n) $3,116.24

(o) $259.87

(p) $637.98 (Table A7–4, 12.409)

(q) $275,227.23 (Table A7–1, 5.604)

(r) $324,357.12 (Table A7–2, 337.872)

Willie Winkle

(a) $76,276.80 (Table A7–4, 10.594)

(b) $89,344.80 (Table A7–4, 12.409)

(c) $79,939.60 (Table A7–4, 15.373)

(d) $30,494.40 (Table A7–2, 6.353)

(e) $9,019.20 (Table A7–2, 5.637)

(f) $25,740.80 (Table A7–1, 2.854)

(g) $24,070 (Table A7–1, 2.407)

(h) $305,369.27 (Table A7–1, 3.820)

(i) $3,681,984 (Table A7–2, 767.080)

(j) $1,610,073.83 (Table A7–1, 52.799)

(k) $144,030 (Table A7–1, 4.801)

(l) 20.8 (Table A7–3, .208)

(m) $765,852.67 (Table A7–3)

Lyle and Nyla

(a) $49,282.80 (Table A7–2, 5.867)

(b) $20,293.20 (Table A7–2, 5.637)

(c) $884.33 [($112,424.00/10.594)/12]
(Table A7–4, 10.594)

(d) $754.98 (Table A7–4, 12.409)

(e) $885,160 (Table A7–2, 442.58)

(f) $436,176 (Table A7–2, 136.305)

(g) $1,871,870 (Table A7–1, 10.285)

(h) $3,352,258 (Table A7–1, 18.419)

(i) $176,000 (Table A7–1, 7.040)

(j) $286,675 (Table A7–1, 11.467)

(k) $22,528 (Table A7–1, 7.040)

(l) $10,438.40 (Table A7–1, 3.262)

Monty Markowitz

(a) $29,505 (Table A7–1, 1.967)

(b) $25,589.20 (Table A7–2, 4.921)

(c) $1,158,116.94 (Table A7–2, 45.258)

(d) $2,381,049.47 (Table A7–2, 93.049)

(e) $4,833,185.74 (Table A7–2, 188.876)

(f) $336.34 (Table A7–4, 4.212)

(g) $523.81 (Table A7–4, 12.409)

(h) $76,497.60 (Table A7–2, 15.973)

(i) $274,915.20 (Table A7–2, 57.274)

(j) $2,124,384 (Table A7–2, 442.58)

(k) $347,584 (Table A7–1, 21.724)

(l) $623.05 (Table A7–4, 8.560)

(m) $203,004.61 (Table A7–2, 27.152)

(n) $1,390,182.42 (Table A7–1, 6.848)

(o) $1,015,800 (Table A7–1, 3.386)

(p) $290,406.80 8%
(1,158,116.01 + 2,124,384 + 347,584)

(q) $340,054.80 (Table A7–3, 10.675)

Ben Banks

(a) $169,000 (Table A7–1, 3.380)

(b) $86,922 (Table A7–2, 14.487)

(c) $23,976 (Table A7–1, 3.996)

(d) 9% (85/18 = 4.722) (Table A7–1, 4.722)

(e) 12% (9,228,000/1,200,000 = 7.65)
(Table A7–1, 7.65)

(f) $810,892 (Table A7–2, 337.872)

(g) $1,086,845 (Table A7–2, 434.738)

(h) $869.35 (Table A7–4, 6.710)

(i) $681.46 (Table A7–4, 8.560)

(j) $594.15 (Table A7–4, 9.818)

(k) $518.15 (Table A7–4, 11.258)

(l) $69,920.40 (Table A7–4, 10.594)

(m) $81,899.40 (Table A7–4, 12.409)

(n) 7% (Table A7–3, .2575)

(o) 4% (Table A7–1, 2.0)

(p) $46,610 (Table A7–1, 4.661)

Worksheet 6

(a) 13.765 (Table A7–4)

(b) $99,108

(c) 3.243 (Table A7–1)

(d) $289,745.19

(e) $513,296.71 (Table A7–1, 5.743)

(f) $65,577.60 (Table A7–4, 9.108)

(g) $50,572.80 (Table A7–4, 7.024)

(h) $29,520 (Table A7–4, 4.1)

(i) 1.480 (Table A7–1)

(j) $10,656

(k) $132,230.04 (Table A7–4, 12.409)

(l) $55,953.50 ($132,230.04 − 76,276.80)

(m) $951,209.50 (Table A7–1, 17.00)

8 Marketing: A Customer ••••••• Information Girder

Chapter Objectives

- To emphasize the importance of quality of product and service in a successful, integrated small business marketing strategy.

- To introduce a positioning model utilizing the marketing mix variables with an emphasis on small business.

The functional area of finance is important in understanding the relationships of numbers. It is also a requirement if a business venture is ever to get off the ground. That is not to minimize the importance of the accounting function or the importance of other management and personnel issues. In my interviews with small business owners, almost all of the entrepreneurs explained that to be successful, they had to understand the numbers. They usually began by explaining how they went about marketing their product or service. Marketing is a job that never seems to go away or ever finally be completed. It is pervasive throughout the business. The net result of the marketing effort becomes the initial input number in determining revenue for the income statement and is one of the critical source numbers from which financial ratios are computed, which in turn relate revenue to expense.

In most beginning-level accounting courses we learn that total revenue is found by multiplying the number of units sold by their respective unit price. That definition is correct but is limited in some respects. Another perspective of the revenue equation is to define revenue as equal to the level of acceptance of the firm's products and/or services by the consumer in the marketplace. The implementation of that definition within the context of small business is to make every effort to enhance the level of acceptance of your firm's product or service in your defined market. Such an effort incorporates the marketing concept. It also embodies the bridge model of this book.

One major premise of this book is that for small business, the best competitive position is to produce products or services that are of the highest possible quality. The quality pillars of success demonstrate this premise. The model suggests that high levels of quality are not stand-alone components. A decree by management that quality must exist does not make it happen. Quality is built and is pervasive. Quality is difficult to achieve and difficult to maintain. Quality is more than machines and systems; it must be supported by people. The human relationships pillars demonstrate that for a firm to achieve quality, it must have good human systems grounded on good human relationships both internally and externally.

Externally, a business is supported by suppliers, creditors, the surrounding community, and many other stakeholders. A business must also depend on those outsiders to support efforts to produce the products and services that they produce. Without good external support relationships to support the flow of materials into the production process and to support the flow of finished goods into the distribution system, the quality and timeliness of products to the end user will be interrupted.

The quality of any firm's output begins as a function of the quality of the inputs. The starting point is the quality of the raw materials, followed by the quality of the production process, which in turn hinges on the quality of the internal relationships: worker to worker, worker to management, and management to management. The quality of the internal relationships supports the production and distribution process. High employee turnover, high absenteeism, and low morale are indicators of a strain on internal relationships; they have a negative effect on quality. To do a good job of producing a high-quality product or service, the people producing the product or service need to care about what they are doing. High-quality human relationships supported by high-quality systems tend to produce high-quality products or services, which in turn will support a higher level of acceptance by the consumer in the marketplace, ultimately producing higher levels of revenue and profitability. The firm must still pay heed to the functional areas of business, and from the marketing perspective employ the marketing concept and produce what people need and want.

I would like to propose that from a strategic marketing perspective, quality is even more important to the success of small business than it is to big business.

Small business must generally seek a niche to be successful. A successful strategy often employed by small business is to raise the level of their service to a degree that sets them apart from the competition: service based on a personal relationship with customers, from a level of quality of service and responsiveness to the customer that cannot easily be duplicated, especially by big business, which tends to be somewhat impersonal.

• POSITIONING STRATEGIES · · · · · · · · · ·

Every business assumes a position in the marketplace, and every customer mentally positions a business or a business's product or service in his or her mind. We often refer to this as a firm's image. A product name and a visual image come into your mind, and personal judgment is placed on the product. A firm whose image in the minds of customers is the same as the image they have attempted to project has done a good job of positioning. It should be obvious that it would be extremely difficult to position a low-priced, low-quality product as a prestige item—which is something it is not. Positioning is not just related to marketing but is the culmination and synthesis of all the output generated by a firm. Marketing a firm's output correctly will position the firm's products or services correctly in the minds of the firm's customers.

For most small businesses, and for most large businesses, for that matter, only four main strategies exist with regard to price and quality of a firm's products and services. The following is an attempt to demonstrate that major problems would tend to exist should the small business owner attempt any strategy other than strategy A.

A. High price and high quality
B. Low price and high quality
C. Low quality and low price
D. Low quality and high price

These strategies could be expanded to include a medium-price, medium-quality strategy, or expanded further to a type of continuum with regard to price and quality. They are easiest to comprehend by evaluating the extremes.

A high-price, high-quality strategy (A) is most conducive to the bridge model format of this book. It tends to be the most specialized and the most difficult to replicate by the competition. By design this strategy works well for the type of business that can carve out a market niche through a specialized product or level of personal service. The craftsmen in any of the trade areas who have perfected their skill to the master level fit well into this mode. To be successful, the market need be only large enough to supply work for one person and or a small crew. Demand for the service can often be generated simply by word of mouth, especially if the quality of the work can speak for itself. Premium prices can be charged because substitutes are difficult to find.

The principal advantage of this type of position lies first with the fact that competition is minimized because duplication of the product or service is difficult to produce. Being difficult to reproduce direct competition from major corporate chains and mass marketers is generally not encountered. Being small by nature creates a situation in which mass marketers are generally not interested in pursuing such a small market, leaving the niche open to small business. Along these same lines the small proprietor may be somewhat limited as well, due to the specialized nature of a particular craft. Substantial growth can pose a real challenge for a small business, simply because the success of the business is hinged on a specialized high-quality service, which in turn is difficult to duplicate, even for the small business.

The same strategy can work for small manufacturers and retailers as well. By attempting to find a niche in a high-quality premium-price position, head-to-head competitive conflict with most major competitors can usually be avoided. If an analysis of the restaurant industry were done, the findings would support the fact that the majority of outlets in the nation are franchise or corporate chain outlets. Individually owned outlets tend to survive by niching. They generally offer something distinct and unusual in menu, decor, or location. Rarely will people recommend an eating establishment to friends because the food is cheap. Word-of-mouth advertising usually goes something along the line: "If you like barbecued ribs, so and so has the best ribs in town."

Price is undoubtedly a factor, though, and cannot be ignored. In attempting to adopt a premium price, coupled with a high-quality product or service strategy, the value must be such that the customer is willing to pay the premium price. In the exchange relationship, a trade-off exists. As long as consumers perceive the exchange to be fair and equitable, they usually don't mind paying a premium. In part, customers need to be educated as to what they are receiving in the exchange and why your product or service commands the price that is being charged. Customers must be made aware that they are receiving a good value. Value shopping is becoming more and more prevalent, and quality becomes the major component when considering the value of a product or service.

Marketing for small businesses is in so many ways different than marketing for a major enterprise. Similarities exist, but much of what is taught from the textbook corporate perspective is beyond the financial realm of the small proprietor. Yet without finding a way to get the message out to a pool of potential customers in a way that will induce them to use your product or service at a high enough level to make a profit, your business will fail. The trick is to find "the way" to reach your customers economically. Every small business struggles to solve that equation.

In the course of my work as a tax representative with the state Department of Labor, I received many phone calls from people who were contemplating starting a business. Recently, I received a call from a gentleman who had lost his job due to downsizing. He had 36 years of experience and was very competent in his line of work. A market does exist for his particular type of service and he was calling for information about the requirements to start a business. In the course of our conversation I asked him if he had a customer list, or how he was going to find clients. He indicted that he was thinking of running an ad in the local shopper. He intended to run a pretty big ad, at least 2 column inches. He thought that running one ad in one paper one time would inform the world that he was open for business and that customers would just start to call his home for appointments. I don't know how many times I have heard similar comments, and I know those people don't really believe that marketing is going to be that easy or that simple. The small business owner must accept the fact that marketing is ongoing, pervasive throughout everything the firm does, that there is a constant search for effective means to reach customers. With history or time in a business, word-of-mouth advertising might be sufficient, but it very rarely is for the new proprietor.

Strategy B embraces a position of offering a high-quality product and a low price. This sounds like the marketing concept at work. Identify what the customer wants or needs, and then find a way to provide it. Most customers would agree to the terms of high quality and low price. The terms of the exchange relationship are not complete unless the exchange is acceptable to both parties. The seller must be able to receive an adequate level of profit if they are to remain in business. The strategy in question boils down to addressing the financial feasibility of implementing such a strategy.

A high-quality, low-price strategy can work under certain conditions. It should be apparent that the seller in this relationship is willing to operate on relatively low profit margins on a per item basis. Ratio analysis would imply that for net profit to be respectable on low markups, inventory turnover must be high. The nature of this strategy dictates the presence of high volume. To maintain high volume and high quality in a manufacturing setting would indicate the likelihood of high operating leverage in the form of capital-intensive investment in plant and equipment with a high degree of mechanization. By definition this type of strategy is best suited to a mass manufacturer, which for the most part means a big business.

For the small proprietor to compete in this type of environment, they generally must have a competitive advantage built into their cost structure. Major corporations have the advantage with regard to access to capital, cost of capital, and access to a major distribution network. The usual disadvantages that major corporations face with regard to their cost structure stem from such areas as occupancy costs, sales and administrative costs, and officers' salaries. If the small proprietor can gain enough of a reduction in unit costs from advantages gained in the area of occupancy costs, labor, administrative, sales, and other costs, and if they can maintain access to a distribution system that can keep their production output at near capacity, they may be able to compete effectively.

In reality a number of small manufacturing businesses do compete effectively; many are located in rural and smaller communities throughout the country. Many are component suppliers to larger corporations. As globalization continues to expand, export markets are also opening up to the smaller manufacturer. Access to mass markets through the Internet and cable television is also being utilized to maintain product demand. Many government contracts are awarded to small businesses, and contract assistance is available through many state economic development agencies and small business development centers.

Many smaller communities and cities have established economic development offices, and financial assistance is available for small manufacturers that offer employment opportunities in their communities. A trade-off exists: The communities attempt to offer a competitive position to a manufacturer, who in turn adds to the economic base and stability of the community. Site-selection studies for many communities have been done by local economic development agencies, and assistance is a phone call away.

The high-quality, low-price strategy can be utilized in the service industry as well. Again some sort of cost advantage must usually be present. Service tends to be labor intensive, and high-quality service tends to necessitate some degree of specialization and training. It would seem that volume would be somewhat restricted and the cost of producing the service somewhat constant. Yet franchising in the service industry is rising, creating standardization of service levels. If the level of service can be standardized at a high degree of quality and through efficiencies produce a cost savings, the profile of this strategy is met.

The more typical outcome of such a strategy tends to degenerate from one of high quality, low price to a strategy of low quality, low price. There are two main reasons for this degeneration: forced first by the volume of activity, which initially rises by accepting additional work at a lower price to maintain full capacity or to beat out the competition, which in turn forces lower and lower prices as the competitive situation progresses. The higher level of activity requires more equipment or strains existing equipment, shortening its useful life. The higher level of activity strains the human resources to the point where additional help is required. A difficulty can arise in maintaining the level of quality as new personnel are added—the tendency is for quality to suffer. Not always, but a dimension for quality deterioration exists. As the equipment wears out, the possibility of breakdown grows, and the quality of output tends to lessen with the use of older equipment. Strained resources—financial, human, and production—begin to make it difficult for the small business owner to upgrade equipment continually and to establish proper training to maintain high-quality personnel, which reflects the quality of output. Thus the business has deteriorated into a low-price, low-quality strategy, which is the third strategy.

Strategy C employs a low price coupled with low quality. A market always seems to exist for the lowest-cost producer. This strategy seems to fit the profile of a third-world or emerging-world manufacturer in a market where labor is cheap. Coupled with a labor-intensive process and cheap material inputs, the output can be generated at a very low per unit cost. Certain products, such as clothing, and certain industries, such as the textile industry, seem to have provided opportunities for many foreign firms to capitalize on their cost structure advantages.

For the small proprietor to take advantage of this strategy seems difficult but can be done on the basis of cost, and if demand existed for lower-quality service or merchandise, the situation could be taken advantage of. I personally can think of only a single example where I encountered a small business that knowingly adopted this strategy. This business positioned itself as the low-cost producer in the fast-food burger industry. They do not totally fit the profile of low quality because they position themselves as a bigger and better burger at a lower price. Unit cost reductions were obtained because the outlets are all corporate (small corporation) owned. Facilities are all drive-up and walk-up, with no interior seating; thus occupancy cost savings exist, as do economies in layout, which in turn reduces labor costs on a per unit basis. Advertising and promotion are primarily local in nature using radio and billboard as the primary media.

I have not had the opportunity to review this firm's financials. It appears that they are remaining profitable, but the jury is still out. It will be interesting to see how well this firm can maintain its physical facilities and production equipment. The acid test of almost any low-price strategy occurs in the hidden cost of accelerated asset utilization and the firm's ability to replace means of production in the form of plant and equipment.

Strategy D is one of low quality and high price. For this strategy to work, almost monopolistic conditions must be present: a situation where a captive clientele exists, in a situation of near-zero competition with relatively strong demand, with few if any substitute products. The best example I can think of is the circus, often a charitable event, where trinkets and toys are sold at a relatively high price but with a quality standard such that many do not survive long enough to make it through the parking lot and the trip home. Most consumers knowingly enter into this exchange relationship due to the special circumstances, but taking such a position in a competitive setting such as a mall would probably result in failure.

I cannot see a situation where it would be wise for the small proprietor to employ this type of strategy, even under a situation where location is everything, such as a state fair or ballpark. This strategy is sometimes employed by traveling carnivals, where repeat business is of minor concern, but a broad-based use of this strategy would seem difficult at best.

• MARKETING DYNAMICS · · · · · · · · · · · · ·

Positioning begins with the identification of your target market and customer profile. Once you know who you are selling to, you can begin to focus on a marketing strategy. You must have an idea of which group of people will best accept your product or service within the context of your specific competitive environment. It is that customer base which will allow you to be most profitable, and it is to that customer base to which your focus, position, and energies should be directed.

If the critical elements in a marketing strategy could be synthesized into a single statement, that statement would revolve around the dynamics between a company that produces a product or service, the customers who buy those products or services, and the competition and substitute products that also vie for those customers. In this dynamic triad, each company and each product is struggling for a competitive advantage that will allow it to prosper and profit. The following is an attempt to model these dynamics to address your firm's position, what your firm is offering, and how your firm can best reach its intended customers.

```
Your firm
Your customer
Your competition
Your positioning strategy ──→ Product
                              Price
                              Place
                              Promotion ──→ Inside sales
                                            Outside sales
                                            Direct mail
                                            Other channels
```

Your Firm

The scope of this analysis is to attempt to answer some critical questions. Why should a customer buy from you? What are your capabilities? What is your competitive advantage? It might be helpful to view your firm from the perspective of the factors of production: land, which includes real estate in the form of buildings and also entails raw material inputs; capital, which implies your financial capability; labor; and entrepreneurship. From these four elements, define your strengths and weaknesses. From the perspective of your strengths, begin to build a competitive position. For small businesses in general, strength usually stems from location or access to a specific group of customers; they may often have a special knowledge or skill or may have formed personal relationships with a group of potential customers.

Define a firm's capabilities first, in the sense of human and financial resources, along with the strengths associated with those resources, which gives the proprietor a good idea of what the upper limit might be in a sales forecast and begins to define the scale of the proposed operation. Based on specific skills stemming from the human resources available in yourself and those you intend to hire, the type of product and/or service mix you will offer can begin to emerge. The quality of the products or services can also begin to be defined. The product or service that you ultimately choose to produce must somehow give you a competitive advantage or position you such that enough customers will accept your products or services for you to survive. Your company and/or your product must be unique enough and/or offer specific benefits to your potential customer base. Does your firm possess such a capability? How, and in what form?

Your Customer

Based on the identification of a target market or market segment, a detailed and ongoing study of your customer is necessary to answer some critical questions, of which the following are examples:

- What do your customers need and want?
- What products do they buy now?
- Where do they buy?
- How much do they buy?
- When do they buy?
- Why do they buy the product they are now buying?
- What benefit does the customer receive from the product they are now buying?
- How often do they buy or repeat the purchase?
- How much do they spend?
- What services do they expect?

If you are to convince your target market to buy from your firm, these types of questions need to be answered. The more you understand about your customer, the more closely you can position your firm to meet these customer needs. Traditionally, the field of marketing has defined the buying process as moving from a stage of need awareness or want to a stage of evaluation or selection based on a set of buying criteria or standards and culminating in a decision and purchase stage. An understanding of this process is paramount to understanding customers' buying habits.

A customer profile is required as a starting point: an understanding of demographic issues such as age, gender, income, or any other common trait of your market segment. The point of the research is to find out what the common buying characteristic is.

Define what the purchase criteria are. Your target market may have certain requirements as to convenience, price, quality, service, availability, support services, and a host of other factors. Customers may buy because they are comfortable and feel safe in a particular environment. They may buy at certain times of the day, night, or week. The customers will perceive some benefit from every purchase. If you can identify what that benefit is, you can identify the motivation for the purchase and can position your product or service to match that motivation. These issues can simply take the form of satisfying a basic human need, or may evolve into an issue of meeting some emotional need in the form of a prestige product. On the other hand, it may be that credit and credit terms are the motivating force. Product features such as dependability or reliability may act as the desired benefit. The spectrum concerning the customers' perceived benefit and ultimate motivation to buy can be wide indeed. Your firm cannot be all things to all people; you must therefore know and understand your customer and gear your firm's energies and resources to that customer or risk that most of these resources and energies will be wasted.

A part of understanding your customers' buying habits addresses the issue of who actually does the purchasing and who actually makes the decision to purchase. This is especially true in dealing with commercial customers. In my own experience on several occasions a service was sold to one representative of a company, only to have that sale fall through at the last minute because some other executive in the organization had made a commitment to a competitor. Only when you understand that decision-making and buying process can you direct your marketing efforts to the right person or group. In the consumer market many a husband or boyfriend has been sent to the supermarket by a wife or girlfriend to make a purchase of a specific item. It does the grocer little good to attempt to alter or upgrade that purchase decision at the point of sale, because the decision on what to buy was made by someone else well beforehand. In the same way, as a entrepreneur you need to understand how the purchase decision process is made for your product or service.

The information gathered from the customer concerning what the customer buys will help the entrepreneur make decisions regarding his or her product mix and product quality, as well as the array of services to be offered and to some extent the quality of those services. Information gathered concerning how the customer buys will have implications on the marketing channel or channels used. Information concerning when the customer buys will help determine the store hours for a retail establishment or the hours of operation in a service business. It may mean that operating a 24-hour service hotline will best meet customer needs. How much customers are willing to spend will have product quality implications. How frequently the customer buys will help determine inventory levels. Where customers get their information will help answer questions regarding advertising and promotion issues.

Discussing what type of questions to ask and what type of information to seek is helpful, but the entrepreneur is left with the task of uncovering and discovering that information. Two broad categories exist for that type of information. The first, *secondary information,* is public information that is not specific in nature. Secondary information stems from governmental studies and/or statistics or information relating to another type of market or customer in general. The library is the starting place. Secondary information is general in nature and not specific to your customer.

The other type of information, *primary information,* is market or customer specific in nature. This is the type of information required to answer most of the direct questions concerning your customers. Primary information tends to be the most difficult to attain. If you are already in business, a wealth of information is probably available from your internal records as to what the customer is buying, when they are buying, in what quantities, and so on. If you were to hire a marketing research firm to help answer some of the primary information questions, that marketing research firm would generally begin with a study of the business's own internal information.

Other marketing information can be gleaned from talking to your cutomers on a one-on-one basis. If the customer knows you are the owner, or if the customer is caught offguard, the information given may be biased. For example, how many times have you had a substandard meal at a local restaurant, but when the manager asked how your meal was, did not tell the manager your true feeling concerning its quality? Even though the meat was undercooked, the potato was cold, and the vegetables were soggy, our tendency is to reply that everything was fine.

Questionnaires can be used as another source of primary information, as can small focus groups and telephone inquiries. Observation can also be used to assist in the information-gathering function. If you have employees, they can be a great source of information, as can the employees of your competitors. Another proprietor in a different geographic market could provide real insight. Often the chamber of commerce and different fraternal organizations will have guest speakers, some of whom may be in the same or a similar line of business. Personal experiences can also be relied on to some degree. It is one more reason why it is so important to have some experience in the type of business you are attempting to enter before making the plunge.

Whatever the source or method used to gather primary information, a concerted effort should be made to obtain valid and reliable information. In creating questionnaires, the wording and meaning should be as clear and concise as possible. Every attempt should be made to eliminate bias by the wording of questions and the manner of soliciting the questions. Certain biases are inherent within the sample itself. It is helpful if more than one method of obtaining information is used. In the end, though, the best way to discover what your customers' wants and needs are, or your customers' perception of your firm's product or service, is simply to ask them.

If your firm is already in business and is serving a customer base, they are your best source of information with regard to your firm's position and the level of satisfaction those customers are experiencing from your existing product mix and level of service. That customer base should be considered a part of your information system, and a method of obtaining information from that source and then utilizing that information should be implemented. Included in that customer base are the customers whom your firm has lost. If a business owner had a clear understanding of why each lost customer was lost, a much clearer focus on what is important in customer service and product mix would rapidly emerge.

Your Competition

To begin to understand how your firm is positioned in the marketplace must entail a thorough and honest assessment of the competition. It does matter what the competiton does, because what the competition does affects your position. The customer has accepted your competitors, which affirms that what they are doing is right. To understand your competitors it is helpful to develop a profile of them. In so doing you may discover some shortcomings as well as some competitive strengths in your own firm. It is also good to have a handle on how your competitors have differentiated themselves in the marketplace and how you compare or match up or fit in the overall market.

The competitors you are most concerned with are those who are targeting the same customers as yourself. It is generally common knowledge who those competitors are. Your customers know them and so do your employees. It is not uncommon for employees to voice negative comments about competitors. This is rarely accurate competitor information but usually the articulation of an employee's loyalty or sometimes inner fear for the organization.

The type of information you need concerning your competition is basically the same information you want on your own firm. It would be nice to know and be able to compare from a financial perspective: an understanding of the competitor's cost structure, to help define a competitive advantage and/or disadvantage; an understanding of what they offer in the form of promotions, incentives, and value-added services to induce customers to buy from them; an analysis of location, product mix, price, promotion, level of service, and quality of product and service. It might be beneficial to know who your competitors use as suppliers, where each competitor attempts to sell, and how they go about selling their products and services—in short, to understand your competitors' strengths and weaknesses. An answer to the questions stated above can help gain an understanding of what their capabilities really are and how best to position your firm in relation.

An analysis of the competitors must be a realistic and honest evaluation of how your firm stacks up against them. This may well require a customer perspective. Your customers are already evaluating and comparing you with the competition. It would be beneficial to know why your customers chose you and why they chose a competitor.

The information gathered begins to define how you are perceived as different from your competitors. It is not necessary that you attempt to emulate them; in fact, it is this information that will help you differentiate from your competition.

Your Positioning Strategy

In addition to what has already been discussed about the broad choices available in choosing a positioning strategy based on your product's quality and your product's price, as an entrepreneur you must further differentiate yourself within the category of price and quality. It is a foregone conclusion that your products and/or services will not be alone in their respective category. If you are alone because you were the first to capitalize on a new innovation, your success will inevitably invite competition, and those competitors will generally attempt to copy your products and service.

Your goal is to get customers and to keep customers. Some of the new customers you obtain are exactly that—new customers. They might be new to the area, or they might be young adults who are newly employed or just married. In part the new customers you are getting are coming from the competition. You must give them a reason to come over to you. In the same way, you must give those customers a reason to keep coming back to you. This is done primarily through what you have to offer the customer, which may be what they cannot get elsewhere. It is the essence of what makes your business different and what makes your business special.

The positioning strategy you employ should attempt to be unique, and an attempt should be made to make it difficult to copy. It is my preference that for small business a strategy that supports a premium price and a high level of quality is the optimum position from which not only to differentiate but also to survive in. A major cause of small business failure is that the firm cannot charge enough for a product or service, which in turn forces that business into a situation where the break-even volume is sometimes beyond its capacity. Such a situation is doomed from the start. The critical issue is to have product or service features and qualities that can demand a higher price from the onset.

One of the elements that will support a premium price is a low level of competition, or better yet, no competition. For this situation to exist, something must be keeping new competitors from entering; a barrier to entry must exist. Major corporations have gone to great lengths to create barriers to entry for their competition and have spent millions through advertising and product development and packaging to be different and unique. Major corporations through product development will often possess patents and processes that new competitors do not possess or cannot use, thus creating a strong barrier to entry. In addition, the progressive use of a new process creates a barrier of entry, due to progression through the learning curve.

Small business can also have developed a patent or process that creates a special advantage. Such an advantage could be temporary if a major competitor views the market segment as large enough to warrant going after. If a large company is willing to expend the resources to develop a patent similar to the one already in existence, new competition could soon be on the way. This reality should motivate the entrepreneur to use the window of opportunity gained through innovation to develop a loyal customer base and to cultivate strong channels of distribution, which are supported by those elements that create a perception of value in the minds of the customer. In essence, begin to build market share from the onset from a high-quality position.

Quality is the key element that will support a premium price and at the same time differentiate a business or product from the competition. It seems that quality is also becoming the byline of many ad campaigns and the current strategy of many corporations. Quality is easier to define than to accomplish. Quality can also mean the level of workmanship. When a master craftsman produces workmanship that is difficult to duplicate, it should be clear that such workmanship can demand a premium price.

In a manufacturing setting, quality in workmanship is a function of the production process. That process incorporates the use of high-quality inputs, beginning with materials. That is why many manufacturers today who believe in quality will bring their component suppliers into a partnership relationship and share information to develop high-quality components. Such a relationship involves a move away from low bidding and creates a more stable form of relationship. In the same way, suppliers of raw materials are sought who can provide consistent high-quality input materials. Less emphasis is placed on cost alone.

The second phase in the manufacturing process is the process itself. The manufacturing process consists of two components, the first equipment based and the second stemming from the human element. It is the human element acting on the input materials with the use of plant and equipment that produces the level of quality inherent in a particular product. The equipment must first have the capability to produce consistent output. A machine that is machined improperly and cannot remain in calibration cannot produce consistent output. High quality implies that investment in high-quality equipment that can produce high-quality output is in place.

The human beings who use the equipment must have the training and skills to utilize the equipment to produce the type of quality ouput desired. The more complex the process, the higher the skill level required by the employee operating that equipment. This itself can be difficult to achieve. The personnel officer's job is to find employees with the basic skills required to perform a particular function, but if the firm does not have in place a system to support and train that worker to achieve a high level of performance, the quality of the output will suffer. To take this process one step further, it does not matter what a worker's skill level is—if he or she does not have the proper attitude and motivation to want to do a good job, quality can suffer.

The same issues exist for small business but on a smaller scale. Quality workmanship is a differentiation strategy that is difficult to duplicate. That is why it works, but your firm must have the capability to create that quality itself. Quality differentiation may well have implications concerning the rate your firm can grow and the level of capacity it can handle and still maintain high-quality workmanship. From the perspective of the customer, quality is often measured in the reliability and durability of the output. It may be measured by appearance or features as well, but fundamentally, quality deals with how well a product performs in relation to the customers' expectations of that product.

The goal is to obtain and keep customers. Your firm can do that by offering something competitors don't offer. Quality itself, though difficult to achieve, can go a long way toward doing that, but customers must be able to perceive the difference in the quality of your output versus that of your competitors. Customers must not only be able to perceive that difference—they must value it enough to remain loyal to your firm. You can help customers perceive that difference by adding a feature or component that is unique to your product.

Take a moment to look at television ads and try to analyze how major companies attempt to sell consumers on how their product is different and somehow better because of that difference. The competition in breakfast cereal is a classic example. With only five grains—wheat, corn, oats, barley, and rice—and only a few main processing methods, cereal manufacturers have differentiated their product in a number of ways. They can pop it, flake or roll it, then shape it, coat it, and flavor it, add complementary ingredients, package it, and put it on the shelf. You can almost get lost in the product mix, and cereal dominates a major aisle in most grocery stores. Fortunately, most product categories are not that saturated, so feature differentiation is a little easier to achieve.

Another function of quality stems from the service element. The quality of service can stretch across a continuum, from almost nonexistent to a level of high quality. It is a way to differentiate and can be a strong reason why customers should patronize your establishment instead of the competition and provide a reason for customers to remain loyal and return to purchase again.

Service begins at the point of sale. Even though a strategy of high quality is adopted, and the necessary expense and energy are expended in the production process, complemented by special features to differentiate your product from the competition, much of that effort, energy, and expense can be lost or destroyed at the point of sale by your attitude or that of the employee who first comes into contact with the customer. Good customer relations are a part of a pillar in the model presented in this book because that relationship is critical to the success of an enterprise. Check your attitude at the door. Your personal problems and those of your employees can quickly color or taint a customer relationship. Most of us can recall a sour encounter with a salesclerk or cashier at some time or other. High-quality service at the point of sale should leave customers with a feeling that they have just left a human encounter that was enjoyable, one that they would like to repeat, and one that they would feel welcome to come back to whether or not they made a purchase. This is especially important if your product would be considered a shopping type of good, because that customer will not buy until he or she has completed a personal evaluation of a competing set of goods.

High-quality service at the point of sale goes beyond being warm and friendly. If high quality is the defining feature of your product, your front-line employees should be aware of those product qualities and features to inform and educate the customer of the same, at or before the point of sale. For a sale to occur, a reason must exist that creates value in the mind of the customer. The fact that value exists is by itself of little value unless the customer is aware of the existence of that value. Sometimes the only thing that the customer will perceive is that the product carries a premium price. Training and product knowledge on the part of the front-line employee become an essential part not just of sales, but in truly providing high-quality customer service at the point of sale.

Service can be differentiated through convenience, which in turn is a function of location, and accessibility. Part of that accessibility is established through the hours of operation. It is important to understand the buying habits and lifestyles of your customers to accomodate them effectively in terms of store hours. Expanded hours may be an easy way to differentiate yourself from your competitors.

A position of high quality in service may imply a broad base of services, one of which may be delivery service. Delivery itself is not something that can easily differentiate your business; it is to easy for your competitors to duplicate. If delivery is something that your customers require, it may be required to complement your position. Credit services are much like delivery services, in that it is difficult to differentiate simply on credit services alone, and like delivery service, it may well be something the customer expects.

Service differentiation truly can begin to be established in the area of support. If your product is a high-maintenance product, after-sale support can be a very important feature to offer the customer. If the product is very technical in nature, the follow-up service may be more important than the overall product features. If a product is custom made, or one of a kind in nature, service may be unique to your firm. After-sale support may be critical. For large-ticket items, after-sale support may be paramount to maintaining good customer relations.

In the examples above, many of the customers may be commercial in nature. The product you sell may well be involved in the production or operational functions of that customer's business. From the perspective of human relationships, products and services are a integral part of maintaining relationships between various groups. Businesses use and need to maintain the integrity of those relationships. A violation of the commitments made can erode those critical relationships. Your products or services to a commercial customer can be an important element in helping the customer maintain the relationship. Thus the level of service you offer in support of your products can become critical in the circle of relationships. The quality of support and assistance that you offer can further strengthen the bonds of trust between supplier and user. You can create for yourself a link in this chain of relationships.

The consumer type of customer has a series of commitments as well, not in the form of customer supplier relationships but of commitments to family, job, and community. Time and performance are the cornerstones to keeping those commitments. To the same degree, the performance of your product and the quality and level of your support services may be critical in allowing your consumer customers to maintain the integrity of their commitments. In providing a high level of support and providing high-quality service, you may be able to differentiate your firm or product from the competition and create a relationship of trust, which in turn creates a link in the lives of your customers.

After an analysis of a firm's capabilities, customer base, competition, and positioning strategy, all of which act together in a dynamic environment, an entrepreneur will probably have a pretty good idea of what type of product or service he or she is going to produce and a pretty good feeling for how the product should be marketed. In most cases the enterpreneur probably had an inkling of the outcome prior to undertaking the study in the first place. Yet as with most detailed studies, there are usually some surprises and refinements of the original premise. The outcome of the study doesn't necessarily define what to produce or sell, or how and where to market the product or service, but the information gathered can identify weaknesses in the original concept and act to modify and strengthen the marketing strategy.

Product

When starting a small business, multiple steps or phases are progressing simultaneously. One of those phases, which begins very early, is the concept of product development. In fact, the product or service idea may have been the original impetus for going into business in the first place.

Most major corporations define product development as containing a series of steps, beginning with idea generation. For the typical enterpreneur, the idea generation phase was the original itch that began the process of looking into starting a business. The next step in the progression involves some type of screening or concept testing phase, which is followed by some type of business analysis. These steps are what we have been talking about in the positioning strategy. The results are also part of the business plan. The questions that must be answered first begin with: Does a market exist? How large is that market? How much of that market can we capture? How do we reach our share of that market? How much does it cost to produce and deliver that product or service? How much should we charge for that product or service? Ultimately, how much profit can be generated by providing that product or service? These questions have been on going from the beginning. The final steps in the product development cycle involve some mode of test marketing and implementation or commercialization of the concept.

A larger question that should be addressed concerns the product life cycle. A very real danger to a small business can often exist if a single product or a single service is being produced. Some analysis and monitoring of the product life cycle may be in order. The product life cycle must be long enough for the entrepreneur to recover the initial investment in plant and equipment. If the product life cycle is short or intermediate term, good management would dictate that resources be expended to develop a second generation of products or services, or the business itself may terminate at the end of the initial product's life cycle.

The percentage of businesses that survive for a generation is very low. I roughly define a human generation as 25 years. Those that eventually become multigenerational firms must possess a product mix or provide a service that has a long life cycle. That is not to imply that management decisions concerning products and service are static. In fact, it would be difficult to find many businesses that produce and sell the same product or service that they did 25 years ago. We live in a rapidly changing society. A business must have the adaptability to change within the context of a technologically driven world if that business is to survive. It is that technological change which to a large extent is a force that tends to shorten the product life cycle of many products.

In conducting research concerning the size of the target market, which in turn will result in an estimated level of demand for your product or product mix from a customer base, the research may well modify your original concept of the product or product mix. It is essential that the demand be high enough to support your operation. It is best if your projected market share is relatively low: If a total market produces $100 million in sales in a market trade area, for your business to do $1 million in sales, you need only capture 1 percent of the market. That is more achievable than if you needed to capture 80 percent of the market to sustain your business.

If you were the only provider in a small market segment, you may well capture 100 percent of that market, but if a new competitor entered that market, your share might well drop to 60 percent. On the other hand, if you are in a small market where you need an 80 percent market share to meet your forecasts and the market is growing at 3 percent a year due to population growth, growth for your firm will be somewhat slow. Contrast that situation with a total market of $100 million which also experiences a 3 percent growth in overall size—the potential for growth is enormous. A small change in market share can translate into enormous business growth.

Price

In one sense, price is restricted by your competition. If your company and product position is the same as those of your competitors, it will be difficult to charge perceptibly more than your competitors. This sounds like a contradiction. I have been touting premium pricing. Now I sound like I am touting competitive pricing. I am, but restricted to or limited to the specific realm of direct competition from that competitor who is positioned where you are. This of course depends on the product and the price elasticity levels of the product. It also depends on a host of other variables. If all variables are equal, competition will influence the price you can charge. Thus the degree to which variables differ reduces the influence that competitors have on price. This is the essence of differentiation.

Price is but one component, and not necessarily the most important component in the buying decision process. Yet there is a strong urge for many small business owners to attempt to increase sales by cutting price. Stop for a moment and think about the image you conjure up when thinking of the lowest-cost producer of any good or service. Then ask yourself if you would want to be that low-cost producer. Generally, the image is not good, and as indicated earlier, the low-cost, low-quality position is somewhat difficult to operate in profitably.

So what is the right price to charge? The right price lies somewhere within a definable range. On a number of occasions I have asked a group of my students to define the "right" price. Invariably the response is "the price that will maximize sales." That would be a correct response if your objective were simply to maximize sales. The lowest price that could be charged and allow you to remain in business would best accomplish that objective. Profit would approach zero, however. The objective, then, is to maximize profit. If you ran a lawn-mowing service and charged $1000 to mow a lawn, you would need to mow only 100 lawns over the summer to make a very nice living. The likelihood that anyone would accept that $1000 mowing price is extremely low. Competition and substitutes will act to restrict price no matter how you differentiate. Thus the upper limit is set by what the market will bear given demand, customer need, and competition, including substitute products.

The lower end of the price range is driven by cost. In a competitive environment, cost structure becomes a critical element. In a head-to-head competitive marketing situation, big business tends to have a cost advantage. This is the logic behind the idea that small businesses should segment and niche to avoid head-to-head competition. A lower cost structure depends in part on the level of debt and the cost of capital inherent in a firm's capital structure. The degree to which operating leverage is incorporated in a firm's capital structure also influences cost. High operating leverage is determined by the degree to which capital intensive automation and mechanization is used in the production process. This tends to lower unit costs at high volume, due mainly to reduced labor costs at higher levels of production. The size of the market and level of sales volume in relation to production capacity also influence cost structure on a per unit basis.

A strategy that allows for segmentation and differentiation, particularly through higher levels of quality, can demand a higher price. This allows the producer who is not the low-cost producer to compete effectively. This does not eliminate the need for a concerted effort to control costs within the financial and operational structure of the firm. Cost savings that can enhance bottom-line profitability should be pursued aggressively but be constrained by the focus of maintaining quality in product and service. The goal is not to be the lowest-cost producer but to reduce waste as much as possible.

For the small business manager to be able to price effectively, a detailed understanding of his or her cost structure is a requirement. Knowledge of what each unit cost is provides the manager the information required to bid effectively. An informed manager can tell you what it costs to operate his or her business on an hourly or daily basis. Such knowledge enables proactive decisions to be made. The bottom limit concerning the "right price" begins with an understanding of cost; from that point return on investment and profit projections can be added in.

Price is, in one sense, a management tool. Volume and market share are influenced by price, which in turn influences the rate at which the business grows. Price is not the only variable influencing the rate of growth, but it is a factor. Raising the price can slow growth in a market where some price sensitivity exists. Raising prices deliberately to slow growth may have some very beneficial consequences for small business, especially if a position of high quality coupled with a premium price is taken. Rapid growth can sometimes deteriorate quality. If your systems are not in place to accommodate rapid growth, it may be wise to slow growth to maintain a high level of quality. Raising prices when costs are constant will widen profit margins, thus making more capital available for debt reduction and/or capital improvements, which in turn can act to lower costs further, or to enhance quality, further strengthening the firm's position. A position where demand increases in the face of increasing prices is a very enviable position to be in. A more common position requires diligence to control costs and support price levels through marketing and promotion.

Place

The research done concerning your position, your product, and your customer will greatly influence the location and/or place from which you conduct business. If your product and/or product mix is such that your customer is a retail consumer, location becomes very important. If your customer is an institution and you reach that customer through an outside sales force, location of the office and warehouse is less important.

In my interview with Mr. Barlow of the Burlington Restaurant,[1] location was cited as the prevailing factor in the success of the business. In a retail establishment, location may well be one of the most critical decisions influencing the success of the business. In general, the more accessible the location, the more expensive will be the occupancy costs associated with that location. In a sense a trade-off exists; a prime location will, by its nature, attract and draw in customers. A less desirable location will cost less to occupy, but due to its poorer accessibility and convenience, customers must be drawn to that location through more aggressive advertising and promotion. To maintain an equivalent level of sales, the cheaper location from the perspective of occupancy may in fact cost more when the costs of the additional advertising and promotion are factored in.

In areas such as a mall location where demand for retail space is very high and consequently very expensive, it may not be feasible for certain businesses to survive. A cost/volume analysis must produce figures that are feasible. A coffee shop of 1800 feet of retail space at $15 per foot per month would create an annual occupancy cost of $27,000. If the coffee and the labor to make and serve that coffee cost $0.22 and a price of $0.80 is charged, leaving a gross profit of $0.58, then $27,000/$0.58 = 46,551.72 cups of coffee must be served each month just to cover the rent portion of the operation. Divided by 30 days, that amounts to 1552 cups per day, and if the mall hours are such that they operate 12 hours per day, they must sell 129 cups per hour to meet the rent obligations. Other costs would also need to be factored in, as well as a projected margin of profit. This situation does not seem very feasible, especially if seating exists for only 40 or so patrons.

One solution would be to raise the price and recompute. It is easy to see the connection between cost and price. It is should also be easy to expand that interconnection to include product, customer, competitor, location, and volume.

Promotion

Promotion deals with the multifaceted issues of reaching the customer. At the on-set the business concept in the form of a product or service and a potential target market began as a visualization. As research progresses, the visualization becomes more and more refined until it reaches a stage of implementation and eventually reality. A complete marketing concept involves the development of a firm's image. Early on, a business name and business logo are developed, which often incorporates that business concept into a specific design and often incorporates distinctive colors or color combinations as well. The purpose of such a distinction is part of the concept of differentiation. An attempt to build a presence in the marketplace by creating an image that is distinctive and recognizable to the customer helps to mar-ket your product or service.

This is why many firms will use the same design and colors through all facets of their promotional campaign. The color of their service vehicle fleet may re-semble their packaging and billboards. Sales invoices, packing slips, stationery, and other documents carry the same colors and logo.

Promotion and advertising are usually considered separate but related activi-ties. Advertising is viewed more from a perspective of "out there someplace." Ad-vertising is an activity and a process of getting the word out that your firm exists, and the message you wish to convey is broadcasted to a target audience through se-lected media, while promotion deals more with in-store merchandising and mar-keting. The two types of activities support each other.

Promotion is multifaceted but deals primarily with a visual presence: eye ap-peal and the attention-getting aspects of the physical structure, equipment, mer-chandise, and personnel who make up the physical elements of your enterprise. Promotion begins with the facility itself and the grounds surrounding the facility. The image that those facilities convey should be viewed as contributing to your firm's image. A junkyard often looks and conveys the image of a junkyard. A retail outlet that looks like a junkyard would have a difficult time marketing itself as a place to buy premium-quality merchandise. A neat, clean, and well-maintained physical structure should be an obvious requirement. The window displays and sidewalk message boards are part of the promotional mix. Many major retailers spend enormous time and energy to attract customers into their stores through the attractive use of window displays. In high-traffic retail settings such as a mall, many prospective customers walk by the store. It is the window and merchandise displays within the potential customer's line of sight that attract and influence store traffic. Window banners, signs, posters, and the like, which influence a store's image, are all a part of developing the customers' first impression.

Major retailers have spent enormous amounts of money attempting to maxi-mize sales through store layout, shelf, and gondola arrangements. Product and/or company representatives are available to provide information, assistance, and sup-port for you to take advantage of the work and research done by their firms to help set up your store. Many manufacturers will supply stationery and sometimes mov-ing displays and end-of-aisle displays. Many suppliers will offer to set up end-of-aisle displays in your store.

How you display your merchandise reflects on the image of your store. Keep-ing your merchandise looking fresh and clean is a time-consuming task. Keeping an inventory that appears to be new and bright can be assisted with adequate light, wide and spacious aisles. Keeping your inventory interesting often requires that dis-plays be moved and changed frequently. Even a store's price tag is part of the pro-motional effort and conveys a message to the patron. It is easy to see the extensive use of point-of-sale displays near the checkout counters of nearly every major retailer. Point-of-purchase displays tend to offer impulse items and account for substantial increases in sale levels. Even a business such as a machine parts store or automotive replacement parts store can increase sales at the point of purchase by emphasizing merchandizing. Another avenue used to increase the level of impulse buying of patrons is through the use of vending machines. Their presence and appearance are also a part of the promotional activity and contribute to the image of the business.

Whatever the promotional mix employed, it should support the firm's image, not contradict or detract from the positioning strategy that the firm has adopted. Keeping a retail outlet as fresh and appealing as the plate layout of a five-star restaurant is a demanding activity. It requires a great deal of energy and a lot of creativity to maintain a good promotional mix.

What advertising is really about is information. Somehow the entrepreneur must get the word out and inform the public, particulary the target market. The advertising message should contain information about who and what the business is about and what product or service is offered. The presentation of this information should create at least an interest and ultimately a desire in the consumer to try that product or service. Promotional efforts ideally are efficient and effective. Unfortunately, promotion is rarely a simple thing. Promotional costs can be very high and the potential exists to expend resources on media that reach the wrong audience at the wrong time and in the wrong way. Getting it right is a continuous process.

After a name and logo are developed to help create a specific image, probably the best promotional tool is the product or service itself. One of the most effective marketing tools is word of mouth from one satisfied customer to that person's circle of family, friends, and associates. Quality of product or service is best established before the first day of business. If you can imagine a business where the service became a fiasco and the product quality ebbed to a low level, the damage to the firm's image could be irreparable. It is much easier and cheaper to keep existing customers than to replace customers continually with new ones. A product and/or service with a high level of quality can be a real asset in maintaining customer loyalty.

• QUESTIONS FOR DISCUSSION········

1. Define the four main positioning strategies.
2. Discuss the merits and disadvantages of each of the four main positioning strategies.
3. Discuss the main issues an entrepreneur should understand about his or her competitors.
4. Discuss the main issues an entrepreneur should understand about his or her customers.
5. Do you agree with the premise of differentiation in the text? Explain how an entrepreneur can gain a competive advantage through differentiation.
6. What is the main concern in establishing a price for a product or service?
7. How can location affect a small businesses advertising and promotional budget?
8. The bridge model implies that two of the pillars supporting a successful small business are a high-quality product and high-quality service. Do you agree or disagree with this premise? Explain.

9 Opportunity-Based Marketing and Marketing Research

Chapter Objectives

- To demonstrate various ways in which a strategic marketing advantage can be obtained through realization of a marketing opportunity.

- To introduce the marketing research function and to generate an awareness of some of the marketing research resources available to the new entrepreneur.

- To provide an introductory analysis of various advertising mediums through the eyes of an advertising agency.

- To generate an awareness of the marketing research issues and provide some additional tools to conduct a more accurate revenue forecast and to support that forecast with a targeted marketing approach.

Marketing for would-be entrepreneurs is usually thrust on them. Proprietors know what they want to do. They have experience in a specific area, or they have always wanted to own one of those coffeehouse businesses or some other endeavor. That is the first step, but from that point forward the prospective business owner must develop an action plan. Before a lending institution will consider a loan, a business plan must be submitted and within the context of the business plan, some type of marketing plan must exist to support the forecast.

The marketing plan will strive to define what is possible given a certain level of investment. What is possible will be constrained by the firm's maximum income-generating productive capacity, given that initial level of investment, and correlated to the level of customer acceptance of the firm's product or service. To answer the question of customer acceptance will depend on factual information regarding not just your own business but the competitive environment around your business. What is the potential market in your trade area? How do you go about defining and measuring that market? How do you define the portion that you expect to reach? What and who is the competition? Who are their customers, and why do they buy from them? Why should those customers buy from you? What is it that your customers want? What you are attempting to do by entering that market is offering your potential customers an opportunity to buy from you. The degree to which they respond will determine your success or failure. To increase the odds in the favor of success begins with information. The marketing plan begins with the collection of that type of information.

• OPPORTUNITY-BASED MARKETING · · · ·

It often seems that the single most important difference between a true entrepreneur and the masses of people is the way they gather and process information. Most successful entrepreneurs are constantly gathering and absorbing information, which is filtered internally to identify possible opportunities.

We live in a very dynamic economic environment, which is constantly changing and ever evolving, driven by technology, demographics, and a host of other forces that alter the demands of the marketplace and the needs of individuals. The ability to perceive these changes and foresee the implications and changes in the marketplace are at the heart of marketing and marketing information.

Let me explain it this way. If you asked the typical person what would be a good business to start, they might say a restaurant or a convenience gas station. It is true that many such businesses exist, and therefore a need must exist, which is demonstrated by the very existence of those businesses. That part of the equation is true, but their existence does not validate the need for your restaurant or your convenience store. In fact, the successful existence of those other businesses already in place indicates that to a great extent, the need has already been met. An opportunity does not necessarily exist, unless there is compelling evidence that your new business can offer something the market needs or wants and is currently not getting. The implication is this: Through information gathering and processing the would-be entrepreneur attempts to anticipate change and act on that change ahead of the event, so that when the need is present in the marketplace, the entrepreneur's business is present to fill the need.

Opportunity, then, is to a large extent need driven. Adequate market potential must exist for an enterprise to be successful. A need-driven approach attempts to capitalize on an unserved or underserved market segment. An unserved market segment is created through the changing forces of a dynamic economy, a change in technology such as the commercialization of the VCR, which created a ripple effect through the marketplace. This new technology created a myriad of opportunities. Video stores opened all over the country, seemingly almost overnight. In reality, a window of opportunity was opened that existed for a year or two at the most. The gap between consumer want and service availability was soon filled.

A video rental business had a much better chance of survival if it was opened early in this new product phase rather than at the latter stages, after the gap in customer need had essentially been filled. Correct timing is a critical component in small business success. As in the video market, as that market continues to mature, the number of new entrants continues to grow until a saturation point is reached. Once a saturation point has been reached, it typically will be followed by a shakeout. During the shakeout phase, predatory pricing may emerge, and almost certainly competitive pricing, which cuts into profit margins. The customer base or total market is not large enough to support all the players. The natural evolution in a free-market system means that the weakest firms will go out of business.

Competition begins to evolve in many forms as the free-market system acts to find the best, most economical way to fill consumer need. In the example of the video rental business, as video rental services began to mature, those services soon became available in grocery stores, convenience gas stations, and other outlets. Videos also became available for purchase in retail outlets, especially mass merchandisers and discount stores. The price the public paid for videos was initially high enough that most consumers would rent rather than buy, but as prices were reduced through mass marketing and competition, video ownership became commonplace. A secondary market for video sales continues to emerge, evolve, and expand. Videos are now available in pawn shops, at garage sales, and in a number of other places.

To survive in the video rental business, an early entrant would obviously have a better chance of success than a late entrant. Early profits can help sustain the latter leaner times and can help recover some of the early input costs. The early entrant can best select the prime location and build a customer base, which hopefully exhibits some loyalty.

Identifying an unserved market can create a window of opportunity, but as the video rental example demonstrates the window generally closes quite quickly in a mature economy such as our own. It is also common for extreme competition to follow in the wake of that opportunity. It behooves the entrepreneur somehow to establish a position that will enhance his or her chances of survival. A secondary plan of action that is flexible enough to change with the changes in market demand may be in order. Adaptability has long been the mainstay of small business.

In some instances the best time to exit a business might be at the top, although identifying that top is another issue entirely. In a technology-driven society, many new products are generated by technology. The application of technology can quickly create product opportunities, but the downside of this rapid change in technology can often mean that product life cycles can be very short. Adaptability and flexibility are supposedly the forte of small business, but rapid change makes economic nimbleness a requirement for survival.

An unserved market can sometimes be created by something as simple as changes in traffic patterns. In a growing community, information concerning the city's long-range plans to build streets and highways can create an opportunity based on location. As traffic patterns change, a new best site for a restaurant or convenience store to reach this new group of commuters will have changed. Anticipation and information can create opportunities.

An underserved market can be created by changes in population demographics. As population grows in a community, the need for essential services grows as well. At some point a given population base will support another grocery store, liquor establishment, Laundromat, and so on. Success often is hinged heavily on the "right location" when attempting to open such an outlet.

Demographical changes with regard to the age of a given population base can create underserved market opportunities. The graying of the United States will increase demand for elderly day care, recreational activities, and medical services. This concept is not new. The marketing concept premise explains that the product must be created to meet the consumer's need. For the small business proprietor it is even more important that the need exist and be in place beforehand to create the opportunity, because only limited resources are available to educate their public to a given product or service. At the same time that the need emerges, an opportunity to fill that market niche must be acted on because the window of opportunity tends to close quickly. If your business does not meet the need, another firm will soon move in on the turf.

The marketing information process must somehow identify and measure the needs of the marketplace before attempting to meet the needs of the consumer with a specific product or service. Given that a need exists, the marketing information can be turned into a business opportunity only if the entrepreneur can identify a course of action that will bring the product or service to the marketplace in such a way that a competitive advantage is realized. A competitive advantage will increase the odds of success, especially if a sector shakeout situation occurs down the road.

A competitive advantage can be gained as an early entrant into a new technology or through the application of a new technology. The old adage of being "the first with the mostest" applies. Being first allows the entrepreneur to cultivate a loyal customer base. An advantage in market share once realized is easier to maintain than attempting to build market share by taking customers away from competitors.

The early entrant can often gain an advantage in location. In many business enterprises, location is everything. It is much easier to find the right location by being on the scene first, or nearly first. In the fast-food hamburger industry, the best sites have already been taken by McDonald's, Burger King, and Hardee's. It would be difficult to build a new burger barn next door to those existing chains and expect to do well. Site selection studies have been done by the predecessors and the best sites are taken early.

A competitive advantage can stem from a special knowledge, or a patent, which can help to create barriers of entry for future competitors. This has been addressed earlier but bears repeating. A special knowledge or skill can set a business apart from the competition and can be difficult for competitors to duplicate, as explained in the section concerning segmentation and differentiation. A special process or formula such as the carefully guarded secret of the Coca-Cola formula can create a competitive advantage that is difficult for competitors to duplicate. What this really does is buy time for the product life cycle curve to establish itself while few participants are competing for market share. Once that cycle begins to approach the mature stage, it becomes difficult for new entrants to break into the market, or if they do break into the market, it increases the difficulty they have in making substantial inroads.

Once the mature stage of the product life cycle is reached, there is a tendency for the market to solidify. Little change in market share seems to occur, and if the market share does change, it is usually gradual in nature. Such an assertion needs to be qualified a little. In the case of the small business enterprise, the entrance into a market by a major corporation as a competitor could dramatically affect a particular firm's market share. A small business owner may tie up a local market to some extent and create barriers to entry on a local scale, but this does not preclude major corporations from taking a run at that particular market. Survival for the small business may in fact hinge on the degree to which a competitive advantage can be created.

Such logic concerning the creation of barriers to entry is more applicable to large corporations, which have the resources to build production capacity and develop distribution networks, as well as the advertising campaigns to build product awareness and market share quickly. The major corporations are often more able to erect formidable barriers to entry, but some of the logic also works for small business. A specific market can be somewhat tied up; certainly a specific location or locations can be acquired.

A competitive advantage can come from an advantageous cost structure. Again the early entrant will often obtain an advantage by finding equipment or real estate that is undervalued in the marketplace, for which the entrepreneur finds an alternative use. Once that local resource is used up, new competitors must purchase new equipment or build to suit, but doing so will leave them at a serious cost disadvantage. The entrepreneur who was there first thus obtains a wider profit margin spread and can more easily afford to be the low-cost provider if need be, or by design, build a dominance in the share of the local market. Such a cost structure advantage also makes it difficult for a major corporation to move in and be competitive.

Another source of a cost structure competitive advantage can come from building supplier networks and relationships: finding alternative sources of supply that can somehow create a quality premium which allows the entrepreneur an opportunity to offer a higher-quality product for the same or less money. The other side of this issue is attempting to create a cost structure advantage by obtaining equipment or resource inputs at a lower price than that being paid by competitors, which translates into a cost structure advantage.

Let me try to explain this with a personal example from my first business, Sentry Safety. One source of lowering the cost structure for the entrepreneur can be through the use or modification of alternative equipment. The oil field service industry used specially built equipment trailers in which were loaded a bank of air bottles tied together with a system of high-pressure air hose run through a regulator to reduce the air pressure to appropriate levels. The gross weight of this air bottle cascade was around 1200 pounds. The trailer also needed to be equipped with compartments to hold various types of air packs, safety equipment, air hose, signs, and other equipment. Most firms in the industry used specially built trailers that were manufactured by various machine shops. At the time most of those units ran about $4000 each.

Having grown up on a farm and ranch in southwestern North Dakota, I knew that most of the ranchers in the area used various types of livestock trailers to haul more than just livestock. The industry was supplied by a number of manufacturers. Using the *Thomas Business Directory,* I was able to locate several manufacturers in the midwest. I explained the needs and equipment requirements to several manufacturers, who came up with a modified version of the livestock trailer which worked excellently. The cost came in around $1700, which encouraged me to look further for additional savings. Finding alternative equipment to meet equipment and supplies requirements begins as an information-gathering process. The more people you can bring into the problem-solving picture, the more creative you become.

In a recent visit and interview with Joe Hurly[1] of Hurly's Candies, Joe explained his need for a corn syrup storage tank and the fact that his supplier of corn syrup really wanted him to buy corn syrup by the truckload or partial truckload. Joe was thinking of having a trailer built with a tank mounted on it and then adding tank storage to a building he was going to need. After some discussion I suggested that he contact several local dairy suppliers. With the continued trends in the concentration of almost the entire agricultural sector, many small dairy farmers either quit or expanded, and a supply of small 300- to 500-gallon bulk milk tanks were available. These are stainless steel, with refrigeration units, which could be converted to heating units if need be. Most of these tanks had an original cost of over $3000 but could be purchased for as little as under $100.

Yet another approach to creating an advantage in cost structure can stem from a supplier network. If a cost advantage cannot be created, care should be taken not to create a cost disadvantage. As an example I again relate to my experiences with Sentry Safety. Within the context of the oil field safety service business, Sentry Safety, like other firms, used thousands of feet of low-pressure air hose with Hansen quick couplers to hook hose together without an air loss and without becoming unhooked. Most firms in the industry used various safety supply distributors to purchase their hose. The usual cost of air hose was about $1.10 per foot. Again using the *Thomas Business Directory* I found a regional distributor of Gates 214 B low-pressure hose, the hose I was already using. By establishing Sentry Safety as a bulk user, the firm was granted a dealer discount, which allowed Sentry Safety to purchase hose for $0.35 per foot. The Hansen quick couplers were located at a firm in Rochester, Minnesota, at a price of $5.35 a pair. Thus Sentry Safety's cost for air hose was $0.4035 per foot as opposed to $1.10 per foot for the majority of firms in the industry.

Pursuing dealerships and bulk discounts is nothing new for corporate America. Many firms employ full-time purchasing agents and have a purchasing department. The purpose of a purchasing department is to ensure that quality, quantity, and timeliness specifications are met so as not to impede the production operation of an organization. Some firms are very concerned about cost and can have an advantage in buying direct, but the small business owner can with diligence create a cost advantage through supplier networks and through the use of alternative equipment and/or used equipment. A word of caution: It is not worth it to save a few dollars at the expense of sacrificing quality or productivity.

A competitive advantage can also be built on relationships. In the end it does not matter what type of product or service is being provided in the marketplace, the production of that product or service is based on human relationships. As the bridge model indicates, the quality and caliber of a firm's internal human relationships determine to a great extent the quality of the output. A specially skilled team can create higher quality and higher levels of productivity that can become difficult to duplicate. Thus even under ideal conditions, a new entrant would have a somewhat lengthy learning curve to overcome before they could become truly competitive in the marketplace. Such a situation can buy a firm time in the evolution of the product life cycle to gain an advantage in market share and cost economies.

Cost advantages can be created within the context of external relationships as well. A special relationship with a customer base can easily lead to sales and service agreements in the marketplace. Just as the production of any type of product or service is dependent on the quality of human relationships within a firm, in every order or sale of those products or services, a human element is involved. Thus the quality of the external relationships between the firm and its customers can influence the level of sales. A competitive advantage can be built on the quality of customer relationships.

In my personal experience in the oil field service industry I realized this many times. Sentry Safety had a number of clients who were not concerned with price, although Sentry was price competitive. The customer wanted the personal services of Sentry Safety personnel and would often request a field safety representative by name. Such relationships make it difficult for a competitor to make inroads. Relationship marketing creates a competitive advantage and is something on which you can build a business. Such customer relationships provide a degree of predictability and stability in a firm's cash flows and provide a firm with the time required to build a broader customer base, which in turn diversifies the firm's cash flow to improve the firm's stability and predictability of cash flows even further. The opposite is also true. If your competitor has established firm human relationships with their customer base, it becomes increasingly difficult to take customers away from them.

A competitive advantage can also be cultivated with supplier relationships. If a competitive environment exists, inputs can become critical to meet customer demand, as in an environment of shortages. The maintenance of a satisfied customer base for your firm could well depend on the quality of supplier and/or vendor relationships. Good supplier relationships may result in a competitive advantage.

An example of a such a situation could easily occur in a business like the propane gas business. Each year in late summer or early fall the local propane gas distributors load up on inventory in preparation for the grain-drying season and for consumer heating requirements. If the supply is short, the quality of the relationship between a local distributor and their supplier can have a direct impact on market share and on profitability.

A similar result can occur in the event of a price hike. If a distributor has a good relationship with a supplier, a little friendly advice to stock up on inventory or to lock in a purchase price prior to the price hike can create a cost advantage.

You may know a salesperson personally, who right before you make a purchase tells you to wait a day or two because the item is going on sale, or gives you the sale price anyway. The same thing happens in the business community. In a situation where supply is scarce or prices are rising, personal relationships influence outcomes favorably for preferred customers.

One final thought in regard to opportunity-based marketing. Even with a competitive advantage in the marketplace, the small business owner will have an enhanced chance of survival and success if two other conditions are present in the environment. First, the customer base should be increasing, not decreasing. Even a good-quality product coupled with high-quality service will have a difficult time growing in the face of a declining customer base. The level of growth or lack of growth in the customer base may be a direct result of growth in the community or neighborhood or may be the result of other demographical changes.

The second condition, which has already been discussed, has to do with the timing or phase in the product or service life cycle. It is easier to support growth in sales when the product life cycle is young and in the growth phase. If the total market is expanding capacity to meet demand, it is much easier to enter the market and carve out a share.

The opposite is also true. If the product life cycle is in the declining stage, revenue growth is difficult to achieve because overcapacity generally exists and price cutting is a natural outcome of overcapacity. As suppliers struggle to maintain at least a level revenue stream, they must increase market share to do so. Price cutting usually results due to overcapacity and too large an inventory. It should be obvious that it becomes more difficult to enter the market as a new entrant at this phase.

PROFILES IN ENTREPRENEURSHIP: JOE HURLY, HURLY'S CANDIES[2]

Joe Hurly was a 33-year-old accountant working in a CPA firm who hated his job. Joe knew a lot about numbers, and he knew how to analyze numbers. He also knew that he didn't want to keep doing books for other people's businesses. What he really wanted was to be doing books for his own business. The really pressing issue, though, was what business? Joe didn't have a clue what type of business he should start; he just knew he wanted to start and run his own business.

In one sense Joe is probably typical of a lot of people: Many people are not satisfied with their jobs or where they are at in their careers, nor are they satisfied with what they are doing. It's that itch driving people to create or to do something. For Joe Hurly the search for something from which to launch a business was shared with his friends and family. At one point he considered starting a business to make homemade ice cream. Ben & Jerry's had been successful in that area, but when Joe crunched the numbers, it just didn't seem to him that an ice cream venture would pan out.

The beginning for Joe dates to a day while he was off work and was at home taking care of the Hurly children. He began whipping up a batch of homemade caramel candy from a recipe handed down from his mother. Joe's landlord happened to drop by just as Joe had finished his batch of caramels. Being hospitable, Joe offered a piece to his landlord, who thought they were the best thing he had ever tasted and exclaimed that those caramels were so good that Joe should consider going into the candy business. Although his landlord probably wasn't really serious about it, the lights went on for Joe. From that moment forward he began to give the candy business serious consideration, and in fact that recipe became the flagship of Hurly's Candies. This butter sweet caramel mixed with nougat was later named the Swirly Hurly.

Joe studied the numbers for the next nine months, attempting to project sales forecasts and determining unit costs, marketing strategies, equipment needs, and capital requirements. In the end he decided that the candy business could work, and began from there. According to Joe, it wasn't that he was any more enchanted with the candy business than with any other type of business. It was just that he knew he could work twice as hard and twice as long for his business than he could for someone else's business and still not be as physically tired.

Joe talked to his mother about the idea, and she was in favor of the concept. In fact, Joe's mother purchased stock in Hurly's Candies. Financially, Hurly's was launched with that stock equity and a line of credit from the bank. Joe's dream to be in business for himself was fast becoming a reality.

Joe's mother had taught Joe to make candy while he was growing up. They never made caramels at home, but had made English toffee and other types of candies. Joe was typical in the sense that the types of businesses that people start are usually an extension of themselves. The idea genesis often stems from a hobby or pastime that evolves into a special talent. For Joe Hurly it just happened to be making candy.

Almost immediately the learning curve began for Joe. He had to make the leap from producing a 3-pound batch of caramels in a kettle on top of the kitchen stove to a production batch that had to have a shelf life of five months. In hindsight Joe says, "If I were talking to a young person today about going into business, I would tell him or her that there is no way you can know too much about your business before starting out." Joe went on to explain that the copper ions from the kettle in which he was making caramels would, in minuscule quantities, mix in with the candy; even those few particles were enough to ruin a batch. Joe said he soon had to become a chemist and a lot of other things.

A lack of specific experience really caused some problems for Hurly's Candies. Joe recalls his "baptism by fire," as he calls it. "It takes a lot of perseverance to make it, and with even a little experience a lot of mistakes could be avoided. Like the time I purchased a wrapping machine for $11,000 and it never wrapped a single piece of candy. That single mistake just about put me under financially. I finally traded that machine off for $4000—that hurt. I learned a lot about packaging, and I have since learned a lot about equipment. It's all those little mistakes that can really add up to a lot of money."

Joe began to develop the production and packaging systems required to do production-type candy making. In part by trial and error. Joe began to dig through confectionary magazines and books about candy making. Today, Hurly's Candies is currently expanding into chocolates, but according to Joe, "this time I'm going to slow it down. I'm not going to put my fanny in the fire like I did with caramels."

I asked Joe why he thought he was successful. Joe explained: "Everybody brings something to their business. What I brought was a real knowledge of numbers." In addition to being a CPA, Joe was also a level one Certified Financial Planner. Joe not only knew how to put financial reports together; he also knew how to read some meaning into those numbers. Joe felt that his real strength lay in the application of financial information to the management of his business. Although he lacked "proper experience" in candy making, which he had to acquire, Joe also felt he had a real weakness in mechanical aptitude. The installation, calibration, maintenance, and repair of specialized equipment was proving to be very costly. Joe was finding that he also had to learn to be a Mr. Fix-it. His repair bills have since declined dramatically. Joe reflects: "I'd rather have the accounting knowledge than the fix-it knowledge. I think you can acquire the mechanical and production know-how a lot easier than you can pick up the accounting knowledge of the business. Although I almost undid any advantage I had with the accounting knowledge by making a mistake on that wrapping machine, that one almost did me in."

Joe went on to elaborate on the countless little decisions that had to be made on a day-to-day basis. He explained that with so many decisions to be made, errors were inevitable. Joe readily admitted that a lack of experience really hurt. In fact, he said, "You know, if I'd had another $50,000 on top of what I already had to start this business, I think I'd be worse off today than I am." What he meant was that mistakes which are made when you are small are less costly than if you attempt to step the business up to a higher level. Along the same line, if you do not have money, you are forced at first to go a little slower, which gives you time to learn and you are forced to seek creative solutions. Joe added: "I think that if you have a lot of money, you are tempted just to throw money at the problem, which doesn't really solve anything—it just burns up money. Money doesn't buy success, and money cannot solve problems."

(continued)

(*continued*)

Joe Hurly believes that entrepreneurs who succeed are those who have good product ideas to begin with, and who persevere. "If anybody thinks that he or she is going to start a business and be successful, and work just 40 hours a week, I think they're nuts." Then Joe went on to explain how he and his wife Lori spent the first year in business. Joe said he would often work over 100 hours a week. I asked Joe how many hours he puts in now, and he explained that things have now kind of slowed down for him—he said he probably puts in 50 or 60 hours a week. Joe went on to tell me that those hours don't really seem like work, though, and work was hard to define. "You know—making phone calls, mopping the floor, lots of little things that you do which are actually work, but it doesn't seem like work. It's a lot different when your working for someone else, where the employer will have defined the things that are work. In accounting we had to have a time sheet to bill out every job. This is different, although during the holidays things get a little nuts—we put in 100-hour-plus weeks. The candy business is seasonal by nature and it will probably always be this way."

Joe talked about how being his own boss was a compelling reason for going into business, but at the same time elaborated on how being in business still doesn't give you control over your own time. The demands of running a business often means that your time is required, and therefore you also give up things in your life. An avid hunter and fisherman, Joe says that he no longer has time to hunt and seldom has an opportunity to go fishing.

I asked Joe what his greatest challenge has been, and his response did not really surprise me. He indicated that trying to balance business and family seemed especially difficult. Hurly's Candies has been operating out of the basement of Joe and Lori's personal residence and has done so since the inception of the business some three years ago. The Hurlys have three children. Joe said that one of the things he and Lori agreed upon early in the business's formation was that if Joe was to be working out of the house, the first priority would be the children—that Joe would be a Dad and father first and a business owner second. Joe said, "It's nice to be at home working and having the kids around, but sometimes it's hard to get anything done."

Joe's wife Lori works as a night-shift nurse, and according to Joe, Lori is the reason why Hurly's Candies is still in business. Lori's income supports the family while Hurly's Candies revenue can be reinvested in materials and equipment. Joe and Lori can see that Hurly's Candies has a future, but it has already been several years in the development. Growth potential exists but cannot be realized until production and packaging problems can be solved so that customer demand can be met. Those systems continue to improve and evolve.

A major hurdle revolved around the wrapping function. Joe purchased an older, used candy wrapping machine from a major manufacturer. The machine works, but there remain problems with proper sizing of the caramels. After Joe cooks a batch of caramel, it is poured out onto a cooling table, a stainless steel table with a water jacket through which cool or warm water is circulated through a system of coils. The result is a constant temperature that cools the caramel gradually until it is workable. The caramel is then cut into ropelike lengths with a roller-type cutter, and the caramel rope is then hand-fed into one end of the wrapping machine. The wrapping machine helps to size the caramel rope, cutting the rope into sizable pieces. Currently the machine creates too many rejects—the system needs refining.

Another major problem that Joe and Lori were forced to solve came in the area of packaging. Hurly's Candies is positioned as a premium product. Joe is adamant about quality. Only the best ingredients go into the product. All odd-shaped or poorly wrapped product is not sold. The type of packaging that Joe wants for Hurly's Candies should reflect the premium quality of the product. In an attempt to match the product with the package, Joe tried an order of decorative bags. He ordered thousands of this decorative bag, which had a clear window to display the product and a gold tie to tie off the end of the bag. The package looked beautiful when neatly filled by stacking the square caramels in an oblong fashion. The only problem was that there was no convenient mechanized way to fill these bags. Joe finally resorted to a metal tray that was open on both ends. By hand stacking the tray, then sliding the tray into the bag and neatly hand tying the bag with the gold tie, he and Lori utilized this shipment, but it took hundreds of hours to package the product.

Needless to say, Joe did not reorder those bags. The packaging problem is nearing a solution through utilization of the Lions' Sight and Service Center. Joe is considering contracting with this facility on a per unit basis. The really good news about this arrangement is that it allows a high degree of flexibility in output. The Lions' Sight and Service Center has the personnel to gear up for a seasonal rush, and they have the facility already set up. This does away with personnel issues and further creates a known cost situation. A piecework contract makes cost control much more achievable.

With the packaging problem solved and most of the wrinkles out of the wrapping machine, the production capacity constraint is beginning to go away. As Joe solves these glitches, his production capability will reach a new level. The time is fast approaching when Hurly's Candies will need to think of hiring that first critical employee. As is typical for small businesses, growth often comes in stages and in incremental steps. The basement that Joe has been operating out of is fast becoming too small.

What Joe really needs is a shop building where he can put storage tanks, because his suppliers of corn syrup are becoming less and less willing to sell him 5-gallon buckets of syrup. They have been hinting strongly to Joe that he really should be buying in bulk. Joe is considering several alternatives, one of which is possibly mounting a tank on a trailer to transport the syrup. Another is to acquire several stainless steel bulk milk tanks to hold the syrup and have it delivered in bulk. A shop building will also enable Joe to set up his stove, mixing kettles, cooling table, feed table, wrapping machine, and finished product storage units in an almost continuous process system. This will allow production to take a quantum leap forward, but such a system will require an employee.

A quantum leap in growth will require additional financing for Hurly's Candies. Joe is considering those financial requirements. One possibility is an SBA loan, but Joe is not ready for that step yet. Money has been offered by family members who want to invest in Hurly's Candies. Joe has

(*continued*)

(*continued*)

mixed feelings about accepting that offer because it adds another dimension of stress into the equation. An obligation to perform and to return a profit will be expected even if those expectations are not articulated. Yet without additional financing, Hurly's Candies will take a long time to grow to the point where performance begins to meet expectations and plans.

The building, additional equipment, and the employee will probably all come together in a relatively short span of time. Joe has tentatively been searching for that employee. He has a real concern that the first hire will be a good fit for his personality. He wants a person with complementary skills. Joe has a good handle on the financial end but feels weak in the mechanical end. He is looking for someone with good aptitude in that area, but also someone he can work with in a variety of tasks, and someone he can bounce ideas off.

I once asked Joe if running his business was lonely. He responded that it was. He expressed some difficulty in that the only person he had to bounce ideas off was his wife, Lori, and that sometimes she just wasn't up to listening to business anymore. In that sense Joe is hoping to fill a void in his life with an employee. Joe went on to tell me that he was a type A personality, and he knew that whomever he hires will need to be a low-key person to offset his high-strung tendencies.

I asked Joe about the growth of Hurly's Candies and where he wanted sales revenue to be. He responded that $100 million would be nice, at first joking but then serious. "You know," he said, "I usually don't like to mention those kinds of numbers because most people just say that can't be done. In part, the negativism comes from an internal belief that they themselves cannot do that, so if they can't, you can't either." Joe went on to elaborate that such levels will probably take 75 years to accomplish, if they are accomplished at all. With the current production problem constraints, large markets cannot be pursued, but one by one these problems will be resolved and then the next level can be reached—one level at a time.

I asked Joe how he intends to market his candy to reach his goals and how he is marketing now. Joe indicated that he had put a link on the Internet for a two-month period by linking to someone's home page. He acquired one customer. "In my opinion the Internet is highly overrated, although that will change; somebody is going to figure out how to utilize that system. It is a powerful tool, but the problem is that if you do a search for candy, there are 10,000 candy companies on there already." For Hurly's Candies the Internet is a marketing tool that bears a longer-range perspective.

Joe also talked about one day possibly utilizing the televison cable QVC network. QVC is also a marketing tool whose time has not yet come for Hurly's Candies. The vehicle has tremendous potential to move huge amounts of product. That is the problem for Hurly's Candies. Production capacity must be increased to a level where they could withstand the demand. According to Joe, one of the worst things that could happen to Hurly's Candies would be to create a huge demand for the product and not be able to meet that demand.

Starting as a home-based business, what Joe and his wife Lori have been attempting to do is to market through referrals and through word of mouth. They use many of the rejects as free or low-cost samples. Joe explained: "That's not free advertising either, but it is still a good value. The idea is that when people hear of Hurly's Candies, they have probably also tasted Hurly's Candies."

Hurly's candies are distributed through a number of retail outlets in the city of Sioux Falls and in the surrounding region. Hurly's caramels are positioned as a premium candy. Joe Hurly firmly believes that people buy Hurly's because of the taste. The taste is a result of the quality, which begins with the best ingredients. If the recipe calls for cream, Joes uses cream, not a cream substitute—that and the proper process builds quality in. You have to taste Hurly's caramels to appreciated them. This is the logic behind the sample marketing strategy that Joe has been utilizing. Joe believes that the money will follow the quality. "Quality of the product must come first; the money will always follow the quality. You cannot cost-cut your way to profitability." Joe voices some criticisms of the accounting profession. He says that the accountant's logic is to keep lowering costs to make profit higher. The error in that logic occurs at the point where quality is sacrificed for the sake of a reduction in cost.

The second most important reason why Hurly's customers choose the product is a result of the packaging. Joe explains, "Packaging is huge. It's the presentation, and that includes you yourself. If people like you, they will buy from you."

Joe is very careful about the positioning of his candy product. He is not interested in using a distribution system that will detract from the gourmet image he is trying to convey with his caramels. Friends have suggested to him that he attempt a vending-type distribution system. His response is that he does not want his product associated with a generic piece of candy. Joe is not interested in the grocery market for similar reasons. Yet he has a long-range view of perhaps distributing a product to put into that market someday. In fact, Joe already has a candy that he believes to be superior to anything out there in the market now and would consider pursuing that market someday. The investment required to enter the mass market is very large. Joe priced a single piece of equipment at nearly $1 million.

Hurly's Candies has also used product representatives. According to Joe, the product representatives must believe in the product or they will not push it. In fact, he attributes the majority of his retail outlet customers to a single product representative who has aggressively pushed the product. Hurly's Candies usually packages a free sample bag along with orders to their wholesale customers. This type of promotion is effective if the store owner will place the samples out front and promote the candy. It is not effective if the candy gets left in the back room. Nor does this type of promotion work if the distribution of the candy is not limited in some way. It works best if the samples are priced cheaply so that people will try a Hurly's caramel, after which many will buy them.

Some months back, Hurly's Candies was featured in the local newspaper as a special-interest story. A feature story in the Sioux Falls *Argus Leader* moved some 43,000 bags of candy in a week. Joe and Lori even lost some sales because they could not keep up with the demand.

• COLLECTING MARKETING RESEARCH INFORMATION · · · · · · · · · · · · ·

Before a marketing plan can be developed, the entrepreneur must begin to gather marketing information. Step one is to get some help. Use the resources around you. Talk to a marketing research firm—just a visit may provide some direction in conducting your own marketing research. Visit with governmental agencies at all levels: the SBA, the Department of Commerce, the Small Business Administration Development Centers. Also contact the office of economic development at the state and city levels, and the local chamber of commerce. Contact your local library and visit with the resource librarian. The SBA offers SCORE (Senior Corps of Retired Executives) personnel free of charge. Contact your nearest college and visit with the dean of the business school, who may be able to assign several students to you on an internship. Visit with several business professors; many are looking for real-life projects to complement their course work. A marketing research class I was teaching put together a marketing survey for a local firm, whose marketing department adopted our attitudinal survey format. Suppliers, trade groups, and other sources of information exist.

Business is about people. The more people you know, the more people you network with, the more information you gather. It is the sum of that information that will direct your decisions. The information you need to make informed decisions is out there—you just need to find it. I mentioned earlier that the information available is basically in two forms. The first form is public information, sometimes referred to as secondary information. It is information that has already been gathered. That type of information is available through those public entities. The problem is that general information rarely answers specific questions. For example, if you are interested in opening a coffeehouse, knowing how many already exist in the nation or even in your state doesn't answer the question of what type of demand you can expect on the corner of 9th and Vine in your city. General information can, however, tell you if demand is growing or declining for that industry due to a change in consumer attitudes about coffee consumption.

The second type of information, primary information, is much more specific but is also not available directly. You must discover this information on your own. The essence of marketing research is the investigative work behind primary research. Most of us are aware of marketing research by means of the survey method, since most of us have been solicited by phone for our opinion on certain products or on certain political candidates or political issues. Such telephone surveys are one means of primary research but not the only means of conducting primary research.

Collecting primary information sounds expensive, and for many firms it can be expensive, but it need not necessarily be cost prohibitive for the small business entrepreneur. Primary research answers specific questions that cannot be answered adequately through general information sources. To address the issue of marketing research for the prospective small business owner more accurately, I felt that for this book to address this issue validly, I should take the same steps that I would take were I starting a new enterprise. I would visit with a marketing research firm.

There are over 5000 marketing research firms in the United States, of which some 160 are members of the Council of American Survey Research Organizations (CASRO). I discovered one member, Robinson & Muenster Associates Inc., in Sioux Falls. I called this organization and explained what I wanted and was referred to their director of marketing, Rick Bauermeister, who graciously agreed to be interviewed over lunch.[3]

For the prospective business owner, the process could well be the same. Call the nearest reputable marketing research firm in your area. Arrange an appointment with their marketing director or sales manager to discuss what they have to offer you. It need not be over lunch, although I like doing business over lunch because it takes people off their own turf, provides a congenial relaxed setting, and establishes limits to the time committed. In this way, if you feel you want to pursue the issue further, you can make another appointment, the next time at their office or yours.

The agenda I had set for Mr. Bauermeister was simply to find out what a marketing research firm could do for the small business entrepreneur, and second, what was this going to cost. Is marketing research cost-effective?

Mr. Bauermeister explained his background. He had a degree in speech communications and had an extensive background in both radio and television. He had worked for a number of ABC affiliates and held positions not just in sales as an account executive, but also as a reporter, anchor, and photographer. As a sales manager he had worked extensively with the marketing and advertising side of business, not just from the perspective of the affiliate he was working for but more important, from the perspective of their client base, of which many were small businesses.

Rick Bauermeister explained that like most people, he brings to the job a bias based on past experience. He explained that because of his years in radio and television, particularly in the sales end of advertising, he believed that the best approach for a business to increase sales was simply to increase their volume of advertising—more or less the shotgun approach. Mr. Bauermeister now admits a bias toward marketing research but explains that attitude has evolved due to experience and his knowledge of what good marketing research can do for a firm. From the small business perspective, where an advertising budget of $400 or $500 a month is a lot of money, you cannot waste those dollars in a shotgun approach to advertising, because that amount of money just doesn't buy you a lot of advertising. It is therefore even more essential for the small business owner to be effective with those advertising dollars. Marketing research can help make the advertising dollars effective by identifying who the customers are and narrowing that group to a target market. Marketing research adopts a micro approach to advertising versus the macro approach that some mass merchandisers can utilize.

The other critical element outside the realm of advertising a marketing research firm can offer is that they can define what the total market is in a given area, an analysis of the competition, and what position in the market those competitors have taken. The marketing research can begin to define what part of that total market can be gained given a level of capital investment and advertising push. Part of the market share analysis defines what your competitive position could or should be to best attain that market share—in essence, defining the market niches that are available.

Having information as to how large that potential market share can be allows the entrepreneur to make an informed decision regarding the correct size of the new business. If a business startup is too small, it leaves room for yet another competitor or concedes market share to the existing competition. If the startup is too large, that investment in the market segment leaves you with excess capacity, which in turn forces your cost structure up. Excess capacity creates an environment in which success is dependent on taking additional market share away form existing competitors, who will in turn respond to that aggression in the marketplace. In essence, this marketing research information is a feasibility study. It may be that after the marketing research project is completed, the information gathered supports the conclusion that the market just is not there, or it is not large enough to support your investment in that market.

This is the issue that most startup businesses really struggle with. It goes back to the business plan and that all-critical initial forecast. That forecast is the number the bank will scrutinize to determine whether it is realistic and achievable. A degree of credibility is introduced if a reputable marketing research firm is involved in the analysis of the numbers. The lender is very concerned about the feasibility of your forecasted projections.

At the same time that the market feasibility study is being undertaken, information is being gathered that begins to define your prospective customer's profile. The demographic characteristics of the market area are defined, and the demographic factors pertaining to the target market begin to emerge. Those lifestyle characteristics provide invaluable information not only as to who these people are and what they buy, but also when and why they buy. With this information on the target market's buying habits, an effective targeted advertising campaign can be put together. The new business can put together the correct product mix and have an image concept that is in synchronization with the target market.

At the core of the marketing research process, at least concerning the customer base, are the gathering and analysis of information that answers why people purchase what they are currently purchasing from competitors. Such information helps determine which product traits and characteristics the customer deems important. Knowledge concerning what competitors' customers like and dislike about the products and service they are receiving can help a business in positioning itself to capitalize on those identified weaknesses. This information is important and is reflected in the message that the prospective entrepreneur wants to convey to those customers in an integrated marketing program.

Mr. Bauermeister talked about planning in business. He said he was amazed at the small amount of planning that goes into most businesses. He referred not just to small businesses but also to some larger firms. Mr. Bauermeister explained that people often go into business because they have a specific knowledge or a specific skill, and based on that, launch an enterprise. Having a specialized skill is a good thing, but too often a venture is launched without knowledge of whether the intended customer wants the particular product or service. The implication is that the venture is launched without any of the information that marketing research could provide. What is truly amazing is that some of these firms are successful. Unfortunately, most of us are only aware of the survivors; we forget about the large number of firms that failed by such methods.

According or Mr. Bauermeister, market research provides a degree of protection against business failure. It does so by defining the size of the market and potential market share. It defines who the customer is and assists in putting together a marketing program. Informed decision making is much better and the chances of success are enhanced—versus shooting in the dark, so to speak. One of the projects that Robinson & Muenster Associates is often charged with is to conduct a research project for a site location.

I asked Mr. Bauermeister how he goes about doing a marketing research project. He explained that the first step is to sit down and visit with the owner to gain an understanding of exactly what it is that the entrepreneur wants. Often, that is something different than what they are saying. In learning about the business and the problem the business is faced with can help establish the scope and scale of the research that needs to be conducted. Marketing research projects are unique and customized to each client's needs. A great deal of time is sometimes required to be able to reduce that problem into a quantitative format. This creates a unique situation in trying to price a project for the client, because each project is often so different.

The cost of a research project is a negotiated item, depending on the depth and complexity of the project. The spectrum of clients can run from a single independent insurance agent to a Wal-Mart. In fact, Robinson & Muenster Associates did do the site-selection work for Wal-Mart when they located a store and a Sam's Club in Sioux Falls. Price is not something that can be quoted after the first meeting.

One tool often used by this and other marketing research firms is to establish a focus group. Typically, a focus group is made up from a cross section of individuals, usually about 10 to 12 people, who may consist of current or prospective customers. They may include customers who have been lost. It is not unusual to keep these focus group members in the dark as to who the client is. Focus groups are used to look for qualitative information, such as attitudes, buying habits, income, lifestyle, and other items that will explain who, what, when, and why they buy. The outcome of using a focus group could easily be a survey instrument that will be used to sample a broader population. The mechanism utilized may be direct mail, telephone surveys, or face-to-face interviews. This is raw research in gathering the information required to define a customer profile.

I asked Mr. Bauermeister what his recommendations would be for the new business entrepreneur. His response was for the budding entrepreneur to take the first step by contacting a marketing research representative to visit with. That visit won't cost anything, but a lot of useful information for the entrepreneur could come out of that meeting. Even if a research project is not done for them, they will know a lot more about where to begin gathering the required information than they knew before they walked in the door. Another thing such a visit will provide is that the problem will begin to be defined for the entrepreneur. Cost certainly is an element, and only a limited-scale project could feasibly be completed, but much of the research could be done by the entrepreneur. This leaves the door open to more of a consulting relationship with the marketing research firm. If a marketing research professional could define and direct the efforts of the entrepreneur, those efforts would certainly be more productive.

Few people ever think of using a marketing research firm. They either think that they are too expensive or that they are only for very large firms. Probably more often than not, the would-be entrepreneur is not even aware that such a firm exists. Too often the entrepreneur enters into business with a production focus. In college we learn about accounting, finance, production, and to some degree, marketing. It is difficult to teach and to learn how to be successful in small business. A starting point, though, is making decisions from an informed position. Mr. Bauermeister emphasized that if he were starting a business on his own, he would spend as much as 25 percent of the available startup capital in marketing research. That seems incredibly high, yet he argues that without the right information, the capital expenditures could be invested the wrong way. Failure will cost 100 percent of those startup dollars. The decisions that are made in the startup phase of a business are critical. It is not hard to see how good information to direct those capital-intensive decisions is necessary. The issue is where to get that information, and to make every effort to ensure that the information is accurate and reliable.

Mr. Bauermeister also emphasized that marketing research does not end; it is ongoing. It is a part of life and a part of business that you constantly lose some customers, and therefore you must gain others. It costs in the neighborhood of six times as much to acquire a new customer as it does to maintain an old customer. Marketing research information will assist you in maintaining your old customers by being informed about their likes, dislikes, and attitudes about your product and/or service. Marketing information will assist you in directing and targeting your advertising and promotion dollars to acquire those critical new customers.

One other area where marketing research may be helpful is in the area of information systems management. Most organizations that have been ongoing for any period of time already have a wealth of customer and marketing information within their existing records. Whether that information is usable and in a retrievable format is another question. Firms like Robinson & Muenster Associates provide assistance in this arena as well. The organization and retrieval of existing information is often a starting point for this firm when called to conduct a research project. Understanding a firm's existing customer base is an important element in retaining satisfied customers. Much of that type of information is already available. Information is available from the sales invoices, the computer database, packing slips, billing invoices, and accounting records: information about who the firm's customers are and where they are from; what they buy; when they buy; how often they buy; and a host of other information about those customers. It is just a matter of organizing and analyzing the existing information. The next step is to modify the information system to ensure that the right kind of information is being gathered and to put the systems in place so that information can be retrieved and utilized.

Mr. Bauermeister discussed some of his experiences and some of the conclusions he has drawn from those experiences. He indicated that it wasn't until he went to work for a marketing research firm that he really began to understand the scope and value of marketing research. He indicated that a lot of public information is available, and for the small business person that is really a starting point. He also reiterated that small business owners can do much of the marketing research on their own; sometimes all they need is a little direction. They can develop their own focus groups and form their own surveys, although creating a nonbiased marketing research instrument is no easy task. Information can be grossly biased, nonetheless, a lot of useful and valuable marketing information can be gathered by the business itself.

Mr. Bauermeister talked about the importance of direct selling—that in a society like ours, face-to-face contact between the business owner and the client is very powerful. It sends a message to the customer that they are important, and knowing that the owner will take the time out to visit with them does good things for customer relations. In some businesses you simply cannot get away from direct selling, nor can you substitute for direct selling. The business owner can bring to that relationship a degree of credibility and confidence. A sense that the business owner can get things done, and that decisions made and agreements entered into will be honored. He talked about how important honesty was in relationships between the business and the customers, and that there is no substitute for doing what you say you are going to do and delivering when you say you are going to deliver. If that is done, a customer will be maintained for life. He said that it is not price that is number one on the customer's list as to why one firm is patronized over another. What customers want is someone they can rely on, someone who is dependable, especially in the service sector. The customer wants prompt service, they want competent service, they want professionalism, and they basically want a fair deal. If customers can get those, they are willing to pay a premium price. Businesses really need to understand that.

After having visited with Mr. Bauermeister, I began to reflect on some of the business experiences I have had and some of the decisions that I made upon entering into business. In hindsight, I believe it really is true that most prospective business owners jump into an enterprise without proper planning and without enough information. I, like others, entered the enterprise in a production frame of mind, thinking that if I purchase the equipment and have the resources to enter a business, the market will make room for me. That assumption is not always true. I also realized that I did do marketing research on my own, but had I knew then what I know now, I would have approached it a lot differently. I now believe that a little direction and guidance from a marketing research firm would be the most cost-effective way to get the job done.

Mr. Bauermeister showed me a client list that looked like a who's who in the midwest. It was not surprising that one of the clients happened to be the company that owns the major radio and television stations in this area. It makes sense that those firms who are in business to sell advertising would certainly have a need to obtain detailed market research within their trade area. It makes sense that much of the general information concerning the demographical attributes of the trade area would have already been gathered by a marketing research firm for the advertising media's client base. The television and radio stations, as well as the major retail firms and retail support firms like the mall, would also already have much of this information at their disposal.

The next logical step in pursuing marketing research information would be to contact one of these firms to see what was available, the logic being that if as a new business you are going to do a degree of advertising to launch your enterprise, bringing the advertiser into the information loop early on could prove quite beneficial. That advertising firm can also act as a valuable resource. They could provide you with much of the secondary and some of the primary information you will require to conduct your marketing research and to assist you in establishing a credible forecast for your business plan.

In pursuit of this concept I contacted Mary Simmons, who is the sales manager for KELO, a major radio and television station in the Sioux Falls metro trade area.[4] Ms. Simmons explained to me that she had a degree in business and marketing and had worked primarily in sales and marketing for television and radio stations around the country. She did a stint with a station in Fargo, North Dakota, and later worked for another firm in Green Bay, Wisconsin, followed by a position in Boise, Idaho, then Spokane, and finally, Sioux Falls. Mary explained that she has always worked in the sales and marketing area. Moving around the country has given her a breadth of experience in the radio and television industry.

After explaining to her that my focus was on small business, I asked her to elaborate on how she and her firm could assist a would-be entrepreneur in the startup phase of a business venture. Ms. Simmons explained that she and her team at KELO have a lot of data at her fingertips[5]:

> First I would sit down with this new business owner and ask them just what is your market. What is your target as far as the geographical area that you are marketing to? First understand what that geographical area is. Number two, what is the demographic group that you're going after? Number three, what is the lifestyle group of your target customer? Once we've got that identified, we've kind of identified who our customer is. We've identified geographically where that customer lives. Then, based on what type of business you are in, I would look up the industry percentages to give us an idea of what should be spent on advertising based on your revenue projections.
>
> That advertising budget could vary, depending on your product, from as little as 1 percent to as much as 5 percent. These percentages come from published industry codes, which make recommendations. Then we take that percentage, which is the basis for determining your advertising budget. From that I would ask what your delta flow is. A delta flow takes a look at your business from a bell curve perspective and flows your forecast through the year to identify your sales peaks and valleys. That process will give you a projected sales forecast for each month throughout the year. Once you know what your projected revenues are, you can break that down into a monthly budget. The next step involves choosing the medium that is going to be the most affordable and the most effective for you to use, and there are lots of choices out there. If your

budget is fairly good size, television is something you would probably want to look at using. If you are looking at a fairly large geographical area, television is something to consider; similarly, if you are attempting to reach a mass audience, television is a medium to consider. There is, however, an expense associated with using television.

Newspaper is another medium you can look at; however, the newspaper trend is that they seem to be losing circulation and readership nationally. They are dealing with rising costs, especially the cost of paper, which is causing a lot of consolidation in the industry. Meanwhile, they must pass on their cost to you, the advertiser, so while their cost is going up, at the same time their efficiency is going down. When you are determining what the newspaper costs you, the rule of thumb is measuring reach in costs per thousand. What does it cost you to reach 1000 people?

Usually, you can measure reach in newspapers by taking their circulation and multiplying that number by about 25 percent, and that comes to the true number of how many people are seeing your ad. That cost is usually quite high. The reach is also affected by the size of your ad. A full-page ad will reach more people than a quarter-page ad. Normally, reach for a newspaper is in the 20 percent range with a frequency of 1. That is, over 20 percent of the circulation base will see your ad once.

If you were to compare newspaper to television, say, for $1000 of advertising, in our local network buying ads primarily during news programs, you would reach a lot of adults primarily ages 25 to 54 and should obtain a reach of around 35 to 36 percent with a frequency of 1. If you were to spend that same dollar amount with radio, you are looking at a reach of 40 or 50 percent with a frequency of 5 or 6.

What is the bottom line in comparing all these types of media? You cannot just look at cost per ad or cost per spot. You must ask yourself what percentage of your market this medium will reach and at what frequency? From that information determine what your best buy is and budget accordingly.

The real advantage of radio is not only the reach but the frequency. In this day and age, when we have so many similar products in the marketplace, where so many are competing for their own little niche in the market and so many people are trying to set themselves apart as different from the rest, the only way you can make yourself stand out is that (1) you need to reach the masses in a very creative way, and (2) you need to buy a medium that can give you frequency. To actually motivate someone to buy your product, you need to reach that customer at a very minimum three to five times, depending on what they know about your product or service. If it's a product like McDonald's, the public already knows what that product is and a frequency of three can work, but if you are selling a new product you are going to have to reach those potential customers a lot more than three times to get them to buy the product.

There is a scientific model for radio called OES (optimum effective schedule). That model indicates that if you are in advertising and you are going to buy radio, you need to buy based on the number of people who listen to radio. To do a minimum impact schedule on radio, you will need to run as many spots as it will take to reach a minimum of 35 percent of those listeners with a frequency of 3.2 times. If you want a higher impact for that week, it will take more radio spots. That reach and frequency vary among stations, due to the amount of listenership.

I asked Ms. Simmons how she would go about marketing a product like Joe Hurly's premium caramel candy. Her response was[6]:

For something like that, one avenue might be event marketing. What event marketing consists of is going into an event, for example we have a Kid Fest, which will attract families with children. There would be an opportunity for a candy company to get a lot of exposure by participating in a show like this. What a show like this does is offer mass exposure, where a lot of people would have an opportunity to sample his product. Event marketing can give you this exposure for very little money. You could buy a booth and give away free samples. We are expecting over 10,000 people in just two days. Where else can you spend just $500 and get mass exposure to a very targetable audience? If your budget is limited, you can just buy a booth. That sample approach could be supported with a discount coupon campaign or some other means to make that product available through retail or direct mail after the show is over. For a product like candy, it would be especially effective if this were done right before Christmas.

Another advantage of event marketing is that it can expand your vendor list. For a product like Joe Hurly's candies, a trade show can create an opportunity to meet other retailers or wholesalers who might be interested in marketing your product. So with event marketing you kind of get two birds with one stone—you are reaching the direct customer, and also have an opportunity to do some business-to-business selling. Event marketing can be backed up with additional forms of advertising to increase the impact of the event. For some products, like Hurly's Candies, event marketing is a good fit.

I pressed Ms. Simmons with a question concerning the percentage of business she does with small business, and whether that segment was growing.

A very large percentage of our business is from small businesses, because radio is one of those mediums which can be very affordable for the small business. The other thing that makes radio such an attractive medium for small business is that they can grow their business with radio. We have a saying, that as goes retail in Sioux Falls, so goes radio. We work hand in hand; if retail is not doing well, we are not doing well. Radio is a big part of their advertising budget because radio is what has kept them alive, allowed them to stay in business and to grow. As they grow they begin to add television and more things into their advertising campaign, which is good. We think radio gives them a good solid base to build on.

I asked Mary Simmons about costs, to which she responded: "Well, you don't have to pay anything for production costs, because that is all part of the customer service that we provide. To give you an example, an OES schedule on KELO AM or FM, which are adult oriented, with a 60:40 split women to men. If you want to reach at least that minimum OES, you should not need to spend over $500 in a week's time."

That dollar figure is going to vary from market to market, depending on listenership and size of the market. In subsequent interviews with advertising agencies and marketing research firms, the consensus seemed to be that if you are going to use radio as an advertising medium, do not use the cheapest station. You should use the premier station to maximize reach and frequency. Ms. Simmons continued:

The only way I would recommend going with less than $500 in a week for radio advertising is if they were going to lay out a long-term plan over a three- to six-month period. Normally, we like to sit down with people and plan out at least 13 weeks; we find so many people who just kind of plan month to month. We like to see them plan for at least 13 weeks and stick with that plan, at least see if the advertising program is working for you. You need to figure out what is working for you. Once you've gotten a 13-week advertising campaign under your belt, you can begin to back off it a little. It depends on the client. Every business and every product is different, so in doing our consulting we try to take a look at the individual situation.

The amount and frequency of the advertising that any particular business or product must do to be effective is going to depend in part on how many people you have in the marketplace and how many competitors you have. If you have a lot of competition in your product area it is more important to stay in the top of that market situation. There are ways you can do this more affordably. One method is to buy, say, weather sponsorship, which will give you a 10-second positioning message. These types of spots are popular with many of our smaller customers. A weather sponsorship in this market works out to be about $5.25 apiece—that is very affordable.

In this market 80 percent of the workforce is working mothers; this is indicative of the nation, but South Dakota has the dubious distinction of being at the top of that scale. That segment is a target group which does not have time to read the newspaper and they do not watch the six o'clock news. These working women are too busy to read the paper or watch the news; they have too much going on. So the logical medium to reach them is radio. Our research indicates that our listeners at work are a high percentage of these working women. For most retailers that is a principal target market. They are either doing the buying or are involved in the buying decisions with their husbands. Especially for high-ticket items, both are involved. Today, women are often buying their own cars, getting them fixed, and doing a lot of the purchasing that was predominantly male territory. They have become very independent consumers. Another market is the aging baby boomer, age 35 to 45. We attempt to identify our listener and gear our programming to the groups just mentioned. KELO stations target the higher-income zip codes.

I asked Ms. Simmons if KELO does its own marketing research.

No, we subscribe to different marketing research firms. They provide us with up-to-date information, which we have on computer. We can log on and get just about any type of marketing research information that we want for just about any type of business. So my salespeople can come in and talk to you and tell you about your business. Based on our marketing research we can tell you what your customer's buying habits are, when people buy, how much they spend, how frequently they buy, and almost anything you would want to know about that customer. All of that information is available at our fingertips and we can make that information available to our clients as we help develop an advertising program for them. All of that is free of charge. Our people are trained not just in radio, but can act more as marketing consultants to work with many of the small business owners, especially retailers.

The small business owner doesn't really have anyone to consult with, so we provide that as part of our service. If we can bring those business owners some really good information so that they can make wise decisions, then everybody wins. In addition to all of that, we can offer the small business person many promotional ideas. If we know that May is a big month for your business, we can offer those promotional ideas to give you that little extra push.

At their fingertips the radio and television marketing staff has information about the customer demographics, the customers' buying habits, and other critical marketing information. Realize, of course, that this information was not gathered specifically for your enterprise, but was gathered to support and better serve the radio or television station's clientele.

Sioux Falls is like most markets in the nation; in fact, it is often utilized as a test market for national retailers and other national chains. So the type of information gathered will have a bent toward those types of potential customers who are supposedly typical in a market that is supposedly typical. Much of the marketing information gathered is generic in nature, but some will have specific application to a business like yours. Your community will likewise be served by radio and television stations that have similar marketing information regarding a specific trade area.

The implication here is that for those advertising dollars within your budget which you were going to spend on some type of advertising and promotional push to launch your enterprise, you can have access to a wealth of marketing information. In addition, the marketing staff can help you develop an advertising and promotional campaign that can have an impact on your target market. In addition the marketing staff has available experience and expertise in the area of product promotion. If you are going to spend advertising dollars, you want to maximize the impact of those dollars. One way to increase your impact is to launch a promotional campaign simultaneously. Help is available in developing that program from the radio advertiser as well. Ms. Simmons indicated that as a radio advertiser she felt that they brought a lot of added value to the table, in the form of marketing information and assistance as well as promotional support.

There is another source of help and information in the marketing area, which is to get professional help from an advertising agency. It may be that your community does not have a marketing research firm, but there are thousands of advertising agencies. The American Association of Advertisers will have a list available. That information should be available at your local library, or look in the Yellow Pages.

An advertising agency is a firm that helps develop an advertising campaign for firms. They must have detailed information concerning their local market as well. They also contract a marketing research firm to supply that market information or will conduct marketing research on their own. At any rate, these firms are marketing specialists who specialize in the local market. Their client base is generally larger firms, but they also serve smaller businesses.

For the small business owner, marketing research defines the total market size, which is then reduced further to a potential market segment or percent of market share, which is feasible given the entrepreneur's inputs. This is again the baseline of the sales forecast, which is plugged into the business plan. Once financing has been obtained, equipment and inventory are purchased, with the latter displayed at the site selected. The personnel are hired and trained, and finally, the entrepreneur is ready to open the door for business. What then? What will make the customer come into your establishment to buy from you? The answer is obvious: The entrepreneur must promote, sell, and advertise!

• ADVERTISING AND PROMOTION • • • • • • • •

Most people do not give advertising much thought until they have something to sell, even a person who wants to sell, say, a used car. The first thing they do is clean it up. Why? To make it as attractive to the buying public as possible. The second thing they do is put a for sale sign in the window and put the car in an area of high traffic. The third thing they do to sell the car is to advertise. Maybe some 3 x 5 cards are made up and posted, or maybe a classified ad or e-mail ad, or other electronic ad is run.

In business the steps are the same, except they are much more complex. The first element, similar to cleaning up the car for the individual, relates to the in-store sales and merchandising for the business. Assume that the marketing research has been done to identify the site selected as a high-traffic area, which is especially important if you are engaged in any type of retail trade. The entrepreneur must then set up his or her business to display the merchandise for sale inside the store.

Help is available from the manufacturers and suppliers of the merchandise. In some instances suppliers will have display racks and promotional items, battery-powered signs and displays that move, banners, posters, and a host of other promotional items. Manufacturers spend hundreds of thousands of dollars on these items and on learning the best possible way to stack a shelf so that the right number of facings, which is usually the maximum number of facings, can be placed on a shelf and the height and eye level that will most attract customers' attention, to maximize sales.

Take a moment to observe a company's shelf display in a grocery store. When I was a Frito-Lay delivery driver one summer, the majority of the training I received was in the area of shelf stocking and display as well as product rotation. The firm spent enormous numbers of dollars in promotion and display research, and a system of merchandising had evolved. My experience took place a number of years ago, but when I observe the Frito-Lay grocery displays, they are still roughly the same: corn chips at the left, because that was the company's flagship and original item, potato chips next, first plain and then flavored, stacked by size vertically from smallest to largest. The company knows and understands the importance of placing their items properly on a shelf for display and sale.

If you watch you will see additional signs, tags, or stickers on many retail items which act to further promote the goods. Those types of promotional items are also available from suppliers and manufacturers. The retailer will attempt to expand sales even more by making additional supporting purchases easy and convenient. For Frito-Lay those easy-to-reach little racks in front of the Doritos encourage the shopper to grab a can of chip dip as long as the customer has already stopped to shop in that area.

Once the shopper's cart has moved beyond that shelf space, the selling opportunity is gone. Frito-Lay does not give up easily, though, and as you turn your shopping cart around the end of the aisle you are greeted with an end display, which almost shouts out "buy me." The end display is usually a portable display which promotes a particular item through a special price. Frito-Lay may offer the $\frac{3}{4}$-pound Nacho Doritos at a reduced price, and that item is stacked top to bottom on the display. The idea is to get as many facings as possible to attract shoppers' attention.

Even after the shopper has moved past the end aisle, firms like Frito-Lay will make one more attempt to make a sale to the shopper with a point-of-purchase offer. At the checkout counters the aisles are stacked with a multitude of impulse items. Frito-Lay participates in this type of marketing with a line of snack items, which include an assortment of snack-sized versions of their chips. They are easily recognizable because of the consistency of their packaging. You know that red package contains Nacho Doritos.

It is unlikely that you will be selling and displaying chips, but the same principles apply to most retail items. The fact that the shelves are stacked in a neat and orderly fashion and such that visibility is high helps to increase sales. Profits are maximized by offering those higher-profit items in an easily accessible way, promoted through stickers, banners, and promotional tags. Even in an outlet like an automotive parts store there are ways to display the merchandise attractively and items that are conducive to end-of-aisle displays and point-of-purchase displays. Certainly, you also need to buy a can of vinyl cleaner, gasoline additive, or a spark plug gap gauge before you leave the store. Attractive displays help sell merchandise. The design layout and atmosphere of the store is all part of a firm's image. Good lighting and clean and attractive displays help make customers feel like shopping and buying.

The merchandise on the shelf is just one aspect of in-store product promotion; many retail outlets will use window displays, outside signs, and banners or posters to help promote and entice potential customers to stop and shop. A great deal of creativity is required to keep the store front and window displays attractive and inviting. It is sometimes surprising how a little creativity can increase traffic flow.

I stopped at a restaurant one day because the proprietor had hung banners and balloons all over the front of the store. I listened to patrons keep asking the firm's employees what the occasion was. These customers were stopping out of curiosity and were expecting a grand opening or some other type of celebration. They were, instead, greeting a clever promotion. The balloons were given to those patrons who stopped.

In-store advertising and promotion can also be facilitated through the use of technology and electronics, such as electronic displays that assist and educate customers about a product or product use. Customer-activated audio or video displays are being used effectively by more and more outlets. These devices can sometimes be accessed outside the store to help sell the store's merchandise. Customers often enjoy hands-on demonstrations of unique and interesting merchandise. Creating a learning experience or a fun place to shop and browse can increase store traffic and ultimately increase sales.

In continuing my research into marketing research and advertising media I felt it important to round out the search with a visit with an advertising agency. Many marketing research firms will also provide advertising agency services as part of their total customer service. As a prospective small business person, help is available from the professionals associated with the various advertising media. Still, to obtain a more balanced view of the advertising media available to the small business owner, I felt it appropriate to contact an advertising agency. I chose to contact Paul Schiller of Lawrence and Schiller, a regionally recognized full-service advertising agency located in Sioux Falls. Mr. Schiller invited me into his office for a visit. The following is a recap of Mr. Schiller's experience and wisdom in the advertising field.[7]

Before you can sell the customer something inside your store, you must somehow make the customer aware that you exist, and then somehow favorably manipulate the potential customer's attitude toward your firm and or your products so that they will at least try it. By definition that is what advertising is. Advertising manipulates the market favorably. Advertising cannot, however, force anybody to buy anything they do not need or desire. Proof of that fact is in your home. Your cupboards are not stacked with food you do not like to eat, your closets are not full of recent purchases of clothes you do not wear, and so on. Advertising must be supported by a customer's basic need for the product.

Advertising is an inescapable part of American life and is endemic to the free-market system. Advertising is the vehicle by which the public becomes aware of your firm and/or product or service. Advertising can lower your per unit costs by increasing volume, which in turn lowers per unit fixed-cost components. But the most important thing about advertising for the small business person is to stay with the basics. Advertising acts as salespeople functioning in the paid space and time of the media, print or radio. Advertising cannot sell a product to someone who does not have a basic need for that product. Advertising cannot sell a product to someone who does not have the ability to buy that product.

Advertising can convince a logical prospect to try your product once. That means that you had better have your product or service in shape before you advertise. That positioning strategy includes all the components that make up your product's unique features, of which the quality of product and service are critical. This book argues that those features are pillars that support your firm's success. If advertising can convince a prospective customer to try your product one time, you have one opportunity to demonstrate to that customer your level of quality—and that quality is why the customer will want to buy again. If your product quality is poor or the level of service is not up to standard, an effective advertising campaign could do your firm irreparable harm. Advertising is a powerful tool, and its power should be respected. Advertising can kill a poor product quickly. It is therefore very important that you be ready to serve all logical prospects when they come into the door the first time through a high level of quality in your product and service. Failure to do so destroys your credibility. The customer will not believe your ads in the future. The basic premise in this book is the value ethics, of which honesty, truth, and integrity are integral parts. If the customer does not believe you because you did not meet the truth-in-advertising criterion, it is very difficult to overcome that barrier in the marketplace, particularly for the startup firm which has only potential customers at the onset.

If the initial advertising campaign to launch a new enterprise is successful, it is important to maintain a continued presence in the market through additional ongoing advertising. Mr. Bauermeister of Robinson & Muenster[8] indicated that he would recommend a marketing research budget of up to 25 percent of startup capital, which would include the first year's advertising budget. Most advertising agencies would recommend a first-year advertising budget of around 10 percent of forecasted sales to launch the firm, and then around 3 to 4 percent of sales to maintain the firm's market share. These are estimates, not hard-and-fast rules, but it should be obvious that a startup business needs more advertising to get its name out in front of the public, while the established enterprise needs to reinforce its presence to maintain and hopefully, to increase, its market share.

If a firm fails to continue to advertise in face of competitors who do, it will be difficult to maintain the firm's market position. Your customers are being bombarded with messages from competing products and services. Your customers must be reminded of you and your firm through continuing advertising.

When the small business owner is establishing an advertising budget, several things need to be taken into consideration. First, it takes a larger percentage of sales for a small business than it does for a large business. This is especially true if the entrepreneur is running a single outlet. There are no advertising economies of scale for the small proprietor; therefore, a larger percentage of sales for the advertising budget is required. The second point to remember is that it requires a larger advertising budget to launch a new enterprise than is required to maintain an existing business. It takes a lot of marketing effort for the new entrepreneur to get his product or service into the minds of the consuming public and to make an impression on that potential customer base. A third element that will influence the advertising budget not only of the new business but also for existing firms, is the level of competition. If competition is strong, it takes a greater marketing effort to keep those customers coming into your store and/or using your product or service. If you need to increase your market share to maintain your level of sales or to support growth, you must increase your advertising budget because you must convince a larger number of the potential customer pool to switch from the competitor to your business. Your advertising campaign must be very convincing to get that customer to try you and eventually become a loyal customer.

What an advertising budget can really do for you is allow you to buy better. You have a specific number of dollars, determined in part by your sales forecast. The advertising budget is part of your overall marketing plan. Having a plan forces you to concentrate more on the marketing decisions that are to be made now and in the future. The quest is for an effective advertising campaign that delivers value in the form of accomplishing your goals, which may be expanding sales and or expanding your customer base or market share.

It does not take long to discover that advertising is expensive. Just because you spend a certain percentage of dollars in advertising does not guarantee the desired effect. Your advertising budget should be spent with the same level of scrutiny with which you make other purchasing decisions. Many advertising promotional deals exist where if you buy such and such a package you will receive a free trip or a free television. The impact of an ad that is aired at two o'clock in the morning is close to zero. If you want a trip, contact a travel agent for your best value in travel, not a marketer of advertising media. You need to maximize the impact of those dollars by targeting prospective customers with an appropriate message, through media or a medium that will reach those customers as often as possible. Industry standards indicate that a potential customer needs to be reached or hear or see your message between five and seven times for that message to register and get through to the potential customer.

The other side of finding a deal in advertising is that many media firms will offer a discount if you will agree generally in the form of a contract to purchase a specific amount in a given period of time. This can amount to thousands of dollars, but those decisions should be made as part of a well-thought-out marketing plan and within the context of your advertising budget.

If you are in business, it will not take long for charitable groups or agencies to find you. You will be asked to donate to various agencies and organizations, often in the form of putting an ad in an organizational journal such as *Peace Officers*. These types of ads and promotions such as calendars, pens, and a thousand little giveaway trinkets generally do not constitute real advertising dollars. A word of caution: Don't burn up your advertising budget with these types of promotional items. If you choose to donate to these organizations, call those expenditures donations, which they generally are. Your advertising dollars should be spent to generate traffic or to generate a response in the marketplace. One other point about the advertising budget is that it is the easiest to get cut and is often the last to get increased. It is the easiest category to tap for other expenditures.

The advertising message should be geared to that unique feature or unique advantage that separates your product from the competition. Why your customers use your product should be broadcast to the target market of potential customers. This type of advertising campaign provides the entrepreneur a consistency of messages about image and positioning strategy.

The message should consist of three fundamental ingredients: first, a clear and concise description of your product's unique features or qualities; second, a clear statement of information about the product or service; and finally, your ad should stand out and be noticed among all competing ads. Part of that concise and clear message should include where the potential customer can actually buy the product. Advertising is worthless if no one sees or hears your message. Before a sale can occur, the customer must know who you are, what your product or service is, and where they can obtain the product or service.

In execution of the advertising message, two rules prevail. The first is to keep it simple; your message should be clear and simple. It should be easy to read, or memorable if you hear it. Essentially, an advertising message can convey one thought. You will never be able to tell everything about your product or service in one ad, so synthesize your message into its simplest form. Second, your ad must be believable. Truth and honesty in advertising are part of the ethical integrity of your firm. A third element could be added here, which is be sure to make the product the hero, not the advertising. The focus of advertising should be the product, not the personality of the business owner. Ego should not detract from good advertising. Some ads that feature the owner of a business are well done, but many are done simply to put a personality on television or radio.

Advertising supports merchandising and packaging. The advertising process consists basically of eight elements. The starting point is the marketing plan, which includes advertising and an advertising budget. An advertising plan should be made at least a year in advance. If a business has a history, comparisons can be made as to the cyclical nature of the firm's sales. The type of product or service will to a great extent determine the degree to which sales are seasonal in nature. A key element to remember is to advertise before the customer is ready to buy. It is difficult to sell snowshoes in July, no matter how great the price or how much you advertise.

An annual advertising plan helps the entrepreneur budget the advertising campaign. This plan is supported by marketing research. It is critical to know who your potential customers are and why they buy, in order to choose a medium and a message that will reach those customers effectively. The final three elements—sales promotion, merchandising, and internal communications—deal with more internal elements of the firm. Identifying the eight elements of the advertising process can be a little confusing, so I have listed them below.

Eight elements of the advertising process

1. The advertising plan
2. The advertising budget
3. Marketing research
4. The advertising media
5. The advertising message
6. Sales promotion
7. Merchandising
8. Internal communications

It does little good for the business owner to set up this process, go through the expense and effort involved in the first seven steps of the advertising process, and then fail to inform and train the employees. It is the firm's front-line employees who are meeting the customer in a one-on-one setting. The degree to which employees can meet the needs of customers will or will not translate into a sale. The amount of product knowledge employees have and the degree to which employees are aware of the products' attributes and how those attributes have been marketed to meet the needs of prospective customers will greatly affect the success of an advertising campaign. All eight elements tie together to focus on a targeted customer base to use the advertising budget most effectively.

How many times have you gone into a store and asked an employee where a sale item is, only to have them respond with a strange look and say "I don't know." If the product is not on hand, and if the employees are not aware of the promotion, the expense to get potential customers in the door is all for nothing.

Advertising is an inexact science. That truism makes marketing and advertising in general much more difficult. Advertising does work, and that is why it exists. In fact, it has been proven to work; it's just that a specific formula for success does not exist. The acid test for advertising is: If it works, it must be right. We all have a good idea what good advertising is and we generally can agree on what a good ad is when we see or hear it. Similarly, we generally recognize bad advertising when we are exposed to a bad ad.

Your advertising campaign should be consistent with your firm's image and with the way you have positioned your firm and your product or service in the marketplace. Advertising helps to build and support your firm's image and your positioning strategy in the marketplace. The clearer your firm's image and market position are in the minds of your target market, the easier it is for your advertising to continue to reinforce the message, and thus the more effective your ad campaign can be. To take effective advantage of those advertising messages that reinforce your firm's image requires a degree of consistency and a degree of market penetration through repetition.

The average person is exposed to somewhere between 600 and 1600 ads per day. In an average morning before the typical person gets to work, he or she is exposed to 50 newspaper ads, 30 radio ads, and at least 20 billboards. As a small business owner it is extremely difficult to get your message through this barrage. It takes a long time to create that image connection in the minds of your potential customers. For example, if I asked you what product you would associate with the statement "It's the real thing," most people would know that it is Coca-Cola.

Consider for a moment what Coca-Cola is trying to say. They are saying that as far as soft drinks are concerned, Coke is the real thing. It will quench your thirst, it is better than every other soft drink, and all others are but poor imitations of the real thing, which of course is Coke. Suppose that the maker of a substitute product such as a flavored tea came out with an ad campaign touting their product as "the real thing." What would Coca-Cola's reaction be? In all likelihood they would file a lawsuit. Why? Because Coca-Cola has spent millions of dollars to position their product in your mind with that slogan. They did that because it meets the acid test of advertising. It works.

Can advertising also create an image and position a small business in the minds of a local market? The answer is yes, but it takes consistency and a degree of repetition. According to Paul Shiller of Lawrence and Shiller: "The first person to tire of a creative concept like a slogan is the person who is buying the advertising. The second person to get tired of it is the person who created it. By the time both these people are tired of the concept, is about the time the consuming public is beginning to recognize it." That is not the time to quit the ad campaign. When you advertise, you know when and where that ad will appear. The moment it is aired or put in print, you immediately recognize it as yours; you are in tune with it. Your assumption may be that the rest of the audience is as attentive to that ad as you are. Not true. The consuming public is being so bombarded with messages that it takes a period of time to get your message across. Your message is competing with hundreds of ads daily, so it takes a certain amount of market reach to get the message across to potential customers.

Everyone has a perception about specific products and specific firms. That perception in the minds of consumers is your firm's image. How you attempt to position your firm in the minds of the consumer will influence three things: your firm's name, your advertising image, and the media you choose to advertise in. The marketing research you have done will help you identify what market position should be workable, based on the current competition and on the needs and wants of the potential customer. That is the starting point for marketing, and the advertising campaign helps develop and support that position by developing a product and/or company image. Your firm's name and logo are part of that position and also help position the firm correctly. That one advertising medium is better suited to accomplish that positioning strategy by reaching the customer base you are targeting more effectively and efficiently should be obvious.

The place to advertise does affect a firm's image. The businessperson should attempt to appeal to the right audience with the right message using the right medium. If the entrepreneur knows who the customer is, the choices become much easier. Some media can be very effective in reaching a specific type of customer.

Newspapers

If possible, place your message in the headline of your news or print media. The headline should tell the whole story. Use the headline to flag your prospect. Select your audience by appealing to the reader's self-interest. It is important to grab the prospective customer with the headline so that they stop and take the time to read the advertisement. The competition for attention is so intense that often all the reader scans is the headlines. The headline should also offer a benefit to the potential customer. Tell the customer why they should come see you or use your product. It may require a long headline to accomplish this task. If a long headline is required, use a long headline. Other things you can do to grab attention is to inject news into your headline: something new or improved, or that you just moved. Research indicates that long headlines sell more than short headlines.

The print media message should be positive: that is, concentrate on the positive attributes of your product. Avoid negative ads. Look for story appeal in your illustrations. Let the illustration work in concert with the headlines. Use photos rather than drawings. Photography tends to increase sales by as much as 26 percent. Photos make a point much better than words. This is the place for those before and after pictures. Photos act like a demonstration. Your car is wrecked and it looked like this—now after *OUR Body Shop* repaired it, your car looks like this.

Use a simple layout; don't clutter the page. One single photo with a caption can grab the reader more effectively than an entire page of photos. Use color carefully; color can be very effective. Testimonials can add believability to your ads; testimonials lend credibility to products and make an ad more memorable and persuasive. Develop a single advertising format. Adopt a look and a type style and stay with it. Change will make you look like 10 different companies and few people will remember any of them. It goes back to the issue of the repetition of a message that is required to get the consuming public aware of your existence and to convince that pool of people to try your product or service. Don't confuse the customer; get to the point where the public can recognize the look of your ads. That look may require professional help to develop.

If you are running a promotion, tell the public about the promotion. If you are running a sale on an item, have that item available and at the front of the store so customers can find it as soon as they walk into the store. That is what brought them in; don't make them look for it and don't run out of the item—you'll just make them angry.

Television

Brand and store identification should be made early in a television ad, preferably in the first 10 seconds of the commercial. Flag your customer in the first few seconds of the ad, either with music, visuals, or some other means. If you do not grab the viewer in those critical first few seconds, they will be off to the refrigerator or just tuning out. It is usually a good idea to show the customer what they are buying; show them the product. The focus here is on local retail or service advertising. If you are in the food business, the more appetizing you can make the food look, the better chance you have of bringing customers in to try the product. The same is true of other products—you can make your product or service very desirable. Make your product look good. Television is a very powerful medium. If you spend the money to go on air, you want to do it right because a poorly done ad could affect your image adversely. By its nature television can strongly help shape your firm's image.

Make your product the center of attention. If you can't say anything about your product, sing it. Music can be use very effectively, as can sound effects. Impact the senses of the viewer to make your message memorable. Voice-overs or on-camera talent are more effective than the proprietor going on camera. The small business owner generally should not go on camera and attempt to look like a professional. On the national scene many corporate CEOs do go on camera. Some are excellent; others would probably do better if they left television to the professionals. The same is true for small business; television is generally best left to the professionals. Most television stations can locate local talent to perform on camera, or the ad can be shipped out of the local market to have an ad professionally done at a larger affiliate.

Work hard at creating a format and then stay with it. As with the newspaper, it takes repetition to become remembered. Like most mediums, keep it simple. A single idea that looks good is more memorable than jamming a 30-second ad with information. Notice the Budweiser ads; often the only idea or concept they are pushing is the word *Budweiser,* although a national product leader is in a different position than a small entrepreneur. The small entrepreneur is not doing much in the way of test shoots, nor can they afford to.

Billboards

Billboards are often an underutilized medium. It is a very bold type of advertising. The number one rule is to keep it simple. If you feel you are limited by print or electronic media, you are really limited in the amount you can say on a billboard. You could fit a lot of words on a billboard, but it would be difficult to read without stopping. Few potential customers would take the time, unless out of curiosity. The average message on a billboard should be five to seven words.

Billboards tend to be a reinforcing type of medium. A combination of radio and billboards can be very effective. A billboard has a tremendous reach potential for a short period of time. The majority of those who will notice a billboard will notice it in the first week to 10 days. Roughly 45 percent of households will be reached the first day the billboard goes up. They gradually begin to lose their effectiveness after the initial impact. Thirty days is about as long as you want to keep a billboard up, unless it is along an interstate highway and you are advertising a hotel or similar business or service that pulls traffic off the highway. Billboards should generally be backed up by another medium.

Bold type and a bold message should be used. For a letter to be readable at 200 feet it must be at least 6 inches high; at 400 feet the letters must be at least 1 foot high. The most readable color combination is black and yellow. The message must be simple because if you have only five to seven words to work with, the big idea is all you can hope to get across. The cost of billboards is relatively high, but they are a very effective way to announce a new product or a new store opening, and if that message is backed up with print and radio or television campaigns, it can be very effective. Again the entrepreneur is trying to reach potential customers in the target market from five to seven times.

Yellow Pages

The Yellow Pages can be very effective for certain types of businesses. The type of service that is best served by the Yellow Pages falls into several categories. The first is the type of service that is purchased without shopping; an emergency service fits this category. Most people do not think about their furnace, air conditioner, or plumbing until something goes wrong. If the sewer is backing up onto the carpet, we usually don't shop for the cheapest service. You grab the phone book and call until you can find someone who will respond—now. The same is true for a tow service or other emergency service.

The second category of businesses that normally advertise in the Yellow Pages are simply service businesses in general: often things you don't think about, but services that are required from time to time—a flower shop, a garbage service, a photographer, and the like. Some of these services may be purchased based on convenience or location; other services will be shopped for.

Professional services fall into this category, along with other shopping goods. We might shop for an attorney, CPA, dentist, and/or physician. We also shop around for large-ticket items. If your car is involved in an accident, you will need several estimates. Most people do not know the names of the autobody shops in their community. The Yellow Pages are where many people look for that type of service. Mortgage lenders are another service for which people may shop around for rates. Customers may check first with their local banks, but chances are that they will at least check with one other institution before committing to a mortgage rate.

Many businesses advertise in the Yellow Pages, but the ads are certainly more conducive to some types of business than to others. That level of importance determines the size of ad the entrepreneur would want to place. Many communities have competing classified ad publications. Should you advertise in one or all? My opinion certainly, if you advertise in any, be sure to do so at least in the premier publication.

Direct Mail

Direct mail can be an extremely effective means of advertising, especially to your loyal customers. Direct mail can be utilized in a campaign to obtain new customers as well. If you are using a direct-mail campaign, it is very important that you know who the target market is. You had better understand who should receive a direct-mail piece from your firm because it can cost as much as 20 times more to reach that customer through direct mail as it would to reach them with a 30-second radio spot. However, that assumption depends on a number of variables. In another sense, it costs less to use direct mail to contact, say, your best 30 customers with a special thank you and an offer on a future purchase than it would cost to reach those customers in almost any other way. In that sense, direct mail cannot only be cost-effective but can be very personal as well.

The general perception the business community has about direct mail is that it is expensive. In truth, direct mail can be very expensive if a shotgun approach is taken with its use. Direct mail is a precision advertising instrument and should be directed at a very specific customer base. In that sense direct mail can be very effective, and response percentages can be greatly enhanced because every recipient is a potential customer in a very real sense.

Most people associate direct mail with junk mail. In fact, billions of dollars are spent annually by publishers of magazines trying to get you to subscribe to magazines. Promotions like the $10 million Publishers Clearing House sweepstakes are from many recipients' perspective part of the junk mail they receive. From the perspective of the publishers of those magazines, this is an effective form of marketing. They use direct mail because it works—as do catalog firms, food stores, department stores, record and CD clubs, book clubs, and so on.

There must be obvious reasons to use direct mail or it would not be used to the extent that it is. Some of its advantages utilized by major retailers and others can also apply to small businesses. One of the key advantages of direct mail is that research has found that customers acquired through direct mail tend to be loyal and are a good source of repeat business. As I indicated earlier, direct mail can provide a vehicle to target your most likely customer base with precision and accuracy. You are restricted much less in your layout and the type of message you can deliver to your customers. In most print media, space is a critical restraint, but with direct mail you have the space to get your message told. You have the ability to include brochures, coupons, and even samples. Samples can speak volumes. In the buying decision process pyramid, that point where the customer decides to buy the product to try it out is quite far up; in fact, the majority have already screened out your product. A sample almost guarantees that the prospective customer will in fact try your product and will probably recognize and remember your product.

You can be very creative in your direct mail. Video and audio tapes can be mailed. Your selling can be very personal in nature; you can greet someone by name. You can mail specialty items as gifts to arouse the curiosity of the recipient to induce them to open your piece and read it. You can control the timing of the mailing, which can give you the ability to monitor that campaign. You can reach people out of your geographical trade area, where radio and other print media will not reach. Other advantages exist in addition to those mentioned, but I think it is easy to see that if done right, direct mail can have a positive impact on sales and revenue for small business owners and should be considered in their marketing strategy.

Once you have decided that a direct marketing campaign should be part of your marketing program, the first step is to narrow your focus by identifying specific objectives you wish to accomplish. Obviously, conducting a direct sales campaign could be an objective, but so could increasing store traffic. You might want to identify customers who have been lost or who have not patronized your firm for a while and use a direct-mail approach to get some of those customers back. You could also use direct mail to solicit new customers. Direct mail could be used to sell your customer base an expanded service or attempt to increase the frequency of purchases. Direct mail can be used to just say thank you for being our customer, which in turn can do a lot to strengthen customer loyalty. Building product or service awareness can also be achieved through direct mail. The direct-mail objective is influenced by the type of business and the product mix.

With a specific objective in mind, the message must be developed to coincide with the objective. Creativity will play a big part in the development of the message and in the type of package that message is delivered in. Response rates will hinge on how well that process is done. The message will usually be centered around some type of offer. Your message will tell your customer creatively about the benefits they will gain in using your product or service. The goal is to make the message look as or more appealing than the product itself, without straying from the truth. The customer does not know your product like you know your product; therefore, the message is educational and informational in nature. You have an opportunity to tell the customer why your product is better than competitors' products and how it is different due to certain features. Your product may offer certain advantages over the competition, which is what your product and market segmentation strategy is all about. The message could include a special promotion or sale or whatever.

Packaging of the direct-mail piece must be creative to ensure a high response rate. If the prospective customer doesn't take your piece seriously but relegates it to the realm of junk mail, it could easily wind up in the garbage unopened. The envelope must entice the prospect to open and read it. A phrase like "Free Offer Inside" can grab attention but is an overused technique. Personalized letters are more frequently read, but with computer technology that technique is also getting overused. This is where the inclusion of a free sample or specialty gift item can be beneficial. Creativity and imagination are requirements in conducting a successful direct-mail campaign, both for the message and for the messenger.

If it is important to have the right message and the right package for that message, it is even more important to deliver that message to the right mix of prospects. Developing and maintaining the mailing list are probably the most critical components of the direct-mail marketing tool. The critical step in any direct-mail campaign is centered around the list itself. Depending on the scale of direct marketing for your firm, lists can be used to segment the market in different ways. The obvious is from existing and former customers, but you can also reach groups with certain demographical characteristics. Your marketing research can identify those segments, based on geographical, educational, gender, lifestyle, income, and a host of other characteristics.

What you are looking for is a high degree of correlation between a particular demographic variable and the use of your product or service. Such a correlation is not always easily discernible. The use of zip codes to segment by neighborhoods with the implication of similar lifestyle and incomes may be useful. Lists can sometimes be obtained from organizations and many other sources, but you must understand your customer before you can build a profile and attempt to associate behaviors or lifestyles or any other demographic variable with a positive response to your direct-mail offer.

One more time: Your target market consists of the who, what, when, why, and where approach to your customer base and your products and services. Who are your customers, what are they buying, when are they buying from you, and why are they buying? When do they make the decision to buy? Where do these people live? If you can answer why the customer should buy from you as well as answering the other questions stated above, you are well on your way to being able to develop a direct-marketing campaign that will hit the right mix of customers with the right product at the right time in the right way and for the right reasons.

Direct mail is a precision marketing instrument. You have the ability to select who receives your message. It is therefore critical to first define the customer and understand that customer at the micro level. If your direct mail as well as the rest of your marketing strategy is to be successful, you must understand your competitors as well. Who they are? What is their market position and their marketing strategy? With this understanding you can design you message to fit your marketing strategy and market position.

It is imperative in any direct-mail campaign that you have something to offer the customer. Customers must perceive a benefit or they will not respond. The degree to which you obtain a positive response will correlate to the degree to which you are offering customers what they need and want, and that the benefit offered is perceived to be a good value.

One would expect that with the advances in technology and the increased costs of direct mail, that direct mail would be on the decline, and possibly on the way out, but according to Paul Schiller, the opposite is happening. Direct mail is actually on the increase. The use of direct mail is on the rise because marketers are becoming more sophisticated in use of the direct-mail tool. That sophistication is grounded in a firm's ability to target customers. Mailing lists stemming from certain databases are more able to profile a particular customer. The marketer has the ability to search those databases to identify that customer profile either within a select market or within a broader market. Computerization has fed into the development of the databases; direct mail is an extension of that.

The really powerful function of mailing lists works something like this. You can research your customer base to identify a typical customers' profile and lifestyle. For some product categories the correlation between product use and lifestyle segmentation is very high. The next step would be to contact a list broker who has compiled or can compile through their database a list of customers whose profiles match your existing customer segmentation profile. In this way, if you were operating in city A, you could expand your customer base to city B and city C through direct mail. Those cities could be within the region or anywhere in the country or the world.[9]

The example above should crystallize the importance of maintaining a good database, which is an integral part of the customer information system. The database should be kept up to date and revised periodically because of customer changes. With the costs associated with direct mail, a clean customer list is more efficient. The database is built initially from within the store. The reason behind many of the within-store drawings or giveaway promotions is to build the database. Information is gleaned off billing statements, warranty cards, credit card applications, in-store VIP cards, and a host of other sources. Many firms ask for personal identification at the cash register, which is entered into the store's computer database.

Telemarketing

Closely associated with direct mail because of the personal nature of the method is use of the telemarketing tool. It would seem that with the sophistication of communication systems, including such things as caller identification and answering machines, the effectiveness of telemarketing would be on the decline. Another similarity that telemarketing has with direct mail is that telemarketing also depends on computerization and electronic sophistication to enhance its effectiveness as a marketing tool. Technology is providing the telemarketer with some new tools as well, not just from the standpoint of better access and better utilization of customer information systems, especially databases, but from new tools such as predictive dialing. Essentially, what that does is dial a phone number in advance of the telemarketer getting the call. It actually contacts the potential customer first, then transfers the call over to the telemarketer in a short period of time. If a disconnect or answering machine is contacted by the computer-assisted dialer, that number is kicked out of use, which increases efficiency by about a third.

Firms such as Lawrence and Schiller are looking to double and or possibly triple their telemarketing capability because of the increased demand for those types of services. Yet even with the increased efficiency of the telemarketing systems, telemarketing is not cheap. In quizzing Mr. Schiller about costs for their services, he estimated about $30 an hour for telemarketing services. If you have a good list, a good script, and a competent person on the phone, telemarketing can be a very productive tool. A lot of variables come into play as to the effectiveness of any particular campaign.

Telemarketing mirrors direct mail in another way, and that is it has more precision. Where the radio and broadcast media take more of a shotgun approach in reaching a broad market, telemarketing is individual-specific, based on a set of predetermined variables. Like direct mail, the response will be affected by the offer.

One other factor to consider as we go through this list of advertising and marketing media. They can all be stand-alone media but rarely are. They are most effective when used in conjunction with another form. If a series of ads were first run on radio and/or television, followed by newsprint, followed by direct mail or telemarketing, the mass media forms would increase the response and the effectiveness of the targeted media such as telemarketing and direct mail.

Like all mediums, telemarketing can only get the customer to try the product once. The product and the service must be ready to grab customers and hold them. If the product is not in shape, a good marketing campaign will kill it permanently.

Radio

Radio is one of the most used media for small business. Radio can stretch the listeners' imaginations. Radio requires creative writing. What is important is to include the advertising media firm in the advertising process. Providing information concerning your product, your firm's positioning strategy and image, as well as the goals identified in your marketing plan will result in better ads, ads that are more consistent with your firm's objectives.

A typical 30-second radio ad can deliver a message that is roughly 60 to 70 words in length. That is it. You cannot tell the whole story about your company in 70 words or less. You cannot even explain all the features about one product in that time frame. What you can do in 30 seconds is have the ads professionally done to get the most impact. You should mention the name of your company or firm several times in your ad. If you don't, the consuming public won't know where to get the product or service you are selling. If they can't find you, they won't spend a lot of time looking for you and that sale has been lost. You should tell the public about your product or service, but you cannot say everything, so stick to a main feature and keep it simple. The feature or concept or theme that you stress should be consistent with why the consumer is buying or using your product. The message should fit your target market.

Look for a memorable sound or a memorable idea and use it. If an ad works or if you have found the right message, keep using it. Keep the message simple. Buy the time periods that reach your target market. This holds true for every medium. This time may be more expensive, but if that is the time when your target market is listening, to be effective you want your message delivered in that time frame. Radio offers many different formats, which makes it a somewhat flexible medium, because it has segmented the market somewhat already.

People tend to be more attentive as drivers of a vehicle than as home listeners. Commuting hours are good times to reach working people. Radio and television stations are rated by the number of viewers or listeners who are tuned in to the station. Their advertising rates will be geared to those ratings.

With advertising you want to reach your potential customer somewhere between five and seven times to maximize your impact. Radio is a good medium with which to do that by itself or in support of or in conjunction with another type of advertising.

The Internet

Relatively new on the scene, the Internet becomes one more tool to be added into the advertising mix equation. It is difficult to project the impact that Internet access will have on the way that people make purchases and the way that marketers market their product and/or services. The information available is already so enormous that it is easy to get lost, even when searching for a specific type of information. It is also true that a marketer who places a message out there can easily have the message get lost.

Remember that the Internet is a medium just like radio, television, or print and has a role in the marketing and customer information system. The role that the Internet should play within the marketing context is the role where Internet's unique strengths can be utilized. It is a remarkable tool but is not the be all and end all of marketing. We are still learning how to use it.

The Internet has some key strengths that are unique and difficult to replicate in any other type of medium, and as a result the Internet will be a tool of expanding use as time goes on. The first major advantage that the Internet has over existing media is that it acts not only as an advertising and marketing medium but also acts as part of the distribution system. Not unlike direct mail, a potential customer can respond with a direct order, but with the Internet the offer can be changed immediately. If a particular item is not selling well, a marketer can lower the price. If an item is sold out, the marketer can delete the item. The Internet acts like the word processing of direct marketing, with the added feature of instantaneous billing and inventory control. The Internet provides a reach that direct mail and other media could not reasonably achieve. Yet at the same time the reach the Internet provides is limited to that part of the population currently on line. Various estimates have been undertaken, but at the time of this writing the most optimistic estimates are still under 25 percent of the population. Certainly those numbers will grow rapidly, but segments of the population will be slow to embrace this new technology: the poor, who cannot afford the hardware and/or the monthly fees associated with Internet access, those who are not computer literate, and others.

One of the Internet's primary strengths lies in the fact that it is such a versatile and flexible tool. A company can design a new look and or change the look it already has very quickly. The design of a home page may be geared to business-to-business marketing, while links may be created to key in on the consumer end of the business.

Mr. Schiller indicated that the marketing research industry is telling him that to have an effective Internet site, it should be 10 seconds long and 10 minutes deep. Not unlike a television commercial, an Internet site must grab prospective viewers and hold them. If the message doesn't grab them instantly, you've lost them. That means that the site must be fresh; the site must be changed regularly.[10]

One implication of the Internet is that the life span of ideas has become shorter and shorter. This poses a special problem in the marketing function. It means that more effort must go into generating new and creative marketing concepts. In many ways the Internet is representative of what is happening in our society, which is being driven by technology and information. The product life cycle of many products has become condensed into shorter and shorter time frames. A Web page is just one such element.

• QUESTIONS FOR DISCUSSION········

1. In an opportunity-based marketing strategy, the focus is to take advantage of an underserved or unserved market. What is the difference between these markets?

2. Explain what causes a market to be unserved.

3. What would cause a market to be underserved?

4. The importance of being an early entrant into a business to take advantage of an opportunity created by a shift in technology has been emphasized. Explain why being an early entrant is important.

5. An opportunity can be gained in a market by taking advantage of a number of situations. Identify these situations.

6. Why is is important that the total market for the product or service that a small business is entering into be expanding?

7. In the small business profile, Joe Hurly made a comment that if he had had an additional $50,000 with which to launch his new business, he felt that he would be worse off than he is today. Explain what he meant.

8. In the interview with Mr. Bauermeister, he indicated that as much as 25 percent of a new startup business's total budget should be expended conducting marketing research. Do you agree with that statement? Explain.

9. Mr. Bauermeister suggested that for the prospective business owner, very early on the person should contact a marketing research firm at least for a visit. Explain the merits of that suggestion.

10. In the discussion with Ms. Simmons, she recommended that for some small businesses an excellent marketing tool is a concept called *event marketing*. Define that concept. Include an example of the type of product that would best be marketed through event marketing.

11. Where can a small business go for assistance in building a promotional campaign?

12. Under what conditions can advertising do more harm than good to a small business?

13. Why must a new business be more aggressive and expend more advertising dollars than an established firm?

14. Identify the principal advantages and disadvantages of each of the following advertising media.
    (a) Radio
    (b) Television
    (c) Newspaper
    (d) Direct mail
    (e) Billboards
    (f) Telemarketing

15. For what type of business would it be most advantageous to advertise in the Yellow Pages?

• BEYOND THE CLASSROOM: RECOMMENDED ACTIVITIES · · · · · · · · · · ·

1. Contact the following firms in your area, either individually or in groups, to request a visit or to conduct an interview:
   (a) A marketing research firm
   (b) An advertising agency
   (c) The sales manager of a local radio station
   (d) The sales manager of a local television station
   (e) The sales manager of a local newspaper

2. Conduct a site-selection analysis.

3. Attend a trade show.

4. Visit a major retailer to identify and list the corporate-sponsored promotional items used in their displays.

• APPENDIX: MODEL MARKETING PLAN · · ·

Not unlike the business plan modeled after the five C's approach, which will tend to be unique to the entrepreneur's business, the marketing plan will also be unique to the business. Like the business plan, in which it is not imperative that the entrepreneur model the plan after the five C's approach as long as all the critical elements are presented in a manner acceptable to the financial institution, so must the marketing plan submitted contain all the critical elements. That does not mean that your marketing plan will contain every element identified in the plan outline below. Your marketing plan may not require certain elements. It is possible that other elements may need to be added to adequately address your specific situation.

In the five C's approach, the third C represents cash flow, which deals with the projected financial statements, of which the revenue forecast is the most critical assumption in the entire plan. That revenue figure and expense projections, or rather the accuracy of those projections, will often determine the success or failure of the enterprise. The marketing plan's entire focus is to refine and support those critical revenue forecast numbers and expense projection numbers. The entire marketing plan will dovetail with the business plan at that point. In the end the banker will ask the entrepreneur, and the loan committee that reviews and approves the loan will ask and attempt to determine, what the degree of confidence is in that revenue forecast. As demonstrated earlier, we can use sensitivity and scenario analyses to massage the numbers a little and play with some of the what-if's, but ultimately it boils down to a few critical assumptions. Ninety-nine plus percent of our efforts should go into supporting and firming up those assumptions. That is why Mr. Bauermeister suggested that as much as 25 percent of the revenues available in a startup enterprise should be expended in proving those critical assumptions.[11]

The marketing plan presented here will probably not address every contingency and may need to be modified for a particular business. The plan here will attempt to synthesize the preceding two chapters and address the critical issues as I see them.

Marketing Plan

Business name:
Name, address, and phone number of the entrepreneur:

Abstract. Provide a short summation identifying the product, the size of the market, the proposed market share, the strategic position, and the competitive advantage. Identify what your business will offer the community and why the consumer will use your firm.

Step 1. Identify why a need exists for your product or service. Identify the size of the total market. Total market size may be regional or from a local perspective if that is the scope of your enterprise. This forecast number will normally require some support and documentation from your marketing research.

Step 2. Identify in detail your proposed share of the market. It is here where you can support with marketing research the rate at which the total market is expanding and the rate at which you expect to increase your total revenue, first by sharing in the total market expansion, and second, by increasing your market share of the total market, if such is in your plan.

Step 3. Identify your positioning strategy. If you chose to adopt a premium-price, premium-quality strategy, define and demonstrate how you can achieve the premium quality in your product or service. Attempt to demonstrate the level of acceptance of your product or service. Your level of acceptance by the customer could be supported by letters of commitment, attitudinal studies, or some other means of marketing research.

Step 4. Address the following in detail:

(a) *Your firm.* Define your business's capabilities as to production output and its quality component. Identify the types and levels of service your firm is capable of providing. Here you can identify your firm's strengths. Define how you are going to differentiate based on the strengths of your firm. Attempt to demonstrate why customers will buy your product or service and why you are competitive, and that does not just mean price if you adopted a premium-price, premium-quality position. Define your niche.

(b) *Your customer.* Identify your target market: why they buy, what they buy, when and how much they buy, where they are buying now, and why they will buy from you. Identify the customer attitudes. Support your statements and assumptions with market research and provide customer demographic data. In brief, identify who your customer is and how you will reach that customer.

(c) *Your competitor.* Identify the major competitors. Develop a profile of each and state why their customers buy from them, what their marketing positioning strategies are, and what their market share is. Identify each competitor's strengths and weaknesses. Show how your price and quality match with those of your competitors and demonstrate the overall positions in the market. Identify any substitute products. Define your competitive advantage and disadvantage with regard to each competitor. Address the issue concerning the prospects of new competitors or the likelihood of the exiting of existing competitors.

Step 5. Address the marketing mix variables.

(a) *Product.* In detail, describe what it is and how it provides value to your customer. Define in detail what service components exist with your product or as part of your product. Identify your product's life cycle and its ability to adapt and remain technologically current, why the customer wants or needs your product and/or service, why they will buy it from you, and how your product has differentiated. Define the raw material and labor inputs and the probabilities of shortages or price fluctuations in those components, if applicable.

(b) *Place.* Describe your location. Support your location study with population statistics, traffic pattern data, and so on. Address future issues that can affect your site, such as street construction and general growth, city plans for expansion, zoning changes, public access, parking, sign availability and restrictions, licenses, interstate access, loading and unloading access for shipping, and any other pertinent issues.

(c) *Price.* Identify how you are positioned as to price. Address the feasabilities of future price pressure or the probability of price increases. Detail the price elasticity associated with your product. Detail the threat posed by substitute products.

Step 6. Describe your plan for promotion. Detail how you are going to market your product or service and which advertising or sales media you will use. Identify what your advertising budget will be and who, what, and how those dollars will be spent. Describe your initial marketing effort, and address any special or extraordinary advertising, sales, or promotional campaigns. Address your continuing marketing research efforts, and define your customer information systems.

Step 7. Identify your market-based opportunities: Describe in detail any market-based opportunities that provide your firm with a competitive edge. Define how you will capitalize on that advantage, and how you can expand the scope of your competitive edge. If your specific location is important, your site study data can be used to support your location advantage. Identify any special access to customers that you might have. If access or cost advantages exist in raw materials, identify that advantage. If a special skill or knowledge creates a special advantage, mention those elements here. A plan to develop relationships internally and externally which can lead to a competitive edge can be mentioned. If an advantage already exists or if you have a plan to improve quality and service, that should be defined as well. Define all cost advantages, marketing advantages, or any other factor that gives your firm a leg up on the competition, and explain in detail how your firm can capitalize on that.

Step 8. Conduct a complete environmental scanning. Address any legal, political, social, technological, or environmental issue that could evolve into a threat.

Step 9. Develop a contingency plan. If the market does not develop or does not develop in the time frame anticipated, describe as best you can and in as much detail as you can what corrective action you will take, what cost-saving measures you will pursue, and what revenue-enhancing strategies you can employ.

Step 10. Describe your planned control mechanism. Describe in as much detail as possible how you will measure and monitor the progress of the marketing plan. This could well entail an annual budget with benchmark revenue and expense projections. It might include graphs with sales quotas or targets broken down incrementally by quarter, month, week, and day.

10 Small Business Accounting ● ● ● ● ● ● ● ● ● ● ● ● ●

Chapter Objectives

- To introduce an expedient streamlined accounting method. To demonstrate the importance of sound accounting practices.

- To describe the federal forms required to file personal income tax for the small business owner.

- To introduce a payroll accounting system, payroll reporting forms, and payroll reporting requirements.

- To provide an understanding of the importance of determining employee versus independent contractor status.

- To introduce multiple ownership forms available to a small business owner and to demonstrate some of the major tax implications associated with each.

During the last decade I have had the opportunity to consult with virtually hundreds of small business owners. In the performance of my duties as an unemployment tax representative, I was often present at the startup phase of a business within my assigned territory and again at its termination. The cause of each particular business failure was as individual as its proprietor, but if a single common thread could be found among businesses that failed, it would probably be associated with the accounting function. This is not just my assessment alone. I often posed that question to many of the accountants and CPAs I worked with, and they seemed in general agreement. In short, many business failures were caused because the small business owner simply did not completely understand their cost structure. In some cases the proprietor underestimated what the revenue inflow would be, and in many other cases they were unable to collect on their accounts receivable.

It was not unusual for entrepreneurs to reach the point of realizing that their businesses were in trouble or for a proprietor to realize that he or she was in way over his or her head. At that time they would contact a CPA firm in a last-ditch effort to save themselves, or more frequently, to deal with the IRS or other governmental agency.

In visiting with members of the accounting profession whom I knew personally, the accountants and CPAs seem in general agreement in their amazement that people continue to jump into enterprises without a clear business concept and without understanding the basics of accounting. I'm certain that the bankers involved have a similar perspective, although they may describe the situation as the proprietor's lack of understanding the numbers.

• IMPORTANCE OF AN ACCOUNTING SYSTEM ·

In writing this book I interviewed a number of small business owners. I asked each one what he or she thought was the most important principle in being successful. Each had a separate version of what was required to be successful in a particular industry, but they all agreed that one had to understand the numbers to make it.

Just because a person is a bricklayer or carpenter and a demand exists for those services doesn't mean that the bricklayer or carpenter can start a small business, become a contractor, and make money. It seems so simple. If a carpenter can charge $25 per hour for his services and can hire help for $12.50 an hour, the remaining $12.50 should be his profit. Right?

The real world is a little more demanding. First, the $12.50 he pays for labor is not just $12.50 but more like $16 an hour, due to payroll taxes and benefits. (More on that later.) The employee wants to be paid every hour he works, but a problem arises in being able to charge out to a customer for every hour the employee is on your time clock. Some of that time is spent waiting on the plumber, electrician, concrete crew, or sheetrock crew, or waiting for lumber or other supplies. All these delays cause an interruption in your revenue-generation activity, but the expense side of the equation, at least as far as payroll is concerned, continues unabated.

A second major problem facing the small contractor stems from situations in which a mistake is made and something must be torn up and redone. Who stands that expense? If it's the contractors fault, you can be sure that he will have to stand it, including materials. A problem exists in the area of bidding. The contractor estimates a job to take 60 hours and it takes 90 hours; the job becomes a wash at best. If a job is bid on materials plus labor, another realm opens up with the estimation of materials and incidentals. We haven't talked about additional overhead, such as transportation expenses, insurance expense, communications expenses, office, legal, equipment rental, and a host of others.

Each type of business has its own set of problems and pitfalls. The successful enterprises in each segment of our economy have evolved. They are successful for a reason, and most did not become a success overnight. For many, the business is already a multigenerational firm. They have developed a customer base. They have specific experiences in all phases of the industry and have developed a level of competence that the marketplace has accepted. The very reason they still exist indicates that they have been able to utilize this customer base and deliver a product or service at a level acceptable to their customer base and to show a profit doing it. The successful enterprise has seen much of its competition fall by the wayside over the years. It is into this environment that the new enterprise seeks to compete.

Year after year new businesses leap into the marketplace to compete with older, established firms in an attempt to take enough market share away from the competition to survive and thrive. My point remains the same: Failure to understand the cost structure of a business will generally result in the failure of that business. Similarly, failure to understand how revenue flows into a business and the lack of a fairly accurate forecast of that revenue inflow will generally result in the failure of that business. Ignorance of such matters will not cause them to go away; it will only magnify the critical issue. Accurate and timely information becomes critical because you base your financial decisions on that information. Failure to develop information systems because you are too busy or just don't like paperwork is like operating blind. You have nothing on which to base your decisions. You are therefore guaranteed to make mistakes, and the summation of those mistakes can easily cause the business to fail.

I am convinced that one personality trait that an entrepreneur needs is courage. Knowing what the numbers say is often very frightening. The tendency often is to just not look, particularly when a entrepreneur is flying by the seat of his pants, so to speak. Even when operating under the premise "if there is money in my checkbook, I'm making money," deep down the proprietor knows that a problem exists but too often doesn't want to face it. It is hard when someone pumps all the assets he or she has in world into an enterprise which demands 70- or 80-hour weeks just to stay alive; then, after putting in so many hours, that the entrepreneur must spend another 10 hours or so a week to determine exactly how much money the business is losing or how little it's making. Such a scenario should give the word *depression* new meaning. Yet without that critical cost and revenue information, decisions cannot be made that attempt to correct the situation. Nor can the proprietor recognize when to pull the plug on the business if corrective action doesn't work.

Even more depressing than knowing exactly how little you are making or knowing what your losses are would be a situation where a enterprise is able to hang on for 20 years with the owner still working 70 or 80 hours a week and then finally, going broke. If anything is going to get better, the proprietor needs to know and understand the numbers.

In practice, accounting tends to be a little bit different than textbook theory. I knew a university student with a major in accounting who later went to work for a local CPA firm. I asked her if work was like school, to which she responded, "not even close." The business world generally stays pretty close to standard accounting procedures, but many develop shortcuts or design specific applications for their business.

For most entrepreneurs time is at a premium, so the accounting function needs to be streamlined and/or automated. This raises yet another issue. Many small business managers dislike keeping track of "the books," so they buy a computer to do it for them. The problem doesn't change; it just becomes automated. Now in addition to needing to understand some basic principles of accounting, the business owner must also understand the computer software and hardware. If the proprietor doesn't understand the cost structure or accounting information generated, having computer-generated information won't help. It also creates the chore of inputting the information, and in many cases that probably isn't getting done either.

The first step in setting up an accounting or record-keeping system is to recognize that the accounting function is a part of the management information system. Ask yourself what information you need to make informed decisions. Who else needs information about the business? In what form does the information need to be? The answers to these questions begins with you. You need the financial information, but so does your banker and so do several governmental agencies.

The information you need should be the most detailed, because it is management information. You need to make day-to-day decisions regarding pricing, production, marketing, promotion, purchasing, and a host of other decisions that require reliable information. The banker wants profit and loss statements or income statements, aging of accounts receivables, and balance sheets, preferably on a quarterly basis, but the banker doesn't need the detail that you require. The information generated for financial institutions and governmental institutions is more summary in nature. The government is going to want reports on and for sales tax, income tax, and payroll tax, for both state and federal agencies.

The accounting systems that have evolved have for the most part been developed for major corporations, to ensure absentee owners that a system of checks and balances is in place. It is this type of accounting that is taught in most college courses. The sole proprietor does not necessarily need such an elaborate system yet. The accounting system that you set up for your business should be unique to your enterprise, designed to provide you with the specific types of information you need, while allowing designated others the ability to interpret them as well.

Begin designing your accounting system by addressing the issue of how money will flow into the firm. If your business is a retail establishment, most of your revenue inflows will be cash, whereas a service business will tend to have more accounts receivables. If you have accounts receivables, you need to design the invoices on which you are billing those services. If you think for a moment where this revenue inflow information needs to go, you soon realize that it will not only be a source document for the income statement, but also flow into the income portion of schedule C for income tax reporting. In addition, the invoices themselves need to become part of your accounts receivables and need to be tracked on an aging report, for collection and credit purposes. To facilitate good managerial decision making, regarding from what activity or sales items your revenues are coming, you need to have that type of detail built into your invoices.

If we were to interview an established firm about their invoices, it would not be uncommon to hear that their invoices have evolved along with their business. When information requirements change, so must invoices. In many retail establishments paper invoices have been replaced by computerized cash registers, but whatever the mechanism, it still acts as the original source document at the time and point of sale. The means may have had to adapt to supply whatever the new information requirements are that have been placed on the system by management's demands or need for that information.

Look at cash inflow from a retail perspective, using McDonald's as an example. When you walk into McDonald's for lunch, the person at the cash register greets you and attempts to sell you an extra value meal, but you opt for a Big Mac, small fries, and a large Coke. The clerk pushes three keys on the cash register, which immediately records the sale and simultaneously sends it back to the cook. These same keystrokes add the order and provides change information for the clerk. This sales information will eventually become a part of McDonald's income statement. In fact, they have every item on the menu programmed into the cash register. They know which cash register the order was made at, what time of day, and at which store location the sale took place. Management can tell you how many small fries were sold between the hours of 11:00 and 12:00 A.M. at an outlet in Austin, Texas, and compare that outlet with one in Green Bay, Wisconsin, or anywhere else in the world. This type of detailed and timely information enables management to make pricing decisions, menu decisions, purchasing and inventory decisions, and so on.

The small proprietor needs the same type of information but on a smaller scale, to make the same decisions but on a smaller scale. The design of your invoices or the programming of your cash register will be your source document to generate the same type of detailed and timely information. Again start by asking the question of who needs what type of information. In a small business where the owner performs all the functions, this type of cash inflow or revenue information needs to be gathered and assimilated into a usable format with the least amount of effort and time, because running a small business is demanding in other ways, and you just won't have large blocks of time to devote to this function.

• ACCOUNTS RECEIVABLE · · · · · · · · · · · · ·

If the nature of your business is such that most of your revenue is in the form of accounts receivable, a system is required to keep track of receivables. You are going to want to know who owes what and how long they have owed it.

First visualize the system from a manual perspective. If you can understand what input and output you want, it will be easier to automate. This may simply be a generational quirk. One of the easiest methods from a manual system perspective is to set up a card file (manual or computerized) preferably 5×8 cards, with the appropriate information pertaining to each customer: name, address, phone number, credit rating, and any other information that is deemed necessary. In this way as receivables are generated, they can be entered on the account card, and when paid, marked off. This allows you to view at a glance the sales and payment history of each customer. This can be helpful in reviewing credit terms. It can also be helpful in identifying your best customers, who should be rewarded with special attention and a special thank you. A Christmas turkey may generate more goodwill and additional sales from your best customers than could be generated by a $5000 advertising campaign.

An aging of accounts receivable record should also be maintained. That is, periodically, but at least monthly, go through the cards, list all the accounts receivable that are 30, 60, 90, and over 90 days old. (Computerized systems are good at generating these types of reports.) Before you begin to grant credit and charge to a customer, you probably want some references and certainly want to establish expectations and policies. It is not uncommon for many industries to bill out for services at month's end with payment due within 15 days or possibly, 30 days. Define your billing cycle, then pay a great deal of attention to your accounts receivable. Remember that your accounts receivable are really your money. You expect to be paid and should not be shy about asking to collect your money from your customers. If an account is past due, a phone call is in order, sincere and tactful at first, with increasing firmness and increasing levels of consequences such as suspension of services, followed by liens, small claims court, or some other legal recourse. The graveyard of failed businesses is well represented by firms that failed due to uncollected accounts receivable. Tight control in this area will help you reduce the time of your business cycle. It will free up your cash to expand your enterprise or reduce debt. If your firm is growing, you will tend to be short on operating capital for a long time. You simply cannot afford to allow your cash to remain tied up in accounts receivables.

Uncollectible accounts receivable are rarely those under the 30- or 60-day aging column. If you persist and stay on top of your accounts receivable, there is less chance that they will age to 120 to 150 days and over past-due column. These aged accounts are the receivables that easily turn into uncollectibles.

A physical card system may be cumbersome. If you have many clients, it is easy to see the expedience that computers bring to the accounting function. It is important, however, to understand what you're expecting of your accounting program and be sure that it is generating the documents required.

• SCHEDULE C

Total revenue figures are compiled from daily cash sales and from accounts receivable, the totals of which will be input figures for the income statement and will be reported for income tax purposes. For tax purposes a sole proprietor will file a form 1040 and attach a schedule C. Examine the schedule C in the appendix to this chapter (Figure A10–1). Part I of schedule C requests income information on your business. This can simply be a total of your four quarterly income statements. The IRS doesn't need the detail you yourself require; they simply need the year's annual taxable total. The bottom portion of part II of schedule C lists the expenses generally associated with a small business. It is convenient to use schedule C as a starting point in numbering your expenses for your chart of accounts. You can use the same numbers as shown on part II of schedule C, although the account numbers are in single or double digits. For example, advertising expense is reported on line 8. It might be helpful to assign an expense account number of 208, or you can use your own numbering system. In either event you will probably need to expand the number of expense accounts to provide you with the detailed information required to make informed decisions.

If your business is a retail firm or if your firm requires inventory of any type, you will need to complete part III of schedule C before you can complete part I. Part III identifies another critical element of your accounting system, your inventory control system and cost of goods sold. Schedule C requests your beginning-year inventory plus your purchases, less any purchases used for personal use less your ending inventory, which will calculate the cost of goods sold figure for a retail firm. If you are in manufacturing, you start with beginning inventory, then add your manufacturing, labor, material, and supply, and other costs that make up manufacturing overhead, calculate the cost of finished goods, subtract your ending inventory, and again compute your cost of goods sold figure.

Again, what is adequate for tax purposes will not provide you with the decision-making detail required for good management. Once again you must design your own system. Good inventory management is going to require that you don't overstock or understock. It will require that you are able to track your input costs due to price changes. You will want to make sure that your physical inventory is not being pilfered. You will want to ensure that perishable inventory does not spoil and that your inventory does not become obsolete.

A starting point is to identify your business cycle, list the material inputs required for a day's activity, then a week, a month and so on, through the time frame of your business cycle. This will give you an idea of what minimum amount of inventory you must have on hand to conduct business. From that point you may need to add an adequate level of safety stock, depending on reorder lead times. You will need to evaluate quantity discounts as well. Managing inventory levels requires a certain amount of personal discipline, due to the fact that most of your suppliers will hire a sales staff to call on your firm. These are professional salespeople and they will do their best to induce you to purchase. There is rarely a shortage of suppliers.

I was recently asked by a prospective new business owner where they were going to find a supplier. I found it almost humorous. It will generally take very little effort on your part to find a supplier, although there are exceptions depending on the type of business you plan to run. Generally, they will find you. Once word is out that you are in business, various salespeople will call on you, often unannounced and at very inconvenient times. After you have screened your suppliers, from that point forward it might be helpful to establish a policy not to talk to a sales representative without an appointment, including the ones you have approved to be on your vendors' list. This will save you time. It is also helpful to schedule your vendors. My preference was to schedule all my suppliers on the same day, 15 minutes apart. This mandates that each vendor has 15 minutes and only 15 minutes. To make economical use of their 15-minute block of time, the conversation was all business and saves on the niceties. If you elect to build a personal friendship with a particular vendor, you can schedule that vendor last or give the person a different day or time slot.

I found that once the sales representatives who called on you realized what you were doing, they appreciated the efficiency you introduced into their day as well. They would tend to get down to the business at hand. If they were going to write an order that day, it would be done within that 15-minute time frame and they were on their way to their next sales call. If for some reason a salesperson was wasting your time, when the next sales representative arrived I found it easy simply to stand up, thank the person for their time, and greet the next sales rep. The former salesperson would usually pack their things hastily and head out the door.

Inventory control begins with purchasing. A simple system that worked in my restaurant enterprise was to list inputs on a clipboard. Pareto's law states that 20 percent of your inputs will account for 80 percent of your costs. Start by listing the date and price of each item you wish to track. When meeting with your supplier, you simply need to ask for a price quote, compare it with previous prices listed on your clipboard, jot down his quote, and at a glance compare price movements.

You will help prevent pilferage by keeping the delivery doors locked and always controlling the keys to that door so that only one or two people have access. Someone should check the delivery in, comparing items ordered and shown on the packing slip with actual items and quantities actually delivered. This should be done at the time the delivery is made. This is also the time to rotate your inventory. When putting your inventory away, put the new purchase in the back and the old product is pushed to the front of the shelf—you not only have product rotation but a FIFO (first in, first out) system.

This system does not address the problems associated with product mix for the retail firm. What how much to stock is an ongoing dilemma. At the end of each quarter a physical inventory will be required to compute your cost of goods sold figure, which is needed to complete a profit and loss statement. Not every firm will need to perform a physical inventory at the end of each quarter; they may perform one at year's end only. For a service enterprise, inventory may be a minor issue, but by nature if little physical inventory exists performing a physical inventory becomes a simple task.

• CHECK REGISTER· · · · · · · · · · · · · · · ·

With completion of the cost of goods sold portion of schedule C, we can compute our gross profit. We then move down the schedule to part II, where we are asked to identity our expenses. To streamline the accounting function, it is easiest to begin with your checkbook. I would recommend the large-type format shown in the appendix (Figure A10–2). Your bank can assist you in choosing a check design that meets your needs. It is also possible to have checks designed and printed from outside suppliers. After you create your chart of accounts, you can tape a copy of account numbers to the inside front cover of your checkbook. Then when you write a check, simply jot the corresponding account number in the margin. If a check is written that is part of several types of expenses, break it apart, and list the corresponding expense accounts in the margin. For example, suppose that in a food service business you created an expense account with number 237 to represent your food costs while paper products were given the number of 239. You happen to run out of onions and napkins, which you purchase at the local grocery store. For simplicity, the onions cost $4.50 and the napkins were $3.00. The check you wrote was for $7.50 and was check number 101. In your checkbook you will write on the stub, acct. #237 $4.50 and acct. #239 $3.00, a total of $7.50, which you enter in as the total of the check written. On the grocery invoice you simply note the date and check number written, which will be filed in a manilla folder dated by month and year.

Periodically, you can enter the expense information from your check stubs into your check register; if you are computerized, you can enter the information into a integrated system. I found it easiest to create two main files on my desk, one filled with bills paid, another with bills payable. The grocery slip for $7.50 would remain in my bills paid file until that information was entered into the check register, at which time I would review the physical slip before filing it in the monthly accounts payable file. Done monthly, this was a relatively simple task.

Again, if you understand a manual system, you can make sense of a computerized accounting system. Most integrated accounting software packages will generate a check register. The check register simply tracks and categorizes all the expenditures run through a checking account for a period of time. See the appendix (Figure A10–3) for a simple manual check register.

Once a check is written, the expense receipt should show the date and the check number with which you paid this expense. These receipts should be filed in a manilla folder or a large envelope date with the month and year. In this way if a receipt must be found, you can glance in your check register, find the date and check number, locate the corresponding file, and you will only need look through only one month's receipts to locate the particular receipt. This type of information may be required in the event of a question arising from an audit, or you may need it for internal reasons.

The check register can be totaled by expense type at the end of each quarter to provide the input information for completing the quarterly income statements. The annual totals can go directly onto the schedule C for income tax purposes and into an annual income statement.

When compiling quarterly or annual income statements and for income tax purposes, schedule C, it is important to remember that not all the business's expenses will be compiled on the check register itself. Certain expenses will come from outside sources; for example, it is common to set up a separate payroll register for payroll expenses. In addition, loan repayments are not considered expense, except for the interest component. Similarly, expenses associated with your checking account will not be in the check register, because a check was not written for those charges; they will therefore need to be added in as a separate item. In addition, depreciation expenses will not be present in the check register either. A separate account should be set up for capital expenditures: that is, any type of equipment that must be depreciated. For this type of expenditure it is useful to create a depreciation schedule for the entire life of the asset. In this way one can simply add up the depreciation expense allowed in a particular year for each asset or group of assets. You can also keep track of your taxable basis should you sell an asset or trade it in. See the example in the appendix (Figure A10–4).

It may at first seem confusing and a bit overwhelming, but if you are to make informed decisions from a tax perspective, you need to understand the consequences of each capital expenditure. The alternative to this situation is to hire a competent accountant to perform this function for you, although that will generally cost $75 to $100 per hour. The dilemma that exists with farming out your accounting function is that you still do not understand the process. I have come to two truisms regarding small business: "Nobody knows your business like you know your business" and "Nobody cares about your business quite like you care about your business." That includes your accountant, who is busy running his business, which just happens to be an accounting practice. It also includes your attorney, your banker, and anyone else you care to add into this equation. So why depend on someone from the outside with no way of knowing if a critical area of your enterprise is being handled correctly and in your best interest? If you understand the accounting function and then grow to the point where delegation becomes a necessity, at that point you can delegate the accounting function but will be able to supervise and communicate about the accounting process from a knowledgeable and informed position.

Should you reach the point where you contract the accounting function out to an outside firm, it is important that someone is watching or overseeing the accountant! Yours would not be the first case of embezzlement by an accountant or bookkeeper. Yours would not be the first case where the proprietor thought federal and state reports were filed, only to find they were not. In either case, the consequences will be borne by the proprietor. You cannot delegate duties that you don't understand. You don't have to be an expert, but you do need a basic understanding. The opposite is also true: that if you are internalizing the accounting function, some system of oversight is advisable. It would be equally advisable to have your tax forms and records looked over, if not audited, by a reputable accounting firm. This should help prevent errors and oversights on your part.

Like every other facet of small business, small business accounting will tend to change and evolve. At the point where multiple people are performing different tasks, the need for more traditional accounting practices grows. The very reason for double-entry accounting practices is to provide a system of checks and balances. Regardless of the accounting system in place, it becomes imperative that oversight capability exists as soon as a second person has access to any part of the accounting function. One rule of thumb exists, though; I can see almost no circumstance in which a small business owner would relinquish the checkbook and delegate check writing to a second person except under very limited situations. This is my personal bias, but I believe the practice of maintaining control over the purse should be a carefully guarded function, especially in the early years of business growth.

• SELF-EMPLOYMENT TAX (FORM SE)···

Going back to schedule C again. Once you have calculated gross profit and then having subtracted out the expenses in part II of schedule C, you have computed net profit, which is transferred to line 12 on the form 1040 individual tax return. The net profit figure must also be placed on line 2 of the form SE (self-employment) tax form (Figure A10–5).

If you've ever had a job where you were identified as an employee, you received a W-2 at the end of the year. You probably noticed that on your pay stub your employer withheld FICA or social security tax, as well as medicare tax, which your employer also matched. In addition, your employer probably withheld money for federal and state income tax. As a self-employed person, no one is matching the withholding for FICA and medicare; therefore, you must pay the full rate. What would have been the employer's portion is now all your responsibility as a self-employed worker. That self-employment tax is handled by form SE (Figure A10–5).

The way self-employment tax is computed begins with the net profit figure from schedule C, which will be transferred to line 2 of form SE assuming that you have a profit. Net profits must currently be $400 or greater before a self-employment tax liability begins. This net income figure is then multiplied by 0.9235, or 92.35 percent, assuming that net profit is greater than $400. The result of multiplying the net income figure shown on line 2 by 0.9235×0.124 and $\times 0.0295$ for a combined total of .153, which is the self-employment tax owed. The self-employment tax owed often is no small matter, and many business owners or independent contractors are horrified by their self-employment tax bill at year's end.

Early each year the Internal Revenue Service sends you a form 1040 booklet, which includes the tax forms that you have filed in your recent past. Once you file your first year's return with a schedule C and form SE, you will receive those forms in your booklet to file along with your form 1040. In the back of the form 1040 booklet, you may have noticed a number of pie charts showing the federal budget. The pie chart identifies the sources of revenue and a breakdown of expenditures (Figure A10–6). The shift in who pays the $1.7 trillion required by the federal government has been toward the individual wage earner and sole proprietor. Tax law is another issue and will not be dealt with here, but it is important to understand the tax implications as a small business owner. Note the amount of revenue collected from employment tax and medicare and the amount paid out as benefits. The aging of America, coupled with rising health care costs, has created a dilemma for the medicare industry. As a self-employed person you will be doubly affected by any increase in self-employment tax rates. This issue bears monitoring.

Take just one short example. Suppose that a single person is operating a small business which is this person's sole source of income. If schedule C shows a $20,000 profit, that amount would go to line 12 of form 1040 (see Figure A10–7). The $20,000 profit figure would flow through to line 32, where the $20,000 would be reduced by the standard deduction of $4150 (single filing status for 1997, assuming no itemized deduction). The remaining $15,850 would again be reduced by the personal exemption of $2650 leaving a taxable income of $13,200 which would be shown on line 38. This income is taxed at a current rate of 15 percent for a total income tax liability of $1980 ($13,200 $\times$ 0.15 = $1980). The $20,000 net profit figure from schedule C must also flow to line 2 on the short form SE, which in turn is multiplied by 0.9235, which reduces the $20,000 to $18,470. This figure is then multiplied by 0.153, which amounts to $2,825.91, which along with your federal income tax of $1980 from line 39 of the 1040 is your total tax bill, which is

$4805.91, an amount for most people that is too much to dig up as an afterthought at the end of the year.

In addition to the federal income tax and federal self-employment tax, most states impose a personal state income tax. Most state departments of revenue generally begin as a spin-off of line 32 of form 1040, from which the state applies a formula derived from the revenue department of the particular state where you reside.

• 1040-ES ·

At this point these figures are just academic. They will have real meaning to you only when you must reach for your checkbook and attempt to write the check from your account. The IRS knows that people will have a very difficult time coming up with this much money at the end of the year, so they have mandated that you must pay as you go in the form of a quarterly tax estimate form 1040-ES (Figure A10–8). In those cases where you expect to owe more than $500 the IRS expects you to deposit payments using payment vouchers (Figure A10–9) which are part of form 1040-ES[1] The payments you make are supposed to be within 90 percent of the tax owed on form 1040 and form SE combined. An estimated tax worksheet is included with form 1040-ES to assist you in making your estimate.

This text is outlined in the bridge model format. The model is grounded in ethics. People generally act on their beliefs, and there is no better place to test those beliefs than in the area of taxes. Many people do choose to illegally alter their income statements at this point. Some are caught by the IRS, while others seemingly get by. A dilemma exists. If you would be willing to cheat on your taxes, where do you draw the line? The outcome here is money. Would you then be willing to cheat a stranger in a business deal for money? How about a supplier? An employee? A partner? How about your own mother? Some people have in fact regressed to the point where they have actually cheated their own mothers.

The original premise of the model of this book is that business is based on internal and external human relationships. You begin to lose personal credibility as soon as you start making rationalizations that it's okay to violate those relationships. To violate those external relationships will generally lead to a violation of internal relationships as well, which in turn creates a climate of mistrust, which in turn gradually erodes the foundation that holds the business community up. With enough erosion, the system itself will crumble and fall.

Another problem exists with altering your records for tax purposes. If you alter them, do you begin to make decisions based on altered information, or do you risk having two sets of books, which provides written documentation of how you are cheating? If you make decisions from altered information, your decisions are likely to be altered. If a flaw exists in your business concept, if a mistake is being made or a critical issue is not being recognized, cheating on your taxes will only hide the issue for awhile, it is not going to make it go away. Cheating on your taxes will never make you rich, nor will it save your failing enterprise. At best it will delay the inevitable. If your business is failing, face it. Identify the problem, find a solution, and move on or else close it down. You need accurate reliable information to make realistic decisions which support good results. As with most forms of dishonesty, cheating on your taxes has a price. The pressure associated with the fear of getting caught can make you unhappy and moody. A prolonged state of internally realizing that you are less than totally honest will often lead to a situation where you begin to project your mistrust on everyone around you. Rarely will cheating save a failing business, but it will certainly cheapen you in the eyes of those you care about and in your own self-concept. Once you give in, it will forever take away from your personal dignity and integrity. Americans like to win, but not by cheating. Why should the world of business be any different?

We have not yet addressed the balance sheet. If you have ever applied for a bank loan, your banker required you to fill out an application in the form of a financial statement, which is nothing other than the bank's format of a personal balance sheet. With a business loan the bank may require you to submit a balance sheet on a quarterly basis, which for management purposes you would want anyway. By the nature of its format, the balance sheet breaks down the asset section into current and long-term assets; it breaks the liabilities down the same way. The difference between total assets and total liabilities is equity. The balance sheet provides the user with information regarding the makeup of the asset section. It identifies the current assets in terms of liquidity and allows for contrast between current liabilities and current assets at a glance. The balance sheet identifies the makeup of the long-term assets, which are generally fixed in nature, and again provides a contrast between long-term assets and liabilities, as well as total assets and total liabilities. The equity portion is stated as total assets less total liabilities. At a glance the user knows the size of this operation, the approximate debt ratio, and a good guesstimate of cash requirements. The banker is interested in changes in these positions. You should be also. Detail is again in order. The balance sheet should be designed to provide you with the detail required to make management decisions.

Even with a streamlined approach to the accounting function, a considerable amount of energy goes into compiling the information required for the income statement and the balance sheet, to say nothing of all the forms required by state and federal governments. If the reports are to be of much use from a management perspective, they must be analyzed. It is helpful to take the income statement and convert every line and every item on the statement to percentages. In this way you can obtain another view of your revenues and expenses.

Pareto's law can again be applied (20 percent of your inputs will account for 80 percent of the expenses, and 20 percent of your customers will result in 80 percent of your revenue). You have a basis for comparing your revenue and expenses to those of your competitors and to industry standards. It doesn't matter if your competitor is 100 times larger than you; comparisons can be made. To do this total revenue is equal to 100 percent, with every other item in the income statement making up a part of that total, including profit. Thus if revenue is $100,000 and delivery expense is $2000 your delivery expense comprises 2 percent in relation to your total revenue. Such a calculation can put you on the same plane as your competition for comparison purposes; thus if your competitor has a delivery expense of 3 percent in relation to their total revenue, you can identify a competitive advantage.

The next question to answer once the percentages have been computed and comparisons made is: Why? Why is that expense the way it is? What can you do better? What can you do to take advantage of this situation? Which expenses are low, and which are high? This type of analysis can help in identifying waste and also in identifying efficiencies that can be taken advantage of. It also helps in setting goals and targeting projections. A percentage analysis helps to identify cost creep so that controls can be put in place to keep expense items from getting out of control. The next logical step is to calculate ratios to compare with your business's projections, to compare with your business's past, to compare with industry averages, and to compare with your key competitors. Chapter 7 deals more fully with ratio analysis and other tools of financial statement analysis.

A major step in small business ownership is hiring that first employee. You may be purchasing an existing business which already has employees and are assuming them along with the operation. It is important, though, to address this issue from its beginning. A substantial percentage of the approximately $1.7 trillion in the federal government's annual budget comes from employment taxes (Figure A10–6). For most small business the employment taxes are far greater than their income tax liabilities. It has been my experience that a failure to understand payroll costs, and a failure to budget for them, resulting in a failure to stay current with those tax liabilities, has been a major cause of business failure and foreclosure.

• FEDERAL IDENTIFICATION NUMBER (SS-4 FORM)· ·

Assume that you are a sole proprietor, have never had employees and have reached a decision to hire. The first step is to file for a federal identification number. This nine-digit number identifies you to the IRS as a specific entity. You are required to have an EIN (employer identification number), sometimes referred to as a federal ID number, if you are an employer. You may be required to file for one even if you are not an employer, but as an employer you are required to have one. This number, once received, is not transferable. If you form a partnership or corporation, you will be required to file for a new EIN. Note also that on schedule C, box D asks for your EIN.[2]

To file for an EIN, you file a form SS-4 (Figure A10–10). As a sole proprietor, if you were to run multiple businesses, you will need only one under that type of ownership. You would be required to file multiple schedule C's (but they would all use the same EIN), but a single form SE would be filed combining the net profit and/or losses from the three businesses for self-employment tax purposes. You can also file for a EIN by phone. See pages 2 and 3 of form SS-4 for the number in your area. By filing for the EIN, you inform the government that you are a reportable business entity, which in turn initiates the wheels of the governmental bureaucracy. The IRS will mail you an information packet. They will generally include a coupon payment booklet for making payroll deposits. You will also receive preprinted form 941's, a form 940, and a packet at year end to file W-2's.

• W-4 FORM, I-9 FORM· · · · · · · · · · · · · · · · ·

Having filed form SS-4, let's assume that you have interviewed and are about to hire your first employee. The first day on the job you would have the employee fill out form W-4 (Figure A10–11). Basically what this form does is provide you with the information you will need to make out a paycheck. The W-4 provides information so that the employer can withhold the proper amounts for federal income tax. The W-4 also provides you with the information required to provide the employee with a W-2 at year's end. The required information includes the employee's correct social security number and a current mailing address. It's important to have the employee fill the W-4 out immediately, because if you do not, there is a tendency not to get it done. Also, employees have been known to quit without notice, and you have a legal obligation to mail a W-2 to them, but to comply with that requirement, you need to know where to mail it. Start a personnel file on each employee you hire and the W-4 should go into that file.

As long as you are having your employee fill out form W-4, have them also fill out form I-9 (Figure A10–12), required by the Immigration and Naturalization Service to document that the person you are hiring is not an illegal alien. Section 1 of form I-9 is completed by the employee, and section 2 is filled out by you, the employer. Note you will need to examine one document from list A or one document from both lists B and C. Form I-9 indicates that you as the employer are to examine the appropriate documents, but it would be my recommendation that you attach a copy of those documents to form I-9, all of which should go into the employee's personnel file.

• NEW HIRE REPORTING · · · · · · · · · · · · ·

On August 22, 1996, President Clinton signed into law the Personal Responsibility and Work Opportunity Reconciliation Act of 1996 (PRWORA). The law includes comprehensive child support enforcement provisions that gives states and the federal government additional tools to locate parents, establish paternity where necessary, and increase the collection of child support payments. The law expands the existing Federal Parent Locator Service (FPLS) by adding two new components: first, a National Directory of New Hires (NDNH), which will house a database of all new hires, unemployment insurance claims, and quarterly wage reports, and a Federal Case Registry (FCR), which will house a database of all new and modified child support orders. The office of Child Support Enforcement at the Administration for Children and Families has the responsibility for implementing these two new federal databases. The NDNH must be ready to receive inputs from the states by October 1, 1997, and the FCR must be established no later then October 1, 1998.

What is behind this new legislation is the fact that more than 15 million children in the United States are living in single-parent households. In more than half of those households the custodial parent is receiving little or no child support. Many of these children are going without basic necessities. As a result, the custodial parent is forced to rely upon public assistance, thus becoming a burden on the taxpayer. In each state literally millions of dollars in welfare and medical benefits are spent to support these children.[3]

The new hire database will help track down delinquent parents and provide social services with another tool to locate and collect from parents who are delinquent in child support payments. The states will be required to implement a mechanism to comply with the new hire reporting requirements by October 1, 1997, although for those states that need to enact new legislation a grace period may extend that requirement to January 1, 1998.

The employer requirements are stated as follows:[4]

- *Who must report?* Each employer must report to the State New Hire Reporting Center. All employers must report all new hires, including any employee that is hired whether full time, part time, student or temporary worker. It the employer is required to give an individual a W-2 form the employer must meet the new hire reporting requirements. This requirement will create an incentive for those who are on the run from Child Support Enforcement to attempt to become independent contractors to avoid W-2 reporting. This will create another issue to be aware of, as a small business owner.
- *What information must be reported?*

  The Employee Name, Address, and Social Security Number
  The Employer Name, Address, and Federal Identification Number

  The report must be sent to the New Hire Center in the State in which the newly hired employee works.

- *When do employers report this information?* This report must be sent to the NH center no later than 20 days after the date of hire, but states may enact stricter requirements.
- *How can employers report?* Information reporting format is specified under federal law. Reporting must be made on either a W-4 form or, at the employer's option, an equivalent form defined by the employer. The state of South Dakota currently accepts a W-4 form by fax or mail. They also accept a printed list with the required information mailed to NHRC. An employer can call the information in using a 1-800 number or fax the information in using a 1-800 fax number. Magnetic cartridge or diskette reporting is acceptable and/or reporting via the Internet.

    States may determine where to house the SDNH. Options include child support agencies, state unemployment security administration, the department of health and human services, department of revenue, or even contracting to an outside agency. [It would be my guess that most states will use the state unemployment office.]

- *Why have a National Directory of New Hires?* A Multistage Employer Registration has been created which allows many employers the option of reporting all new hires to only one state. Contact the New Hire Center in your region for details. Information entered in each State Directory of New Hires will be forwarded to a National Directory of New Hires. It is estimated that over 30 percent of child support cases involve parents who do not live in the same state as their children. By matching this New Hire data with child support participant information at the national level, the Office of Child Support Enforcement will be able to assist states in locating parents who are living in other states.
- *Who will receive and view this information?* Information sent to the NHRC is strictly confidential. In addition to the use for child support enforcement, the Department of Labor will use the information to verify that unemployment benefits are paid only to workers who remain unemployed. The Department of Social Services will also use it to prevent unlawful or erroneous receipt of public assistance payments.
- *Are there penalties for employers who do not report New Hires?* All employers are required to report new hires on a timely basis. Any employer who intentionally fails to comply with any duties imposed by the New Hire law commits a petty offense. This may result in a monetary penalty for each violation. [South Dakota imposes a $25 penalty.]
- *What other information will the NHC request?* States may require information in addition to the six elements mandated above by the federal government, but must then do so under the authority of the state legislature. You can almost be assured that due to the newness of this program that it is bound to evolve. Changes are very likely to require additional information on the part of the employer. Be advised to stay on top of this issue. States who request optional information design such requests to improve fraud detection and administration. States might ask for information regarding Date of Hire, State of Hire, Employee Date of Birth.

At first glance this may seem like another intrusion by government into the free-enterprise system. It is just something to get used to and to facilitate within the accounting function. It used to be advisable to have the new employee fill out a W-4 upon hiring; that process is now mandatory. The reporting time frame will depend on the particular state. I would expect most states to require reporting within 15 days, which would generally be around the end of the first pay period for most employers.

If one of your employees is found to be delinquent in child support payments, it is likely that with this new reporting system, the child support enforcement agency may require you to withhold child support from your employee's check. If that is the case, the office CSE will direct you as to how much and where and when to make those deposits.

The state where you operate your business can provide you with complete information and instructions regarding all aspects of the new hire program. For information regarding your responsibilities as an employer, the following list of phone numbers has been added for your convenience. You can also find new hire information on the Internet at http://www.afc.dhhs.gov/programs/cse/newhire/docs/q-apam2.htm#MULTISTAGE.

Alabama	334-353-8491	Montana	406-442-7278
Alaska	907-269-6832	Nebraska	402-471-9160
Arizona	602-252-4045	Nevada	702-687-4744
Arkansas	501-682-6039	New Hampshire	603-271-4427
California	916-657-0529	New Jersey	609-588-2355
Colorado	303-866-3936	New Mexico	505-827-7728
Connecticut	860-424-5044	New York	800-972-1233
Delaware	302-577-4815 (ext. 249)	North Carolina	919-571-4114 (ext. 304)
District of Columbia	202-645-7500	North Dakota	701-328-3582
Florida	904-922-9590	Ohio	800-208-8887
Georgia	404-657-2498	Oklahoma	405-522-2550
Guam	9-011-671-475-0101	Oregon	503-373-7300 (option 2)
Hawaii	808-587-3695		
Idaho	800-627-3880	Pennsylvania	717-787-6466
Illinois	800-327-4473	Puerto Rico	787-767-1500
Indiana	800-437-9136	Rhode Island	401-277-2302
Iowa	515-281-5331	South Carolina	800-768-5858
Kansas	913-296-3237	South Dakota	888-827-6078
Kentucky	502-564-2285 (ext. 466)	Tennessee	615-313-4880
		Texas	800-252-8014 (option 5)
Louisiana	504-342-4787		
Maine	207-287-2886	Utah	801-536-7739
Maryland	410-347-9911	Vermont	802-241-2194
Massachusetts	617-577-7200 (ext. 30488)	Virgin Islands	809-775-3070
		Virginia	800-979-9014
Michigan	517-373-3190	Washington	800-562-0479
Minnesota	800-672-4473	West Virginia	800-835-4683
Mississippi	601-359-4315	Wisconsin	888-300-4473
Missouri	800-859-7999 (option 3)	Wyoming	307-777-6448

• PAYROLL LEDGER, CIRCULAR E • • • • • • •

It is now time to set up your payroll ledger. There are many computer programs written to handle payroll, if you can understand the manual method, you will understand the computer-generated output. The key is to keep it simple. I would suggest using a hard 5 × 7 card or a columnar ledger. The idea is to keep each employee separate on a single page, not run transactions sequentially as in a general journal. Running transactions sequentially creates a cumbersome situation where you jump from page to page attempting to total a particular employee's wages and withholding. Many office supply stores sell payroll ledger forms. The recommended type would be loose leaf, which lists two quarters on the front and two quarters on the back.

The format to set your payroll up with is to identify the salary or wage input information used to calculate gross wages. Normally, those inputs begin with hours worked times rate of pay plus any overtime, tips, and so on, if applicable for a specific time frame. If time is an element and it usually is, avoid paying weekly; instead, pay every two weeks or bimonthly. By reducing the number of times you must make payroll, you also reduce the chance of error as well as cutting the amount of time spent on preparing payroll. You will need to calculate the deductions for FICA (social security tax), medicare, and state and federal income tax withholding. See Figure A10–13 for a sample payroll ledger sheet. You design or set up your payroll according to your type of business.

In its simplest form, as of each payroll ending date, multiply the employee's hourly rate × hours worked to equal gross pay. To calculate the FICA deduction, take gross pay and multiply it by 6.2 percent. To calculate the medicare deduction, again take gross pay and multiply it by 1.45 percent. To calculate federal income tax withholding, refer to circular E[5] and your state department of revenue should be able to provide you with guidelines for state income tax withholding. If the office of child support enforcement requires you to deduct child support, simply create a column to accommodate that as well. To compute the net pay, simply take the gross pay figure, subtract the FICA deduction, subtract the medicare deduction, subtract federal income tax withholding, subtract state income tax withholding, subtract child support, and the remaining is net pay, which is amount you actually cut the check for.

It is helpful to put the W-4 information, name, address, social security number, and withholding of filing status at the top of the payroll sheet so that you don't have to run to the personnel file every time you want to make payroll. The amount of federal income tax to withhold is found in a circular E table based on gross wages, filing status, and weekly, biweekly, or monthly payroll frequency. Your particular state department of revenue will have specifics on figuring state income tax withholding. These are guidelines; each employee will have a different tax situation and you can tailor their state and federal income tax withholding to meet the employee's needs.

Suppose, for example, that John Doe worked 40 hours per week and is paid at a rate of $9.00 per hour and payroll is biweekly. Gross wages are calculated as $80 \times \$9.00 = \$720$, FICA is calculated as $\$720 \times 6.2$ percent $= \$44.64$; medicare is calculated as $\$720 \times 1.45$ percent $= \$10.44$; federal income tax withholding will come from the appropriate table in circular E. Assume that the employee is filing as single with one exemption $= \$131.32$. Assume a state income deduction of 7 percent: $\$720 \times 7$ percent $= \$50.40$. Total the deductions: $\$44.64 + \$10.44 + \$131.32 + \$50.40 = \$236.80$. Subtract this sum from the $720 gross and the net pay is $483.20.

The fact that a check for $483.20 was cut for payroll does not indicate that your payroll expense for that two-week period was just $483.20. Remember that the $236.80 was withheld, and that amount will not only be due the respective agencies, but the FICA and medicare will be matched by the employer: you. Thus the employee payroll costs for that period are in fact $483.20 plus the $236.80 deducted, to equal the original gross pay of $720.00, plus the employer FICA and medicare match of $44.64 and $10.44, respectively, for a total of $775.08. In addition, we must also include workers' compensation and state and federal unemployment insurance, covered later in the chapter.

• FORM 941 ·

The way the employer reports the wages paid and the federal payroll taxes due is as follows. The federal government requires that an employer's quarterly federal tax return be filed (form 941, Figure A10–14) to report these wages and liabilities. The 941 report is due the last day of the following month after the quarter ends. For instance, the first quarter ending date is March 31; the 941 report is due on April 30. The second quarter 941 is due July 31, and so on. It is helpful to have the payroll card or ledger set up so that at the end of each calendar quarter a line can be drawn and a quarterly summary computed. You can further expedite payroll reporting by simply subtotaling the gross wage column and the federal withholding column. Calculating FICA and medicare is simple math based on the total FICA and medicare wages paid. It is not necessary to subtotal the medicare and FICA columns and then double the amount for 941 reporting purposes. You increase your chances of error by doing so, and you have a multiplied rounding effect and will inevitably be off several cents per report.

• PAYROLL TAX DEPOSITS (FORM 8109) ·

Even though the IRS requires that you submit a form 941 for each quarter, you generally will have to make monthly or semiweekly payroll deposits throughout the year. First let me explain the deposit rules and how to make the deposits. If you will not have a total employment tax liability of more than $500, you need not make periodic deposits under current IRS rules. You may elect to submit payment either with a deposit coupon or with form 941-V (Figure A10–14). Form 941-V is a payment voucher attached to the form 941 you receive from the IRS or which you can pick up at a local IRS office. The 941 reports are due by the due dates listed in circular E. For all new employers with an employment tax liability for the quarter over $500 but under $100,000 you will make deposits according to the monthly lookback rule for your first year. Under the monthly rule, employment and other taxes withheld on payments made during a calendar month must be deposited by the 15th day of the following month. In your second year of business and thereafter, the IRS has two deposit schedules: a monthly and a semiweekly schedule based on a four-quarter lookback period, which is July 1 to June 30. If you reported less than $50,000 of employment tax liability for the lookback period you are a monthly depositor, but if you exceed the $50,000 liability you are a semiweekly depositor. The IRS will notify you each November which of the two categories you fall under. Circular E will provide you with more specific details if you should require further information. Most small business owners fall under the monthly deposit rules.[6]

To deposit the payments, use federal tax deposit coupon, form 8109. (Figure A10–15). You should receive a coupon booklet from the IRS after filling your SS-4 EIN or federal ID number request. If you do not receive a federal tax deposit coupon booklet, you can request one by filing form 4417-A (Figure A10–16), which is a request for federal tax deposit coupon books. To make a deposit, first calculate the liability, then use a soft lead pencil to darken the appropriate form number (Figure

A10–15), (section 3). Then darken the appropriate quarter to which you want to apply the tax (section 4). Finally, fill in the amount of the deposit you are making (section 7). You may make a deposit at any Federal Reserve Bank or other authorized depositories; check with your bank. You make the check out in the name of the bank and give them federal tax deposit coupon, form 8109. See circular E for additional details concerning penalties for required deposits not made timely.[7]

Note in form 941 (Figure A10–14), that line 2 asks for the total wages paid in a quarter. The total wages figure is for all employees combined. If your payroll card or payroll ledger is set up, one need only subtotal the gross wage column for each employee in the quarter reporting for, then add those totals together, and input the figure into line 2. Line 3 asks for the amount of federal income tax withheld, simply add the federal income tax withholding column up for each employee and add the totals for the same period and input into line 3. Line 6 asks for social security wages, which without flex benefits would be the same as gross wages as reported in line 2. Multiply by 12.4 percent, which is where you pay the FICA match (6.2 percent + 6.2 percent = 12.4 percent), put the sum on line 6a, then do the same for line 8, gross wages × 2.9 percent, which includes the employer's match for Medicare, and put the sum on line 8. The total of lines 3, 6, and 8 will be the total taxes due on line 11, assuming no adjustments. Compare the amount due on the 941 with the total amounts deposited with your coupon form 8109. If additional dollars are due, use another coupon form 8109 to bring your deposits up to match your liability. Remember to darken the appropriate quarter and appropriate type of tax. If you have overdeposited in a quarter, you may elect a refund or transfer the overage to the next quarter's liability.

• W-2 AND W-3 TRANSMITTAL · · · · · · · · ·

Upon completion of the calender year's payroll, W-2's will be required for each employee the business has employed throughout the year. As indicated earlier, an assumption of cash basis accounting was taken. This requires that income must be reported when received, not when earned, and also that expense is reported when paid, not when incurred. This is generally a minor issue except at year end. As far as payroll is concerned, if an employee is paid every other week and the pay period ends on December 31, the payroll is not made until after the New Year's holiday. Then from a cash basis point of view, the payroll expense did not occur until the following year and that final paycheck goes into the next year. One could do this and be correct. The other option would be to hold the checkbook open for a few days, writing checks dated December 31 for those payroll checks that close out the year. In essence, the same thing could have been adopted for the 941 and state unemployment reporting purposes throughout the year. Consistency is the rule. Adopt a method and stay with it. If an IRS audit or one by a state agency is conducted, the normal rule is to recognize wages when paid, but generally the agency will accept your system if you are consistent.

In my personal business, I always made sure that if payroll ended at the end of a quarter or at the end of a year, the check was dated on that date. It would be difficult for an agency to prove that this check was or was not received on that date. To a large extent, I feel this is splitting hairs and is a minor issue, but bureaucracy being what it is, there are instances where it makes a difference, as in computing an unemployment insurance benefit, which is based on quarterly income.

The end of the year, when W-2's are computed, is also the time to reconcile payroll for the year to verify that your payroll cards or payroll ledger is accurate.

For each employee one could add up all the paycheck gross wage figures that have been earned throughout the year. The total, assuming that section 125 and 401(k) pretax plans are not in force to alter the totals, would be input in box 1 of the W-2 (Figure A10-17), wages, tips and other compensation. The same figure would be input in box 3, to report social security wages, and in box 5, to report medicare wages and tips. The same figure as total gross wages reported in box 1 will be reported in all three boxes unless limits for social security wages have been reached, or as previously mentioned, a pretax 401(k) or pretax section 125 cafeteria plan is in force. Consult circular E for the social security maximums, as they do change each year. Medicare wages currently do not have a maximum.[8]

The income tax withheld for federal purposes can be tallied similarly; the annual total withheld for each individual will be entered in box 2. Box 4 asks for information concerning the amount of social security tax withheld. Simply multiply the social security wages in box 3 by the social security rate of 6.2 percent and enter the figure. It is easier to calculate that figure mathematically rather than doing the addition. You are responsible for the tax; it has all been paid in on the 941, and you will almost always be off by pennies due to rounding. The same technique can be applied to box 6, which asks for information concerning medicare withholding. Multiply the medicare wages reported in box 5 by a rate of 1.45 percent, the medicare withholding rate, and input the number.

Box b requests your federal identification number, box c requests your mailing address (this tells the IRS and Social Security Administration who the W-2 originated from), box d requests the employee's social security number, and box e requests the employee's name and address. This information should have been provided you on the form W-4 and form I-9 and should be in the employee's file. You should have required those forms as a condition of employment. It is at this time that you will often discover why it should have been a requirement. Some of those people are no longer in your employ, and you have no idea where they are. The IRS mandates that you make a reasonable effort to deliver these W-2's, a requirement satisfied by mailing them to the employee's last known address. If the W-2 is returned undeliverable, you are required to hold that W-2 for a period of four years.[9]

If you live in a state that also has a state income tax, your state reporting number is required in box 16, your employees' total wages are reported in box 17, and the amount of state income tax withheld is reported in box 18. That figure should be also accessible by totaling the appropriate column on the payroll card or ledger.

Current IRS regulations require that copy A of the W-2, with the entire first page of the W-3, transmittal of wage and tax statements, be filed by February 28. Extensions can be granted, but the extension must be requested. Copy A should be sent to Social Security Administration, Data Operations Center, 1150 East Mountain Drive, Wilkes-Barre, PA 18769-0001.

Send copy 1 of the W-2 to your state, city, or local tax department. For more information concerning copy 1, contact your state, city, or local tax department, usually under the department of revenue. Keep copy D with your copy of the W-3 for your records. Furnish copies B and C and copy 2, of the W-2 to your employees, generally by January 31. You will meet the "furnish" requirement if the form is properly addressed, mailed, and postmarked on or before the due date. This is one reason why it is important to maintain a file for each employee and to make sure that a W-4 and a I-9 are completed prior to cutting the first payroll check for that employee. If the employee's W-2 comes back as nondeliverable and that employee is no longer in your employ, you are required to keep for a period of four years the copies that you tried to deliver.

If an employee leaves your employ prior to the December 31 year end, you may give the employee a W-2 any time after employment ends. If the employee requests a W-2, that form should be delivered within 30 days. Information regarding form W-2 is available in an IRS publication, "Instructions for Form W-2."[10]

The W-3 transmittal is a summary form (Figure A10-18). It coincides box number by box number with the W-2. For example, if the totals of all the W-2 forms, box 1, that are to be submitted were added up, that figure would be entered in box 1 of the W-3, and so on. The first page of the W-3 transmittal form, which is printed in red ink, should act as the cover sheet for copy A of the W-2's, also printed on red ink, which are submitted to the Social Security Administration. These forms are important because they act as the raw input data for SSA to compile the wage earnings of each employee for future retirement and other benefits. These forms also provide the IRS with information to cross-reference those employee's personal income tax returns.

• FEDERAL UNEMPLOYMENT INSURANCE (FORM 940)· ·

In addition to the 941, an employer may be liable for state and federal unemployment insurance, federal unemployment form 940 or 940-EZ (Figure A10-19). The rules for federal liability are that an employer owes who pays out $1500 in gross wages in any calendar quarter. This is the total gross wages of all employees combined, including part-time help. The rules for liability for domestic help or agriculture are different and are spelled out in circular E. If one is a sole proprietor, you are not considered an employee and thus any draws you take are not considered wages. There are also certain exempt employees, specifically one's spouse, children under the age of 21, and one's father and mother. These exempt employees are only for a sole proprietorship; for a partnership or a corporate form of ownership, different rules apply. If $1500 of gross wages are not paid out to reportable employees in any calendar quarter, you are not liable to file federal unemployment insurance unless you meet the second criteria for liability, if you have employed someone for any part of a week for 20 different calendar weeks within the year. That is, if you hire someone to work some part of a day for 20 different weeks in a year, and do not pay out $1500 in gross wages in any quarter, you will be liable if you meet the 20-week rule. If you become liable to file federal unemployment, you become liable to file state unemployment.[11]

The federal unemployment tax liability is 6.2 percent based on the first $7000 of wages paid to each person each year. A credit is given for timely filing with the appropriate state unemployment insurance agency. That credit is 5.4 percent, so the effective federal unemployment tax rate is 0.8 percent, or 0.008, on the first $7000 per employee: thus $0.008 \times \$7000 = \$56$ maximum per employee. If a worker only earns $2000, the federal unemployment liability would be $16 ($0.008 \times \$2000$). The wages are reported on form 940-EZ (Figure A10-19) or on the long form, which is form 940. Either form is due January 31; however, if you have already deposited all the tax due, you have until February 10 to file the form.

The 940-EZ automatically calculates the 5.4 percent federal credit and is used by employers who had employees in only one state, paid these taxes by the due date, paid wages that are not subject to the state unemployment laws of a credit reduction state, and that all wages that were taxable for FUTA purposes were also taxable for your state's unemployment tax. Otherwise, use form 940. Most small proprietorships that operate in only one state can use form 940-EZ, which is less complicated. It should be noted that the employer pays all of the unemployment tax; nothing is withheld from the employee's paycheck for unemployment tax.

For deposit purposes, figure the FUTA tax liability quarterly. This is done by multiplying the taxable base (that is, the first $7000 per employee per year) or that part of the base paid in that quarter by 0.008. If your liability for any calendar quarter exceeds $100, which includes any underdeposited taxes from prior quarters, you will be required to make a deposit. Again you use form 8109 (Figure A10-15). You complete the coupon by darkening the appropriate quarter with a lead pencil, darken form 940, complete the dollar amount, and make a deposit at an authorized depository. It is easiest to make a deposit at the end of each quarter, irregardless of the requirements, because it's too easy to forget to make this deposit. Even if you owe less than $100, by making the deposit you are sure to stay current and thus avoid needless penalty and interest charges. Note part II of form 940-EZ (Figure A10-19). You are required to maintain a record of your quarterly tax liability for FUTA. If you make the deposits at the end of each quarter, you have an easy record of your liability.

The taxes that you pay into federal unemployment are used for administration of the state and federal unemployment agencies. The tax dollars are also used to assist states, especially in times of economic disaster. If a certain region is hit hard by an economic recession and many of the workers have exceeded their 26 weeks of state unemployment eligibility, the federal unemployment insurance agency may elect to extend those benefits for an additional 13 weeks. Those dollars come from federal unemployment, for form 940 or 940-EZ.

• STATE UNEMPLOYMENT INSURANCE···

All 50 states have state unemployment insurance agencies; most dovetail their regulations with the federal government. The regulations, tax rate, tax base, and liability requirements vary from state to state. Most states will have two or more rate structures, based on industry. Typically, construction industries will have a higher rate than retail or other types of industries, due to the seasonal nature of the business. It is common for the state to use a taxable base that exceeds the $7000 taxable base used for FUTA. You will need to contact your state unemployment insurance division for specifics. They usually have a representative attached to the local job service office.

All states will have an application form, which will result in the assignment of a state unemployment account number. This form will need to be filled out at the onset of liability. The application is made not unlike the SS-4 (federal ID number application), only once with each type of legal entity. The form generally ties into the federal ID number and is cross-referenced with the form 940 by federal ID number. This process validates and certifies that the 5.4 percent credit taken on either the 940 or 940-EZ is authorized. If the taxable wages reported to the state do not match the taxable wages reported for FUTA, aside from recognized discrepancies stemming from 401(k) and section 125 benefits, the 5.4 percent credit may be denied. See Figure A10-20 for form DOL-UID-001 used by the state of South Dakota.

The states' reporting requirements are a little different than for federal unemployment. A database is kept which requires that every covered employee have their name, social security number, and gross wages reported to the unemployment insurance division on a quarterly basis to maintain this database. Thus if an employee is laid off, they just need to tell the unemployment office their name and social security number and the unemployment representative can with a predetermined formula calculate what the person's weekly monetary benefit will be assuming that the eligibility requirements are met. From the employer's standpoint, a quarterly contribution and wage report must be filed. See Figure A10-21 for an example of a quarterly report for the state of South Dakota. Most states have a similar format. The individual information is listed on the bottom half of the report and on adjoining pages or attached computer printouts, or a computer disk may be enclosed. The individual totals are transferred to the top of the page; line 3 requests a gross wage figure, line 4 the excess (that amount over $7000 for all employees in that quarter), and line 5 is the taxable wages multiplied by two separate rates. Note that South Dakota does match federal unemployment on the $7000 taxable base. It can be somewhat confusing when calculating the excess wage portion of the form, because the state views the wages from a quarterly perspective. Thus an employer must track that employee through multiple quarters to the point where they reach the excess wage point and from that point on remain in excess.

For example, suppose that John Doe has wages of $720 biweekly at the end of the first quarter, March 31; $4320 (6 × $720) of wages has been paid to date. The first-quarter report will show John Doe with $4320 of wages on line 17, nothing in line 18. By June 30 the second-quarter report will show John Doe with $5040 ($720 × 7) on line 17 but now has earned $9360 for the year; $9360 less $7000 = $2360. Thus $2360 will be shown on line 18 as excess wages. In the third and fourth quarters, $4320 and $5040 will be reported on lines 17 and 18, respectively, because the $7000 base was met in the second quarter. If we look at the wages at the end of the year, $18,720 was paid in wages, of which $7000 was taxable and $11,720 was excess ($2360 + $4320 + $5040), which should and does match the 940. With the state unemployment return, the tax itself is submitted along with the quarterly report.

As in the case of the 941, if no wages were paid in a particular quarter and you receive a form from an agency, you still must file the form, even if nothing is due. If you fail to file, the agency will consider you delinquent and will take progressive action against you. Be aware that each state dictates what the taxable base is and what the tax rate is on that base. It may vary according to industry, and most states will grant an experience rate. An experience rate is a rate reduction based on each employer's history of wages and account balance. For example, the state of South Dakota currently assigns a total rate of 1.9 percent to first-year nonconstruction employers, a second- and third-year rate of 1.7 percent, and thereafter an experience rate based on the last three years' total taxable payroll divided into the account balance, which results in a decimal amount, which in turn is applied to a table that will correlate to a specific rate.

• WORKERS' COMPENSATION INSURANCE

If you have employees, you will be liable to provide workers' compensation coverage on those employees. Each state will have different requirements, so you will need to contact the workers' compensation agency in your state for specifics.

Workers' compensation is an insurance program that pays medical and disability benefits for work-related injuries and diseases. This coverage is paid for by the employer. Workers' compensation protects both employees and employers. The workers' compensation law is administered by the Division of Labor and Management of the Department of Labor. Each state has a section in the codified law relating to workers' compensation, and some irregularities between states exist. Again you will need to contact the agency in your particular state for specific regulations. That said, in a general sense if you are a sole proprietor, you are not required to cover yourself nor are you required to cover certain family members. Generally speaking, if you are a closely held corporation, you can elect to take an officer exclusion. Check with your state workers' compensation office for specifics. Some states underwrite the workers' compensation coverage through the state agency, while other states require that you acquire coverage through your business insurance agent. In the latter case an endorsement is added to your business liability policy. Premiums are based on an industry rating and or an experience rate, which is then multiplied by the estimated annual gross payroll less any workers excluded. There is generally a minimum premium, and premiums are often required to be paid up front. In some cases, particularly if underwritten by the state, they are paid on a quarterly basis. Some states will have reporting forms somewhat similar to unemployment reports. Some states charge premiums on a taxable basis. Like unemployment insurance, workers' compensation coverage is 100 percent employer borne. You do not deduct anything from the employee's pay.

• INDEPENDENT CONTRACTOR VERSUS EMPLOYEE STATUS · · · · · · · · · · · · · · · · ·

Independent contractor versus employee status is a major issue with the IRS, Department of Labor, workers' compensation board, and employers. Each year many disputes wind up in hearings and many in a court of law to sort out and make a determination.

It is not uncommon to see workers' compensation premiums in the range of 12 to 15 percent, again depending on the industry. Clerical help would tend to have lower rates, while something like a moving and storage firm could well have much higher rates. It is little wonder that one of the biggest issues facing the IRS and the business community is the definition of employee versus independent contractor. It doesn't take long for an employer to realize that the total payroll expense far exceeds the actual cost of the employee's paycheck. If you have an employee earning $10.00 per hour, by the time you add 6.2 percent for the FICA match and 1.45 percent for the medicare match, plus 1.9 percent or more for state unemployment, and another 0.8 percent for federal unemployment, and say 10 percent for workers' compensation, the total is 20.35 percent.

Suddenly the $10.00 an hour employee costs $12.35 per hour without adding any other fringe benefits, such as vacation pay, sick leave pay, or retirement. The actual costs you incur will depend on the rates assessed for unemployment and workers' compensation. The fact remains that employees are expensive, and worker productivity is of paramount importance. Little wonder that corporate America is reconfiguring using more capital investment and downsizing personnel. To a large extent, it is also what is behind the expanded use of temporary labor pools.

If a person is an independent contractor, all of the above is a mute point. The pay is $10.00 per hour, period. An independent contractor is responsible for his or her own taxes. Too often employers who make the employee/independent contractor decision tend to hear or read what they want to hear or read. The result is a lot of confusion and misunderstanding concerning who is, in fact, an independent contractor and who is an employee.

In defining someone as an independent contractor, the implication is that the person is a business. The distinction or classification is of critical importance to both parties. If a business erroneously determines one to be an independent contractor and the IRS overturns that classification, the 941's were either not filed or were filed incorrectly. Not enough wages were reported, and amended returns will be required along with the additional tax due plus a penalty and interest for late payment of those taxes. To make matters worse, the employee's portion of the social security and medicare taxes were never withheld. In addition, all the payroll forms will be required to be amended to all the agencies (state and federal unemployment, workers' compensation, state department of revenue, 941's, and W-2's) as well as the additional monies due with penalty and interest charges associated with each form.

Consider a situation where a business paid out $50,000 per year to independent contractors for a period of three years and had that classification overturned. The total bill could easily reach $50,000 and could mean financial ruin for a small enterprise.

A problem exists in defining an independent contractor. Each state will have a definition by statute for unemployment insurance purposes and also for workers' compensation purposes. A common definition is that an independent contractor is free of direction and control and is engaged in an independent trade or profession. Both criteria must be met. The agency performing the ruling will look at how the person was paid. Was a contract or bid used, or was the person paid by the hour, week, or month? Was the person told when to come and go? Was the person told how to perform the work in any way? Does the employing unit provide training, or support services, tools, transportation, materials, supplies, samples, office space, or telephone? Who inspects the work? Are any reports required to be filed? Who supervises the work? Is the worker eligible for vacation, sick leave, bonuses, and so on? Does the person perform these services for others? If so, who? Has this person been treated as an employee in the past?

Answers to these and other questions are used to establish the control issue. Questions relating to engagement in an independent trade or profession will go along this line. Does this person have a federal identification number? State identification number? Sales tax or excise tax number? Does the person have a business liability insurance policy? Is the person bonded? Does the person have a place of business? Does this business advertise? Where? Is the firm listed in the phone book? Does the person have an investment in this business? How much, and what type? Is this investment at risk? Does this business have employees?

An independent contractor is a business or profession that presents itself to the public as a business or profession. Rulings are usually performed on a case-by-case basis. In some situations the independent status is easily defined; in other cases such a status tends to become a bit gray and difficult to determine.

The IRS defines an independent contractor through common law, based on precedence. They use 20 common-law factors (Figure A10-22). The questions asked and conclusions drawn are generally similar to the state agency's criteria, yet cases exist, though rare, where state agencies and the federal government disagree on interpretations and rule differently.

How are you supposed to know, if governmental agencies cannot always agree? You could get a ruling up front. Do not just call the IRS or stop in at a local office and ask the local representative. The IRS does not recognize verbal information provided by its own employees. If you act on advice given by the IRS, make sure you get that decision in writing. An SS-8 form (Figure A10-23) can be submitted to the IRS for a decision, or your state unemployment office should be able to provide a decision as to your status. If you elect to use legitimate independent contractors, I recommend keeping a file on each one and to have them fill out some type of data sheet prior to their acceptance on any job. See Figure A10-24 for a sample data sheet.

The correct classification and use of independent contractors is not only a legal issue but also an ethical one. Cases exist in which the employee is turned into an independent contractor by forced circumstances, often without their own knowledge or understanding of the consequences. The employee becomes a business for income tax purposes and is treated as being self-employed. They will be required to file and attach schedule C to their 1040 personal tax return and will also be required to file as a self-employed person and will be required to attach form SE and pay social security and medicare at the full combined rate of 15.3 percent. It also stands to reason that since independent contractors are not reportable for state and federal unemployment insurance, nor are they reportable for workers' compensation, they are not covered by those programs either. The misclassified person will be treated as an independent contractor for tax purposes unless an appeal is made to the IRS or the Department of Labor to investigate this relationship.

If for this business to survive, a business owner feels compelled to misclassify his or her employees as independent contractors, much like tax evasion it will probably only delay the inevitable. The real issue is an error in the business concept, or a problem exists in one of the function areas. It may be that this concept will not survive. Universally, businesses are faced with situations in which they must solve a problem or seek a solution to a troublesome situation. The existence of the business often hinges on the successful resolution of that situation. These situations tend to be fundamental in nature: finding additional capital, finding new markets or new products, finding new production methods to cut cost, or a similar problem. Cheating your employees or the government will not make those issues go away.

• 1096 AND 1099 · · · · · · · · · · · · · · · · · ·

Form 1099-MISC (Figure A10-25), miscellaneous income, must be filed for each person to whom you have paid (1) at least $10 in royalties or broker payments in lieu of dividends or tax-exempt interest (box 8); (2) at least $600 in rents, services (including parts and materials), prizes and awards, other income payments, and medical and health care payments; or (3) fishing boat proceeds. In addition, use form 1099-MISC to report that you made direct sales of at least $5000 of consumer products to a buyer for resale. You must file form 1099-MISC for each person from whom you have withheld any federal income tax under the backup withholding rules, regardless of the amount of the payment. Report only payments made in the course of your trade or business. Remember, though, you do not use form 1099 to report payments made to your employees, such as business reimbursement expenses; you generally report those payments on form W-2, unless the payments were made in an accountable plan.

When reporting payments on form 1099, be sure to report those payments in the proper box. The IRS uses that information to cross-match and verify that the recipient has properly reported the payment.

When the following situations exist, you do not need to report payments to the IRS on form 1099: (1) when the recipient is a corporation, except for payments required to be reported in boxes 6 and 8, (2) payments for merchandise, (3) payments of rent to real estate agents, (4) wages paid to employees (use form W-2), and (5) business travel allowance expenses paid to employees. Note this list is not all-inclusive; see the IRS instructions for form 1099 for additional information.[12]

Generally, payments made to independent contractors are reportable on form 1099-MISC in box 7. Generally, amounts reportable in box 7 are subject to self-employment tax. If payments are not subject to this tax and they are not reportable elsewhere on this form, report the payments in box 3. A payment is generally considered nonemployee compensation (box 7) if the following four conditions are met: (1) you made the payment to someone who is not your employee; (2) you made the payment for services in the course of your trade or business; (3) you made the payment to someone other than a corporation (you would give a form 1099 to an individual or to a partnership); and (4) you made payments to the payee of at least $600 during the year. Again, consult the IRS instructions for form 1099 for additional information.

The relationship between form 1096 (Figure 10-26) and the attached 1099's are similar to the relationship between the W-3 and the attached W-2's. Form 1096 acts as a summary of all the 1099's attached. Please note that there are a number of different 1099's, such as 1099-DIV for reporting dividend distributions, 1099-INT for reporting interest payments, and many others. It is important to remember that a separate 1096 is required as a summary report for each type of 1099 issued. Thus an organization may issue several form 1096's, each with its appropriate attached 1099's of the same type. Thus a 1096-INT would summarize the attached 1099-INT documents issued, and so on, but only one 1096 of a specific type will be issued. A separate 1096 is required only for each different classification of payments made.

• PAYROLL REVIEW···············

Payroll reporting seems overwhelming and confusing for many people, at least the first time through. It helps to see the big picture in the sense of a payroll summary. Most accounting firms will run such a summary to ensure that the year is closed out without oversights and to tie all the payroll reports together.

To begin, an annual summary is done on each employee: on a separate page or separate computer run, date paid, gross wage, federal income tax withheld, state income tax withheld, social security withheld, and medicare withheld. The totals of these columns are compared with the payroll ledger and are used as the input numbers for the W-2's. Every other report must somehow tie to the W-2's and the W-3 transmittal. Assuming that a 401(k) or other payroll pretax retirement is not in use, the federal taxable totals will be the same as the social security and medicare totals as long as earnings do not exceed the limits for social security withholding. Medicare has no such upper limit.

The total amount of federal income tax withheld, added to the total amount of social security withheld, plus a 6.2 percent match, both those added to the medicare withheld, plus the 1.45 percent match should be equal to the total of all 941 deposits made with your deposit coupons, form 8109. Depending how your state handles state income tax, your withholding for the state department of revenue must match the amount sent in to that agency.

The totals of all the W-2's are transferred to the W-3 on a line-by-line basis. The W-3 total for line 1, total taxable wages paid, should match the total wages paid figure on the 940 or 940-EZ form on line 1, asking for the total of wages paid.

On a quarterly basis, if totaled, the 941's should match the total wages in box 1 of the W-3; that figure should also match line 1 on the 940. Totals of the social security and medicare wages of all four quarters should match the appropriate box totals on the W-3: box 3, for social security wages, excluding tips, which is reported in box 7, and box 5 for medicare wages. The totals of the federal income tax withheld should tie into box 2 on the W-3. Similarly, add the four 941 totals for social security tax submitted divided by 2; this should tie into box 3 on the W-3 and box 7 for tips. The same would hold true for medicare tax submitted divided by 2;

this should match box 5 on the W-3. If you add the totals of line 11 (total taxes) on the four 941 forms, you should tie into the total of all 941 deposits on form 8109 deposit coupons.

The quarterly state unemployment reports should tie into the federal forms in much the same way. The totals for wages paid on each of the four reports should match the 941's. The totals of the four reports should tie into box 1, total wages on form W-3, and also match line 1 on the 940-EZ form. The wages in excess and taxable wage totals will probably not match the 940-EZ, because the taxable base for unemployment in most states does not match the $7000 base charged on the 940 or 940-EZ.

· 401(k) PLANS ·

The small sole proprietorship generally is not concerned with 401(k), at least not initially. As the firm grows, some type of retirement plan may be incorporated into the benefits package for employees. I therefore chose to leave 401(k) out of the mix and to simplify payroll reporting as much as possible. But it might be beneficial to understand the logic and the tax consequences of pretax retirement plans.

Historically, nothing was available in the way of pretax or tax-deferred investments until the late 1970s, when tax-deferred annuities came on the scene. Prior to that the only way to delay or in some cases avoid income tax was through the use of life insurance policies, where the death benefit was paid to heirs on a tax-free basis.

During the 1970s the nation came to grips with a pending crisis in social security. Both the public and the government began to realize that social security benefits would be inadequate to totally fund retirement for the working class. Not that social security was ever intended to be the sole source of retirement income, but the perception by the public was often construed to believe that social security would be adequate. At the same time, the government was acutely aware that under the current structure, social security would soon even be incapable of funding current benefits, much less future benefits. A multitude of political fixes ensued.

The first step was legislation that would incrementally raise the rate of withholding from the then 10.2 percent to the current 15.3 percent combined social security and medicare rate. The base for social security withholding was also raised dramatically, to its current base of $62,700, as of 1996. This base will be adjusted upward continually on an annual basis. A second crisis occurred and continues to evolve in the area of medicare. A legislative fix was to separate medicare wages and taxes from social security, as it is today. A second phase of that legislative alteration was to separate the wage base subject to medicare, which currently is unlimited. This issue is not over yet. At the time of this writing the debate goes on over how to fix social security and medicare. The choices seem to be raise more money or to limit benefits. For social security the current drift seems to be toward limiting benefits at first in part by using a less sensitive index to estimate the rates of increases in costs of living adjustments. For all practical purposes, medicare seems to be on the verge of being out of control and continues to be a real challenge for recent administrations.

To back up a moment, back in the late 1970s the first legislation that provided a mechanism for the person to gain some control over his or her retirement income through the use of tax-deferred investments began to emerge. The insurance industry lobbied hard and won the right to sell tax-deferred annuities. The banking industry and brokerage industry quickly responded with a push to create the Individual Retirement Account (IRA) for individuals and the Keogh for self-employed people, which actually gave a tax credit in the form of reducing a person's adjusted gross income. At the onset everyone was eligible for one or the other; today one must be both eligible to participate and also income eligible for the deduction. Those adjustments are currently made on line 23 of form 1040 for IRAs and line 27 for the Keogh. The tax consequences are as follows if you are eligible to participate and eligible for the deduction. In the case of an IRA, the social security and medicare tax have been withheld from your paycheck; a reduction in adjusted gross income occurs on form 1040 on line 23. A $2000 deduction would in most cases result in a tax savings of $300.

By the early 1980s the federal government as well as those in the financial industry began to realize the economic consequences of this pool of tax-deferred retirement savings. Political lobbying resulted in the current systems we have in place. The managed 401(k) and the multitude of similar plans are a pretax payroll deduction. The end result is the same as a deduction under an IRA except that the $2000 limit can be exceeded. The taxable salary base is reduced immediately. In the case of a person who participates only in a 401(k), the end result on this employee's W-2 will be that line 1 taxable wages will be less than line 2 social security earnings by the amount of the 401(k) deduction.

The implication of these plans is enormous. In January 1997, a record $29.39 billion was invested in stock mutual funds alone, primarily through 401(k) deductions.[13] The cumulative total is in the trillions of dollars. The net result is that we will have many Americans who will retire with substantial sums of money in their 401(k) accounts, which in turn will have a large impact on the future economy of the nation. It is also very good for the brokerage industry and those professional money managers who manage and control this tremendous wealth.

• SECTION 125, CAFETERIA PLANS·····

Cafeteria plans are the result of legislation to assist individuals and employers in funding the skyrocketing costs associated with medical care in this nation. The political solution is to attack the problem through tax legislation, the most recent of which is to allow tax-free withdrawals from IRA and other retirement funds to pay for medical bills. The payroll implications are dollars that are withheld from the employee's paycheck to pay a variety (thus the name *cafeteria*) of insurance premiums and medical expenses, including through the use of a pretax spending account. Those eligible dollars will not be taxed for income tax purposes, nor will they be taxed for social security or medicare. Thus, participation results in a lower figure in the appropriate boxes on the W-2. The employer benefits by offering employees an opportunity to participate in cafeteria plans because a reduction in social security and medicare wages results in a reduction of the employer's payroll tax contributions.

• OWNERSHIP FORM················

The perspective of this book is that of the sole proprietorship. Most businesses start out as a sole proprietorship because it is the easiest and simplest form to use. One thing to remember is that once your business elects a form of legal ownership, to change that ownership is very similar to the sale of the business in the eyes of most agencies. If you change ownership form, every agency must be notified of the termination and startup dates. Some of your identification account numbers can simply be transferred; others will require new numbers. In almost every instance, paper documentation will be required in the form of new applications and/or transfer forms. It is advisable to make any change of ownership at the end of a year and the beginning of the following year. If that is not feasible, the next best thing would be to make those changes at the end of a quarter.

Before anyone begins an enterprise, he or she should identify which agencies require reports to be filed and what licenses will be required. The easiest perspective to take to assess who might have requirements is to view your business from the aspect of control. In our society, certainly, the federal government has the broadest jurisdiction; each of us falls under federal mandates in one form or another. The state would cast the next largest net of jurisdiction, followed by the county and the city. If you are in a profession of any sort, those professional organizations have lobbied to put in place certain regulations and restrictions in the form of legislation at various levels to place limits and controls within the industry. These limitations can act as a barrier to entry for that profession, which is striving to protect their economic turf, although most would argue that such restrictions protect the public. In some cases that is a valid argument.

It doesn't matter why requirements were imposed; it only matters that they have been imposed and are enforced. This requires new entrants to identify what is required and to ensure that they are in compliance. Failure to be in compliance will almost always result in a financial penalty, or worse.

To identify what is required in the way of licensor, permits, and agency reporting begins by working backward. In other words, begin with a microview of jurisdiction and expand to the macroview. Start with city government. Your local telephone directory will list the city offices and departments for your city, including the office of the mayor. It would also be advisable to contact your local chamber of commerce and your city's economic development office. If zoning restrictions apply, or if building permits or a professional license or registration is required, they should be able to supply you with that information.

The county commissioners should be able to advise you of any requirements on the county level. The telephone directory also provides a list of county offices and departments. At the state level, the governor's office of economic development should be able to direct you to the correct departments and agencies at the state level. As indicated earlier, all 50 states have small business development offices, and they may be of some help in identifying filing requirements. At each level ask the agency representative if they know of any other agency with which you need to file. In this way you cross-check yourself. It is difficult to find any bureaucrat who has the knowledge to put together the entire picture for you, but most are aware of at least one other agency with which you will be required to at least notify. The state agencies should be able to direct you to the appropriate federal agencies as well. Most state agencies that have jurisdiction over certain types of activity will have a federal counterpart. At a minimum the Internal Revenue Service must be contacted.

The first major decision that a new businessperson must make is that of the form of ownership. Most people recognize that the choices are sole proprietorship, partnership, or corporation; in a general sense that is true, but there are a number of different partnerships and corporate forms. The tax consequences can be very different. A decision to adopt any type of form should at least have the input of a competent attorney and a competent accountant. I would recommend the use of both, not one or the other, and both professionals should be in communication, to avoid duplication, omissions, errors, and oversight.

Once the decision is over and an ownership form established, changes can be made down the road, although the appropriate issues need to be addressed. Generally, it is easier to go from a sole proprietorship to a partnership or corporation rather than the reverse. It is important to understand that ownership form can be changed and adjusted to meet the needs of the business owner and the business organization that he or she has created. Just bear in mind that good planning and informed decision making is the best remedy.

Advantages and disadvantages exist for each form of ownership. The critical issues are the simplicity or complexity of the organizational form, along with the tax consequences and the ability to manage the business and your personal tax liability. The other major issue stems from the legal ramifications and liability associated with your business and personal risk exposure as it pertains to your specific form of ownership.

Sole Proprietorships

Most businesses begin as sole proprietorships because they are the easiest to form. You are already a sole proprietor. All that is required from the IRS perspective is that you are engaged in some income-producing activity and that you report that income and expense on your tax return, first on a schedule C, which in turn is transferred to form 1040 for income tax purposes and form ES for self-employment taxes in the form of social security and medicare. The key element in the simplicity of the sole proprietorship is that you have nothing to form and that the only tax return you need to file is your own.

From a tax standpoint the main advantage stems from the fact that schedule C may allow you to deduct certain expenses that the working person usually cannot deduct. The depreciation expenses associated with your business's capital expenditures will tend to reduce your taxable income substantially, which also reduces your self-employment taxes. You can employ your children, and as long as they are minors under the age of 18, they are exempt from social security and medicare, yet the wages are deductible. From the perspective of workers' compensation and unemployment, they are not deemed taxable employees. You may elect to pay your spouse, and she also is considered an exempt employee for workers' compensation and state and federal unemployment, but social security and medicare must be withheld and reported. See circular E for specifics.[14] Generally speaking, from a strictly tax perspective, if your business is relatively small, the sole proprietorship is usually the most advantageous form of business ownership.

A self-employed person may elect to set up a Keogh or IRA. Pretax retirement savings are limited to the maximums under one plan or the other, but either a Keogh or an IRA is relatively easy to set up and administer. The effective income tax rate paid by the sole proprietor may be as low as zero but in other cases may be higher than would be paid under another type of ownership.

If a rule of thumb exists, it would be that if you and or your business is making money, or if you have a large asset base to protect, look into another organizational form. If you or your business is exposed to high levels of liability risk, it might be wise to look into another type of ownership form.

In a sole proprietorship, you own 100 percent of the business, and you control the business. That, in turn, means that you are at risk: first, financially for the business risk to which you are exposing yourself (if the business loses money, you will be held personally accountable for those dollars), and second, if your business is sued, there is no distinguishing the business from you. You have unlimited liability exposure.

Partnerships

Partnerships are usually formed when two or more people enter into a business relationship or venture together. They are not precluded in a partnership form, but it is an optional form of ownership for them. Under a partnership agreement the members come together to carry on in a business activity. The formation of a partnership is set forth in a partnership agreement, which falls under the codified laws of the Uniform Partnership Act, which has been adopted by most states. Most states will require the partnership to register with the office of the secretary of state.

Partnerships are formed for the purpose of operating a business for profit and generally fall under two broad classifications. The first is a *general partnership*, which is the most common type of partnership and the type that most people are familiar with or relate to when speaking about a partnership. A general partnership has all the partners sharing equally in the ownership, management, and responsibilities of the partnership.

This type of arrangement allows members to pool their resources for the purpose of conducting a business. It is advantageous to those who do not have sufficient capital resources to undertake a venture of their own. In addition, being a student of small business management, you can appreciate the complexity of running a business. In a partnership the management responsibilities are shared, which allows for a delegation of duties, or a team approach to solving the management and operational problems.

A key distinction of the partnership business ownership form stems from a business's legal status. The IRS will consider the partnership a separate ownership form, but only in the sense that the partnership must have a federal identification number. Other agencies that may require filing or a license will usually tie the partnership's identification to the federal identification number, although they will also require the names and addresses of the partners. From a tax standpoint the partnership will file form 1065, which is a partnership tax return. This tax return is an information return only. The IRS will consider each partner to be a self-employed person whose self-employment takes place in a partnership. Thus the profits of the partnership are allocated to the partners based on each one's percentage of ownership, which is in turn reported by each partner on his or her personal tax return form 1040 and form SE (self-employment). Tax is therefore reported at the personal tax rate. The implication of forming a partnership is that the services of a competent attorney will be required to write up the partnership agreement, and that multiple tax returns must be filed: the 1065 and the personal 1040's for each general partner.

From a legal standpoint, in most states a partnership cannot be sued on its own. The general partners as individuals are responsible for the partnership's financial obligations and for any legal obligations that the partnership may incur. To take this a step farther, each partner is wholly and totally responsible for the obligations of the partnership. That means that if you enter a general partnership relationship with others, and they do not or cannot meet the partnership's obligations, you individually will be required to meet the entire obligation on your own.

It is important that you know, trust, and understand the other person or persons with whom you are entering into a partnership agreement. Compatibility is a critical element, since each party is individually and jointly responsible for the financial and management affairs of the partnership. It is not uncommon for a partnership to be formed and to operate a few years and then be dissolved, due to conflicts that have arisen between the partners. Disagreements over capital expenditures, pressure due to debt loads, disagreements regarding the delegation of duties, or conflicts over employees can all help create a situation that makes continuation of the enterprise seem intolerable.

Another type of general partnership is the *joint venture*. In a joint venture the duration may be limited. A joint venture is formed by two or more partners to undertake a specific project, such as a joint venture between a real estate broker and a residential construction firm for the purpose of developing a subdivision. After the completion of that project, the partnership would be terminated. Joint ventures may be formed to be ongoing, but the scope of the business may be limited to a specific area. For example, a major manufacturer may form a joint venture with a supplier for the sole purpose of building a plant to supply a component part needed in their normal line of business. The application to small business may be of a similar nature. A person may join a larger entity as a partner in a joint venture to supply a needed product or service. By entering such an arrangement, capital needs may be met.

The second type of partnership is a *limited partnership*. Under a limited partnership, the general partner assumes the management duties and responsibilities. The general partner is also held personally liable for all financial or legal obligations incurred by the partnership. There may be more than one general partner. The other limited partners act as investors and have a limited role in the affairs of the partnership. The limited partners are called by that name because their obligation is limited to the extent of their investment; they are not personally held financially or legally liable for the partnership's obligations beyond that investment.

Limited partnerships also file a 1065 partnership tax return. The 1065 acts as a profit and loss statement for the partnership. Should there be any income or expense not specific to the type of business the partnership is in, such as rental income, that income or loss will be reported on a schedule K. The net profit reported on the 1065 and schedule K is then broken down, or segmented, to the partners involved through the use of additional schedule, the K1. Each K1 reports the proportionate income of each partner's income, and a copy of the K1 is attached to that partner's personal 1040 to report the partnership income. As mentioned earlier, self-employment tax is reported on form SE.

Corporations

Corporations take various forms. Corporations tend to be the most permanent type of business form in that they can be set up to be perpetual entities. A corporation is a separate legal entity. A charter must be filed, and once granted, an annual report must be filed with the office of the secretary of state to maintain the corporation's good standing. A corporation exists separate and apart from its stockholders. Put another way, if you form a corporation, you do not own it. You cannot own a corporation; it is a separate legal entity. You can own the stock of the corporation, you can control the assets of the corporation, and you can control the corporation's activity, but the separate legal form is always present.

It is the nature of that separate form that is often the greatest reason behind the formation of a corporation. It creates what is often called the *corporate shield* for liability purposes. If through the activities of the corporation, a liability suit is filed, the stockholders cannot be held liable. This insulates or shields the people who formed the corporation and protects their personal assets. It should be noted that if a stockholder is also a corporate officer and if negligence is proven, that is a separate issue; corporate officers can be held liable for their actions. This may sound like a contradiction, but in fact, the corporate form does provide considerable personal liability protection. If liability protection is a primary consideration in adopting a corporate form, the services of a competent attorney should be sought prior to setting up a corporation.

The corporate form of ownership is not something that should be taken lightly. Corporations are relatively easy to form but can be quite difficult to get out of. Corporations should be formed for the right reasons. In other words, the corporate form of ownership should be entered into for the right reasons, of which tax considerations are just one issue. As mentioned previously, corporations do provide a degree of liability protection. Many businesses adopt the corporate form for this protection. One bit of elaboration: It might be assumed, then, that this limited-liability aspect extends to creditors as well. It does, but only to some degree. Most lending institutions and major creditors require a personal guarantee from the corporate officers for debts incurred. Some governmental agencies will require a personal guarantee or have provisions within the law to enable the agency to pierce the corporate shield. These provisions have evolved due to the fact that unscrupulous people have used the separate legal status of the corporate form to strip the corporation of its assets and then attempt personally to avoid liability for debt obligations incurred under the corporate ownership. Restrictions and limitations have therefore been imposed.

A corporation generally is formed under the guise of perpetual life. The implication then is that the type of business which should be incorporated is the type of business that conceivably would also tend to have a perpetual life. A corporation formed to buy a piece of equipment, which itself has a limited life, does not make good business sense. If the corporation was formed to enter into the equipment rental business, that more closely complements the concept of a perpetual existence. If the life of the enterprise is limited, a different form of ownership or possibly a limited-liability company might be a more appropriate form of ownership.

The perpetual-life concept has tremendous implications for estate planning. This continuity can be extended from generation to generation and can take the form of stock transfers. This is a good business reason for forming a corporation.

Suppose, for example, that a business exists that is already multigenerational. Grandpa started it and still works in the business, but most of the responsibility of the day-to-day operations has already been transferred and taken over by the sons. The third generation is now beginning to work in the business. The value of the assets, being large, will create some estate problems.

In such a situation, great flexibility and a broad latitude of options are available in the corporate form. If this business is now being incorporated, it would seem obvious that the intent would be something like the following. First, grandpa would not want to be saddled personally with existing debt obligations incurred by the business. He would want to be provided with a secure income for the duration of his life. The type of assets that the corporation could provide under these conditions could be primarily in the form of debt and income securities. When that personal estate is passed on, the inheritance by the family members would be in the form of bonds and preferred stock. The continuity of the corporation itself goes on uninterrupted by the death of its original founder.

The sons who are actively managing the business would probably be concerned with maintaining the control they now exercise over the business and its activities. This position could easily be protected by issuance of a voting class of stock. In this way, even though a minority interest were held by the second generation, the business could be controlled and managed by that group. Thus decisions concerning executive compensation and management control would remain.

The grandchildren and the third generation's interest in the business would best be served by the incorporated business's continual growth, which could possibly provide a lifetime employment opportunity or a source of personal wealth through stock ownership. This generation could be provided with shares of common stock, which in turn could provide the mechanism for that potential growth. If new members are added to the family, they in turn could be gifted shares of common stock in whatever percentage or numbers are deemed appropriate. In turn, subsequent generations can inherit shares of stock and ownership interests as long as the business remains successful.

The example above should clarify any doubt that may have existed concerning the need for a professional team throughout the formation period of a corporation. The concept and intent of the founders must be well thought out and articulated so that those considerations and issues are implemented properly.

You probably already realize that the formation of a corporation can facilitate an easy transfer of ownership of a business. That ownership transfer would take the form of a common stock sale and can represent a whole or partial transfer of ownership. This raises some other issues. First, if a business enterprise is being formed and owned by more than one person, a sole proprietorship ownership form is basically excluded as an option. That reduces the choices to either a partnership or corporate form of ownership. The corporate form can leave some unsavory consequences under certain conditions.

First know with whom you are going into business. The model of this book is based on ethics and human relationships. If you enter into a corporate form of ownership, the ethical standards and the trust within those internal human relationships had better have been established and proven prior to formation of the corporation. The central issue is control. If a closed corporation is formed between two people where one class of stock exists, and one person has 49 percent of stock and the other stockholder has 51 percent, who controls the company? It does not matter than the paid-in capital is $49 as opposed to $51 or $4.9 million as opposed to $5.1 million. If a policy concerning the sale of assets, the acquisition debt, the compensation of officers, or the paying of a dividend is brought to a vote, who will cast the deciding vote? Many horror stories exist concerning the economic abuses stemming from such a relationship, where the minority stockholder is basically powerless as far as control of the corporation is concerned.

The opposite side of the control issue allows minority stockholders to own a segment of a business without concerning themselves with management or control issues. The corporate form is ideal in a situation where investors can be added almost at will. If the business concept is such that growth is anticipated, and huge growth potential exists, the corporate form of ownership is ideally suited to accommodate that type of growth. For some business owners the goal is eventually to become a publicly traded entity. To become a publicly traded company, a corporate form of ownership is required.

Going public through a primary offering is one reason to adopt a corporate form. To go public the first step would be to contact an investment banker. A registration will be required with the Securities and Exchange Commission and a filing with the secretary of state will be required to authorize the sale of those securities in each state in which the securities will be sold.

Two more issues need to be addressed when considering a corporate form of ownership. The first relates to the costs associated with a corporation. The costs stem primarily from the fees associated with the professionals involved in setting up the corporation. The accounting and legal fees will depend on the size and complexity of the business being incorporated. I am reluctant to estimate a cost. The low end would tend to be in the neighborhood of $1000 and the high end of the range could be substantial. From the perspective of small business, should you decide to incorporate, the fees should not be more than a few thousand dollars. The legal fees associated with a corporation I had formed were $500 although that was a decade or so ago. The accounting fees were more than three times that amount. In addition to the professional fees, a filing fee or registration fee will be assessed, and an annual filing fee will be charged as well.

Once the corporation is set up, costs are associated with filing a corporate tax return each year. In addition, you must maintain a record of your corporate minutes. This is often done and/or held by your attorney or possibly by your accountant. If they are maintained by you, certainly a copy should be provided to those on your professional team. In addition, someone will be required to make the annual filing with the secretary of state to keep the corporation in good standing.

The second issue ties in with the first. Forming a corporation will complicate your life. This is a guarantee. Documentation will be required to maintain your corporate status, and documentation will be required to support expense and capital expenditures necessary to compile and support your tax deductions. This requires not only time and energy but often entails expense in maintaining and compiling the records. The tax laws of corporations are different than those for individuals, and this in itself creates an element of complication. The year end in a corporation can be different than the fiscal year end associated with your personal tax return, which can further complicate life. It may seem that you are constantly preparing for a tax return.

From the perspective of tax, corporations have a multitude of implications. A quick overview will be given here, but again if a corporate form is pursued, a good accountant and a competent attorney should be brought into the circle early and maintain lines of communication between the two professionals.

The Internal Revenue Service will recognize the corporation as a separate entity, distinct from the stockholders. In doing so the IRS will require the corporation to file for a federal identification number and to file a separate tax return. Corporations are treated differently for tax purposes, and an understanding of the tax consequence is of paramount importance prior to embarking on this form of business ownership.

C Corporations

The C corporation or regular corporation is the form most people are aware of. It is the form that corporations listed on Wall Street have adopted. These are perpetual entities whose lives go on outside the lives of the stockholders. There are estate and business succession issues here. The C corporation files its own tax return and pays its own income tax. You as an officer of the corporation are considered an employee. Wages taken from the corporation are subject to payroll taxes, and the corporation issues you a W-2 just as if you were any other employee. The corporation deducts those officer wages and the corporation's share of the payroll taxes as an expense item, thus lowering the corporation's income tax liability. Officer wages and salaries are a major tax planning tool used to limit the corporation's tax liability. In my work as a payroll auditor, I have seen many W-2's that were in excess of 1 million. The IRS does have restrictions on officer salaries and may require that dividends be paid. I do not profess to be an expert on corporate tax; competent counsel is advised.

Dividends are taken after the corporation pays its own income tax. Dividends are thus subject to double taxation. First, income is taxed at the corporate rate, then it is reported again as personal unearned dividend income on the personal tax return form 1040.

A major tax advantage under the corporate form of ownership stems from those employee fringe benefits that are a deductible expense for the corporation. Because the corporate officer is deemed an employee, should the corporation pay the premiums for health insurance that becomes a deductible expense, as do premiums for group term life insurance, with certain limitations. In the area of pretax retirement plans, the corporation will generally have a tax advantage. Careful planning regarding corporate officer compensation and benefits can save substantial sums in the form of tax savings.

Because the corporation pays tax as a separate entity. The corporation begins paying tax at the beginning corporate tax rate. In essence, the business income can be proportioned between the stockholder's personal tax rate and income transferred in the form of employee or officer wages. Thus the individual's tax liability can be limited by the amount of compensation transferred. At that point the corporation pays on the remaining profits by starting to pay income tax based on the corporation's lowest tax rate and then working its way up. For example, if a business generated $60,000 of income, $30,000 could be transferred to the individual tax return through officer wages. Thus the current personal rate would be 15 percent after a standard or itemized deduction and personal exemptions were subtracted. The other $30,000 would be taxed at the corporation's beginning tax rate. Had the entire $60,000 been earned in a sole proprietorship, a full 15.3 percent would have been assessed for social security and medicare on form SE for self-employment tax. The $60,000 would have placed the individual in the 28 percent tax bracket, and a portion of that income would have been taxed at a higher rate than it would have been taxed by splitting the income between two entities. Bear in mind that the corporation would have had to match the social security and medicare expenses at a combined rate of 7.65 percent on the $30,000 in wages paid to the corporate officer, and those wages would also have been subject to federal and state unemployment insurance. The overall tax paid in the example above would have been less in a corporate structure. How much less it would be for a particular business will depend on the circumstances.

I touched on this topic earlier, but when forming a corporation, some sound planning in regard to the mix of debt and equity financing used to establish the corporation's capital structure can do much to minimize taxes and facilitate the transfer of assets from the corporation back to the individual. The IRS has restrictions, and a competent accountant and attorney should be used to ensure that the IRS requirements are not violated. Since debt instruments require the corporation to pay interest expense, those forming the corporation can loan money to the corporation and have the corporation pay them interest. This then flows back to the corporate officers as unearned income. When the note comes due, the loan is repaid from the corporation back to the corporate officers, and no tax liability is incurred from that repayment. It should be easy to see the favorable benefits from a tax point of view of such a structure. The IRS can see those benefits as well and has imposed restrictions to limit such tax-free exchanges.

Another major tool used to limit the corporate tax bite is for the people forming the corporation to hold some assets outside the corporation and not capitalize everything they own, thus making those assets part of the corporation. It is common for individuals to hold the real estate and/or major pieces of equipment personally and then lease or rent those assets to the corporation under a lease agreement. Again, the corporation will deduct those payments as an expense, and the person will receive those payments as unearned rental income, and offset that income in part through depreciation. Such an arrangement can allow the corporate officer to take a lower rate of salary, especially in the early years, to help the corporation build an asset base. How a person capitalizes the corporation can be extremely important.

From both the perspective of tax and liability, some people will layer corporations, that is, form multiple corporations. This is common in the construction trades, where an operating corporation is formed. This corporation has minimal capitalization, but is exposed to the financial and liability risk inherent in the nature of their work. This corporation will probably need to be bonded to meet the requirements of specific project bids. Payroll is also run through this corporation. A second corporation may be set up which owns the physical equipment and leases that equipment to the first corporation. In this manner the operating corporation rarely shows much of a profit. The intent is to keep the operating corporation thinly capitalized. A third corporation may be set up to own the real estate or other types of assets. The intent is to spread the income and wealth through a number of corporations and individuals in an attempt to insulate and protect the wealth from undue tax and liability claims. With the right advice from the professionals involved, corporate structure can add a dimension of flexibility that can be designed to fit the needs of the businesses involved.

The corporate structure can also act as a two-edged sword. By its nature the corporation requires multiple tax returns as well as the time and energy that must be expended to keep appropriate records and to keep the corporation current. To make maximum use and to obtain the most benefit, a C corporation form is best suited to a situation where the business will survive a very long time. That business should also be one in which the asset base is relatively large and the cash inflow from operations quite substantial. Businesses tend to evolve; so does the business form. The C corporation structure tends to be on the opposite end of the spectrum from the sole proprietorship.

Having personally owned a C corporation, I'd like to give a few words of advice. First, don't form a corporation until your business is ready for that structure. Second, not all attorneys and accountants are equal. Make sure that the professionals you are using are familiar with corporate structure. Use a professional team; do not attempt to file and structure a corporation on your own. Finally, before you form a C corporation, study the tax laws that apply to corporations. Do not depend exclusively on the professionals to do everything in your best interest. If you can discuss your situation from an informed position, your time and theirs will be more productive and the chances of obtaining the intended outcome are vastly improved.

Subchapter S Corporation

The subchapter S corporation is a corporation in every sense of the word from a legal viewpoint. Like a C corporation, a corporate charter is filed with the office of the secretary of state. An annual report must be filed to maintain the legal status. Stock is authorized and issued, officers and directors are elected. Liability protection in terms of the corporate shield exists also. A subchapter S corporation or small business corporation is the same as a C corporation except in a few very important ways.

First, some minor restrictions apply as to class of stocks and number of stockholders. Second, to be a subchapter S corporation, an application must be made and status granted by the Internal Revenue Service. Your accountant can facilitate this, but if you want subchapter S status, you must apply. The critical difference between a C corporation and the S corporation is in the tax treatment. The S corporation files a 1120S tax return, which in many ways acts much like a partnership, which files tax return form 1065, with one key distinction, that being self-employment tax. The activity of the S corporation is reported on the 1120S itself like the partnership return; any outside income or expense is reported on schedule K, with the income or losses from the tax return being prorated to form K-1, like the partnership return. The principal difference is that the K-1 income flows back to the 1040 as dividend income and is not subject to self-employment tax.

Unlike a C corporation, in which an attempt to minimize the double taxation of a dividend distribution, officer wages are often maximized, in an S corporation, officer wages are often minimized and dividend distributions are maximized to avoid the payroll taxes on the spread between what has been declared as a wage and what the social security limits are (assuming that net income is substantial).

Officers are deemed employees of the corporation and if payroll is taken, a W-2 is required and payroll is treated as if the corporate officer were the same as any other employee. A line is segregated on the 1120S tax return to identify officer wages. The IRS is concerned that officer wages are being paid, due to the unearned status of the dividend distributions. Corporate officers are deemed employees for purposes of state and federal unemployment. Officers in many cases can elect an officer exclusion for worker's compensation.

The tax rate for an S corporation is the personal tax rate of the individuals involved. Since the S corporation files an information return only, taxable income flows back to the people who own the stock of the corporation. This is the principal advantage of the S corporate structure. You avoid double taxation—that and the savings associated with minimizing self-employment taxes.

Variations of the subchapter S corporation have evolved. Many professionals form professional corporations, which use a similar structure. In addition, a variation called the limited liability corporation (LLC) is a legal business form in most states. The LLC is structured more closely to a partnership than a subchapter S corporation is. In an LLC the principals are deemed members, not officers. They are treated as partners, not as employees.

It is easy to see how quickly one can require the use of professional help when addressing the issue of ownership form, particularly when moving beyond the structure of a sole proprietorship. This is intended to be a brief overview and has not been intended to be all-inclusive concerning the implications involved in the corporate structure form of ownership. Tax laws continue to change and evolve. Legal issues are also evolving and changing, due to changes in statutes due to legislation, and court case precedent continues to change and modify the interpretation of laws. The only way to find out what the implications are for your business would be to consult a professional to address your specific issues. I will address corporate structure again later in the book to identify some of the advantages and disadvantages of corporations.

• WHEN YOU ARE AUDITED · · · · · · · · · · · ·

As a small business owner your actions cross into the domain of a multitude of state and federal regulatory agencies. As indicated earlier, many of the agencies that exist do so because of past abuses. If no one ever polluted the air, land, or water, there would be little need for the Environmental Protection Agency. This is a free country which espouses the concepts of free enterprise, but as the old saying goes, your freedom ends where the other guy's nose begins. The governmental agencies act to enforce the rights of the other guy's nose.

The state department of revenue, which oversees the collection of sales and excise tax, is an agency very likely to conduct an audit. Their authority to audit and enforce the state revenue code has been granted to them by the state legislature and the state century code which created that agency and charged it with the duty of levying a tax structure to generate revenues to pay for the general and administrative duties of the state. The agency will be backed by the attorney general's office. The department has the authority to issue sales and excise tax licenses to firms that wish to conduct business in the state. Generally, there are few problems for the small business owner in obtaining a license that is a required to conduct business.

Don't be surprised if the revenue department requires you as a new proprietor to post a cash bond in your name and in the name of the department of revenue. This practice has evolved over the years, and from the experience of having business come and go and in the going fail, or be unable, to pay the sales or excise tax owed. That tax is not a part of any sale; it is a fee collected by the state and is rightfully the state's revenue. Failure to collect this fee and failure to remit all that is owed will be taken seriously by the department of revenue. Thus posting a cash bond ensures a degree of compliance and gives the department something to which they can readily attach a claim. This bond may be released after a predetermined period of time in which the new entrepreneur has had an opportunity to establish his or her creditworthiness by collecting and paying sales or excise taxes in a timely manner.

Since the money that is being collected rightfully belong to the state and/or city department of revenue, they also have the right through an audit to check that their revenue is being collected correctly. In an audit the auditor will attempt to determine that the collection of sales and excise tax is being done correctly (that everything which should be collected has been collected), and that the correct amount has been remitted in a timely manner. An audit should not be considered harassment, although it sometimes feels that way. What right do they have to come into my place of business, take up my time, and examine my books with the threat of assessing additional tax, penalty, and interest? The answer is, because it is their money and they have given you the privilege of conducting a business, trade, or profession within their jurisdiction. The roads, streets, and infrastructure that you require in order to conduct business is paid for by that revenue. You are the medium of collection.

If you are in business, expect to be audited. My experience was that I was audited at least once a year by some agency. To ease the stress of an audit is simple: Do it right the first time. If you have a question concerning what you should be collecting or withholding, go to that agency for assistance. Get answers to all your questions directly from the agency. Do not count on your accountant to do it right. Understand the process first, then farm it out. An audit should be a confirmation that your systems are correct, not a threat.

The state department of labor will audit your business for unemployment insurance purposes to ensure that the proper wages have been reported to their agency and to the IRS. In the state of South Dakota the department attempts to audit every employer at least once in seven years. Their recent policy was to audit a new business employer in their second year of employment. The issues audited for are proper reporting and proper employment classification, especially independent contractor versus employee issues.

Workers' compensation personnel will perform audits as well. In some states, workers' compensation is underwritten by the state. You can expect that the agency regulating workers' compensation will perform audits to ensure that the correct premiums are being submitted. They, too, will be concerned with independent contractor versus employee issues. In other states workers' compensation is underwritten by an insurance carrier and is attached or endorsed onto the business insurance package. In that case you can expect to be audited annually by the insurance company. They have vested interest because premiums are a function of payroll. In some cases the business insurance premiums are a function of sales revenue, in which case the insurance company will perform an annual audit to confirm your sales or revenue levels to adjust their premiums for the next year.

An audit with workers' compensation or with the department of labor is not a cause for alarm. Like the department of revenue, they are looking to ensure that the correct premiums or taxes have been paid. The best course of action is to maintain accurate records and to pay what is owed up front.

Ironically, as a tax auditor for seven years with the department of labor, on a percentage basis I gave refunds more often than I collected additional taxes. At first glance that sounds good, but whether the business being audited paid too much tax or too little, the fact remains that they paid the wrong tax. A case in point: I once audited an employer with about 80 employees. I discovered that his computer program was picking up the wrong amounts from the payroll program. After making the corrections, I met with the proprietor. He asked how he came out, after which I informed him that he was going to obtain a combined state and federal refund of over $2500. His response was "That's great," to which I responded, "No that's not so good." He asked me to explain why getting money back was not a good thing, so I explained that his refund was due to an error in his computer program. I explained that I was handing him several thousand dollars due to errors buried in his accounting system, of which he was not aware. I then asked him what his degree of confidence was in the accuracy of his accounts receivable. To which his response was simply, "Oh."

As an auditor I did not keep accurate statistics of the percentage of times I discovered errors within the accounting systems of those I was auditing. Quite regularly, though, I discovered serious errors in areas I was not auditing, which leads me to believe that their incidence is quite high. Once discovered, the proprietors were grateful for that information. Which leads to the point that a number of people who were notified of an audit called to inform me that they welcomed the audit because it was a test of the integrity of their systems. The point is that as a business owner your accounting systems should be accurate enough to withstand an audit.

No one welcomes an IRS audit. At the core of the problem with an IRS audit is the tax code itself, which is too complex. There simply are too many gray areas that are open to interpretation. Not all IRS auditors are fully trained. Add to that the perceptual differences between the auditor and the entrepreneur, which creates a situation where the differences could be substantial. All these issues combined can create a difficult situation indeed.

I experienced an IRS audit as a small business owner. I was awarded a slight refund, but I do not relish the thought of another audit. Yet if you keep accurate records, along with documentation, and use consistent procedures, an IRS audit should not be a major cause for alarm. In many cases the audit will be limited to a specific area. As long as you are not pushing the limits of the law and or the interpretation of the law, there is little to fear from any type of audit. These agencies have gotten a bad reputation in part from a small percentage of incompetent bureaucrats who work for the agencies, and in part from people who through ignorance, or knowingly, did not pay their full taxes and got caught. The baseline for the entrepreneur is to keep good records, not only for management purposes but for the tax purposes as well. If the small business owner does that and reports income and expenses accurately, there should be no major problems should an audit occur.

Again, acting in an ethical manner is one way in which you as a small business owner can help ensure that your business will be allowed to stay in business. As citizens we all need our government, and as a citizens we are bound to contribute our fair share, even if we do not always agree with the way in which our government acts.

• QUESTIONS FOR REVIEW ·············

1. Calculate the actual out-of-pocket expense for a small business employer to hire an employee for $10.00 per hour for a 40-hour week. Include deductions from the following: FICA, medicare, workers' compensation at a rate of 9 percent, state unemployment at a rate of 2.1 percent, and federal unemployment at the standard rate.

2. In the text it is stated that many entrepreneurs find it difficult to look at the numbers. Do you agree or disagree? Explain.

3. Why is it important that financial statements include as much detail as possible?

4. Maintaining and managing inventory levels requires a degree of personal discipline. Do you agree with that statement? Explain.

5. Why is the self-employment tax owed generally higher than the personal income tax liability for the entrepreneur?

6. The new hire program was recently established. Explain the purpose of this program.

7. Explain how many form 941's are filed by the employer in a year's time. On what form does the employer make the payroll tax deposits? Where are those deposits made?

8. Explain the issues concerning payroll that ends at the quarter or at the end of a year.

9. Why is it so important to distinguish between an employee and an independent contractor?

10. How can you obtain a ruling on an independent contractor's status?

11. Explain the difference is between a 401(k) plan and a section 125 cafeteria plan.

12. Explain the difference between a C corporation and an S corporation from an income tax standpoint.

13. What is the best defense against being subject to substantial additional tax and penalties in the event of an audit by a state or federal agency?

• BEYOND THE CLASSROOM: RECOMMENDED ACTIVITIES ···········

1. Visit your nearest IRS office.

2. Attend an IRS-sponsored small business workshop.

3. Visit your local unemployment insurance office and consult a representative concerning small business reporting.

4. Contact a CPA firm and set up an interview concerning small business tax reporting.

5. Contact your local representative from the state department of revenue concerning small business reporting.

SCHEDULE C
(Form 1040)

Department of the Treasury
Internal Revenue Service (O)

Profit or Loss From Business
(Sole Proprietorship)
▶ Partnerships, joint ventures, etc., must file Form 1065.
▶ **Attach to Form 1040 or Form 1041.** ▶ **See Instructions for Schedule C (Form 1040).**

OMB No. 1545-0074

1996

Attachment
Sequence No. **09**

Name of proprietor

Social security number (SSN)

A	Principal business or profession, including product or service (see page C-1)	**B Enter principal business code** (see page C-6) ▶
C	Business name. If no separate business name, leave blank.	**D Employer ID number (EIN), if any**

E Business address (including suite or room no.) ▶ ....
   City, town or post office, state, and ZIP code

F Accounting method: **(1)** ☐ Cash **(2)** ☐ Accrual **(3)** ☐ Other (specify) ▶ ....

G Did you "materially participate" in the operation of this business during 1996? If "No," see page C-2 for limit on losses. ☐ **Yes** ☐ **No**

H If you started or acquired this business during 1996, check here .... ▶ ☐

Part I Income

1	Gross receipts or sales. **Caution:** *If this income was reported to you on Form W-2 and the "Statutory employee" box on that form was checked, see page C-2 and check here* ▶ ☐	1	
2	Returns and allowances	2	
3	Subtract line 2 from line 1	3	
4	Cost of goods sold (from line 42 on page 2)	4	
5	**Gross profit.** Subtract line 4 from line 3	5	
6	Other income, including Federal and state gasoline or fuel tax credit or refund (see page C-2) . . .	6	
7	**Gross income.** Add lines 5 and 6 . . . . ▶	7	

Part II Expenses. Enter expenses for business use of your home **only** on line 30.

8	Advertising	8		19 Pension and profit-sharing plans	19	
9	Bad debts from sales or services (see page C-3) . .	9		20 Rent or lease (see page C-4):		
				a Vehicles, machinery, and equipment .	20a	
10	Car and truck expenses (see page C-3) . .	10		**b** Other business property . .	20b	
11	Commissions and fees . .	11		21 Repairs and maintenance . .	21	
12	Depletion	12		22 Supplies (not included in Part III) .	22	
13	Depreciation and section 179 expense deduction (not included in Part III) (see page C-3) . .	13		23 Taxes and licenses	23	
				24 Travel, meals, and entertainment:		
				a Travel	24a	
14	Employee benefit programs (other than on line 19) . .	14		**b** Meals and entertainment .		
15	Insurance (other than health) .	15		**c** Enter 50% of line 24b subject to limitations (see page C-4) .		
16	Interest:					
a	Mortgage (paid to banks, etc.) .	16a		**d** Subtract line 24c from line 24b .	24d	
b	Other	16b		25 Utilities	25	
17	Legal and professional services . .	17		26 Wages (less employment credits) .	26	
				27 Other expenses (from line 48 on page 2)		
18	Office expense	18			27	

28	**Total expenses** before expenses for business use of home. Add lines 8 through 27 in columns ▶	28	
29	Tentative profit (loss). Subtract line 28 from line 7	29	
30	Expenses for business use of your home. Attach **Form 8829**	30	
31	**Net profit or (loss).** Subtract line 30 from line 29.		
	• If a profit, enter on **Form 1040, line 12,** and ALSO on **Schedule SE, line 2** (statutory employees, see page C-5). Estates and trusts, enter on Form 1041, line 3.	31	
	• If a loss, you MUST go on to line 32.		
32	If you have a loss, check the box that describes your investment in this activity (see page C-5).		
	• If you checked 32a, enter the loss on **Form 1040, line 12,** and ALSO on **Schedule SE, line 2** (statutory employees, see page C-5). Estates and trusts, enter on Form 1041, line 3.	**32a** ☐ All investment is at risk.	
	• If you checked 32b, you MUST attach **Form 6198.**	**32b** ☐ Some investment is not at risk.	

For Paperwork Reduction Act Notice, see Form 1040 instructions.   Cat. No. 11334P   **Schedule C (Form 1040) 1996**

FIGURE A10–1

Part III	**Cost of Goods Sold** (see page C-5)		

33 Method(s) used to
value closing inventory: **a** ☐ Cost   **b** ☐ Lower of cost or market   **c** ☐ Other (attach explanation)

34 Was there any change in determining quantities, costs, or valuations between opening and closing inventory? If
"Yes," attach explanation . . . .   ☐ **Yes**   ☐ **No**

35	Inventory at beginning of year. If different from last year's closing inventory, attach explanation . .	35	
36	Purchases less cost of items withdrawn for personal use	36	
37	Cost of labor. Do not include salary paid to yourself	37	
38	Materials and supplies	38	
39	Other costs	39	
40	Add lines 35 through 39	40	
41	Inventory at end of year	41	
42	**Cost of goods sold.** Subtract line 41 from line 40. Enter the result here and on page 1, line 4 . .	42	

Part IV	**Information on Your Vehicle.** Complete this part **ONLY** if you are claiming car or truck expenses on line 10 and are not required to file Form 4562 for this business. See the instructions for line 13 on page C-3 to find out if you must file.

43 When did you place your vehicle in service for business purposes? (month, day, year) ▶ .... / .... / ....

44 Of the total number of miles you drove your vehicle during 1996, enter the number of miles you used your vehicle for:

   a Business ....   **b** Commuting ....   **c** Other ....

45 Do you (or your spouse) have another vehicle available for personal use? . . . . ☐ **Yes**   ☐ **No**

46 Was your vehicle available for use during off-duty hours? . . . . ☐ **Yes**   ☐ **No**

47a Do you have evidence to support your deduction? . . . . ☐ **Yes**   ☐ **No**

   b If "Yes," is the evidence written? . . . . ☐ **Yes**   ☐ **No**

Part V	**Other Expenses.** List below business expenses not included on lines 8–26 or line 30.		
	....		
	....		
	....		
	....		
	....		
	....		
	....		
	....		
48	**Total other expenses.** Enter here and on page 1, line 27	48	

✪ *Printed on recycled paper*   *U.S.GPO:1996-407-198

FIGURE A10–1   (*continued*)

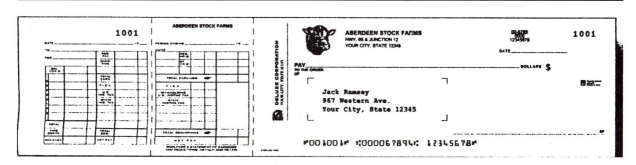

FIGURE A10–2   Payroll check

#	Date 1998	Chk#	Description	110 Food purchaces	120 Supplies	130 Paper towels	140 Candy	150 Chef's equip.	160 Advertizing	170 Utilities	180 Rent	190 Misc.
1	8 25	101	Kuhlman	5220								
2	8 25	102	Farner		8012							
3	8 25	103	Braungers									
4	8 25	104	Braungers	33023								
5	8 25	106	ARA			8260						
6	8 25	107	Dick Codington				20045					
7	8 25	111	Hobart					26565				
8	8 25	112	Farner Broken		25000							
9	8 28	114	Harkers	80952								
10	8 28	115	Sioux City Journal						3080			
11	8 29	116	Braungers	40650								
12	8 29	117	Farners Broken		6725							
13	8 29	118	Kuhlman	5280								
14	8 29	119	Western Paper			8240						
15	8 29	121	Tristate Refuse							9000		
16	8 30	150	Culligan							811		
17	8 31	153	Sioux City Journal						7000			
18	9 1	154	Braunger	45086								
19	9 1	156	IPS							62000		
20	9 1	157	Kuhlman	7560								
21	9 1	158	Farner Broken		19176							
22	9 1	159	Farner Broken		5000							
23	9 5	164	McCook Properties								30000	
24	9 5	165	Braungers	49528								
25	9 5	166	Farner Broken		25000							
26	9 5	167	Harker	87528								
27	9 5	168	Means			9223						
28	9 6	187	Farner Broken		20729							
29	9 7	189	Western Paper			3389						
30	9 7	190	Business Supply			700						
31	9 7	191	Rf Supply		2400							
32	9 7	192	McCook Properties								80000	
33	9 11	194	Braungers	8350								
34	9 11	196	Farners		25000							
35	9 12	197	Sioux City Journal							11200		
36	9 12	198	Harker	42094								
			Sub Total	405271	137042	29812	20045	26565	10080	83011	110000	

FIGURE A10–3   Make Believe Cafe check register

Date	Description	Chk #	Amount
5-15-96	Hobart Deep Fat Fryer	117	5,500.00

DATE PLACED IN SERVICE	MACRS METHOD	RECOVERY PERIOD	CONVENTION	CLASS LIFE
5-15-96	200%	GDS	Mid 2nd Qtr.	7 years

Depreciation

Year	Rate	Deduction
1996	17.85%	$ 981.75
1997	23.47%	$1,290.85
1998	16.76%	$ 921.80
1999	11.97%	$ 658.35
2000	8.87%	$ 487.85
2001	8.87%	$ 487.85
2002	8.87%	$ 487.85
2003	3.33	$ 183.70
		$5,500.00

FIGURE A10–4   Depreciation schedule

TABLE A-3, 3-, 5-, 7-, 10-, 15-, and 20-Year Property
Mid-Quarter Convention
Placed in Service in Second Quarter

| Year | Depreciation rate for recovery period | | | | | |
	3-year	5-year	7-year	10-year	15-year	20-year
1	41.67%	25.00%	17.85%	12.50%	6.25%	4.688%
2	38.89	30.00	23.47	17.50	9.38	7.148
3	14.14	18.00	16.76	14.00	8.44	6.612
4	5.30	11.37	11.97	11.20	7.59	6.116
5		11.37	8.87	8.96	6.83	5.658
6		4.26	8.87	7.17	6.15	5.233
7			8.87	6.55	5.91	4.841
8			3.33	6.55	5.90	4.478
9				6.56	5.91	4.463
10;				6.55	5.90	4.463
11				2.46	5.91	4.463
12					5.90	4.463
13					5.91	4.463
14					5.90	4.463
15					5.91	4.462
16					2.21	4.463
17						4.462
18						4.463
19						4.462
20						4.463
21						1.673

Self-Employment Tax

▶ See Instructions for Schedule SE (Form 1040).

▶ **Attach to Form 1040.**

OMB No. 1545-0074

1996

Attachment
Sequence No. **17**

Name of person with **self-employment** income (as shown on Form 1040)	Social security number of person with **self-employment** income ▶	

Who Must File Schedule SE

You must file Schedule SE if:

- You had net earnings from self-employment from **other than** church employee income (line 4 of Short Schedule SE or line 4c of Long Schedule SE) of $400 or more, **OR**
- You had church employee income of $108.28 or more. Income from services you performed as a minister or a member of a religious order **is not** church employee income. See page SE-1.

Note: *Even if you had a loss or a small amount of income from self-employment, it may be to your benefit to file Schedule SE and use either "optional method" in Part II of Long Schedule SE. See page SE-3.*

Exception. If your only self-employment income was from earnings as a minister, member of a religious order, or Christian Science practitioner **and** you filed Form 4361 and received IRS approval not to be taxed on those earnings, **do not** file Schedule SE. Instead, write "Exempt–Form 4361" on Form 1040, line 45.

May I Use Short Schedule SE or MUST I Use Long Schedule SE?

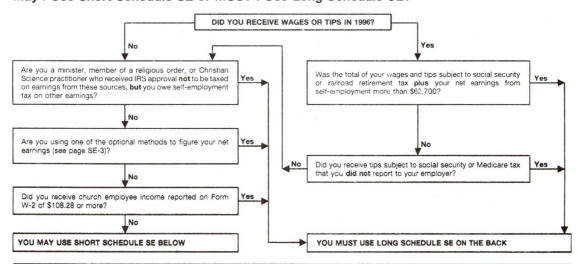

YOU MAY USE SHORT SCHEDULE SE BELOW

YOU MUST USE LONG SCHEDULE SE ON THE BACK

Section A—Short Schedule SE. Caution: *Read above to see if you can use Short Schedule SE.*

1	Net farm profit or (loss) from Schedule F, line 36, and farm partnerships, Schedule K-1 (Form 1065), line 15a	**1**	
2	Net profit or (loss) from Schedule C, line 31; Schedule C-EZ, line 3; and Schedule K-1 (Form 1065), line 15a (other than farming). Ministers and members of religious orders see page SE-1 for amounts to report on this line. See page SE-2 for other income to report	**2**	
3	Combine lines 1 and 2	**3**	
4	**Net earnings from self-employment.** Multiply line 3 by 92.35% (.9235). if less than $400, **do not** file this schedule; you do not owe self-employment tax . . . . ▶	**4**	
5	**Self-employment tax.** If the amount on line 4 is: • $62,700 or less, multiply line 4 by 15.3% (.153). Enter the result here and on **Form 1040, line 45.** • More than $62,700, multiply line 4 by 2.9% (.029). Then, add $7,774.80 to the result. Enter the total here and on **Form 1040, line 45.**	**5**	
6	Deduction for one-half of self-employment tax. Multiply line 5 by 50% (.5). Enter the result here and on **Form 1040, line 25**	**6**		

For Paperwork Reduction Act Notice, see Form 1040 instructions.   Cat. No. 11358Z   **Schedule SE (Form 1040) 1996**

FIGURE A10–5

Name of person with **self-employment** income (as shown on Form 1040)	Social security number of person with **self-employment** income ▶	

Section B—Long Schedule SE

Part I   Self-Employment Tax

Note: *If your only income subject to self-employment tax is **church employee income**, skip lines 1 through 4b. Enter -0- on line 4c and go to line 5a. Income from services you performed as a minister or a member of a religious order **is not** church employee income. See page SE-1.*

A   If you are a minister, member of a religious order, or Christian Science practitioner **and** you filed Form 4361, but you had $400 or more of **other** net earnings from self-employment, check here and continue with Part I . . . . . . ▶ ☐

1	Net farm profit or (loss) from Schedule F, line 36, and farm partnerships, Schedule K-1 (Form 1065), line 15a. **Note:** *Skip this line if you use the farm optional method. See page SE-3* . .	**1**	
2	Net profit or (loss) from Schedule C, line 31; Schedule C-EZ, line 3; and Schedule K-1 (Form 1065), line 15a (other than farming). Ministers and members of religious orders see page SE-1 for amounts to report on this line. See page SE-2 for other income to report. **Note:** *Skip this line if you use the nonfarm optional method. See page SE-3.*	**2**	
3	Combine lines 1 and 2	**3**	
4a	If line 3 is more than zero, multiply line 3 by 92.35% (.9235). Otherwise, enter amount from line 3	**4a**	
b	If you elected one or both of the optional methods, enter the total of lines 15 and 17 here . .	**4b**	
c	Combine lines 4a and 4b. If less than $400, **do not** file this schedule; you do not owe self-employment tax. **Exception.** If less than $400 and you had **church employee income,** enter -0- and continue ▶	**4c**	
5a	Enter your **church employee income** from Form W-2. **Caution:** See page SE-1 for definition of church employee income **5a**		
b	Multiply line 5a by 92.35% (.9235). If less than $100, enter -0-	**5b**	
6	**Net earnings from self-employment.** Add lines 4c and 5b	**6**	
7	Maximum amount of combined wages and self-employment earnings subject to social security tax or the 6.2% portion of the 7.65% railroad retirement (tier 1) tax for 1996	**7**	62,700 00
8a	Total social security wages and tips (total of boxes 3 and 7 on Form(s) W-2) and railroad retirement (tier 1) compensation. **8a**		
b	Unreported tips subject to social security tax (from Form 4137, line 9) **8b**		
c	Add lines 8a and 8b	**8c**	
9	Subtract line 8c from line 7. If zero or less, enter -0- here and on line 10 and go to line 11 . ▶	**9**	
10	Multiply the **smaller** of line 6 or line 9 by 12.4% (.124)	**10**	
11	Multiply line 6 by 2.9% (.029).	**11**	
12	**Self-employment tax.** Add lines 10 and 11. Enter here and on **Form 1040, line 45**	**12**	
13	**Deduction for one-half of self-employment tax.** Multiply line 12 by 50% (.5). Enter the result here and on **Form 1040, line 25** **13**		

Part II   Optional Methods To Figure Net Earnings (See page SE-3.)

Farm Optional Method. You may use this method **only if:**
- Your gross farm income[1] was not more than $2,400, **or**
- Your gross farm income[1] was more than $2,400 and your net farm profits[2] were less than $1,733.

14	Maximum income for optional methods	**14**	1,600 00
15	Enter the **smaller** of: two-thirds (⅔) of gross farm income[1] (not less than zero) or $1,600. Also, include this amount on line 4b above	**15**	

Nonfarm Optional Method. You may use this method **only if:**
- Your net nonfarm profits[3] were less than $1,733 and also less than 72.189% of your gross nonfarm income,[4] **and**
- You had net earnings from self-employment of at least $400 in 2 of the prior 3 years.

Caution: *You may use this method no more than five times.*

16	Subtract line 15 from line 14	**16**	
17	Enter the **smaller** of: two-thirds (⅔) of gross nonfarm income[4] (not less than zero) **or** the amount on line 16. Also, include this amount on line 4b above	**17**	

[1] From Schedule F, line 11, and Schedule K-1 (Form 1065), line 15b.   [3] From Schedule C, line 31; Schedule C-EZ, line 3; and Schedule K-1 (Form 1065), line 15a.
[2] From Schedule F, line 36, and Schedule K-1 (Form 1065), line 15a.   [4] From Schedule C, line 7; Schedule C-EZ, line 1; and Schedule K-1 (Form 1065), line 15c.

✿ Printed on recycled paper   ☆ U.S. GPO: 1996-43-1410168/407-219

FIGURE A10–5   *(continued)*

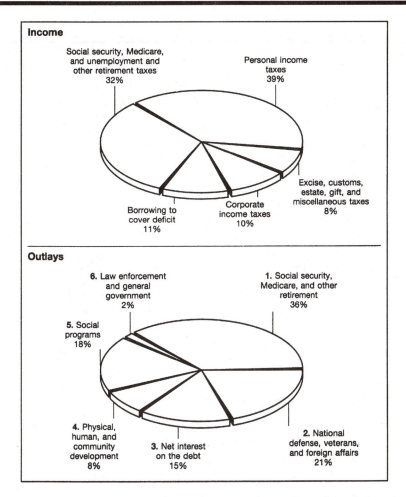

Income

Social security, Medicare, and unemployment and other retirement taxes
32%

Personal income taxes
39%

Borrowing to cover deficit
11%

Corporate income taxes
10%

Excise, customs, estate, gift, and miscellaneous taxes
8%

Outlays

6. Law enforcement and general government
2%

1. Social security, Medicare, and other retirement
36%

5. Social programs
18%

4. Physical, human, and community development
8%

3. Net interest on the debt
15%

2. National defense, veterans, and foreign affairs
21%

FIGURE A10–6 Income and outlays: These pie charts show the relative sizes of the major categories of federal income and outlays for fiscal year 1995.

Form 1040

Department of the Treasury—Internal Revenue Service

U.S. Individual Income Tax Return (U) **1997**

For the year Jan. 1–Dec. 31, 1997, or other tax year beginning , 1997, ending , 19

IRS Use Only—Do not write or staple in this space.

OMB No. 1545-0074

Label

(See instructions on page 10.)

Use the IRS label. Otherwise, please print or type.

L A B E L H E R E

Your first name and initial | Last name | Your social security number

If a joint return, spouse's first name and initial | Last name | Spouse's social security number

Home address (number and street). If you have a P.O. box, see page 10. | Apt. no.

City, town or post office, state, and ZIP code. If you have a foreign address, see page 10.

For help in finding line instructions, see pages 2 and 3 in the booklet.

Presidential Election Campaign (See page 10.)

Do you want $3 to go to this fund? . . . .

If a joint return, does your spouse want $3 to go to this fund? . . . .

Yes | No | Note: *Checking "Yes" will not change your tax or reduce your refund.*

Filing Status

Check only one box.

1 Single
2 Married filing joint return (even if only one had income)
3 Married filing separate return. Enter spouse's social security no. above and full name here. ▶
4 Head of household (with qualifying person). (See page 10.) If the qualifying person is a child but not your dependent, enter this child's name here. ▶
5 Qualifying widow(er) with dependent child (year spouse died ▶ 19). (See page 10.)

Exemptions

If more than six dependents, see page 10.

6a ☐ **Yourself.** If your parent (or someone else) can claim you as a dependent on his or her tax return, **do not** check box 6a . . . .

b ☐ **Spouse** . . . .

c **Dependents:**

(1) First name Last name	(2) Dependent's social security number	(3) Dependent's relationship to you	(4) No. of months lived in your home in 1997

No. of boxes checked on 6a and 6b

No. of your children on 6c who:
• lived with you
• did not live with you due to divorce or separation (see page 11)

Dependents on 6c not entered above

Add numbers entered on lines above ▶

d Total number of exemptions claimed . . . .

Income

Attach Copy B of your Forms W-2, W-2G, and 1099-R here.

If you did not get a W-2, see page 12.

Enclose but do not attach any payment. Also, please use **Form 1040-V.**

7 Wages, salaries, tips, etc. Attach Form(s) W-2 . . . . | 7
8a **Taxable** interest. Attach Schedule B if required . . . . . | 8a
b **Tax-exempt** interest. DO NOT include on line 8a . . . | 8b
9 Dividends. Attach Schedule B if required . . . . | 9
10 Taxable refunds, credits, or offsets of state and local income taxes (see page 12) . . | 10
11 Alimony received . . . . | 11
12 Business income or (loss). Attach Schedule C or C-EZ . . . . | 12
13 Capital gain or (loss). Attach Schedule D . . . . | 13
14 Other gains or (losses). Attach Form 4797 . . . . | 14
15a Total IRA distributions . | 15a | b Taxable amount (see page 13) | 15b
16a Total pensions and annuities | 16a | b Taxable amount (see page 13) | 16b
17 Rental real estate, royalties, partnerships, S corporations, trusts, etc. Attach Schedule E | 17
18 Farm income or (loss). Attach Schedule F . . . . | 18
19 Unemployment compensation . . . . | 19
20a Social security benefits . | 20a | b Taxable amount (see page 14) | 20b
21 Other income. List type and amount—see page 15 --------- | 21
22 Add the amounts in the far right column for lines 7 through 21. This is your **total income** ▶ | 22

Adjusted Gross Income

If line 32 is under $29,290 (under $9,770 if a child did not live with you), see EIC inst. on page 21.

23 IRA deduction (see page 16) . . . . | 23
24 Medical savings account deduction. Attach Form 8853 . | 24
25 Moving expenses. Attach Form 3903 or 3903-F . . | 25
26 One-half of self-employment tax. Attach Schedule SE . | 26
27 Self-employed health insurance deduction (see page 17) | 27
28 Keogh and self-employed SEP and SIMPLE plans . | 28
29 Penalty on early withdrawal of savings . . . . | 29
30a Alimony paid b Recipient's SSN ▶ | 30a
31 Add lines 23 through 30a . . . . | 31
32 Subtract line 31 from line 22. This is your **adjusted gross income** . . . . . ▶ | 32

For Privacy Act and Paperwork Reduction Act Notice, see page 38.

Cat. No. 14087D

Form **1040** (1997)

FIGURE A10–7

				33	
Tax Computation	33	Amount from line 32 (adjusted gross income)			
	34a	Check if: ☐ **You** were 65 or older, ☐ Blind; ☐ **Spouse** was 65 or older, ☐ Blind. Add the number of boxes checked above and enter the total here . . . . ▶	34a		
	b	If you are married filing separately and your spouse itemizes deductions or you were a dual-status alien, see page 18 and check here . . . . . . ▶ 34b ☐			
	35	Enter the **larger** of your: { **Itemized deductions** from Schedule A, line 28, **OR** **Standard deduction** shown below for your filing status. **But** see page 18 if you checked any box on line 34a or 34b **or** someone can claim you as a dependent. • Single—$4,150 • Married filing jointly or Qualifying widow(er)—$6,900 • Head of household—$6,050 • Married filing separately—$3,450 }		35	
If you want the IRS to figure your tax, see page 18.	36	Subtract line 35 from line 33		36	
	37	If line 33 is $90,900 or less, multiply $2,650 by the total number of exemptions claimed on line 6d. If line 33 is over $90,900, see the worksheet on page 19 for the amount to enter .		37	
	38	**Taxable income.** Subtract line 37 from line 36. If line 37 is more than line 36, enter -0-		38	
	39	**Tax.** See page 19. Check if any tax from **a** ☐ Form(s) 8814 **b** ☐ Form 4972 ▶		39	
Credits	40	Credit for child and dependent care expenses. Attach Form 2441	40		
	41	Credit for the elderly or the disabled. Attach Schedule R .	41		
	42	Adoption credit. Attach Form 8839	42		
	43	Foreign tax credit. Attach Form 1116	43		
	44	Other. Check if from **a** ☐ Form 3800 **b** ☐ Form 8396 **c** ☐ Form 8801 **d** ☐ Form (specify)_____	44		
	45	Add lines 40 through 44		45	
	46	Subtract line 45 from line 39. If line 45 is more than line 39, enter -0- . . . . . ▶		46	
Other Taxes	47	Self-employment tax. Attach Schedule SE		47	
	48	Alternative minimum tax. Attach Form 6251		48	
	49	Social security and Medicare tax on tip income not reported to employer. Attach Form 4137 .		49	
	50	Tax on qualified retirement plans (including IRAs) and MSAs. Attach Form 5329 if required		50	
	51	Advance earned income credit payments from Form(s) W-2		51	
	52	Household employment taxes. Attach Schedule H		52	
	53	Add lines 46 through 52. This is your **total tax** . . . . ▶		53	
Payments	54	Federal income tax withheld from Forms W-2 and 1099 . .	54		
	55	1997 estimated tax payments and amount applied from 1996 return .	55		
	56a	**Earned income credit.** Attach Schedule EIC if you have a qualifying child **b** Nontaxable earned income: amount ▶ _____ and type ▶ ----------------	56a		
Attach Forms W-2, W-2G, and 1099-R on the front.	57	Amount paid with Form 4868 (request for extension) . . .	57		
	58	Excess social security and RRTA tax withheld (see page 27)	58		
	59	Other payments. Check if from **a** ☐ Form 2439 **b** ☐ Form 4136	59		
	60	Add lines 54, 55, 56a, 57, 58, and 59. These are your **total payments** . . . . . ▶		60	
Refund	61	If line 60 is more than line 53, subtract line 53 from line 60. This is the amount you **OVERPAID**		61	
Have it directly deposited! See page 27 and fill in 62b, 62c, and 62d.	62a	Amount of line 61 you want **REFUNDED TO YOU** . . . . ▶		62a	
	▶ b	Routing number _____ ▶ c Type: ☐ Checking ☐ Savings			
	▶ d	Account number _____			
	63	Amount of line 61 you want **APPLIED TO YOUR 1998 ESTIMATED TAX** ▶	63		
Amount You Owe	64	If line 53 is more than line 60, subtract line 60 from line 53. This is the **AMOUNT YOU OWE.** For details on how to pay, see page 27 . . . . ▶		64	
	65	Estimated tax penalty. Also include on line 64	65		

Sign Here

Keep a copy of this return for your records.

Under penalties of perjury, I declare that I have examined this return and accompanying schedules and statements, and to the best of my knowledge and belief, they are true, correct, and complete. Declaration of preparer (other than taxpayer) is based on all information of which preparer has any knowledge.

Your signature	Date	Your occupation
Spouse's signature. If a joint return, BOTH must sign.	Date	Spouse's occupation

Paid Preparer's Use Only

Preparer's signature	Date	Check if self-employed ☐	Preparer's social security no.
Firm's name (or yours if self-employed) and address			EIN
			ZIP code

FIGURE A10–7 (*continued*)

1997 Estimated Tax Worksheet (keep for your records)

1	Enter amount of adjusted gross income you expect in 1997 (see instructions)	**1**	
2	• If you plan to itemize deductions, enter the estimated total of your itemized deductions. **Caution:** If line 1 above is over $121,200 ($60,600 if married filing separately), your deduction may be reduced. See Pub. 505 for details. • If you do not plan to itemize deductions, see **Standard Deduction for 1997** on page 2, and enter your standard deduction here.	**2**	
3	Subtract line 2 from line 1	**3**	
4	Exemptions. Multiply $2,650 by the number of personal exemptions. If you can be claimed as a dependent on another person's 1997 return, your personal exemption is not allowed. **Caution:** If line 1 above is over $181,800 ($151,500 if head of household; $121,200 if single; $90,900 if married filing separately), see Pub. 505 to figure the amount to enter	**4**	
5	Subtract line 4 from line 3	**5**	
6	**Tax.** Figure your tax on the amount on line 5 by using the 1997 Tax Rate Schedules on page 2. DO NOT use the Tax Table or the Tax Rate Schedules in the 1996 Form 1040 or Form 1040A instructions. **Caution:** If you have a net capital gain and line 5 is over $99,600 ($85,350 if head of household; $59,750 if single; $49,800 if married filing separately), see Pub. 505 to figure the tax	**6**	
7	Additional taxes (see instructions)	**7**	
8	Add lines 6 and 7	**8**	
9	Credits (see instructions). Do not include any income tax withholding on this line	**9**	
10	Subtract line 9 from line 8. Enter the result, but not less than zero	**10**	
11	Self-employment tax (see instructions). Estimate of 1997 net earnings from self-employment $....................... ; if **$65,400 or less,** multiply the amount by 15.3%; if **more than $65,400,** multiply the amount by 2.9%, add $8,109.60 to the result, and enter the total. **Caution:** If you also have wages subject to social security tax, see Pub. 505 to figure the amount to enter . .	**11**	
12	Other taxes (see instructions).	**12**	
13a	Add lines 10 through 12	**13a**	
b	Earned income credit and credit from **Form 4136**	**13b**	
c	Subtract line 13b from line 13a. Enter the result, but not less than zero. **THIS IS YOUR TOTAL 1997 ESTIMATED TAX** . . . . ▶	**13c**	

		14a		
14a	Multiply line 13c by 90% (66⅔% for farmers and fishermen) . . .			
b	Enter the tax shown on your 1996 tax return (110% of that amount if you are not a farmer or a fisherman and the adjusted gross income shown on that return is more than $150,000 or, if married filing separately for 1997, more than $75,000)	**14b**		

c	Enter the **smaller** of line 14a or 14b. **THIS IS YOUR REQUIRED ANNUAL PAYMENT TO AVOID A PENALTY** . . . . ▶	**14c**	
	Caution: Generally, if you do not prepay (through income tax withholding and estimated tax payments) at least the amount on line 14c, you may owe a penalty for not paying enough estimated tax. To avoid a penalty, make sure your estimate on line 13c is as accurate as possible. Even if you pay the required annual payment, you may still owe tax when you file your return. If you prefer, you may pay the amount shown on line 13c. For more details, see Pub. 505.		
15	Income tax withheld and estimated to be withheld during 1997 (including income tax withholding on pensions, annuities, certain deferred income, etc.)	**15**	
16	Subtract line 15 from line 14c. (**Note:** If zero or less, or line 13c minus line 15 is less than $500, stop here. You are not required to make estimated tax payments.)	**16**	
17	If the first payment you are required to make is due April 15, 1997, enter ¼ of line 16 (minus any 1996 overpayment that you are applying to this installment) here and on your payment voucher(s)	**17**	

Page 4

FIGURE A10–8

Form 1040-ES
Department of the Treasury
Internal Revenue Service

1997 Payment Voucher **4**

OMB No. 1545-0087

Calendar year—Due Jan. 15, 1998

File only if you are making a payment of estimated tax. Return this voucher with check or money order payable to the **"Internal Revenue Service."** Please write your social security number and "1997 Form 1040-ES" on your check or money order. Do not send cash. Enclose, but do not staple or attach, your payment with this voucher.

Amount of payment	Please type or print	Your first name and initial	Your last name	Your social security number
		If joint payment, complete for spouse		
$...............................		Spouse's first name and initial	Spouse's last name	Spouse's social security number
		Address (number, street, and apt. no.)		
		City, state, and ZIP code. (If a foreign address, enter city, province or state, postal code, and country.)		

For Paperwork Reduction Act Notice, see instructions on page 1.   **Page 5**

FIGURE A10–9

Form SS-4
(Rev. April 1991)
Department of the Treasury
Internal Revenue Service

Application for Employer Identification Number

(For use by employers and others. Please read the attached instructions before completing this form.)

EIN

OMB No. 1545-0003
Expires 4-30-94

Please type or print clearly.

1 Name of applicant (True legal name) (See instructions.)

2 Trade name of business, if different from name in line 1

3 Executor, trustee, "care of" name

4a Mailing address (street address) (room, apt., or suite no.)

5a Address of business (See instructions.)

4b City, state, and ZIP code

5b City, state, and ZIP code

6 County and state where principal business is located

7 Name of principal officer, grantor, or general partner (See instructions.) ▶

8a Type of entity (Check only one box) (See instructions.)

☐ Individual SSN _____
☐ REMIC   ☐ Personal service corp.
☐ State/local government ☐ National guard
☐ Other nonprofit organization (specify) _____
☐ Other (specify) ▶ _____

☐ Estate
☐ Plan administrator SSN _____
☐ Other corporation (specify) _____
☐ Federal government/military ☐ Church or church controlled organization
If nonprofit organization enter GEN (if applicable) _____

☐ Trust
☐ Partnership
☐ Farmers' cooperative

8b If a corporation, give name of foreign country (if applicable) or state in the U.S. where incorporated ▶

Foreign country

State

9 Reason for applying (Check only one box.)
☐ Started new business
☐ Hired employees
☐ Created a pension plan (specify type) ▶
☐ Banking purpose (specify) ▶

☐ Changed type of organization (specify) ▶
☐ Purchased going business
☐ Created a trust (specify) ▶
☐ Other (specify) ▶

10 Date business started or acquired (Mo., day, year) (See instructions.)

11 Enter closing month of accounting year. (See instructions.)

12 First date wages or annuities were paid or will be paid (Mo., day, year). **Note:** *If applicant is a withholding agent, enter date income will first be paid to nonresident alien. (Mo., day, year)* ▶

13 Enter highest number of employees expected in the next 12 months. **Note:** *If the applicant does not expect to have any employees during the period, enter "0."* ▶

Nonagricultural	Agricultural	Household

14 Principal activity (See instructions.) ▶

15 Is the principal business activity manufacturing? If "Yes," principal product and raw material used ▶ ☐ Yes ☐ No

16 To whom are most of the products or services sold? Please check the appropriate box.
☐ Public (retail)   ☐ Other (specify) ▶   ☐ Business (wholesale)   ☐ N/A

17a Has the applicant ever applied for an identification number for this or any other business? ☐ Yes ☐ No
Note: *If "Yes," please complete lines 17b and 17c.*

17b If you checked the "Yes" box in line 17a, give applicant's true name and trade name, if different than name shown on prior application.

True name ▶   Trade name ▶

17c Enter approximate date, city, and state where the application was filed and the previous employer identification number if known.

Approximate date when filed (Mo., day, year) | City and state where filed | Previous EIN

Under penalties of perjury, I declare that I have examined this application, and to the best of my knowledge and belief, it is true, correct, and complete. | Telephone number (include area code)

Name and title (Please type or print clearly.) ▶

Signature ▶   Date ▶

Note: *Do not write below this line. For official use only.*

Please leave blank ▶	Geo.	Ind.	Class	Size	Reason for applying

For Paperwork Reduction Act Notice, see attached instructions.

Cat. No. 16055N

Form **SS-4** (Rev. 4-91)

FIGURE A10–10

Form **W-4**	**Employee's Withholding Allowance Certificate**	OMB No. 1545-0010
Department of the Treasury Internal Revenue Service	▶ **For Privacy Act and Paperwork Reduction Act Notice, see reverse.**	19**96**

1 Type or print your first name and middle initial	Last name	2 Your social security number

Home address (number and street or rural route)	3 ☐ Single ☐ Married ☐ Married, but withhold at higher Single rate. **Note:** *If married, but legally separated, or spouse is a nonresident alien, check the Single box.*

City or town, state, and ZIP code	4 If your last name differs from that on your social security card, check here and call 1-800-772-1213 for a new card . . . . . . ▶ ☐

5 Total number of allowances you are claiming (from line G above or from the worksheets on page 2 if they apply) . | **5** |

6 Additional amount, if any, you want withheld from each paycheck . . . . | **6** | $ |

7 I claim exemption from withholding for 1996 and I certify that I meet **BOTH** of the following conditions for exemption:
- Last year I had a right to a refund of **ALL** Federal income tax withheld because I had **NO** tax liability; **AND**
- This year I expect a refund of **ALL** Federal income tax withheld because I expect to have **NO** tax liability.

If you meet both conditions, enter "EXEMPT" here . . . . ▶ | **7** |

Under penalties of perjury, I certify that I am entitled to the number of withholding allowances claimed on this certificate or entitled to claim exempt status.

Employee's signature ▶ _____ Date ▶ _____ , 19 ___

8 Employer's name and address (Employer: Complete 8 and 10 only if sending to the IRS)	9 Office code (optional)	10 Employer identification number

Cat. No. 10220Q

FIGURE A10–11

U.S. Department of Justice
Immigration and Naturalization Service

OMB No. 1115-0136
Employment Eligibility Verification

Please read instructions carefully before completing this form. The instructions must be available during completion of this form. **ANTI-DISCRIMINATION NOTICE.** It is illegal to discriminate against work eligible individuals. Employers **CANNOT** specify which document(s) they will accept from an employee. The refusal to hire an individual because of a future expiration date may also constitute illegal discrimination.

Section 1. Employee Information and Verification. To be completed and signed by employee at the time employment begins

Print Name: Last	First	Middle Initial	Maiden Name

Address (Street Name and Number)	Apt. #	Date of Birth (month/day/year)

City	State	Zip Code	Social Security #

I am aware that federal law provides for imprisonment and/or fines for false statements or use of false documents in connection with the completion of this form.

I attest, under penalty of perjury, that I am (check one of the following):
☐ A citizen or national of the United States
☐ A Lawful Permanent Resident (Alien # A _____)
☐ An alien authorized to work until ____/____/____
(Alien # or Admission # _____)

Employee's Signature	Date (month/day/year)

Preparer and/or Translator Certification. (To be completed and signed if Section 1 is prepared by a person other than the employee.) I attest, under penalty of perjury, that I have assisted in the completion of this form and that to the best of my knowledge the information is true and correct.

Preparer's/Translator's Signature	Print Name

Address (Street Name and Number, City, State, Zip Code)	Date (month/day/year)

Section 2. Employer Review and Verification. To be completed and signed by employer. Examine one document from List A OR examine one document from List B **and** one from List C as listed on the reverse of this form and record the title, number and expiration date, if any, of the document(s)

List A	OR	List B	AND	List C
Document title: _____		_____		_____
Issuing authority: _____		_____		_____
Document #: _____		_____		_____
Expiration Date (if any): ___/___/___		___/___/___		___/___/___
Document #: _____				
Expiration Date (if any): ___/___/___				

CERTIFICATION - I attest, under penalty of perjury, that I have examined the document(s) presented by the above-named employee, that the above-listed document(s) appear to be genuine and to relate to the employee named, that the employee began employment on (month/day/year) ____/____/____ and that to the best of my knowledge the employee is eligible to work in the United States. (State employment agencies may omit the date the employee began employment).

Signature of Employer or Authorized Representative	Print Name	Title

Business or Organization Name	Address (Street Name and Number, City, State, Zip Code)	Date (month/day/year)

Section 3. Updating and Reverification. To be completed and signed by employer

A. New Name (if applicable)	B. Date of rehire (month/day/year) (if applicable)

C. If employee's previous grant of work authorization has expired, provide the information below for the document that establishes current employment eligibility.

Document Title:_____ Document #:_____ Expiration Date (if any):___/___/___

I attest, under penalty of perjury, that to the best of my knowledge, this employee is eligible to work in the United States, and if the employee presented document(s), the document(s) I have examined appear to be genuine and to relate to the individual.

Signature of Employer or Authorized Representative	Date (month/day/year)

Form I-9 (Rev. 11-21-91) N

FIGURE A10–12

290

LISTS OF ACCEPTABLE DOCUMENTS

LIST A		LIST B		LIST C
Documents that Establish Both Identity and Employment Eligibility	**OR**	**Documents that Establish Identity**	**AND**	**Documents that Establish Employment Eligibility**

LIST A
Documents that Establish Both Identity and Employment Eligibility

1. U.S. Passport (unexpired or expired)

2. Certificate of U.S. Citizenship (*INS Form N-560 or N-561*)

3. Certificate of Naturalization (*INS Form N-550 or N-570*)

4. Unexpired foreign passport, with *I-551 stamp or* attached INS Form I-94 indicating unexpired employment authorization

5. Alien Registration Receipt Card with photograph (*INS Form I-151 or I-551*)

6. Unexpired Temporary Resident Card (*INS Form I-688*)

7. Unexpired Employment Authorization Card (*INS Form I-688A*)

8. Unexpired Reentry Permit (*INS Form I-327*)

9. Unexpired Refugee Travel Document (*INS Form I-571*)

10. Unexpired Employment Authorization Document issued by the INS which contains a photograph (*INS Form I-688B*)

OR

LIST B
Documents that Establish Identity

1. Driver's license or ID card issued by a state or outlying possession of the United States provided it contains a photograph or information such as name, date of birth, sex, height, eye color, and address

2. ID card issued by federal, state, or local government agencies or entities provided it contains a photograph or information such as name, date of birth, sex, height, eye color, and address

3. School ID card with a photograph

4. Voter's registration card

5. U.S. Military card or draft record

6. Military dependent's ID card

7. U.S. Coast Guard Merchant Mariner Card

8. Native American tribal document

9. Driver's license issued by a Canadian government authority

For persons under age 18 who are unable to present a document listed above:

10. School record or report card

11. Clinic, doctor, or hospital record

12. Day-care or nursery school record

AND

LIST C
Documents that Establish Employment Eligibility

1. U.S. social security card issued by the Social Security Administration (*other than a card stating it is not valid for employment*)

2. Certification of Birth Abroad issued by the Department of State (*Form FS-545 or Form DS-1350*)

3. Original or certified copy of a birth certificate issued by a state, county, municipal authority or outlying possession of the United States bearing an official seal

4. Native American tribal document

5. U.S. Citizen ID Card (*INS Form I-197*)

6. ID Card for use of Resident Citizen in the United States (*INS Form I-179*)

7. Unexpired employment authorization document issued by the INS (*other than those listed under List A*)

Illustrations of many of these documents appear in Part 8 of the Handbook for Employers (M-274)

Form I-9 (Rev. 11-21-91) N

FPI-RBK

FIGURE A10–12   (*continued*)

Payroll Ledger

James Jones
1257 East Ave.
Anytown NY
     12345-1234

Filing Status - Single
Exemptions - 1
SSN 111-22-3333

Date of Hire:
Pay Rate:

Date 1998	Pay Rate	Hours Worked	Gross Pay	6.2% Fica	1.45% Medi C	Federal Inc Tax	State Inc. Tax	Net Pay
9-15	10.00	80	$800.00	49.60	11.60	85.00	40.00	613.80
9-30	10.00	80	$800.00	49.60	11.60	85.00	40.00	613.80
10-15	10.00	80.00	$800.00	49.60	11.60	85.00	40.00	613.80
10-30	10.00	80.00	$800.00	49.60	11.60	85.00	40.00	613.80
11-15	10.00	80.00	$800.00	49.60	11.60	85.00	40.00	613.80
11-30	10.00	80.00	$800.00	49.60	11.60	85.00	40.00	613.80
12-15	10.00	80.00	$800.00	49.60	11.60	85.00	40.00	613.80
12-30	10.00	80.00	$800.00	49.60	11.60	85.00	40.00	613.80
Qtrly Totals			6400.00			680.00	320.00	

FIGURE A10–13   Payroll register

Form 941
(Rev. January 1995)
Department of the Treasury
Internal Revenue Service (O)

4141

Employer's Quarterly Federal Tax Return
▶ See separate instructions for information on completing this return.

Please type or print.

Enter state code for state in which deposits made . ▶

Name (as distinguished from trade name)

Date quarter ended

Trade name, if any

Employer identification number

Address (number and street)

City, state, and ZIP code

(see page 3 of instructions).

OMB No. 1545-0029

T	
FF	
FD	
FP	
I	
T	

If address is different from prior return, check here ▶

IRS Use

1 1 1 1 1 1 1 1 1 1   2   3 3 3 3 3 3   4 4 4

5 5 5   6   7   8 8 8 8 8   9 9 9   10 10 10 10 10 10 10 10 10

If you do not have to file returns in the future, check here ▶ ☐   and enter date final wages paid ▶

If you are a seasonal employer, see **Seasonal employers** on page 1 of the instructions and check here ▶ ☐

1	Number of employees (except household) employed in the pay period that includes March 12th ▶	
2	Total wages and tips, plus other compensation	**2**
3	Total income tax withheld from wages, tips, and sick pay	**3**
4	Adjustment of withheld income tax for preceding quarters of calendar year	**4**
5	Adjusted total of income tax withheld (line 3 as adjusted by line 4—see instructions) . . .	**5**
6a	Taxable social security wages . . . . $ × 12.4% (.124) =	**6a**
b	Taxable social security tips . . . . $ × 12.4% (.124) =	**6b**
7	Taxable Medicare wages and tips . . . . . $ × 2.9% (.029) =	**7**
8	Total social security and Medicare taxes (add lines 6a, 6b, and 7). Check here if wages are not subject to social security and/or Medicare tax . . . . ▶ ☐	**8**
9	Adjustment of social security and Medicare taxes (see instructions for required explanation) Sick Pay $ _____ ± Fractions of Cents $ _____ ± Other $ _____ =	**9**
10	Adjusted total of social security and Medicare taxes (line 8 as adjusted by line 9—see instructions)	**10**
11	**Total taxes** (add lines 5 and 10)	**11**
12	Advance earned income credit (EIC) payments made to employees, if any	**12**
13	Net taxes (subtract line 12 from line 11). **This should equal line 17, column (d) below** (or line D of Schedule B (Form 941))	**13**
14	Total deposits for quarter, including overpayment applied from a prior quarter	**14**
15	**Balance due** (subtract line 14 from line 13). Pay to Internal Revenue Service	**15**
16	**Overpayment,** if line 14 is more than line 13, enter excess here ▶ $ _____	

and check if to be: ☐ Applied to next return   **OR**   ☐ Refunded.

- **All filers:** If line 13 is less than $500, you need not complete line 17 or Schedule B.
- **Semiweekly depositors:** Complete Schedule B and check here . . . . ▶ ☐
- **Monthly depositors:** Complete line 17, columns (a) through (d), and check here . . . . . . ▶ ☐

17	**Monthly Summary of Federal Tax Liability.**			
	(a) First month liability	**(b)** Second month liability	**(c)** Third month liability	**(d)** Total liability for quarter

Sign Here

Under penalties of perjury, I declare that I have examined this return, including accompanying schedules and statements, and to the best of my knowledge and belief, it is true, correct, and complete.

Signature ▶   Print Your Name and Title ▶   Date ▶

For Paperwork Reduction Act Notice, see page 1 of separate instructions.   Cat. No. 17001Z   Form **941** (Rev. 1-95)

FIGURE A10–14

Form 941-V

Department of the Treasury
Internal Revenue Service

Form 941 Payment Voucher

For Paperwork Reduction Act Notice, see Form 941 instructions.

OMB No. 1545-0029

19**95**

1 Your employer identification number	2 First four characters of your business name	3 MFT	4 Tax period		5 Transaction code
		0 1	*0* 1st Quarter *0* 3rd Quarter		6 1 0
6 Name and address			*0* 2nd Quarter *0* 4th Quarter		

7 Enter amount paid with return . . . . . $ _____

● Make check or money order payable to the Internal Revenue Service. Do not send cash.

● Include, but do not staple, your payment with this voucher and Form 941.

FIGURE A10–14   *(continued)*

TAX YEAR
MONTH ➡

EMPLOYER IDENTIFICATION NUMBER ➡

BANK NAME/
DATE STAMP

Name _____

Address _____

City _____

State _____ ZIP _____

Telephone number (_____) _____

0 941   *0* 945   *0* 1st Quarter

0 990C   *0* 1120   *0* 2nd Quarter

0 943   *0* 990-T   *0* 3rd Quarter

0 720   *0* 990PF   *0* 4th Quarter

0 CT-1   *0* 1042

0 940   35

FOR BANK USE IN MICR ENCODING

Federal Tax Deposit Coupon
Form 8109-B (Rev. 1-94)

FIGURE A10–15

Request for Federal Tax Deposit Coupon Books

(See reverse for instructions)

1. Type of entity *(check one)*
☐ Sole proprietor
☐ Partnership
☐ Corporation

Note: After completion, please forward this form to the appropriate district office or service center for processing.

2. Employer Identification Number	3. Quantity *(Max. 8 bks)*	4. Fiscal Month	5. Name
			6. Trade name

☐☐☐☐☐☐☐☐☐ ☐☐ ☐☐

7. Street address	8. City	9. State	10. ZIP code

11. Name of requester	12. Phone number

Reasons for Request

13. *(Check applicable box(es))*

☐ Name change   ☐ Coupon books received, but lost   ☐ Quantity increase

☐ Address change   ☐ Coupon books not received   ☐ New requirement

14. Name of preparer	15. Date

Form **4417-A** (Rev. 10-89)   Cat. No. 22910R   Department of the Treasury — Internal Revenue Service

FIGURE A10–16

b Employer's identification number		**1** Wages, tips, other compensation	**2** Federal income tax withheld
c Employer's name, address, and ZIP code		**3** Social security wages	**4** Social security tax withheld
		5 Medicare wages and tips	**6** Medicare tax withheld
		7 Social security tips	**8** Allocated tips
d Employee's social security number		**9** Advance EIC payment	**10** Dependent care benefits
e Employee's name (first, middle initial, last)		**11** Nonqualified plans	**12** Benefits included in box 1
		13 See Instrs. for box 13	**14** Other

	15 Statutory employee ☐	Deceased ☐	Pension plan ☐	Legal rep. ☐	Hshld. emp. ☐	Subtotal ☐	Deferred compensation ☐
f Employee's address and ZIP code							

16 State Employer's state I.D. No.	17 State wages, tips, etc.	18 State income tax	19 Locality name	20 Local wages, tips, etc.	21 Local income tax

Cat. No. 10134D

Department of the Treasury—Internal Revenue Service

Form **W-2** Wage and Tax Statement **1997**

Copy A For Social Security Administration

For Paperwork Reduction Act Notice, see separate instructions.

Do NOT Cut or Separate Forms on This Page

---

a Control number	22222	Void ☐	For Official Use Only ▶ OMB No. 1545-0008	

b Employer's identification number		**1** Wages, tips, other compensation	**2** Federal income tax withheld
c Employer's name, address, and ZIP code		**3** Social security wages	**4** Social security tax withheld
		5 Medicare wages and tips	**6** Medicare tax withheld
		7 Social security tips	**8** Allocated tips
d Employee's social security number		**9** Advance EIC payment	**10** Dependent care benefits
e Employee's name (first, middle initial, last)		**11** Nonqualified plans	**12** Benefits included in box 1
		13 See Instrs. for box 13	**14** Other

	15 Statutory employee ☐	Deceased ☐	Pension plan ☐	Legal rep. ☐	Hshld. emp. ☐	Subtotal ☐	Deferred compensation ☐
f Employee's address and ZIP code							

16 State Employer's state I.D. No.	17 State wages, tips, etc.	18 State income tax	19 Locality name	20 Local wages, tips, etc.	21 Local income tax

Cat. No. 10134D

Department of the Treasury—Internal Revenue Service

Form **W-2** Wage and Tax Statement **1997**

Copy A For Social Security Administration

For Paperwork Reduction Act Notice, see separate instructions.

FIGURE A10–17

DO NOT STAPLE

a Control number	33333	For Official Use Only ▶ OMB No. 1545-0008		

b Kind of Payer ▶	941 ☐ Military ☐ 943 ☐ CT-1 ☐ Hshld. ☐ Medicare govt. emp. ☐	**1** Wages, tips, other compensation	**2** Federal income tax withheld
		3 Social security wages	**4** Social security tax withheld

c Total number of statements	**d** Establishment number	**5** Medicare wages and tips	**6** Medicare tax withheld

e Employer's identification number	**7** Social security tips	**8** Allocated tips

f Employer's name	**9** Advance EIC payments	**10** Dependent care benefits
	11 Nonqualified plans	**12** Deferred compensation
	13	
	14	

g Employer's address and ZIP code

h Other EIN used this year	**15** Income tax withheld by third-party payer

i Employer's state I.D. No.				

Under penalties of perjury, I declare that I have examined this return and accompanying documents, and, to the best of my knowledge and belief, they are true, correct, and complete.

Signature ▶ _____ Title ▶ _____ Date ▶ _____

Telephone number ( )

Form **W-3** Transmittal of Wage and Tax Statements **1997**   Department of the Treasury
Internal Revenue Service

Paperwork Reduction Act Notice

We ask for the information on this form to carry out the Internal Revenue laws of the United States. You are required to give us the information. We need it to ensure that you are complying with these laws and to allow us to figure and collect the right amount of tax.

You are not required to provide the information requested on a form that is subject to the Paperwork Reduction Act unless the form displays a valid OMB control number. Books or records relating to a form or its instructions must be retained as long as their contents may become material in the administration of any Internal Revenue law. Generally, tax returns and return information are confidential, as required by Code section 6103.

The time needed to complete and file this form will vary depending on individual circumstances. The estimated average time is 25 minutes. If you have comments concerning the accuracy of this time estimate or suggestions for making this form simpler, we would be happy to hear from you. You can write to the Tax Forms Committee, Western Area Distribution Center, Rancho Cordova, CA 95743-0001. **DO NOT** send the form to this address.

Changes To Note

Household Employers.—All household employers, even those with only one household employee, must file Form W-3 with their 1997 Forms W-2.

Boxes 13 and 14 Eliminated.—Entries are not needed for *Adjusted total social security wages and tips* (formerly box 13) and *Adjusted total Medicare wages and tips* (formerly box 14).

Need Help?

For information about the Information Reporting Call Site, Bulletin Board Services, substitute forms, and how to get forms and publications, see page 1 of the 1997 **Instructions for Form W-2.**

Where To File

Send the entire first page of this form with Copy A of Forms W-2 to:

Social Security Administration
Data Operations Center
Wilkes-Barre, PA 18769-0001

Note: *If you use "Certified Mail" to file, change the ZIP code to "18769-0002." Also see* **Shipping and Mailing** *on page 2 for additional information. If you use a* **carrier other than the U.S. Postal Service** *to deliver this information, add "1150 E. Mountain Dr." to the address and change the ZIP code to "18769."*

Cat. No. 10159Y

FIGURE A10–18

Form **940-EZ**

Department of the Treasury
Internal Revenue Service (O)

Employer's Annual Federal Unemployment (FUTA) Tax Return

▶ For Paperwork Reduction Act Notice, see page 2.

OMB No. 1545-1110

1996

	T	
	FF	
	FD	
	FP	
	I	
	T	

Name (as distinguished from trade name)   Calendar year

Trade name, if any

Address and ZIP code   Employer identification number

Follow the chart under **Who May Use Form 940-EZ** *on page 2. If you cannot use Form 940-EZ, you must use Form 940 instead.*

A Enter the amount of contributions paid to your state unemployment fund. (See instructions for line A on page 4.)▶ $ _____

B (1) Enter the name of the state where you have to pay contributions . . . . ▶ _____
(2) Enter your state reporting number as shown on state unemployment tax return ▶

If you will not have to file returns in the future, check here (see Who Must File on page 2) and complete and sign the return . . . . . ▶ ☐

If this is an Amended Return, check here . . . . ▶ ☐

Part I   Taxable Wages and FUTA Tax

1	Total payments (including payments shown on lines 2 and 3) during the calendar year for services of employees	**1**	
		Amount paid	
2	Exempt payments. (Explain all exempt payments, attaching additional sheets if necessary.) ▶ _____ _____	**2**	
3	Payments for services of more than $7,000. Enter only amounts over the first $7,000 paid to each employee. Do not include any exempt payments from line 2. Do not use your state wage limitation. The $7,000 amount is the Federal wage base. Your state wage base may be different	**3**	
4	Total exempt payments (add lines 2 and 3)	**4**	
5	**Total taxable wages** (subtract line 4 from line 1) . . . . ▶	**5**	
6	**FUTA tax.** Multiply the wages on line 5 by .008 and enter here. (If the result is over $100, also complete Part II.) .	**6**	
7	Total FUTA tax deposited for the year, including any overpayment applied from a prior year (from your records)	**7**	
8	**Amount you owe** (subtract line 7 from line 6). This should be $100 or less. Pay to "Internal Revenue Service." ▶	**8**	
9	**Overpayment** (subtract line 6 from line 7). Check if it is to be: ☐ **Applied to next return, or** ☐ **Refunded** ▶	**9**	

Part II   Record of Quarterly Federal Unemployment Tax Liability (Do not include state liability.) Complete only if line 6 is over $100.

Quarter	First (Jan. 1 – Mar. 31)	Second (Apr. 1 – June 30)	Third (July 1 – Sept. 30)	Fourth (Oct. 1 – Dec. 31)	Total for year
Liability for quarter					

Under penalties of perjury, I declare that I have examined this return, including accompanying schedules and statements, and, to the best of my knowledge and belief, it is true, correct, and complete, and that no part of any payment made to a state unemployment fund claimed as a credit was, or is to be, deducted from the payments to employees.

Signature ▶   Title (Owner, etc.) ▶   Date ▶

DETACH HERE   Cat. No. 10983G   Form **940-EZ** (1996)

FIGURE A10–19

UNEMPLOYMENT INSURANCE DIVISION OF SOUTH DAKOTA   **BOX 4730**   Aberdeen, South Dakota 57402-4730

Form DOL-UID-001 (11/92)   EMPLOYER'S REPORT TO DETERMINE LIABILITY

This Report is to be completed whether or not you are liable for contributions under the South Dakota Unemployment Insurance Law, and returned to the Division within ten (10) days.

IF ADDITIONAL SPACE IS NEEDED FOR ANSWERING ANY QUESTIONS, PLEASE USE THE COMMENT SPACE ON THE REVERSE.
INSTRUCTIONS ON REVERSE (BOTH SHEETS)

Enter your Federal Identification Number: _____

SUBMIT ORIGINAL

DO NOT WRITE IN THIS SPACE		
REGISTRATION NUMBER		
C-	**Employer Liability Begins**		
No. 21a	Applicable Rate:		
	Reviewer's Initials:		

1. OWNER(S) _____

   BUSINESS NAME _____   PHONE (___) _____
   Area Code

2. MAIL ADDRESS _____
   Street Address   City   State   Zip Code

   BUSINESS HEADQUARTERS ADDRESS _____

3. **TYPE OF ORGANIZATION:** (Check One)   1. Individual ( )   3. Corporation ( )   5. Other ( )
   2. Partnership ( )   4. Association ( )   Explain: _____

   IF A CORPORATION, complete the following questions:
   State of Incorporation: _____   Date of Incorporation: _____   Date qualified in S.D.: _____
   Name of Statutory Agent: _____   Address: _____
   IF YOUR BUSINESS IS A NONPROFIT ORGANIZATION, did you employ four (4) or more persons in twenty (20) weeks during any Calendar Year?
   Yes ( )   No ( )   Under what section of the Internal Revenue Code were you granted an exemption as a nonprofit organization? _____

4. **IDENTIFICATION OF OWNER(S), CORPORATION OFFICERS, PARTNERS, ETC.**

Social Security Number	Name (Given name must be shown in full)	Title	Residence Address

5. Have your previously made a report to the Unemployment Insurance Division?   Yes ( )   No ( )
   If Yes, enter name _____   Account Number _____

6. Does this report cover all establishments owned and operated by stated ownership?   Yes ( )   No ( )

7. **WORK LOCATIONS** (List Additional Locations in Comment Section)   **NATURE OF BUSINESS**

	City	County	Primary Activity	Principal Product/Service
(a)				
(b)				

8. Date of first employment in S.D. _____   **ENTER THE TOTAL WAGES PAID IN EACH CALENDAR QUARTER:**
   19 _____   1st _____   2nd _____   3rd _____   4th _____
   19 _____   1st _____   2nd _____   3rd _____   4th _____

9. **WEEKLY RECORD OF EMPLOYMENT:** Enter the number of individuals performing services for you in the day in which you employed the largest number within each calendar week ending at midnight Saturday. (For instructions of completion of item 8, see reverse.)

WEEKS IN EACH MONTH CURRENT YEAR 19	JANUARY	FEBRUARY	MARCH	APRIL	MAY	JUNE
	JULY	AUGUST	SEPTEMBER	OCTOBER	NOVEMBER	DECEMBER

WEEKS IN EACH MONTH PRIOR YEAR 19	JANUARY	FEBRUARY	MARCH	APRIL	MAY	JUNE
	JULY	AUGUST	SEPTEMBER	OCTOBER	NOVEMBER	DECEMBER

10. **PREDECESSOR**, if any, from whom your business was acquired. (See item 9 on reverse.) If none, enter "None" _____
    Name _____   Address _____
    Date Acquired _____   Employer Account No. _____

    ** It was agreed between the **EMPLOYER** and the **FORMER OWNER** that: ALL ( )   NONE ( )   PORTION ( ) of the Employer's Experience Rating Account shall be acquired with assets and liabilities following the account as provided in Section 61-5-33 SDCL.

11. **COMPANY STATUS:** Is the covered establishment(s) PRIMARILY engaged in performing services for other units of the Company?
    YES ( )   NO ( )   IF YES, please indicate in the comment section the nature of these services.

12. Are you required to file the **EMPLOYER'S ANNUAL FEDERAL UNEMPLOYMENT TAX RETURN**, Treasury Form 940, for either the current or preceding year?
    Yes ( )   No ( )   Which Year? _____

THIS REPORT MUST BE SIGNED BY THE OWNER, A PARTNER, or AUTHORIZED OFFICIAL. (See certification on reverse side)

DATE	By (Signature)	TITLE
	X	

FIGURE A10–20

EMPLOYER'S QUARTERLY CONTRIBUTION, INVESTMENT FEE, AND WAGE REPORT

DOL-UID-21 (6/96)

Unemployment Insurance Division of South Dakota

P.O. Box 4730 • Aberdeen, South Dakota 57402-4730 • Phone (605) 626-2312

Account Number

Please use Black Ink Only.
Completion instructions are on the back of the employer copy and below.

EXAMPLE: TYPE characters THROUGH boxes

`Machine Print`

EXAMPLE: PRINT characters IN boxes

`H A N D   P R I N T`

3. Total gross wages paid in this quarter	
4. Wages in excess of $7,000.00 this year (see instructions)	
5. Taxable wages	
6. UI contribution rate % x line 5	
7. Investment fee rate % x line 5	
8. Total due (add lines 6 & 7)	
9. Adjustment from prior quarters (explain on reverse or attachment)	
10. Interest: Line 8 x 1.5% per month from due date	
11. Penalty for late filings: $5.00 per month	
12. Penalty for late payments: $5.00 per month	
13. Total remittance (Add lines 8, 9, 10, 11 & 12)	

Quarter/Year   Due Date

1. For each month, report the number of covered workers who worked during or received pay for the payroll period which includes the 12th of the month.

If none, enter "0"		
1st month	2nd month	3rd month

2. Does this account operate in more than one location in South Dakota?   Yes ☐   No ☐

14. If your business in South Dakota has changed in any way, please complete Item 14 on the back side of this page. If the ownership changed during this quarter, a separate report must be submitted by each ownership.

Make remittance payable to the South Dakota Unemployment Insurance Division

15. Employee's Social Security Number	16. Employee's Name (Last, First)	17. Total Gross Wages Paid	18. Excess Wages This Quarter

I certify all information on this report is complete and correct.

Signature

Title   Date

Prepared by   Telephone

19. Total Gross Wages This Page	20. Total Excess Wages This Page

21. Total Gross Wages All Pages	22. Total Excess Wages All Pages

FIGURE A10–21

Who are employees?
Generally, employees can be defined either under common law or under statutes for special purposes.

Common Law Employees
Anyone who performs services that can be controlled by an employer (what will be done and how it will be done) is an employee. This is so even when the employer gives the employee freedom of action. What matters is that the employer has the legal right to control the method and result of the services.

Generally, people in business for themselves are not employees. For example, doctors, lawyers, veterinarians, construction contractors, and others in an independent trade in which they offer their services to the public are usually not employees.

If an employer/employee relationship exists, it does not matter what it is called. The employee may be called a partner, agent, or independent contractor. It also does not matter how payments are measured or paid, what they are called, or whether the employee works full or part-time.

1. **Instructions.** A worker who is required to comply with other persons' instructions about when, where, and how he or she is to work is ordinarily an employee. This control factor is present if the person or persons for whom the services are performed have the right to require compliance with instructions. See, for example, Rev. Rul. 68-598, 1968-2 C.B. 464, and Rev. Rul. 66-381, 1966-2 C.B. 449.

2. **Training.** Training a worker by requiring an experienced employee to work with the worker, by corresponding with the worker, by requiring the worker to attend meetings, or by using other methods, indicates that the person or persons for whom the services are performed want the services performed in a particular method or manner. See Rev. Rul. 70-630, 1970-2 C.B. 229.

3. **Integration.** Integration of the worker's services into the business operations generally shows that the worker is subject to direction and control. When the success or continuation of a business depends to an appreciable degree upon the performance of certain services, the workers who perform those services must necessarily be subject to a certain amount of control by the owner of the business. See United States v. Silk, 331 U.S. 704 (1947), 1947-2 C.B. 167.

4. **Services Rendered Personally.** If the services must be rendered personally, presumably the person or persons for whom the services are performed are interested in the methods used to accomplish the work as well as in the results. See Rev. Rul. 55-695, 1955-2 C.B. 410.

5. **Hiring, Supervising, and Paying Assistants.** If the person or persons for whom the services are performed hire, supervise, and

(*continued*)

FIGURE 10-22

(continued)

pay assistants, that factor generally shows control over the workers on the job. However, if one worker hires, supervises, and pays the other assistants pursuant to a contract under which the worker agrees to provide materials and labor and under which the worker is responsible only for the attainment of a result, this factor indicates an independent contractor status. Compare Rev. Rul. 63-115, 1963-1 C.B. 17 with Rev. Rul. 55-593, 1955-2 C.B. 610.

6. **Continuing Relationship.** A continuing relationship between the worker and the person or persons for whom the services are performed indicates that an employer-employee relationship exists. A continuing relationship may exist where work is performed at frequently recurring although irregular intervals. See United States v. Silk.

7. **Set Hours of Work.** The establishment of set hours of work by the person or persons for whom the services are performed is a factor indicating control. See Rev. Rul. 73-591, 1973-2 C.B. 337.

8. **Full Time Required.** If the worker must devote substantially full time to the business of the person or persons for whom the services are performed, such person or persons have control over the amount of time the worker spends working and impliedly restrict the worker from doing other gainful work. An independent contractor, on the other hand, is free to work when and for whom he or she chooses. See Rev. Rul. 56-694, 1956-2 C.B. 694.

9. **Doing Work on Employer's Premises.** If the work is performed on the premises of the person or persons for whom the services are performed, that factor suggests control over the worker, especially if the work could be done elsewhere. Rev. Rul. 56-660, 1956-2 C.B. 693. Work done off the premises of the person or persons receiving the services, such as at the office of the worker, indicates some freedom from control. However, this fact by itself does not mean that the worker is not an employee. The importance of this factor depends on the nature of the service involved and the extent to which an employer generally would require that employees perform such services on the employer's premises. Control over the place of work is indicated when the person or persons for whom the services are performed have the right to compel the worker to travel a designated route, to canvass a territory within a certain time, or to work at specific places as required. See Rev. Rul. 56-694.

10. **Order or Sequence Set.** If a worker must perform services in the order or sequence set by the person or persons for whom the services are performed, that factor shows that the worker is not free to follow the worker's own pattern of work but must follow the established routines and schedules of the person or persons for whom the services are performed. Often, because of the nature of an occupation, the person or persons for whom the services are performed do not set the order of the services or set the order

infrequently. It is sufficient to show control, however, if such person or persons retain the right to do so. See Rev. Rul. 56-694.

11. **Oral or Written Reports.** A requirement that the worker submit regular or written reports to the person or persons for whom the services are performed indicates a degree of control. See Rev. Rul. 70-309, 1970-1 C.B. 199, and Rev. Rul. 68-248, 1968-1 C.B. 431.

12. **Payment by Hour, Week, Month.** Payment by the hour, week, or month generally points to an employer-employee relationship, provided that this method of payment is not just a convenient way of paying a lump sum agreed upon as the cost of a job. Payment made by the job or on a straight commission generally indicates that the worker is an independent contractor. See Rev. Rul. 74-389, 1974-2 C.B. 330.

13. **Payment of Business and/or Traveling Expenses.** If the person or persons for whom the services are performed ordinarily pay the worker's business and/or traveling expenses, the worker is ordinarily an employee. An employer, to be able to control expenses, generally retains the right to regulate and direct the worker's business activities. See Rev. Rul. 55-144, 1955-1 C.B. 483.

14. **Furnishing of Tools and Materials.** The fact that the person or persons for whom the services are performed furnish significant tools, materials, and other equipment tends to show the existence of an employer-employee relationship. See Rev. Rul. 71-524, 1971-2 C.B. 346.

15. **Significant Investment.** If the worker invests in facilities that are used by the worker in performing services and are not typically maintained by employees (such as the maintenance of an office rented at fair value from an unrelated party), that factor tends to indicate that the worker is an independent contractor. On the other hand, lack of investment in facilities indicates dependence on the person or persons for whom the services are performed for such facilities and, accordingly, the existence of an employer-employee relationship. See Rev. Rul. 71-524. Special scrutiny is required with respect to certain types of facilities, such as home offices.

16. **Realization of Profit or Loss.** A worker who can realize a profit or suffer a loss as a result of the worker's services (in addition to the profit or loss ordinarily realized by employees) is generally an independent contractor, but the worker who cannot is an employee. See Rev. Rul. 70-309. For example, if the worker is subject to a real risk of economic loss due to significant investments or a bona fide liability for expenses, such as salary payments to unrelated employees, that factor indicates that the worker is an independent contractor. The risk that a worker will not receive payment for his or her services, however, is common to both independent contractors and employees and thus does not constitute a sufficient economic risk to support treatment as an independent contractor.

(continued)

(continued)

17. **Working for More Than One Firm at a Time.** If a worker performs more than de minimis services for a multiple of unrelated persons or firms at the same time, that factor generally indicates that the worker is an independent contractor. See Rev. Rul. 70-572, 1970-2 C.B. 221. However, a worker who performs services for more than one person may be an employee of each of the persons, especially where such persons are part of the same service arrangement.

18. **Making Service Available to General Public.** The fact that a worker makes his or her services available to the general public on a regular and consistent basis indicates an independent contractor relationship. See Rev. Rul. 56-660.

19. **Right to Discharge.** The right to discharge a worker is a factor indicating that the worker is an employee and the person possessing the right is an employer. An employer exercises control through the threat of dismissal, which causes the worker to obey the employer's instructions. An independent contractor, on the other hand, cannot be fired so long as the independent contractor produces a result that meets the contract specifications. Rev. Rul. 75-41, 1975-1 C.B. 323.

20. **Right to Terminate.** If the worker has the right to end his or her relationship with the person for whom the services are performed at any time he or she wishes without incurring liability, that factor indicates an employer-employee relationship. See Rev. Rul. 70-309.

Form **SS-8**

(Rev. July 1996)

Department of the Treasury
Internal Revenue Service

Determination of Employee Work Status for Purposes of Federal Employment Taxes and Income Tax Withholding

OMB No. 1545-0004

Paperwork Reduction Act Notice

We ask for the information on this form to carry out the Internal Revenue laws of the United States. You are required to give us the information. We need it to ensure that you are complying with these laws and to allow us to figure and collect the right amount of tax.

You are not required to provide the information requested on a form that is subject to the Paperwork Reduction Act unless the form displays a valid OMB control number. Books or records relating to a form or its instructions must be retained as long as their contents may become material in the administration of any Internal Revenue law. Generally, tax returns and return information are confidential, as required by Code section 6103.

The time needed to complete and file this form will vary depending on individual circumstances. The estimated average time is: **Recordkeeping,** 34 hr., 55 min.; **Learning about the law or the form,** 12 min.; and **Preparing and sending the form to the IRS,** 46 min. If you have comments concerning the accuracy of these time estimates or suggestions for making this form simpler, we would be happy to hear from you. You can write to the Tax Forms Committee, Western Area Distribution Center, Rancho Cordova, CA 95743-0001. **DO NOT** send the tax form to this address. Instead, see **General Information** for where to file.

Purpose

Employers and workers file Form SS-8 to get a determination as to whether a worker is an employee for purposes of Federal employment taxes and income tax withholding.

General Information

Complete this form carefully. If the firm is completing the form, complete it for **ONE** individual who is representative of the class of workers whose status is in question. If you want a written determination for more than one class of workers, complete a separate Form SS-8 for one worker from each class whose status is typical of that class. A written determination for any worker will apply to other workers of the same class if the facts are not materially different from those of the worker whose status was ruled upon.

Caution: Form SS-8 is not a claim for refund of social security and Medicare taxes or Federal income tax withholding. Also, a determination that an individual is an employee does not necessarily reduce any current or prior tax liability. A worker must file his or her income tax return even if a determination has not been made by the due date of the return.

Where to file.—In the list below, find the state where your legal residence, principal place of business, office, or agency is located. Send Form SS-8 to the address listed for your location.

Location:	Send to:
Alaska, Arizona, Arkansas, California, Colorado, Hawaii, Idaho, Illinois, Iowa, Kansas, Minnesota, Missouri, Montana, Nebraska, Nevada, New Mexico, North Dakota, Oklahoma, Oregon, South Dakota, Texas, Utah, Washington, Wisconsin, Wyoming	Internal Revenue Service SS-8 Determinations P.O. Box 1230, Stop 4106 AuCC Austin, TX 78767
Alabama, Connecticut, Delaware, District of Columbia, Florida, Georgia, Indiana, Kentucky, Louisiana, Maine, Maryland, Massachusetts, Michigan, Mississippi, New Hampshire, New Jersey, New York, North Carolina, Ohio, Pennsylvania, Rhode Island, South Carolina, Tennessee, Vermont, Virginia, West Virginia, All other locations	Internal Revenue Service SS-8 Determinations Two Lakemont Road Newport, VT 05855-1555

Name of firm (or person) for whom the worker performed services	Name of worker
Address of firm (include street address, apt. or suite no., city, state, and ZIP code)	Address of worker (include street address, apt. or suite no., city, state, and ZIP code)

Trade name	Telephone number (include area code) ( )	Worker's social security number
Telephone number (include area code) ( )	Firm's employer identification number	

Check type of firm for which the work relationship is in question:

☐ **Individual**   ☐ **Partnership**   ☐ **Corporation**   ☐ **Other** (specify) ▶ ....

Important Information Needed To Process Your Request

This form is being completed by: ☐ Firm   ☐ Worker

If this form is being completed by the worker, the IRS **must** have your permission to disclose your name to the firm.

Do you object to disclosing your name and the information on this form to the firm? . . . .   ☐ Yes   ☐ No

If you answer "Yes," the IRS cannot act on your request. **Do not complete the rest of this form unless the IRS asks for it.**

Under section 6110 of the Internal Revenue Code, the information on this form and related file documents will be open to the public if any ruling or determination is made. However, names, addresses, and taxpayer identification numbers will be removed before the information is made public.

Is there any other information you want removed? . . . .   ☐ Yes   ☐ No

If you check "Yes," we cannot process your request unless you submit a copy of this form and copies of all supporting documents showing, in brackets, the information you want removed. Attach a separate statement showing which specific exemption of section 6110(c) applies to each bracketed part.

Cat. No. 16106T

Form **SS-8** (Rev. 7-96)

FIGURE A10–23

This form is designed to cover many work activities, so some of the questions may not apply to you. **You must answer ALL items or mark them "Unknown" or "Does not apply."** *If you need more space, attach another sheet.*

Total number of workers in this class. (Attach names and addresses. If more than 10 workers, list only 10.) ▶ _____

This information is about services performed by the worker from _____ to _____
(month, day, year)   (month, day, year)

Is the worker still performing services for the firm? . . . . ☐ **Yes** ☐ **No**

- If "No," what was the date of termination? ▶ _____
(month, day, year)

1a Describe the firm's business ....
b Describe the work done by the worker ....
....

2a If the work is done under a written agreement between the firm and the worker, attach a copy.
b If the agreement is not in writing, describe the terms and conditions of the work arrangement ....
....
....

c If the actual working arrangement differs in any way from the agreement, explain the differences and why they occur ....
....
....

3a Is the worker given training by the firm? . . . . ☐ **Yes** ☐ **No**
- If "Yes," what kind? ....
- How often? ....
b Is the worker given instructions in the way the work is to be done (exclusive of actual training in 3a)? . ☐ **Yes** ☐ **No**
- If "Yes," give specific examples ....
c Attach samples of any written instructions or procedures.
d Does the firm have the right to change the methods used by the worker or direct that person on how to do the work? . . . . ☐ **Yes** ☐ **No**
- Explain your answer ....
....

e Does the operation of the firm's business require that the worker be supervised or controlled in the performance of the service? . . . . ☐ **Yes** ☐ **No**
- Explain your answer ....
....

4a The firm engages the worker:
☐ To perform and complete a particular job only
☐ To work at a job for an indefinite period of time
☐ Other (explain) ....
b Is the worker required to follow a routine or a schedule established by the firm? . . . . ☐ **Yes** ☐ **No**
- If "Yes," what is the routine or schedule? ....
....
....

c Does the worker report to the firm or its representative?. ☐ **Yes** ☐ **No**
- If "Yes," how often? ....
- For what purpose? ....
- In what manner (in person, in writing, by telephone, etc.)? ....
- Attach copies of any report forms used in reporting to the firm.
d Does the worker furnish a time record to the firm? . . . . ☐ **Yes** ☐ **No**
- If "Yes," attach copies of time records.
5a State the kind and value of tools, equipment, supplies, and materials furnished by:
- The firm ....
....
- The worker ....
....

b What expenses are incurred by the worker in the performance of services for the firm? ....
....

c Does the firm reimburse the worker for any expenses? . . . . ☐ **Yes** ☐ **No**
- If "Yes," specify the reimbursed expenses ....

FIGURE A10–23 *(continued)*

6a Will the worker perform the services personally? . . . . ☐ **Yes** ☐ **No**

 b Does the worker have helpers? . . . . ☐ **Yes** ☐ **No**

- If "Yes," who hires the helpers? ☐ Firm ☐ Worker
- If the helpers are hired by the worker, is the firm's approval necessary? . . . . ☐ **Yes** ☐ **No**
- Who pays the helpers?   ☐ Firm ☐ Worker
- If the worker pays the helpers, does the firm repay the worker? . . . . ☐ **Yes** ☐ **No**
- Are social security and Medicare taxes and Federal income tax withheld from the helpers' pay? . . ☐ **Yes** ☐ **No**
- If "Yes," who reports and pays these taxes?   ☐ Firm   ☐ Worker
- Who reports the helpers' earnings to the Internal Revenue Service? ☐ Firm ☐ Worker
- What services do the helpers perform? ....

7 At what location are the services performed? ☐ Firm's ☐ Worker's ☐ Other (specify) ....

8a Type of pay worker receives:
   ☐ Salary   ☐ Commission ☐ Hourly wage   ☐ Piecework ☐ Lump sum ☐ Other (specify) ....

 b Does the firm guarantee a minimum amount of pay to the worker? . . . . ☐ **Yes** ☐ **No**

 c Does the firm allow the worker a drawing account or advances against pay? . . . . ☐ **Yes** ☐ **No**

- If "Yes," is the worker paid such advances on a regular basis? . . . . ☐ **Yes** ☐ **No**

 d How does the worker repay such advances? ....

9a Is the worker eligible for a pension, bonus, paid vacations, sick pay, etc.? . . . . ☐ **Yes** ☐ **No**

- If "Yes," specify ....

 b Does the firm carry worker's compensation insurance on the worker? . . . . ☐ **Yes** ☐ **No**

 c Does the firm withhold social security and Medicare taxes from amounts paid the worker? . . . . . ☐ **Yes** ☐ **No**

 d Does the firm withhold Federal income tax from amounts paid the worker? . . . . ☐ **Yes** ☐ **No**

 e How does the firm report the worker's earnings to the Internal Revenue Service?
   ☐ Form W-2 ☐ Form 1099-MISC ☐ Does not report ☐ Other (specify) ....

- Attach a copy.

 f Does the firm bond the worker? . . . . ☐ **Yes** ☐ **No**

10a Approximately how many hours a day does the worker perform services for the firm? ....

 b Does the firm set hours of work for the worker? . . . . ☐ **Yes** ☐ **No**

- If "Yes," what are the worker's set hours? _____ a.m./p.m. to _____ a.m./p.m. (Circle whether a.m. or p.m.)

 c Does the worker perform similar services for others? . . . . . . ☐ **Yes** ☐ **No** ☐ **Unknown**

- If "Yes," are these services performed on a daily basis for other firms? . . . . . ☐ **Yes** ☐ **No** ☐ **Unknown**
- Percentage of time spent in performing these services for:
   This firm .... % Other firms .... %   ☐ **Unknown**
- Does the firm have priority on the worker's time? . . . . ☐ **Yes** ☐ **No**
- If "No," explain ....

 d Is the worker prohibited from competing with the firm either while performing services or during any later period? . . . . ☐ **Yes** ☐ **No**

11a Can the firm discharge the worker at any time without incurring a liability? . . . . ☐ **Yes** ☐ **No**

- If "No," explain ....

 b Can the worker terminate the services at any time without incurring a liability? . . . . ☐ **Yes** ☐ **No**

- If "No," explain ....

12a Does the worker perform services for the firm under:
   ☐ The firm's business name ☐ The worker's own business name ☐ Other (specify) ....

 b Does the worker advertise or maintain a business listing in the telephone directory, a trade journal, etc.? . . . . ☐ **Yes** ☐ **No** ☐ **Unknown**

- If "Yes," specify ....

 c Does the worker represent himself or herself to the public as being in business to perform the same or similar services? . . . . ☐ **Yes** ☐ **No** ☐ **Unknown**

- If "Yes," how? ....

 d Does the worker have his or her own shop or office? . . . . ☐ **Yes** ☐ **No** ☐ **Unknown**

- If "Yes," where? ....

 e Does the firm represent the worker as an employee of the firm to its customers? . . . . ☐ **Yes** ☐ **No**

- If "No," how is the worker represented? ....

 f How did the firm learn of the worker's services? ....

13 Is a license necessary for the work? . . . . ☐ **Yes** ☐ **No** ☐ **Unknown**

- If "Yes," what kind of license is required? ....
- Who issues the license? ....
- Who pays the license fee?

FIGURE A10–23   *(continued)*

14 Does the worker have a financial investment in a business related to the services performed? . . . . ☐ **Yes** ☐ **No** ☐ **Unknown**
- If "Yes," specify and give amount of the investment ....

15 Can the worker incur a loss in the performance of the service for the firm? . . . . ☐ **Yes** ☐ **No**
- If "Yes," how? ....

16a Has any other government agency ruled on the status of the firm's workers? . . . . ☐ **Yes** ☐ **No**
- If "Yes," attach a copy of the ruling.

b Is the same issue being considered by any IRS office in connection with the audit of the worker's tax return or the firm's tax return, or has it been considered recently? . . . . ☐ **Yes** ☐ **No**
- If "Yes," for which year(s)? ....

17 Does the worker assemble or process a product at home or away from the firm's place of business? ☐ **Yes** ☐ **No**
- If "Yes," who furnishes materials or goods used by the worker? ☐ Firm ☐ Worker ☐ Other
- Is the worker furnished a pattern or given instructions to follow in making the product? . . . . . ☐ **Yes** ☐ **No**
- Is the worker required to return the finished product to the firm or to someone designated by the firm? ☐ **Yes** ☐ **No**

18 Attach a detailed explanation of any other reason why you believe the worker is an employee or an independent contractor.

Answer items 19a through o only if the worker is a salesperson or provides a service directly to customers.

19a Are leads to prospective customers furnished by the firm? . . . . ☐ **Yes** ☐ **No** ☐ **Does not apply**
b Is the worker required to pursue or report on leads? . . . . ☐ **Yes** ☐ **No** ☐ **Does not apply**
c Is the worker required to adhere to prices, terms, and conditions of sale established by the firm? . . ☐ **Yes** ☐ **No**
d Are orders submitted to and subject to approval by the firm? . . . . ☐ **Yes** ☐ **No**
e Is the worker expected to attend sales meetings? . . . . ☐ **Yes** ☐ **No**
- If "Yes," is the worker subject to any kind of penalty for failing to attend? . . . . ☐ **Yes** ☐ **No**
f Does the firm assign a specific territory to the worker? . . . . ☐ **Yes** ☐ **No**
g Whom does the customer pay? ☐ Firm ☐ Worker
- If worker, does the worker remit the total amount to the firm? . . . . ☐ **Yes** ☐ **No**
h Does the worker sell a consumer product in a home or establishment other than a permanent retail establishment? . . . . ☐ **Yes** ☐ **No**
i List the products and/or services distributed by the worker, such as meat, vegetables, fruit, bakery products, beverages (other than milk), or laundry or dry cleaning services. If more than one type of product and/or service is distributed, specify the principal one ....
j Did the firm or another person assign the route or territory and a list of customers to the worker? . . ☐ **Yes** ☐ **No**
- If "Yes," enter the name and job title of the person who made the assignment ....
k Did the worker pay the firm or person for the privilege of serving customers on the route or in the territory? ☐ **Yes** ☐ **No**
- If "Yes," how much did the worker pay (not including any amount paid for a truck or racks, etc.)? $ ....
- What factors were considered in determining the value of the route or territory? ....
l How are new customers obtained by the worker? Explain fully, showing whether the new customers called the firm for service, were solicited by the worker, or both ....
m Does the worker sell life insurance? . . . . ☐ **Yes** ☐ **No**
- If "Yes," is the selling of life insurance or annuity contracts for the firm the worker's entire business activity? . . . . ☐ **Yes** ☐ **No**
- If "No," list the other business activities and the amount of time spent on them ....
n Does the worker sell other types of insurance for the firm? . . . . ☐ **Yes** ☐ **No**
- If "Yes," state the percentage of the worker's total working time spent in selling other types of insurance .... %
- At the time the contract was entered into between the firm and the worker, was it their intention that the worker sell life insurance for the firm: ☐ on a full-time basis ☐ on a part-time basis
- State the manner in which the intention was expressed ....
o Is the worker a traveling or city salesperson? . . . . ☐ **Yes** ☐ **No**
- If "Yes," from whom does the worker principally solicit orders for the firm? ....
- If the worker solicits orders from wholesalers, retailers, contractors, or operators of hotels, restaurants, or other similar establishments, specify the percentage of the worker's time spent in the solicitation .... %
- Is the merchandise purchased by the customers for resale or for use in their business operations? If used by the customers in their business operations, describe the merchandise and state whether it is equipment installed on their premises or a consumable supply

Under penalties of perjury, I declare that I have examined this request, including accompanying documents, and to the best of my knowledge and belief, the facts presented are true, correct, and complete.

Signature ▶   Title ▶   Date ▶

If the firm is completing this form, an officer or member of the firm must sign it. If the worker is completing this form, the worker must sign it. If the worker wants a written determination about services performed for two or more firms, a separate form must be completed and signed for each firm. Additional copies of this form may be obtained by calling 1-800-TAX-FORM (1-800-829-3676).

✪ *Printed on recycled paper*   *U.S. Government Printing Office: 1996 — 405-493/40147

FIGURE A10–23 *(continued)*

Independent Contractor Data Sheet

Your Name _____

Your Firm Name_____

Your Mailing Address _____

_____

_____

Your Federal ID Number _____

Your Social Security Number _____

Your Sales Tax or Excise Tax Lic. Number _____

Name of your Business Liability Insurance Carrier

_____

_____

Name of your Insurance Agent _____
Agent's Address   _____
                             _____
                             _____

Agent's Phone Number   _____

Do you carry workmen's compensation insurance ? _____

If so who is the insurance carrier?   _____

References: List the Name and Address of three firms that you have performed similar services for.

_____

_____

_____

FIGURE A10–24

9595 ☐ VOID ☐ CORRECTED

PAYER'S name, street address, city, state, ZIP code, and telephone no.		**1** Rents $	OMB No. 1545-0115	
		2 Royalties $	**19 97**	**Miscellaneous Income**
		3 Other income $	Form **1099-MISC**	
PAYER'S Federal identification number	RECIPIENT'S identification number	**4** Federal income tax withheld $	**5** Fishing boat proceeds $	**Copy A**
RECIPIENT'S name		**6** Medical and health care payments $	**7** Nonemployee compensation $	**For Internal Revenue Service Center**
Street address (including apt. no.)		**8** Substitute payments in lieu of dividends or interest $	**9** Payer made direct sales of $5,000 or more of consumer products to a buyer (recipient) for resale ▶ ☐	**File with Form 1096.**
City, state, and ZIP code		**10** Crop insurance proceeds $	**11** State income tax withheld $	For Paperwork Reduction Act Notice and instructions for completing this form, see **Instructions for Forms 1099, 1098, 5498, and W-2G.**
Account number (optional)	2nd TIN Not. ☐	**12** State/Payer's state number	**13** $	

Form **1099-MISC** Cat. No. 14425J Department of the Treasury - Internal Revenue Service

Do NOT Cut or Separate Forms on This Page

9595 ☐ VOID ☐ CORRECTED

PAYER'S name, street address, city, state, ZIP code, and telephone no.		**1** Rents $	OMB No. 1545-0115	
		2 Royalties $	**19 97**	**Miscellaneous Income**
		3 Other income $	Form **1099-MISC**	
PAYER'S Federal identification number	RECIPIENT'S identification number	**4** Federal income tax withheld $	**5** Fishing boat proceeds $	**Copy A**
RECIPIENT'S name		**6** Medical and health care payments $	**7** Nonemployee compensation $	**For Internal Revenue Service Center**
Street address (including apt. no.)		**8** Substitute payments in lieu of dividends or interest $	**9** Payer made direct sales of $5,000 or more of consumer products to a buyer (recipient) for resale ▶ ☐	**File with Form 1096.**
City, state, and ZIP code		**10** Crop insurance proceeds $	**11** State income tax withheld $	For Paperwork Reduction Act Notice and instructions for completing this form, see **Instructions for Forms 1099, 1098, 5498, and W-2G.**
Account number (optional)	2nd TIN Not. ☐	**12** State/Payer's state number	**13** $	

Form **1099-MISC** Cat. No. 14425J Department of the Treasury - Internal Revenue Service

Do NOT Cut or Separate Forms on This Page

9595 ☐ VOID ☐ CORRECTED

PAYER'S name, street address, city, state, ZIP code, and telephone no.		**1** Rents $	OMB No. 1545-0115	
		2 Royalties $	**19 97**	**Miscellaneous Income**
		3 Other income $	Form **1099-MISC**	
PAYER'S Federal identification number	RECIPIENT'S identification number	**4** Federal income tax withheld $	**5** Fishing boat proceeds $	**Copy A**
RECIPIENT'S name		**6** Medical and health care payments $	**7** Nonemployee compensation $	**For Internal Revenue Service Center**
Street address (including apt. no.)		**8** Substitute payments in lieu of dividends or interest $	**9** Payer made direct sales of $5,000 or more of consumer products to a buyer (recipient) for resale ▶ ☐	**File with Form 1096.**
City, state, and ZIP code		**10** Crop insurance proceeds $	**11** State income tax withheld $	For Paperwork Reduction Act Notice and instructions for completing this form, see **Instructions for Forms 1099, 1098, 5498, and W-2G.**
Account number (optional)	2nd TIN Not. ☐	**12** State/Payer's state number	**13** $	

Form **1099-MISC** Cat. No. 14425J Department of the Treasury - Internal Revenue Service

FIGURE A10–25

DO NOT STAPLE ᒷ9ᒷ9

Form **1096**	**Annual Summary and Transmittal of U.S. Information Returns**	OMB No. 1545-0108

Department of the Treasury
Internal Revenue Service

19**97**

A T T A C H   I R S   L A B E L   H E R E

FILER'S name

Street address (including room or suite number)

City, state, and ZIP code

If you are not using a preprinted label, enter in box 1 or 2 below the identification number you used as the filer on the information returns being transmitted. Do not fill in both boxes 1 and 2.

Name of person to contact if the IRS needs more information

Telephone number
(　　　)

For Official Use Only

1 Employer identification number	2 Social security number	3 Total number of forms	4 Federal income tax withheld $	5 Total amount reported with this Form 1096 $

Enter an "X" in only one box below to indicate the type of form being filed. | If this is your FINAL return, enter an "X" here . . ▶ ☐

W-2G 32	1098 81	1099-A 80	1099-B 79	1099-C 85	1099-DIV 91	1099-G 86	1099-INT 92	1099-LTC 93	1099-MISC 95	1099-MSA 94	1099-OID 96	1099-PATR 97	1099-R 98
☐	☐	☐	☐	☐	☐	☐	☐	☐	☐	☐	☐	☐	☐

1099-S 75	5498 28	5498-MSA 27
☐	☐	☐

Please return this entire page to the Internal Revenue Service. Photocopies are NOT acceptable.

Under penalties of perjury, I declare that I have examined this return and accompanying documents, and, to the best of my knowledge and belief, they are true, correct, and complete.

Signature ▶　　　　　　　　　Title ▶　　　　　　　　　Date ▶

Instructions

Purpose of Form.—Use this form to transmit paper Forms 1099, 1098, 5498, and W-2G to the Internal Revenue Service. *(See **Where To File** on the back.)* DO NOT USE FORM 1096 TO TRANSMIT MAGNETIC MEDIA. See **Form 4804,** Transmittal of Information Returns Reported Magnetically/Electronically.

Use of Preprinted Label.—If you received a preprinted label from the IRS with Package 1099, place the label in the name and address area of this form inside the brackets. Make any necessary changes to your name and address on the label. However, do not use the label if the taxpayer identification number (TIN) shown is incorrect. **Do not prepare your own label. Use only the IRS-prepared label that came with your Package 1099.**

If you are not using a preprinted label, enter the filer's name, address (including room, suite, or other unit number), and TIN in the spaces provided on the form.

Filer.—The name, address, and TIN of the filer on this form must be the same as those you enter in the upper left area of Form 1099, 1098, 5498, or W-2G. A filer includes a payer, a recipient of mortgage interest payments (including points), a broker, a barter exchange, a creditor, a person reporting real estate transactions, a trustee or issuer of an individual retirement arrangement (including an IRA, SEP, or SIMPLE) or a medical savings account, and a lender who acquires an interest in secured property or who has reason to know that the property has been abandoned.

Transmitting to the IRS.—Send the forms in a flat mailing (not folded). Group the forms by form number and transmit each group with a **separate** Form 1096. For example, if you must file both Forms 1098 and 1099-A, complete one Form 1096 to transmit your Forms 1098 and another Form 1096 to transmit your Forms 1099-A. You need not submit original and corrected returns separately. **Do not** send a form (1099, 5498, etc.) containing summary (subtotal) information with Form 1096. Summary information for the group of forms being sent is entered only in boxes 3, 4, and 5 of Form 1096.

Box 1 or 2.—Complete only if you are not using a preprinted IRS label. Individuals not in a trade or business must enter their social security number in box 2; sole proprietors and all others must enter their employer identification number in box 1. However, sole proprietors who do not have an employer identification number must enter their social security number in box 2.

Box 3.—Enter the number of forms you are transmitting with this Form 1096. Do not include blank or voided forms or the Form 1096 in your total. Enter the number of correctly completed forms, not the number of pages, being transmitted. For example, if you send one page of three-to-a-page Forms 5498 with a Form 1096 and you have correctly completed two Forms 5498 on that page, enter "2" in box 3 of Form 1096.

Box 4.—Enter the total Federal income tax withheld shown on the forms being transmitted with this Form 1096.

For more information and the Paperwork Reduction Act Notice, see the 1997 Instructions for Forms 1099, 1098, 5498, and W-2G. Form **1096** (1997)
Cat. No. 14400O

FIGURE A10–26

• INSTRUCTOR'S NOTE · · · · · · · · · · · · · ·

The material contained in this chapter could well be a bit overwhelming without some form of application. Comprehension and retention of the material contained in this chapter are critical for those who attempt self-employment as a career choice. I suggest setting up an individual or group project where students begin by writing a series of checks, creating a chart of accounts, and transferring that information into a check register and then filing a simple 1040 tax return with a schedule C and form SE. The second phase of this project would be to set up a payroll ledger, compute a fictitious payroll, and file all the payroll reports.

11 Selected Topics in Small Business Management

Chapter Objectives

- To introduce special management issues associated with the business cycle upturn and downturn.

- To introduce methodologies associated with social security benefit programs and to stress the importance of proper retirement planning for the small business owner.

- To discuss some of the techniques used in a risk-exposure assessment and some contemporary issues surrounding the insurance industry.

Management is the process in which the firm's resources, human and financial, are organized and directed to achieve the goals of the firm. It also involves that process in which the manager identifies, establishes, and/or implements the control systems that allow the manager to maintain control of the organization. The management function for major corporations and small business is essentially the same as far as the intended outcome is concerned, but the implementation and practice of management are vastly different. For the small proprietor management is just one of the duties the owner must perform.

Small business management differs from corporate management in several different ways. In some ways corporations have some major advantages over small business. Although this book is not concerned with corporate management per se, it is worthwhile to contrast the differences and define the advantages of big businesses, because the small business owner must operate among the corporate giants.

Generally, the small business owner is also the manager. Corporate management spends and controls vast sums of other people's money. The small proprietor spends and controls very limited sums of his or her own money. This epitomizes the differences between the two.

One fundamental advantage that big business has over the small entrepreneur is the availability of capital. A lower cost of capital, particularly of debt capital, is generally available. This can be a deadly combination should the small proprietor get in a position of head-to-head, capital-intensive competition. The standard logic is that small business should not challenge large corporations. Generally that is true, but exceptions exist.

A striking difference between major corporations and the small proprietor is the time frame in which the two operate. An advantage that corporations possess is that they are publicly traded companies and have a perpetual life. Many corporations in the United States have been around for 100 years or more. Some small businesses have been in a family for 100 years, but it is more difficult to maintain such longevity. Estate taxes and the transition from generation to generation take a real toll on small businesses. This acts as an impediment to the continuation of what originally was a successful enterprise. This is not to say that small business succession cannot be accomplished, and using a corporate structure, business can flow smoothly; that is, ownership and the asset base can be transferred smoothly. Yet it is common that with the passing of one generation, the business is often piecemealed to create estate equity. More often than not, the surviving business is placed in debt, so that one heir may buy out the remaining heirs.

The greatest problem a small business faces in the context of transition from generation to generation rests with management, when the son or daughter lacks the experience and/or technical skills of the parent who founded the firm. Unless the child or a key employee has been groomed in a management position with the intent of taking over the reins of senior management, the future success of the firm is often in doubt. In a major corporation, succession is not as major as issue, as there are usually several competent candidates for the position of president and CEO. Major corporations can easily expand the pool of eligible senior management candidates by recruiting outside the firm. Perpetual life for a corporation is thus accomplished in a natural manner.

Perpetual life implies perpetual growth. Most major corporations are large because they have had a very long time to grow large. A firm with a 100-year history has had 100 years to expand their revenue through developing a product mix and expanding their distribution systems. They have had the opportunity to take the net profit for 100 years and reinvest through retained earnings. Little wonder that many firms have become international oligopolies.

The small business owner tends to operate in a very limited market with limited capital, the nature of which creates some advantage. Small size enables the proprietor financial and marketing nimbleness, which in turn allows them to operate within a niche. Smallness allows a small business to operate in markets too small for the large firm to take advantage of profitably. The key is to recognize and capitalize on those advantages. The contrast is one of economies of scale and mass markets for corporate America versus defining and operating within that defined niche for small business.

Another major difference in management stems from the fact that corporate America is usually managed by "hired help," all the way to the CEO and board of directors. The term *hired help* trivializes the organizational chart. Corporate management is identified by the firm's organizational chart where managerial duties are broken down into functions and departments, each filled by professionals within that specialty. Within each department a staff exists, and decisions are often the outcome of a team approach or a group consensus. The team leader is generally an experienced person with a great deal of expertise and is ideally supported by a staff of bright, up-and-coming junior executives. Decisions are then channeled upward in the organizational chart for further review and modification before authorization is granted and implementation is undertaken by the department.

The small business owner is often alone in the decision-making process, alone not simply in one functional area but often alone in all the functional areas. It is difficult to have a level of expertise and competency in all areas. Herein lies a critical difference, often a critical disadvantage faced by the small entrepreneur. It is the manager's weakest functional skill or gap, which often creates constraints and limits to growth in an organization. This aspect is often overlooked when contrasting a small business with major corporations. When the two are pitted in a head-to-head competitive situation, the big corporation usually wins. We tend to attribute this dominance in the marketplace to the big corporation's size, which generates certain economies of scale, which along with their financial strength easily overwhelm the small proprietor. A major part of corporate America's dominance stems from the availability and depth of their professional management team.

The small business owner must and does compete, sometimes very well, operating in market segments too small for corporations to go after. Small businesses tend to thrive in specialized and personalized service business. Small business also does well in unique specialty businesses. Small business and the entrepreneurial spirit are often the impetus that leads to new technological developments, particularly in computer software and other high-technology areas. Many innovative products come out of the workshops of individuals and are brought to the marketplace.

Large corporations have many advantages over small business. Another of their main strengths lies in their ability to bring products to the marketplace. Corporations are, by their nature, designed for mass marketing, and mass production. Their size and the complexity of a national or multinational firm creates a degree of rigidity. Even with the aid of state-of-the-art technologies, large corporations tend to be less adaptable and less responsive than a small business can be. Corporations have recognized this and have made huge gains in narrowing the response gap through the use of state-of-the-art technologies and through improvements in organizational structure and the decision-making process. Nonetheless, this drawback is an advantage that can be capitalized on by small business.

Small business management is the focus of this book. What many small business managers do is develop and implement the components of their control systems within the context of the bridge model. This separate chapter on management provides an additional approach to the topic of management as a function by itself, even though it is integrated throughout the book. It also provides an opportunity to discuss some of the topics that are not addressed specifically in the chapters covering the functional areas.

• THE MANAGEMENT FUNCTION · · · · · · · ·

Management implies the ability to control. For many small business owners, management begins with the recognition and acceptance that not everything is in the realm of their control. In fact, once a business is set into motion and the original capital is expended, the business is often led as much as it is controlled. Forces greater than and beyond the control of even the best manager dictate the direction in which a business will go. The manager operates within the context of a greater environment.

So what can managers do? They can, first, read the signs of the times—by being informed and understanding what is going on around them. At the onset of a business, the accuracy with which the new proprietor perceived the current economic conditions around him or her, recognized an opportunity, and acted on that opportunity dictates a business's initial level of success. If the proprietor's vision was outside reality, in the sense that things as he or she saw it were not as they actually were, the business will probably be in jeopardy from the beginning.

To some degree a contradiction exists: On one hand, small business is very flexible and adaptive; on the other, it is very rigid. To a large extent, beginning a small business is a very creative act. It begins with a unique interpretation of the surrounding environment, from which an opportunity is perceived, not unlike an artist who stands back and views a landscape before beginning the creative act of putting that vision on canvas. The entrepreneur has the ability to stand back and view an opportunity before he or she puts that view or perception into motion by creating a business. The action of creating a small business entails the expenditure of capital. A danger exists in the sense that once the business is in motion, the daily battle gets so intense that the proprietor no longer has the time or energy to detach occasionally, to again stand back to view the panorama. The result is a stifling of those very creative energies that brought the business into creation in the first place. A constantly changing dynamic environment demands creative solutions. Creative solutions demand the ability to stand back lest we are not able to see the forest for the trees.

The initial vision must not only be accurate but must be broad enough to survive. For a business to survive it must have enough volume. I indicated earlier that it is not the cost of capital that threatens the survival of a small business as much as the cost of living. It would be difficult for almost any business to operate on a gross revenue of $10,000 per month, even a service business. The expense of operating and the costs associated with maintaining a public presence are high. Occupancy costs, advertising, communications, transportation, insurance, production, and distribution expenses all need to be met, to say nothing of interest on loans, and the biggest expense of all, which is usually payroll. All this before you take a draw for living expenses. The accuracy of the business concept is but one requirement; sufficient volume is another.

Management's next job is to identify the input needs of the business and to purchase those inputs. The accuracy of the forecast is imperative to prepare accurately for the production function. The entrepreneur's initial vision or concept is put into reality at this stage. The initial purchases of plant and equipment and the layout and design will determine and define the business capacity, efficiency, and to some degree its cost structure. A good job of distinguishing between what is wanted and what is needed can make the difference between success and failure. Having had experience in the business you are entering will make this process much easier. Once the decisions are made and the capital sunk, the situation becomes rigid. You are stuck, at least initially, with those decisions.

For most startup businesses a severe capital rationing situation exists. A firm's needs usually outstrip the organization's cash. A danger exists in choosing a cheaper alternative but one that in the end costs more in terms of lower productivity and lost revenue. The purchase of plant and equipment is closely interwoven with your firm's image. Will the equipment purchases do the job? Can you maintain those external relationships with your customers, and what impact will those purchases have on the relationships you must maintain internally with your employees? Your plant and equipment are a part of your ability to be competent, reliable, and dependable, and to affect the quality of your product and/or service.

A balance needs to be obtained between extravagance and your ability to compete cost-effectively. Every business wants to be a first-class operation and have the best in equipment and facilities, but it is a small group that can afford it and perhaps a smaller group who can justify it.

I recently visited with the owner of a small trucking firm that hauls bulk milk. The owner who had been hauling milk for 30 years was talking about his equipment. "I'd like to run new trucks," he said, "but with what they want for new equipment these days, a guy could never pay for it. All you'd ever do is make truck payments. I guess I'll just keep running the ones I've got." He went on to explain the competitive structure in the industry and the costs associated with his operation, indicating that repairs on older equipment were higher than they would be on new equipment but that he could afford a lot of repairs for what he'd have to lay out for truck payments.

A proprietor's age and personality can have an impact on a person's willingness to accept new debt and the time frame that is associated with that debt. Experience can also reflect how difficult it is to pay off that debt, and how profit can be squeezed.

The new proprietor is faced with the management decisions to buy new or used, to weigh function over form, or vice versa. Can equipment be rented; if so, should equipment be rented? How about the use of subcontractors in lieu of equipment purchases? The new manager must weigh and balance the firm's needs with the availability of capital. The purchasing decisions are most critical initially but remain a management responsibility throughout the life of the business. Management must have the equipment in place to meet the demands of their customers and to maintain and support a large enough volume without overspending to the point of inflating the cost structure or having undo idle capacity. Many small business owners and managers have gotten themselves into real financial trouble by spending themselves into a financial corner when times are good. When the business cycle turns and times get tough, those excess expenditures can cause financial failure.

Having committed themselves through the purchase of plant and equipment, management will then need to design the processes or layout and use of the plant and equipment. The manner in which equipment is utilized and deployed affects the business's productivity, efficiency, and ultimately, their profitability.

An excellent example of good design and layout is the grocery industry, which has traditionally operated on very small margins; success is a function of volume and efficiency. The grocery industry has evolved to where it is today. The most efficient stores are quite large. The next time you go into a grocery store, notice the line of checkout lanes. The design allows for maximum flexibility and adaptability to volume. During slow periods, most of the cashiers are either not scheduled or are performing stocking functions or some other duty. If the store gets a temporary rush of customers, they quickly adapt, first by monitoring the line until it reaches a predetermined length, and then by issuing a call to open the next lane, then the next, and so on. In this way customer service levels are maintained at all times without overstaffing.

The small proprietor cannot totally replicate the grocery store industry in layout and design. An attempt should be made, however, to structure within the proprietor's design and layout an ability to adapt to volume or demand fluctuations and a degree of flexibility in the use of personnel and equipment. The acid test for any system occurs at peak demand. Can the equipment, production function, and layout handle peak demand without bottlenecks? In a hurry-up society such as ours, customers will generally not wait very long for products or services. If a wait occurs, under normal conditions it is almost a sure bet that our systems are costing our business customers.

Another critical element within the proprietor's span of control lies in the way decisions are made. Everyone makes decisions based on past experiences and personal perspectives. That personal view or perspective is what makes the entrepreneur so unique. Decisions are supported and greatly influenced by the information available. Management's job is to create and put in place information systems to support decision making with dependable, reliable, valid real-time information. The more accurate the information, the better the decision.

The bridge model that supports this book attempts to demonstrate that information, and information systems support the functional areas, especially the area of management. This topic is covered in more detail in another chapter, but information systems need to be in place throughout the startup phase and forward throughout the life of the enterprise.

Example of the Management Function

I would like to share part of a personal story at this time. In the late 1970s I started an oil field safety business called Sentry Safety. The logo depicted a colonial-type soldier standing guard in front of an oil drilling derrick. This was a service business that served the oil exploration and development industry by providing electronic detection equipment for hydrogen sulfide gas, the gas that posed such a danger after the Gulf War, when Iraqis destroyed and set fire to over 2000 oil wells when pulling out of Kuwait. Sentry Safety also rented and provided safety equipment. The types of equipment were of several classses, the first being the type that would allow the crew to escape in event of an oil well fire or exposure to hydrogen sulfide gas. The second class was equipment that allowed personnel to work under exposure to the gas. The third type was equipment that would allow for the rescue of a downed worker. In addition, electronic detection and alarm equipment were provided as well as on-site training and on-site consulting services, which were provided during drill stem tests and other hazardous operations.

Sentry Safety was not a typical service business in that it was so specialized, but it was typical in that it served a major industry and was tied to that industry. By its very nature, the oil field industry is a boom-and-bust industry. My business begain with an $80,000 SBA loan and was started out of my basement and in an old barn that was an outbuilding near my house in Gladstone, North Dakota. Gladstone was somewhat central to the Williston Basin, an oil field that covered most of western North Dakota, eastern Montana, and the northwestern corner of South Dakota.

Sentry Safety was extremely difficult to start. Breaking into an industry that was dominated by large firms was difficult. One of the most difficult aspects during the startup phase was to become an authorized vendor, or being on the vendor's list of the major oil firms. Sentry Safety had a difficult time obtaining the appropriate liability insurance to meet the requirements set by the oil drilling firms of all their vendors. It took the assistance of the State Insurance Commissioner's office and a tour with an insurance underwriter to demonstrate for the insurance underwriter that the liability exposure was not as great as it first appeared.

I have visited with many small business owners who have faced some seeming insurmountable problem to getting their firm going. It almost always seems like there is some type of initial trial to test your level of commitment, resolve, and persistence. Once off the ground, Sentry Safety experienced a geometric rate of growth.

My forecast for my startup year was $180,000, or $15,000 per month. The first three months' revenue was zero, due to the insurance and vendor list delays. Sentry had very little left in the way of cash reserves by the end of the first quarter of operation. Fortunately, the next three quarters exceeded the initial forecast and the first year ended with an annual revenue of $230,000. Revenues grew to a peak of $69,000 per month by February 1983; then came the oil field bust. Net profit usually ran around 42 percent, but by the end of May 1983, just 90 days later, total revenue was down to $8900 and the end of the industry decline was not yet in sight. Remarkably, Sentry was still in the black at that level and had never posted a monthly loss, except for the first three months of operation.

It was at that point that I pulled the plug and liquidated the firm. At that time Sentry Safety had an equipment replacement cost of $550,000. Actual equipment purchase costs exceeded $350,000; when the firm's equipment was finally liquidated, it was for around $70,000. Sentry Safety had over $100,000 in accounts receivable and very little debt at the time the decision was made to liquidate the firm. That decision was based on the current market condition, which constituted massive overcapacity and a short and intermediate outlook that offered little hope for an industry recovery.

In hindsight, liquidation was the best choice, because the downturn lasted over 10 years. It was a very difficult thing to do, but the correct thing to do under the circumstances. Of the competitors and others in the oil field service industry that attempted to remain, only a fraction survived. Many businesses went into bankruptcy, and the financial repercussions of the oil industry slowdown were felt not only on Wall Street but throughout the country.

The type of management skills demanded during a boom-and-bust period are multifaceted. My personal experience and the experiences of others who have shared similar situations have led me to attempt to set forth some guidelines or recommendations for managing during the ups and downs of the business cycle.

• MANAGING SUCCESS: THE BUSINESS CYCLE UPTURN····················

For the small business manager, many of the business management principles learned in college are not applicable. Textbook theory is invariably from the perspective of big business; the training is designed for cogs in the corporate wheel.

I wish to elaborate on two opposing sets of outcomes for the entrepreneur. Often, just due to the business cycle or changes in the environment beyond the span of control of the manager, the proprietor's business is either very good or very bad. These extremes can easily happen to the same business over a period of time. Most long-time successful businesses will at one time or another have to face adversity and at other times will have had banner years. Different sets of management principles and practices apply to those extremes.

When things are going great, let prudence prevail. Your information system and management control systems should be able to identify why things are good, at least in the sense of why your customers are saying yes to your product or service. Attempt to identify a cause and a time frame for prosperity. Be conservative in your estimate.

Upturn principle 1: Identify your key strategic success variables. Articulate why your customers are using your product or service. Once defined, develop a system to measure and monitor those success variables. Develop a time line or a time frame. Your market will remain good for a specific period of time. How long will that be?

With Sentry Safety I visited with dozens of oil field business people, consultants, engineers, tool pushers, and so on, to attempt to get a handle on how long the boom would last. In business school you might identify such an approach as an executive survey. The best guess at that time was that the boom would last for seven years. I structured my debt and all midrange planning for five years. Reality was three years.

I identified Sentry Safety's key strategic success variables to contain two critical elements. The first was tied to the industry. As long as oil exploration activity was prevalent in the Rocky Mountain region, more specifically in the Williston Basin, Sentry Safety would be able to maintain at least its market share. The level of oil exploration activity was a function of the total of the authorized drilling budgets of all the oil companies operating in the region. Supporting information came from seismograph activity, lease activity, new oil discoveries, drilling location permits, drilling rig count, and similar information.

The second element stemmed from the fact that Sentry Safety was hired not just because of the quality of work and service, although every effort was made to maintain high standards. Nor was Sentry hired because of price, although every effort was made to remain competitive in price. Sentry Safety was hired because of the human relationships developed between Sentry Safety's personnel and the personnel of the oil companies or drilling companies authorized to make the hiring decision. The service was sold based on who was going to be on the job site. Specific requests for a particular person to be present was not uncommon. This had nothing to do with price or the caliber of the equipment placed on that well. This is also not just indicative of the oil field but of many industries.

Measuring and monitoring drilling budgets was easy. I also had the advantage of having a former classmate working for Mesa Petroleum in their regional office in Denver, Colorado. Weekly phone conversations provided not only much appreciated leads but critical information on what was going on inside a major participating oil company. The human relations element was more cultivated than monitored. Yet personal relationships were given a priority and were the primary responsibility of my key salespeople who were given a minority stock position in the firm.

Upturn principle 2: Let prudence prevail, be conservative. If your niche is exceptionally profitable, you can be sure that others will notice and will enter your market. When Sentry was started, it was the third safety firm in the region and the first independently owned safety firm in the area. Three years later my competitors numbered 17. It is difficult for a small entrepreneur to tie up a market or create barriers of entry to prevent competition from moving in. With the current boom and prosperity one is tempted to scramble for market share and grow exponentially to serve an ever-expanding list of customers. As difficult as it is to resist, now is the time to really step back and review your original goals for starting this business in the first place. If you have achieved your goals at the level you are currently at, what will accelerated growth accomplish for you?

Limiting growth is sometimes easier said than done. It was my intention to limit Sentry Safety to a three-person operation and to run no more than seven safety trailers. This would have ensured a small, tightly controlled, high-quality, highly profitable operation. It would have begun generating a large cash reserve instead of increasing capital expenditures for more equipment. My goals had been met. It was my plan to stay at that level.

One day when the firm was operating at total capacity a call came in for another unit, which I tried to decline. But the call came from my original customer, the man responsible for hiring the first safety trailer put out by Sentry. He wanted us and no one else; expansion resulted from that phone call. In hindsight a mistake was made. Growth could have been limited by raising my prices. Even though my customers were focused on the personnel, price still played a role in the industry.

I once performed an audit on a small liquor business in a midsized city. I spent several days on this audit because I was having trouble verifying and believing the numbers I was seeing. This business had a design and layout that required a minimum of two people on staff at all times. Total annual payroll was less than $5,000, which by my estimate just couldn't be done. I also had questions pertaining to ownership structure. I pulled the tax returns, sales tax reports, canceled checks, deposits, and other supporting documents. I pulled these records for three years. I interviewed the accountant, the attorney involved, and finally, confronted the proprietor. The records and statements confirmed that this business was surviving on a shoestring and that the proprietor's family and friends were donating labor to keep this business afloat.

Several months later a change in legislation legalized limited gambling in liquor establishments. This business was on the right side of the river, bordering another state. In months this owner went literally from rags to riches. Approximately a year later I caught up with the proprietor again, only to discover that he had added onto his first business, spent in excess of $500,000 building a second business, and was contemplating buying a third. He didn't have time to talk, as he literally ran in an attempt to keep up with the demands of vendors, contractors, personnel, and so on. When we finally were able to spend five minutes together I asked him if he was happy. He gave me this funny look and said, "I don't know, I don't even have time to go to the bathroom." I reminded him that a year ago all he really wanted to do was make enough money so that he could pay his mother, his girlfriend, and himself. Why, then, all this expansion?

It is easy to forget the value of a dollar: how hard money is to earn and how difficult it is to save. When prosperity is happening, it always seems almost endless. When it does change, it usually changes rapidly.

Upturn principle 3: Get your financial house in order. When things are good, do not assume that they will remain that way forever. Set your financial priorities. Get your debt down to a manageable level. Create a cash reserve. Look for ways to increase profitability through the purchase of plant and equipment. For example, if you were renting a building, perhaps buying or building your own might be a better choice. Do not throw dollars at something, though, if all it will do is save dimes. Set up a screening process—a set of criteria you use to evaluate those capital expenditures. Compare the outcomes against a cash reserve invested in an income-producing account. Consider, for example, an outlay of $50,000 to replace a piece of equipment because the newer unit would save $4000 a year in operating costs. The effect on net income would be identical if you put that $50,000 in corporate bonds with an 8 percent yield. The latter would have the effect of diversifying income and be more certain.

The traditional capital budgeting process can be beneficial in evaluating and comparing competing investments. It does set up the screening criteria and establishes the hurdle rates. Depending on the nature of your business, it may warrant a higher degree of caution than corporate America applies. From a traditional finance position, a small business is usually viewed from a stand-alone risk perspective. The point remains: Get your financial house in order and proceed with caution.

Upturn principle 4: Maintain discipline; avoid cost creep. When business is good, it is imperative that you manage it. This is the time in your business's life cycle to really make money. To do so, you need to stay on top of your ratios and profitability margins. It is easy to say yes to the barrage of salespeople who come calling. With success comes notoriety and solicitations to buy promotional items, office supplies, office furniture, tools, and so on. Your business name is sold from lists. A filing as a corporation or a filing with Dun and Bradstreet will result in a barrage of solicitations by mail and phone. Maintain your budget and do a cost–benefit analysis on everything you do. As your sales volume increases, your expenditures will tend to increase proportionately, but you should also be reaping some economies of scale and operating efficiencies. A 98 percent level of capacity should increase your profit margins. If profits are not increasing when you are operating at or near capacity, question where expense creep is occurring.

Your employees will also pressure you for more equipment, supplies, and so on. Some of this is valid, but ratios need to be maintained. Measure your expenditures from a cost–benefit perspective and measure how these expenditures will affect your image and what impact they are having on your success variables.

One element of Sentry Safety's image was a silver and black color combination, displayed by the firm's vehicles and equipment trailers, which gave us immediate recognition and visibility. That, along with bug deflectors embossed with our name and logo, created a lot of exposure and generated positive comments throughout the oil patch. Almost immediately I could sense that Sentry was being sized up by our customers in the sense that they knew Sentry was making money but they didn't know how much. A display of high-priced pickup trucks, a status symbol on the back roads of the oil country, could backfire by causing feelings of exploitation and/or jealousy. Sentry needed to maintain an image of dependability, reliability, and professionalism. Our equipment needed to reflect that image, not flaunt purchasing power.

Upturn principle 5: Control your lifestyle. Every small business owner wants to be successful, and once success seems eminent, many want to show it. One of the greatest dangers is to place too great a financial strain on a small emerging enterprise by saddling the business with a huge salary or draw to support the owner's lifestyle. The big house on the hill, new furniture, a new car, vacations, the country club. To support such a lifestyle requires a substantial income. Large draws can jeopardize the future of the business as easily as extravagance within the business itself. The most conservative approach is to grow your business with cash. The same is true of your lifestyle. When the business can afford it, pay for those luxuries as you go if they are a priority for you. If a cutback is required, that big house with the large mortgage will be sold, and usually in a depressed market if the business downturn affects the entire area.

Controlling your lifestyle is probably the most difficult of all the principles that I've laid out so far. It seems to be also the most abused of the principles set forth. It is amazing how a business owner can set in place all the control mechanisms to keep a business profitable, only to jeopardize that business by an extravagant lifestyle.

It is difficult to write about this area without instilling a bit of regret and pain. I hate to make mistakes, but I did make a mistake in this area. With Sentry Safety my first concern was to pay my bills and be able to make good on my debts. All growth was financed with cash, and once my accounts receivable exceeded my total outstanding debt, I felt I was out of the woods financially. I did want to reward myself, and particularly reward my salespeople with an increase in personal earnings for the work and risks involved in making the business work.

At the onset I took a modest salary of $1200 per month and soon raised that to $1500, which was equivalent to the base pay of most workers in that industry. That wage quickly rose; I soon took $4800 per month and paid my salespeople and vice president $3200 per month, itself not way out of line, but triple what others were earning at the time. Such a salary did not jeopardize the business, but a more conservative approach would have been to take a modest raise and save the rest, which placed in a mutual fund would have funded my retirement by age 40.

The problem with raising one's income is that most people immediately raise their standard of living. Such a substantial raise was therefore not reflected in my personal savings. Personal savings could have been accomplished had I not locked myself into a higher lifestyle by purchasing the proverbial big house.

My original residence was too small to accommodate our growing family. I had built a new shop building on property that adjoined my residence and was having difficulty separating my personal life from my business life a problem very common with home-based businesses. At the time I considered and could have paid my house off for $32,000 and built an addition on for about $20,000 more, all of which could have been paid for in 18 months. I chose instead to buy a huge home in Dickinson, North Dakota. I put a up a substantial down payment and did another $10,000 of repairs and updates. We lived in this home less than two years, until the oil industry crashed. My immediate response to the crash was to list this home for sale well under the market. I took a $30,000 loss on top of dropping another $20,000 in payments and considered myself lucky to have gotten out from under a debt that could have created a severe financial hardship. As a side note, the housing industry in that region was tied to the oil industry. The oil bust took with it thousands of high-paying jobs, which created a glut of homes on the market, with few if any buyers. Real estate values dropped by as much as 80 percent.

Conservatism in one's personal lifestyle is the lesson I hope to relate in this story.

Upturn principle 6: Plan for your retirement and for your future. Plan as if the business did not exist; assume the perspective that you are an employee of someone else. Fund your IRA, Keogh, or SEP and include your spouse. With those dollars in a tax-deferred retirement plan, they should be safe even under a worst-case scenario. If you are using a subchapter S corporation form, to limit earned income it is important that you aggressively fund an alternative source of retirement income. Similarly, you are somehow able to hold net taxable income down in your sole proprietorship, you should aggressively fund an alternative source of retirement income. The result of holding your next taxable income down will also be to lower your self-employment taxes. This is a goal that many small businesses attempt to accomplish, but in so doing you also limit your social security earnings, which in turn will limit your social security retirement benefits. If this is the case, it becomes even more imperative that alternative retirement plans be funded. Social security is not a great retirement plan, but unfortunately, it is the main source of retirement income for many people.

If it sounds like I am beating on this topic, I am. I have seen, through my work as a tax investigator, too many instances where people worked their entire lives in a business which at one time may have been prosperous, only to reach their retirement years near financial ruin. Through careful tax planning such people were able to dodge most of their tax liability. They failed to fund an alternative retirement because their retirement was funded through the business's assets they were accumulating. But they lost those assets, or never really accumulated them, due to debt and business losses. In the end they have neither business assets nor a retirement fund. To make matters worse, their social security benefits will be minimal because little was paid in. You may see such a person stocking shelves at your local grocery store. I would hate to see my father doing that, and I don't want to do that myself.

If you are in a prosperous business, deal with the issue of your retirement while the business is prosperous. The simplest and easiest way to fund retirement is through an individual retirement account (IRA). For a couple working in a family business the spouse must earn at least $2000 per year to qualify for an IRA. I recommend that the spouse be paid at least $6000 for social security reasons (see the benefit formula below).

Here is an example of a funded IRA portion of a retirement plan with the assumption of $2000 paid in for 35 years, with an average return of 10 percent (using future value interest factors for a $1 annuity table): $2000 × a factor of 271.018 = $542,036, which of course is in future dollars. If inflation were to remain at about 3 percent, each of those dollars would have a purchasing power of 0.355 (based on the table of present value interest factors for $1). This means that the $542,036 saved would have a purchasing power, or would be worth in today's dollars, $192,422.78 ($542,036 × 0.355 = $192,422.78). If this amount were in turn invested in an 8 percent corporate bond, it would generate $15,393.82 of annual income ($192,422.78 × 0.08 = $15,393.82). If this annual income were adjusted by 3 percent to compensate for future inflation ($15,393.82 × 97 percent = $14,932), based on these assumptions ($14,932/12 = $1244) this program would generate the equivalent of $1244 per month in today's purchasing power indefinitely and leave the asset base intact for your estate.

It may seem strange to be talking about social security at your age. The reality is that social security will probably still be around when you reach retirement age, but it may not be in the same form. It is extremely doubtful that you will be excused or released from the obligation of paying into social security and medicare. It behooves you, then, to know a little about the system and to manage your benefits as best you can. The self-employed have more control over managing their incomes and their self-employment tax than almost any other group in the United States.

Social Security Benefits

Social security provides a number of benefits: a nominal death benefit, disability benefits, retirement benefits, medicare benefits, and disability and survivor benefits for your family. The eligibility for each type of benefit is based on specific criteria, but a certain number of years of covered employment and a minimum number of credits are required to qualify for benefits. Social security keeps a record of the amount of earnings reported each year under your name and social security number. When you apply for benefits, they check your record to see if you worked enough over the years to qualify.

In 1997 you get one credit for each $670 of your covered annual earnings, up to a maximum of four credits for the year, no matter when you work during the year. Most people need 40 credits or 10 years of work to qualify for benefits. Younger people need fewer credits for disability benefits or for their family members to get survivor benefits if they should die.

You can request a personal earnings and benefit estimate statement by mailing in a request. Forms are available at your nearest social security office. You can also call 800-537-7005 and request a form.

Disability Benefits

Disability benefits are paid if you become totally disabled before you reach full retirement age. To get disability benefits, three conditions must be met:

1. You need a certain number of work credits and they had to be earned during a specific period of time.
2. You must have a physical or mental condition that has lasted, or is expected to last, at least 12 months or to end in your death.
3. Your disability must be severe enough to keep you from doing any substantial work, not just your last occupation.

Survivor and Disability Benefits for Your Family

Benefits may be payable to:

- Your unmarried children under age 18 (age 19 if in high school) or 18 and older if disabled before age 22
- Your spouse who is age 62 or older or who is any age and caring for your qualified child who is under age 16 or disabled
- Your divorced spouse who was married to you for at least 10 years and who is age 62 or older and unmarried

Usually, each family member qualifies for a benefit that is up to 50 percent of your retirement or disability benefit, subject to certain limits.

If you should die your unmarried young or disabled children may qualify for monthly payments. Your widow or widower, even if divorced, may also qualify for payments beginning at age 60 or at age 50 if disabled (if divorced, your marriage must have lasted 10 years or more). Your widow or widower may qualify for benefits at any age if caring for your qualified child who is under age 16 or disabled. Your spouse or children are eligible to receive a one-time death benefit of $255.

Medicare Benefits

When you earn credits for social security benefits, they also count for medicare. However, if you have government earnings on which you pay medicare taxes but not social security taxes, those are considered "medicare-qualified government earnings." Those earnings give you credits for medicare but do not count for social security benefits.

Medicare hospital and medical insurance is a two-part benefit program that helps protect you from the high cost of medical care. Hospital insurance benefits (plan A) help pay the cost when you are in the hospital and for certain kinds of follow-up care. Medical insurance benefits (part B) help pay the costs of doctors' services. If you have enough work credits (currently you need 40 credits of work) you may qualify for medicare hospital insurance at age 65, even if you are still working. You may qualify before age 65 if you are disabled or have permanent kidney failure. Your spouse may also qualify for hospital insurance at 65 on your record. You must pay a monthly premium for medical plan B benefits.

Social Security Retirement Benefits

To get social security retirement benefits, you need 40 credits of work. It is the earnings on your record, not the amount of taxes you paid or the number of credits you have, that is used to figure how much your monthly benefit will be. Social security benefits are calculated on your average earnings over your entire work life. For most retirement benefit estimates, they will average your 35 best years of earnings. Benefits are also adjusted based on your actual age when you begin taking benefits. You can get reduced benefits as early as age 62 or get full retirement at age 65. By the year 2027 this age will gradually increase until full retirement begins at age 67. Your benefits may be higher if you delay retirement until after full retirement age.[1]

The following is the format currently used by the Social Security Administration to calculate retirement benefits.

1. SSA gets a record of all earnings you have had since 1951 (this calculated for retirement in 1996) in jobs and self-employment where you paid social security taxes.

2. SSA converts all of the earnings you had from 1951 until the year you turned 60 into amounts that are approximately equal to what the earnings were worth in the year you turned 60. This is done by multiplying your real earnings by yearly *indexing factors* that are based on the changes in average wages each year.

3. From this list of converted earnings, SSA will choose the 35 years with the highest amounts and disregard the rest of the years. If you do not have 35 years of work on your record, SSA will use years with zero earnings to complete the total of 35 years.

4. SSA then will add up the earnings for the 35 years and divide the total by 420, the number of months in 35 years, to get your average monthly earnings.

5. SSA then applies a formula to the average monthly earnings. For people born in 1934 (this advances each year and the formula is modified slightly each year as well) the formula is as follows:
   - SSA multiplies the first $477 of your average monthly earnings by 90 percent.
   - SSA then multiplies the next $2398.00 of your average monthly earnings by 32 percent.
   - SSA then multiplies any remaining amount by 15 percent.

The example that SSA gives is for someone with indexed earnings of $3000 per month (SSA Pub. No. 05-10070; see Figure A11–1).

$$
\begin{aligned}
\$\ 477.00 \times 90\% &= \$\ 429.30 \\
2,398.00 \times 32\% &= \$\ 767.36 \\
\underline{125.00} \times 15\% &= \underline{\quad 18.75} \\
\$3,000.00 \qquad\qquad & \quad \$1215.41
\end{aligned}
$$

A maximum benefit is allowed. The dollar amounts of the formula change each year. SSA will figure your benefits using the formula for the year you turned 62 even if you delay retirement until later. Currently, full retirement is age 65, but that will gradually change to age 67.[2]

It may seem absurd for college students to be thinking about social security and retirement, but if you are 22, add 35 years and you will be 57, which will leave you only 10 years of low or no social security earnings before they begin to add zeros to your total. As a retirement system that is required, it behooves you to stay informed concerning changes in the system and to manage that part of your retirement as you should be managing the other parts of your retirement plan.

One other consideration concerning social security. If you are a couple both working in the family business which is being operated as a sole proprietorship, it may be wise to pay one spouse a wage reported as W-2 income with the other spouse considered self-employed paying self-employment taxes on form SE. The net cost of that wage will be minor considering it a business expense, which reduces net profit and taxable income. The spouse's wages will similarly reduce the self-employment taxes, but the savings will be paid out as social security and medicare withholding and the employer's match. The important aspect here is that you can to some degree control who gets how much of the social security wage credits. It would seem prudent to at least pick up the 90 percent portion and qualify your spouse for the other benefits by obtaining 40 quarters' worth of credits.

Sentry Safety existed before 401(k)'s came into being. Principal retirement vehicles that did exist were IRAs and Keoghs. After some consideration I chose to fund IRAs, even though this meant that those funds were under the employee's name and they were in a sense 100 percent vested immediately. Using IRAs and funding them as a bonus was very easy and straightforward, with no federal regulations to worry about. Those dollars paid to all concerned were earned and deserved; I had no problem justifying some type of vesting criteria.

Upturn principle 7: Maintain a degree of humility, a sense of gratitude, and give something back to your community and to those who helped you. The self-made man or woman is a fallacy. Every person who ever accomplished anything did so with the help of others: parents, community, teachers, mentors, employees, and others. Most of these people we can never repay; the gift they gave you lives within you. Does it not seem that a duty exists to return the favor by passing your gifts on to others?

It is easy to get a big head. Success breeds a sense of credibility and validates one's judgment. People look to you for advice and seek out your opinion. A danger exists in developing a false sense of invincibility. It seems that as soon as we begin thinking that we are so intelligent, that we can't make a mistake, we make one.

Finally, a personal note, which is more than just a principle of management, but a code of conduct. That which you give away cannot be lost or taken away. My accountant had a hard time understanding why I chose to fund charity like I did.

Estimating Your Social Security Retirement Benefit
For Workers Born In 1936

This worksheet shows how to estimate the Social Security monthly retirement benefit you would be eligible for at age 62 if you were born in 1936. It also allows you to estimate what you would receive at age 65, excluding any cost-of-living adjustments for which you may be eligible. If you continue working until age 65, your additional earnings could increase your benefit amount.

Step 1:
Enter your actual earnings in Column B, but not more than the amount shown in Column A.

Step 2:
Multiply the amounts in Column B by the "index factors" in Column C, and enter the results in Column D. This gives you your "indexed earnings," or the approximate value of your earnings in current dollars.

$_____

Step 3:
Choose from Column D the 35 years with the highest amounts. Add these amounts.

$_____

Step 4:
Divide the result from Step 3 by 420 (the number of months in 35 years). This will give you your average indexed monthly earnings.

$_____

Step 5:
a. Multiply the first $477 in Step 4 by 90%.

$_____

b. Multiply any amount over $477 and less than $2,875 by 32%.

$_____

c. Multiply any amount over $2,875 by 15%.

$_____

Step 6:
Add a, b and c from Step 5. Round down to the whole dollar. This is your estimated monthly retirement benefit at age 65.

$_____

Step 7:
Multiply the amount in Step 6 by 80%. This is your estimated monthly retirement benefit at age 62.

$_____

Year	A. Maximum Earnings	B. Actual Earnings	C. Index Factor	D. Indexed Earnings	Year	A. Maximum Earnings	B. Actual Earnings	C. Index Factor	D. Indexed Earnings
1951	3,600		9.26		1975	14,100		3.00	
1952	3,600		8.72		1976	15,300		2.81	
1953	3,600		8.25		1977	16,500		2.65	
1954	3,600		8.21		1978	17,700		2.45	
1955	4,200		7.85		1979	22,900		2.26	
1956	4,200		7.34		1980	25,900		2.07	
1957	4,200		7.12		1981	29,700		1.88	
1958	4,200		7.05		1982	32,400		1.78	
1959	4,800		6.72		1983	35,700		1.70	
1960	4,800		6.47		1984	37,800		1.61	
1961	4,800		6.34		1985	39,600		1.54	
1962	4,800		6.04		1986	42,000		1.50	
1963	4,800		5.89		1987	43,800		1.41	
1964	4,800		5.66		1988	45,000		1.34	
1965	4,800		5.56		1989	48,000		1.29	
1966	6,600		5.25		1990	51,300		1.23	
1967	6,600		4.97		1991	53,400		1.19	
1968	7,800		4.65		1992	55,500		1.13	
1969	7,800		4.40		1993	57,600		1.12	
1970	7,800		4.19		1994	60,600		1.09	
1971	7,800		3.99		1995	61,200		1.05	
1972	9,000		3.63		1996	62,700		1.00	
1973	10,800		3.42		1997	65,400		1.00	
1974	13,200		3.23						

Social Security Administration
SSA Publication No. 05-10070
March 1998 *(March 1997 edition may be used)*
ICN 467100
Unit of Issue - HD (one hundred)

Printed on recycled paper

*U.S. Government Printing Office: 1998 - 433-327/60053

FIGURE A11-1

Today, almost two decades after the demise of the oil industry, Sentry Safety no longer exists, but the windows I purchased for a local church remain, as do other charitable acts. "Do not lay up for yourselves an earthly treasure. Moths and rust corrode; thieves break in and steal. Make it your practice instead to store up heavenly treasure, which neither moths nor rust corrode nor thieves break in and steal. Remember, where your treasure is, there your heart is also" (Matthew 16:19–21). You may not share my Christian value structure, but giving helps to maintain a sense of humility and is in itself an expression of gratitude. The act of extending a helping hand to the less fortunate without prejudgment does good things for us as well.

I cannot adequately portray in words the tragedy of the thousands of small businesses that were devastated by reversals of fortune in the oil industry. It is difficult to deal with a business failure or even, as in my case, the decision to quit voluntarily. For those entrepreneurs whose total lives, fortunes, and identity were tied up in their businesses, the emotional costs were very high. It is easier to recover from such an experience if your heart is not totally in your business. My recommendation remains: If you are favored by fortune, be generous.

• MANAGING THE BUSINESS CYCLE DOWNTURN · · · · · · · · · · · · · · ·

As indicated earlier, most businesses will go through periods of prosperity and periods where the business experiences a downturn and business is not so good. Some businesses survive this period; others fail or choose to quit. What makes the difference? Sometimes just the timing of the downturn dictates success or failure—Timing in the sense of the business's life cycle. A mature business is generally more able to withstand a business downturn than is a firm in the infant stage. The severity of the downturn, the duration, and the speed at which the downturn occurs are all factors in a business's ability to cope and survive. A firm's current financial structure, especially the level of debt, can be a major determinant in success or failure. The accuracy and reliability of the business's information system and the manager's willingness to act on that information are also important contributing factors in a business's ability to survive.

A reversal of fortunes can come from many directions. Your information system needs to answer some pressing questions:

- Why the downturn?
- Is just your business affected, or is the downturn industry-wide?
- How are other industries being affected?
- How severe and how long will the downturn last?
- Is the downturn temporary, or does it represent a permanent shift in demand due to changes in technology or customer wants?
- What are your customers telling you?
- What are your suppliers telling you?

Once the questions above and any other pressing issues are answered, define what you are going to do.

A vulnerability analysis should be a part of every firm's information system. That will define and articulate those factors or elements that could threaten the future success of your firm. Once identified, develop and put into place those systems that will measure and monitor those threats.

In preparing a vulnerability analysis for Sentry Safety, I discovered several areas that could threaten the firm's existence. First, the entire industry was created due to the presence of hydrogen sulfide gas, which was sometimes found mixed with the oil, gas, and water discovered in the exploration process. A single OSHA regulation created the requirement for safety services. I did not foresee the removal of that regulation posing a serious threat, yet the possibility of governmental regulation or the lack of it existed.

I have previously mentioned our dependence on the continued funding of exploratory drilling in the Williston Basin. This posed a threat but was already being monitored. A major concern was the boom-and-bust nature of the industry. An executive survey had predicted a seven-year boom period, but I was planning on five. Sentry had been formed primarily to serve the oil exploration phase of the industry. This left Sentry in a vulnerable position.

To protect Sentry Safety from the effects of an eventual slowdown in the industry, an effort was made to establish a position in the oil production segment. The production phase would still be in the area for years. All the oil wells discovered would be put into production, and those wells would also need to be maintained. An emphasis was placed on procuring contracts to provide rental equipment and services on tank batteries and to work with the production companies. This type of loose rental was increased to account for about 20 percent of revenue, and revenue from production contracts on workover rigs increased to account for another 20 percent of revenues. With a total of 40 percent of revenues coming from production, Sentry was positioned to withstand a bust period.

A final element in Sentry's vulnerability analysis dealt with the technological aspects of the industry. At the heart of the safety service was an electronic detection monitor that triggered alarm systems when a predetermined gas level was exceeded. A change in technology, especially if initiated by the drilling fluids suppliers, could jeopardize the safety industry. Mud loggers maintained a manned 24-hour surveillance of the drilling activity. They had monitors to detect any sign of hydrocarbons. It would be a small step for those firms to add the safety element to augment their existing services—Another reason for Sentry to diversify into the production phase.

With a vulnerability analysis complete and the information systems in place to monitor those critical elements, if a downturn occurred, the existing information system should be able to answer the critical questions. As a manager you need to be able to determine what to do.

Downturn principle 1: Define reality. The first and most important step is to define reality. Distinguish between what is true and what is rumor and speculation. Then evaluate what you want to do, and define what is possible. Evaluate what your customers want, and merge those desires into what is possible.

In my experience with Sentry Safety, the downturn was immediate and drastic. In March 1983 the company was in an expansion mode. I was setting the groundwork to grow by 75 percent in one stroke. This expansion plan began by establishing a line of credit to purchase the equipment required and to expand the operating capital as needed. Phase 2 was to sell enough work to exceed current capacity by 75 percent. This phase was complete at the time of the oil industry bust. Phase 3 was to add equipment and personnel to move on the job site as required. Phase 4 was to open a new branch in Evanston, Wyoming. Phase 5 was to sell the business.

By March 1983, jobs were being delayed and/or canceled. An unprecedented state of confusion and uncertainty began to emerge, which is uncharacteristic in an industry that exudes action. My guess was that field personnel were out of the information loop. My contact with Mesa Petroleum in Denver informed me that high-level meetings were going on in the Amoco building in Denver. Hours later I had the news that the industry was changing its strategic plan. The major oil companies would change from being domestic oil producers to oil importers. All domestic exploration would be reduced by 90 percent. Most firms would finish the wells they were on and then basically shut the industry down to a near standstill. Domestic drilling costs had gotten too high, the state and federal taxes were too high, and global oil prices were falling.

The impact would be industry wide. The duration of the downturn would be dictated by global oil prices, which appeared to be indefinite. My estimate was a minimum of five years, probably as long as seven years; the reality was a period of over 10 years. At first I believed that Sentry could survive at a reduced level because of the planned diversification into oil production rentals. I had cultivated such a position by having rental equipment on producing oil wells.

I believed that the information I had was valid and reliable. This information was verified in part by the fact that 90 percent of the work I had sold was canceled. The next step was to attempt to verify this information further. I did so by a drive through three oil field states. I talked to everyone I came across associated with the industry in different capacities. No one knew what was happening other than that the demand for their services had dried up.

Once reality is defined, it must be believed. Honesty with yourself is of paramount importance. In my personal experience I believe my information system provided me with an early warning, yet even months later, denial within the oil field service sector was rampant. Business owners refused to believe what was happening to them, convincing themselves that the downturn was temporary. Such delays caused a great number of bankruptcies and exacerbated losses.

A word of warning here also. When circumstances create an atmosphere of desperation, even good managers will sometimes grasp at straws. It is also a time when the unscrupulous see an opportunity and seek to prey on the desperate.

Several months into the industry meltdown, when the oil industry slowdown was common knowledge, I went to pick my mail up at the post office. One letter, printed on very expensive stationery, had a return address of Colonel so and so at a box number from a city in Oklahoma. (The title *colonel* is a military rank but is also a title used by auctioneers.) I smelled a rat. Upon opening the letter I found a solicitation. This person supposedly had connections to Arab oil money, foreign investors who were anxious to invest in the U.S. oil industry. For a fee the Colonel could arrange for loans all the way up to $5 million. Just enclose the appropriate graduated fee—you know the story.

I initially threw the letter in the trash but then fished it back out, knowing that somebody would respond out of desperation. So I called Consumer Labs, an agency in North Dakota that looked into consumer fraud. They asked me to mail the letter to them. Several weeks later I received a phone call from the State Banking Commissioner thanking me for bringing this to their attention and informing me that the Colonel would not be doing any business in the state of North Dakota.

Downturn principle 2: Act quickly. With valid information, do what you have to do. Your business probably has your first loyalty. If your debt structure has been put in an acceptable position before the downturn occurred, management is a little easier. A business recession will reduce your volume, so cut back. Management in a downturn requires that you adjust to a new level of activity. Corporate America has gone through a number of downsizing cycles. If your business has grown to the point where you can downsize, do the difficult. At some level there is little or no room to cut back. You must adjust your forecast to reality. Your ratios need to stay in line, and the goal of management is to maintain those levels and remain profitable.

You need to act quickly because time will eat up your existing cash, and your accounts receivable will be used up as well as the rest of your current assets. Once expended, your financial structure may be such that recovery is not possible. Take immediate control of your accounts receivable; at this time they become a critical part of your balance sheet. Care must be taken to ensure that most, if not all, will be collected. Do not allow undue aging at this point. With an industry under financial pressure, you must make every attempt to collect what is owed.

With Sentry Safety, I arrived back in Dickinson after my road trip. I immediately contacted the bank and warned them of the industry collapse. I then called a meeting and brought all my employees in. I told them the truth and gave all but my key employee a two-week notice. I left the meeting with the advice that everyone would be forced to move (and basically they all would) to attempt to sell their houses immediately. The impact on the community would result in a glut on the housing market, and high unemployment.

Downturn principle 3: Take command and be proactive. By downsizing I conserved the firm's financial resources. My current operating expenses were in excess of $40,000 per month. I set a goal to reduce them to $7500, the absolute floor, within 30 days. By letting the accounts receivable flow in, I had enough cash to be totally debt free. The only thing left to do, then, would be wait for the competition to go broke and pick up the pieces.

Success may be redefined as being able to pay your bills. Free up cash by reducing inventory and supplies. Cut your expenses in every conceivable area without jeopardizing customer loyalty. Prioritize your payables. Reduce and control your accounts receivable; ask your customers for advance payments or early payments. Go to your creditors and ask for extensions or whatever help they can give you. In a survival mode the business owner-manager should take control of the critical elements. Cash flow can become critical.

Go to your employees and everyone involved in your business. Tell the truth. Your employees know your business as well as you do in many cases. During a crisis they may think more clearly than you, because the emotional pressure is not as great. Go to them not only to tell the truth but for ideas and assistance. They have a stake in your business. They may offer a cut in wages, reduced hours, or have ideas to create new business, or save money.

Downturn principle 4: Ask for help. Get help from your SCORE representative, your CPA, and others. Form a support group with other business owners, to share information, and to evaluate each other's business.

With Sentry Safety, I went to everyone I could think of in the industry for advice and counsel. I went especially to my customers to solicit work. I found sympathetic ears, but most were in no position to hire anyone, and many were getting their pink slips as the industry downsized almost universally. Industry capacity was five times greater than demand. Prices for services crashed as firms desperate for cash flow slashed prices, then slashed them again, in an attempt to get work. I found the safety industry had slashed prices by as much as 90 percent.

My decision to shut down totally came when my principles were violated. I was at the time providing safety services for several hundred tank batteries which were on some of the deadliest wells in the United States. I was called by a company vice president who wanted me to cut my prices to a level where I could not provide adequate service. I informed him that to do so would cost someone his or her life. His response was: "If you won't, I'll find someone who will." I pulled my equipment the following day and began the liquidation process. As it turned out, not two months later a truck driver died on top of one of those tanks from exposure to hydrogen sulfide gas.

Downturn principle 5: Check your attitude at the door. The world may seem like a dark and foreboding place to you, but you do not want your customers to pick up on that gloom-and-doom attitude—it's bad for business. Maintain an upbeat, "can do" attitude. Your employees should be required to do the same. Concentrate on the positive. List those things that you are grateful for and those things that are positive. Start with your family. Do not make your family sacrifice unduly during this phase. The stress on family life can be enormous during hard times. One of the saddest things that can happen is that the proprietor loses not only his business but also his family. Anyone who has been involved with small business for any length of time can name people who have lost both.

There is an old adage that it is lonely at the top. It is never more true than during hard times. The bills, responsibilities, and type of decisions small business owners are required to make during times of survival are not fun. These can be very tough times. It requires a strength of will and will test your character. The emotional strain is great. As the manager, accept what is happening, move quickly with your corrective action even when those decisions are difficult. You must buy time for this cycle to turn, or you must downsize to retain a degree of profitability. Do what you can do, keep the faith, and accept the consequences. Be a leader and maintain your personal integrity.

• LEADERSHIP QUALITIES· · · · · · · · · · · ·

Being a small business manager and owner is lonely. If you have employees, they look up to you for direction and leadership. The actions you take determine the success or failure of the business. You are therefore deemed a leader by your very position. The topic of leadership warrants some discussion. An attempt to define leadership and an attempt to describe what a leader does can give the prospective entrepreneur a starting point.

Much has been written about leadership over the years, and the definition has changed and evolved with the times. Historically, the view of a good leader was synonymous with a strong personality: the Manuel Noriega type, beating a machete on the podium and screaming at the top of his lungs. In the factory the shop boss was a tough authoritarian type. Employees did what they were supposed to do out of fear. No one spoke up to give an opinion or a suggestion. There was only one way to do things, and the employees did what they were told, when they were told to do it.

One of my favorite authors on the subject of leadership is Mary Parker Follet (1868–1933). She was way ahead of her time, especially remarkable because at that time women were not recognized as having much to contribute. Mary Parker Follet never held a management position and never worked in a factory. She did understand management, though, and the role that leadership played in management. In a series of lectures she presented at the University of London in 1933, she set forth some of the principles of leadership:[3]

1. Leaders are not born, they are made. It is a learned skill. Aggressiveness is not a requirement of good leaders; in fact, it is often a detriment.

2. Leadership usually has some type of authority attached to it. Thus leadership is granted or authorized by position. In the corporate world the supervisor is granted authority over the subordinates. In small business management authority stems from the fact that you hire and write the paycheck for the employee. This grants authority and places the proprietor in a leadership position, but that is not a complete definition of leadership. On the contrary, it is more a definition of legal authority.

3. Leadership also has a personality component. If I asked you to recall your grade school years and to identify the group of kids you hung around with, and then asked you to identify the leader of that group, you could probably give me the person's name. This is probably the root of the historical inference that aggressiveness is related to leadership. The outspoken, the strong personality, will often assume an informal leadership role.

4. The group grants leadership to the leader. This is true whether the leader has formal authority granted by position or whether the group just looks to a certain person for direction. The person they look to is usually someone the group trusts and has confidence in. Often, this comes from a special ability or knowledge. Sometimes leadership is situational. For example, suppose that an automobile mechanic picks up a group of doctors to haul to the airport. On the way the car engine quits. Who will the group look to for a solution to this situation? The chief surgeon may look under the hood but will accomplish little. Eventually, if not immediately, the group will turn to the mechanic. Why? Because he knows what he is doing in that situation. If one of the members had a heart attack on that trip to the airport, I doubt that the mechanic would say, "Step back, I'll handle this; I'm a mechanic you know."

Leadership, then, can stem from position, personality, or expertise. This does not qualify or identify the characteristics of a good leader. Mary Parker Follet lists several prerequisites for successful leadership:[4]

1. A leader must have a thorough knowledge of the job.

2. A leader must possess the ability to grasp the total situation in order to organize all the forces in the enterprise to pursue a common goal.

3. The leader must possess the ability to see the evolving situation in order to direct the future.

4. A leader should have a spirit of adventure.

A dynamic situation exists between leaders and followers. I mentioned before that the followers concede or grant the leadership role to the leader. For those dynamics to work, dialogue must be allowed. The best solutions are found when the followers participate in the solution process. This is why authoritarianism is so dysfuntional; it allows only one solution or set of ideas. The follower should be allowed to make suggestions, and they should be able to express their frustration and explain the problems they are having. The employee has a part in the solution and problem-solving process.

Mary Parker Follet laid down principles in 1933. It has taken management theory until recently to put this type of management style into practice. Notice the ads in your local paper or at your college placement office. Firms are seeking team players—participative workers—but some entities, governmental as well as for profit, still operate on authoritarian management principles even when they speak the language of the team concept.

Historically in the United States, management theory has been advanced by the aerospace industry, in large part due to the nature of the task at hand: in situations where there is a great deal of ambiguity, as there is in research and development work. Solutions need to be discovered and problems solved. The teams consist of highly trained professionals. This type of environment is most conducive to an open, participative style of management. The leader makes the team, facilitates and utilizes the resources, and keeps the team on track and focused.

The best example I can think of is shown in the movie *Apollo 13*. If you have not seen that film, review it from a management perspective. The emphasis on the team concept is pervasive. The outcome could not have been achieved without a concentrated team effort. The space program has long recognized that the team concept produces the best solutions and produces those solutions the most quickly.

The application to small business management stems from the fact that from the start, as the business grows, careful attention should be given to the creation of a team. Those first hires are critical to the future success of the organization. Care should be taken to bring people into the organization that are compatible and that bring complementary skills. People should bring something with them that can create a synergy. In this way the advantages that corporations have over small business through the use of functional experts begins to diminish.

In my interview with Mr. Barlow at the Burlington Restaurant, he called his management style a family-type style. He indicated that his first priority was to bring people into his business who were honest. Arden indicated that honesty had to come first, then a sense of trust could begin to develop and the trust be reciprocated. Once mutual trust is established, a family atmosphere can evolve. He could have just as well used the word *team* in describing the type of relationship he was striving for in his organization. Trust and mutual respect are the foundation on which a team is built.

Throughout our visit, Mr. Barlow talked about his business. He synthesized the reasons for his success into several critical areas. First was his experience; he felt it critical that to be a good restaurant manager and to be successful, you had to know how to do every job in the place. From a practical sense that is true because you never know when turnover or an illness can leave you short of staff and you may need to fill a gap. From a leadership point of view, how can you train employees and direct their activities without a thorough knowledge of each position? The same is true for designing layout, purchasing equipment, and implementing control systems. You need to have a degree of expertise in each area of your enterprise.

The Burlington was also successful due to its location. Mr. Barlow did not choose that location by chance. Notice the second and third elements that Mary Parker Follet describes as prerequisites to leadership. Mr. Barlow was able to recognize a situation and saw that location as an opportunity. He met all the prerequisites of leadership that Follet set forth. In addition to the second and third elements mentioned, Mr. Barlow had 30 years of experience and had the personal courage to take advantage of the situation. This is not to equate the qualities of successful leadership with success in small business. It is to say that most small business owners need to be leaders to be successful. Leadership ability, therefore, is a requirement for small business success. It should not be a surprise that a good deal of correlation exists between leadership and ability and small business success.

In some respects management can be reduced to specific duties or functions. It is the responsibility of a small business manager to manage the cash inflows or revenue side of the business. That begins with an accurate achievable forecast. The small business manager must control and monitor the sales activity and marketing activity of the business to ensure adequate revenue for the survivability of the firm. Revenue must be adequate to meet the expenses and profit projections of the firm. That is management's responsibility. Just as a revenue shortfall can be detrimental to a firm, so can the expense side of the ledger. If expenses exceed projections, profits can soon be eroded and the firm can be put in a difficult position. It is management's job to monitor and control expenses. Those two issues are givens in the realm of small business management.

Too often the small business owner does a good job of managing the revenue and expense side of a business but experiences severe cash flow problems which sometimes cause a business failure. Many firms experience cash flow problems, and cash flow management is another one of those management duties that fall on the shoulders of the small business owner and manager. At the heart of cash flow management are the credit and collection policies. Almost every business owner must wrestle with the problems associated with credit. If credit is a part of doing business, some collection problems are sure to follow. I wish to address those two issues in more detail here.

• MANAGING CREDIT POLICIES · · · · · · · · ·

For most business operating today in the United States, credit and the extending of credit are almost necessities. What credit really means is that you have a belief in your customer and that you trust that customer to repay the credit extended to them. It is an affirmation of the customer's good character and reputation. It is a demonstration that a trusting relationship exists. Trust between you and your customer is a pillar in the bridge model of this book. I stand by that premise, but trust must be reciprocal and trust must be earned. In our private financial lives we must earn our credit rating, and we do so by demonstrating our trustworthiness by paying those who have extended credit to us. As a business owner and manager there is a powerful urge to grant whatever terms are asked to make the sale. It is often the main focus of the entrepreneur to concentrate on the revenue and sales side of the management equation.

If credit is to be extended, the entrepreneur will need to develop a credit policy early on. It would be very difficult to find any business which extends credit that has not experienced some credit and collection problems. A good credit policy begins with the credit application. You will want to make sure that the credit application you use or design will provide you with the information you will need to implement your credit policy. First, information will be required to make an informed decision as to whether or not you should extend credit to that customer, and second, to what extent and under what terms. You also need information that will support your efforts in the collection process should that customer turn out to be a bad credit choice.

The credit application has three primary functions, which coincide with three different levels in the collection and credit process. The first function, and the first level, is that the application should be used as a tool for screening the applicant for creditworthiness. Embedded in the application will be those questions that will gather the information from which the entrepreneur makes the decision to grant or reject credit to the applicant. On a secondary level, the application is a tool that will aid in the collection process should this particular applicant deteriorate to that level. Should the situation worsen to the third level, the application will then become a tool to be used in attempting to extract a judgment from the creditor, and from the judgment the collection process begins anew. Inherent in this credit application and review process, it should be apparent that the best time, and in many cases the only time, the entrepreneur will have to gather the information required is at the time the application is taken. It goes without saying that a good application design is the starting point, supported by good information systems to keep the aging of accounts receivables up to date and to keep your client database as current as possible.

Step one in the credit-information-gathering process is to get the information on the application that will enable you to find that customer should you need to do so. Too often, someone who defaults on his or her bills leaves town or moves somewhere else within the community. Most applications would require a business address and phone number if credit is being extended to another business. Where credit is being extended to an individual, a residence address with a phone number is customarily asked for on the application. In cases of credit default, the address and phone number may be of little value, but in an attempt to determine and measure how stable a person's financial background is, a question is often included to determine if the applicant is a homeowner or a renter. Homeowners are less able and less likely to disappear. Homeownership is a sign that the person has a stake in the community and has been granted some rather serious credit from a lending agency. Many credit applications will include a line asking how long the applicant has lived at this residence and where his or her previous residence was. The same process could be applied for a business applicant as well, requesting how long the business applicant has been at his or her current address. The probability of continued financial survival of a business that has already survived in the business community for five years is much greater than for a business that has been operating for only 60 days. If any additional information is deemed useful, the place to acquire it is on the credit application itself, at the time the application is first filled out.

If some detective work must be done to locate a credit applicant, what type of information would you want to have to assist you in tracking the person down quickly and easily? A social security and driver's license number certainly would be helpful, especially if the account were to be turned over to a collection agency. The department of labor, social security division, department of transportation, and other agencies can track individuals by social security number. As an individual you cannot normally have access to those databases, but a collection agency might have a way to use that information. An employer's name, address, and phone number might enable you to call the person at work, provided that they have not changed employment. Even then, in many cases that employer's personnel officer may have conducted an exit interview and know where the person is currently working, although such information is not always released. Another often-asked request on a credit application is for the name, address, and phone number of at least two close relatives. Families generally know where other family members are living and working, and it might be possible that a parent or brother would inform you where you might be able to locate your delinquent creditor.

In the case of an incorporated business that is applying for credit, other issues arise. Much more care should be exercised in granting a closed corporation credit than an individual or sole proprietorship, because of the corporate shield afforded the corporate structure. This type of business can be much more difficult to locate and to collect from. In the case of bankruptcy, it is usually the unsecured creditors that are harmed the most. With the existence of a corporate shield, the situation becomes even more difficult. Still, reliable information obtained on the application can help not only screen corporate applicants but help in the collection process itself should an account turn bad. On a corporate credit application you will probably want to get more information than you would for an individual. In many states when a corporation files for a corporate charter, the secretary of state will accept a post office box number as a legitimate address. That box number could even be at a agency such as Mail Boxes Etc., which creates another barrier to information access.

The credit application form should identify the officers of a corporation and the directors as well, although they are usually the same. In addition to the identity of the principals, it would be wise to obtain the residence addresses and phone numbers of these corporate officers as well. In the banking community some hard lessons have been learned concerning the extension of credit to closely held corporations. Most lines of credit extended to such entities now require a personal guarantee by one or more corporate officers. If such a guarantee were included on your credit application, that signature would allow you to hold that corporate officer personally liable for the credit debt incurred. The officer's signature would go a long way toward piercing the corporate shield in a collection case. It is certainly worth considering the merits of including such a line on any credit application used. Requiring one of the corporate officers to accept personal responsibility for any credit debt by signing a personal guarantee will tend to give payment of that bill a priority. Without a personal guarantee by a corporate officer in a situation where a firm's corporate customer refuses to pay, and if the corporation does not have any assets, little can be done down the road in the way of collection, and the creditor has little if any recourse.

Recall the five C's approach to the loan review process. The same standards can be applied in establishing the screening process within your credit policy. The issues that identify the applicant's character should just jump out at you. If your firm is extending credit to people of high moral character who operate their business and their personal lives from an ethical set of standards, you will have little trouble. If the people to whom you extend credit also have the capacity to pay, you will have even less trouble with collections. In many respects since the type of credit you are issuing is unsecured credit, not backed by a specific claim on any asset except possibly the one you are selling, the credit standards you impose should be relatively high.

How do you identify the character and creditworthiness of an applicant? Again, employment history is a start. The applicant who has a stable employment history is less likely to have fallen behind on other bills than the applicant who bounces from job to job or has employment broken up by periods of unemployment. There is a reason that mortgage lenders like to see their loan applicants have had at least two years with the same employer. Now is the time to gather other pertinent financial information regarding the person or the business applicant. The extent to which such information is gathered will depend on the type and extent of the credit being applied for. An authorization to do a credit search at the credit bureau may be excessive, but that depends on the level of credit granted and may be something that should be considered. It is a given that any credit applicant with a jaded credit history will not highlight those situations. In fact, every credit applicant will attempt to put themselves in the best light possible. It is unlikely that a person with past credit problems will identify those problems on the credit application. Incomplete or incorrect information is the most likely response. In hindsight, many of those applicants would have been screened out by a credit check with the local credit bureau.

Almost every credit application is going to ask for credit references. A minimum of three credit references should be requested, and the references should be checked. Many applications will request a list of current outstanding creditors. What you are really looking for is information to verify that the applicant has been granted credit by others in the past and that the credit extended has been repaid. In essence, that is the task the credit bureau performs. If your firm elects not to use a credit bureau, this function is internalized. Individuals are routinely granted credit by utility companies, cable firms, landlords, and others, many of which will verify a credit history.

Should a credit applicant deteriorate into a collection, it might be a good idea to have information available concerning the applicant's financial position. The detail will be determined by the extent of credit you are extending. Information regarding the name of the applicant's bank should be obtained, although in asking for a credit reference you may not get reliable information from the bank. If that bank has extended a loan, they will probably give a positive credit reference, even if that business person has a poor credit history which was somehow hidden from the bank. It may be that the bank is unaware of their client's credit problems because the secured loan they extended is kept current. If the applicant has credit problems at the time of making the application with you, it is unlikely that you will get a list of everyone they owe, nor will you get current credit references.

If you are dealing with a business credit application, one way to help ensure valid credit references is to ask the applicant to sign two or three credit reference authorization forms. Because of the Rights and Privacy Act, many businesses and virtually all governmental agencies will deny access to information without written authorization by the individual or corporate officer. Recommended sources of reliable credit references are the state unemployment office and the department of revenue. If a business is not delinquent on their unemployment tax or sales tax, chances are that they are current on their other bills as well. If you can develop a liaison between your firm and those governmental agencies, you can quickly verify your applicant's credit standing. You would normally also want to verify that your applicant is in good standing with those other businesses that were listed as credit references. It would probably be surprising to discover how many credit references are not checked, but for most enterprises the road to minimizing collection problems begins with obtaining good credit information on the application and verifying the accuracy of that information.

One other consideration when compiling credit information on your client base is that you can build into that database a framework not only for tracking those who are past due by over 30, 60, and 90 days but also those who are current and remain current. This list is a prime source conducting a direct-mail campaign with a special thank you and offer. For those who are past due by over 30 days, a progressive system to collect those funds needs to be developed. Each account is unique, but a follow-up will be required. This first action certainly should be mild; for those who are a few days to 30 days overdue, a statement that acts as a reminder is the normal course of action. It is your choice how long after purchase you expect payment. Local and industry standards may dictate that a full 30 days is given, or it may be that 15 days is all that is allowed before a statement is mailed.

The majority of your accounts will respond to that first billing notice, especially if the applicants were screened for creditworthiness from the onset. After the 30-day notice has been sent, and for those who do not respond, it might be a good idea that when the account reaches 45 to 60 days past due, the friendly reminder gives way to a telephone call. That phone call gives you an opportunity to ask the customer specific questions about the past-due statement. With such questions as "Why hasn't the bill been paid?" and "When can we expect payment?" you can begin to ascertain whether future credit should be suspended and if this account will be a continual problem. It may be that the decision to put this customer on a cash basis only will save a lot of headaches down the road. It may also be that such a decision will cause you to lose this customer, but if you believe that the problem is chronic, this is one customer you might want to send to the competition. You may want to wait until the account is 90 days past due to respond should there be extenuating circumstances.

Whatever you decide to do after the phone calls you make, those phone calls will inevitably result in the collection and payment of a percentage of those outstanding accounts receivable. When an outstanding account reaches 90 days, a phone call is in order, with a specific time frame such as seven days, after which some action will be taken. If you make such a phone call and establish a consequence, your credibility requires that you follow through. When I was a tax investigator, I found that adults can act much like children, notably those adults who did not grow up to be responsible. I found that sequential consequences usually got results. As a business owner you cannot issue subpoenas and have individuals arrested. I'm not sure that you would want to follow that course of action even if you could if you are trying to maintain a for-profit business. You can, though, take those delinquent accounts to small claims court, turn them over to an attorney for collection, or use a collection agency.

If the accounts receivable is a large amount, you may file a lien. This is very common in the construction trades where a job was not done properly or where a supplier or subcontractor was not paid. A lien will impair a deed from being transferred until all liens and encumbrance are taken care of. Such an action may do nothing in the immediate future, but that property will not sell without raising your collection issue.

You must also weigh the cost-effectiveness of your actions. How much time can you afford to spend on collections? Is the account worth going to small claims court over, or turning it over? In some cases it might be wise just to cut your losses and let it go. You could respond with a letter to the credit bureau.

The most important factor in minimizing collection problems is to establish a policy for extending credit, verify that credit information, and finally, follow the credit policy that you have imposed. Credit and collection problems take needed cash flow out of your business; they also take time away from your business—time that could be better spent soliciting new business.

One other possibility available to the entrepreneur when developing a credit policy is to allow everyone and anyone to purchase your product or service on credit but to transfer the risk of the credit sale to the credit specialists. The easiest way to transfer credit sales payment and collection risks is to transfer the risk to the credit card companies. They have established a format for screening credit applicants, and they have developed collection procedures and techniques.

In a small business the customer usually can readily understand an explanation that cash flow is tight and that we just can't play the role of being a banker also. Instead, what your firm can offer and facilitate is a charge to your credit card. If the customer does not have a credit card, having several credit card applications available might help. Many manufacturers offer credit terms that can be passed on through to the customer, which essentially does the same thing. It puts the cash from the sale into your account and transfers the credit issue to someone else. Some customers will balk at the idea of being forced to transfer the purchase to their credit card. Of those who refuse to do business with you, a high percentage will probably refuse because they cannot get credit, or the credit they have been granted is maxed out. Those within either of these groups would not be good credit candidates from your perspective.

If initiated from day one of business, a credit risk transfer policy would be most accepted and tolerated by your customer base. Some sales and revenue may be lost. The receptiveness of a no-direct-credit policy will depend on the product, service, and type of customer. The individual customer will be more receptive than if your client base is a business. Extending credit between businesses is more common. That does not preclude you from offering a split policy, where you extend credit to the business community and require cash or transfer the credit with your retail customer.

• COLLECTIONS ·

If credit is a part of your business, then just as integral to your business will be collection. Rare indeed is the business that extends credit and has few collection problems. In my oil field service business I was very fortunate in that there were a very small percentage of uncollectibles, which was especially significant since 100 percent of my business was on credit. In the restaurant business I had more of a collection problem than I did in the oil industry. This was especially troubling because in the restaurant business, 95 percent of my business was cash; only about 5 percent on credit. Uncollectibles were still a minor problem. It was the nonsufficient funds checks that turned out to be the biggest problem in the restaurant business as far as credit was concerned.

As a manager you are ultimately responsible for the collection of past-due accounts. If you are not doing that function yourself, you want to make sure that a competent person is performing the collection function. For most managers, collections is not a task that is number one on their to-do list. In fact, it is easy to procrastinate and put it off because it is confrontational and unpleasant by nature. Yet if you are not doing the collections, it is advisable to make sure that someone is; either way, you still need to stay on top of the task. Those past-due accounts are not very likely to come look you up. The old adage that "the squeaky wheel gets the grease" applies. Chances are that the people who are delinquent with you are also delinquent in other places. They will usually pay those who are most aggressive in hounding them for payment.

Aggressively pursuing accounts receivable and debtors who have not paid is often required to get them to pay, but the Federal Trade Commission (FTC) has placed restrictions on collection practices, and certain actions are prohibited under the law. You may contact a debtor in person or by mail, telephone, telegram, or fax, but you cannot contact a debtor at unreasonable times or places. Unreasonable times usually indicate before 8:00 A.M. or after 9:00 P.M., unless they agree. You generally may not contact a debtor at work if you know that the debtor's employer disapproves. If the debtor writes you a letter forbidding you to contact him or her further, you must comply except to acknowledge receipt of that request and or to notify them of a specific action you are taking.

As a collector you may not harass the debtor. Following is a list of recognized restrictions imposed by the FTC.[5] You may not:

- Use threats of violence or harm against a person, property, or reputation.
- Publish a list of creditors who refuse to pay their debts (except to a credit bureau).
- Use obscene or profane language.
- Use the telephone repeatedly to annoy the debtor.
- Telephone the debtor without identifying yourself.
- Advertise their debt.

You may not make or use any false statements in your collection procedures, such as:

- Falsely imply that you are an attorney or governmental representative.
- Falsely imply that the debtor has committed a crime.
- Falsely represent that you operate or work for a credit bureau.
- Misrepresent the amount of the debt owed.
- Misrepresent the involvement of an attorney in collection of the debt.
- Indicate that papers being sent to the debtor are legal forms when in fact they are not.

You may not state that:

- The debtor will be arrested if he or she does not pay the debt.
- You will seize, garnish, attach, or sell their property or wages unless you intend to do so and can do so legally.
- You are initiating actions such as a lawsuit, which legally you may not do, or if legal, you do not intend to do.

In short, you are restricted from misrepresenting yourself, and you are restricted from making false statements and or statements that could be deemed harassment. The following actions would also be deemed as unfair by the FTC.

- You may not collect any amount greater than your debt, unless allowed by law.
- You may not deposit a postdated check prematurely.
- You may not force the debtor to pay for collect calls or pay for telegrams.
- You may not seize or threaten to seize property unless this can be done legally.
- You may not contact the debtor by postcard.

What happens if you violate the law? You may be reported to the Federal Trade Commission. You may be reported to the attorney general's office in your state, which may have additional debt collection laws. Those agencies will not intervene in any dispute, but a complaint may initiate action or an investigation by the FTC. The debtor could sue you in state or federal court. If they win, damages can be awarded up to $500,000 or 1 percent of your net worth, whichever is less, and you may be required to pay the court costs and attorney fees of the debtor who sued you. Additional information is available through the FTC, which may be contacted by telephone at 202-326-3650 or you can contact them on the Internet at http://www.ftc.gov/WWW/bcp/conline/pubs/credit/fdc.htm.

From the perspective of the small business owner, these restrictions may seem excessive. It seems absurd that someone can come into your business and cheat you out of money and/or merchandise, then refuse to pay you—and after refusing to pay what they rightfully owe, turn around and file a lawsuit against you for harassment and be awarded financial damages. It may seem like the situation has deteriorated to the point where the criminal appears to have more rights than the victim. From the perspective of the debtor, I'm certain that past abuses have taken place. It is generally an outcome of past abuses that causes the government to put in place legislation to place some controls on those excesses and to create and fund the agency required to administer and enforce that legislation.

In your credit collection policies, you must stay within the law. The best approach is to establish policies and procedures. A systematic documented methodology. The debtor was and perhaps still is a customer, yet if the person owes you money, it is your money and you have a right to collect it. Credit that has been extended and then not paid back usually is not paid back for a variety of reasons. This is true whether credit has been extended to a person or a business. The most obvious reason that a debtor doesn't pay is simply that he or she cannot pay. The debtor doesn't have the money and/or doesn't have the financial resources that give the person the ability to pay.

As a small business owner, the first response to the person or business who isn't paying should be to review your firm's credit application. Was adequate information gathered, and was the screening process correct? Should you adjust your credit policy? Should you adjust your credit screening criteria? The second response should be to make a decision as to what you are going to do about the debtor. Do you go after this person or business in an attempt to resolve the issue? If so, how? Is the issue worth pursuing in time, energy, and money? The third response is: Who do you inform about the collection problem? Certainly whoever is responsible for extending credit should be informed. Do you or do you not want your sales staff to continue to sell to this firm or business on credit? Internally, your staff needs to know. You may also consider informing the credit bureau.

Debtors who cannot pay, cannot pay for several reasons. They may have been poor credit risks from the start. The debtor had no money when credit was extended and had no way of getting money to repay the debt. Regardless of the intention of that debtor, if credit was extended to that type of person or business, a mistake was made and an adjustment of your credit system is required. Often some adverse event occured which put the debtor under some financial hardship, which in turn prevents him or her from being able to pay back money owed. The debtor may have lost his or her job, or a medical emergency occurred, or his or her business was affected through no fault of his or her own. People in this group generally want to pay their bills and would pay what is owed if they could. As individuals they may feel bad about the situation.

If you can contact people who fall into this category, there is a relatively good chance that you will be able to collect from them down the road when their financial situation improves. It will, though, require your firm's attention and monitoring in the form of maintaining contact, or they will often fall through the cracks and become uncollectibles that will eventually need to be written off. Often a reasonable time delay or a payment plan can be arranged. A rule of thumb used by most collectors is to get at least a token payment right away. Don't walk away from that meeting without a check in hand and a payment plan. A promise to pay $25 a month or even $10 is better than nothing. The biggest problem the entrepreneur will face with this group is finding them.

When bad things happen to people, their entire lives are often disrupted. The job information, residence information, phone numbers, and so on, obtained on the original credit application are often invalid by this time. A search using the city directory or credit bureau information may be helpful. This is where the information about relatives becomes important.

Another group of debtors will fall into the classification of being fraudulent. They knew at the time of the credit charge that they either didn't have the money or never had any intention of paying the bill. This is the person who often gives a phony name, address, phone number, and so on. This applicant should have been screened out in the screening and credit verification process. If credit was extended, an adjustment to the credit policy will be required.

Still another group, although relatively small in number, has the ability to pay. In fact, sometimes such people and/or businesses seem to have plenty of assets and cash but refuse to pay. A reference search may reveal a chronic complainer. The person wants a deal and wants an adjustment on everything he or she buys: the miser type who has to be taken to small claims court to extract payment. A cash-only policy for such a person may or may not cost you this customer. Many businesses maintain a list of customers who are cash only. It is important to keep personnel informed of the status of who is on that list.

In other cases a customer who seemingly has the ability to pay but refuses to pay is a customer who was mishandled and mistreated, and their refusal to pay immediately is deliberate, to send a message to management that something is wrong. This customer deserves a thank you, and retribution. Such a situation should be taken seriously and considered a red flag. A thorough review of all of your systems is in order, especially those systems that affect product and service quality.

It is useful to gain as much understanding as possible about customers who turn into a collection issue. The information gained can be used to adjust and adapt the credit application and screening process to further minimize future problems. This is a dynamic, ongoing process, and one more duty that the small business owner is faced with. A systematic methodology of collecting needs to be developed and followed. The collection process should have a specific time frame. In most accounting courses it is a known that the longer a collection goes uncollected, the more difficult it becomes to collect and the less likely the debt will be collected. Your banker will request an aging of accounts receivable for that very reason. A decision point must be reached concerning your collections which you have not collected after a certain period of time. You have several alternatives. First you can continue to attempt the collection on your own. For those who are on some type of payment plan, you may want to retain that function. Others you may retain but write off. Some minimum amount may deem the collection process too expensive to pursue.

A second alternative would be to turn the uncollected accounts over to a collection agency. Most collection agencies will offer their services on a percentage basis or a fee basis. All collectors will want those accounts receivable as early as possible. The truism concerning the aging of accounts receivable also holds true for the professionals. The sooner they get them, the better the chances are of collecting them successfully. A common mistake that business managers make is to hold their accounts receivable and/or collectibles too long before turning them over. If the business owner has done all that he or she can do within 90 days or 120 days, why not take the next step?

One advantage of turning debtors over to a collection agency is that a collection agency specializes in the collection function. For the entrepreneur where collections is but one facet of a multitude of duties, the collection agency should be able to do a better job. A good collection agency can employ the tricks of their trade to collect what the person cannot. If used, a collection agency should provide you with progress reports on a regular basis. If their services are unsatisfactory, change to another agency. You will need to notify the agency in writing that your relationship is being terminated, but switching agencies should not be a problem.

A collection agency should be more able to find debtors than an individual proprietor can. They have the ability to pursue remedies that might be cost prohibitive for the individual. Most agencies employ an attorney who can access the civil court process. The collection agency may opt to take the debtor to small claims court to obtain a judgment on behalf of the entrepreneur. This may be helpful where the small business owner does not want to confront the debtor personally.

The fact that the collection agency is an impersonal entity can be effective and can take a burden off the entrepreneur. Sometimes the fact that the agency is a third person is helpful. There are situations where personalities clash and the debtor simply cannot or will not deal with the business owner. A collection agency can act as a mediator. The same is true in situations where debtors feel they have been wronged, and the collection agency may be better able to facilitate a settlement.

Be aware that just because a debtor has been turned over to a collection agency, no guarantee exists that the account will be collected. Some people are almost judgment proof. Similarly, the agency will not be able to collect from every debtor but should meet with more success than you can as a business owner. If they cannot, consider a different collection agency. Be aware also that once turned over, you will not recover all that is owed to you, due to the fees associated with use of the collection agency. One major problem for many small business owners is the debtor who skips town and moves out of state. It becomes increasingly difficult and expensive to continue to pursue that collection. The collection agency will generally belong to an association and can assign collection to a representative in the city and state that the debtor lives in. The fact that collections are eventually turned over will help send a message to your customers that collections will not be written off summarily.

• SMALL CLAIMS COURT[6] • • • • • • • • • • • •

Small claims court is another recourse available to the small business owner. Small claims court offers distinct advantages and disadvantages. What small claims court is stems from a legislative authorization that allows a state supreme court to adopt rules for an informal process to handle claims efficiently that stem from contract or tort, with some exceptions. The amount of the claim is limited; in the state of South Dakota the limit is currently $4000. Small claims court was created to keep many of these cases out of the formal side of the court system, which is already overburdened with cases. Small claims court will resolve cases where there are monetary damages within the limits of the court. The remedy that small claims court can grant is financial and only financial. The court is not going to grant equity relief, and the court will not require performance in a contract. All the judge can do is award financial damages. The court is limited in its jurisdiction, first from the perspective that financial damages is all it can award, and second, those financial damages, if awarded, are limited by statute. If your claim can be reduced to meet those criteria, small claims court may be a workable option.

Small claims court is informal, which means that you do not need an attorney. Many of the judges who preside over small claims court discourage the presence of an attorney. The idea is to move the case along. The judge will ask the questions in an informal procedure. That means that small claims court is relatively inexpensive. A fee schedule is available at the clerk of courts office in your county. In my local county, the fees range depending on the dollar amount of the claim and upon the number of parties being sued. Fees in my area of South Dakota currently range from $9.09 to $25.09 if an award at the maximum limit $4000 is sought. If you win, the fees are recoverable. In addition, a fee of $2.77 for postage may be added because service of the notice is by registered mail. That fee is also recoverable through the judgment. The small claim's fee schedule in your county probably will not differ drastically. Note also that there may be slight variations in how small claims court is conducted in your area, due to the fact that it is the state supreme court that establishes jurisdiction.

In this county it is fairly simple to access small claims court. To file a claim, the plaintiff must provide a written statement describing how he or she was harmed financially, including in the statement the nature and extent of the loss. Second, all supporting documentation must be included. If a collection is involved, a copy of the invoice and copies of any subsequent billing notices are required. Third, the plaintiff must pay the appropriate filing fees. Finally, the plaintiff must provide the court with the correct spelling of the defendant's name and a current mailing address. The defendant will be served by certified mail.

A court date is set ahead roughly six weeks; again, that will depend on the locality. If the certified letter is not claimed by the defendant, he or she may be served by the sheriff's department or by the constable's office, which adds yet another fee. That fee is added to the amount of the claim. You as the plaintiff will have to pay the fees initially and then attempt to recover that fee after a judgment is obtained.

Once the fees have been paid by the plaintiff, the clerk of court sends out the notice to the defendant. The defendant has an opportunity to respond. They in turn can attempt to deny the claim, but a written response must be submitted explaining why the claim should be denied or damages reduced. The defendant may decide to remove that case from small claims court. From a practical standpoint, if someone receives a notice that they are being sued in small claims court, the person may contact an attorney. That attorney, knowing that his or her presense is not welcome in small claims court, may convince the client to remove the case from small claims with a petition to go to the formal side of court. The attorney can do this by filing an affidavit claiming that circumstances exist that require this case to be heard in formal court. Such a request may or may not be granted, but as a practical matter, that type of request is often granted, and you, as plaintiff, just escalated this proceeding up to a civil court case. However, the defendant must pay the appropriate fees. If that happens, you do not need to hire an attorney immediately; you can represent yourself.

The defendant has several other options upon being served. Instead of attempting to deny the claim, the defendant might attempt a settlement. In a statement to the small claims judge, the defendant might explain that services were not rendered satisfactorily and that instead of owing, say, the $1500 that was billed, the job was really worth only $500. The defendant also has the right to file a counterclaim. For example, suppose that an auto repair shop worked on a vehicle and the defendant was billed $800 for repairs, for which he would not pay. A small claims suit was filed. The defendant countersues, stating that he or she not only does not owe the $800 that he or she was billed for. Instead, the mechanic ruined the vehicle's engine, for which the overhaul repair bill will be $2000. The defendant then countersues for $2000, and if the evidence demonstrates the former statement to be correct, the defendant does stand a chance of winning that suit. That counterclaim will be heard at the same hearing for which your original suit was scheduled.

At the time set for your small claims trial, the small claims clerk will determine who appeared or failed to appear before the court. If you, the plaintiff, fail to appear at the appointed time, your case will be dismissed; you lose your case. If the defendant fails to show up, you win and will be awarded a default judgment, which means that you are entitled to receive your money. If you get a default judgment, you can notify the defendant that you have been awarded the judgment and that you will allow them 10 days or a reasonable period of time before you proceed with a writ of execution. If the defendant does not contact you and or attempt to make an arrangement for settlement, you may be forced to follow through with execution of the judgment.

Many small claims cases, sometimes the majority of the cases, are dismissed due to one of the parties not showing up. When the judge enters the courtroom, the first order of business is to look through the denials that have been submitted, prior to calling the cases forward. The judge will ask the questions. On a collection, the judge may ask the defendant why he or she is there. Is there a reason why the defendant feels that he or she does not owe the money? If it is simply an issue of an unpaid account, the judge may ask the defendant if they have the means to pay the sum. The judge attempts to find the facts of the claim. If the judge rules in your favor, you are awarded a judgment and you are entitled to a writ of execution, but certain time constraints may be imposed. You may be required to wait 30 days prior to proceeding to a writ of execution.

If you are not paid within that specified grace period, you may return to the small claims clerk and obtain an execution, which is an order requiring the constable or sheriff to attempt to find money and other property to satisfy your judgment. There will also be a fee associated with obtaining a writ of execution. In my local county that fee is currently $5 but it varies from county to county and from state to state. Constables' and sheriffs' offices have certain rules and make certain charges for attempting to collect your judgment. These charges may be recovered from the judgment debtor in addition to the amount of the judgment.

By this stage of the process it is easy to recognize that at some point, paying fee after fee in an attempt to obtain monetary satisfaction or to recover that old accounts receivable, good money is being thrown after bad. Just because you can obtain a judgment does not mean that you are going to be able to recover damages. Some people are literally judgment proof. They don't have any money, they don't have any assets, and they have no real way of getting money. It will be difficult to collect from this group. The court document that can be obtained through the small claims court process just means that you are entitled to the money. No guarantee is given by the court that you will obtain the money. The court itself does not collect the money for you; it only grants the judgment.

In cases where a judgment is granted and the defendant comes up with the money and pays off the judgment, whether in a lump sum, through an installment agreement, or through a settlement where you agree to accept an exchange or partial payment, you, as plaintiff, have an obligation to notify the clerk of courts office that you have been paid. The judgment is then taken off the books and you are no longer a lien holder. Failure to do so could leave you open to a liability suit.

Judgments can be transferred or filed in counties other than the one in which you are residing. You have the right to renew a judgment; the credit bureau will carry judgments for seven years. The problem with obtaining a judgment from someone who cannot pay lies in keeping track of the person. How much time and energy can you afford to expend in your collection efforts? It is often those people who are nearly judgment proof who seem to be the most transient in nature. If they move out of the county in which the judgment was issued, you can file the judgment in the county and/or state to which the debtor moved, but the filing fees and the logistics become exceedingly prohibitive. At some point a decision needs to be made either to write the debt off, or to turn it over to a collection agency. If the latter is the case, the earlier the collection agency receives the account, the better their chances are of collecting.

The principal advantages of using small claims court is that it is relatively quick, especially when compared with the formal side of the court system, relatively inexpensive, and relatively easy to use. You do not need an attorney; in fact, the use of an attorney is discouraged, because small claims court is designed to be expedient.

Some judges presiding over small claims court will require that any attorney present refrain from speaking unless a party to the case. The principal advantage is that small claims offers a medium in which to pursue claims that you could not afford to pursue in the formal court system.

The principal disadvantages of small claims court stem in part from the decisions rendered. First, the judge has very limited knowledge of the circumstances of the case. Due to the expedient nature of the process, the judge must shoot from the hip, so to speak, and make a snap judgment based on limited information. The incidence of error, then, would tend to be higher than would be expected from the formal side of court. The disadvantage stemming from that decision is that it is final. There is no appeals process in small claims court. A small claims decision by a small claims judge is final. The judge does have the right to take the case under advisement and study the circumstances before rendering a decision, but from a practical viewpoint that is not done, due to time constraints. The second principal disadvantage is the fact that a judgment does not necessarily turn into a collection. The court does not guarantee performance. The debtor will not be sent to jail. You can obtain an execution and in some cases wages can be garnisheed. There are restrictions on the garnishment of wages and many jurisdictions do not allow wages to be garnisheed. The third disadvantage of small claims court stems from the fact that in a collections process you are in fact suing a customer. In many counties the official county newspaper, the one that publishes the legal notices issued by the county, often publishes the small claims court proceedings. Your name and the name of the defendant will appear in the paper. Your other customers will know that you are suing. Taking a customer to court cannot do good things for customer relations, but on the other hand it puts your customers on notice that in the event of a debt problem, they also can expect to be taken to small claims court. The final disadvantage stems from the time and expense involved. Even though the small claims process is relatively inexpensive, if you go very often, the fees do add up.

The best possible outcome is first not to extend credit to those who cannot or will not pay, which is easier said than done. The next best possible outcome is to obtain a settlement outside the court system. Be that as it may, small claims court remains a possible alternative in the collection process.

• RISK MANAGEMENT · · · · · · · · · · · · · · ·

The area of risk management has the potential to rise to the highest priority for the entrepreneur. Unfortunately, that usually occurs after the fact. If appropriate insurance coverage is not in place at the time of a major loss, the future of the business could certainly be put in jeopardy. At issue for the small business manager is identifying what insurance is needed—how much coverage is needed without going broke from paying excessive insurance premiums. The types of insurance that a small business will need depend on the specific type of business and the unique nature of the risks to which the firm is exposed. At one level, certain types of insurance coverage is mandatory under law, while other types of coverage are optional or elective.

The most common concern for the business owner when thinking of risk management is property coverage, because property usually represents the largest major investment the entrepreneur has in his or her business. Most entrepreneurs can relate to property protection because of its similarities to residential home insurance. Property is very tangible and it is a natural response to want to protect that investment against loss. The most important point to be aware of when addressing business or commercial property insurance is that it is not like residential homeowner's insurance in many important ways.

The first issue concerning commercial property insurance is the type of coverage: actual cash value or replacement cost. Actual cash value coverage covers a building for the value of its depreciated state. Replacement value coverage will replace the building with similar construction, or repair the building to its original condition. This difference between actual cash value and replacement cost is significant. Most property losses that occur are not a total structure loss but damage to a property. In the case of, say, damage to a roof that has been in place for 20 years, replacement coverage will replace the roof less any applicable deductible. Actual cash value may pay only one-third the cost of replacing the roof if it is determined that a roof has a useful life of 30 years.

The first step in risk management is to perform a risk assessment. A risk assessment begins by identifying the types of exposures for the small business, which stem from three major sources: property, liability, and personnel. A second approach is to view the exposures from the perspective of direct or indirect loss.

For the small business owner a risk assessment is usually not a difficult concept to apply in the area of property coverage. Once a risk exposure has been identified, the business owner will need to evaluate the levels of exposure and obtain appropriate levels of coverage, or determine if another response is appropriate. In conducting a property risk assessment, the business owner will start by identifying the real property owned or rented. It is not just the structure itself, but the contents that must be covered. The property loss exposure, along with the contents in the form of equipment, fixtures, inventory, and the like, would be considered a direct loss should a loss occur.

Most businesses would suffer economically from indirect consequences as well. Things like business and income interruption could be devastating, not only in the lost revenue that would occur while the structure and contents were being replaced, but the lost customers due to the shutdown could have long-term consequences. In addition, many paper documents, especially accounts receivable and customer records, could well be lost for good.

The second major area of risk exposure stems from liability. Those liabilities may stem from the structure itself should a customer or employee be physically harmed while on the premise. Liability can also stem from a firm's equipment, products, or services. Fiduciary issues, malpractice, and other liability issues may be a concern as well.

The third major area of loss exposure deals with personnel issues. Death to the proprietor may mean the end of the business as well. The business could suffer real financial loss should a key employee die or become disabled: health insurance issues, disability, unemployment, retirement, and so on.

Normally we don't give the risk management function much attention, but much like the production and personnel functions, risk management can sometimes be classified as a critical function. The focus of this book has been on the big three—marketing, finance, and accounting—but the other areas of a business can and in many cases do rival the big three in importance. Certainly, all functional areas can be critical to the success of the organization. This section was included to address specifically some of those specific managerial functions which if overlooked could potentially put you out of business. A mistake or more accurately an oversight, followed by an unforeseen event, has the potential to ruin a business financially. Constant review and upgrading of a business's risk protection are in order.

As indicated above, risk is associated primarily with losses to property, to people, or in the arena of liability. The small business-person must first be able to identify the types of risk to which the business is exposed, followed by some measurement of the extent of that exposure, and finally, the proper response to the exposure, not all of which is coverable by insurance.

A starting point is to establish a personal relationship with a reputable insurance firm. Be aware, however, that the insurance industry has changed dramatically over the years. The local insurance agent used to know his or her customers by name and knew the types of coverages that were written for those clients. Like other segments of the economy, the insurance business has had to become more efficient, due to competition and the increased costs of doing business.

To deal more fully with the issue of risk management, I called an old friend of mine, Mark Gary, who manages an insurance agency.[7] He told me that his one-man office with a single secretary who he shares with a real estate agency costs him over $4000 a month. Computer costs are substantial to remain technologically in the game, as are telephone systems. His client portfolio is over 1800 clients.

Mark Gary of Gary Insurance indicated that the business has changed. He complains that he no longer can recognize his customers' voices over the phone, and that in turn is frustrating to his customers. "They call and ask what type of coverage they have on their vehicle and expect me to know off the top of my head. I've got 1800 clients; I can't even tell you the coverages that are written for the folders on my desk. I've got to look in the file."

Gary Insurance is a small town agency. Mark has years of experience and is a very competent agent. Yet some serious implications exist for the small business-person because this industry has become so intense. The implication is that small business owners had better be more aware of their own risk exposure and become less dependent on their insurance agent. Mark indicated that he cannot remember the last time he sat down for a noon meal; eating is always on the go. That lifestyle is reflected by the fast-food industry which is now developing what they call dashboard food.

Mark indicated that the agencies he represents require an insurance audit every three years. The purpose of such an audit is to review the coverages and to bring coverages up to date so that in event of a loss, the client is not left under-insured. It is also designed to review the exposures and ensure that the right coverages are in place.

I asked Mark where he starts with a new business client. "The first step is a needs assessment, and then we branch out from there." The needs assessment phase attempts to identify specific exposures a business might have. The typical exposure assessment format will fall into three categories: property losses, liablility losses, and losses associated with personnel. The property loss category is the easiest to address and to understand. The physical assets start with the buildings. Mark indicated that the first question he asks a new client is whether he or she owns the business or are leasing. Then he asks if they own the property, the building the business is in, and the land it sits on. If the building is owned, coverage will be required, as an owner risk exposure exists to hazards such as fire, smoke, explosion, hail, wind, riot, vandalism, flood, water, and earthquake. For the small business owner the property coverage element is easy to identify. It is doubtfull that a physical structure will be forgotten and left off an insurance schedule, but it is important to attempt to identify the hazard exposures and write as broad a form as close to an all-risk policy as possible. The danger for the small business person in this realm is under-insurance. First, if your business is doing well and expands in the physical structure, the expansion needs to be included in the coverage as soon as it is completed. An under-construction endorsement should be considered while under construction. A key problem area for the small businessperson is that property insurance coverages are allowed to lag. That is, property improvements and the impact of inflation can cause a property to be underinsured. The three-year insurance audit is designed to close that gap, but as a small business manager, it is your responsibility to keep coverages current by notifying your agent of any changes.

The risk to the small businessperson is that undercoverage in the event of a loss could result in enormous out-of-pocket expenditures. The insurance won't cover the loss, which could put a firm out of business. To date, property insurance in the country has been a real value, but with increasing costs in construction and the labor associated with construction, along with the seemingly increased losses due to severe weather patterns, underwriters are taking a second look at their losses. It is a safe bet that property insurance rates will rise significantly in the next decade.

Having addressed the real property, a risk assessment will next identify the contents of the structure. As a small businessperson it is imperative that you remain involved in this process: first from the standpoint that your firm's physical contents are likely to change frequently, and second, because you as the manager are the one most aware of those changes and are in a position to document alterations in inventory and equipment. It is easiest to begin by identifying that part of the contents which is most static, such as office equipment. The next phase is to identify fixtures, equipment, tools, and so on, used in the course of your business and a part of the contents of the structure. The inventory should be addressed. If this is a retail firm, inventory will be substantial. Inventory may consist of different types. For example, an inventory of office supplies may be maintained as well as inventory for resale. Office equipment and other equipment tools will require a detailed inventory to be kept with serial numbers and/or model numbers off each piece of equipment. In event of a single item loss, you will be required to show proof of that loss. A camera, or better yet, a videotape of the contents, with supporting documentation such as a depreciation schedule or purchase invoices, should be kept at a secure location. Equipment is generally endorsed in a commercial insurance policy. The better your records are, the more accurate your coverage can be. When equipment is replaced and/or added, the insurance coverage needs to reflect those changes.

With physical contents, additional exposures exist. Coverage for burglary, robbery, and theft, including employee theft and/or fraud, may be added. If the contents of the structure includes a boiler, a special endorsement may be required to cover it. Glass may also require a separate endorsement.

In the event of a loss, especially a loss involving major structural damage to the property, certain indirect losses may occur as a result whether or not you own the building: losses resulting from business interruption and loss of profits. Generally, losses associated with these types of coverage must be substantiated in the form of demonstrated profits. If profits did not exist in the past, it is unlikely that a loss can be proven. Indirect losses are those due to rents, temperature changes, or damage caused by the loss of utilities or valuable papers such as accounts receivable. Your agent can assist you in identifying the types of indirect loss exposure you may have and can write the appropriate coverage.

Liability is the next major area of risk exposure. With physical assets loss can be more easily defined and measured. For example, the loss of a structure has a definite maximum value, being the replacement cost of the structure. The inherent problem with liability protection is that loss limits are not so clearly constrained. The trend in this country has been to award higher and higher damages, especially when punitive damages are added on. Part of that trend has to do with a basic societal frame of mind. It seems that few people want to take responsibility for their own actions—that if something bad happens, it must be somebody else's fault. When disaster hits, even caused by the weather, somebody has to pay—if not the insurance company, then the government. This was not the case 50 years ago. I am not passing judgment that this is good or bad—it just is, and the fact that this type of attitude prevails has an affect on liability insurance, even to the point of the absurd.

The outcome of this attitudinal shift makes it more imperative that the small business owner carry adequate liability coverage and that the limits are high enough. Mark Gary indicated that he does not like to write any liability coverage limits of less than $1 million for his clients. The first type of general business liability provides protection against claims resulting from some type of accident that occurs on the premises or on the property of the business owner. A more common type of liability coverage which can be added is products and completed operations coverage, which protects against claims resulting from harm or damage caused by customers' use of the products sold or services rendered: for example, if a gas station sells gasoline that was mixed incorrectly and or had water in it, and use of that gasoline by the customer caused a vehicle's engine to be ruined. The products and completed operations policy will compensate the injured parties for the damages incurred. If the workmanship or service provided caused harm to a customer's property or person, that liability is also insured against in this type of policy.

Liability exposures can come from professional services in the form of errors and omissions. If your firm is a manufacturer, product liability exposure exists. Construction firms will have specific liability exposures. Other types of liability exposures are associated with the equipment and asset structure of a particular firm: for example, ownership of an elevator, aircraft, water craft, heavy equipment, and vehicles. Liability can stem from malpractice or fiduciary responsibilities. Specific performance of your organization may require bonding. Liability can stem from your employees or principals in the business. It is difficult, if not impossible, to address all the types of liability exposures for a particular business. What most businesses do is write a general liability policy, plus specific liability coverage, and then an umbrella policy over the top of that to protect against any gaps that were left in the coverage and to add additional limits to the scope of the policy. This is especially important because of the propensity for courts to award punitive damages and to award for pain and suffering in liability cases. The presence of either can easily tap out the limits of a liability policy.

It is important to understand that most policies have what is called split limits: a limit for property damage and a limit on damage to a person. They also have limits for each occurrence and limits in aggregate. For example, you may have a $500,000 limit per occurrence and a $1 million aggregate. If two people were involved in the claim and each was awarded $500,000, you have maxed out your policy on both the occurrence limits and the aggregate limit. If a third person was involved in the award, coverage has been exceeded and that part of the award would be stood by the business owner. It is for this reason that many insurers will recommend that an umbrella policy be attached to go over the top of the policy to expand and extend your coverage. A typical umbrella endorsement will add between $1 million and $5 million in additional liability coverage to the policy. If you need more than $5 million in umbrella liability protection, the insurer proceeds with extreme caution, due to the size of the potential claim. The underwriter is going to take a close look at your organization, and they will not normally write that level of liability coverage without your business being backed by strong financial statements, in part due to the practicality of the judicial system. If a small business with a net worth of $125,000 is engaged in a liability suit and the business has liability protection of $2 million, chances are that the defendant will settle for $2 million, but if the business has $10 million in liability coverage, the defendant may well attempt to recover $10 million. The deep pockets rule prevails, and it is the insurance company's pocket that the defendant's attorney is trying to pick. The $125,000 net worth of the proprietor is incidental.

From the insurance company's point of view, they will be reluctant to expose themselves to undo risk by writing excessive liability limits. As those limits rise, the underwriter will become more and more cautious. My oil field safety business, which provided training and leased detection and protective equipment to oil well drilling and completion companies, had a high degree of liability risk exposure. Those major exploration and production companies who were using the services of companies like my own were doing so in part to transfer the risk of such high levels of liability exposure away from themselves and onto an outside firm. The point I'm trying to make is that obtaining adequate levels of liability coverage in this type of business was incredibly difficult. The underwriters were understandably wary. I first obtained coverage through a specialty insurance broker and then with the help of the North Dakota state insurance commissioner was able to identify the main underwriters in the region, personally take an underwriter on a tour of my facility, and demonstrate the equipment and meet some of the personnel involved, to give them first an understanding of the industry and a feel for the liability exposure they would face. In that case the underwriter agreed to write the policy, although the rate was on the high end of their rate scale.

According to Mark Gary, the majority of liability cases that he sees his clients involved in are completed products cases. The big liability exposures stem from product liability cases or from bodily injury cases stemming from such events as automobile accidents. It should be noted that automobile liability is not covered by your business liability coverage. Vehicles are specifically excluded because that coverage is specific to a vehicle policy.

If you are operating a business for profit in a generally recognized trade or occupation and are using a vehicle in that business, you will need to obtain specific commercial auto insurance to cover the vehicle. That coverage can be endorsed and added to your commercial policy, but commercial coverage applies.

It is also important to realize that if you are operating a business from your home, your homeowner's insurance policy does not extend its liability protection to your business. For example, if a client comes onto your property and slips and falls, resulting in injury, that incident is not covered because of the business relationship that exists. In the same manner, your investment in tools, equipment, and/or computers, along with the valuable papers and information used in your business, are excluded from coverage in your personal homeowner's policy. It is important to obtain separate home business coverage, and many agencies write that type of coverage for reasonable rates.

The third major classification of liability exposure that Mark Gary would address for the small business person extends to the individual proprietor himself or herself. Adequate life insurance should be in place in event of death so that sufficient funds are available to pay the debts of the business and provide for the personal needs of the survivors. Just as important a potential risk exists for the entrepreneur should he or she become disabled and unable to carry on the business activity. As a self-employed person those risks are exacerbated because worker's compensation coverage is often not present, nor is there a company disability policy. Health insurance is also a requirement. For the self-employed there is no employer-paid health policy unless assistance is obtained through the employer of a spouse. The lack of health insurance could put the business in jeopardy should a major accident or illness occur. A self-funded retirement plan has been addressed earlier but deserves consideration here again. In addition to these issues being present for the entrepreneur himself or herself and their families, the personal liabilities extend to their employees as well. In many small business entities, management is often the joint effort of the small business owner and a small core of key employees, some of which would be difficult to replace and whose loss in the form of disability or through loss of life would cause financial harm to the firm. It may be in the business's best interest to insure the life of those people.

The insurance industry has evolved over many years. The key principles of the insurance industry are built on contract law and the law of large numbers. The industry is built on the statistical prediction of losses incurred through the pooling of standardized risks. This works well for policies like life insurance and even homeowner's insurance; the units are somewhat standard and the losses definable. The policies are standardized because life insurance can be reduced to costs per thousand, and the contract requirements established by the regulating agencies can be applied uniformly. To the same degree, housing units and/or personal automobile policies can be standardized. To some degree commercial insurance can be somewhat standardized, but it is much more difficult for the industry to move into the commercial realm because businesses are somewhat unique in the types of liability exposure each faces, and the limits of exposure are also not consistent. As a result, commercial insurance is much more flexible and is broken down into major lines of insurance, with each line consisting of a number of forms or endorsements of coverages with flexible limits. In this way, the small business owner can put together the lines and endorsements that fit his or her operation. The policy becomes much more customized.

The major lines of coverage begin with a commercial package policy and a declaration page, and is followed by a policy condition page. The first line covers commercial property; the second line addresses commercial liability, followed by crime, inland marine, boiler, and machinery, commercial auto, and farm. The type of business you are in and the risk exposures your business will face will determine which lines you will need.

Once you have identified the types of risk exposure you are faced with, the second natural step is to somehow attempt to measure the exposure and define the exposure in a dollar amount. Once done you can make a determination as to which risk exposures you will insure, which you will self-insure by not insuring, and which you will attempt to avoid or transfer to someone else.

At first glance most people would think that it is quite difficult, if not impossible, to avoid risk. To some degree that is true, but there are ways to spread the risk, to minimize the risk, to transfer risk, and to some degree avoid risk completely. Begin with the premise and the perception of a manager with a fiduciary responsibility. The first rule and objective is to preserve the asset base that you have been charged with managing; in short, don't lose what you've got. The purpose of this discussion is to help you do just that. The second rule is to maximize returns. The first rule puts reasonable limits on the second.

Having conducted a thorough risk assessment with your agent, it may be that certain risk exposures are unacceptably high. The costs associated with that exposure may be such that little profitability will be left. You can avoid this exposure simply by not doing the activity. In many cases, the input can be purchased from the outside.

A more accurate description of the scenario above is risk transfer, but in many ways the concepts of risk avoidance, risk transfer, and risk minimization are tied together. In the case of farming out an activity or process to an outside firm, the majority of the risk associated with that process is also transferred. In my oil field safety business, I was keenly aware that the major exploration companies were subcontracting the safety function over to firms like mine because of the risk associated with that industry. It did not make sense for them to expose themselves to that level of risk. In the event of an accident, the deep pockets theory would in all likelihood prevail and the oil company would have been named in the liability suit, but their first line of defense would have been that they were not liable because they were not performing the service. It makes it more difficult for the plaintiff to prove negligence and also would probably limit damages due to contributory negligence. I'm not professing to be learned enough to write a legal opinion, but from a practical armchair point of view, I believe that is the way the scenario above would play out.

For many organizations one often-used method to transfer risk is to subcontract certain functions out to another firm. A city does not send out its employees to build a bridge; they contract it out, in part because of the liability. If the bridge collapses, the contractor and the materials suppliers will be brought into the liability suit. The city's liability is minimal. This is especially true if the city engineer who was overseeing the project took reasonable steps to ensure that the project was completed according to specifications. The fault would then point to negligence on the part of the contractor, or faulty materials, which were outside the control of the city engineer. The risk would have been much greater had the city used their own employees in the construction. The blame and the negligence would rest with them, and their defense would have to be aimed at proving that the collapse was caused by something like a truck that exceeded weight limits, or faulty materials.

From a practical point of view, risk is minimized by doing the right things: conducting inspections to recognize and monitor potential hazards; using the right type of construction methods and materials to minimize damage due to fire, tornado, wind, earthquake, and so on; lighting and security systems to prevent theft burglary and help ensure the safety of customers and employees; putting deicer down when side walks are icy; training employees in safety and providing them with safe equipment. This means that guards and shields are in place, safety goggles are available and used, electrical outlets are covered, and so on. Each type of business has unique hazards and a program to minimize first, the number of occurrences, and second, the scope of the loss, should be in place.

Another perspective of risk minimization stems from the structure of the organization and the policies and procedures in place. First the procedures. It makes sense to back up your computer files in case the system crashes and/or in the event of a fire. A dual set of records would be nice. A policy to back up records routinely, and the procedure that on Friday nights before locking the business for the weekend, the backup file is taken home by the comptroller or owner. A look at all systems and procedures to minimize loss is part of what a risk manager does. In small business it is the owner-manager who wears that hat.

Another approach to the risk transfer, risk avoidance, risk minimization approach is to rethink what it is you want to own. If property insurance and deductibles reach a point where that becomes a factor in your capitalization and occupancy costs, one approach would be not to own that structure, but to rent. The same is true for equipment and fixtures. The downside of such an approach is that if the cost is high for you, it will also be high for the owner of that asset, and the costs will eventually be reflected in rental prices. Understanding those risks and the costs associated with them is the basis for good decision making. As I indicated earlier in my interview with Mark Gary, one area in the insurance business that is having a tough time due to excessive claims is the property end of the business. The result will be higher premiums, tougher adjusting, and higher copayments and deductibles. In the end a loss will cost you more money, and that might be money that your business cannot afford. Rental would transfer that risk to the owner of the structure. The cost becomes more than the passing on of the premium alone.

In my work as a tax investigator I would often audit businesses that were layered with corporations. The logic behind this was risk minimization as well as tax minimization. In the military, when a unit goes into combat, the supply officer who is in charge of bullets, beans, and bandages does not put all the bullets in one truck, the bandages in another, and the beans in another. It makes sense not to do this, because if one truck is destroyed, you are out of one of the three critical elements required to stay in the field. It makes sense to put one-third of each type of supply in each truck, so if you lose one or even two, the unit can still function. Business operates in much the same way. You do not risk everything in a single venture or a single firm (rule 1 is preservation of the asset base).

Successful companies will create a separate corporation for each business they open. For example, I have a friend who is part owner of a number of convenience gas stations. Each station has its own corporation. In the event of financial or legal disaster, that corporation stands on its own. Another firm, which is a construction contractor, has a separate corporation that owns the real estate, another firm owns the equipment, which it rents to yet a third corporation, which acts as the operating company. The third corporation is bonded, and the majority of the payroll is run through this company. Why? Because if the bridge collapses and liability is assigned to the contractor, it would be difficult for a defendant to penetrate through the equipment leasing company and even more difficult to get to the real estate holding company. Thus a worst-case scenario preserves most of the asset base.[8]

To summarize the risk management function, the small business owner needs to stay informed, and have a constant awareness of potential risk hazards, levels of risk exposure, and attention to risk minimization details. Keep coverages up to date. Since the agent you will probably be working with is more than likely under an information overload, you will be required to take the lead in keeping your agent informed of changes in your asset structure so that coverages are in place. Use risk transfer strategies that protect your asset base, and avoid exposure to the "big one" that can potentially put your firm out of business. You cannot know too much about your business. Like a good attorney, banker, and accountant, a good insurance agent is an integral part of running a business. Cultivate a relationship with your agent. Friends tend to look out for each other. A good agent fits into the model of external relationships.

• SUMMARY ·

In many respects what small business management boils down to is making the best possible use of time, energy, and resources of the firm. It is being able to identify what is critically important and to prioritize the firm's resources and direct the firm's activities to maximize and/or capitalize on the advantages the firm has. The small business manager must also be aware of an attempt to minimize the risk from a threat. Sometimes the activity and energies of the small business owner must be in the realm of damage control or attempting to thwart that which could undermine the health of the business.

In many ways the small business owner-manager has an advantage over major corporations, simply due to the fact that every person in a small firm is involved directly in income-producing activity. This type of enterprise with a working manager does not have the high overhead associated with professional managers, who require office space, office staff, and support equipment and fixtures. The small business entrepreneur need not require the status symbols that often go along with a position in a major firm. I mention this because one of the dangers for small business entrepreneurs is to get caught up in buying too many of the good things too early, before the business can comfortably afford such luxuries. It is important to understand the market position of the business, especially from the perspective of the life cycle of the product or service provided. A business cycle downturn can and often does happen. The best defense is to maintain proper management controls and a more conservative financial structure. When things are good, use the time and resources to firm up the business's underpinnings.

The small business manager is faced with many functional areas of decision making. At the onset of starting a business enterprise, the most difficult aspect for most entrepreneurs is coming up with the finances to get the business up and off the ground. Once the initial financing has been obtained, most entrepreneurs struggle with obtaining enough money to keep the business alive and thriving. This cash flow is for the most part generated by marketing the products and services that brought them into business in the first place. The marketing function goes on and on, hopefully developing into a system that fuels continual growth. The entrepreneur must keep track of the financial resources to make good decisions and must also meet certain legal requirements. For many entrepreneurs the accounting function is the final one of the big three functions.

For the entrepreneur, mastering the big three small business functions—accounting, marketing, and finance—can take them along way toward managing a successful enterprise, provided that they do not encounter a critical problem which could jeopardize the survival of the firm. One such danger area alluded to earlier was a situation where the owner-manager spends the company broke. The second critical area dealt with earlier addresses issues concerning the accounts receivable and collection functions. It does little good to generate sales only to sacrifice the profits to uncollectibles. In fact, it is extremely dangerous, because an illusion can easily be created in the financial statements. The income statement reflects the sales revenue and the profitability. The balance sheet reflects the current asset of the accounts receivable. Decisions are made for capital expenditures based on the financial health of the firm. Failure to collect can quickly cause a firm to run out of operating capital, which in turn can jeopardize the external and internal relationships that keep the firm in business.

The small business manager has many jobs, the synthesis of which would be putting in place systems that will allow the business to be successful. That process is never complete but is ongoing. Along with doing the things that make the business successful, the entrepreneur must also do the things that will protect the firm against major calamity, of which risk management is a major part.

• QUESTIONS FOR DISCUSSION · · · · · · · ·

1. How is management in small business different from management of a large corporation?
2. How is management of a small business similar to managing a large corporation?
3. During times of prosperity for the small business, identify and discuss the principles that should guide management.
4. During a period in which a business is experiencing a business downturn, what suggestions would you have for the business manager?

5. What are the major benefit programs offered under the Social Security Administration?

6. What is the likelihood that social security will still exist when you retire?

7. What are the main personality characteristics of a good leader?

8. Do you think good leadership qualities are important to the success of a small business? Define the qualities of a good leader.

9. What type of criteria should be established before extending credit?

10. What is the maximum penalty if your collection practices are deemed harassment or unfair by a state or federal court?

• BEYOND THE CLASSROOM: RECOMMENDED ACTIVITIES··········

1. Contact the local telephone company in your area and obtain a price list of what it would cost to have your business name listed in:
   (a) The white pages
   (b) A 2 in. by 2 in. ad in the Yellow Pages
   (c) A quarter-page ad in the Yellow Pages

2. Locate and obtain the names, addresses, and phone numbers of equipment rental companies in your area.
   (a) Obtain a price list from a local equipment rental company.
   (b) Price the daily rental rate of three pieces of equipment that you might use in your business.

3. Contact your nearest social security office and obtain form SSA-7004-SM-OP1, request for earnings and benefit estimate statement. Fill the form out and mail it to the SSA.

4. Contact the clerk of court in your county and obtain information concerning the cash limits and the procedures for initiating a small claims process.

5. Attend a small claims hearing.

6. Call or visit an insurance agency and ask the agent to discuss or demonstrate how a risk assessment is conducted.

12 Management Information Systems: The Other Information Girder

Chapter Objectives

- To provide a model of a management information system based on information needs.

- To demonstrate the importance associated with document design and to introduce document imaging and retrieval systems.

- To demonstrate the integration of control systems within the context of a management information system.

- To demonstrate the multifunctional scale of a management information system.

If you will note the placement of the management information system (MIS) within the bridge model, you will notice that it runs through the functional areas. The MIS function does so to signify the importance of information, and even at that, the model does not do MIS complete justice as to its importance. Success or failure depends as much on mastering a firm's information system as any part of the model.

I hope I have made the point that for a small business to succeed it must master the critical areas of production, accounting, finance, and marketing, and maintain the human relationships that make the organization operate successfully. It is the focus of the management information system, which provides the information necessary to make informed decisions, and provides guidance and direction for the firm to remain successful. Start making poor decisions, and regardless of how good the original business concept was, the firm's profitability will suffer and failure is almost imminent.

To appreciate the importance of a good management information system, it might again be helpful to look at the decision-making process. People in general, and managers in particular, base all their decisions on several variables. Decisions are in part a function of our personalities, which in turn are formed in part by our genetic makeup. I like to make the analogy of an electronic system. Our biological makeup is comparable to the internal circuitry of a computer. Based on that hard wiring we have certain capabilities and predispositions, which in turn influence how we perceive and interpret the information received. We cannot change that part of the decision-making process. A second element that makes up how we interpret information stems from the total of our experiences, which includes our education, work experience, family background, and so on—the socialization process, if you will. That part of us which represents the past also cannot be changed; we simply need to recognize how and what impact the past has on our current decision making.

A third critical element that influences current decision making is related directly to the situation at hand, which includes the emotions and feelings that go along with the immediacy of the situation. Decisions based on emotion are rarely correct; that is why many managers have learned to step back and give the situation some time to cool off before making a decision. If you want a bit of evidence concerning situational decision making, look at the cooling-off period which has been mandated by law surrounding major purchases such as real estate. In small business a manager makes lots of decisions, sometimes without the benefit of a cooling-off period, only to regret the decision made in haste because it was based almost solely on the moment or the situation. As a manager we can learn to protect ourselves from emotional decision making, but recognize that the current situation has a lot to do with decision making, as we are trying to perceive what the future will bring based on present-day variables.

The fourth element influencing decision making comes from the information we currently have on hand. It is this element that generally has the most weight in the decision-making process. It is therefore quite critical that we have valid, reliable, and timely information on which to base our decisions. As small business managers we are attempting to perceive what will happen in the future with present information, or we are attempting to respond to a current situation. If our perception and interpretation of information and events is correct, we stand a good chance of making the correct decision. If we misinterpret that information and continue to misinterpret subsequent information, the survival of the business will be in question.

As small business managers we have a degree of control over this information-gathering process. We decide what type of information to gather and how we gather it: in short, what is critical and what is not. The information we gather comes from within the organization itself: that is, internally. Information is often buried within the internal documents, paper and electronic transactions that occur as the daily process of conducting business marches on. It is up to the management information system to accumulate, access, and evaluate that information. Other aspects of the information system must come from external sources, which is also part of the responsibility of the small business manager, who must decide what type of external information is important and how that information should be gathered.

• THE INFORMATION-GATHERING PROCESS ·

A starting point is to determine what is critical. In my own experience and in dealing with other small business managers, it does not seem difficult to determine what is critical. Begin by identifying the key strategic success variables of the firm—why your customers use your product or service: in short, why your business is successful. That success will be a function of a few activities or variables. Those are the critical success variables. Those variables are what you as a manager will want to measure. It should also be what you base your reward systems on. It is sometimes more difficult to design an information system that will measure a particular variable than it is to identify the variable itself.

The opposite of the key strategic success variables is the identification of major threats. A vulnerability analysis is a process in which the manager identifies those elements that could cause the greatest harm to the enterprise. Once identified, an information system is designed to measure and monitor those variables that act as a threat. From that information the small business manager can begin to develop a contingency plan for the event, which will lessen the economic impact should the event occur. Again, the difficulty lies more with establishing a good source of information and information systems than with identifying the threats.

Information may be internal and external to the organization. That may mean that both internal and external sources of information may need to be compiled to gather the type of information required to make informed decisions. The management information system itself consists of all the information and information-gathering techniques used by a particular business. That information system is more than just a network of computer hardware and software, although computerization has become more and more a very integral part. The system of gathering raw data includes the types of paper invoices used to conduct business, as well as electronically based transaction information. Information is also verbal, and a system to document and collect information from employees and customers may need to be put into place. Information may be industry specific or it may be public information, such as that associated with a governmental policy. If something affects your business, and if that effect is significant, an information system may be a requirement.

Internally, each and every functional area of a business generates information and requires information to make decisions regarding that function. All businesses sell a product or a service or both. There are issues concerning, costs, unit costs, production capacity, utilization rates, scrap, constraints, slack, and a host of other issues concerning the production and delivery of that product and/or service. The following is a list of some of the questions you might want answers to within the production function:

- What is the total unit cost of your output?
- What is the cost of raw materials?
- What is the labor cost?
- What is the manufacturing overhead?
- What is the variance in tolerance of output?
- What is the efficiency of each machine?
- What is the efficiency of each operator?
- How much scrap or waste is created?
- How many items are returned due to malfunction or flaw?
- How do the material inputs differ in quality from supplier to supplier?
- How do the material inputs differ in price from supplier to supplier?
- What is the production capacity?
- What is the production capacity utilization?
- What are the constraints to capacity?
- What are the constraints to quality?
- What are the costs of additional units of the constraining variable?
- What are our slack variables?
- How much slack exists for each variable?

The answers to these types of questions or information requirements will ultimately lead to more questions, such as the following, which are information based but require human creativity and decision making to capitalize on:

- If we have slack variables, which are unused resources, how can we generate revenue from that slack?
- Should we buy replacement equipment, or lease equipment?
- Should we update any of our production equipment?
- Do we need to change suppliers?
- Do we need to change input materials?
- Do we need to train production personnel in any facet of the operation?
- Which employee or group of employees is most productive? Why?
- Which group of employees is least productive? Why?
- Should we increase our sales efforts to increase capacity utilization?
- Should we lower price to increase plant utilization?
- Should we raise prices because we are at capacity?
- Should we add capacity? If so, how?
- How do we increase quality?
- How do we increase productivity?
- How do we increase efficiency?
- How do we decrease scrap?

The above are but a sample of the types of questions that can be asked in the production function. The information requirements are going to be business and industry specific. The issues that Joe Hurly faces in the production of caramels is a lot different than the problems that Jan and Pat Garrity face in the raising of fruits, vegetables, and other products at their Prairie Gardens. What is important for the entrepreneur is to have a complete understanding of the business that they are in, which will enable the entrepreneur first, to ask the right question, and second, to figure out a method to access the information readily, that is, internally within the organization.

It should be somewhat self-evident that information relating to a particular function is not always stand-alone information. By that I mean that a bit of information which causes an improvement to be made in the quality or performance of a product will affect the other functional areas of the firm. Sales and customer satisfaction levels may well rise because of that improvement, which in turn will increase profitability and affect other financial ratios positively as well.

Much of the internal information generated within the functional areas can best be gathered, sorted, and accessed through electronic means. In fact, more and more businesses are information driven. That information would not and could not be assimilated without the use of technology. It would probably be a safe assumption to say that those who master the use of technology in the operation and management of their businesses will be those who survive. It should be fairly obvious that if you have the answers to production questions, you will make better decisions, which will allow your firm to be more productive, more profitable, and more competitive.

Other information is external. Earlier I emphasized the importance of some of that external information, such as information regarding customer awareness and levels of satisfaction are important to the marketing effort. So is information regarding those critical issues, such as why the customer uses your product or service—specifically what they like about your product or service. Just as important and more difficult to ascertain is why past customers no longer patronize your establishment and why they use your competitor. We already discussed the advantages associated with marketing research, which like MIS begins with internal information and expands to external or secondary information sources.

External information is most prevalent from a strategic management point of view and environmental scanning. External information systems are much more difficult to establish. It is not easy to find a reliable source of information concerning what your competition is doing or how changes in social attitudes will affect your business. It is also difficult to find reliable sources of information to track what changes in governmental policies will affect your business and how. Changes in the greater economic environment also affect us as individuals and affect most businesses. This type of information is external to the business itself and requires external information sources.

Example of Information Management

It may be helpful to attempt to develop an example of a management information system. As a model I will use a dairy farm: first, because I am familiar with this type of enterprise; second, because the information requirements are somewhat simple and somewhat limited; and finally, because this type of enterprise is primarily production based, a function we have thus far avoided in this book.

The information requirements of any business is first related to the key strategic success variables of the business. It is somewhat easy to identify what those success variables are if we first look at the revenue function of the business we are in. In the dairy industry, revenue follows the accounting definition: Revenue is equal to the number of units sold multiplied by the price per unit. In the dairy industry the unit sold is milk, which is sold by the pound or hundreds of pounds. The producer has virtually no control over price and a very limited choice over where the raw milk will be marketed unless the dairy producer is large enough to handle the processing and distribution function himself or herself.

Since dairy production does not normally deal directly with the marketing function, there is little concern for gathering market information except at the macro level: a perspective that would view what the trends are in the consumption and production of the milk product, and how these trends affect price. In the dairy industry, as in any business that concerns itself with the production of a commodity, whether agricultural or industrial, the functions under the control of the manager are limited. This is a critical assessment. As a small business manager, certain elements of your business are under your control, certain elements can be influenced, and certain elements are for the most part beyond the span of your control. Your time and financial and energy resources are best spent on those elements that can be controlled or influenced, but your information requirements should cover the entire realm.

The first variable to be measured and monitored in the dairy industry is the level of production, both as a total and on a per animal unit basis. For the manager to effect some control over the quantity of milk produced, it is essential to understand the factors affecting milk production or the functions of production.

It might be helpful at this point to provide a general background of the dairy industry. A dairy cow reaches maturity at around two years of age. A cow reaches production age and enters the producing herd after giving birth to a calf, which triggers the lactation or milking cycle. At the onset of lactation good dairy animals cannot eat enough forage and grain to maintain their body condition, due to the amount of milk they are producing. It is possible for these animals to produce as much as 100 pounds of milk in a single day, and in some cases even more, which translates to roughly 23 half-gallon cartons in the store. A mature cow is able to consume roughly 60 pounds of feed per day, although that could easily reach 80 pounds if corn silage or some other high-moisture feed is used in the ration. So feed intake will vary within a range, but there are limits to how much food a cow can ingest.

If one were to track a dairy cow's production on a curve, the curve would go up very rapidly, reach a peak, and then drop off gradually. A cow will normally remain in the milking herd for 9 or 10 months, at which time the animal will be taken off the lactation cycles through a process called drying up. During the dry phase the animal is usually given a rest period of about two months before beginning another cycle of calving and lactation. The dry rest period allows the cow to regain body condition and to recharge for the next lactation cycle.

What makes a good dairy cow is the animal's body efficiency, which allows it to convert the forage into milk while maintaining a degree of body condition. Body condition is important because the cow must be able to breed and conceive in order to produce the next calf while at or near the peak of the lactation cycle. If the animal cannot breed back, its lactation cycle becomes extended, which will lower its overall lifetime production. It may also lead to the animal being culled from the herd.

The better the animal's body efficiency, the better able it is to maintain a high level of production. A good production curve would be one that reaches a high level, stays high for a long time, and then drops off very slowly or drops somewhat and then levels off with a very slow decline. Good dairy cows will produce 20,000 pounds or more of milk in a lactation cycle, which is amazing since their body weight is something like 1300 pounds.

An animal's ability to produce milk is influenced and affected by a number of factors. Cows are very individual and exhibit individual characteristics and disposition. A dairy cow's ability to produce milk is influenced by its genetic makeup. Milk production is heavily influenced by the quality of the feed the animal is eating. The ration itself, especially the quantity of grain that the animal is eating, affects milk production. Grain normally is the more expensive part of the ration and normally is reduced as the production curve drops off. The animal's health affects its ability to produce milk as does the point on the lactation cycle. External factors such as weather affect the cow's ability to produce. For example, if the weather is too hot, the animals feel stress and are less likely to eat as much as when it is cool. If the weather is very cold, especially in the northern parts of the country, more energy is required to maintain their body heat, and thus milk production is reduced. Cold is generally not as detrimental to milk production as heat, because most modern dairy farms provide housing for their animals. Cold weather will, however, tend to have more of an impact on the animals' health. There are a few other minor factors affecting the milk production of dairy cattle, but for our purposes we have described the main variables.

As in any business, a clear understanding of the factors influencing the outcome of each function acts to identify what to measure. As in our example above, it is important for the dairy producer to be able to track the production curve of each cow in the herd. That means that information requirements include the daily milk production of each animal. Knowing what to measure leads to the next question, and that is how to measure a specific element. In the dairy industry individual production measurement can be done with a manual scale or electronically, but either method means isolating each animal's milk output. The information requirements must be balanced with the availability of technology, the cost of that technology, and the time and human energy required to acquire the information.

The measurement of milk production itself is the outcome or the result of the other factors of production: feed quality, quantity and ration mix, point on the lactation cycle, and genetic makeup. The management information requirements must provide the manager with the type of information required to make decisions. Thus the feed inputs need to be measured and evaluated. Modern technology allows for a computer worn around the animal's neck with a magnetic docking apparatus that allows each animal's feed input needs to be programmed into an automated feeding system. Individual records must be maintained on each animal as to how long into the lactation cycle each animal is. That means that records need to be maintained as to the date of calving. Since the birth of a calf triggers a new lactation cycle, physical pregnancy checks are made to verify whether or not a particular animal has been bred back. This type of information will support decision making as to which cows are to be culled from the herd and how many replacements will be needed.

The future genetic makeup of the dairy herd is dependent on the breeding program. Each animal can be evaluated as to a specific set of traits, and sires can be selected based on a similar set of traits, with the intended offspring hoped to be an improvement on the current generation. The use of artificial insemination has long been a commonly used technique to improve herd genetics.

A management information system begins with the design of all the systems of an enterprise. A dairy is primarily a system of production, and the information requirements stem primarily from that function. If marketing is also a major function, the information requirements of that function must also be incorporated into the information system. The manager must understand the costs and benefits of the capital inputs into any system being developed. The feasibility and profitability of the business must always be at the forefront of the decision making process.

Internal information in the dairy industry comes not just from the production function, but also from the accounting and financial functions. Needs requirements must be balanced with financial resources and profitability projections. Ratio analysis and return on capital must be incorporated into any analysis. In the dairy industry there are certain cost parameters. It takes a specific amount of land to produce the forage requirements of a dairy animal, so each farm will have a specific carrying capacity. To expand that capacity requires additional capital for land, buildings, equipment, and animals. Each dairy farm, given a specific carrying capacity, will have labor and equipment requirements or constraints. The higher the carrying capacity, the greater the labor requirements, which can be offset somewhat by capital expenditures for technologically advanced equipment.

Like other businesses, the size of the operation will dictate certain constraints and requirements. In the dairy industry there are certain variable costs, the main cost usually being feed inputs. If feed is purchased, it can easily cost 4 to 5 cents per pound. As I indicated earlier, a dairy cow can consume 60 to 80 pounds of feed per day; at 0.05 that is $3.00 per day, assuming the lower consumption figure. Add other variable costs and fixed costs such as equipment, buildings, labor, and capital, and the daily cost factor rises further. If, for instance, the total daily costs per animal unit in the lactating production phase is $5.00 and given an arbitrary income of 20,000 pounds/300 days = 66 pounds × 0.12 = $7.92 subtracting the $5.00 expense figure leaves $2.92 per day of profit per cow. On a dairy farm that maintains 60 cows in the lactating cycle, the calculation is: $2.92 × 60 × 365 = $63,948.

These figures are not meant to represent a detailed analysis, nor are they intended to represent any specific cost/revenue structure. The point rests with the process. Internal management information enables the manager to reduce costs and revenue to a daily, weekly, monthly, and annual basis. If the small business manager is going to make decisions regarding capital expenditures, cost and revenue projections need to be made. Each business has a different cost and revenue structure. Each business has a different set of production variables. Each business has different information requirements. It is the manager's job first to determine and understand what those information needs requirements are and then to design systems within the framework of constraints. The management information system is the part that ties the business together and supports the decision-making process with the right kind of information at the right time.

The following is a beginning of the list of internal information requirements for this example.

Aggregate production history

- What is the total annual production of this dairy farm? Graph that production on a monthly basis.
- What is the average monthly production?
- What is the daily average production?
- What is the herd average level of production? Graph that, and calculate percent and rate of change.
- What is the annual historical production of this dairy farm? Graph that history.
- What is the percentage change in historical production? Include the butterfat content of the milk along with the production calculations.
- What is the herd average bacteria count in the milk by month? By year?
- What is the herd average somatic cell count in the milk by month? By year?
- What is the herd cull rate in percentages by year?
- What is the cause of cull? State in numbers and in percentages from the following: mastitis; poor production; health reasons; breeding problems; other.

- What is the overall percentage of live births for the herd annually? Historically?
- What is the percentage of death loss after birth annually? Historically?
- What percentage of live births annually and historically, are female? Male?

Feed history

- How many tons of forage did this farm produce on an annual basis?
- What percentage of forage requirements was produced on the farm annually?
- What percentage of forage requirements was purchased off the farm annually?
- What percentage of grain requirements was produced on the farm annually?
- What percentage of grain requirements was purchased off the farm annually? Forage type? Quality? Protein content? Grain type? Quality? Protein content?
- How many tons of forage did this farm purchase annually? Monthly? Forage type? Quality? Protein content? Price? Grain type? Quality? Protein content? Price? Supplement type? Price? Mineral type? Price? Vitamin type? Price? Other? Price?

Animal history

- What was the date of birth or purchase? If purchased, what was the price?
- What was the birth weight?
- What is the genetic lineage: sire, dame, grand sires, grand dames?
- What is the calving history: date bred, sire, date of delivery, calf ID number?
- What is the health history: vaccination dates and types?
- What were the causes and costs of veterinarian calls?
- What were the date of death and cause, or cull date and cause? What was the cull price?
- What is each cow's production daily, monthly, annually, lifetime, and by lactation cycle?
- What is the butterfat content of each cow? Graph butterfat along with production.
- Graph each cow's production by lactation cycle, by month, and by day.
- What is the somatic cell count on each cow by lactation cycle and by month?

Milk price history

- What is the price history by year? By month? Graph that history.
- What is the butterfat premium history by year? By month?
- What are the discounts from the price, tracked on an annual basis, for the following: hauling; promotion; check off; other?

Equipment

- Model number? Serial number?
- Date of purchases? Dealer or seller? Cost?
- Warranty type and length? Warranty expiration date?

- Depreciation method? Depreciation basis?
- Maintenance record: list of information, such as types of oil and lubricants, filter numbers and types, spark plugs, belts, bearings, etc.
- Date of maintenance? Type of maintenance?
- Date of repair? Type of repair? Cost of repair?
- Date of sale or salvage? Price received?

Accounting Information

A detailed income and balance sheet needs to be prepared. From the income statement, both the income and sources of income should be identified and broken down into a percentage of contribution. It would also be helpful to know what historical rate of change is occurring in these income components. The same is true for the expense segments. Changes in financial position also need to be tracked, as would financial ratios and the change in the ratios.

I think you can begin to get the idea of how to build a management information system. The process begins with asking the right questions, which is nothing other than determining what it is that you need to know and prioritizing into what is most critical. I have no doubt that there are information gaps in the dairy farm example. Like any type of business, the information requirements change and evolve.

• DEVELOPING AN INFORMATION-GATHERING SYSTEM · · · · · · · · · · · · · · · ·

The good manager is always asking questions and looking for sources of information. The part of the management information system that is the most difficult stems from information the proprietor is unaware of. To state this another way: The most troubling aspect of a management information system stems from the question that was not asked. I have said before that business is sometimes very unforgiving. Ignorance provides no legitimate excuse in the profit and loss statement. Your business either survives by making a profit, or it goes broke for a lack of profit. Your management information system is an integral part of how you make those profits.

I think you can appreciate that as a business grows in size and complexity, the information requirements will seem to grow almost exponentially. In the dairy farm example, it would be feasible to meet most of the information requirements through a manual method, although it would be very cumbersome and time consuming. As a business's information requirements grow, it becomes almost mandatory that the proprietor seek help in the form of technologically based information equipment. Not unlike the accounting function, I think it is beneficial for an emerging small business to be able to change its information-gathering techniques and methods from a manual method to an electronic technologically based method. This may just be a generational bias, but I think one can avoid some costly mistakes if information equipment purchases are part of an evolutionary process. I should qualify that statement somewhat because there are situations where information needs are evident at the onset and technologically based information equipment should be designed right into the system from the onset.

It is doubtful that many of my readers will be entering the dairy industry, but I believe the example provides a clue as to the importance of understanding the information requirements of a specific business. If you were to act as a consultant to a new business startup, what degree of confidence do you think you would have in identifying the information needs of that client? The answer would depend greatly on the degree of experience you had in that particular business or industry. My point is again to emphasize the importance of having adequate experience in the business you are entering.

The starting point in setting up a management information system is to ask the right questions, which in turn depends on understanding the business, which in turn depends to a great extent on the right experience, including education and technical training. To take this line of thinking one step farther, suppose that you had the right experience and were acting as a consultant to a startup as to the design of their management information system. What degree of confidence would you have that your recommendations would be adequate to meet the information needs of this enterprise for the next three years? I believe the answer to that question hints at the types of demands a new business should make on the technological information equipment that is put in place.

Regardless of what the initial management information needs are for a business, it is almost a certainty that those needs will change. When the first personal computers (PCs) came out, they had 640K of memory. Users kept demanding more and more memory and more and more capability. In the same way, the small business manager will demand more and more information to support decision making. Information systems are almost certain to evolve with a business. That evolution will generally include issues such as capacity, capability, and speed. Information systems tend to evolve as well in complexity and cost.

Some basic questions to consider before putting management information equipment and systems in place are as follows:

- Can this system handle peak demand?
- What if we double the current demand; can the system handle that new information load?
- Is this system adaptable; that is, can we query for different information than we are currently asking for?
- Is this system upgradable? At what cost?
- What are the constraints of this system; that is, where is the first bottleneck likely to be?
- Can this system give us the information we need currently?
- How far into the future do you project the current system can take us?

I am not referring just to computer technology but to the entire management information system and the demands placed on that system by all functional areas of the business. In some instances evolution of the system will simply involve new external sources of information or a change in the way documents are designed.

In my own experience I discovered that invoice design was instrumental in the organization and retrieval of information. In visiting with other entrepreneurs there seems to be a general consensus that forms and paper invoices evolve continuously. Sometimes paper documents need to be simplified. In an interview with Tom Mahoney of a data and retrieval firm,[1] a comment was made that because graphics require more storage space and computer time, it is more cost-effective to simplify documents.

For many firms, business documents are the lifeblood of the management information system. Both paper and electronic documents can create a very complex web and a massive data storage and retrieval problem. For any business in which the database is large, stemming from a multitude of products, customers, clients, or transactions, and where an interrelationship exists between documents and customers, a real-time information requirement is created.

An example of such a complex system might be a large hospital or clinic where physicians need to access a client's medical file to check a medical history, previous test results, medications, or the like. That patient file needs to be an interactive part of a database to enhance customer service. Access to portions of a patient's file may be required by others in the organization, such as the pharmacy, business office, receptionist, nurse, and so on. The file may need to be archived due to a time lapse, or death of the patient, yet regulation and policy would make it mandatory that those records be accessible and retrievable, even though real-time accessibility would no longer be a requirement. Now suppose that this hospital has more than 8000 employees, a cumulative patient list in the hundreds of thousands, and a 100-year history. The information system requirements begin to get a little overwhelming.

Many small businesses have the same or similar information needs but on a smaller scale. Information to track inventory, sales history, client history, credit information, billing information, and so on, are all requirements of running an efficient and effective business. The more real-time capability that a business has, the faster and more accurate decisions can be made. Real-time point-of-sale product information and customer information can greatly enhance customer service.

As technology enables us to compile, sort, and access information more readily, the more information we seem to create and demand. For many organizations the bulk of paper files is becoming a very real cost. That cost has created a need for businesses that provide data storage and retrieval, beginning with document management. The first step obviously is to determine the various needs of the organization. Most firms will need to store archival information. A cost-effective approach to that problem begins with a document imaging system. Like every other facet of the technological revolution, document imaging or scanning equipment continues on an evolutionary course. Current technology uses scanning technology to take the document image and store it on a medium such as a CD or some type of magnetic disk or disk pack, which in turn can be accessed. This permits a massive economy of storage; a room full of file cabinets filled with paper documents can be reduced to a single drawer in a single file cabinet.

Depending on the system, the retrieval of mass information can be reduced from hours or minutes to seconds. The way in which document information is stored must be well thought out, because it will affect how the information can be retrieved, which in turn is influenced by the work flow that created the information. Most data imaging systems are highly flexible and can be highly customized. The information to be stored will be indexed. The business manager will need to determine how the information will be indexed, although multiple indexes can be used, which will help to query information later.

For a new business for which the costs to purchase document imaging, storage, and retrieval technology are prohibitive, but which still face the expenses associated with document storage, an outside firm can be hired to come into a business, scan their documents, create indexes, and store the documents on CDs. Although CDs are somewhat slower to access than other technologies, they are cheaper because the information can be accessed using existing PCs, which already have CD drives. The key to using this technology is to understand what your real needs are beforehand. One advantage of using an outside firm for document management purposes, at least initially, is that you also have access to the experience of the data storage staff. Setting up a good document storage and retrieval system the first time will prevent you from having to redo the system later. Your document storage and document management needs will undoubtably grow and evolve as your organization grows.

It may reach a point where these services will need to be internalized and the investment in equipment will be justified. With existing technology I use a figure of approximately $10,000 as a minimum of what it would cost to make the equipment purchase. Obviously, a wide price range exists depending on the needs of a particular business and the capability you want in your system. With firms available that can provide document storage services at a cost of less than what it would cost to buy filing cabinets to store the paper documents in, the decision to internalize the function is difficult. It will often be based on a need for increased capability, especially document interactive capability, rather than simply on the cost of the document storage and retrieval function.

As more forms and documents become part of an information database, there is increased use of bar codes. By including a bar code on a document, the document can be preconditioned to an indexing format. For example, if a sort by customer is important, customer identification can be coded on the document, or if document type is the sort query, a bar code can identify the document type. A real advantage of bar codes is the codes' ability to cut down on manual data-entry errors. A key advantage of using document imaging systems is that they are adaptable to changes in the documents and to the information needs of a firm. The greatest advantage, however, stems from the systems' ability to store enormous amounts of information. A normal-sized document will take up about 30,000 bits or 30K, so a single gigabyte of storage capacity will store thousands of documents.

I asked Tom Mahoney what recommendation he would make to a small business owner who came to him for advice and assistance. "The first step would be to ascertain the needs of the business. The second step would be to identify what the document load would be—how many documents the business produces in a year's time. The document load would determine what type of system package would be best to configure with that document load. A part of the systems package determination would consist of an analysis of what type of filing system currently exists and how the business is interacting with that system. This would be followed by a determination of what type of capability the firm would like. In one sense, if a current system is working for a business, why change it? If we can keep it the same, there is less of a learning curve for the customer. If we find inadequacies, we make recommendations for change. We follow with a proposal such as this hardware with this software will give you this capability. It depends on what the client wants."

I asked Mr. Mahoney what type of businesses their client list consists of now. He listed mostly document-intensive firms such as medical services, law offices, governmental entities, and the like. I asked about retail, to which he replied that few retail firms were using their services at this point. Document imaging technology is geared more strongly to the service industry.

Mr. Mahoney talked about the history of document imaging technology. He felt that changes in the software side of the technology seemed to be slowing a bit—that real change in the industry was driven by changes in hardware. He felt that on the hardware side, the product life cycle was as short as six months. Mr. Mahoney suggested that if you were buying state-of-the-art hardware, it might be best to wait a little while. By that he meant not to invest in cutting-edge technology because many new systems have a few glitches that need to be worked out. He felt that one would be better off to lag behind the technology curve a little bit, simply because it would be better to have an older system that worked well than a state-of-the-art system that still had a few bugs to be worked out. The rate of change in the hardware side is so fast that a firm will be on the cutting edge only a short while with current state-of-the-art equipment. A far better approach is to meet the information management needs of your firm with proven equipment. He felt that it was also important to stay with mainline manufacturers so that maintenance, parts, add-ons, and upgrades will be available down the road. The obvious conclusion, then, is that the lowest initial cost, may not always provide the greatest value, and in fact may not represent the lowest cost in the long run.[2]

With a service business the documents that represent customers and client files are the base of the management information system. With a retail establishment the baseline of the information system revolves around the product and service mix that is sold and the customers' level of acceptance of the same. Management information systems in such an establishment are geared to track the transactions that occur. It is important to answer all marketing function questions related to in Chapter 8: things like who is buying what, when, and in what quantities.

The heart of such a management information system will often center around a computerized cash register, which acts not only as a control system but also as an information system. To answer questions such as: Which product is selling best; worst? How many of those products are being sold will affect how many we should order and when we should order them. It will also provide information as to what the level of inventory should be. If we purchased 100 and we sold 90 but have only six left in inventory, what happened to the other four? Do we have theft or pilferage? Do we have items going out without being billed? Did the service department use inventory internally?

Good information systems help us refine our control systems. If we can isolate what or where our errors are occurring, we can fine-tune the system to reduce and eventually eliminate them. I once did an audit on a small businessperson who ran several beer-retailing establishments from the basement of his residence. He had all hired help. His realm of responsibility centered around management and accounting. This person told me that he was so confident in his control systems that when he hired personnel, he would dare them to steal from him.

What he did was to set up a system whereby he could isolate and monitor the activities of the businesses, particularly the employees. His management information system and controls began with an intimate understanding of the business. With a computerized cash register system, he knew which employee was keyed into the system on which day and at which times. He also knew how many kegs of beer were purchased in a week, month, and year. He knew how much inventory he had on hand and how many kegs had been consumed. By using constant-size glasses and pitchers, coupled with historical information, he knew how many ounces of beer had been consumed. His computer printouts would show this information to the hundredth of an ounce, and variances were tracked.

Detailed information like this has many applications. It provides a micro view of any shifts in market demand. This information system provided detailed information on what was sold and when, and who sold it. It provided costing information to the hundredth of a penny per transaction and in cumulative totals. It provided information for employee shift scheduling. It provided information on employee performance. For example, if total volume on a shift was $900, and Kay sold $700 worth of product and Bob sold $200 worth, who is doing all the work? Who is hustling and who is not? If the cash register checkouts are long or short, it can be traced to a specific shift, generally to a single person. If product shows up short, it will be noticed quickly.

A computerized cash register integrated into a management information system can be a very powerful tool. In all types of retail establishments, use of these types of systems is a critical component. Not unlike other applications of computer technology, the capability of computerized cash registers continues to evolve.

In the end, though, the design of any information system is hinged on the entrepreneur's understanding of what type of information he or she wants to get out of the system. It depends on identifying which information is most critical and how that information should be compiled, organized, sorted, and retrieved. Advances in technology expand and change how information is collected, sorted, and retrieved, but people must determine what is important and what is not. Human beings must also choose the systems and determine how the information technology will be integrated. The rate of change in technology does nothing to make that job easier; if nothing else, change has raised the level of importance of the management information function.

• QUESTIONS FOR DISCUSSION·········

1. Identify and explain the four primary elements influencing the decision-making process.
2. What should a good management information system attempt to measure?
3. In the text it was indicated that the paper documents, invoices, and the like tend to change and evolve over time. Explain why this happens.
4. When designing and developing a management information system, why is it important to have the right experience in that type of business?
5. Explain how a computerized cash register can be a part of the management information system.

• BEYOND THE CLASSROOM: RECOMMENDED ACTIVITIES··········

1. Contact a business office supply firm. Ask them to demonstrate the various types of electronic cash registers and explain their capabilities in providing management information.
2. Contact a business machine outlet and seek a demonstration of the following:
   (a) Computer hardware and software available for the small business
   (b) Document scanning and imaging equipment
   (c) Document storage and retrieval equipment

13 The Environment in Which We Operate

Chapter Objective

- To provide a broad and general perspective of some environmental implications for small businesses.

The economic environment in which we live has at least one constant element—change. The economic environment is a dynamic environment, but a number of forces are present that will continue to influence and shape the economic environment, not only on a local and national level but on a global level as well. One should realize, though, that the economic environment is only one part of the larger picture, which includes both governmental and societal forces, which in turn are acted upon by yet another multitude of forces.

Such issues as natural disasters, the ozone layer, the proliferation of nuclear weapons, and the increase in illegal drug use, to name just a few, all affect the world in which we live. Sometimes the lines between what is economic and what is political or what is the beginning of a change in society begins to blur a bit, because in reality they are interconnected.

For example, the global population has nearly doubled in the past 25 or 30 years, which results in greater and greater strain upon natural resources, particularly nonrenewable natural resources such as mineral deposits and petroleum-based products. As the global population uses up more and more of these resources, and as the rate of use increases as a result of increase in the global population base and the emergence of many third-world economies, the entire world is bound to experience at least spot shortages, which in turn could have a major economic impact. Many emerging nations require greater quantities of nonrenewable resources to continue to build their infrastructure and support their growing industrial base. In addition, developed nations such as the United States, which have used up great quantities of their natural resources, must cast a wider and wider net in search of the raw material inputs required to sustain our economy. We can no longer support our needs domestically; we must import. This was not nearly as true 50 years ago.

So must every other developed nation import raw materials or finished goods to support and sustain their economies. Access to critical raw material inputs has always been a major concern of nations, but today and into the future, maintaining adequate supplies of inputs will become increasing complex and difficult to maintain, which creates an ever-present possibility of spot shortages and price spikes, inflationary pressures, and the like.

Nations that are no longer self-sufficient in raw materials create a climate of international dependency, which in turn spurs a real need for international trade, which has grown dramatically over the last several decades and will continue to grow. Another contributing factor behind the increased international trade and commerce is that fact the our standard of living has improved, as has the standard of living of many other nations. The consuming public's tastes and ability to pay can and do demand such things as fresh fruit in January, and coffee and other products that are not grown or manufactured domestically. The marketplace thus far has provided those products.

This global situation creates just that: an ever-increasing global interdependence between nations. That international interdependence is but one of the underpinnings supporting a globalized economy. The stage has been set to force firms to go abroad to find the raw material inputs that make up one of the factors of production. It is a short step in logic for a firm to realize that if they must go abroad for any factor of production, they could just as easily go abroad for any or all of the factors of production. Within the context of a global economy, this has become a fact of life. Even for small business, an international capability exists not only to acquire products or inputs, but also to market on an international scale. The flip side of that coin is also true. Just as a small U.S. business has increased international capability, so can a foreign firm compete in our backyard. As they say at Chrysler Corporation, "The rules have changed."

The very crux of the issue, then, for big business and to somewhat a lesser degree for small business is that a firm's products and services must be globally competitive. For the small business owner globalization brings not only a broader market, but changes in the nature of competition. Small business owners must concern themselves with competition from abroad. Competition from big business has always been present, but major corporations have a distinct advantage in their capability to tap into the lower cost factors of production on a global scale. This requires the small business person to maintain a competitive position among a broader base of competitors.

A globalized economy could not have evolved to its current level based simply on the possibility of spot shortages of raw materials or other inputs alone. Globalization had to be supported by technological improvements in the fields of telecommunications, transportation, and computerization. In addition, the political and social climates had to evolve to facilitate a more interdependent world as well. Capital requirements for many new multinational firms took a quantum leap forward with the emergence of a global marketplace, which in turn required new and additional sources of capital. Global oligopolies are beginning to emerge as giant multinational firms battle it out in the marketplace for dominance in market share. Governmental regulation, both domestically and internationally, continues to evolve to adopt legislation dealing with the changes brought about by these forces which are driving the U.S. economy as well as that of other nations.

One particular bit of legislation that is of prime importance to the small business community is the level of funding for the SBA, which is a major source of capital for small startups. The Federal Reserve, which sets interest rates and monetary policy to control inflation, affects the economic environment as well.

Foreign exchange rates, availability of inputs, and access to markets all affect the greater economic environment. The structure of the economic system itself needs to be monitored. It seems that to be in business, one needs a license for everything. Industries and professions are busy protecting their turf, in part through a licensing process. Licensing does maintain a level of competence within industries and professions and does much to protect the public. Licensing also restricts access to the marketplace. For example, a city may allow only so many taxicab companies to be licensed to operate within a specific market. A more common example is the limitation on the number of liquor licenses a city will grant. Is this the sign of a mature economy, or is it a way to protect economic turf?

The economic environment that we live in seems in many ways to be less secure. It costs more and more to live, and it costs more and more to do business. The result is a fast-paced and complex society where things continue to become more complex, moving faster and faster and changing faster and faster, creating shorter and shorter product life cycles. All of this tends to create an economic climate where it is increasingly difficult for a small businessperson to maintain an economic balance.

To win in this type of environment means that a business must improve constantly, incorporating training to help in the search for better, cheaper, and faster ways of doing things. Access to the right information becomes a requirement that makes management more demanding and more difficult.

An armchair futuristic look at the economic environment begins with a prediction or an educated guess of where and what the economic future holds. It is my belief that we are headed for a world economy dominated by global oligopolies, huge multinational firms with hundreds of billions of dollars in financial resources and hundreds of billions of dollars in annual sales. They will dominate their respective industries with huge economies of scale in marketing capability. With their maturity they will refine their distribution systems to the point where their products can literally be purchased almost anywhere in the world and at almost any time. They will be formidable competitors with huge political clout and financial clout, enabling them to create barriers to entry that few will be able to penetrate.

Such is the scenario for traditional products and services. A case in point are the global soda wars. Pepsico and Coca-Cola are slugging it out both across U.S. air waves and around the world. Pepsico conceded in Venezuela but will win somewhere else. The battle for market share and bottlers to fill the distribution pipeline goes on and on, one nation and one market at a time. When this battle is over, there will be Coke and Pepsi—but how many others? Probably a few others at first, who in turn will be purchased until only two or three giants remain. Thus globalization will bring oligopolies. With current antitrust laws extending only to our borders, and with lucrative political coffers, there will be little incentive for government to push for global regulation to limit monopolistic powers. That may change in the future, but domestic authority has limitations in a global economy.

So will go the soft drink industry. One advantage for soft drink companies is that technological change does not affect their basic product. The changes in technology may change how they do business, but it doesn't change the basic formula. Carbonated water and caramel-flavored corn syrup remain the basic ingredients. It is a lot different than for a PC manufacturer, where the life of a memory chip may be as short as 18 months and survival depends on bringing the next generation to the marketplace in time. Yet even in the high-tech and biochemical industries, those who can dominate are those who have the financial resources available to pour into research and development. Those financial resources and their availability were addressed in Chapters 4 and 5. It is primarily major corporations that are capable of the majority of the initial public offerings, which utilize the new capital brought to Wall Street. The mechanism that brings in all that capital, currently about $1 billion every working day, is the pretax 401(k) plan. Once again, as the Chrysler ad says, "The rules have changed."

Major corporations are in a race to lock down market share by increasing production capacity to fill their new and growing distribution systems. It is a race because once globalization is essentially completed, there will probably be little change in market share between competing oligopolies. Change in market share from that point forward will come only through a slugfest in the marketplace, fought by traditional marketing means such as advertising, promotion, price, and place utilities, all of which are very expensive. Gains in market share will come either in that way or by buying out minor competitors. Once the globalized oligopoly dominance is complete, the barriers to entry will be overwhelming—and they are already substantial.

All nations are in this economic fray; in fact, many foreign-owned companies are already household names in the United States. The big economic winners will almost inevitably be the oligopolies and those who act as suppliers to these multinational firms.

To take yet another perspective, one more local in nature and typical of almost any U.S. city, it is my opinion that many of the changes that have occurred on the main streets of many of our cities have to do with the continual maturing of our economy. In the city where I live the grocery business is dominated by three major players and the gas station business is dominated by another three major players, corporations or individuals whose companies have been in the grocery or gas station business for a long time. As both the city and their asset base grew, they were able to meet the needs of the marketplace with another outlet, such as a convenience-type gas station. A major contributing factor is that the banking community is more likely to participate in financing growth in an existing, already proven firm than they would be in financing a competitor for an existing client. The same holds true for city hall. Local government is far more likely to grant a building permit, zoning variance, or beer and wine license to someone they already have a relationship with, or someone who has proven to be responsible. There is less risk for the municipality or financial institution in granting expansion capital or authority to an existing firm than in granting it to a new entrant. In addition, the existing firm has the advantage that the processes of licensing and expansion become smoother and easier the second time around. The end result is that often we see communities being dominated by their own mini-version of oligopoly-like competition.

From a financial perspective it takes more and more money to live and to operate a business. It only stands to reason that to be successful a business needs to grow. Standing still is a guarantee of gradual obsolescence, and sometimes a not-so-gradual shift to loss of profitability. Not that businesses cannot achieve a "right size," but generally, businesses must grow to remain successful. The gas station convenience store that remained on the corner, did not add a new outlet, and did not remodel will often reach a point at which they just seem to be hanging on. Almost every community has at least one business like that.

One conclusion that can be drawn is that to start up a new business, it will be increasingly difficult to compete with these oligopolies. Most traditional knowledge agrees with that statement. Yet we've been in this globalization process at least a decade already. One would think that such an environment would be very restrictive for a small business startup, yet the number of new business ventures is growing, not shrinking. Windows of opportunity are always created with change. It may be difficult for the small business to compete in many of the traditional products and/or services. For example, you will have a tough time starting a long-distance telephone company from scratch, but other opportunities abound. A technologically driven society creates opportunities where none existed before. For people who are computer literate and who have the ability to be on the cutting edge in software development and other applications, many opportunities exist. If we look back even five years and count the number of businesses that could not have existed earlier because the technology did not exist, it is astounding.

Small business has always lived between the cracks, so to speak: utilizing their very smallness and their ability to capitalize quickly on opportunity and adapt quickly to change. The economic environment is intricately tied to the technological environment. The future has always belonged to those who could anticipate and adapt to change, but the time frame has been compressed. In some respects, that compressed time element has made opportunity greater, but in other ways it has made it a more dangerous economic world. You can see some of the same effects in the workplace because big businesses are not immune to this economic environment, and many of their employees can feel the pressure.

Another realm of opportunity exists for small business in a mature economy dominated by oligopolies. Those opportunities are very traditional in nature and much as they have been since the advent of major corporations. For corporations it becomes almost mandatory that a market must have a certain size to be taken advantage of. Where a major corporation cannot take advantage of a market because it is too small or too specialized, the market is then left to the entrepreneur, who must find a new way to adapt products and services to meet the needs of that market niche. Adaptability and responsiveness are some of the things most closely related to small business.

In some ways, once the globalization process has become essentially complete, I predict that a degree of stabilization will occur in the marketplace. Technological change will probably still be the main driving force in the economy. We are all a part of his process, whether we run a small business or work for an oligopoly. Only time will tell whether my speculations are correct.

• GOVERNMENTAL IMPACT: THE LEGAL AND REGULATORY ENVIRONMENT······

Viewing government's impact begins with the perspective of governments acting as collectors of funds, which they collect from individuals and businesses alike. Currently, the federal government collects roughly $1.7 trillion annually. When all the state, city, and county taxes collected each year are added, government can be seen as a huge economic player in society.

Who these taxes are collected from and in what form have a tremendous impact on how citizens of the country and the states conduct their business. Tax legislation has as much to do with government's policy and agenda as it does with collecting revenue. If it were just a function of collecting revenue, a much simpler system could be devised. Tax legislation has more to do with encouraging the "right" type of capital investment to move the country's agenda forward. On occasion, tax legislation is passed to reward or pacify a constituent or group of constituents.

One example of tax legislation passed to move forward the country's political and economic agenda dealt with the oil embargo of the early 1970s. When the oil embargo hit the government responded with a multifaceted approach. The tax laws incorporated a tax credit and a preferential depreciation basis for energy-conserving investments. Depletion allowances for oil and mineral mining operations were incorporated and/or expanded in the tax code. By the early 1980s the oil embargo was a distant memory. The government then imposed a windfall profits tax, which hit many oil companies. At the same time, many state governments increased their oil and gas extraction taxes. The combination of the two did much to put the brakes on domestic oil exploration and was a contributing factor to the oil bust of the early 1980s.

Tax legislation can fan the flames of a particular industry or douse it with cold water. The most recent tax legislation to spur an agenda is the education tax credit and loosening of, and changes in, IRAs, geared specifically to help Americans pay for higher education. Why? Because the administration recognizes that for the United States to remain dominant militarily and economically and to maintain a high standard of living, we need to educate the populus. Is this a good thing or a bad thing? It depends on how you are affected individually and how it affects the nation in general.

The second part of the government's economic impact comes from how they disperse that $1.7 trillion or so that they collect. During the oil crisis in the early 1970s the federal government allocated several billion dollars to the Department of Energy to issue in the form of energy grants, money for research and development. A program was set up by the Department of Energy whereby citizens could apply for grant money. Someone with a concept of how to build or develop sources of alternative energy and or energy-conserving devices could be awarded funding to launch that concept. Many ideas were submitted, some bizarre, some not so bizarre. With some of those funds, Exxon worked on a project to extract oil from oil shale rock, and Tenneco and others funded a huge coal gasification plant in North Dakota.

In the same way, should the government recognize a military threat, they respond with a military buildup. Today the threat is not so much from a single source, but from any source, and the keys to military dominance are technology and high-tech weaponry. Congress and the Senate are currently debating funding a new generation of weaponry, in the form of state-of-the-art fighter aircraft, with a price tag of $200 billion plus. Who wins in an atmosphere of whims of governmental decision making? That depends. If your business is in the right economic sector at the right time, you and your business might win. For example, if you are in the road construction business and government decides that the nation needs more and/or better roads, and funds a program to repair and build those roads, business will be very brisk. But government can pull funding just as quickly. The flow of federal dollars into certain sectors of the economy is like standing at the ocean shoreline. The economic tide can sweep you up on shore or can pull you out to sea, depending on the direction of the tide. You can be helped or hindered economically in much the same way.

From the federal perspective, small business is most aided by the funding of the Small Business Administration. The SBA not only provides loan guarantees, without which many small entrepreneurs could never find the funding to launch their enterprises, but it also provides a lot of support services to the small business community. For the entrepreneur this is a critical piece of the economic pie.

In many communities local and state governments have taken a proactive position toward their economic future. Many communities have economic development foundations. In some instances communities are assisted by the governor's office of economic development in conjunction with federal help from the state's senators and or representatives to locate, aid, and support a corporate partnership in a community. Government is interested in protecting the local economic base with the support of corporations in the form of a plant in their backyard to ensure an employment base. Government expends funds in those efforts, not only in granting tax concessions but also in underwriting business in direct or indirect aid in one form or another.

Aside from the direct economic impact that governments have on business in general and small business in particular, probably the biggest impact that government has on business and how business is conducted stems from the regulatory arm of government at all levels. Many people feel that government impedes business and the free-enterprise spirit and infringes on our individual rights as citizens. Before we condemn government as having too much of a big brother perspective, it is helpful to stop and think about government's role in our economy and to look back at what has happened in our economy in the past. If big business decided to trample on the rights of their employees, competitors, community, and other stakeholders, who other than government could stop them? Who could muster the resources required to mount a legal challenge? If as an individual you are violated or harmed by a corporate giant, who can you run to for assistance if not the agency that regulates such activity? Generally speaking, each governmental agency was created as a response to a problem in that area.

The state insurance commissioner's office was created out of the need for a regulatory and oversight body to represent the millions of policyholders in the country. In the early years of the industry, policies were written with named perils only, so if your house was destroyed by a tornado and your policy covered fire only, you stood the loss. Some of these policies were sold by agents who were either ignorant or who mislead the client. In the end a regulatory body was required to standardize the contracts and to authorize the use of insurance contracts.

Governmental regulatory agencies are far from perfect and can be difficult to work with, comply with, and in some instances can be a real economic burden on a business, but who else has the ability to protect our air, water, soil, and standard of living? The regulatory function of government is not going to go away; if anything, it will continue to increase. An increasingly complex world and competition for resources will continue to strain issues between free enterprise and the interests of other stakeholders in our society.

One major impact that governmental regulation has on small business is to increase its complexity. The government's position remains that ignorance is no excuse when it comes to compliance with a regulatory branch of government. The small business person must first be aware of the governmental regulations under which they fall. The only insurance against noncompliance is to remain informed. Secondhand information does little good if it is wrong. It is always best to go to the source for information and assistance and to be some what proactive in seeking out information regarding your responsibilities as a businessperson.

Like the analogy of the economic tide of government, a regulatory tide exists as well. With passage of the Americans with Disabilities Act, some businesses were hurt while others were helped economically by the regulation. Such a regulation created an entire industry, the making and installation of wheelchair lifts. It enhanced business for elevator manufacturers and service firms. It provided opportunities for construction firms. On the other hand, if your business was forced to comply, which required renovation of an existing structure, an economic hardship could have been placed on your business. New standards in construction made some buildings obsolete because they did not comply to the new regulations. With each new regulation the complexity of being in business increases. Once you are in business a new regulation is just one more thing to comply with, but for the startup enterprise the culmination of past and present regulations may seem overwhelming. In my experience as a tax representative I have heard people say that they won't hire a new employee because of all the paperwork. Underlying that statement was frustration and exasperation with regulatory expense and red tape.

A new concept is evolving between business and government. More and more, a cooperative stance is assumed. In a global economy our government has a vested interest in supporting and helping U.S. industry compete. This filters down to the local level in the ability of a specific plant or a specific local business to remain healthy. Governmental assistance is increasingly available in the form of accessing markets and accessing information to support U.S. business.

Prior to globalization it was less critical to government who won or lost a particular market because both competitors tended to be domestic and in many cases local. Today, a lost market could well mean a lost market for a very long time, possibly forever, especially if that market is lost to a foreign competitor. It is not an anomaly that at the very time that U.S. business is showing record profits, Asian nations are feeling a real economic pinch. Governments around the world are attempting to support their national industries in a global economy.

If government is supporting business and if that support is important, it stands to reason that a business that can muster governmental support has an increased chance of survival. The implication becomes that business which has access to governmental support will ultimately have the best chance of survival: access to monetary support and access to information and other types of assistance, such as help getting through the regulatory maze, technological assistance, licensing authorization, and on and on. Government is a very active player in our economy.

Access to governmental support begins for many firms and for many organizations with the formation of a unified front—an organized lobbyist effort. The grease that oils the political machine is campaign money. A political action committee that is well financed contributes not only financial support to a variety of candidates but also contributes to the agenda the candidate will support. A strong voice in Washington can have an impact on how and what legislation is drafted. Such legislation can impede competition and/or enhance a firm's competitive advantage.

For the small business person, such access and such assistance from government is somewhat difficult. The ante has been raised, so to speak. The impact of such an environment is more restrictive to small business. By design it takes large capitalization to compete globally at the level that is of interest to big government. Fortunately for small business, the SBA was created. Small business has also banded together in the form of various national associations, such as the National Chamber of Commerce and others.

Concerning the issue of governmental access, the debate continues as to what constitutes legal and illegal campaign financing. The debate goes on as to how political candidates can and should raise money for election campaigns. The truth remains that political campaigns are expensive and continue to become more expensive. Money buys influence directly or indirectly. It could be argued that it also buys access to the political process. Rightly or wrongly, that is basically how the system works. As a small business person, one must operate within that environment.

Governmental support and access do not always mean that one must have access to government at the highest levels. For the small business person, governmental access can mean building a liaison network with governmental agencies at the lower levels. If nothing else, these people who work within governmental agencies can be dispensers of information within the context of that agency's function in society. Assistance and information can often be gained from the bottom up. All governmental agencies are bureaucratic in nature in the sense that they are governed by regulation and policy that has evolved over the years. It often takes the personal involvement of someone inside the system to move a process through the system—in short, to access the resources of a particular agency.

Access to local and state government is generally much easier to obtain than access to central government. One can drive to the state capital or call a department. Generally, the red tape and bureaucracy is much less in state and city government than in the federal government. A personal relationship with people inside agencies that are most critical to your business can do a lot to facilitate access to those agencies' programs and resources. If such an approach is not feasible, most agencies will put on training seminars for the public. Many are sponsored by the local chamber of commerce, or contact the agency directly to obtain a list of public forums. The Internet is becoming a real resource tool to access information from agencies as well.

• THE SOCIAL AND CULTURAL ENVIRONMENT · · · · · · · · · · · · · · · · · ·

Social and cultural changes are what marketers and marketing research firms attempt to monitor and anticipate, in an attempt to identify the likes and dislikes, the needs and wants, of the consuming public. The marketing research firm can hope to anticipate the needs of the marketplace and have a product in place as the need for that product emerges. The essence of the marketing concept is a proactive response to the sociocultural forces in our society.

Demographically, many changes are occurring that will certainly affect the marketplace. The better your information, the more able the small business person is to meet emerging demand. Being ahead of the curve is becoming more important due to the increased cost of doing business. Anticipating is much better than guessing. The importance of good marketing information is growing.

As we look back and then look ahead, the basic needs of humankind have not changed, but the technological advances in our society have changed the product and service mix drastically. Still we all need food, shelter, and clothing, but how we get those necessities and define those necessities has changed dramatically. It should also be noted that just identifying societal shifts in attitudes is only the starting point; capitalizing on those shifts in attitude is more difficult.

This book is not designed to identify those changes in our society and our culture but to emphasize the importance of recognizing how cultural shifts affect the marketplace and to impress on you the far-reaching consequences. For example, let's consider for a moment the changes that affect our food supply: what we eat and how we obtain what we eat. In the early days of this nation we were primarily an agrarian society. The vast majority of the nation's population was involved directly in raising the agricultural produce that we required to meet our basic necessities. The industrial revolution, with the mechanization that followed, required fewer and fewer people to be involved directly in raising those agricultural products. The current system is able to raise more food, of better quality, with only a fraction of the personnel, due to increases in genetics and other technological improvements. The downsizing in agriculture has continued through the emergence of a service economy and into the information age. The mechanization process that began with the industrial revolution has not stopped; it has continued to evolve, in many ways facilitating and supporting the service and information age which is evolving at the same time. A modern combine can harvest in one day the amount of grain that required a season to harvest in the early days of the industrial age.

The result is that fewer people in our society are directly involved in agriculture. Today, the farm population is a little over 1 million—a change from farm life as a way of life to agribusiness, very capital intensive, supported by technology and chemicals. Our food supply used to be raised by a large number of people on a small scale but is now raised by a few people on a very large scale. The process used to be somewhat organic, but it has become very chemical intensive. The implications are many. Many rural communities, particularly in the midwest, are experiencing population drains. The small towns and rural communities are dying because the population and economic base to support them is drying up. On the other end of the spectrum, our nation's cities continue to grow, some at an unprecedented pace.

The intensity of agriculture makes the process very strange and foreign to the mass of our population base. The intensity of agriculture also has a huge impact on our ecology. Chemical-based fertilizers, herbicides, and pesticides, which keep a monolithic crop weed- and pest-free to increase yield, do not always do good things for water quality. That process, which is matched with concentrated livestock raising, which results in tremendous amounts of animal waste, has begun to raise huge environmental questions regarding air and water quality. Agricultural interests are beginning to bump heads with urban interests, environmental groups, and others. Increased governmental involvement and restrictions concerning licensing, zoning, and building permits are sure to follow.

In many respects industrialized agriculture has helped to sustain a higher standard of living. At the same time, the nation's land resources are forced to produce more and more to support a growing population base while that population base is demanding a more diversified diet. Improvements in transportation, communication, and packaging have all helped supply the food chain with a larger variety of products. International trade has supported this trend. Today, we have gourmet coffee beans in the grocery store and exotic fruits that many of us cannot even pronounce, let alone know how to use. Still an undercurrent of concern remains. *E. coli* bacteria outbreaks and other incidents highlight the concern for food safety.

So what does any of this have to do with running a small business? Actually, a lot. Shifts in this segment of society continue to create opportunities. For instance, there is something very basic about owning a small piece of the earth to call home. The dream of homeownership for most people is not just a dwelling. For many people, home includes a lawn and a yard. After working in a high-stress, technological environment for a week, many find comfort in the simplicity of garden work and seek the quiet and seclusion of a home and yard. The lawn care industry is huge. For some, lawn care is a service to be sourced out. There is also a slow but growing trend toward people who recognize that chemically treated, chemically fertilized, manicured lawns are not the best thing for the environment, and are shifting to lawns that consist of natural grasses and natural flowers. A business opportunity exists to educate and assist people in that direction.

There is also something very basic about working in the soil. For many people that desire is translated into various types of gardening. Many people take pride in raising flowers and/or vegetables. Some resort to raising vegetables in part out of concern for the quality of our food supply; for others it is out of a sense of enjoyment. Others prefer raising flowers rather than vegetables, because in part it can be done on a smaller scale, but also because raising food is not always economical and is time consuming. Business opportunities exist in the landscaping and horticulture business. Retail, wholesale, and service businesses exist in this sector already, but different trends continue to emerge.

If you recall the discussion on Prairie Gardens, success did not come until Jan and Pat Garrity realized that rather than attempting to pursue the mass production mode of commercial agriculture, they should sell the farm experience. They recognized the shifts that had occurred in our society, realizing that picking fruits and vegetables in a relaxed atmosphere, and enjoying the outdoors on a quiet family outing, were things to market. The you-pick-it experience provided a value above and beyond the value of the produce itself.[1]

The Garritys are not alone in recognizing this shift in society. Popularity continues to grow all around the country for the you-pick-it concept. Farmers markets continue to gain in popularity, and food cooperatives are starting to emerge. This concept partners the urban with the rural in a food-producing endeavor. There may be several hundred urban people who pay a fee to a grower who has land and equipment, but the work is a joint effort. The grower guarantees a certain number of pounds of produce to each partner in return for their investment and effort. New concepts will continue to emerge in this sector, but all are driven fundamentally by shifts in our society.

Major change in our culture was started initially by the industrial revolution, but change has been accelerated by the information/computer age. It is my belief that the most far-reaching effect was a shift from generalization to specialization and the loss of traditional knowledge, which were exacerbated by the breakup of the extended family due to societal mobility. This results in continuous changes in society, which in turn creates new opportunities.

Let me attempt to explain it this way. Prior to the industrial revolution and the information age, life was fairly stable. The skills that a child would need to survive as an adult were taught to the child by the family and the extended family. Formal education was restricted mainly to the three R's. The real skills, which were mostly trade in nature, were taught primarily through an apprenticeship in a family setting. Thus a shoemaker would teach his son to be a shoemaker, and so on. Girls were taught the art of baking, cooking, canning, sewing, and a host of other gender-related tasks, to prepare them for roles as wives and homemakers. The emphasis was on hands-on skills. Most people had a broad general aptitude for those types of things; if they needed to build or repair something, they did it themselves. Much of the need to do it yourself was economically based. For someone to hire someone, say for the laundry, would be considered wasteful, or only for the wealthy.

The industrial revolution called for a new set of skills. A society based on mechanization and mass production required professional management. The demands of an industrialized society required more emphasis on formal education. If the shoemaker's son went to work at the factory as an accountant, the skills learned in the shoemaking business had little value. It was training and skills as an accountant that enabled the shoemaker's son to keep his job, which supported his family. The shoemaker's son retained most of the apprentice-type traditional knowledge that his father taught him but did not pass it on to *his* son. The shoemaker's son realized that for his son to make a living in this new society he would need a good formal education, and so would his daughter.

When the shoemaker's grandchildren reach adulthood to start their own lives, which often involved a professional career, traditional knowledge was, for the most part, gone. In our society that would be the baby-boomer generation, and for their children, many of whom are now starting out on their own, traditional knowledge is often just something to read about in a book.

A member of the baby-boomer generation, I can remember both my grandfathers. Neither had much formal education, something like the third grade, but I wish I had their skills. Both were farmers, but my mother's father especially was a skilled craftsman. He also made the best sausage I ever tasted. My point is that some of those general skills have now become specialized skills and are quite valuable. For example, a few generations ago many people knew how to shoe a horse. My grandfather had a blacksmith shop on the farm primarily for that purpose. There are still millions of horses in the United States. Many need to have horseshoes, but very few people know how to shoe a horse, so horseshoeing has become a service based on a traditional knowledge. Much like antiques, one can search the hollows of your family traditions in search of a bit of traditional knowledge that can be launched into an enterprise.

If we are looking at what was lost, it is only fair to look at what we have gained. The industrial revolution and the information age have created a society whose citizens are the most educated in the history of the nation and of the world. People today also possess a very broad range of skills and knowledge. The information age in particular has created a very fast-paced, intense environment. The workplace has become both gender diverse and culturally diverse. Competition is global, and profit is a necessity to remain competitive. In most respects we live in a high-stress, high-pressured society. There is no going back, only forward. This is the time in which we live, and the world in which we live.

Our needs are different than they were in previous generations, and those needs continue to evolve. Previous generations may have been a hands-on do-it-yourself group. Today, most people not only lack the know-how but also the proper equipment and the time to do most major projects. In our modern society time is money. That is why business is capital intensive; it is difficult for the individual to justify major investment in tools and equipment for an occasional need. The option of doing things manually is often closed just due to time constraints. A Saturday on the roof with a hammer and nail pouch will not shingle a roof. The combination of these factors and others has ushered in a growing service sector in our economy and in our society.

Complexity is another hallmark of our modern society. It is no small matter to tinker on a vehicle, other than some routine maintenance. In past generations the backyard mechanic would putter and fix a vehicle that was strictly mechanical. Today, even the shade-tree mechanic often admits that he takes his car in for service and repair. The modern vehicle is engineered to be more sophisticated and is becoming more and more electronically based, calling for computerized diagnostic equipment. Customers demand more of their vehicles, and the customer base is becoming farther and farther removed from possessing a technical understanding of how the equipment works. Customers expect their cars to run when they jump in to fight the freeway; thus manufacturers race to build stylish, fuel-efficient, environmentally friendly, safe, comfortable, and maintenance-free automobiles. Many vehicle price tags reflect the sophistication of the product.

The dual-income family has put some stress into modern society that grandpa never knew. It is difficult to juggle two careers, which calls for some middle ground in residence location. It also requires two automobiles. Day care is of critical importance for families with small children. Logistical problems exist for those with older children, and the phenomenon of latchkey kids raises all kinds of concerns and special problems. Parents look for supervision controls and mechanisms. Parents need quick, convenient meals and snacks. Restaurant chains such as Boston Market cater to the need to take home carryout dinners.

As life continues to become more fast paced, and as certain segments of society become more and more affluent, the range of products and personal services will continue to expand. Personal shoppers, maid services, nanny services, and lawn services are just a few. The downside of the convenience of those increased personal services is that the ante has been raised. It costs more and more to live because of all the electronic niceties and personal services that make life so comfortable, which in turn makes us run faster and faster to make more and more money. Our society and our culture pays a price, and a trade-off exists for our modern way of life which leads to another trend of our times. Some people are beginning to say no. They are rejecting the faster pace and in some cases are turning down promotion and transfer, and/or are stepping down in the organization or even quitting, for a slower life. For some the personal price has gotten too high, and they are willing to do with less to preserve some of what was traditional family life.

Demographic indicators hint at a future with labor shortages, especially if U.S. companies continue to win in global competition. Already many sectors of the economy want more overtime from existing employees. It is almost a contradiction; first they have a downsizing blitz, then a labor shortage.

Employees are expensive; the training curve is sometimes long. It is beneficial for firms to run lean, but they still need the flexibility to expand quickly and the option to contract quickly as well. This opens the door for productive employees who wish to take a reduced role to fill some of those gaps. Rather than leave a firm completely, more opportunities are being created to participate by telecommuting, on a contractual basis, or through flex time.

Issues and trends like these in our society create demands for different products and services. For the person with information and foresight, the next step is to capitalize on that shift in society.

• TECHNOLOGY · · · · · · · · · · · · · · · · · ·

Of all the forces that operate in the greater environment of small business, or for that matter all business, the most powerful force seems to be technology. Those who understand and can master the use of the rapidly changing technology have a distinct advantage over those who cannot. Technology creates a realm of opportunity and threat simultaneously. To lag behind technological innovations for too long can render a business obsolete and uncompetitive. Such obsolescence can create a drain on profits, which if allowed to go on too long makes it difficult to raise the needed capital to reinvest to regain competitiveness.

Another way to view the dynamics of technology as it affects a business, particularly a business whose products or services are technology based is to view the cash inflow generated by the sale of the product/service mix as a representation of not of money alone but also of time—time as a segment of the product life cycle. If your product/service mix is acceptable to your customers given a technological environment, but then the environment changes, all you have left is the revenue generated in the past to buy time for your organization to adapt to the new environment with a new product/service mix. If you fail to have the right product/service mix in the developmental pipeline to smooth out this process, revenue inflow will be more chaotic. In the chaotic environment described, one product or service miss could destroy the firm economically. Obviously, not every firm is that dependent or susceptible to changes in technology.

Change and the rapidity with which change occurs have raised the bar, so to speak. Technology has changed the cost structure of an organization. For many firms investment in new technology is leading capital expenditure, exacerbated by the fact that the product life cycle is so short on technological products, requiring reinvestment to stay current. Technology has created recurring expenses that were not even present a decade ago. Cellular phone service, Internet access charges, and other technology-based products and services have raised the cost of doing business, which in turn requires that firms be more efficient and/or do more business to offset the increased costs, and this cycle is repeated over and over in the marketplace.

The increased use and application of technology can create a dilemma for the startup enterprise. With the use of technology as a requirement to do business, and with the cost associated with that technology, the new enterprise must enter the market at a higher level to survive. It only stands to reason that if the cost of doing business has risen, the introductory phase for the new enterprise has been shortened. At one time it was acceptable to operate a small business at a loss for the first few years before really getting it off the ground and showing a profit. The introduction of technology has done much to take that luxury away, or at least shorten the time horizon.

On the other side of the coin, technology has created some very real opportunities for those who have a grasp of how to gain an advantage with its use. For others, the fact that they are entering the marketplace with a new capital investment provides them with an opportunity to begin with the current technology, which may be something their competition cannot readily afford; thus they begin with a competitive advantage based on technology.

Arguably, the single most powerful force driving business today is the change that is occurring in technology and the pace of that change. It creates whole new realms of opportunity while making obsolete old ways of doing business. To further demonstrate the effects of technology, it might be helpful to take a more micro approach, as in how technology affects a specific business or industry.

First take the travel agency business. What defines that industry is the ability to put together a network and access information: information concerning flight departure times and arrivals, and the ability to compare ticket prices between competing carriers. The service traditionally provided was to plan a trip for a client by providing access to the information and then making recommendations as to which carrier could accommodate a client for the best possible price. The travel agency service would also coordinate vehicle transportation as well as hotel accommodations. Through the change in technology, most of the traditional customers can now do all that on the Internet. A change in technology that makes information available to everyone can alter permanently how business is done. An executive secretary can now perform many of those services on-line, reducing the need for the traditional travel agency.

The survival of the travel agency business depends on not doing business as usual. The window of opportunity will close as the masses of people discover access to on-line travel information which used to be the exclusive realm of the travel agent. As the public becomes comfortable with the use of that information, the traditional customer base of the travel agency could erode. Travel agencies will have to scramble to provide value-added services and or to renegotiate with carriers so that certain ticket discounts are available exclusively through their network of agencies.

Another example is in the brokerage industry. The Internet has made available information such as real-time quotes, which were once the sole domain of a networked broker available to the public. It is a short step to opening an account with a discount brokerage firm and simply entering buy and sell orders on-line at a fraction of the cost. What, then, do full-service brokers do? They must scramble to provide a value-added service to those customers who are not computer literate, but like the travel agent's clientele, those numbers are rapidly becoming a vanishing breed.

The full-service broker must concentrate on performing and providing more research and other types of services. The game has changed and will continue to change as technology continues to move us into the information age. Or full-service brokers could respond by moving into the turf of the discount broker, by adding those types of services.

It becomes increasingly difficult for the small business owner to stay on top of changes in technology. Even with effort, most managers are lagging behind on the technological curve. It creates other dilemmas as well, the most significant being the impact on the decision time horizon, which is constantly shrinking. The need for current information and technologically current equipment drives the capital budgets of many organizations. The time frame in which that investment keeps the organization in the mainstream and ahead of obsolescence is relatively short.

Technology is multifaceted. We are not just talking about computers and computer software and systems when we talk about increases in technology. We must include the continual improvement brought on by the industrial revolution: new and better machines, which often are made better by the computer and information revolution. We must include advances in communication and bioscience, as well as advances in every other facet of our environment.

For most businesses to remain consistently profitable depends on a willingness to adapt to the use of new technologies. Ignoring technological advances will render you uncompetitive, not because your cost structure has changed, but because that of your competitors has. What technology should do is raise your productivity, thus lowering your per unit costs. Technology allows people using equipment or software to produce better output more efficiently.

Let me explain this concept more fully with a personal example. When I returned to graduate school I had a wife and two children, with a third child on the way. Supporting a family and going to school full time turned out to be a lot more expensive than I had originally thought. One day as I was driving down the highway, the local livestock sales barn was on the air to liquidate a herd of dairy cows.

Having grown up with beef and dairy livestock, I recognized that these cattle were selling for a very low price. At the time I happened to own a small farm with a set of old buildings which we had purchased as an investment. I convinced my wife that this would be an opportunity to profit on undervalued assets as well as a good part-time job. A week or so later, another dairy liquidation sale occurred. I purchased a semiload of dairy cows, all which were two or three months away from having calves, which would trigger the milking cycle for those dairy animals.

The plan was to gain a competitive advantage by using virtually no debt, by entering with a very low cost structure, to be more labor intensive and less capital intensive. New buildings and new dairy equipment are very expensive. I renovated some very old buildings and purchased equipment that was commonplace 20 and 30 years earlier. This type of equipment could be purchased for almost nothing. In fact, my total equipment and renovation expenditures amounted to less than $5000.

The reality of entering any type of business is that the asset base, particularly the income-generating assets, which could be viewed as a technological variable, tends to lock your enterprise into a certain revenue and cost structure, at least temporarily. That is, a set of physical assets has the capability of producing only so much income while incurring a fairly definable amount of expense. New investment in new technology can shift and change that cost structure, generally lowering the cost structure.

Another way of looking at technology is from the perspective of the financial demands placed on capital investment. That investment must return the original cost and show a profit. Profits are generated by producing more revenue than expense. One of the biggest dilemmas associated with using obsolete equipment in a small business is that the profit generated often is not large enough to meet expenses and make a living. It is the increase in productivity gained from new technology that allow us to maintain and increase our standard of living. If inflation were just 4 percent, the cost of living will increase by a factor of nearly 2.2 times in just 20 years and over 3.2 times in 30 years. That was the situation I was in with my dairy enterprise. I had to be roughly $2\frac{1}{2}$ times more productive than my father's generation just to make a living. In the dairy industry, as in many other industries, the gains in productivity were not just mechanical. Better genetics had increased dairy animals' production capability. So had advances in understanding nutrition. Those types of advantages could help offset the mechanical disadvantages. Still if one were to remain successful in the dairy industry, capital investment in buildings and equipment would be a necessity, which in turn would require even more production through an increase in the number of dairy animals to offset the increased costs of plant and equipment. More dairy animals would increase the need for land and/or feed, which puts more demands on cash flow. Each increase in technology forces an increase in the overall output, which usually means an increase in size. It is easy to see why the agricultural population has decreased over the years as acreage sizes of farms are forced to increase. Most industries are faced with similar circumstances.

If you accept the implications of technology, it would seem logical that some type of planning process should be in place to analyze the technological needs of your business. If a need exists, a plan to raise the capital needs to be incorporated. In part, new technology may reduce certain expense costs, which can help offset some of the capital costs.

Productivity gains through the use of new technology does not occur automatically through the acquisition of new equipment or the implementation of new processes and procedures. Productivity increases are achieved through human interaction with those new technologies. Your technological plan will need to address how personnel gain proficiency with new technology. New technology is often very expensive; sometimes it is necessary, and other times an investment in personnel training can create gains out of the old equipment. Similarly, implementing better systems can create huge gains. It is not always just the equipment but the system in which people interact with equipment. Sometimes modifications of existing equipment can upgrade its capabilities to near the level of current technology. This is especially true with computers and software. A faster modem, a memory upgrade, or a new version of a software package can create new capabilities from an older machine.

Technological improvements can come from the outside, while for some firms, technological development is their product development. Whatever the source, the entrepreneur must be wary that he or she does not rush headlong to embrace a technological solution to remedy a systems problem. The technology that is purchased should be truly needed and bring with it a benefit that outweighs the cost. On the other hand, the entrepreneurs dare not bury their heads in the sand and deny the advances and advantages that technology brings, or they risk falling so far behind that they lose their ability to compete.

One thing that is certain about the technological environment—the difficulty with perceiving what direction it will take. If we look back and compare the types of business opportunities and jobs that exist today with those of just 10 years ago, it is amazing how much things have changed. If we then project 10 or more years into the future, it is difficult to imagine what things will be like. The change is partly driven by product and technological improvements. Those things we can project somewhat. Issues such as the geometric growth of the Internet will continue to affect the way we conduct business. As small business owners we can ride the wave and utilize the technology for information and marketing. The technological innovations that are difficult to project are the ones that have not yet been realized. Innovative breakthroughs in any field of science can render products and markets obsolete.

How does one defend against the adverse impact of technological change? In part, a firm can try to stay on the cutting edge of technology. In marketing there is a concept that views acceptance of a new product by placing people on a continuum, from the innovator and early adapter to the laggard on the other end. To remain healthy, most small business owners need to be somewhat on the innovator end of the continuum. Most small business owners are not involved in the development of new technologies, but they can be early users of technology. An attitude of openness and adaptability instead of resistance can do much to ease the transition—an open system of management where everyone in the organization shares information. A system in which management listens and is willing to learn from subordinates creates an organization more able to adapt to a changing environment.

Another area in which small business owners can help protect themselves against the adverse affects of technological change is to stay informed. To the best of their ability, entrepreneurs can establish information systems that will track changes in critical technological areas. A network of information that includes suppliers can help tip you to impending changes coming down the road. Often, a cut in price of an input can tip you that a newer version is just around the corner, because the supplier wants to run out of the old before they introduce the new. A price cut in input costs is generally a good thing as long as it does not deteriorate your competitive position.

If yours is a business that is easily affected by a particular technology, especially if that technology is changing rapidly, it might warrant a shorter product life cycle for capital expenditures. If, for example, a software package is a critical component in your operation, capitalizing that software over 18 months instead of three years may make sense. The cost is increased within that time frame, but there may be a greater cost associated with not upgrading. Awareness, adaptability, and information are some of the keys to survival in a changing technological environment.

• COMPETITION· ·

In operating a small business it goes without saying that one needs to monitor the competition in several broad areas. Within the context of every market, the competitors carve a market share out of the whole. Who gets what share depends on a number of factors, including capacity; the firm's distribution system, including the number and type of outlets; the extent and quality of advertising and promotion; the firm's product and service mix; and the quality, reputation, and image the firm has. Other factors may also come into play, but within each market the players divide up the existing market. The total market may expand with increased competition and with a total increased product availability, but generally for one firm to increase its sales revenue, those increases must come either from an expanding total market or from an increase in market share.

It is for those reasons that it is a good idea to stay on top of what the competition is doing. As a manager you want to know who is winning in your market and why, and who is losing market share in your market and why. It is also helpful to know and understand your competitors' cost structure and how it compares to yours. Answers to these types of questions can help determine what your position is in the marketplace and what your advantages are over your strongest competitors.

We looked at competition earlier but now revisit the subject from a more strategic point of view. Major corporations enter a market attempting to gain an advantage through economies of scale and access to distribution channels. To some extent the major firms are concerned with product differentiation, especially when they do not dominate the market. Other forces are at play as well, but our concern here is how the small proprietor can scan the competitive horizon and react to the forces of competition. Conventional wisdom suggests that head-to-head competition with major corporations is best avoided.

I suggested earlier that the best approach to competition was grounded in a differentiation strategy, preferably one based on quality of product and service. The bridge model of this book was designed to stress the importance of internal and external relationships, none more important than the relationship that a small business has with its customer base; building customer loyalty through quality service, quality products, and personal relationships. If that is the accepted and implemented strategy on which an entrepreneur bases the success of a business, the critical element in measuring success relates to measuring how well those objectives are being met. From an external environment perspective, it is also critical how well the competition is meeting the same criteria. In other words, how well is the differentiation strategy working? Does the customer perceive the firm's products and service quality in the same light? To monitor those variables is a key element of measuring the impact of competition.

It is one thing to identify your local competitors, but to understand and monitor the competition entails understanding their success strategies: how they differentiate and what their marketing strategy is, especially the quality of their product and service mix. The small business owner must be concerned about a number of forms of competition, even with a differentiation strategy, first the competition stemming from major corporations. Should they attempt to move onto your turf, your business will be affected. Monitoring their product and service mix and attention to their advertising campaigns can provide strong evidence of their marketing strategy. Often the most dangerous threat from major competitors stems from a marketing strategy where they offer your product or service as a loss leader, or add it as a peripheral segment to their marketing mix. For example, when the grocery industry began offering deli services which often included dine-in, carryout, and catering service, many small proprietors gained a formidable competitor. A somewhat similar situation occurred in the video rental business, which experienced a proliferation of competition from large and small businesses alike: grocery and discount stores, gas stations and movie theaters, all trying to expand their product mix with the same added service.

The second major area of competition that the entrepreneur faces comes from other small firms. Most small businesses possess similar competitive advantages. They tend to specialize in a particular product and/or service. They tend to key on a particular advantage or two, such as location, personal service, quality of product, or cost advantage due to lower labor or occupancy costs. Competition from the small business sector can come from an increase in the number of new entrants or from the growth in size of an existing competitor. As a small proprietor your external locus of control over other small competitors is limited or nonexistent. The one thing you can do is monitor who is doing things right and who is not, measured not only by the level of business they are doing but by their profitability. For example, it is not uncommon in the building trades for a particular competitor to underbid the competition consistently; the strategy is to get work, to keep new competition out, and to put pressure on current competition, but such a strategy is worthless if profitability is sacrificed in the process. Such competitors are not winning even though they are gaining in market share. It is important to understand the difference, lest you be drawn into a bidding shootout with such a competitor.

The competitive environment can be adversarial, or it can be cooperative, especially between small business competitors. An adversarial environment is one where the players do their best to keep what they are doing a secret and adopt strategies to try to drive the others out of business or at least to erode the competitor's market share. A cooperative approach accepts the local competition as a part of life and adopts an attitude that there is room for everyone. The competitors themselves determine their own competitive environment based on their marketing activities. I suggest a cooperative approach because an adversarial approach generally begins with negative advertising and cost cutting, which in turn forces a response from the other local competitors, which can start a price war in which profits are difficult to maintain, let alone expand.

The third competitive realm that warrants the small business owner's attention comes in the form of substitute products, which can be tied to changes in technology, changes in consumer tastes, or as a customer response to perceived high prices. Contraction of the total market can signal a change in customer preferences, which could signal a permanent downtrend in the market. Such an event would warrant modification of the product or service mix. A dynamic technological environment could easily make this area a major threat simply because products and markets can change so rapidly.

• ENVIRONMENTAL SUMMARY · · · · · · · ·

Depending on the type of business, the environment that we operate in may include elements other than those discussed here. It should also go without saying that this is a brief overview and not a complete analysis of the operating environment. A starting point in establishing an information system to deal with the operating environment originates with an analysis of what your key success variables are and what your vulnerability analysis discovers. Those are the areas to focus on in establishing what is important to monitor and what is not so critical.

The most difficult aspect of environmental monitoring stems from the area of management information systems. Finding dependable, reliable, and timely information is a never-ending task. Good information on which to ground good decision making is the mark of a good manager. Good information coupled with an understanding of what is important, mixed with a little emotional stability, gives the small business manager the ability to maintain a focus that enables decisions to be based on fact rather than hearsay.

As a small business owner, it often seems that you are standing alone. Your employees often do try to help, but often they are acting out of emotion or partial information. It is also sometimes difficult for the proprietor to determine what information is important and how to acquire that information because so often the process is unique to your enterprise. Sometimes there just isn't anyone to model your business after. Environmental scanning can be unique in much the same way, but it is a critical function because the information you gather and how you interpret that information will have a profound effect on the decisions you make. The total of those decisions will determine whether your business succeeds or fails, and you alone will bear the fruits of your success or failure.

The success of a small business depends on so many things. It must be fundamentally sound—that is, have competence in all the functional areas. A small business must be conceptually sound—that is, the business must bring something to the marketplace that is needed. The need for your product or service must be real, and it should be growing, in order to have long-term survivability. A successful small business should meet the requirements set forth in the bridge model's pillars of success: that human relationships are formed and maintained based on trust, honesty, and integrity, and that the business produces products and services that are of high quality. The successful small business manager steers the business's future from an informed position, through the customer information systems and management information system that are in place to provide reliable, valid, and timely information. As part of that, the small business manager must scan the horizon constantly, always aware of what is going on within and around the business—a demanding task, indeed.

Endnotes ●●●●●●●●●●●●●●●●●●●●●●●●●●●

Chapter 1

1. Jeffrey L. Alvey, Assistant Vice President, First National Bank, 100 South Phillips Avenue, Sioux Falls, SD 57117; interview, February 1997.
2. Paul Hawken, *Growing a Business,* Simon & Schuster, New York, 1987.
3. Arden Barlow, President, Rails Inc., The Burlington Restaurant, 1917 West 41st Street, Sioux Falls, SD 57105; interview, March 1997.

Chapter 2

1. Arden Barlow, President, Rails Inc., The Burlington Restaurant, 1917 West 41st Street, Sioux Falls, SD 57105; interview, March 1997.
2. Paul Schiller, Partner, Lawrence & Schiller, 3932 South Willow Avenue, Sioux Falls, SD 57105; interview, August 1997.
3. Jan and Pat Garrity, Owners and Managers, Prairie Gardens, 30661 444th Avenue, Mission Hill, SD 57046; interview, June 1996.
4. Jan and Pat Garrity, *Garden News,* Vol. 1, June–December 1994.

Chapter 3

1. Carolyn Downs, Director, The Banquet, 300 North Main Avenue, Sioux Falls, SD 57104; interview, September 1997.

Chapter 4

1. Jeffrey L. Alvey, Assistant Vice President, First National Bank, 100 South Phillips Avenue, Sioux Falls, SD 57117; interview, February 1997.
2. Ibid.
3. D. Tim Wenzel, 530 North Franklin Avenue, Sioux Falls, SD 57103; interview series, November 1997.

Chapter 5

1. U.S. Small Business Administration, *Profile: Who We Are, What We Do,* 3rd ed., 409 Third Street S.W., Washington, DC 20416, May 1996.
2. U.S. Small Business Administration, *Programs & Services,* 409 Third Street S.W., Washington, DC 20416, May 1996.
3. Ibid.
4. U.S. Small Business Administration, *LowDoc Quick & Easy Small Business Loans,* 409 Third Street S.W., Washington, DC 20416, September 1996.
5. U.S. Small Business Administration, *The Facts about Micro Loans,* 409 Third Street S.W., Washington, DC 20416, January 1996.

6. U.S. Small Business Administration, *Borrower's Guide,* 409 Third Street S.W., Washington, DC 20416, May 1996.

7. U.S. Small Business Administration, *How to Buy or Sell a Business,* 409 Third Street S.W., Washington, DC 20416, September 1996.

8. Mortgage Associates, 411 North Minnesota Avenue, Sioux Falls, SD 57103, February 1997.

9. Ibid.

Chapter 6

1. *Uniform Franchise Offering Circular,* South Dakota Department of Commerce, Division of Securities, 118 West Capital Avenue, Pierre, SD 57501, April 1993.

2. Robert L. Purvin, Jr., *The Franchise Fraud,* Wiley, New York, 1994.

3. *AAFD Member Guide & Service Directories,* P.O. Box 81887, San Diego, CA 92138-1887, January 1997.

4. Ibid.

5. Bernard Schramm, Chairman, Park-it Market, Inc., P.O. Box 88707, Sioux Falls, SD 57109; interview, May 1997.

Chapter 8

1. Arden Barlow, President, Rails Inc., The Burlington Restaurant, 1917 West 41st Street, Sioux Falls, SD 57105; interview, March 1997.

Chapter 9

1. Joe Hurly, President, Hurly's Candies Inc., 2010 First Avenue South, Sioux Falls, SD 57105; interview, May 1997.

2. Ibid.

3. Rick Bauermeister, Director of Marketing, Robinson & Muenster Associates Inc., 1208 Elkhorn Street, Sioux Falls, SD 57104; interview, April 1997.

4. Mary Simmons, General Sales Manager, Midcontinent Radio, KELO Radio, 500 South Phillips Avenue, Sioux Falls, SD 57104; interview, May 1997.

5. Ibid.

6. Ibid.

7. Paul Schiller, Partner, Lawrence & Schiller, 3932 South Willow Avenue, Sioux Falls, SD 57105; interview, July 1997.

8. Rick Bauermeister, Director of Marketing, Robinson & Muenster Associates Inc., 1208 Elkhorn Street, Sioux Falls, SD 57104; interview, April 1997.

9. Paul Schiller, Partner, Lawrence & Schiller, 3932 South Willow Avenue, Sioux Falls, SD 57105; interview, July 1997.

10. Ibid.

11. Rick Bauermeister, Director of Marketing, Robinson & Muenster Associates Inc., 1208 Elkhorn Street, Sioux Falls, SD 57104; interview, April 1997.

Chapter 10

1. U.S. Department of the Treasury, Publication 17, *1996 Tax Guide For Individuals,* 1996, p. 48.

2. U.S. Department of the Treasury, Publication 15, *Circular E, Employer's Tax Guide,* January 1997, p. 7.

3. Department of Social Services, Child Support Enforcement, 700 Governor's Drive, Pierre, SD 57501, July 1997.

4. SD New Hire Reporting Center, P.O. Box 4700, Aberdeen, SD 57042, August 1997.

5. U.S. Department of the Treasury, Publication 15, *Circular E, Employer's Tax Guide*, January 1997, pp. 36–55.

6. Ibid, pp. 18–22.

7. Ibid, p. 17.

8. Ibid, p. 23.

9. U.S. Department of the Treasury, *Instructions for Form W-2, Wage and Tax Statement*, 1997, p. 2.

10. Ibid.

11. U.S. Department of the Treasury, Publication 15, *Circular E, Employer's Tax Guide*, January 1997, pp. 27–31.

12. U.S. Department of the Treasury, *Instructions for Forms 1099, 1098, 5498, and W-2G*, 1997, pp. 20–24.

13. *Wall Street Journal*, No. 41, February 28, 1997, p. C1.

14. U.S. Department of the Treasury, Publication 15, *Circular E, Employer's Tax Guide*, January 1997, p. 8.

Chapter 11

1. Social Security Administration, *Publication 7005-SM-OR*, May 1996.

2. Social Security Administration, Publication 5-100070, *How Your Retirement Benefit Is Figured*, May 1996.

3. Mary Parker Follet, *Freedom and Coordination*, Pitman, London, 1949, pp. 47–60.

4. Ibid.

5. Federal Trade Commission, Bureau of Consumer Protection, *Facts for Consumers: Fair Debt Collection*, Washington, DC 20580, August 1996.

6. Clerk of Courts, County of Minnehaha, State of South Dakota, *Guidelines for Small Claims Court*, Sioux Falls, SD 57103, August 1997.

7. Mark Gary, Gary Insurance Agency, 632 Main Avenue, Garretson, SD; interview, August 1997.

8. Ibid.

Chapter 12

1. Tom Mahoney, Active Data Systems Inc., 2504 West 46th Street, Sioux Falls, SD 57105; interview, September 1997.

2. Ibid.

Chapter 13

1. Jan and Patty Garrity, Owners and Managers, Prairie Gardens, 30661 444th Avenue, Mission Hill, SD 57046; interview, June 1997.

Index